Arctic Circle

16

17

Tropic of Cancer

Equator

Indian Ocean

Tropic of Capricorn

9

13

2

Antarctic Circle

COME HELL &
HIGH WATER

COME HELL & HIGH WATER

Extraordinary Stories of Wreck, Terror and Triumph on the Sea

JEAN HOOD

CONWAY

For my mother and parents-in-law,
and in memory of my father,
with love

A Conway Maritime book

© Jean Hood, 2006

First published in Great Britain in 2006 by Conway,
an imprint of Anova Books, 151 Freston Road, London W10 6TH
www.anovabooks.com   www.conwaymaritime.com

All rights reserved. No part of this publication may be reproduced, stored in a retrieval system,
or transmitted in any form or by any means electronic, mechanical, photocopying, recording or
otherwise, without the prior written permission of the copyright owner.

Jean Hood has asserted her moral right to be identified as the author of this work.

British Library Cataloguing in Publication Data:
A catalogue record for this book is available from the British Library

ISBN 10: 1844860345   ISBN 13: 978144860340

Edited by Jonathan Dore
Design and layout by Stephen Dent
Printed by MPG Books Ltd, Bodmin, Cornwall

Contents

Acknowledgements

It is a truth universally acknowledged that an author writing a book of this scope must owe much to many people, and I am no exception to the rule. A single long list seems to devalue contributions, and so I have decided to mention people individually in the sources and bibliography for each story. If anyone has been missed out, please believe it was through carelessness, not ingratitude.

There are, however, those people and institutions whose assistance spanned more than one chapter. Once again I find myself indebted to the resources and staff of the British Library, the National Archives, Manchester Central Library, Merseyside Maritime Museum and my local library at Sandbach, not to mention Barbara Jones and her colleagues at *Lloyd's Register*, who were marvellous. I'm also very grateful to the staff at the Service Historique de la Défense at the Chateau de Vincennes, who made me so welcome, and Jean-Michel Brunner and colleagues at the Musée de la Marine, Paris, for turning around enquiries so efficiently. Across the pond, the United States Naval Institute, the Naval Historical Center and the National Archives and Records Administration were likewise very helpful.

This is probably a good place to acknowledge two authors whose invaluable reference books must enjoy pride of place on any maritime historian's shelf: Peter Kemp for *The Oxford Companion to Ships and the Sea* (OUP, 1976) and John Harland for *Seamanship in the Age of Sail* (Conway Maritime, 1984)

Translations from foreign texts, excluding Russian, are almost entirely my own, and I want to thank Jean-Yves Le Lan, Andrea David Quinzi, Ann Armstrong, Elinor Van Mierlo, and Louise Kerr for helping with some difficult phrases.

Nor should I forget Steve at Compurite, who dropped everything when my computer self-destructed at New Year, and the Map Shop at Upton-on-Severn, who seem to have maps of everywhere and dispatch them immediately.

This leaves five very large bouquets to hand out. The first goes to John Lee at Conway for offering me a project so close to my heart; the second, to Judy, Peter and Sarah for the spare room close to London. The third is for my marvellous husband, George, who not only found himself press-ganged into helping with the research but even drove me round the Paris Peripherique. Number four goes to the book's designer, Steve Dent, for services above and beyond the call of duty. My editor, Jonathan Dore, who had the unenviable task of waving a magic wand over a very unwieldy manuscript, easily deserves the fifth. I am grateful to him not just for spotting errors and inconsistencies but for helping to resolve them, and for his enthusiastic, rigorous commitment. All remaining mistakes are, alas, my responsibility.

Jean Hood, Sandbach, 2006

Introduction

COME HELL AND HIGH WATER: a meaningless cliché for an increasingly urbanized population? A throwaway phrase that devalues the hundreds of thousands killed or injured in pursuit of trade, exploration, exploitation, travel, prosperity, war and freedom? Or a subconscious recognition that for centuries the oceans have tested the courage, ingenuity and resilience of man – who is, after all, 'a helpless and perishable creature' when out of his depth?

We do not know the date or location of the first shipwreck, let alone the circumstances, or names of the unlucky victims, but the chances are that it involved a log, a stretch of inconveniently deep water and at least one curious, scared or hungry human who was willing to take a risk. Since then, man has worked long and hard to find a safe and efficient means of conquering or exploiting the rivers and seas, incorporating additional refinements such as comfort, cargo space, life-saving equipment and weaponry along the way. Yet despite the centuries of marine technology which have seen the humble log give way to the nuclear-powered submarine, the VLCC and the floating palace, worse things still happen at sea.

If our first unlucky mariner succeeded in struggling back to land, he would have had a good yarn to tell his friends, and so our fascination with the subject began, soon extending from fact into fiction. The sea was both familiar and alien, an element where the extraordinary could and did happen. Homer's *Odyssey* pits the hero against the terrifying perils of Scylla and Charybdis during his long voyage home. Shakespeare tapped into that excitement when he created the storm and shipwreck that opens *The Tempest*, or when the Captain tells Viola, in *Twelfth Night*, how her brother had tied himself to a floating mast after their vessel went to pieces. In Bernardin de Saint Pierre's 1788 novel, *Paul et Virginie*, the drowning of the heroine was, in its time, the equivalent of Jack Dawson's death at the end of James Cameron's film *Titanic*, while the biblical story of Jonah and the whale invokes the same awe of the sea as Coleridge's *Ancient Mariner* or Wolfgang Petersen's film adaptation of *The Perfect Storm*.

Shipwrecks are powerful metaphors, and maritime dramas have long been used to illustrate the preoccupations of their time, teaching anything from resignation, faith and chivalry to resourcefulness, national superiority, class distinction and the perils of human arrogance. Stereotypes, therefore, abound. The man who fills his pockets with gold – while everyone else is building rafts or rescuing the ship's kitten – *always* drowns. Foreigners generally panic unless too stupid to recognize their peril. Captains who go down with their ship do so by choice, standing erect on the bridge. Until recently, women either shriek hysterically or confront death with perfect calm. Heroic naval victories bought at a price are the stuff of recruitment ballads.

Individual narratives, published as pamphlets, were popular in the eighteenth century, and in some cases remain the only detailed documentation of a particular incident. The nineteenth century saw publishers board the nautical bandwagon brandishing whole collections of shipwreck narratives. Little attempt was made to put them into context for the reader who did not know her starboard from her mizzen, or whose idea of maritime geography barely extended beyond his own coastline. The commemoration of specific dramas in poetry and song arguably reached its peak in that century, and at the same time, newspapers were feeding their readers' appetite for death, disaster and heroism on the high seas. In addition to reporting events, they used accidents or near-misses to call for health-and-safety legislation. The advent first of radio and then of television in the twentieth century allowed everyone to keep up to date with an unfolding crisis until footage of a crew being winched to safety by helicopter became all but routine. February 2006 opened with TV and internet images of distraught and angry families converging on Safaga demanding the list of survivors of the Egyptian ferry *Al-Salam Boccaccio '98*, which had just sunk with the loss of some 1000 of its 1400 passengers.

Countries that consider themselves seafaring nations are proud of their maritime heritage and mindful of the disasters that are part and parcel of it. It pervades their language and, by extension, their culture, invoking admiration for the courage of those who risk their lives on the seas, respect for the shipbuilders and awe at the power of the elements. Even incidents of incompetence, cowardice, defeat, bad luck, arrogance and criminal culpability usually yield something positive: examples of endurance, individual courage, sacrifice or resourcefulness.

When *San Francisco* passenger Lucia Eaton wrote that 'one could see human nature to perfection on that wreck', she was thinking primarily of its negative aspects, but take the remark at face value and it explains precisely why the best maritime dramas are so riveting. A group of people – occasionally an individual – is isolated in an alien and inhospitable environment under the most intense mental and physical stress, in a situation where, even if survival is possible for some, it may not be so for everyone. Who has that right to live, and how much can the human body or mind endure in order to survive? Will help come from outside, and in time, or is the group left entirely to its own resources?

This collection of 17 maritime dramas – the term is used deliberately to include more than shipwrecks – is a personal choice, spanning 250 years and several countries. What links them is their power to move, shock or amaze – sometimes all three – regardless of date or nationality.

If the omissions are surprising, that is intentional. There was no point in including merely the obvious, and several ships were left out because they have been the subject of recent in-depth treatment. So no *Lusitania*, *Birkenhead*, *Forfarshire*, *Grosvenor*, HMS *Hood*, *Lancastria* or *Sultana*. No *Winterton* either. Instead, there is room for ships far less familiar to an English-speaking audience today, such as the French *Méduse* and the Italian *Sirio*, which have their own place in history.

Titanic, surely a ship about which too much has already been written, is here for a special reason. Ask the person in the street – whether in Rome, Paris, London, New York or Sydney – to name a famous ship and the answer is likely to be *Titanic*. Ask them to name the greatest maritime drama, and the answer will probably be the same. However limited its maritime stock, every bookshop offers books about that ill-fated liner. Is it, therefore, heresy even to suggest that the loss of the *Titanic* may not stand head and shoulders above all the others? Perhaps the ordeal of the holidaymakers on a small ferry out of Liverpool can compete with that of the millionaires on the *Titanic*. And maybe the protracted horror, heroism and suffering of France's most infamous maritime disaster eclipses everything else.

In writing about such events, English reveals an unexpected deficiency. While French, Italian, Spanish and German each contains a precise word for someone who has been shipwrecked – *naufragé*, *naufrago*, *náufrago* and *Schiffbrüchiger* respectively – the best English can manage is *castaway*, which has other connotations.

Caveat Lector: A Note on Speech and on Distances

The majority of speech is either set down verbatim or reconstructed from reported speech. However, in the interests of dramatic scene setting, some liberties have been taken, mainly at the start of chapters, and in the case of the *Dodington* speech has been modernized. Therefore, anyone using this book as part of serious research is advised to consult the primary sources or contact the author.

All figures for 'miles' at sea in this book are given in nautical miles, which are defined as one-sixtieth of one degree of a great circle. This means in practice that 1 nautical mile is the equivalent of 1.14 statute miles, or 1.85 kilometres. Speed at sea is measured in knots, which are nautical miles per hour.

1

The Floating Bomb

Prince

1752

Then rose from sea to sky the wild farewell —
Then shriek'd the timid, and stood still the brave,
Then some leap'd overboard with dreadful yell,
As eager to anticipate their grave.

BYRON, *DON JUAN* (CANTO II, STANZA 52)

WHEN DR ROBERT STÉNUIT, the Belgian marine archaelogist, wrote that when it comes to shipwrecks, the East Indiamen are in a league of their own, he was referring as much to the events surrounding their demise as what might be in their broken, silt-filled bones. Whatever their nationality, they were the largest merchantmen afloat in their day, and carried the most valuable cargoes as well as acting as passenger ships. From the public's point of view, they were frequently lost in exotic and remote locations in circumstances that required courage, endurance and resolve for the survivors to reach their destination or return home.

The story of the *Prince* goes beyond this, raising that awkward question about the right to survive which, 160 years later, would be a subject of bitter controversy.

It began with a grey wisp, slinking out from the edge of the dark tarpaulin before dissolving into the wind. The Breton seaman on his way aft paused, wondering if his eyes were playing tricks. He bent down to the hatch cover, sniffed, and isolated an acrid smell. Apprehensive, he straightened up and stared. Another curling ghost escaped and was snatched away. He looked up at the quarterdeck where the second lieutenant, de Lafond, was taking a quadrant reading to calculate the ship's position, then thought better of shouting. Hastily he made his way to the ladder and climbed up to make his report.

'Monsieur, there's a fire in the hold.' He pointed down into the ship's waist.

'You are certain?'

'Yes, Monsieur.'

The second voyage of the *Prince*[1] was turning into a nightmare that the Sieur Pierre de Lafond de Braux would never forget.

She had looked so magnificent when he joined her the previous autumn. All the carving around her stern and quarter galleries had been cleaned and re-

Dramatis Personae

Jacques Aubert : master

Jean Corentin le Gal : seaman

Dom João da Costa de Brito : general of the Portuguese fleet

Baltasar Grispe : bosseman

Nicolas Henrio : first pilot

Joseph Clovis Houdemen : seaman

Pierre de Lafond de Braux : second lieutenant

Bernard-Nicolas Morin des Mézerets : captain

Julien de la Mothe : seaman

Saturnin Plumer : seaman

Laurent Ochu : chaplain

Jean Richard : first lieutenant

Joseph Ruche : seaman

Monsieur Le Prevost de la Touche : lieutenant colonel

Mathurin Tottevin : seaman

Monsieur du Vernay : French consul

gilded, the windows in the stern cabins gleamed golden in the autumnal sun,
and the royal blue paint on the upper works was smart and fresh, an arresting
contrast with the rich honey brown of her hull and the duller blue of her stern
and waterline. Her portholes were open to give light to the men working inside
– she was pierced for 44 guns, which made her more powerful than anything
that Britain's East India Company could send to sea – but she was only mounting 20 of them this time, and that was enough to see off any trouble in peacetime. The less guns and powder, the more cargo and the more profit. A couple
more months and she would be sailing from Port de l'Orient, at the confluence
of the rivers Scorff and Blavet.

Literally, the name of the Breton town – now Lorient – meant *Port of the
Orient*, though it translates better as *Gateway to the East*, because it was from
there that, for just over a century, the magnificent ships of the Compagnie des
Indes left for India and China to bring home the silks, printed cottons, spices,
teas and porcelain that were in such demand in France, as elsewhere in Europe.
The CdI had been established in 1664 by Louis XIV's influential minister
Jean-Baptiste Colbert, 64 years after England's Honourable East India
Company (HEIC) had shown how to cut out expensive middlemen and gain
direct access to the eastern spice trade. The Dutch had immediately followed
the English example and at various times during the seventeenth and eighteenth centuries Denmark, Spain, Austria, Sweden and even Scotland had
established similar but smaller rivals.

A home was needed for the new French Compagnie des Indes, as well as an
imposing headquarters in Paris. Channel ports were discounted because of
their vulnerability to the Dutch and British in time of war, and the company
finally turned to the Port Louis roadstead in south-west Brittany. Largely unde-
veloped, it offered a deep-water channel opening onto the Atlantic, and a
formidable defence in the new, star-shaped Citadelle de Port Louis. The Île de
Groix sheltered the mouth of the roadstead, and the banks of the Scorff could
comfortably accommodate the shipyards that would be needed. Entry and exit
from the port required care and expertise in navigation to keep in the channels
and avoid the hazards, but that was knowledge for French captains to acquire,
and enemies to learn the hard way.

Despite the yards on their doorstep, it was not until 1730 that the CdI built
its own ships. Then, under the direction of Gilles Cambry, a golden age began.
He created a better-proportioned vessel with a shallower draught, much
stronger construction, shorter masts and less sail. With those changes came a
dramatic increased in the size of the ships. The first 900-ton vessel came off the
stocks in 1741, a time when the HEIC's ships averaged around 500 tons.
Another of that new generation, the *Prince* – 141 feet (43 metres) along the keel
and 37.4 feet (11.4 metres) in the beam – was launched on 29 September
1746. She arrived home from a difficult, sometimes exasperating three-and-a-

half year voyage in November 1750, and late summer 1751 found her at her mooring at Lorient making ready for the next.

Yes, even at anchor, a magnificent ship. True, she had been surpassed in size in the few years since her launch: the new 1500-ton *Centaure* lay close by her, but there was nothing outside her own fleet to touch the *Prince*. De Lafond was no impressionable youth: he had spent 18 years at sea and was, by his own admission, well past his youth,[2] one of France's minor nobles who had hoped to make his fortune in the company's service but who had never achieved more than a living and the cachet of belonging to an elite corps of officers.[3]

Scheduled to sail around the middle of November, the *Prince* was loading alongside another dozen Indiamen in various states of preparation.[4] Careful loading was vital to keep the ship trimmed, make the most of the space and to avoid cargo shift. Heavy water casks were stored forward in the hold, the shot locker for the cannonballs was situated amidships, and into the aft hold went the barrels of biscuit, flour and black powder – the latter in a secure room to guard against the dreaded risk of fire. Outward-bound ships carried a heavy cargo of supplies for the company's outposts, including copper, lead, coal, iron, wine, spirits, medicines and paper. Canadian ginseng was another sought-after commodity because, being so much cheaper than Chinese, it could be traded at greater profit. There were the spare masts, spars, anchors and canvas to keep the ship in repair throughout the long outward and homeward voyages, and the food for the crew, the captain's table, soldiers and the sick.[5] With half her guns, removed there was room on the lower deck for cargo, animal pens and fodder – Indiamen carried meat on the hoof – as well as the crew's quarters, cabins of the petty officers, and the surgeon and the sick bay. Up on the poop deck, above the captain's cabin and the roundhouse, went the chicken coops.

Then the human cargo started to arrive: soldiers who had to sleep on the main deck, and passengers with cabins at the stern, close to the Great Cabin, where they dined with the captain and his officers. In general, the passengers consisted of military officers, senior administrative staff, a few relatives of men already established in the eastern outposts, and a steady stream of clerks to replace those who succumbed to the diseases and climate of the East.

On the evening of 19 November 1751, Captain Bernard-Nicolas Morin des Mézerets gave the order to weigh the anchor and the *Prince* glided cautiously into the channel of the Scorff. It was high tide, but the water on either side shallowed rapidly onto the mudflats. With the helmsman keeping a careful eye on the rock known as the Chapeau de Quintrec on the starboard, the *Prince* came up and along the north side of the Île de St-Michel, steering south-west by west to avoid the Banc du Turc that extended out for some distance in front of the island. It was hard work for the crew, testing their speed and efficiency right at the start of the voyage, no matter how experienced they were. The passengers stood on deck, torn between staring aloft to watch the orders translate into rapid action and gazing wistfully at the lights along the soft, darkening coastline.

The sudden change of wind took everyone by surprise. The ship had barely passed the island when it shifted. Next moment the *Prince* had veered across, bumped, groaned and shuddered to a stop with a heavy beating of sails and shaking of her masts. Slowly the wind and the weight of spars and canvas pushed her over until the muzzles of the port battery dipped into the water.

The saving grace was that the full length of the keel was aground, protecting the laden hull from stress, but it was a humiliating situation. A blazing distress signal brought out the port commandant, who decided for safety to unload the chests and most valuable cargo into the ship's boats. Sails, spars and topmasts were taken down and weight shifted to the starboard. All through the night they worked frantically, and had their reward when the morning tide began to flow and floated them off. Heartily relieved, they anchored nearby in the Port Louis roads, under the grey walls of the low fort, where any hopes of being able to put to sea and resume the voyage were soon dashed. The *Prince* was taking on water – not so much that the pumps could not cope with it, but enough to proclaim a problem. For eight days she discharged her cargo into barges, and then returned to port where she was stripped of the rest and properly careened – laid over on her side so her bottom could be examined and repaired. At the same time, they decided to give her a new wooden sheathing – copper had not yet come into use – against the teredo worm that played havoc with hulls in tropical waters. Usually a French Indiaman was careened after three voyages, but the long first voyage in the Indian Ocean had not been far off the equivalent of three normal ones.

The original passengers and soldiers doubtless dispersed to other ships. It is unlikely they could have afforded to wait at Lorient until the beginning of March 1752, when the *Prince* was finally ready to leave again. The cargo was once again stowed on board, a new detachment of military recruits was rowed out, but as fast as the passengers were arriving on board with all their trunks and cabin furniture, the *Prince*'s crew was deserting with its own baggage, leaving lieutenants de Lafond and Jean Richard to look for replacements. Other crewmen who had signed on earlier died, reported sick or found some other reason for remaining behind. Captain Morin even had to ask his masters for a new clerk. On 10 March he finally gave the order to set sail. His ship carried 168 crew, including officers, 18 passengers (five of them young women, including two young cousins of the captain), and 122 soldiers. Chief among the passengers was Lieutenant Colonel Le Prevost de la Touche, a veteran of military activity in Pondicherry. Possibly already a personal acquaintance of the captain's, he was soon on equally easy terms with all the ship's officers, including de Lafond, who had followed his career in India and had the highest respect and liking for him. They thought their bad luck was behind them.

The route took the ship past Madeira, the Canaries and the Cape Verde Islands without any problem. Forty-seven days into the voyage, at midday, when de Lafond took over as officer of the watch, they were around 250 nautical miles (460 kilometres) east of Pernambuco (now Recife) on the Brazilian coast.[6] There was nothing unusual about the route: it was a way of making use of favourable winds, but what did come as a terrible shock to de LaFond as he was taking that noon observation was the urgent arrival on the quarterdeck deck of a crewman with a disconcerting report of fire.

Speed was everything. First Lieutenant Jean Richard, who was in charge of the keys to the hold, commanded that all the hatches be opened to find out what had caused the accident and where the seat of the problem lay. It was an obvious, yet ultimately fatal, decision. In the meantime de Lafond gave his own orders.

'Get all the sails and tarpaulins you can lay your hands on and soak them!' They would be needed to cover the hatches and starve the fire of any oxygen. To Richard, he said: 'We ought to flood the tween-deck. If we can get a foot of water into it, that will cut off the air.'

The lashings were cut, and the heavy tarpaulins dragged off. Anxious fingers turned the heavy locks and men heaved up the hatch covers. Thick clouds of black smoke surged out as the inrushing air roused the fire. Summoned from dinner in the Great Cabin, Captain Morin had arrived on deck, and he issued the orders that de Lafond was already putting into practice.

The rumour of fire had easily outrun the first traces. Now the billowing smoke spread incipient panic. Nowhere on a burning wooden ship is safe, and the *Prince* was carrying gunpowder.

'Get the yawl out of the way!' Morin cracked out the order so that the waist could be cleared. 'He turned to de la Touche, who had likewise abandoned his dinner to come on deck. 'Colonel, would you have your men take up arms.' If he could not keep the crew calm, at least the presence of sixty-odd men with swords would keep them at their stations and give him a chance of extinguishing the blaze. It was fortunate to have the experienced military man at his side.

The pumps were manned with frantic energy, their sleeves directed into the hold . Buckets were lowered over the side and filled with water to throw onto the fire; even water jars were pressed into service, yet there was no sign that they were gaining on the flames. Smoke continued to increase; the crackling spread. Everyone was up on the deck. Men were rigging up a tackle to one of the lower yards in order to raise the yawl, swing it over the side and lower it.

Hardly was the boat in the water than four seamen, led by the bosseman (a petty officer with responsibilities similar to that of a boatswain), abandoned their duties and climbed down to take possession of it. Only then did it dawn on them that they had no means to manoeuvring it.

'Throw down some oars!' they shouted, and it was the perfect excuse for three more to leave. They swam out to the yawl with the oars and once in the boat refused to return.

'We have no rudder!' they shouted, by way of excuse. 'Throw us an anchor!' But they could see only too well that the smoke was getting worse and had no choice but to back water, while the ship herself, still underway, went ahead of them.

Courage remained on board, even though hope was fading. Morin ordered the powder kegs to be brought up and thrown overboard, but though the aft hold was clear of fire the suffocating smoke defeated the most intrepid. Jacques Aubert, the ship's 29-year-old master, fought his way down the ladder into the main hold to see what might be done, only to be beaten back by the savage heat that singed his clothes. Blackened and coughing until he could hardly breathe, he struggled up to the deck in agony, and men threw buckets of water over him.

He did not get out too soon. Spurts of flame burst from the hold into the decks above, devouring all remaining hope.

'Lower all boats!' Morin ordered, but fear was beginning to paralyse the faculties of the crew. They managed to haul the longboat up enough to be in a position to launch it, but the rampaging fire advanced, burning and spitting up the mainmast, attacking the ropes on the port side. The strands parted; the longboat crashed onto the starboard guns, fell on its side, and there was never any possibility of raising it again.

The failure seemed to encapsulate the hopelessness of the situation. Even if all of the boats had been launched, there were insufficient places for everyone on board. Ships' boats at that time were thought of as being for supplying the ship and taking people ashore or to other ships, not lifesaving. Nor was there a single friendly sail on the horizon. They were trapped, without possibility of rescue or even saving themselves, hundreds of miles from the nearest land. Men and women descended into despair, their screams mixed with the heart-trending cries of the dying animals trapped in their pens or running dement-edly around the decks. The smell of burning wood, pitch, fur and canvas was inescapable; the deck was swamped by smoke, Flames climbed the masts and blazed along the whole of the ship's port side, burning the ropes and rigging. Yards and spars went by the board.

'Then everyone,' recalled de Lafond, 'began to raise their hearts and voices towards Heaven. Each person, knowing that death was imminent, wrestled with the sickening alternatives: the fear of both fire and drowning increased the horror of death, and to wrestle with the choice was to suffer the torment of both.'

Faced with that choice, people were throwing hen coops, spars – anything that might float – into the water as the ship began to list to starboard. The ship's chaplain, Monsignor Laurent Ochu, stood on the quarterdeck offering a general absolution, and then went onto the gallery to deliver it to those already struggling in the waves. Some had managed to reach the pieces of wood thrown overboard in desperation, but they were only delaying the inevitable. Overcome by the gravity of the situation, Captain Morin had found some wooden bird-cages and told his two cousins to take off their spreading gowns. Commending them to the care of some sailors, he saw them into the water, then went down into Great Cabin on the main deck. The girls were left clinging to the coops for buoyancy; the sailors supported them with one hand and swam with the other.

The only officer left on the deck, de Lafond gave the order to put the helm to starboard; the ship answered, and it gained them a little more time by preventing the wind from encouraging the fire to spread across the deck, but by this stage it could only be a temporary respite. Many chose to jump, making no attempt to keep themselves afloat. A father[7] snatched his son from the advancing flames, kissed him, threw him overboard, jumped himself, grabbed the boy and then, holding him in his arms, went under. Better to die swiftly and together than drag out the unavoidable.

Not all were so keen to meet their fate. Others clung to the starboard shrouds or crept down the to end of the lower yards; a few clutched ropes or clung together.

The appalling sights flashed past de Lafond, occupied as he was with doing what he could in the line of duty. It came home to him that he, too, was faced with the same fate as the rest. He cast a glance around the chaos of the deck, then turned and went through the doors past the captain's sleeping quarters and into the stern cabin to look for Morin. Smoke clouded the view from the windows, and the panelling on one side was smouldering. Even here, where he had sat so often with Morin to receive orders, make reports or simply enjoy conversation over a glass of Bordeaux, there was no escaping the savage crack-ling of the flames. Now it was empty but for de la Touche, who was on his way out looking remarkably composed.

'Goodbye,' he said, drawing de Lafond into an affectionate embrace, 'my brother and my friend.'

'Where are you going?'

'I am going down to console my friend Morin.' To comfort him and die with him. De Lafond knew then that his own part was done: he could achieve no more for the ship or anyone left on it. It was his duty now to procure what time he could and dedicate it to God, composing his soul to meet his maker. Barely an hour could have passed since the fire had been discovered.

Hardly had he reached the starboard quarter gallery than the flames broke into the two big cabins, shattering the glass and roaring out of the windows. Burned through at its foot, deep in the hold, the mainmast wavered, then fell, tearing the shrouds and stays. Men and women who had taken refuge in the rigging screamed as they were plunged into the sea in the tangle of hemp; those in the path of its fall were crushed or drowned.

As the blaze closed in on his refuge, de Lafond stripped off waistcoat, coat and breeches and made for the yard of the mizzen course, which dipped into the water, but it was already overcrowded with the distraught remnants of those who had stayed on board. He rolled underneath them, made the sign of the cross and, calling on the Virgin Mary to help him, let himself drop. As he rose to the surface, he was grabbed by a soldier making a last attempt to stay afloat. The man was powerful, all the more so in his terror. De Lafond struck out at him with his fists, but still he held on. In desperation, the lieutenant let himself sink down, praying the soldier would let go if he thought he would drown, but he continued to cling on. Lungs bursting, they came up, breaking the surface to gasp for air. As soon as he could, de Lafond once more forced himself down into the green gloom, but his unwelcome companion held on all the tighter, incapable of comprehending that he would be dragged to his death if he clung on.

De Lafond needed to breathe. Hampered by the weight clasping him, he pulled up to the light, dragging air into his lungs again and then struggling to free himself. The soldier fought to keep his embrace, but he had swallowed quantities of water, and his strength was weakening. The officer drew a deep breath and as he went down for the third time, he felt the hands release him. Swimming for a distance underwater, he surfaced well away from the scene of the encounter.

It made him cautious, even of the pitiful dead bodies that floated listlessly on the surface in such numbers that he had to push them aside with one hand. Everywhere he fancied he saw the man who had held onto him and who might grab him again, if only to die with him – and his own strength was beginning to fail. He needed a rest. He found part of the flagstaff and used that to give him some help until he reached one of the studding sail yards. Clutching an end he looked up and saw that a young man had hold of the other, but could barely support himself. De Lafond abandoned it as soon as he spotted the spritsail yard, which had offered a refuge to a group of mainly young soldiers, some naked, others in no more than their shirts. Swimming over to them he asked if they would allow him to join them. Willingly they made room for the newcomer.

"We're really sorry for you, sir," they said, and were so sincere that de Lafond was not ashamed of feeling a lump in the throat.

"I've got more cause to pity you, my brothers. I'm getting on a bit, but you are only beginning your lives," he answered.

Some way astern of the dying ship, the men in the yawl considered their situation. They had the only boat, but were hardly any better off than those clutching the debris in the water. Without a sail, provisions or any idea where they were or where they should go, they had to face up to the likelihood of dying slowly of starvation or dehydration. Impotent, they sat watching events unfold.

From his place on the yard, de Lafond scanned the water to take stock of the situation. People were drowning all around him; the huge mainmast floated a distance away at the whim of the waves, covered in people who saw it as their final hope. Elsewhere, two sailors had perched themselves on a hencoop made from planks of pine.

'My lads!' he shouted, 'get hold of it and swim over to me!'

Followed by a few others who understood their lieutenant's train of thought, they did as they were asked. As soon as they reached the spritsail yard the coop was dismantled and, using the pieces of pine from the doors as oars, the whole group paddled its way over to the mainmast.

Some 80 people now sat or clung to the mainmast, including the master, the first pilot, the chaplain who had lately pronounced absolution and just two of the five girls who had been on board. Now their prayerful resignation offered de Lafond a lesson in faith, even as he recognized ruefully that he had exchanged one scene of misery for another. For what it was worth, however, the mainmast appeared to offer greater security than the small yard he had lately abandoned.

He had not reckoned without a new danger. The *Prince* had turned into a furnace, heating up the barrels of the guns that formed the starboard battery, and even though it was peacetime she sailed with her 12-pounders loaded. One after another each gunport spurted smoke and flame as a ball flashed whistling over their heads; the slightest movement of the burning hulk threatened to lower the trajectory and bring a gun to bear on the mast and the helpless refugees who stared in terror at the broadside, braced for the next explosion.

Sitting in front of de Lafond the chaplain, exhausted, slipped and fell. The lieutenant reached down a hand and dragged him up. Ochu was the younger man, only 29, but he was shattered, and had made his peace with God.

'Let go of me,' he gasped. 'I'm full of water and I'm only prolonging my suffering.'

'No, my brother,' responded de Lafond who had taken considerable spiritual comfort from his companion. 'We will die together, but not until I lose my strength.'

He had spoken his thoughts truthfully enough: he lived for each moment and the possibility of survival had never occurred to him. Resignation to death seemed all that was left as, one by one, those around him began to fall off and drown in the course of three hours leading up towards five o'clock. He remembered seeing one of the girls let go, too tired to hold on any longer, but he was too far away to intervene.

When it was the last thing on his mind, the little yawl rowed into sight, and the all the patient, prayerful stoicism evaporated. Instinctively he wanted to live, not be a martyr.

'I'm your lieutenant!' he shouted over to the men in the boat. 'Would you allow me to share your misfortune?'

They replied in the affirmative. Was that why they had come close in the first place – to see if they could find anyone who might have the single skill they lacked? Only one condition was imposed, and de Lafond was not disposed to quibble. If he wanted the place he must swim to them. If they came to him, the boat would be swamped in the panic, and everyone would die. There may also have been an underlying test: if he was strong enough to swim, he was less likely to die on them.

De Lafond struck out for the boat and hauled himself on board the vessel which, while not the largest of the ship's boats, still could not have been full. Looking back at the mast he had left he saw two men following his example: Jacques Aubert, the master, and his fellow Breton, Nicolas Henrio, the first pilot. Both were useful men, and they were welcomed on board. The newcomers took stock of the crew under the Venetian bosseman, Baltasar Grispe.

Three of them, Joseph Clovis Houdemen, Julien de la Mothe and Joseph Ruche, formed part of the replacement crew signed on shortly before the *Prince* had left Lorient. They could all boast some skill in sail-making, though they were on the ship as seamen. Saturnin Plumer, Mathurin Tottevin – who had lost a cousin or brother in the disaster – and Jean Corentin le Gal were also seamen and, like all but two of the group, Bretons. Most were in their late twenties or early thirties, and all had shown a degree of initiative, and self-interest, in taking the first opportunity to get clear of the burning ship. They were hardly heroes, but de Lafond was not setting himself as a model of heroism, either. At the point when they made their escape he referred to them as 'lucky fugitives,' and now he was sharing their luck as well as their misfortunes.

From their point of view, they had a navigator and two additional solid men to help with the rowing, but their position was far from ideal. They desperately needed provisions, but they dared not go anywhere the ship, and it was not fear of their comrades that induced them to row well out and wait for the inevitable.

It came soon afterwards in a brilliant flash of orange. With a single thunderous roar the explosion blew the ship apart in a ball of fire and dark, acrid smoke, eclipsing the setting sun. Massive chunks of burning wood erupted high and wide. The ten men in the boat watched in stupefied horror as the deadly cascade plunged flaming through the unnatural darkness, dying in the water in crashing, hissing plumes.

Silence – or so it seemed, while the thick smoke slowly dispersed – and they held their collective breath as the scene was revealed. The ship was gone, reduced to a mass of debris, among which floated the crushed human remains of those who had been clinging to the mainmast. As the yawl ventured closer they saw that even after that infernal rain there were a few who clung to the remnants of life, their bodies torn and burned by the blast and falling timbers.

A nineteenth-century engraving of the escape of de Lafond and the other nine survivors of the *Prince*. It is somewhat inaccurate, as all three masts are shown as still standing.

They could not afford to be squeamish. De Lafond may have blessed Heaven for his ability to maintain his self-command when faced by such a sight, but it was the powerful drive for survival that made him tell his comrades they had to go in. Unless they could find some supplies they might as well give up now and join the last expiring souls in the water. There was no time to hesitate: night was coming on. It would be dark around six o'clock in that latitude.

The first barrels proved a bitter disappointment: not food, just the kegs of black powder that had been jettisoned early in the emergency. By the time the darkness closed in, however, they had secured a cask of brandy, around 15 pounds of salted bacon, a piece of scarlet cloth, 20 ells of linen, a dozen staves and some ropes. They had failed to find what they needed most of all – a barrel of fresh water – but it was too dangerous to spend the night riding among the heavy balks of timber and better to start on what they knew would be a long and difficult journey.

Having rowed out to a safe distance from the floating debris, they set about fitting out their vessel as best they could with the skills they could muster between them. Stripping out the boat's internal planking gave them a supply of wood and nails. One of the oars was pressed into service as a mast, and with the boat hook as a yard they were able to set up the red cloth as a sail. A key made an acceptable block for the halyard to raise and lower it. A plank and the sheath of a knife became a rudder; the staves and cloth were used to rig up a weather-boarding along each side. As night fell, de Lafond, who as soon as he came aboard seems to have been accepted – even welcomed – as leader of the survivors, declared that it was as good as it was going to get.

They paused to pray to the Virgin for protection and put themselves into God's hands before hoisting sail on the port tack. With a favourable wind they rapidly left behind the ghastly death and devastation they had evaded. De Lafond's task now was to set a course due west for the Brazilian coast – though without charts, compass or quadrant – and he could not afford to get it wrong. They had to rely on the constellations and the rising and setting of the sun and moon, and had no hopes of sighting land for many days.

Their situation was unenviable. None of them had more than a shirt to keep off the burning sun, and their only food was a daily meal of the bacon. After three days they even gave that up because it caused them to spit blood, while the occasional tot of brandy – all the liquid they possessed – burned their stomach without hydrating them. Flying fish were abundant, but they lacked the means of capturing them and were only tortured by the sight.

Sleep deprivation was taking its toll. The sea was too rough for anyone to relax, and they were too hungry, thirsty and anxious to get any rest. On the sixth day a brief shower of rain gave them a moment of relief as they tried to catch the water in their mouths and hands. They had nothing in which to store any, and when they tried sucking the red sail they found that it was steeped in salt from its earlier immersion. Amid the disappointment the lieutenant found some little consolation: if the rain had been any heavier it might have caused a calm, and if they had lost their fair wind it would have finished them. Yet they were not far off envying the dead they had left behind; just a small flicker of hope kept them going as exhaustion overcame them.

On the eighth night, de Lafond took the tiller for more than ten hours, unable to persuade anyone to relieve him. They were all at the end of their resources, and despair at ever reaching the coast had set in. Dawn was nothing to be welcomed, just the prelude to another day of crippling heat, but as the light strengthened they were suddenly aware that there, on the horizon, was land. It was Wednesday, 3 May.

'You would have had to go through our misfortunes in order to understand how completely our joy changed us. In that moment we were the ten happiest men in the universe. Our strength returned and we took measures so that we would not be carried off course and smashed by the currents. At two o'clock in the afternoon we reached the coast of Brazil and entered Tresson Bay.'

They had sailed into the Baia da Traição – the Bay of Treason, where the first Portuguese explorers to reach Paraiba were killed and allegedly eaten – lying 96 statute miles (155 kilometres) north of Pernambuco in Latitude 6°42′ S, Longitude 34° 54′ W. De Lafond claimed the *Prince* had been lost some 600 miles (1100 kilometres) off the cost of Brazil, but it is highly implausible that they could have covered that sort of distance in seven days in such a small craft with its makeshift sail and exhausted crew. Moreover, 600 miles as the crow flies is considerably longer in actual navigation when currents and winds are brought into the calculation. If, as seems more likely, they were around 250 miles (460 kilometres) off the Brazilian coast in Latitude 8° 30′ S at the time of the explosion, a voyage of some 321 miles (594 kilometres) *as the crow flies* to Baia da Traição, averaging around 1.8 knots, is reasonable.

They had done well to land where they did: a league or so further south and they would have been wrecked on the lethal coastal reefs. Overwhelmed with relief they ran the boat up and threw themselves onto the beach, kissing the sand in an orgy of gratitude before suddenly wondering whether this really was the end of their suffering or whether they would have to endure more privations before finding human assistance. Their appearance was pathetic enough, with just a few soiled rags between them, bearded, with sunken eyes and skin scorched by the sun – and in some cases burned by the fire on the ship. De Lafond tore himself a red belt to mark his leadership should they come across a settlement, and they were on the point of setting out when a body of 50 suspicious Portuguese came to meet them and ask what they were doing.

Reserve turned swiftly to compassion; the newcomers fell over one another to invite the French to their homes, and set off with them. The sight of a stream on the short journey was irresistible: the survivors threw themselves in it, rolling around like animals and drinking their first fill of water for eight days. From that moment on, life did not cease to improve. The leading man in the area took them into his house and provided all of them with linen shirts and breeches while his servants prepared a light meal of fish and cassava. Instead of sleeping they insisted on then going a mile and a half to the nearest church to give thanks for their escape, and once again people were kindness itself. But what they craved was some beef broth to set them up, and the following day they exchanged their remaining brandy for a bullock, not just to satisfy their immediate hunger, but to smoke its meat to take with them on the three-day walk to the nearest town, Paraiba (now João Pessoa). They would have to do it barefoot; shirts were one thing, shoes another.

Two days into their march they were met by the commander of a local fort, who sent them up to Paraiba by boat, where they were presented to the governor. After resting for three days they were given an escort – and de Lafond provided with a horse – for the journey to Pernambuco, where they had the opportunity of falling in with the Portuguese fleet. On arrival, one of the naval captains took them out to meet the general of the fleet, Dom João da Costa de Brito aboard his flagship, the *Nossa Senhora da Nazare*, and once again they met with only commiseration and kindness. De Brito made himself responsible for the men and took de Lafond into his house ashore as his guest, quite overwhelming him with his generosity. His opposite number in the army gave the lieutenant an open invitation to dine with him, ordered his own tailor to make him a suit of clothes, presented him with a sword, and gave the men ten pieces of gold between them. On 15 July the *Nossa Senhora da Nazare* sailed for Lisbon, escorting a convoy, and it took the Frenchmen with it. During the journey, the general even paid wages to the French sailors.

Their good fortune did not end in Lisbon, where hospitality was extended by both the Portuguese and the city's French community, but after a few days de Lafond decided not to trespass upon it any further and took a private lodging with a French landlady close to the port, where he was best placed to learn of a vessel sailing for France. He was evidently ill, and so much attention, however kind, was exhausting. Eventually the Consul du Vernay, the official French representative in Lisbon, procured a passage for him and Aubert on a small vessel sailing for Morlaix; the rest of the men were found places on other ships. Pierre de Lafond disembarked at Morlaix on 2 November and returned to Lorient eight days later, where he spent the next four months in the hands of the doctors, his health completely broken. It is unlikely, given the probability that he was close the age at which officers of the Compagnie des Indes retired – around 53 – that he returned to sea.

The voyage on the *Prince* had been a financial disaster for him. The 'pacotille' system operated by the company, which allowed their employees free transport for a limited quantity of goods that they were permitted to trade privately, offered the possibility of riches, but the officers had to buy the goods they were going to sell when they reached their destination. Either the money came out of their own pockets, or they financed the enterprise by borrowing. The loss of an East Indiaman could therefore make a serious hole in a man's wealth; at worst, it could bankrupt him. By his own admission, De Lafond had come home destitute.

Following his return to Lorient he must have reported the circumstances of the ship's loss to the company, and it has to be assumed, for want of alternative evidence, that his story was accurate. We have no record of the official reaction to his report. Uncorrobarated narratives have to be treated with caution. Nevertheless, beneath the conventions, de Lafond's account has the ring of truth. He laid emphasis on piety and providence, justifying survival as the will of God, almost as if ashamed at having to admit that he lived to tell the tale when so many others perished. Consciously or not, he portrayed himself as a competent if rather too self-effacing officer, and very much a victim – but that might be the consequence of his having written the narrative while still recovering. In any case, what the modern Anglo-Saxon reader might consider an occasional sickly excess of sensibility and gratitude would have fulfilled the expectations of a contemporary audience.

The narrative contains the almost obligatory helpless women and senior officers who confront death with equanimity, but no undisciplined sailors or soldiers who spend their last hour drinking themselves into oblivion and resisting orders. The suffering and faith are as important as the horror of the ordeal.

The publication of his adventure in 1753 was more than likely intended to solicit some form of charity or recompense, but how successful it was remains a tantilizingly unanswered question. However, an undated Dutch pamphlet from the period recounts the story of the *Prince* (closely following De Lafond's narrative), as well as the loss of the VOC's *Rustenwerk* in the same year, suggesting that the little booklet was not unknown beyond the borders of France.

G iven the nature of their long voyages and the state of charts and navigation equipment at the time, East Indiamen had a reasonably good safety record. Between 1730 and 1760, the CdI lost 43 vessels, excluding those captured in wartime. The HEIC lost 32 in the same period. One reason for this success was that the companies did not take short cuts when it came to construction and repairs. Most losses were down to foundering in bad weather or striking rocks.

Fires on all wooden vessels, usually caused by carelessness with lanterns, candles or the fires kept alight in the forge and galley, were not infrequent, but most were minor and swiftly extinguished – the CdI only lost three ships through fire in that 30-year period. If a blaze got out of control, the consequences were horrific. In 1798 the French navy's 110-gun *L'Orient* exploded with huge loss of life during the Battle of the Nile, and two years later off Livorno, HMS *Queen Charlotte* suffered a fate identical to that of the *Prince*, in her case caused when the slow-match used to fire the signal guns set fire to some hay. Many of the boats sent to the scene before she blew up were forced to stand off to avoid the balls fired from her overheated guns. Unarmed merchant ships were at far less risk from explosion, but many damp cargoes were vulnerable to spontaneous combustion, and casks of spirits could give off vapours that were susceptible to ignition. Lightning provided a serious fire hazard. In 1766 it caused the total loss of the French frigate *Modeste* and in 1789 the HEIC's *Royal Charlotte* exploded at Calcutta when lightning travelled down her foremast and directly into the magazine.

If a fire was discovered, ships of the period had only limited equipment: pumps and buckets to direct water onto the blaze and axes to cut away blazing masts and rigging. A few vessels had the luxury of an early form of static fire engine. Prevention, therefore, was the order of the day. In the Royal Navy the master at arms had responsibility for fire security, earning him the nickname 'Fire-and-Lights', and corporals of marines made regular rounds to ensure all was safe. The powder magazine was lined with copper to prevent accidental sparks, a procedure copied by the HEIC.

As late as 1873, Robert White Stevens, in his book on cargo stowage, wrote:

Capt. Sedgwick recommends that when fire occurs in the hold, a recorded number
of auger holes should be bored in the gun-room or forecastle until the water is level

with the beams; one hatch only to be kept open, two will admit a draught and create flame; throw in water daily. When the danger is over, plug all the holes. If bad weather prevails, close every aperture, as a fire may be thus kept smouldering for weeks. Another plan is to bore holes in the deck, over the suspected place, nearly through; plug the scuppers, &c., and fill the deck six or eight inches with water. Then finish the holes, and keep them supplied with water; plug them imme-diately [if] the supply fails or the danger is over. In all cases prepare boats with provisions.

If that advice, not so different to de Lafond's instincts, had been available to Jean Richard, then perhaps disaster might have been averted that day on the *Prince*.

Sources and Bibliography

Sincere thanks to Jean-Yves Le Lan for the digital images, and his help with deciphering the hand-writing and explaining otherwise incomprehensible terms; to Henri Jacquin for his enthusiastic assistance at the Lorient archives; and to Diamantino Videira at the Portuguese Embassy.

Crew list of the *Prince:* Service Historique de la Défence (Marine), Lorient.
Musée de la Compagnie des Indes, La Citadelle, Port Louis.
Boudriot, Jean, *Les Compagnies des Indes, 1720–1770*, 2 vols (Paris: self-published, 1983).
Frayler, John, 'Fire and Lights', in *Pickled Fish and Salted Provisions: Historical Musings from Salem Maritime National Historic Site* 3/6 (October 2002); available online at www.nps.gov/sama/indepth/fish/firelight.pdf
Haudrère, Philippe and Le Bouëdec, Gérard, *Les Compagnies des Indes* (Rennes: Editions Ouest-France, 1999).
Jonkers, A R T, 'Parallel Meridians: Diffusion and Change in Early-Modern Oceanic Reckoning', 2003; available online at www.liv.ac.uk/~jonkers/PARAMER.pdf
Lafond, Le Sieur de: *Relation du Sieur de la Fond, Lieutenant de Vaisseau 'Le Prince'* (n.p.: self-pub-lished, 1753; several briefer versions of Pierre de Lafond de Braux's narrative exist in other sources, including Zurcher and Margollé's *Les Naufrages Célèbres*).
[Morin, Captain] *Twee Rampspoedige Zee-Reyzen, Den Eenen Gedaan Door Den Ed: Heer Capitein Morin Met Een Fransch Oost-Indiesch Compagnie-Schip Genaamt Le Prince ...* (Amsterdam: self-published, [1752]) (The British Library catalogue dates this to 1752 and gives Morin as the author, both of which are impossible, perhaps reflecting a cataloguer's misreading of the title page; its actual author and date are unknown.)
Stevens, Robert White, *On the Stowage of Ships and their Cargoes*, sixth edition, (London: Longmans, 1873).

Notes

1   Technically, her third, but this was her second long-distance run to India.

2   His service record does not appear to have survived, but the officers of the CdI usually joined at 18. In order to progress from one rank to another the officer had to have completed at least two voyages at the lower rank. There were also age limits: the earliest a man could become a second lieutenant was 31. First lieutenants were appointed at about 36, while the youngest captains were 42. De Lafond states that he had 18 years service – meaning 18 years physically at sea – so, taking into account time at home in France between voyages, he was probably in his late 40s.

3   The officers received lower wages than in the merchant service generally – de la Fond would have received some 90 livres a month - , but had the right to a certain amount of private trade allowance, allowing an officer to quadruple his wages.

4   The official records at the Service Historique de la Défense (SHD), Lorient, state that the *Prince* departed on 10 March 1752. Her story has found its way into various old English and French shipwreck anthologies with the departure date of 19 February, but de Lafond's contemporary account (published 1753) states 19 November 1751. This makes considerable sense in the light of the story itself, but represents a very early departure for a ship bound only for India. Usually, the China ships went first.

5   The Compagnie des Indes expected the best food – fresh meat, dried fruits and so on – to be given to the sick.

6   There is a problem in working out the ship's longitude. Latitude 8° 30′ S places them somewhere off Pernambuco on the Brazilian coast, and East Indiamen regularly shaped such a course in order to make use of favourable winds. Longitude 355° E is equivalent as 5° W, but it is necessary to know from which Prime Meridian (PM) that position is being calculated. Between 1760 and the adoption of the Greenwich meridian in 1885, French ships calculated longitude from Paris (and the practice continued unofficially even after that date). Before 1760 it depended entirely on which charts they carried. This was the case even within the CdI, where in 1745 a serving captain, Jean-Baptiste d'Après de Mannevillete, had published the first edition of his book of charts, *Neptune Oriental*, which was based on Paris. Previously, chartmakers of various nationalities favoured PMs running through some of the Cape Verde and Canary Islands because they believed there was little or no magnetic variation. Worse, during a long voyage captains often calculated their positions from the last significant landfall.

   By taking the Greenwich positions of the four most likely PMs and adding the 5° W as calculated by de Lafond, the distance to Pernambuco from the Prince's last plotted position can be calculated as follows. Using a chart based on Ferro (now Hierro, in the Canaries): 696 nautical miles; on Tenerife: 796 miles; on St Jago (now São Tiago, in the Cape Verdes): 254 miles; and on Boa Vista (Cape Verde): 302 miles.

   Later, de la Fond gives an important clue, by stating the longitude of the Baia da Traição, 108 nautical miles N of Pernambuco, to be 348° 15′ E, or 11° 45′ W. From Greenwich, the bay's longitude is 34° 54′ W. The difference between the two is 23° 09′ W, and this suggests that the *Prince*'s charts were based on a map whose PM was based on St Jago/São Tiago, which is 23° 37′ W of Greenwich. It must be stressed that this theory assumes the ship's officers were calculating their longitude correctly. In the days before the nautical chronometer, that is quite a large assumption.

7   Looking at the passenger list it is hard to make an identification.

2

The Phoenix of Bird Island

Dodington

1755

She was stubby and square, but we didn't much care,
And we cheerily put to sea;

CHARLES EDWARD CARRYL, 'NAUTICAL BALLAD'

I F SOME OF THE STORIES of the East Indiamen read like improbable fiction, in the case of the British vessel *Dodington* in 1755, that is very much what it was. After her loss, the diaries of two officers were published, which showed the survivors banding together and working hard for their mutual good. A century and a half later, a third account came to light, written in secret by one of those same officers as events unfolded, and one that painted a darker and more realistic picture of what happened.

In a century cluttered with wars, Britain was just about at peace in 1755. Admittedly, a naval fleet under Admiral Edward Boscawen had just put to sea with the aim of attacking 'any French ships of war that shall be attempting to land troops in Nova Scotia or to go to Cape Breton or through the St Lawrence to Quebec,'[1] but the main hazards the Honourable East India Company had to

Dramatis Personae

Thomas Arnold : captain's servant

Robert Beazly : seaman

Neal Bothwell : quartermaster

Gilbert Chain : seaman

Edward Chandler : captain of the *Rose*

Nathaniel Chisholm : quartermaster

John Collett : second mate

Dysou/Dyson : matross

John Glass : seaman

Norton Hutchinson : captain of the *Carnarvon*

Evan Jones : chief mate

John King : seaman

Daniel Ladoux : captain's steward

John Leister/Lister : matross

John McDugall/MacDowell : captain's servant

Jeremiah More/Moull : seaman

Samuel Powell : fifth mate

Peter Rosenburg : seaman

James Samson : captain of the *Dodington*

Henry Scance / Hendrick Scantz : seaman and smith

Henry Sharp : surgeon's servant

Ralph Smith : seaman

Johanes Taylor : seaman

Richard Topping : carpenter

William Webb : third mate

John Yates : midshipman

(The spelling of these names varies significantly in the various sources, and there are discrepencies as to their positions)

fear that spring were the constants: weather and navigation. On St George's Day a fleet of five Indiamen weighed anchor in the Downs off Deal: the *Streatham*, *Pelham*, *Houghton*, *Edgecote* and *Dodington*. Almost all the British East Indiamen were privately owned by consortia of wealthy individuals and chartered at highly favourable rates to the HEIC. A consortium frequently included at least one significant person such as a nobleman, politician or director of the HEIC, after whom the ship would be named. The *Dodington* was most likely named in honour of George Bubb Dodington, later Baron Melcombe, who in 1720 inherited the estate of his uncle, George Doddington (so spelt), one of the founders of the of the Bank of England.

The fleet was no ordinary one; it is even arguable that it changed the face of the Indian subcontinent. Although the East India Company was formidably powerful, it had not yet achieved the dominance that it wished for, and the French were stubbornly standing in the way of its expansion. As well as the mainland stronghold at Pondicherry, France held the strategic islands of Mauritius and Reunion on the route to India. It was not so long, either, since they had taken Madras (now Chennai), and although they had returned it, they were still a considerable nuisance. The East India Company directors asked its most successful soldier, Robert Clive, to abandon his ill-fated attempt to enter Parliament[2] and to return to India as second-in-command of an expedition from Bombay (now Mumbai) against an Indian potentate who had French support. They threw in a civil appointment that virtually guaranteed his accession to the governorship of Madras, making it an offer he could not refuse.

Clive had wished to travel on the *Dodington*, considered to be the fastest of the five vessels and bound for Fort St George (Madras), but in the end he actually sailed on the *Streatham*, because a change in his orders required him first to go to Bombay. However, he had embarked his personal fortune, valued by him at around £33,000, on board his preferred ship, and that included a chest containing 653 ounces of gold. It was not the only treasure on board the *Dodington*. The company regularly sent out silver to pay its troops and administrative staff, and the *Dodington* was carrying 35,000 ounces to finance the new expedition. Other cargo included copper and field guns.

It was normal for small groups of HEIC vessels to sail in company: the need to catch favourable winds, particularly beyond the Cape of Good Hope, dictated when they could leave, but unless they were under naval convoy during wartime, they tended to string out as the voyage progressed, sometimes meeting at Madeira, St Helena or the Cape to replenish supplies, otherwise gathering at Madras, Calcutta, or, in the case of the China fleet, Canton. Within the week they had cleared the English Channel and were out into the Atlantic, and Captain James Samson of the *Dodington*, in his first voyage as a captain, set course for the Canary Islands.

O n 14 May they passed Fortaventura and the following day sailed between Tenerife and Gran Canaria. From there the *Dodington* headed SSW for the Cape Verde Islands, reaching Boa Vista on 20 May and sighting the *Houghton* on the same day. Both ships anchored before the low-lying harbour-town of Praia, together with the *Pelham* and the *Streatham*, which had arrived earlier. For six days they refilled their water casks, took on fresh supplies and allowed passengers some welcome time on the island.

With her hold full of stores for India and provisions for the voyage, the ship carried over 250 people, for in addition to her crew of around a hundred there were a large number of Royal Artillery recruits and their officers. Mostly aged between 16 and 25, they came from all over England, with a handful from Ireland, Scotland and Wales: labourers, weavers, shoemakers, previously discharged soldiers, and even the odd cutler, glass grinder and curry-comb maker. The HEIC was a private company, and had its own military forces, but where national interests were concerned it had access to His Majesty's troops as well, provided it paid for them.

The crew itself included numerous tradesmen, for East Indiamen, like warships, had to be able to make their own repairs, even extensive ones, on long voyages. The majority was English, with one Italian and a handful of Scots, Welsh and Swedes. Below Captain Samson were five or six mates including Evan Jones, John Collett, William Webb and Samuel Powell. In the 1780s the HEIC would make them and their captain look like naval officers by introducing uniforms for formal and semi-formal occasions. For now, they wore clothes of their own choosing: the fashionable waisted coat with radial pleats at the hip, waistcoat that reached to mid thigh and close-fitting breeches. Collett had his wife with him: they were not returning to Britain but had decided to settle in India, where there was a demand for experienced mariners.

On 26 May, the *Edgecote* arrived in the Praia roadstead, just as Samson and the other captains were making ready to weigh anchor. Leaving the laggard, they set off, but after two days Samson decided his fellows were steering too easterly, and took a more southerly course. With the ship showing off her sailing qualities they had a fine, uneventful seven-week run down to the Cape without ever sighting the other ships, and on 8 July they passed Cape Agulhas and were now steering due east.

Samson intended to take the inner passage – sailing via the Mozambique Channel between the African coast and the island of Madagascar – rather than pass to the east of the island. It was a routine decision, but it had its dangers, particularly because there was as yet no means of calculating longitude with any certainty.[3] A strong westward-flowing current had the effect of deceiving captains into thinking they had sailed further east than they really had. Worse, the charts of the period were frequently unreliable, and those of the coast of southern Africa, based on sixteen-century information, particularly so. They showed the continent cutting northwards much further west than it actually does, suggesting open sea where land, in fact, continues.[4]

The *Dodington* had continued to run due east until Samson's calculations at noon on 16 May allowed him to steer east-north-east. The weather was foul: squally grey weather with the wind gusting from south-south-west to south-south-east and a high sea. Under double-reefed fore and treble-reefed main topsails the ship crashed through the waves. William Webb, the third mate, came off watch at midnight reckoning she had covered 70 miles (130 kilometres) since noon and estimating her position as roughly 34° 45′ S and 31° 30′ E. He went to his cabin and fell asleep.

Up on the storm-lashed quarterdeck, Chief Mate Evan Jones stared into the wild darkness. They were still making between 5 and 7 knots. A voice roared above the wind and surging waves:

'Breakers ahead and to leeward!'

'Helm a-lee!'

The helmsman fought with the wheel; the *Dodington* started to answer, her head coming round almost into the wind. She struck twice, the second time violently; the sea broke over her, smashing boats and sweeping away the crew forward.

Webb's dream disintegrated into an endless deafening crash as he landed on the cabin floor in a tangle of blankets and was hurled against the cabin wall. For an instant he lay paralysed, trying to make sense of the moment. Then he heard the shrieks, and he was out of the door and up the ladder into the melee of breaking surf, rending wood and screams of terror, crawling up the seaswept, listing deck to grab the port rail.[5]

Jones was still hoping she would come round, but the sea was crashing all over her and she struck the rocks again, heavily. The huge mainmast went by the board, bringing down the fore and mizzen, and each successive wave lifted the hull and beat it on the rocks, sadistically tearing it to pieces. The *Dodington* went over onto her starboard side and the waves drove her ever closer to the breakers.

Those who remained alive scrambled up to the port quarter, awaiting the end. Captain Samson huddled beside Jones.

'I judged I was 90 leagues off the land at noon,'[6] he said helplessly to his first mate. 'This has to be an uncharted rock, maybe where the *Dolphin* was lost.'[7]

The East Indiaman went to pieces within 20 minutes of striking. Clinging to the port side of the quarterdeck, Webb exchanged barely a word with the aghast captain before a heavy sea came over and separated them, driving him down into the ship's waist between the fore and mainmast. His arm took the brunt of the impact and he knew instinctively it was broken, but there was no time to worry about it: half-drowned, he had to drag himself back up to the quarterdeck where others had taken some sort of refuge. It was still dark. Later, he would realize he had hardly been off watch for three-quarters of an hour. For the moment he remained totally disorientated as sea and ship united.

'Land!'

Still coughing water out of his lungs Webb looked round to see where the owner of the shout was indicating. There was something out there, but black. It looked too low for land, and was probably only the sea beyond the breakers.

There was no getting out of this alive. It was just a matter of time. The roar of the wave was building; he held on more tightly, praying. Then the water was over him, tearing his hand from its hold; something struck his head.

He came round to find himself floating about on a plank, his shoulder impaled on a nail, and so numb from the cold that he could barely move. The rain was still falling, but there was daylight, and when he raised his head he could see land in the form of some rocks with people on them. Painfully heaving himself clear of the nail he made his way towards the rocky shore and met up with Collett, the second mate, and a few others who had likewise been washed up before him. A little later, the group was reunited with another, led by Evan Jones, and the truth dawned on them that just 23 had survived. The ship had broken up so quickly that most were probably drowned where they slept; many of those who had managed to reach the deck had been swept to their deaths. The fortunate ones were cut and bruised, clothes torn off or ripped to rags; some were more seriously injured, and Collett was inconsolable at the loss of his wife.

The initial reaction was simply to give rein to their shock and dismay, wondering what would become of them and where they could be. The land appeared rocky and barren, covered with guano from the thousands of raucous gannets to which it was home, but gradually they regained their self command and started to think seriously about what they could do to help themselves. A group comprising the uninjured or walking wounded went off on reconnaissance; those who stayed behind decided that if Jones, as the senior surviving officer, would lead them, they would obey. They were under no compulsion to follow orders: this was not the Royal Navy, to which a man was bound until discharge, irrespective of what happened to his ship.

The explorers returned with the news that they were on a low island, one of a small group, and that the African mainland lay, they estimated, some two leagues off. Although they did not know it at the time, the *Dodington* had been wrecked on what was then known as Chaos Island[8] in Algoa Bay (at 33° 50' S, 26° 17' E), considerably adrift of the longitude that calculation and estimation had suggested the day before. At 47 acres (19 hectares), it was the largest of four small scraps of land just 4.5 miles (8.5 kilometres) from the heights of Woody Cape visible to the north and some 33.5 miles (62 kilometres) from the site of today's Port Elizabeth. They were to call it Bird Island, the name it still bears.

The survivors gathered around Jones. Looking at their condition, Jones concluded it would be a month before the whole group was in a fit state to attempt travel. The immediate need was to get a fire going, but rubbing sticks together did not work, so they turned their attention to the wreck of the ship, which lay beyond the rocks with waves breaking over her and dragging out her innards. It was time find out what their resources might be. Their objective was to retrieve as much as possible from the wreck by way of food, fresh water and materials for shelter.

Casks, pieces of wood, and items of clothing washed about in the shallower water or lay tossed onto the rocks; small objects were caught in fissures. Seven pigs had managed to swim ashore and were wandering about looking for something to feed on. Then someone found an escritoire – a writing desk – containing gun flints and a file in its drawers, while the discovery of a cask of gunpowder, some of it still dry, enabled them to start a bonfire round which the wounded could get warm. Other fortuitous finds included a box of candles and case of brandy. Everybody had what Webb described as a dram, though he confessed to knocking back the better part of a pint without feeling the effects.

Collett organized a team to make a tent with sail canvas; Jones went hunting among the rocks and came back with salt pork from a staved-in barrel. There were other casks, but it was too late in the day to do anything about them – and besides, many of the men had consumed far too much spirit to do anything useful for a while. Jones stumbled across Swedish seaman Peter Rosenburg lying in a drunken heap among the debris with the tide beginning to wash over him.

They all spent a miserable night, a foot deep in bird droppings rendered soft and slimy by the unrelenting rain that, along with the wind, soon put out the fire.

The following day was spent in retrieving as much as they could, though many of the barrels were broken and the contents contaminated or washed out by the sea. That night they cooked a hot meal of broiled rashers of pork, but the combination of the driving rain and the pain suffered by those who had been injured made it a depressing occasion. There was nothing that could be done immediately either to relieve pain or dress gashes.

What did give them heart, however, was the fact that the survivors included Richard Topping, the ship's carpenter, and Jones voiced the thought that, if they could but find some tools, there was a good possibility that they could construct a craft from the timbers of the *Dodington*. It was their only chance.

The hope took over their lives and gave a spur to the search, not just for tools and materials but for the food that would have to keep them going until they were ready to sail. Even the omens were good. The other Swedish seaman, Hendrick Scantz, found a pair of bellows on the beach and volunteered the information that he knew something of a blacksmith's work. On the Sunday, when Webb was well enough to go out walking, he came upon two quadrants, and the group found navigation books, carpenters tools, needles for sewing sails, a Common Prayer Book – albeit in French – and a compass card.

Their next discovery was sufficiently grim to wipe out all their satisfaction: the body of Collett's wife. A glance around showed that Collett was too far away to see. Jones quickly went over to him and found some pretext for leading him away behind the rock while Webb, Powell, Topping and three of the others hastily dug a grave in the guano. Webb read the funeral service from the wet prayer book and later passed her wedding ring to Jones to give to Collett when the time came to break the news.

Then they put their energies into the boat. Most of the rocky coastline was un-navigable due to its surf, but there were a couple of small creeks where the water was calm and from which it should be possible to launch a vessel. Beside one of these inlets, now known as Stink Creek, they set up their shipyard.

For the first two weeks, work on the keel and the stern proceeded well with Topping and Chisholm, one of the quartermasters, in charge of construction. The plan was to construct a vessel with 30-foot keel and a 12-foot beam (9.1 by 3.6 metres), large enough and strong enough to take them all north-east to Delagoa Bay in Portuguese-controlled Mozambique, or back west to the Cape. Scantz produced additional tools and repaired kettles, while others of the group busied themselves making good a badly damaged ship's boat they had recovered, and burning pieces of fir from the masts and spars to prepare charcoal for the newly built forge. Henry Sharp, who had signed on as the surgeon's servant, was found to have served his apprenticeship as a comb-maker, and assured the officers that he could turn his hand to saw-making.

Food varied from gannet to pork, and there was fresh water either from the rain or from the odd cask of water. During the voyage, it was usual for sailors to trail a few hooks and lines over the side to try to catch fish, and when some of this tackle was washed up, the decision was taken to put together a catamaran so they could go out to fish. The wounded were recovering remarkably well – at some point they must have improvises splints for those, such as Webb, who had sustained broken bones – and Jones had found the moment to break to his comrade the news of his wife's death. Collett refused to believe it until at last Jones handed him the wedding ring. After that, he went to the grave, built a mound of rocks cemented with bird dung over it, and cut her name and dates into an elm plank.

The first signs of dissension broke out at the end of that fortnight when several of the men were taken sick, including Neal Bothwell and Topping. The former had been sick for much of the voyage and, according to his own account, Jones had taken a good deal of care of him. Concerned now for the health of the carpenter, Collett and Jones went to look for him and found him boiling some pork for himself in the cook's tent. Jones wished him soon better, and was met with an angry response.

'Yes,' Topping answered, 'it's for your own good that you want me well again, but I can see the way things are going here. You're happy to wait on your number three, Bothwell, but I may die and be damned before you offer me any mulled mine or anything else. I'll be damned if I'll put up with such treatment. I know what you're up to, and I won't do another stroke of work until I'm put right in the picture.'

'You've said quite enough,' Jones responded when he could get a word in.

'You'd better explain yourself, because I don't understand what you mean when you say you *can see the way things are going here*. Have you seen anything going on behind your back among the officers or anyone else?'

'No, and you'd soon know about it if I did. I'll be damned before I'll be slighted and insulted by the best of you!'

'I don't think anybody is trying to insult you, and I'm sorry you seem to have taken against me and Mr Collett so strongly just because we assisted a sick man. As soon as we heard you were ill we came to offer our sympathies. We'll gladly do what we can to get you better.' Not receiving any comment, he went on: 'I hope it's no more than a cold, so go to bed with a glass of hot wine.'

Ignoring the attempt at conciliation, Topping responded in a surly tone:

'I want a fair agreement before I do another stroke.'

Collett and Jones went out for a walk, puzzling over the unexpected confrontation. They came to the conclusion that Topping was trying to cover up his inability to build the boat, and, and he later confessed that he did have a problem with one aspect of the stern construction. It would indeed have been something of a miracle if he had not been out of his depth on several occasions: he was charged with building a sea-going sailing ship from the remains of another, with limited tools and inexperienced assistants. But in trying to guess the carpenter's motivation, the officers had not taken into account their unusual situation.

At sea, the people – to use the contemporary expression applied to the seamen and petty officers – relied on the officers for orders and leadership, but the carpenter was significant man, and that was reflected in his monthly wages, which were equal to Collett's. On the island, with all hope invested in the boat, Topping had rapidly become the most important among them, and he felt that he was not being treated with the respect, even deference, that he deserved. He went back to work, admitting afterwards that he never had been ill in the first place. The boat continued to take shape, but the traditional hierarchy was under threat. The conditions did not help: there was no shelter other than the tents they had rigged up for themselves, which were often in danger of being blown down by the strong winds. They spent days up their knees in guano, and while the rain made up for the total lack of fresh water on Bird Island, it soaked them, held up work and helped to nourish discontent. The quantity of food per day was highly variable. Early in August they killed one of the seven pigs because they had been reduced to 2 ounces (55 grams) of bread per day.

A few days later another confrontation blew up over dinner. Jones was faced by indignant complaints from two of the mattrosses (apprentice gunners) who had been helping him out on the wreck, who said that no food was being served to them, nor had even been prepared for them. The cook (it is unclear which of the named survivors this was) had told them that this was by order of Daniel Ladoux.

Early in their enforced stay, Jones had divided the men into two messes in order to make mealtimes more manageable. The officers led one mess, which included Topping, while Ladoux, by virtue of his position on the ship as the captain's steward, appears to have been in charge of the other. Ladoux had decided that what pork he and his mess-mates collected was for them alone to share, a decision in direct contravention of the rule that all food was to be shared equally.

Jones demanded an explanation of Ladoux.

'Mr Collett gave orders to the cook that that any pork he brought to the cook's tent was only to be used for his own mess. So I think I have just as much right to keep whatever I pick up. And in the future, nobody but my mess mates is going to taste a single bit of what I pick up.' He was backed up by those same mess mates in no uncertain terms.

Collett denied issuing any such orders. Jones was sure that the only orders given to the cook had been his own, but his instructions had reflected an unfortunate lack of judgement: the pork was to be shared, he had ordered, but he had added that he expected the best parts for himself. In one sense, this was hardly any different from the situation on board ship, where the officers' food was considerably superior to that of the crew; in practice, the relationship between men and officers was completely changed, as Topping had not been slow to realize. The chief mate was not making things easy for himself, and he was allowing the men to feel as if they were of no account.

Determined that for as long as his leadership was acknowledged he would exert his authority, Jones ordered that from henceforth everyone would make a point of recovering what pork remained to be found, and he appointed Collett as storekeeper with responsibility for seeing it equitably shared.

'Damn me if I pick up another piece while I'm on the island!' retorted Ladoux. 'And I'll have as good a piece as you!'

The incensed officer slapped him a couple of times across the face for his insolence, which had the effect of silencing him and quelling revolt for a short time – until a more serious matter came between officers and men.

Among the items rescued from the ship were the various packets of official letters and other documents intended for the East India Company, and personal letters to be forwarded to its expatriate employees. The three senior officers had taken these to their tent and carefully dried them out. They had also found some plate and one of the chests of silver, and had every intention of ensuring it all reached the Company. They had been open about this in front of the men they trusted, and were taken by surprise when, not long after the Ladoux incident and when they met in the tent for supper, Topping came and asked them when the money and plate was to be distributed. His informant was Bothwell, which came as something of a shock to Jones not just because he felt he had been kind to the man during his sickness on the ship, but because

Bothwell, like Collett, had been intending to settle in India and needed to stand well with the Company.

There was no point in denying his resolve.

'Neither the money nor the plate is to be shared, but instead it will be delivered to the proper authorities when we reach India.'

'And what about those careening blocks you've been taking so much trouble over?'

'Those blocks are highly important to the Navy, and that makes them important to the East India Company in which I am a serving officer. Therefore, as an officer, it is my solemn duty to take care of anything that might be important to the Company, especially whatever it is possible for us to take with us. If anyone even attempts to stop those careening blocks going into the ship I will consider him from now on to be a traitor to his country and unfit to be employed by the East India Company.'

'Damn the King's ships and damn the King's blocks,' snarled Chisholm. The quartermaster was closest to Topping, and was supported by his messmates. 'What do we care about either? Do you think we're building this boat to transport the King's cargo off this island? Them blocks aren't going in that boat, and nor's the money until it's been split between us.' He gave his commander a contemptuous look and added sarcastically: 'You really are an honest man, the way you're insisting the plate won't be shared. It's pretty clear you and Collett just want it for yourselves. Well, since we're all equal now, nothing leaves this island unless it's for all of us.'

Topping had been trying to insert himself into the speech, demanding that the officers give him the respect he deserved and affirming that nothing was going to be embarked on the new vessel without his authority. Concerned at the direction matters were taking, Jones asked them to listen to him, which, between interruptions from the leaders, they did, and he softened his tone slightly.

'Despite what the carpenter says about nothing going in without his agreement, I presume I will be the one in charge of stowing the hold. If I can put the six careening blocks in without inconvenience to anyone – and inconvenience is the last thing I want – I hope none of you will object. But as for sharing out the money, I urge you to think better of it because you would be putting your necks into the hangman's noose.'

Seaman John King and Chisholm were both unimpressed. One of them answered roughly: 'We know the laws of our country just as well as you do, and we're willing to take the risk.' Jones said nothing more, only hoping they would realize the consequences of what they were proposing as time went on .

It had been a trying month. Webb and Jones were both keeping a diary, much as they would have kept a ship's log: noting down the weather and what was done each day, perfectly well aware that those of the crew who could read were scrutinizing it for anything that might later be held against them. The crew did not know, because Jones always kept the papers on him, that the chief mate was also keeping a private account, aware that if it were ever found the consequences for himself might well be grave.

Food was running short, but sitting on rocks and using the pin-hooks and lines they had managed to catch fish, and now they had their first catamaran. They could only go out on it when the sea was calm, which was not every day, but when they did they managed to catch larger fish. On 18 August, pleased with the 14 big specimens brought back, they decided to put together a second catamaran. The following day, despite stronger winds, they sent both fishing vessels out in shifts and were delighted with the day's haul, but at four o'clock, just as Collett and Midshipman Yates weighed anchor to come in with their catch, the wind veered and they were being driven out. Not sure how best to help them, two men went out on the larger craft, but it overturned several times and forced them to swim back. At that moment, Topping sent a message that if they gave him 15 minutes he could get the ship's boat sufficiently watertight for one man to bale. The rescue mission was successful, and, significantly, Topping had acted to save two of the officers.

On 20 August they saw smoke on the mainland.

When the wind was too stiff for sea-fishing, they subsisted on gannets or, as a last resort, killed a hog; on calmer days they continued to bring back supplies from the ship and materials for the vessel that was taking shape. Some turned their hands to making salt, knowing they would have to preserve some meat to provision their ship when they finally went to sea, but their efforts had so far resulted in a metallic-tasting substance that only made people ill. At the end of the month Collett took a couple of men out with him in an expedition to the mainland, but when the weather turned against them he had to abort the journey in order to get home before the surf came up.

The relative peace of the time was disturbed by another outbreak from the carpenter, who had been working steadily on the boat. Jones had gone out on the catamaran, taking with him the ship's boy, Gilbert Chain, in search of any more of the treasure. Chain's usual job was to assist Topping, but on that occasion he had nothing for him to do so the officer did not think it would hold up the work to take him. When Topping found out the purpose of the trip, he vented his anger on Collett.

'He'd be better off spending his time fishing than looking for treasure that'll be no use to anyone here if *he* gets his way. And if I'd been there when that boat went out, Chain wouldn't have been in it ... '

'Mr Jones has the right to take anybody he pleases,' interrupted Collett. 'And anyway, it is his duty to look for that treasure.'

Chisholm was there to back up the carpenter.

'Well, he can save himself the trouble of looking for it. And if I thought that what he'd got already wasn't going to be shared out, I'd carry it on my own back and throw it over the rocks, and that'd be the last you saw of it!'

That treasure remained a bone of serious contention, but before things came to something of a head, another incident took place. On Wednesday 3 September, Bothwell, Rosenburg and Johanes Taylor took the boat out to go across to the mainland, hoping to succeed where Collett had failed. While they were gone four of their comrades went out on the catamaran and succeeded in killing three large sharks and a dog-fish. Meanwhile, on land, Topping cut his leg with an adze and had difficulty in stemming the bleeding. The following day there was still no sign of the ship's boat, but given the gales no one was surprised, and assumed they would stay on the mainland until the wind abated. During the night the larger catamaran broke adrift and was lost.

Friday was spent building a bigger craft, and they fully expected Bothwell's party to return; by Saturday afternoon everyone was anxious. Just as they were about to go into the tent for dinner two of the group came leaping over the rocks shouting that they could see the boat.

Something had obviously gone wrong. Only Taylor and Rosenburg returned, and they were exhausted with heat, hunger and dehydration. A little food was prepared for them, but they were in no state to answer any questions, and none was asked. Only after a good sleep were they recovered enough to tell their comrades what had happened.

They had found the shoreline of the mainland covered with a rough surf, and it took some time to find a place where they thought they could get through, but the boat capsized in the attempt, they lost almost all their provisions, and Bothwell was drowned. They looked for the boat, but by the time they found it they were too weak to drag it up the sand. They had intended to overturn it as a shelter for the night, but ended up having to sleep under a tree. At dawn they went to find the boat, but the surf had been at work and driven it further away. While going after it they spotted a man, but he fled into the woods that came down to the beach, and they made a grisly discovery: Bothwell's body, not just drowned but torn apart by some animal.

Terrified, they got into the boat and would have made for the island at once if they could have got through the surf. In the end, they gave up, dragged it above the high water mark and turned it over, huddling underneath for safety. During the night they were aware of animals around them, which Webb assumed were jackals but which they feared were tigers.[9]

They had another fright in the morning when, from inside the boat, they saw a man's feet in the sand. Emerging from their hiding place, they were beaten and robbed of most of their clothes, but the amaXhosa men afterwards gave them some roots to eat and heeded their pleas not to destroy the boat for the sake of the iron. The following day, the two sailors succeeded in getting the boat out through the surf and reaching the island.

Later, those articles of clothing would be shown to a colonist farmer, Petrus Ferreira, and his friend while they were out elephant hunting. The news that the amaXhosa had met two white men interested him because he had also seen a fire on the island, and the smoke that the *Dodington* people had seen on 20 August was his response. Enquires were set in train by the authorities in Cape Town but nobody actually took a ship out to Bird Island. Only later was the connection with the *Dodington* made.

That Saturday, 6 September, was also remarkable for a 75 per cent solar eclipse during the morning, and it was also the prelude to a few days of high winds that kept the fishermen at home and forced everyone back to a diet of gannets, which Webb wryly called 'penguin broth'.[10] Inevitably it turned fair again, and for three weeks all was well.

The theft was discovered on 28 September when the Swedish smith, curious to know how much the treasure chest weighed, lifted the box and was amazed at how light it was. He was equally surprised to find it had a hole in the bottom.

Jones had no doubt who was behind the theft, no matter how much feigned innocence and indignation was paraded in front of him when the men came to report it to him. Together with Collett and Webb, he secured the remaining 1600 dollars[11] in the store tent and then devised an oath for each man, including themselves, to swear on the Bible. A few of the men were willing to take it, but a significant number refused to do so unless Topping preceded them – which he refused to do. When the others agreed to a cooling-off period of one week, he, Chisholm and Powell sat in silence. Jones begged those who were secreting it to return the silver, trying to make them understand that if they persisted in keeping it they would ultimately be hanged. As an officer, Powell, the ship's fifth mate, might have been expected to stand by his fellow officers, but he had thrown in his lot with the men.

Little work was done the following day, a Monday. The men met together, and the officers suspected that they were planning to elect a new leader, either Chisholm or Powell, both of whom had told Jones to his face that they were competent to navigate. Next day, before getting extremely drunk – so Jones was told by Ralph Smith – the men swore on the Bible to be loyal to one another and to share out the silver. It was turning into a bad week, with the lines clearly drawn between the men and the officers' group. The latter, which comprised the three mates, Yates and the captain's servant, McDugall, decided their wisest course was to try to ignore what was happening. When Jones looked in at the carpenter's tent, Topping met him at the opening and all but head-butted him.

The week passed without the return of the silver. The following Sunday, after a quarrel between Powell and King over a sporting gun that had been recovered, the question of taking the oath was revived.

'I have heard nothing about the money taken from the chest,' the chief mate told the men. 'Will you now follow my example and take the oath?'

'You need nae trouble yourself about it,' replied John Glass, one of the few Scots among them. 'Those that have it will take care of it.'

Jones questioned several of them individually, without success, and then turned to the other matter.

'Do you intend to obey my orders? If you don't, I strongly recommend you appoint someone else to take responsibility for the materials. The sails and rigging are just lying out there, rotting.'

King proposed that Topping should command them, but, though flattered, the carpenter declined. Seaman Robert Beazly spoke in favour of Jones continuing as leader.

'Hold your tongue!' said King. 'I won't obey him unless he agrees to discuss everything with us.'

'I'm not having that.' Jones was adamant. 'If one of you is capable, choose him, and I can wash my hands of the whole business.'

That brought a grudging agreement to keep him as their leader, but with the continued demand from King that, since everyone was now on an equal footing, they had a right to be consulted. Jones left the supper tent thinking that if it had been possible to escape the island without their help he would have done it. Never, he promised himself, would he 'consult with such a parcel of lubbers'.

At the same time as the *Dodington* survivors were perilously close to losing cohesion, the other four ships were watering at St Augustine's Bay, having safely rounded the Cape, entered the Inner Passage and avoided the lethal reefs of south-west Madagascar. The *Houghton*'s log shows the infinite care taken over the navigation. On 25 September they sailed on, the *Houghton* resolving to keep company with the *Edgecote* unless the latter proved too slow. All four ships arrived safely in India, the *Streatham* – with Robert Clive onboard – anchoring at Bombay on 7 November. From the middle of October, after a temporary shortage of food, they were unexpectedly relieved by a new and abundant source. The gannets returned in their thousands for the nesting season, and within a month eggs had become a staple. Webb recorded in meticulous detail the volume of eggs taken each day, which could be up to several firkins.[12] The men became inventive, careful when they scared the birds into the air so that there would always be a reasonable harvest, and then discovering that if they scared the gulls after they had been feeding, the birds would vomit up the contents of their stomachs. This half-digested material, much of it cuttlefish, then became a foolproof bait for the fishermen. The men sometimes crossed to one of the smaller islands in the little archipelago to collect more eggs, naming it Egg Island to go with their own home of Bird Island.

For all the delays, nobody had really lost sight of the main objective, and the boat had continued to take shape. The planking was being cut, the smith made nails, and others attempted to build an oven in which they could bake bread for the voyage. The pork and water in casks was to be reserved for the journey and only broached if the need for water became serious. Fortunately, whenever water supplies ran low the rain came either just in time or in sufficient quantities to refill the casks and give them something for the immediate future.

Relations remained strained, but much less so, and on one occasion Collett went into the carpenter's tent, something none of the officers might earlier have risked. He found Topping and Chisholm drinking watered-down brandy, and was taken aback when they asked him to come and join them. He raised his cup.

'Success to our undertaking,' he offered by way of an unexceptional toast.

'With all my heart!' responded Topping, and they drank together. 'And I am glad that all of us who reached the shore are still alive.'

Not quite understanding what he meant by that, Collett agreed.

'We've been lucky that the climate is so healthy,' he said, 'or some of us would be dead, given the disgusting food we've had to eat on and off.'

'Yes, the air is good, but, putting that aside, you can thank God that you're alive because it's not so long ago that there were plans afoot to kill you and Mr. Jones and the other three.' Collett listened in stunned shock as Topping told him more. 'They only wanted one more to say *yes* and it would have happened, and that was John King. *Over my dead body*, he said. He only told me about it two days ago. Do me a favour, Mr Collett, and don't let on to anyone, and I'll tell you more about it later when we're somewhere else.'

Collett never found him in such a friendly and confiding mood again, so he never did learn who the plotters were.

Although the men had sworn an oath to share out the silver, despite being warned what would happen to them, they refused to accede to the call of one of the mattrosses, Lister, to burn the HEIC's post. Lister feared that the officers might have put their own letters in with the rest of the correspondence – letters that could be used against them. The others, however, were even more afraid that if they encountered one of the company's packet ships, the captain would hang them over it. They may have entertained all kinds of ambitions, they may have swaggered, boasted and threatened, but most of it was bluster: at heart, they were not bad men, and in their position the temptation of the silver must have seemed irresistible. On the day that the ship had gone to pieces, their wages ceased. They had a right to feel aggrieved that the company should get all of its money while they were as good as given the sack while still thousands of miles from home. Now they had a chance to be rich, and all that stood in their way were three officers, men from more privileged backgrounds and far less likely to suffer financially than themselves.

If the officers could be brought into the plot, all would be well, but they staunchly refused to be so and maintained that the money must go to its owners. They were either men of unimpeachable integrity, or else staunchly loyal to their employer. A cynic might say that it was not in their interests to get involved. The East India Company officers chose their careers in order to make their fortunes, and they had plenty of opportunity to do that without putting a rope round their necks. No young man with his eye on the quarterdeck joined the HEIC for the basic wages; he became its *servant* for the opportunities it offered for private trade in a highly regulated market. As in the Compagnie des Indes, a certain amount of space was reserved in the hold for the officers to take out a private cargo to sell to the expatriate population, and then to make a second investment in Indian goods for sale back in London. In fact, there was hardly a man aboard the ship who would not have indulged in private trade according to his means, and the HEIC was known to complain bitterly at the degree to which its marine officers took advantage of it. A life outside the law, exiled from friends and family and in the shadow of the noose, was not an attractive alternative for men with the potential to make a fortune legally.

This apparent incorruptibility among the three leaders and their adherents easily accounts for the plot to kill them, and it left the potential mutineers with the same problem as the crewmen who commandeered the *Prince*'s boat: they needed an officer who could navigate. They were not convinced by the assertions of Powell, a very junior officer, or Chisholm, that they could do it. There was no point in murdering their officers, even if they had the stomach for it, and then foundering at sea in a gale or wrecking themselves one night on a shoal. They must have been bitterly frustrated.

That being the case, it was hardly surprising that small pockets of trouble erupted, particularly as the time crept towards New Year and the prospect of launching the vessel concentrated their minds; but as soon as they flared up they seemed to blow over. King, the man who had apparently saved Collett's life, soon accused him of stealing from the men, calling him the greatest thief ashore. Collett hit him, and at the time McDugall ran from the tent to fetch the chief mate, it looked as though a fight was about to break out. But when Jones arrived, he found the tent empty, and no sign of a scuffle.

The shipwrights were progressing well. The hull was all but finished, and while some of the men shredded rope to make oakum, the smith made a caulking iron. A party had been detailed to start clearing a channel so that the launch, when it came, could be hazard-free. The rudder was soon in preparation. Pumps were fitted and, on shore, the *Dodington*'s canvas was being turned into new sails. By New Year, the caulking was underway: the seams were plugged with oakum before the gap was tarred with hot pitch. Topping did the job alone: a lot depended on it, and not until nearly the end of January was it complete. By filling the hull with water, its watertightness was confirmed.

The final island quarrels sprang up at around that time. One of the crew came to Jones complaining that he had caught Powell with a bottle of brandy that he knew had come out of what they called the sea-stock – the provisions for the now-imminent voyage. Jones asked for an explanation and Powell flew into a rage, denying that he had ever touched a drop of it. Those of the crew who stood by the accusation were prevented by King from speaking, and Powell appeared mortally offended by it.

'You're more likely to have done it than me,' he said to Jones. 'I remember one day when everyone but you and Mr Webb had gone off to collect eggs: you two drank two-thirds of a bottle. I found it under Mr. Webb's hammock a little while ago.'

Astounded by the unfounded accusation Jones hit him. Powell hit back, grabbed hold of his officer and went down underneath him. By the time Topping came on the scene the two had parted, which was perhaps as well. The trouble was far from over, however. Lister, the artilleryman who had become a major troublemaker, turned on Jones, demanding why he presumed to give orders that he and the other gunners should inform on any attempts to take the rest of the treasure.

'You ought to remember that I'm your officer,' Lister asserted, exaggerating his position as a low-ranking army recruit, 'because I'm in the King's service and you're only in the merchant marine.'

Jones thought it beneath his dignity to reply, but as Lister grew rapidly more abusive, he lost his temper.

'Listen, you villain: either you stop your foul language or I'll knock you down with the first thing I put my hand on!'

The response was a contemptuous laugh.

'You're the biggest rogue round here, and I wish you would hit me. There's nothing I'd like more!'

For answer, Jones attacked him. Lister got the first punch in, and before his adversary could reply, Collett and the others had intervened to part them. Chisholm came into the tent demanding to know why the officers were throwing their weight around when nobody wanted their authority.

'I know what to do with that boat once it's afloat,' he informed Jones. 'And if you're looking for an excuse to fight I'll give you one now.'

'Keep your fight, Chisholm, but if you're brave enough to take one of the guns, I'll meet you with the other.'

Chisholm refused, and so, initially, did Topping, who took the challenge to apply to him, too, but after a moment's thought he said he would do it after all, and went out of the tent followed by Jones. Outside in the warm summer air he began to strip off.

'What are you for?' Topping demanded. 'Stick or fist? You see, I'm not scared for my skin.'

Without answering him, the mate returned to the tent, and Topping pursued him demanding to know whether a duel with firearms was the proper way to test a man.

'No' said Chisholm, 'a good stick or fists is the way.' The incident ended without further violence, but the men told the officers they wanted nothing more from them, and went on building the boat, taking their revenge by keeping the officer's group short of cooking pots.

Then events took a more sinister turn. It began with irritations, such as Chisholm and Topping having the careening blocks burnt in the fire they were using to melt the iron out of pieces of the wreck, but it soon became clear that Powell had assumed command. On 11 or 12 February he told Collett that none of the officer group was to be allowed to sail. It was not entirely unexpected news, even though the announcement was made in a fit of anger over an incident involving an empty brandy keg. The officers had anticipated it ever since the last dispute. Wisely, Jones chose not to inflame the situation and left the men to their own devices.

The boat was all but finished. The rudder had been hung on Monday 9 February, and on the following Thursday Topping made the mast, bowsprit, and crossjack yard. For several days, iron ballast was being transferred from the broken hull of the *Dodington* into the bottom of the new vessel.

Two days after Powell's decree, a deputation came to Jones, asking again whether it was right for things to be shared out among them all.

'Have you just come here to torment me?' he said bitterly, 'Don't you think you're punishing us enough by leaving us here on the island?'

'We're not doing anything of the sort,' came the unexpected and indignant answer. 'Don't take any notice of what Powell says: it means nothing. Forget what's happened, please, and take over again.'

Heartily relieved, Jones agreed.

'I've no objection to you sharing out the stuff that doesn't have any obvious owner,' he said, trying to make them see sense now that they were being reasonable, 'but as far as the plate and the treasure goes, I *cannot* agree to share it out. I hope you'll return what was taken from the chest and let things be done as they should be. If you do, I promise you that everything that's happened will be completely and utterly buried in oblivion.'

They said nothing, only went away to the carpenter's tent for a conference. When they returned, it was to say that they had decided to go ahead and share everything, and what did the officers want done with their portion? After some thought, the smaller group decided to accept their shares so that at least something would get back to the HEIC. The stolen money, which had been the focus of so much ill-feeling throughout their stay, had already been secreted in the hold of the boat. During the loading, however, it was spotted by one of those not in the conspiracy. Thwarted, the others removed it before the officers could get their hands on it and, when the moment came, shared it out with the rest of the silver in the chest. Once the money had been divided, the other goods were auctioned off. An uneasy truce prevailed.

Two days later, on Monday 16 February, they launched the vessel into the water, set up the mast and, after loading some more ballast and water, named her the *Happy Deliverance*. Under the expert if ill-tempered midwifery of Topping and his men, the *Dodington* had given posthumous birth to a squat little travesty of herself: broad in the beam, sloop rigged and drawing 5 feet (1.5 metres) of water. She had a hold – and so by definition a deck above – some sort of galley, and it was probable that the off-duty men went below deck to sleep.

The night was spent loading the *Happy Deliverance*, and at the first high tide on Tuesday they hauled her down the channel using grapnels – they were lucky not to damage the ship on the rocks when one of these lost its purchase. Topping blamed Jones, but offered no alternative when asked how he would have averted the mishap. The outburst was the understandable reaction of a man who had just put six months of his life into building a vessel on which all their lives would depend, and who did not seem to have received the congratulation from his superiors that he – and Scantz, too – deserved. It had been a team-effort: those who went down to the wreck to scavenge materials and those who gathered food were vital, but nobody else could have designed and built a seaworthy ship from scratch.

They could finally say farewell to their Bird Island, Egg Island and, the third of the group, Seal Island. Two of those names would find their way into the sea charts and be officially accepted. Egg Island, however, eventually became Stag Island, somewhat inappropriately in terms of its fauna but in honour of HMS *Stag*, which surveyed the archipelago in 1814.

Jones's plan now was basically to head east and then turn north up the Mozambique Channel to make the St Lucia River some 120 miles (220 kilometres) north of modern Durban. From there it should be an easy run up to Delagoa (now Maputo) Bay, some 145 miles (270 kilometres) further up the coast, in Mozambique, where they might expect to find European ships. Unfortunately, they were to find the season was against them, with strong north-easterly currents that set at 2 knots, and variable winds at the tail end of the north-east monsoon.

By 25 February Jones believed they should be more than half-way to the St Lucia River, which was good news as they had already eaten more than half of their rations. However, by dead-reckoning, which took into account the currents and plotted the courses steered and distance run since the last position, he worked out they could only have made 30 leagues (167 kilometres) progress up the coast, putting them a little to the south of modern East London.

Jones's entry for Tuesday 2 March encapsulates their problems.[13]

> The first part fresh gales and squalls, middle calm, latter a fresh breeze. At 5 pm hauled in for an opening which made like a harbour but did not prove so. As we came near the land, met with a large, confused sea which is occasioned by a strong current, for when we were running 4 knots to the eastward (as we thought) we found we drove to the westward by the land at least a knot. As soon as we discovered our mistake, hauled off the ESE in hope to run out of the current, but by my observation find it continues … it made me propose to the people to stand to the southward, but they would not agree to it on any terms, having no wood on board and very little provisions … As have nothing to live on but an ounce and a half of salt pork a day, I proposed putting back to the island to get wood and proceed for the Cape. Accordingly it was agreed and at noon we bore away, latitude observed 33° 03′ South.

They were off East London when they made that decision to turn back and head for the Cape of Good Hope. Less than two days later they met filthy weather from the west, and when they shipped a large sea that nearly swept the watch overboard, Jones recommended they give up the attempt and once more go north-eastwards. They duly bore away to the east, fighting the worst gale in Jones's memory, scudding with just the topsail set. Scudding has its own danger: that of been 'pooped' by a large wave catching the ship up and breaking over the stern. Webb admitted to being scared when 'the squalls were sometimes so violent, that the sea appeared like cliffs under the stern'.

In the early hours of Friday 5 March the gales gave way to fine weather, and on the following Sunday they anchored offshore and sent the captain's African servant, Thomas Arnold, ashore to establish friendly relations.

The surf made it impossible for the *Happy Deliverance* to anchor until they had crept some 4 or 5 miles up the coast into a small bay in Latitude 32° 57′ S, where they took off Arnold and heard his favourable report: after initial suspicion had been overcome, the local amaXhosa were friendly. At once several of the crew insisted on going ashore and coming back with some wood, but no food seems to have been obtained, and the ship resumed her northward progress, unable to land anywhere. The fish refused to bite, and they were down to what Webb feelingly described as 'half an ounce of stinking rotten pork per man per day'.

In fact, not everyone was getting that; the implication is that instead of sharing and rationing the food equally, some had consumed their meagre supply more quickly than others. On Sunday 14 March two of the men who had not eaten for two days (neither account identifies them) begged to be put ashore to take their chance with the local people. They were taken out in the boat, and were lucky not to lose an oar or worse when, as they were getting out,

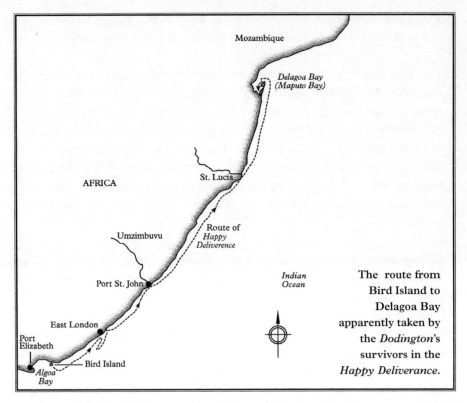

Mozambique

Delagoa Bay
(Maputo Bay)

AFRICA

St. Lucia

Umzimbuvu

Route of
Happy
Deliverence

Indian
Ocean

The route from
Bird Island to
Delagoa Bay
apparently taken by
the *Dodington*'s
survivors in the
Happy Deliverance.

Port St. John

East London

Port
Elizabeth

Algoa
Bay

Bird Island

a shark suddenly grabbed at the blade. The *Happy Deliverance* went a little further up the coast and in the morning they anchored in 5 fathoms (9 metres) and got the small boat out. Four men went ashore to sound out the mouth of the river and look for the other two. The message got back to the ship that the amaXhosa were friendly and willing to sell food.

Exactly where they were at this point is unclear, but very possible in the estuary of the Mzimvubu River, at latitude 31° 37' S, some 215 miles (400 kilometres) around the coast north-east of their starting point on Bird Island, though they had covered far more than that distance to get there.

They had little enough to trade with: brass, buttons, nails and copper hoops made into bangles. Language could have been a problem, but their powers of imitation were good: they held their hands to their heads like horns and made moo-ing and baa-ing noises. Soon their hosts were driving down two bullocks, which they were happy to sell for four buttons and a pound of copper. Milk and wheat came cheaply, and for two weeks the officers and crew spent much of their time ashore, sometimes sleeping on land, visiting the local towns and villages. The two cultures got on well, fascinated by their different ways of preparing food, even if the local taste for raw entrails with the excrement shaken out did not appeal to the visitors. The native tribe, possibly Mpondo, enjoyed visiting the *Happy Deliverance* or going upriver in the small boat; the *Dodington* group admired their hosts' skill with the lance, and undertook to guard their wives and daughters while the menfolk were off in the woods. Webb, who found them very good-natured, described them in some detail:

> They wear little or no clothing in the day time and in the night only a bullock's hide which they dry thoroughly, and make them very supple. Their chief orna- ments are a piece of bullock's tail which hangs dangling down from their rump to their heels with a few small sea shells tied to it. They also wear small pieces of skin tied round their knees, ankles and arms. Their hair they plaster up with a great quantity of tallow or fat, mixed up with a kind of red earth and they rub their bodies all over with grease. They are prodigious active and dextrous with their lances; we often saw them throw a lance thirty or forty yards and hit a small head of corn …

They also had a servant, an obviously European youth with fair hair and very light skin. After a while he was kept out of sight, presumably in case any move was made to take him to the ship.

The survivors had stayed longer than the officers intended simply because the men refused to leave when the idea was first proposed. They obviously felt that their trade was going well, because when Jones wanted to buy an elephant tooth, Chisholm tried to prevent him on the grounds that he would spoil the market. Whether this was because the locals would realize from Jones's ability to pay for the tooth in iron that the visitors were wealthier than they made out is unclear, but Jones did make the purchase, for about 4 pounds of iron, and when he was in the tent they had set up on shore he overheard Chisholm complaining about it to the others. He might have been wiser to let the matter rest, but he emerged into the open and took the quartermaster to task.

Initially disconcerted, Chisholm soon recovered himself.

'Shall we settle it with a good stick, then?' he demanded. It was not what the Welsh officer had in mind, but he agreed to it.

'Alright, then: find a couple a decent sticks and I'll go a couple of rounds with you, even if I do come off worst.'

Chisholm went off, returned with a suitable length and threw it to Jones, then disappeared in search of a second, only to come back empty handed, perhaps deliberately.

'I don't wish you any harm, Mr. Jones,' he said. 'In fact, I'll always wish you well, and,' he added handsomely, 'I'd as soon sail again with you as with any other man.'

Well provided with food, they left on Monday 29 March, and after some concerns about the weather anchored in a river south of the St Lucia on 6 April. They found the Nguni people there civil enough and keen to trade, but less openly friendly: 'a haughty, proud sort of people' according to Jones, and remarkable to him because they were 'very cleanly in their bodies; for the first thing they do in the morning is to wash themselves all over'. Such attention to personal hygiene would not have occurred to the mid-eighteenth century British.

Here they stayed until 18 April, when a strong westerly wind and weather offered a favourable departure. Suddenly, as they approached the bar, nine of the crew hauled down the sail and threw out the grapnel that acted as their anchor, bringing the vessel to a halt. They got into the boat telling the rest that they were scared to go over the bar and that the ship would go to pieces in the rough water.

Whether there was any truth in their explanation – they had, after all, already survived rough weather over a greater distance than they would now have to cover – or whether they feared that they faced death at Delagoa Bay for their seizure of the treasure, is a matter for conjecture. Jones and Webb seemed to think that they would follow the *Happy Deliverance* up the coast on shore, as implied by the fact that those leaving the ship did not attempt to take their share of the treasure. Those who remained on the sloop besides the officers probably included Yates, McDugall and Chisholm, certainly Topping, and possibly Powell.

Leaving the nine men to make their way by land, the *Happy Deliverance* continued to Delagoa Bay, and at 4:00 p.m. on Tuesday 20 April, having survived the perilous shoals and breakers in and around the bay, the remaining survivors of the *Dodington* dropped anchor in the river close to the HEIC's Bombay-based brig *Rose*, whose captain, Edward Chandler,[14] was up-river trading for beef and ivory. Jones sent him a message, and eventually contact was established. Most of the *Dodington*'s people asked for a passage to Bombay when he was ready to leave. Three weeks into their sojourn at Delagoa, during which they remained on the *Happy Deliverance*, moored next to the *Rose*, a small local trading vessel brought them three of the nine who had stayed behind at St Lucia. The others, they said, were on the other side of the bay, waiting for a boat to bring them over.

Collett, Webb and Jones took hasty council together. If the valuable cargo was to get to their masters in India, this was their chance, while the sloop was still under-manned. They found an excuse to send four or five of their men onshore, had two more temporarily locked up on the *Rose* and then, with the help of an armed party from the brig, Jones went back on board the *Happy Deliverance* and took off the Company's money, plate and letters. Amazingly, they recovered everything that had been stolen on the island.

That night, those left on board the *Happy Deliverance*, including Topping, Chisholm and Powell, set sail and slipped away. Webb felt it was to foil another 'unwelcome visit', but it was more than that, for they did go to find their six comrades on the other side of the bay. Three, however, were so ill that they died soon after getting on board, and two more were at death's door. They had planned to go to Anjouan, a sailor's paradise in the Comoros Islands where they could rest, eat well, and enjoy the local company before finding a ship sailing on to India or back to the Cape. But all the doubts about Chisholm and Powell's navigational skills proved well founded, and when they spotted the *Rose* leaving the bay they bore down to her. Topping came on board and negotiated with Captain Chandler to buy the *Happy Deliverance* for 500 rupees. The two vessels then sailed in company for Morondava, a known watering place on the coast of Madagascar. John Collett, Gilbert Chain, Henry Sharp and Lister all died of fever on board the *Rose* before reaching Morondava.

On 14 June, two days after their arrival, they met the HEIC's *Carnarvon* under Captain Norton Hutchinson, a former commander of the *Dodington*, who agreed to give the survivors passage to Madras.[15] The valuables and personal effects were transferred into the big Indiaman.

The fact that the *Happy Deliverance* was good enough to sell speaks volumes for the skill and enterprise of the ordinary seamen in the age of sail. Pierre de Lafond's men likewise managed to make important changes to their boat with very limited means. Topping had, unfortunately, made too good a job of her: when she arrived at Bombay with the *Rose* (probably manned by some of the latter's crew), the HEIC seized her. After all, she had been built from materials that, while not exactly company property, belonged to a ship that they had paid handsomely to charter. With the advent of steamships and iron hulls, however, the ability to improvise the means of survival rapidly diminished.

The *Carnarvon* arrived at Madras on 1 August and, as Webb simply put it: 'we delivered the packets, treasures and other private effects'. It was an outstanding display of honesty and devotion to duty by the officers, and despite all that had gone on, Evan Jones did not publish his damning report, entitled *The Behaviour of the People on Bird Island*, though he did tell the HEIC that, but for King's refusal to be party to murder, the officers would have been killed and the treasure stolen. He must have told Hutchinson sufficient to make him determined to take Powell to Madras. Powell certainly believed so and, afraid for his life, absconded on Madagascar before the Indiaman sailed.

Why did Jones not publish the full truth? On the surface of it, he and the ship's owners may simply not have wished to spoil the impression of harmony and cooperation that the 'official' narratives, by him and Webb, gave to the world. There are two other possible reasons. The first may be that in retrospect he felt that he had not handled things as well as he might in the role of leader, and that the private account did not show him in the best light. But that is probably doing him a grave injustice. When all was said and done, the boat had been built, and built well, and they had been able to get off the island and weather some savage conditions. He owed his life to those same truculent crew members, and it would have been ungenerous to publish the truth, especially as the silver had reached the company in the end. It was enough that they had been through such an adventure.[16] The manuscript only saw the light of day at the end of the nineteenth century when it was found among some old family papers by Sir Richard Carnac Temple, a descendent of the Debonnaire family, which had been a major shareholder in the *Dodington*.

The remains of the *Dodington* were discovered on Bird Island in 1977 by Gerry Van Niekerk and David Allen. The team carried out legal salvage and archaeology for some twenty years and many of their finds can be seen in Port Elizabeth Museum. But one thing they never found was Clive's personal treasure. During that period the South African government woke up to the need to introduce, and then strengthen, legislation to protect the many historic wrecks around their coast from less scrupulous salvors. In 1986 it became an offence to interfere with or disturb a shipwreck or shipwreck material more than 50 years old unless a permit had been obtained. For this purpose South African waters were defined as extending 24 miles (44.4 kilometres) from shore.

In 1997 it was announced that a hoard of 1400 eighteenth-century gold coins, part of Clive's consignment, had been discovered and was to be sold in London. It had allegedly been found in the wreck of a privateer or pirate ship that had been found by sheer chance off the eastern coast of South Africa. Its undisclosed position was conveniently located in international waters.

The whole story appeared highly suspicious, if not totally implausible, to South Africa's National Monuments Council, particularly in view of the complete secrecy surrounding the name and operations of the salvors, and the documentary evidence that Clive's treasure had been stowed aboard the *Dodington*.

The sale was stopped and the auctioneers, Spink and Sons, refused to return the coins to the dealer acting for the unnamed vendors pending legal proceedings. In 2001, a third of the coins, worth £1 million, were handed over to the South African government.

Robert Clive may have lost a fortune, but by embarking on another ship he probably saved his life, and arrived in India in time to set in train the military conquest that laid the foundations of the British Indian Empire.

Sources and Bibliography

Thanks are due to Ms Yvonne Baker of the South African High Commission, London, for identifying the African tribes referred to in the sources accounts.

British Library
IOR/L/MAR/B/619E – wage book, *Dodington*
IOR/L/MAR/B/438H – log of the *Houghton*
IOR/L/MAR/B/605-I – log of the *Streatham*

Allen, David and Allen, Geoffrey, *Clive's Lost Treasure* (London: Robin Garton, 1978).
Gribble, John, *The Dodington Gold Coins*, World Archaeological Congress 4 (Cape Town: University of Cape Town, 1999).
Jones, Evan, *The Wreck of the Doddington, 1755*, preface by R C Temple, (Bombay: Education Society's Steam Press, 1902; this contains the two accounts by Jones).

South African Museum, *Museum News* 10/6–7 (June/July 2006)

Ward, Vincent, and Underhill, Les, *Seabird Sites of South Africa: Bird Island, Lambert's Bay*, http://web.uct.ac.za/depts/stats/adu/birdilam.htm

Webb, William: *A Journal of the Proceedings of the* Doddington, *East Indiaman, from her Sailing from the Downs Till She was Unfortunately Wrecked* ... (in Plaisted, B. *A Journal from Calcutta ... to Busserah, etc.* London: 1758).

The Independent, 18 February 2001

www.divernet.com

Notes

[1] Cabinet Minutes, 10 April 1755.

[2] After returning from India in 1753, Clive had been elected as an MP, but the election was disputed, and it was while the matter was being resolved that he first received the offer from the HEIC. He lost the seat in March 1755.

[3] Even when the chronometer became available mistakes could easily be made by vessels steering for the inner passage, since charts of the area continued to be inaccurate for some time, and the strong currents of the Mozambique Channel continued to confound calculations of distance covered.

[4] It was a problem that, in the 1790s, would occupy the mind of the East India Company's hydrographer, Alexander Dalrymple. At the time of the *Dodington*'s sailing, the finest hydrographer charting the route to the Indies was Jean Baptiste d'Après de Mannevillette, author of the *Neptune Oriental* (a book of charts first published in 1745), who in the 1750s was a serving captain in the Compagnie des Indes at the same time as Dalrymple was part of the HEIC's Indian bureaucracy . The two men went on to become friends and, until the Frenchman's death in 1780, they shared their knowledge. Dalrymple became hydrographer to the HEIC in 1779 and in 1795 he was appointed hydrographer to the Royal Navy. By that time, the chronometer was becoming more widely available, and as new, more accurate charts were produced, ships had a higher chance of navigating safely to their destinations.

[5] In contemporary usage the left side of a ship was referred to as the 'larboard'; since it could easily be confused with 'starboard', the term 'port' arose in the sixteenth century, but was not officially adopted in naval parlance until the mid-nineteenth century. Nevertheless, I have chosen to use 'port' throughout this book as the universally familiar term.

[6] A league is equal to 3 nautical miles, or 5.55 kilometres, so 90 leagues would equal 270 miles, or 500 kilometres.

[7] If Jones, who later recorded his captain's last remark, knew which ship called the *Dolphin* Samson was referring to, it is difficult to determine today.

[8] Nautical charts of the Bay show a 'Doddington Rock' south-west of the island. This was erroneously supposed to be the site of the wreck, but the vessel was lost on the rocks around the island itself. The exact position has not been divulged by the salvors.

[9] There seems to have been a prevalent belief at this time that there were tigers in Africa.

[10] Although jackass penguins are to be found on this coast, Webb was probably referring to gannets, which are overwhelmingly the island's main inhabitants.

[11] Spanish silver dollars, popularly known as pieces of eight, were something of an international currency among the trading nations at this time.

[12] A firkin was a wooden keg with a capacity of 9 (imperial) gallons, or about 41 litres. Webb's exactitude turned his journal into a vital source for present-day ornithologists who used it to calculate the number of breeding pairs on the island and to compare it with the modern population. Bird Island is home to the world's largest breeding population of gannets, and the archipelago has been given national park status (it is also home to other, rarer birds). The *Dodington* activity represented the first recorded exploitation of the island.

[13] Spelling and punctuation has been modernized, and *knot* substituted for *mile*. Note that the date in a nautical log runs from noon to noon, not midnight to midnight as on land.

[14] Jones also refers to the *Rose*'s captain as Chandler Banksale.

[15] According to the receipt book, which was updated at the HEIC offices, these were: Arnold, Beazly, Chisholm, Jones, King, Ladoux, Powell, Scantz, Taylor, Topping, Webb and Yates (it is not impossible, however, that there were one or two more).

[16] Evan Jones made more voyages for the HEIC. He was briefly captain of the little *Syren* and then first mate on the *Winchelsea* in 1757. William Webb served as second mate on the *True Briton*, the *York* and the *Earl of Lincoln*, dying on 2 August 1764.

3

Taken by Storm

HMS *Centaur* and HMS *Ramillies*

1782

They went to sea in a Sieve, they did,
In a Sieve they went to sea

EDWARD LEAR, 'THE JUMBLIES'

NAVIGATIONAL ERROR caused by inaccurate charts or inadequate equipment used to be a common hazard at sea – almost, but not entirely, eliminated now by technology such as the Global Positioning System (GPS). No amount of technology, however, can tame the elements, only issue warnings and create ships capable of resisting them more effectively.

Centuries before any shipping forecast was broadcast, experienced mariners could read the signs of approaching storms and plan how best to cope with them. Hurricane-force winds and high seas are dangerous in themselves, but they also search out any weakness in the design or condition of a vessel, as the Royal Navy found out to its cost in 1782.

It may seem strange that in the 1770s France should have supported Britain's colonies in America in their struggle for an independence founded on principles that were anathema to the *ancien régime* of Louis XVI. She did so out of a desire for revenge on the British, whose navy had enjoyed a crushing and, from the French perspective, unexpected victory during the Seven Years' War (1756–63). From the mid 1760s she embarked on a policy of massive naval

---

Dramatis Personae

Robert Baylis : midshipman, *Centaur*

John Bourchier : captain of the *Hector*

James Clark : surgeon's mate, *Centaur*

William Cornwallis : captain of the *Canada*

Richard Fisher : captain of the *Caton*

Charles Flynn : seaman, *Centaur*

Charles Gallohar : seaman, *Centaur*

Alexander Graham : British consul, Faial

Thomas Graves : admiral

John Gregory : quartermaster, *Centaur*

Theodor Hutchins : seaman, *Centaur*

John Nicholson Inglefield : captain of the *Centaur*

Thomas Larcom : third lieutenant, *Ramillies*

Thomas Matthews : quartermaster, *Centaur*

Charles McCarty : seaman, *Centaur*

Sylverius Moriarty : captain of the *Ramillies*

Christopher Parker : captain of the *Pallas*

Thomas Rainy : master, *Centaur*

Thomas Stevenson : seaman, *Centaur*

Timothy Sullivan : captain's coxwain, *Centaur*

Mr Turnbull : master, *Ramillies*

Woodriffe : carpenter, *Ramillies*

Young : sixth Lieutenant, *Ramillies*

---

building and reform, which left her better placed to take on the British at sea and fulfil her own desire to increase her empire. Outstanding fears that French naval help for the American colonies, if given, would be thrown away were allayed by the victory of the rebels at Saratoga in 1777. It became clear that, given assistance at sea, the American colonies were capable of achieving their freedom, and when in 1781 the Comte de Grasse's fleet prevented admirals Graves and Hood from relieving Yorktown at the Battle of the Chesapeake, a decisive point was reached.

The American war effectively over, the British and the French, the latter with Spanish support, continued hostilities at sea, this time out in the Caribbean, where the French seized islands, including Nevis and Montserrat, and the

British admirals Rodney and Hood blockaded Martinique. On 12 April 1782 the two fleets fought an action between Dominica and Les Saintes (off Martinique), where good fortune deserted the French. Not only did they lose the *Glorieux*, *Ardent* – which they had captured from the British two years earlier – and *Hector*, but de Grasse's magnificent flagship *Ville de Paris* was also forced to surrender. The battle was significant because the British crossed the French line and gained the weather gauge, the tactic that Nelson would employ to more shattering effect at Trafalgar. Five days later, a squadron under Hood pursued the French to the Mona Passage, between Hispaniola and Puerto Rico, and captured two further ships, the *Caton* and the *Jason*.

HMS *Warspite*, Portsmouth, 25 March 1783

The marine sentry paused with his hand on the door to allow Captain Inglefield a moment to flick a hand across his shoulders and brush away any last traces of hair powder from a coat that looked smart but suddenly felt awkward. Glancing down at his shoes to make sure that they remained as clean as when he had put them on, Inglefield nodded with a slight smile that masked his trepidation, not quite trusting his voice. Thinking about the situation rationally, as he had done for weeks, he could convince himself that his actions would bear scrutiny, that he and all around him on the *Centaur* had done their best under the circumstances, yet the closer he had come to the court martial, the more doubts had crept in, and now he was about to learn the verdict of his peers.

John Nicholson Inglefield was 34, and very much a protégé of Admiral Sir Samuel Hood Bt. During the twelve years he had spent rising through the ranks of lieutenants he had served in the *Courageux* and the *Robust* under both Sir Samuel and his brother Alexander, and after promotion to captain in 1780 he was given command of Sir Samuel's flagship, *Barfleur*, which was ordered to reinforce Admiral George Rodney's squadron in the West Indies. The *Barfleur* had taken part in the action off Martinique against the French fleet, warm work with 18 British ships of the line against 26 of the enemy, but hardly decisive. Five of the 41 men killed had been on the *Barfleur*, but the *Centaur* had fared worse, with Captain Nott and his first lieutenant among the dead. Inglefield had found himself appointed to command the third-rate in Nott's place.

'You may go in, Sir.'

He took a deep breath and walked in to confront Commodore Hotham and the twelve captains seated around the table in the great panelled cabin of HMS *Warspite*: old Elphinstone, Fitzherbert, Reeve, Holloway with the long face, all chin; Duckworth's wild brows and perpetually anxious expression; Faulknor, Bertie, Marshall, Clayton, Collingwood, young Luttrell and Cornwallis. Strange to be judged by men he knew, either well or as passing acquaintances, especially William Cornwallis who really ought to be thinking that it was only good fortune that their positions were not reversed. Just a few months ago they had faced one another across a similar table, though on a far less solemn occasion.

HMS *Ramillies*, Bluefields Bay, August 1782

Through the open window a weak breeze moderated the stifling heat of the Admiral's cabin on the *Ramillies*. Between the masts and shrouds of a couple of dozen assorted warships and merchantmen, the view out across the turquoise water to the green-clad mountains of Jamaica was still and fragrant. The ship basked; the ten captains sweated. Sylverius Moriarty, the flag captain, helped himself to a drink of water and pushed the jug towards Cornwallis who poured for himself and for Captain Christopher Parker of the *Pallas* at his elbow.

'Gentlemen,' began Admiral Graves, 'our task here is done, and we are going home. We will have, besides ourselves, the honour of escorting the prizes, and the responsibility for protecting a convoy of not less than one hundred merchant vessels. All being well, we sail on the 15th.'

Convoy duty: a world away from the sulphurous hell of battle, but probably what Thomas Graves was better suited for. His time as Hood's flag captain on the *Barfleur* had taught Inglefield that the fiery-tempered Hood knew the value of urgency and decisiveness. Graves, almost the same age as Hood, was more of a plodder who did everything so strictly by the book that opportunity could be lost, and he lacked Hood's aggressive approach. Years earlier, when commanding the *Sheerness*, Graves had been reprimanded by a court martial for refusing an engagement with a French ship. Sir Samuel would probably not be sorry to see the back of him. He did not always get on with his superior, Rodney, either, but Rodney was a better seaman.

'I'm not complaining about going home,' Cornwallis said afterwards as they stood by the entryport, 'but it will be slow work.'

'The prizes will be slower than the merchantmen. Wilkinson thinks they've patched up the *Paris*, but the *Ardent* ...' Inglefield shook his head at the thought of the former British 74 that, after a couple of years in French hands, they had just managed to retake. 'Lucas says he wouldn't trust her to reach New York.'

'I don't suppose the *Pallas* is much better,' contributed a disconsolate Parker, observing his frigate moodily. 'The sooner we get home for a refit ...'

Inglefield nodded, not entirely happy about his own ship. The 74-gun *Centaur* had been badly damaged the year before, and although repairs had been made she was still leaky enough to need the pumps going. Then again, all the British ships were in poor condition. His consolation was that he had a fine crew.

They weighed anchor on 15 August, and whatever the private reservations of individual naval captains about the state of their own ships, they made an impressive sight, the centrepiece of which was undoubtedly the huge French three decker, *Ville de Paris,* moving in stately glory. She mounted 110 guns – some claimed 120 – and ranked as the world's most powerful warship. Attending on her as though she were the flagship rather than a prize were the three British 74s, the 36-gun fifth-rate *Pallas,* and four of the five captured French warships,[1] with a host of deferential merchantmen spread out across the ocean.

Inglefield's elderly *Centaur* had once flown the *fleur-de-lys* of the Marine Royale. Built at Toulon back in 1746, she had had the misfortune to be last in the line when Admiral Edward Boscawen attacked the French fleet off Gibraltar in '59. A change of flag, new armament and a dab of paint transformed le *Centaure* into the *Centaur,* and at the moment she was a rather leaky ship, though not in as bad condition as the prize *Ardent* whose officers had all declared that she was unseaworthy and who were allowed to take her back to Port Royal. A week into the voyage the prize *Hector,* under Captain John Bourchier, started to drop astern. A fortnight later the *Pallas* was seen to be signalling the flagship, the *Ramillies,* and not long afterwards she changed course with the admiral's permission to make for Halifax. With her went Richard Fisher in the *Caton,*[2] the two ships as watertight as colanders. These were the lucky ones.

The weather had been fine throughout the voyage, but on the evening of 16 September, when off the banks of Newfoundland, they saw the first signs of a gale and Moriarty was quick to set an example to the convoy by bringing the *Ramillies* onto the starboard tack as the south-east wind strengthened and the sea rose. All canvas except the mainsail was taken in, and down came the topgallant yards and masts. Given such precautions, he undoubtedly demanded relieving tackles on the tiller, which connected the rudder to the wheel. From the quarterdeck of the *Centaur* Inglefield gave orders to reef and set the mainsail, strike the top-gallant masts and lower the mizzen yard. By midnight the stronger winds and increasingly heavy seas were causing him acute anxiety as the water deepened in the hold.

'All hands to the pumps,' he commanded, simultaneously asking himself whether to try the ship before the sea – to keep her in the trough of the waves with just enough sail to hold her at the pace of the sea. To do so, however, would be to part company with the convoy he was supposed to be guarding, and the admiral had called the convoy together. If the weather eased, as it felt as though it was beginning to, his decision would be very hard to justify. When the wind dropped appreciably around 2:00 a.m. Inglefield heaved a sigh of relief over that, and over his decision not to lose the convoy, whose distant tossing lamps, glimpsed between the seas, did duty for the stars.

Abruptly the sky was ripped open by a dazzling burst of light. Thunder exploded simultaneously. Rain and spray lashed the deck as the ship pitched and rolled in the reinvigorated gale. As the storm gathered power great fissures of lightning tore into the darkness, and beneath the thunder the wind thrashed the rigging and pounded the solitary mainsail that Inglefield's men now rushed to haul up. Hardly had they finished and regained the deck than the wind swept round, screaming in from the north-north-west.

There was no time to do anything. The *Centaur* crashed over onto her beam ends, hurling men from their hammocks and beds. Naked in the darkness, dazed and disorientated, deafened by the booming wind, the off-duty officers struggled in vain to find their clothes. The men sleeping on the starboard side found their hammocks soaked by the water from the hold that sloshed through the decks; more was forcing its way through the ports as the *Centaur* lay dead.

Inglefield had experienced nothing like it, but he knew what had to be done. Orders cracked out to cut away the main and mizzen masts. Axes hacked into the thick hemp of the lanyards that held the shrouds taut; the mainmast went quickly in an avalanche of rope and rending timber. There was no response from the hull. Then most of the mizzen gave, lurching into the water, leaving a ragged stump, and the hull came back to life, righting itself with a violence that, to the dismay of captain and men alike, sent the foremast and bowsprit the way of the rest, throwing men across the deck like skittles. The force tore loose three of the 32-pounders on the main deck; men who risked their lives to secure them were crushed as they rolled around the deck with every movement of the swell[3]. The cannonballs in the shot lockers had broken free, smashing everything around them.

Within ten minutes of the masts going over, Inglefield was given the worst news: the tiller linking the rudder to the wheel had broken off short in the rudderhead. Before the chocks could be rammed into place either side of it to stop it beating itself to destruction, the rudder had gone too. The ship wallowed, a helpless hulk at the mercy of the storm, riding mountainous dark seas that threatened to broach her at any moment.

The sudden blast that had 'as much disastered as possible' the *Centaur* had wreaked havoc aboard the flagship in mere minutes. Caught aback, her mainmast toppled; her mizzen snapped like a rotten branch; the fore topmast went over the starboard bow and the foreyard broke in the slings that supported its weight. Named after the Duke of Marlborough's great victory against the French in 1706, the *Ramillies* had met an enemy beyond her power to defeat. Dismasted and no longer answering the wheel, she found herself thrown with her stern to the sea, making no way. Behind her, darker than the night, a wave crept up on her as she cowered in the trough, then it flung itself over her, sweeping the deck like chainshot, washing over the sides, cascading into the waist and pouring into the admiral's cabin.

Graves had been in the cot bed suspended from the ceiling when the shock came. He found himself on the flooded cabin floor, groping calf-deep in water for his boots and sodden clothing before he could stagger on deck and take in the situation with Moriarty. Things looked bad; what was the reality?

'Mr Larcom!' Moriarty shouted to the third lieutenant. 'You and Mr. Silly, go below and send me a report on the damage. Keep the men at the pumps. Mr Nash, Mr. Turnbull, cut away this mess and get the deck clear!'

It was vital to chop away the remaining ropes and shrouds that held the broken masts and yards against the side of the hull. Their constant chafing and pounding of the timber was ripping off the copper, allowing the waves to pull out all the oakum in the seams.

The report from below was depressing. The rudder was all but off; the tiller had broken.

The same exhausting work was going on aboard the *Centaur*, where the pumps were at last getting the better of the water, and as dawn slowly broke and the wind moderated, Inglefield stared over a sea of devastation and derelicts. Last night there had been 90 ships, theoretically in columns but in reality more loosely scattered; now he could only count 15. There were two ships of the line to leeward, one – they thought it was Cornwallis's *Canada* – had lost her foremast and bowsprit; the other, probably the *Glorieux*, showed a gap where her mainmast had been. No sign of the *Ramillies*,[4] nor the *Dutton*, a former East Indiaman bought in as a storeship.

They had a reassuring surprise around 7:00 a.m. when, ahead of them, they sighted what could only be the *Ville de Paris*. At least she was in one piece.

'We'll raise a distress signal,' Inglefield decided. 'She ought to see that.' The only spar standing was the stump of the mizzenmast, so the ensign was hoisted on it, union downwards to indicate distress, and the gunner fired one of the forecastle guns to attract attention. The smoke had barely cleared when a last spiteful gesture of the wind tore the flag away, but the ensign had done its job and the *Ville de Paris* was already standing towards them. A few of the merchantmen had come within hailing distance to offer assistance. Inglefield put the speaking trumpet to his lips.

'Thank you, gentlemen – I will rely on the *Paris*. But I would be obliged if you would report our situation to the Admiral.'

He was not to know that the *Ramillies* was no better off than his own ship and likewise surrounded by the dismal consequences of the night. Close by her lay the large storeship, *Dutton*,[5] waterlogged and listing heavily. Her crew were cutting away her masts in an attempt to get her upright, and hoisting her ensign as a distress signal, but there was nothing the *Ramillies* could offer and all the other ships had their own troubles. Further away the *Canada* was down on the lee quarter and missing her mizzenmast and maintopmast; the *Centaur* could just be made out in the far distance. From the vantage point of the *Ramillies* that morning, it looked as if close to three-quarters of the ships in the convoy had either gone down or been scattered far out of sight.

'Sir, Mr Larcom's compliments, and there's six feet of water in the hold and the pumps won't free her.' The young midshipman took a breath. 'He says the sea's worked out all the oakum, and Woodriffe would have you know, Sir, that the beams have almost worked out of the clamps amidships.' It was not the news that Moriarty wanted to hear, particularly the carpenter's assessment. The ship was badly weakened, and they had to find a way of stemming the water. Since the pumps could not cope, they would have to start baling.

'Tell Mr Larcom to keep the men at the pumps. Mr Nash, have the spritsail set on the foremast and a maintopgallant on what's left of the mizzen. Then we will bear up before the wind.'

A difficult situation, and he wondered whether they would be able to keep the ship afloat. But they were not as badly off as the *Dutton*, whose commander, a naval lieutenant, had just leapt into the sea as if well aware that his ship was finished. A dozen other men slid down a rope into one of the ship's boats. For a moment, Moriarty watched the officer, but either he was a poor swimmer or he was exhausted by the night's battle with the elements. His strokes soon weakened, and he went under. Running before the wind, the *Dutton*'s boat was making for one of the larger merchantmen, but those in it had realized they would be unable to heave-to beside her and so shaped course for another vessel. Ropes came snaking down; the small figures heaved themselves up to safety. Lucky bastards. Closer to the *Ramillies* the men still on the *Dutton* were hacking at the foremast rigging in a last-ditch attempt to save her. Then without warning she went down by the head; the last Moriarty saw of her was the fly of the ensign. All that remained was a dying vortex of water choked by swirling timber and debris.

Throughout the day the pumping and the baling went on. Lieutenant Nash, as weary as the men and accompanied by a number of the officers, reported to the quarterdeck.

'Sir, we absolutely must get the guns overboard. We have to ease the ship.'

Left to himself, the Irishman would have seen them heaved overboard with a good will. The mathematics was simple. A 32-pounder weighed 55.5 hundredweight (2.8 tons), and the ship carried twenty-eight of them, plus thirty 18-pounders and sixteen 9-pounders: more than 160 tons of weight they could currently do without, but since the admiral was on board, it would have to be his decision. Moriarty went below to Graves's wet cabin to seek the necessary authorization. Graves shook his head.

'I cannot consent to that, Moriarty. There is still a convoy to protect. Without our guns how will we defend it?'

'Sir, if we don't stop the water soon, we won't have a ship. If we can lighten her, she'll not take it on so fast and that will give the pumps a chance.'

Reluctantly Graves offered a meaningless compromise. The 9-pounders on the forecastle and after-quarterdeck could go – less than 25 tons. Grimly, Captain Moriarty returned to the deck.

The officers of the *Centaur* had no admiral onboard to overrule their captain, but in any case the *Ville de Paris* had responded to their appeals. She was within 2 miles (3.7 kilometres), but to their perplexity she passed them, making no attempt to change course or even acknowledge their distress signal. One of the merchant ships came under the stern of the *Centaur* and offered to carry a message.

'Tell them our condition!' Inglefield shouted. 'Ask them to stand by us!' He watched as the small ship closed on the warship until within hailing distance, but the *Ville de Paris* continued on her tack.

'She's in a worse state than she looks,' he told the disconsolate officers around him. 'Probably lost her rudder. Very well, let's get the guns overboard, and find a way to get her head to the sea.'

On the maindeck and quarterdeck teams of men took off the lashings that had kept most of the guns in place during the storm. With breech tackles rigged to either side of the carriage and a third running between the bulbous pommelion at the breech and a bolt above the port, they raised the gun while others pushed quoins underneath the breech. Using handspikes inserted between the quoins and the breech they levered the guns out. As the ship began to roll, the order was given to open the gun port. Men pushed down on the handspikes, and with the help of gravity the gun slid through its port. Six guns had turned over after breaking loose when the ship righted herself, and they had to be left where they were.

Bringing the *Centaur*'s head to the sea proved impossible, so they were unable to make way and keep the *Ville de Paris* in sight. In the evening they lost sight of her in the haze. They pumped all night, gaining on the water when the wind dropped, losing the battle whenever conditions worsened. The handpumps were regularly choked; the chainpumps worn out. Men and officers were exhausted, and unable to reach any food. Inglefield knew that if by a miracle they managed to save the ship they would have nothing to live on except two puncheons of rum and a little lime juice. They desperately needed water: all were dehydrated, and some men had taken to drinking seawater. Yet despite everything, the crew remained cheerful and followed orders.

That they obeyed the officers is not surprising. They were under the articles of war and disobedience was severely punished. Unlike merchant seamen, they did not sign on for one voyage at a time, able to move from ship to ship. The end of the *Centaur*, if it came, would not free them from naval service. Only the Admiralty could do that, putting men ashore when too infirm to serve or when peace reduced the size of the navy. Their cheerfulness was another matter, and a compliment to Inglefield and his officers.

They had seen one other vessel from the *Centaur*, and she was firing her gun to attract attention, but by the morning of 19 September she had obviously foundered. The winds diminished enough for the pumps to clear one hold sufficiently for some of the seamen to break out a cask of water: dangerous work, but lives depended on it. Everyone but the seamen – officers, passengers and boys – settled to the task of thrumming a sail. This involved sewing short lengths of oakum to the canvas in preparation for hauling the sail on ropes underneath the hull. Water pressure at the leak points would hold the sail against the side, stopping up the hole. It had the desired effect of keeping out some of the water, and Inglefield was able to divide the pumping and baling into two-hour shifts. By the following day the hold was clear of water and the weather fine. If they could rig up emergency steering gear they might be able to make the nearest land. They had raised a jury foremast and thrown over the remaining guns along with anything that would get in the way of baling if it should come to that again. But all through the preparations, Inglefield's most realistic hope was for a ship to come up. When morning came on the 21st, the sky promised a storm.

Things were no better on the flagship *Ramillies*, where the crew had bailed and pumped throughout the night of 17–18 September, only to find seven feet (more than two metres) of water in the hold; the westerly gale did them no favours either. Moriarty's exasperated officers begged for more of the guns to be jettisoned, and once again Graves demurred, finally consenting to the loss of a few 32-pounders and all but two of the quarterdeck guns. With water still continuing to invade, Moriarty ordered Larcom to organize the nailing of tarred canvas and hide from below the ports of the maindeck. The same was done on the lower deck without the captain needing to give any orders, but the ominous sounds coming from below decks convinced the officers that the ship was deteriorating fast, and their pleas to jettison the upper deck guns were heard. With them went most of the shot and whatever heavy stores the crew could get at. The ship was tied together with ropes to ease the strain on her, and nobody was excused pumping and bailing duty. By the evening the water had gone down and Graves began to express hopes of saving the *Ramillies*.

Morning on the 19th brought all the officers to their captain, once again stressing that the ship was still complaining and that the squalls of the night had caused her to settle forwards. The admiral now allowed Moriarty to have the two large bower anchors cut away, and the rest of the day was spent throwing over everything else, including the remaining guns.

'I think, Sir, with all due respect,' the captain said to him that evening while the work was in progress, 'that you should consider your own safety and go on

board one of the merchantmen.' Had he been wishing for his admiral's departure for rather longer, so he could get on with the task of saving the ship
without having to defer to his authority? If the matter had been raised earlier,
the result must have been the same as now.

'Nonsense, Moriarty. You expect me to leave this ship while she can still
swim? It would be unpardonable of me.'

'Sir, your life is valuable to the country. I cannot promise she will last the
night.'

'My dear fellow, what are a few more years of life to me? They are of very
little consequence, but think of the effect on the men if I abandon the ship
while she is in this condition! No, Moriarty, you mean it kindly, I know, but I
will not forsake you. It would be a bad example.'

He was obstinate in his refusal, and the *Ramillies* came through the ensuing
hours no worse than she had begun them thanks to a calm night. They spent
the beginning of the 21st disposing of more heavy anchors. For the first time,
the firmness of the crew wavered. They needed no one to tell them the state of
the ship was critical, and they feared she was going to founder. With 20
merchantmen around them, battered but more seaworthy than their own
vessel, they begged to be allowed to go. Graves, who despite his reluctance to
lose His Majesty's guns had been indefatigable in remaining on deck and
encouraging everyone, got the company together.

'My brave fellows, although I and my officers have the same regard for our
own lives as you have for yours, yet I assure you that we have no intention of
deserting either you or the ship, and that we will stand or fall together as
becomes men and Englishmen.' He fixed them with a firm eye. 'As to myself,
I am resolved to try one more night aboard the *Ramillies*. I hope you will all
remain with me – for one good day, with a moderate sea and our exertions, may
enable us to clear and secure the well from the encroaching ballast; and then
hands enough may be spared to raise jury masts that will carry the ship to
Ireland.' He allowed that optimistic prospect to sink in before continuing, 'The
sight of the *Ramillies* alone, and the knowledge that she is manned so gallantly,
will be sufficient to protect the remaining part of the convoy. But above all, as
everything has been done for her relief that can be thought of, let us wait for
the event; and be assured that I will make the signal directly for the fleet to lie
by during the night.'

Reassured, they went back to work. Moriarty made the signal, and it was
answered by most of the merchant ships. Before dark, he informed them by a
second signal of what was to happen if the need to abandon ship arose. At 3:00
a.m. he was woken by a delegation of officers, men and carpenters with news
that was hardly unexpected. The whole carcass of the ship was giving way.

'We must tread carefully, Moriarty.' Graves warned him 'We will all abandon
ship at first light, but do not tell them that.'

'What may I tell them, Sir?'

'That we are taking off the sick and injured. We will have the merchantmen send us their boats for that purpose. However, I want you to get on deck all the bread and what you can of the beef, pork, flour and the like. We cannot expect these vessels to feed everyone out of their own rations, so we get the food off at the same time as the sick.'

Admiral Graves left for the *Belle*[6] at around 9:00 a.m., when there was 9 feet (2.75 metres) of water in the hold, and he hoisted his broad pennant on the merchantman. Moriarty divided the crew of more than 600 into groups, each with an officer, and saw them into the boats, sending the injured and wounded aboard the transport *Silver Eel*, which had sailed from Bluefields as a hospital ship. With a glow of pride the captain asserted that he observed 'the punctuality, obedience, sobriety and attention of the ship's company to the last moment.' By the time they left, in mid afternoon, the water in the hold had deepened to 13 feet (4 metres).

By 4:30, when the water had risen another foot, the ship was all but deserted. Moriarty said farewell to her and descended into a boat accompanied by Nash and Larcom. Just one officer remained: the sixth lieutenant, Young, who had his orders and for whom a boat was standing by.[7] As they were rowed towards the *Augustus Caesar*[8] they saw the first smoke rising over the derelict; it grew into flames that gained a swift hold. Young had done his job: to prevent the ship falling into the hands of the enemy. Even before they reached Captain Fowler's ship the fire reached the after-magazine, where the powder had been placed as high as possible. Amid a thundering roar, the scene turned orange; timber and burning wood spun up into the sky, falling back in a charred and splintered hail.

And everyone said, who saw them go,
"O won't they be soon upset, you know!
For the sky is dark, and the voyage is long,
And happen what may, it's extremely wrong
In a Sieve to sail so fast!"

The crew of the *Centaur* were alone: they had no reassuring flock of merchant ships huddled around ready to take them off at a moment's notice. Inglefield must have regretted his earlier decision to refuse their help and rely on the *Ville de Paris*. By noon the wind had shrilled into a gale, and the mounting seas forced water into the labouring hulk. The carpenter reported that the overworked pumps were all but useless. Their only chance now was to cut scuttles into the deck so that they could increase the bailing. All day and all night the sailmakers sewed canvas buckets to augment the wooden pails. More holes were discovered in the hull; critically, the sternpost was loose. They had thrummed another sail, but it was useless. The officers shared the arduous duty of pumping with their men, marvelling at their cheerfulness. For two more days they fought for the ship and their own lives, until, during the morning of 23 September, the crew recognized the hopelessness of the conflict and a sudden despair set in. For the first time, grown men began to cry. The carpenter reported to his captain.

'Sir, the water's up to the orlop. She won't hold together much longer. Should I tell the men to start making rafts? Some of them are already asking their mates to lash them into their hammocks.'

'I will speak to them.' He had already noted men changing into their best and cleanest clothes, a sure sign that they thought the end had come.[9] In his address to the company he told them that their only chance now lay in making rafts, though he knew full well that they could not now hope to save everyone. Three of the ship's boats – the yawl, barge and pinnace – were hoisted overboard and provisioned with bread and spirit from which those on the rafts could be supplied. Two responsible men, either captains of the top or quartermasters, were sent into each to guard against a sudden rush. The captain asked his coxwain to get anything useful from the steward and put it into the yawl, the small vessel in which he proposed to embark, rather than his own barge.

All this time the ship was settling lower until she hung, as Inglefield put it, 'suspended in water'. As the weather got up, people realized what their captain had understood much earlier: in such seas, rafts could not save them, and when the ship went down, which it would at any moment, it would drag down anyone around it in the vortex.[10]

At 5:00 p.m. Inglefield came out of his cabin to find the ship's master as the only other officer on deck. Glancing over the side he saw that, contrary to orders, a group of people had forced their way into the pinnace and were in danger of swamping it. He made a swift decision.

> There appeared not more than a moment for consideration: to remain and perish with the ship's company, to whom I could not be of use any longer, or seize the opportunity, which was the only way of escaping, and leave the people with whom I had been so well satisfied on a variety of occasions, that I thought I COULD give my life to preserve them – this indeed was a painful conflict … The love of life prevailed.

'Mr Rainy!' he shouted to the master. 'Follow me!'

He climbed into the mizzen chains and scrambled down into the boat, trying to check the frantic bodies attempting to get into it. As they pushed off, other men were jumping into the water. Robert Baylis, a 15-year-old midshipman, stood in the chains staring after the boat and then plunged in, pulling for it and pleading to be taken in. Inglefield persuaded his comrades to make room. They rowed away from the *Centaur*; within half an hour she was out of sight, leaving them with no idea whether anyone got into the other boats.

The group that found itself in the pinnace was representative of the *Centaur*'s overall complement. With Inglefield, the master and the young midshipman were the surgeon's mate, James Clark; the captain's coxwain, Timothy Sullivan; the quartermasters John Gregory and Thomas Matthews; and five seamen – Charles McCarty, Charles Flynn, Charles Gallohar, Theodor Hutchins, and Thomas Stevenson. It therefore gave the boat strength, leadership, navigational expertise and even some basic medical knowledge.

Those were their advantages. Far less favourable was the state of the boat, which was leaking and had no sail, and the quantity of their provisions: no more than a bag of bread, one small ham, a piece of pork, two quart bottles of water and a few French cordials. Furthermore, in his hasty departure there had been no chance for Inglefield to bring any of the navigational equipment. They would have to steer by the sun and the stars, but assuming that the ship's position had been taken the previous day he must have known that they were in the region of Latitude 42° 48′ N, Longitude 45° 19′ W.[11]

As many had found before them, and others would also discover, escaping a doomed ship in an open boat was the continuation, not the end, of troubles. The seas were heavy, and they had to keep her before the wind, which was blowing from the north-west. That in itself was good news, for the nearest land – the island of Corvo, part of the Azores archipelago – lay east-south-east some 670 miles (1240 kilometres) of their last known position, and when they found a blanket, they were able to make a sail using one of the wooden stretchers from the bottom of the boat against which two of the rowers had earlier been bracing their feet. All night they scudded before the wind, running the continual risk of being pooped by some massive sea, half of them bailing for their lives between each wave, the rest drenched and half drowned in the bottom of the craft.

The long night gave way to a calmer dawn and allowed them a little rest and the chance to plan. The bad news was that the wind had shifted to the south, and if it blew a gale and forced them to scud again they would be heading in the opposite direction. Even their hopes of navigating by the heavens were frequently frustrated by starless nights and entire days when the sun could neither break through the cloud nor even show a trace of brightness. Sometimes they thought they saw land, only to realize it was a fogbank. A run of less than a week to Corvo was now out of the question. For eight days they tried to shape a course for the island, grateful that the southerly wind had desisted from strengthening. Wet through and cold, without coats or cloaks to put over them, their morale was maintained by their captain who kept them singing and telling stories to pass the time and distract from the miserable conditions.

By the ninth day they hoped to spot Corvo, but no land appeared. They feared they had been driven too far north, but had no way of proving it. The first night had taken them south-east; thereafter they estimated they had sailed east-north-east, but it was only an estimate. The sea had ruined most of the bread, and with no idea how long they would have to last before they found land or were picked up, they set a strict daily allowance. From now on breakfast and dinner would consist of one biscuit between 12. The daily water ration dropped to a single glass of water – the glass was the broken-off neck of a bottle with the cork in place – an allowance that, instead of slaking the thirst, only made them realize how dehydrated they were. Most had taken to drinking their urine; and despite knowing the danger, a few resorted to seawater. The songs and stories took the place of supper.

On 4 October, by which time Inglefield's group had been 12 days in their open boat, William Cornwallis brought the battered *Canada* to Spithead, and with her the news of the catastrophe that had overtaken the fleet. Other than those that failed to set out or turned back before the hurricane struck, the *Canada* was to be the only warship, British or French, to survive. The *Ville de Paris*, which inexplicably had failed to answer the *Centaur's* signal, had gone down taking with her Admiral Smith Child's son, Thomas, and the majority of the King's Shropshire Light Infantry. She left just one survivor. Badly mauled during the battle in which some four hundred of her French crew were killed, and no more than patched up for the voyage to England, she must have had damage below the waterline as well as the lost rudder that Inglefield surmised. On 10 October, the *Silver Eel*,[12] which Graves had ordered to make for the first port she could reach, arrived in Falmouth, and in the early hours of the following day the *Augustus Caesar* brought Moriarty safely to Plymouth. One by one the surviving ships were straggling home. On the 10th the unlikely flagship *Belle* came into Cork, where Admiral Graves transferred to the frigate *Myrmidon*.

It rained in the night, and that prolonged lives. They had found a pair of sheets in the boat, though nobody knew how they had got there, and by wringing them out over the kidskin container with which they had been bailing, they managed to secure six quarts of water. They could do nothing about the effects of exposure, or the attrition of the salt water. Their wet clothes rubbed the skin raw, but to remove them was to die of cold. Lack of food, added to the bitter disappointment of not finding land, had sapped their strength, and they were approaching that point where dying seemed less to be feared. A gale from the south-south-west once more forced them to run before the sea, bailing with what little energy remained, until Inglefield and the master reckoned they could be 60 miles (110 kilometres) south-west of Faial – a larger island of the Azores, beyond Corvo, which they had already overshot. Sixty miles: something over a day if only the wind would ease enough for them to steer for it, but it refused.

The following day, 6 October – their fourteenth at sea – the tiny ration was issued. Matthews, the quartermaster, put his piece of biscuit into his mouth, chewed it for a moment and shook his head.

'I can't swallow it, Sir,' he said. 'There's no strength in my throat.' Other men had said as much, but coming from the fittest and most powerful man among them, it was ominous. In the night he took to drinking salt water, and early in the morning he passed away. His death was strangely reassuring to his boat-mates: dying of hunger, it seemed, could be peaceful and painless. What was the point in struggling to prolong life? They did what their captain asked of them, but Inglefield could no longer raise their spirits. They had, in any case, rations for only another 24 hours.

For the first time, the wind was kind to them, blowing the westerly that they been praying for since their last estimate of their position relative to Faial, though it was not until sunrise that they could confirm it. Now they ran before it under their improvised sail, making about four knots. The last breakfast was served: the small piece of stale, damp biscuit that felt and tasted like card, the few sips of rainwater from the sharp-edged bottle-neck glass.

'Look! I can see land!' The exclamation burst from the other quartermaster, John Gregory. 'Look to the South-East!'

They went wild, hugging one another, almost crying, shouting from their parched throats. Inglefield moved to calm then.

'Steady, my friends. Don't get your hopes too high. It may prove to be no more than another fogbank. We've seen those too often before.'

'If that isn't *****land!' shouted one of the men elatedly, ignoring his captain's request not to swear, 'then I've never seen ***** land in my ****life before!'

They set course for it. Inglefield's caution had taken its effect on their confidence, but this time it really was land – 60 miles distant, but land nevertheless. It was a miracle that they had seen it at all, and not only because at such a distance only the top of Faial's 3422-foot (1043-metre) peak would have been visible above the horizon. The rest of the horizon was piled with haze, and only in that one spot had the mist cleared to allow Gregory his precious glimpse.

With the nearby island of Pico buried in cloud they remained uncertain until they came close enough to confirm their hopes. For two hours they ran along the surf-battered coast, so desperate for water that if they had not fallen in with a fishing vessel they would have taken their chance in the breakers. At midnight their guide led them into the harbour, where the Portuguese refused to allow them to land until the health officer had examined them to make sure they were not carrying contagious diseases. In the meantime the fishermen who had found them went off to bring them food, water and wine, and in the morning, formalities complete, they were permitted to disembark.

That was easier said than done: Inglefield and Rainy were in the best condition, but the former was unable to walk unaided, and many of them had to be supported as they made their way through the streets. Alexander Graham, the British Consul, came to their rescue, finding them comfortable accommodation and devoting much of his time to their welfare. It took several days before they began to get better rather than worse, which they initially did – as if their bodies could at last afford the luxury of being ill.

Not until 13 November were Inglefield's party well enough to travel, and even then Clark and two of the seamen were still suffering from badly ulcerated legs. They took passage on a small brig bound for Lisbon, which they reached 13 days later. There Inglefield, Rainy and Sullivan embarked on a merchantman, the *Hannover Packet*, which sailed on 9 December, while the others followed on HMS *Aeolus* under Captain Collins. The *Hannover Packet* entered Falmouth on 23 December, and, knowing that Sullivan's family lived in Plymouth, Inglefield gave the young man leave to visit them while he and Rainy posted up to London, reporting to the Admiralty on 27 December and asking for the court martial to be held as soon as possible.

While waiting for that court martial, he wrote several times to the Admiralty, on 3 January asking permission to publish an account of his experiences and so placate the friends who were urging him to do so. On 11 February he was importuning their lordships to promote or recognize his fellow survivors, pointing out that Rainy had just passed his lieutenant's examination; recommending Sullivan be made gunner; commending Gregory as a 'very excellent, careful sailor'; singling out Baylis as a likely prospect for the future, and expressing satisfaction that Clark had already been promised promotion. He asked that the rest be awarded compensation for the loss of their clothes and suggested that their families should be given Protections against being pressed into the navy.[13]

T he merchant ships had been savagely battered in the storm, but quite how many went down is impossible to determine. Successive editions of *Lloyd's List* tell a miserable tale. Captain T Evers and the crew of the *Withywood* transferred to the *Thetis* before she foundered; the Bristol Jamaicaman *Rodney*, Captain Liscomb, went down, along with Captain Legg's *Ann*, as did the Clyde-bound *Minerva*, Captain Holmes. The surviving Jamaicamen limped back with their stories. One of the first to arrive was Captain C Stuart's 450-ton *Worcester*, which made Plymouth on 1 October despite damage. Captain Fairclough of the 360-ton *Betty* arrived at Hoylake the following day with a vivid description of the storm, which had ripped his sails to ribbons and

put the ship upon her beam ends for two hours, which was the time the storm lashed our decks, full of water, both pumps going, and still the water gained upon us after the storm ceased. I got her before the wind in order to free her, which I could not do before, without cutting away her masts, which I durst not attempt. I am afraid we have lost 30 or 40 hogsheads of sugar washed out; had the storm continued an hour longer I really believe the ship would have foundered. I only saw five sail in the morning, two of which I only [sic] knew, which were the *Mary Ann* and the *Worcester* of London, the former with only her foremast standing, the other with her mizzen mast gone ...

There were just 3 survivors out of 34 from the huge 500-ton *Mentor*. Captain Whiteside told how he had spent seven hours in the water clinging to a yard and a pole while his second mate and a boy held onto the gunwale of the ship's boat. Providentially, the Lancaster-registered brig *Sarah* found them.

The 340-ton *Ellen*, Captain Borrowdale, put into Hoylake on 17 October, where she disembarked 42 of the *Ramillies* crew and reported that she had seen the *Assistance*, Captain Stevenson, a fortnight earlier, and the *John*, Captain Henderson, four days after the gale. Captain D Cottam's Lymington sloop, the *John and Ann*, struggled into Galway leaking and damaged; two others, the *Betsey* and the *Peggy*, put into Cork.

On a happier note, Captain McGill of the *St Lucia*, not part of the fleet, arrived with the news that he had met up with 12 ships and parted with them on 28 September. Also, the French prize *Jason*, which had stayed behind in Jamaica to complete her watering, arrived safely on 11 October.

The French had not been idle. A report from Lorient on 16 October informed the British that a trio of their privateers had captured six ships – the *Jamaica, Dorothea, Hope, Two Brothers, Commerce* and *Swallow* – the last of which had another part of the crew of the *Ramillies* on board. Thirteen days later a French cartel[14] arrived at Portsmouth from St Malo carrying several captains and assorted passengers from various prizes captured homeward bound from Jamaica. They included Captain M Cox of the Liverpool ship *Hector*, who brought news of one of the last sightings of the mighty French flagship. Two days after the gale they had seen the *Ville de Paris* near the Western Islands (of the Canary Islands group). She had only her foremast and bowsprit standing. Thick, blowing weather had separated them.

If history in general is written by the victor, maritime history is written by the survivors. If anyone else managed to leave the *Centaur* on either of the other boats, they perished at sea, and it is sobering to reflect that for every Inglefield or Bligh there must be hundreds of thousands over the centuries who, though surviving their initial shipwrecks, died anonymously in small open boats in a desperate, doomed attempt to reach land, defeated by the elements, lack of navigational skill or equipment, or slowly dying of hunger and thirst.

HMS *Warspite*, Portsmouth, 25 March 1783

He suddenly realized that the men round the table looked relaxed, even smiling. Inglefield drew a sigh of relief even before Commodore Hotham cleared his throat.

'It is', he declared to Inglefield, 'the verdict of this court that you have acquitted yourself as a cool, resolute and experienced officer, and were well supported by your officers and ship's company. Your united exertions appear to have been so great and manly as to reflect the highest honour upon the whole and to leave the deepest impression upon this court that more could not possibly have been done to preserve His Majesty's ship *Centaur*.'

'Surely you were never in any doubt?' demanded Cornwallis as they took a turn on deck afterwards.

'Sometimes.'

'You heard they acquitted Moriarty?'

'Yes.' Inglefield's court martial had taken place four months after that of Moriarty aboard HMS *Dunkirk* at Plymouth. Captain John McBride of HMS *Artois* delivered that court's verdict in similar glowing terms: 'Every possible and laudable exertion was made by Captain Moriarty whose conduct through the whole merits the highest encomiums, nor are the officers and people less deserving of it from Captain Moriarty.'

That was some consolation to Moriarty, who was incandescent with indignation against some petty bureaucrat at the Admiralty who deducted a fee from his wages over some missing paperwork relating to his surveying work in Jamaica with the *Victor*. Nor was that his only grievance: he was furious with Customs, too.

> ... I hope that their lordships will be pleased to think that the manning of the sloop, mostly at my own expense, and raising a number of men in her afterwards for the service, without a single farthing of expense to government, may be looked upon by my affectionate friends as a sufficient balance for the want of a coasting certificate, and that they will in consequence order so ill-judged a mulcting [deduction] to be taken off. As for the *Ramillies*, my papers all went with her, nor was there anything of mine saved except a keg of old rum ... which was seized by the greedy Custom House to enrich His Majesty's exchequer: it was too good to be returned to me, though I went in person to demand it of the commissioners. At my arrival at Plymouth without a stock or handkerchief to put round my neck, a dirty keg was beneath my thoughts. My mind was entirely taken up with the service of my country ... How any office could require a certificate of coasts from a man in the the circumstances I was in, puzzles me to account for ...[15]

Inglefield's subsequent career was not adversely affected by the loss of the *Centaur*. After the trial he was given command of three further ships, and when the French Revolutionary Wars broke out, Hood appointed him to the captured French frigate *Aigle* for the campaign against Corsica. In 1794 he succeeded Sir Hyde Parker as captain of the Mediterranean fleet.[16]

That ships could lose their masts in hurricanes was well understood; that so many had then foundered dismayed the Admiralty. Three more 74s were examined, and their Lordships had a shock. The bolts in the hulls of all were in a dangerous condition thanks to the galvanic activity between the iron from which they were made and the copper plates that covered the hull.

Copper sheathing had only very recently spread across the Royal Navy. Wood sheathing, as used on the French East Indiaman *Prince*, had been the order of the day. Coppering had been proposed at the start of the century, but it was not until 1761 that the Royal Navy treated its first ship, HMS *Alarm*, so that an assessment could be made. The task of the copper was two-fold: to stop the teredo worm from eating away at the wood, and to prevent the ship's bottom from becoming so 'foul' – encrusted with barnacles and weed – that speed and handling were compromised. Trials were favourable, and a few other ships were coppered, but after five years the adverse effects of the copper on the iron bolts were observed, and the programme was halted while a solution was found. That appeared to come in the form of an impermeable barrier of paper soaked in oil of tar and treated with mixture of white lead and linseed oil, which was fixed between the hull and the copper tiles. By 1782 most of the fleet had been coppered with this improved process.

Even the conviction that coppering kept out the teredo worm was to be disproved. Early the following year, Christopher Parker, who had left Graves's convoy to limp the *Pallas* to Halifax, Nova Scotia, was ordered to escort a convoy home to Britain. Once again the *Pallas* began to leak, and on 5 February 1783, following a storm that detached her from her merchantmen, Parker and his crew ran for the Azores, officers and men bailing and pumping day and night. Two days of contrary winds forced them to abandon the attempt to enter the harbour at Faial; with the ship about to founder they ran her ashore on the nearby island of São Jorge on 12 February. What few stores had not been thrown overboard in the exhausting attempt to keep her afloat were unloaded, then she was then set on fire, though not before Parker had had her hull inspected: the wood was found to be riddled by the teredo worm that the copper sheathing was supposed to keep out.

Investigation and experiment later showed that it was not the copper sheathing but the tar-soaked felt that was effective in keeping out the worms – and only then if applied *hot*.

In the same year as the *Pallas*'s last voyage, the navy ended the use of iron bolts on coppered ships, switching to ones made from a specially hardened alloy of copper and zinc.

The disastrous storm that overtook the Atlantic convoy of September 1782 was estimated to have cost the lives of 3,500 naval and merchant seamen, passengers, prisoners and troops. Nevertheless it was eclipsed by another disaster that same summer: the loss of the *Royal George* at Plymouth on 28 August. In attempting to make repairs below the waterline without taking her into dock, she had been heeled over by moving her guns so as to give her the required list. The correct procedure would have been to pull her over with ropes attached to her masts, which offered a 'quick release' if anything went wrong. Unfortunately, too much weight was shifted and the anxieties of the carpenter went unheeded. By the time her commanding officer had been told of her danger it was too late to replace the guns, and she turned over with the loss of almost 1000 lives, including hundreds of visitors and Admiral Richard Kempenfelt. The navy was glad to see the back of 1782.

Sources and Bibliography

This account, allowing for a little dramatic licence taken with Inglefield's court martial, is taken from the accounts of both Inglefield and Moriarty that were placed before the court. Some use has been made by the later account of the loss of the *Ramillies* published over a century later in the *Liverpool Mercury* – but Moriarty's contemporary account has generally been preferred. Thanks are due to John Harland for kindly answering some technical queries.

National Archives
ADM1/1614
ADM1/2123
ADM1/2124
ADM1/1988
ADM1/1791
ADM 1 /5322 (court martial records)
Blackburn, I, 'Brief Biographical Sketches of Men Examined for Lieutenant RN', manuscript (National Archives Library), 2005

Bonnel, Dr Ulane, *The French Navy in the War of Independence* (the author's translation of her own article in *Cols Bleus*, 8/15 November 1975)
Harland, John, *Seamanship in the Age of Sail* (Conway Maritime, London 1984).
[Inglefield], *The Loss of His Majesty's Ship* Centaur *of 74 Guns* (London: Thomas Tegg, 1783).
Landers, H L, *The Virginia Campaign and the Blockade and Siege of Yorktown 1781* (Washington, DC: US Printing Office, 1931).
Liverpool Mercury *The Loss of the Ramillies* (Liverpool: Liverpool Mercury, 1913).
Miller, Nathan, *Broadsides* (New York: John Wiley, 2000).
Monteiro, Paulo, 'HMS Pallas', *Nordic Underwater Archaeology* (January 2001).

Lloyd's List
Lloyd's Register of Ships

Michael and Jane Phillips's *Maritime History* site, www.cronab.demon.co.uk/marit.htm

Notes

1 The *Jason* was left behind because she had insufficient water for the voyage home.

2 The *Caton* and *Hector* were eventually brought to Britain and used as prison ships. Information abstracted by Mr J Rudland Hearn from a journal compiled by Captain Edward Hawkins RN, who in June 1808 was appointed superintendent of the prison ships.

3 A loose cannon on a ship at sea could do formidable damage to anyone and everything around it, hence the adoption of the term, particularly in business and politics, for an unpredictable person.

4 In fact the ship Inglefield tentatively identified as the *Glorieux* corresponds more closely, from its description, to the *Ramillies*.

5 The first Indiaman of that name, not to be confused with the one built in 1781 whose crew was saved in 1796 by the quick thinking of Sir Edward Pellew.

6 The *Belle*, Captain J Foster (or Forster), was a 350-ton, 3-deck ship, built at Stockton in 1764 and trading from London to Jamaica. She carried eight 6-pounders and four 4-pounders.

7 At least one assumes so, since he is known to have survived. In all probability it was Moriarty's own boat that waited for him.

8 *Augustus Caesar*, Captain J Fowler, a 450-ton, 3-deck ship, was built in London in 1774. She carried 14 six-pounders and two 3-pounders. Both she and the *Belle* were given new (wooden) sheathing on their return to England.

9 Although it is nowhere recorded, it is likely that, in the end, no rafts were constructed.

10 George Buchan noted the same when the position of the Indiaman *Winterton* became clear to passengers and crew alike (George Buchan, *The Loss of the Winterton*, Edinburgh, 1820)

11 This is the position given when, after the *Ramillies* exploded, the *Silver Eel* parted from the *Belle,* and the *Centaur* had apparently been visible in the distance.

12 *Silver Eel,* captain T Moore, was a 400-ton single-deck ship, built at Whitby in 1763 and armed with six 6-pounders.

13 Since these men would be the only witnesses at the court martial, Inglefield's motives might appear suspect, but given the lack of papers in the court martial file, it seems as though the trial was only a formality. Nevertheless, no captain could approach a court martial without some trepidation.

14 Cartels are vessels belonging to belligerent nations which are commissioned to carry prisoners who are being exchanged. They may not carry cargo, dispatches or munitions other than one signal gun.

15 After a swift rise to captain in 1781 and his posting to the *Ramillies*, Moriarty's active career stalled. His final appointment was as vice admiral of the white, and he died in 1814.

16 Inglefield's commands after the *Centaur* were the 64-gun *Scipio*, the 44-gun *Adventure* (in which he made several voyages to Africa), and the 50-gun *Medusa*. Later in the same year as his appointment as fleet captain he returned to Britain with Hood in the *Victory,* and held various appointments as a commissioner in the Mediterranean and at Halifax. He retired in 1811, and died in 1828. An unusual sidelight is thrown on his character by his involvement in a marital scandal in 1786, when he attempted to divorce his wife for allegedly having an affair with their African servant. The judge threw out the case because he considered Inglefield loved his wife so much that he had become excessively jealous to the point of imagining adultery.

4

Ice Ship

Albion

1810

Her rattling shrouds, all sheathed in ice,
With the masts went by the board;

H W LONGFELLOW, 'THE WRECK OF THE HESPERUS'

THE DISASTER THAT OVERTOOK ADMIRAL GRAVES'S FLEET was on a vast scale, and the only way to appreciate the human dimension is to zoom in on the individuals who wrote of their experiences. Inglefield clearly felt uncomfortable at leaving most of the ship's company to their fate, but it would be hard to blame him, any more than de Lafond, for taking the chance when it offered itself – and he had the decency to record his honest thoughts on the subject. Crises reveal human nature in every shade from best to worst, and the case of the *Albion*, set against a battle with a very different natural foe, offers striking examples of both, and of the power of human endurance.

A veteran of the Quebec and Montreal trade, John Kirby knew the dangers of the North Atlantic and the Canadian coast in winter: the ice, the storms that conjured up crashing seas, the fog, the blizzards and the pitiless winds that flayed men and ships, but as he tried to load timber in Charlotte County, New Brunswick, he had never experienced such intensely bitter weather as in that winter of 1809–10. His ship, the 242 ton *Albion*, lay at Digdeguash, with lengths of timber rafted alongside to be brought on board, but all work had stopped. The temperatures, always well below freezing, had plummeted further. The water casks on the ship were bursting under the pressure of the expanding ice, and the mouth of the St Croix River was turning white against the backdrop of the frost-capped forests, threatening to drive the timber out into the gleaming expanse of Passamaquoddy Bay and, not for the first time, shackling the ship in the harbour.

There was nothing else to do but have the huge rafts towed on land until the mercury rose. This barely improved the situation: the stacks on the shore froze, gluing the lengths together. Even when the thermometer lifted just enough to open the harbour, the cargo remained solid and had to be laboriously and expensively split apart, re-rafted and towed back to the ship for loading. The *Albion* may or may not have had scuttles cut in her hull to allow mast-length trunks to be loaded horizontally; if not, each piece would have been hoisted and stowed in the hold or on the half-deck by a crew wrapped up and muffled against the cold, fighting against frostbite, breathing air as sharp as glass.

If ships have memories, the Danish-built[1] *Albion*, 92 feet (28 metres) long and 25 feet (7.6 metres) in the beam, three-masted and square-rigged, must have looked back fondly to her early life when, as the *Koffie Boom*,[2] she had traded to Suriname for the Amsterdam merchants who had owned her, returning to her home port laden with coffee and cotton. But Napoleon had put an end to all that when he added the Netherlands to his empire and obliged Dutch ships to fly the flag of the short-lived Batavian Republic. Whether they liked it or not, the Dutch were now de-facto enemies of Britain, and their ships were legitimate prey. Captain Caspar Hansen was south of the Lizard when in 1803 he encountered HMS *Spartiate* and Captain John Manly RN. The *Koffie Boom* was seized and taken into Plymouth Harbour, her fate to be decided in the High Court of Admiralty. A proud burgher of Amsterdam with a stake in the cargo, Hansen argued his case eloquently but in vain. After a long-drawn-out legal battle the *Koffie Boom* and her cargo were sold at auction, bringing in over £29,000. Patriotically renamed *Albion*, she was registered in London at the end of the following year, and the Lloyd's Register surveyor who inspected her later was sufficiently impressed to award her the A1 Classification.

Lightly armed against privateers, she traded to the West Indies, but her best days were behind her, and the bitter aroma of coffee beans no longer impregnated her hold. In 1809, and still only around 11 years old, she came into the possession of Captain John Kirby, originally from Seaton in County Durham but now established in London's Rotherhithe, and his partner Matthew Boyd, a Camberwell rope-maker. Kirby had paid £790 for his one-third share in the three-masted, square-rigged vessel, whose value had halved since she had first been auctioned back in 1804. Her classification at Lloyd's had dropped to E1,

Dramatis Personae

N. Anderson : second mate

Matthew Boyd : co-owner of the *Albion*

Mr. Edwardes : passenger, *Shaw*

W. Fennel : seaman

John Holloway : apprentice

Robert Jackson : captain of the *Shaw*

John Johnson : cook

John Kirby : master and co-owner of the *Albion*

Thomas Loer : sailing master, *Nocton Packet*

William Lyons : first mate

Isaac Osterman : carpenter

Leon Panet : seaman

James Pilmore : apprentice

Richard the American : seaman

J Roallons : putative captain of the *Triton*

James Spears : apprentice

George Thompson : seaman

William Thompson : seaman

further evidence that *Albion* was no longer the smart ship who had plied the lucrative route to the West Indies.

Provided she was sound enough to cope with the North Atlantic, her condition was less important to Kirby and Boyd that it had been to Pole and Pouzelet of Amsterdam. Timber was not a delicate, dry cargo like coffee, spices, silk or sugar, which had to arrive in perfect condition to command a premium when sold or auctioned: lumber was green, cut either square or in the round, and floated downriver to be sold and loaded, much of it exported for the shipbuilding trade. English and Prussian oak was first choice for hulls, and in wartime the Royal Navy had first call on it, but masts and spars for all vessels were made from fir, particularly spruce. Supplies for European seafaring nations had traditionally come from the Baltic countries, but rapidly increasing demand had already led shipbuilders to look further afield, and the vast softwood forests of Canada's maritime provinces offered a seemingly unlimited supply. When Napoleon put a stranglehold on the Baltic trade, Canadian softwood, despite all the logistical difficulties posed by distance and enemy interference, became essential to British shipbuilding.

By Tuesday 16 January Kirby had completed loading, and he made a very curious statement about the process. 'In consequence of the danger attendant on loading of timber cargoes, I was particular that the ends of the timber should not touch the ceiling[3] or ends of the ship.' It suggests he feared the wood might swell during the voyage and breach the hull; but he was carrying green timber that had been brought downriver in the water. It was already as wet as it could ever be. Moreover, the shifting of cargo is the real hazard to be feared, and the way to prevent it is to pack the cargo tightly.

With conditions deteriorating, Kirby had his ship towed down the bay to St Andrews, at the tip of the peninsula between Passamaquoddy Bay and the St Croix, the river that separated the loyalist colonies of what is now Canada from the recently independent United States. The small colonial town, which had been established just a quarter of a century before, was another community heavily dependent on timber for its prosperity.

Mooring with two anchors outside the bar, but less than about 1000 feet (300 metres) from the wharves on Wednesday, in what he described as 'tolerably calm' weather, Kirby found himself in company with a dozen vessels. At least nine hailed from various English ports, including fellow Londoner *Princess of Wales* and the Whitby-registered *Adventure*, an old Whitby collier. which, in her younger days, had flown a naval ensign and accompanied Captain Cook on his second voyage of discovery (1772–75).

There were two Liverpool ships, the *Hero* and the *Lowdon*, the *Friends* from Workington, the Fowey ship *Harriet*, and the *Triton*. This last had undergone recent repairs: there were new planks on her stern and her deck, and her cook's house had new boards that had not been painted. Kirby would have good cause to remember her. Two other vessels, the *Mars* and the *Highlander*, were both stranded.

The crew of the *Albion* put up on shore. The ship had to be provisioned for the return voyage, and this was the opportunity to find warm beds and to meet up with the other crews for a drink and a change of company. Captain J. Shaw of the *Adventure* could guarantee a new audience to whom he could boast of his ship's illustrious past, before he became her master, and if conversation flagged there was always the weather to discuss.

Red sky at night, shepherd's delight; red sky at morning, sailor's warning, runs the old adage, and they awoke on the 18th to find the sunrise reflected in a blazing glow on the town's east-facing windows and dancing on the water. But enough days had already been lost: it was time to prepare for sea. Kirby sent the long-boat out to the *Albion* carrying stores sufficient for the crew of 13: fresh and salted meat, including a whole pig, dried hams, butter, flour, bread, 68 pounds (31 kilograms) of sugar, and an abundance of tea, coffee, rum and porter to go with the barrels of water.

That was all he could accomplish before a savage north-westerly gale set in, accompanied by the fogs that are common to areas round the Bay of Fundy at that season. Braving the savage wind, Kirby stood on the wharf and struggled to make out the distant wraith of his ship, whose topmast cross-trees occasionally emerged above the mist. The temperature plunged; people reported frostbite, and even spirits froze in their decanters.[4]

For three days the storm blew and there was nothing to do but keep indoors around a blazing fire and out of the howling wind-chill. So much ice accumulated in the harbour that those ships who, unlike the *Albion*, were inside the bar of the harbour to load at St Andrews, were unable to leave. Anxious about his ship in her more exposed position, Kirby used his previous experience of St Andrews and the advice of fellow mariners and locals to come to the decision that they would be better trying to put to sea. Later on there would be time to worry about hazards that owed nothing to the weather. He was unlikely to encounter French frigates and privateers so far from home.

On Sunday 21 January the weather showed an improvement, though the fog had not lifted. The four men sent out to find the *Albion* returned to report failure. When Kirby was able to locate and board her the following day, he calculated that she must have dragged her anchors for 1.5 miles (2.75 kilometres). With a broad skirt of ice surrounding her – a good 10 feet (3 metres) thick on her bows – and frost coating her rigging and ropes, she might have passed for a magnificent confection of spun sugar, but for her crew there was nothing romantic in the sight. The same physics that burst a frozen water cask from the inside could crush a ship's hull from the outside or, perhaps worse, leave it strained and weakened for the open seas to exploit.

It took some days to break the ice around her hull, but on the Wednesday Isaac Osterman, the carpenter, inspected the hold. When he reported her tight, Kirby had her moved closer to the bar. A quick spell on the pumps sucked out the bilge water, and at dawn on Sunday 28th, all paperwork completed, the *Albion* weighed anchor. She dropped off her pilot at noon at Head Harbour, and now she was out into the Bay of Fundy. By Monday afternoon she had cleared Machias. Snow and sleet coated her deck and the exposed cargo, freezing a foot thick. The water casks stowed in the open likewise froze and split, forcing the crew to break them open and hack off chunks of ice to melt in the galley for fresh water, but with a light north-easterly wind and a rolling swell the *Albion* made fair progress through the wintry waters for the next few days while the cook ensured a supply of tea, coffee and hot meals to warm the men from the inside.

It was a heterogeneous and close-knit crew, divided into two watches. William Lyons, the first mate, Seaman W. Fennel and two of the apprentices, John Holloway and James Spears, came from London, the last three from Bermondsey. The third apprentice, 14-year-old James Pilmore from

Monkwearmouth Shore was a north-easterner like his captain. There were two
Swedes: Osterman, the carpenter, and second mate N. Anderson from Gotland
Island; one French-Canadian, Leon Panet of Montreal, a seaman known as
Richard the American, and John Johnson the cook, who despite his name
claimed to be from Hamburg. William Thompson came from Fifeshire, but the
origin of the thirteenth man, George Thompson, was not given. Mutual respect
and liking seems to have existed between captain and crew; their ability to pull
together was about to be tested to the full.

The *Albion* had made a little water on February 5, but the problem was easily
repaired. The following day, Tuesday, with the wind at east-north-east and the
ship hove-to in Latitude 41° 46′ N, Longitude 55° 20′ W (where they were 246
miles / 455 kilometres from Sable Island and 315 miles / 580 kilometres from
Cape Race), the crew assembled for breakfast, having just routinely pumped
the ship dry. During the meal the carpenter mentioned that a little water was
coming in every time the ship's stern dipped. It was a minor matter, but he left
the cabin to get his tools.

A moment later he was back with news that left the crew in horrified disbelief. In the time they had taken to eat, the ship had sprung a massive leak. The
half-deck below was already awash: chests stowed on the some of the timber
were floating. At that moment, water appeared at the foot of the cabin ladder,
freeing tongues paralysed by shock.

There was no time to speculate on what had gone wrong. Kirby led the
scramble for the deck. The *Albion* was going down, bow first; time was critical.
So much water moving around in her hull might at any moment change her
centre of gravity and cause her to list. Then the weight of masts and spars
would throw her onto her beam ends. Desperate to keep his foundering ship
before the wind, he gave the drastic order to ease her by cutting away the mainmast, while the pumps were manned in the vain hope of somehow stemming
the rising water. He shouted for the port rigging to be cut. A glance at the men
frantically hacking away at the mainmast showed their axes had made a gash of
barely three inches. They would never do it in time.

At that moment, the *Albion* went over onto her port side in a great crash of
water, rope and canvas. Somehow Kirby recovered, climbed over the lumber up
to the main rigging on the starboard side and, like Inglefield before him, began
cutting it away, Other members of the crew were gathering further aft; he
ordered them to cut away the rigging of the mizzen mast. As they obeyed, a
huge icy sea, so cold it seemed to burn, rolled over them, dragging and driving
them across the rigging. Kirby found himself on a level with the main top.
Thrashing and clawing his way through water, rope and canvas, he got back to
the now-vertical deck and found others who had been swept out likewise
regaining the ship. They climbed up and cut ropes to tie themselves to the rails
and stanchions to which they clung, praying that the ship would not turn turtle.

They were a miserable group, cowering beneath the lash of the wind, bedraggled and soaked through, many with stockings and trousers torn off. Before they could take stock of who might be missing, a second wave struck, ripping away almost everything on the deck: the wheel, compass, binnacle, boats, hearth, almost all the timber. With nothing to hold them, the main and mizzen masts were also swept away, trailing the webs of their severed shrouds.

Freed from the heavy drag, the hull rolled herself almost upright, with a list to port, but now so low in the water that the port gunwale was on a level with the surface of the sea. All that remained of the masts and rigging was the foremast, bowsprit and jib-boom. From the solitary fore-yard flew a rag that had been the fore-course. The frozen and half-drowned crew could at last drag themselves onto their feet. Still stunned, Kirby asked if all were safe, to be told that one of the three young apprentices, Holloway, had been swept to his death. One of the crew suggested they would all be better to gather forward. Beside the foremast – the single mast remaining – Kirby addressed them, urging them to have courage. There was little he could do of a practical nature: all the food and water was below deck, ruined by seawater, or swept away. The twelve survivors huddled together in a body in an attempt to create some human warmth.

Despite having filled with water so quickly, it seemed the ship had reached a point of equilibrium and was not sinking any further, giving one of the crew enough confidence to risk climbing down into the fore-scuttle that provided light and ventilation below deck. Here he found a refuge for them for the night, wet but sheltered.

They began the next day with prayers on the quarterdeck before some of the crew explored the few accessible parts of the ship in search of food. They located a cask of salted beef and pork and another of water, but the sea had got into the water, leaving it useless, and there was no means of making a fire with which to cook the meat. A sail was spotted on the horizon, but the *Albion* wallowed too low to be seen. And now, as the ship passively obeyed the elements, the short timbers loaded onto the half deck became a battering ram, smashing into the bulkhead and the cabins behind it, threatening to destroy her from within.

A laden ship in a heavy sea is bound to work her seams – the narrow gaps between the planking – and the vessel will then take on water. Usually, the pumps will deal competently with it. The speed with which *Albion* had filled, however, and the manner in which she began to go down, suggested a catastrophic failure of the fore-hoods – the horizontal planks rabbeted into the stem to form the bows – rather than mere leaking seams. Those days at Digdeguash, and more particularly off St Andrews, with the stress of the thick ice around the bows, must have had an effect on a vessel no longer in prime condition. Once out of the comparatively sheltered waters of Passamaquoddy

Bay, that weakness had been exposed.

If the *Albion* was to hold together until rescue arrived, they would have to take action now, even if it meant tying her up like a parcel with whatever rope they could find. Captain Moriarty had done something similar with the *Ramillies*. Kirby's plan required getting two swifters round the ship, a recognized form of emergency measure. A loop of cable, large enough to accommodate the hull, had to be put over the stern and dragged along the keel until it reached the desired position, where it could then be tightened enough to take some of strain from the timbers. They found a cable down on the half deck, but hopelessly tangled up with spare canvas and sails, so first they had to rig up a windlass to heave out the remains of the mizzen mast before setting up a tackle to lift the heavy cable – a difficult job for a sodden and frozen crew, most of whom had hardly eaten or drunk anything for a couple of days.

By the end of 8 February they had not finished the swifters, but while searching for rope they had come across a red and a blue ensign, which they hoisted to the top of the mizzen-mast on poles as a distress signal, and they had also located some boards that, when passed through the fore-scuttle, enabled them to create something like a level sleeping platform. Not that any of them were able to sleep in the water that slopped through their new quarters whenever the ship rolled.

Shortly after they had completed the second swifter and manoeuvred it into position, from the fore-top came the news they had longed for. Once again the lookout had spotted a ship, but this one was no mere speck: she was running before the wind towards them. Ecstatically they watched as she reefed her topsails about two miles from them, and from the activity on board it looked as if she was preparing to lower a boat.

Cold, exhaustion, thirst – all were forgotten as the *Albion*'s crew set about preparing for rescue. They attached three buoys to a rope fed over the stern, calculating that the vessel would heave-to astern of them and that her boat would be able to moor by them at the safe distance of 20–30 feet (6–9 metres). All the while their salvation was coming closer.

The varnished black hull with a white streak down each side seemed familiar, and they were both surprised and delighted to recognize her as the *Triton*,[5] one of the ships that had loaded at St Andrews, and coincidentally the only vessel whose captain they had not met. Strangely, however, she was not flying any colours, as if she was waiting to find out what they were before she showed a flag. Kirby had no idea whether she was friend or foe. Now she was within hailing distance, and from her deck a man shouted:

'What do you want?'

An odd question to ask, when the *Albion*'s plight was so obvious. Kirby remembered every detail of the conversation that took place.

'For God's sake, take us out!' he begged. The *Triton* held her course, preparing to pass his stern. The man called again:

'Have you a boat?'

'No!'

They were passing very close to *Albion*'s stern; the helmsman put the helm hard a-port, the fore topsail was filled and the vessel's head came close round *Albion*. Her sails shook and her main topsail came aback. They could see the details of the repairs to her stern. Someone else hailed Kirby with the original question: 'What do you want?' and he returned the same answer as before. The response was swift.

'I will send a boat for you immediately!'

It looked as though some of the crew were already preparing the boat in anticipation of the order, but then their ship filled her sails and reached ahead of *Albion*. However, the sight of men on the lee[7] fore- and main-yards suggested they were about to rig up the tackle to lower a boat on that side.

Kirby's men could barely believe their good fortune, thanking God for their rescue and imagining the warmth and food they would enjoy before dark. There would be hot food, no more cold, wet nights in the fore-scuttle, no clothes freezing to the skin. They were safe.

But the order went out on the *Triton* to set courses and let out the reefs; her sails filled and the distance between the two ships grew until the *Triton* was some 6 miles (11 kilometres) distant. Kirby's crew watched her, puzzled, seeing her sails shake as if she were trying to tack. At last she hauled by the wind on the port tack and came back, passing within 200 feet (60 metres) of the *Albion*'s starboard.

This time the *Triton* made no attempt to communicate with the crippled vessel – she simply maintained her tack and was lost into the horizon, leaving the *Albion* to her fate.

Little wonder if the crew responded to their abandonment with anger and imprecations, or tried to deceive themselves with the hope that the *Triton* would return. Kirby did his best to calm them down; the *Albion* was in well-frequented waters, and if they had sighted two ships in as many days, then there was every likelihood of a third in the morning.

The effect of the abandonment on their spirits was felt the following day. The weather was fine and bright, visibility excellent, but all they could see was the shining dark and empty ocean. No one could fondly imagine that rescue lay close. Their mood ranged from fury against the heartless captain to uncaring lethargy. Kirby shared his opinion of the man freely with them, and admitted that they should have realized quite early on they were not going to get any help from him. The lack of colours and the strange ship-handling should have roused their suspicions. It would be several weeks before they had the answer to the riddle of the *Triton*'s unusual behaviour.

þæt se mon ne wat / þe him on foldan fægrost limpeð
hu ic earmcearig iscealdne sæ / winter wunade wræccan lastum

The man who lives comfortably on land has no idea how I have survived the winter on the icy sea, wretched with anxiety.

The Seafarer, anonymous Anglo-Saxon

Thus far they had held out physically, but over the next couple of days painful boils appeared on their skin, agonizing when touched. They noticed their urine changing colour, and hunger became a rather distant sensation. On Sunday morning, 12 February, less than a week after *Albion* had sprung her leak, came the first death: John Johnson, the cook. They had leisure for grief; the death of one did not assist the survival of the rest, only reminded them of their own mortality, and they said prayers over the body before sending it into the water.

The discovery by William Lyons of some black powder, probably in one of the ship's two three-pound guns, was a boost to morale. If they could only get a fire going they could cook some meat or take a light down into the fore-scuttle. Equally, if a sail was sighted, they could make smoke to attract attention. Lyons took some oakum and put it to dry in the sun before mixing it with the powder. Made from old ship's rope, picked into fibres – often by convicts – oakum was used as a flexible sealant in the seams of wooden ships. They now had tinder, but they needed a flint and steel to make the spark. Kirby remembered putting a flint down while the ship was loading, and by some miracle it was found. A knife did duty for a steel or frizzen, but it took over two hours to make a spark strong enough to catch in the tinder and take firm hold. Kirby even tore off a part of his cotton shirt as spare tinder, just in case it was needed.

Inspired by their success, and cheered by the first warm day of the voyage, they went on to create matches from the pieces of brimstone (sulphur) that Lyons and George Thompson wore next to their bodies in the belief that it prevented the cramp from which they both suffered. Now for the first time since the disaster they had the means to light a fire. At last they were able to broil the pork and beef, and there were some who made a hearty meal of it. Kirby tried, but discovered he could not face it. What should have been delicious just turned his stomach. It tasted off.

The brilliant winter sunshine of day was followed by a heavy swell and a bitter night. While his crew took to the fore-scuttle, the captain went to the top of the foremast, presumably to keep watch, but it was impossible to spend the entire night exposed to the wind-chill and the waves. The heavy seas continued the next day, Monday, putting out the fire, and on Tuesday there was new cause for anxiety. A gale was blowing, driving the helpless hulk, and causing the water inside the hull to surge. Balks of timber in the hold now smashed and battered against the stern, the din mingling with the crescendos of wind and the crash of waves. Down in the fore-scuttle the crew were vainly trying to secure their refuge against the water that poured in through the hatchway. In the evening, defeated by the wet but fearing for the lives of those who chose to remain below, Kirby and one of the seamen went up to the fore-top, where he had placed some canvas to form a kind of small tent. They stayed until the cold drove first one and then the other back down.

Any hopes of the gale blowing itself out in the night were dashed. Heavier seas than before rolled over the directionless *Albion* throughout the Wednesday, and torrential rain turned first to snow and then to hail. Unable to go below, everyone except the two young apprentices, Spears and Pilmore, climbed up the mast, but there was only shelter for three, and the rest had to make do with what little protection they could find on the lee side of the mast, away from the wind. Exhausted from lack of food and sleep, exposed in inadequate wet clothes to such extreme cold for so long, they were losing the ability to stave off death. With nothing to drink, some of them had taken to sucking lead or chewing pieces of spruce and rigging in order to work up saliva in their parched mouths. Lyons continually repeated the desire to leave the fore-top and go below, but he had completely lost the use of his limbs, and nobody was in a position to help him. His captain was all but hanging in an improvised harness, deliberately keeping his arms and legs moving to maintain circulation. Frostbite could lead to gangrene. If that set in, he was a dead man.

From the deck, Panet the Montreal seaman was using his last strength in an attempt to climb up to the tent. He had made it up the lower shrouds and onto the short futtock shrouds. Unable to get further he called weakly 'Thompson, Thompson,' to his comrade, William, huddled in the lee of the canvas. Thompson looked out, saw Panet and went to help him; but before could do anything, the Canadian had lost his hold and pitched backwards, one foot caught in the shroud. He hung there, dead, and Thompson managed to get a rope round the corpse to keep it from falling to the deck or into the sea. Nobody was going to be simply abandoned: the dead were still comrades, and would go into the water with dignity and the prayers of their companions.

Not long afterwards, William Lyons died in the pathetic shelter of the canvas. Devastated by the loss of a quarter of his men in the nine days since *Albion* had gone over, Kirby could find no adequate words to describe his feelings of grief and despair, except to state the stark fact that 'nothing entered our mouths this day but the snow and ice taken from off the canvas, under which my mate lay dead'. Not *the* mate, but *my* mate.

Once again the cold forced him and Thompson down into the fore-scuttle, but though it was less cold than outside, there was still no possibility of sleep. Kirby never said what went through his mind, other than how to keep the crew alive and raise their morale, but he must thought of his family and home, even if the hopes of seeing them again were dwindling. His second wife, Mary, to whom he had been married seven years this month, was a merchant captain's daughter from West Acklam, and like himself had come from County Durham; her younger brother Luke was also a captain, and had briefly commanded the *Albion* the previous year. Had she ever really got used to waiting for the men in her life to come home?

She was 29 when John Kirby married her, and she had given him the one child. William Hansall, named after her late father, was now toddling around their London home in Paradise Street, Rotherhithe. Young William's devoutly Christian father, clinging to life as his crew froze and starved around him, must surely have believed Paradise to be closer than Paradise Street.

Whatever happened, the family would be comfortable if he died. Mary had told him not to waste time making a will, but in March 1809, while at Spithead, he put his intentions into writing. The house, or rooms, in London were rented, but he had a freehold house back in Seaton, and that would keep a roof over his mother's head until her death, after which it would pass to his son along with his share in the *Albion* – except for the £100 invested in the voyage by his brother-in-law Luke, which was to be repaid along with the appropriate percentage profit. Well, the *Albion* was gone, and with her all the profit, but the ship was insured. His father-in-law had left him £100, and he wanted Mary to have that, to do as she pleased with. And she, rather than anyone else, was to bring up little William. He had even decided who should be the boy's tutors: one set if Mary decided to stay in London, another if she preferred to live near Stockton.

All they achieved of any note on 16 February, a Friday, was the burial of Lyons and Panet, but on Saturday Kirby got them working. The fore-scuttle was untenable as an asylum; the crude fore-top refuge too exposed. What they needed to build – and they had the materials – was what sailors referred to as a hurricane house or a weather hut. How their numbed hands managed to rig a tackle to bring up the canvas or fasten it in place around the lower shrouds of the foremast only they could know. It took them two days to accomplish the task, but it gave them a stronger shelter, although it had no roof.

With good weather on the Monday, the ship was quieter, the water below deck less dangerous. Kirby tied a rope round his waist using a bowline knot that would not slip and went through the cabin hatchway to see would could be found in the way of food. There was nothing. The following day, he and the Swedish second mate took a pole and used it to help them dive down the cabin scuttle, undeterred by the consideration that neither could swim. Although they found no food nor sealed liquid, they emerged with some useful objects, including a knife. Best of all they brought up a cask of turpentine, which enabled them to get their little fire going and acted as a dressing for their wounds. And when some seaweed was washed onto the deck everyone saw it as manna from heaven and devoured it.

For some time, Kirby, very much a father-figure to his apprentices, had been anxious about James Spears. Despite all his captain's injunctions, he insisted on drinking water from the casks even though it was contaminated with salt. Kirby had told his crew to stop him, but he was sure that Spears was managing to evade surveillance. On the 21st, Kirby could see he was dying, and that upset the captain perhaps more than any other death. The boy had always been well behaved and able; since the disaster he had showed great maturity in accepting fate. Now he earnestly begged his captain for some of the salty water, and Kirby, taking it as a dying request, sadly consented. Spears died the following day, and was followed by his fellow apprentice, Pilmore, during the night of 23–24 February after a day of swell so heavy that the remaining crew could only move fore-and-aft on the deck by stretching a rope along the ship. They had lost six men, five since the *Triton* had declined to assist them, but on the evening of the Sunday the 24th they spotted a sail on the horizon. Now the turpentine was a blessing: they poured it into their boiler along with rope fibre and got a good fire going, which they maintained through the night, but their hopes came to nothing and they sank back into resignation.

Once again, Kirby had them working: it was useful labour, but it had an added value in taking their mind off their predicament and creating the idea that they were contributing to their survival. They cut the cable to the best bower anchor, the heaviest on board, and got it over the side; later they did the same with the other bower anchor to try to lighten the ship and make her ride higher in the water. They stretched canvas above the hurricane house and caught rainwater, which they boiled up with some spruce bark to make a substitute tea. On both the 26th and 27th they had seen ships, and 'it is needless for me to say, that the joy the poor creatures felt when a sail was announced, was beyond measure: they would cry *glory! glory! glory!* and were in a state almost amounting to frenzy.'

Yet Kirby seems to have started to lose serious hope of being rescued. On the 26th the fire had gone out, and they could not get it going again. His fingers and part of his left foot were suffering from frostbite. There were no more confident speeches, just longer gaps between his recollections of what took place. Osterman, the Swedish carpenter, had lapsed into unconsciousness on the last day of February, and on the night of 1 March he was washed overboard. Death, as Kirby said, had become familiar; worse, most of them were longing for it. Yet he paid a great tribute to his crew for 'the care and attention my deceased fellow sufferers always paid to me whilst alive by placing me in the most secure situation, when, perhaps, they were themselves in most need of it'. Like the survivors from the *Prince*, the crew felt they needed their captain's leadership and it was in their group interest to keep Kirby alive to ensure that some would survive.

Richard the American died on 6 March. George Thompson and Fennel stayed in the fore-scuttle with their dead friend; the other three who remained – Kirby, William Thompson and Anderson – spent the night in the hurricane house where they were joined by Thompson and Fennel after the sea had driven them out half-drowned and choking. Unable to settle, George Thompson wanted to go back again, and the others lowered him down by rope. But as he took off the rope a sea washed over the deck and he was gone. Twenty-four hours later, Fennel too died.

There were just three of them left, so debilitated that it took twenty minutes just to stand up. From 13 March they were confined to the hurricane house not just by their weakness but by huge seas that broke over the ship and reached as high as their refuge. Kirby noted that his vision was dim, and it hurt to look out to sea. Then, on Friday 15 March the weather moderated and Kirby managed to get onto the deck where, using an improvised scoop, he attempted to fish around in the after-scuttle for anything that might be useful. Earlier, he thought he had seen a distant sail, but it had disappeared. Weary of his fruitless search he crawled along the deck on his hands and knees, and he had just reached the forepart when from up in the shelter Anderson's hoarse, dry voice called:

'A sail! A sail!'

Unwilling to allow his hopes to be raised, Kirby was almost sceptical, but when he dragged himself up the rigging to join the other two he saw with his own eyes. It was a brig, a two-masted, square-rigged vessel, and he could make out the steering sail on her fore-topmast. Between pauses to regain what little strength remained to them, the three survivors set up the two ensigns on their poles at the head of the foremast. Below, they attached three red shirts. Any ship spotting those was bound to be curious.

If it spotted them.

All they could do was to wait, and this time they were not to be disappointed. At around 1:00 p.m. they saw the steering sail come down and the brig making directly for them, a red ensign hoisted at her peak. Two hours later she was astern; a voice hailed them and asked how long ago they had lost their masts.

'Thirty-seven days!' Kirby's words emerged in a feeble croak; they could not make out what he said, and he gestured to them to come closer.

'I will send a boat for you!' shouted the captain, and acting on his orders the crew lowered a boat with four men, one of them the vessel's mate. As he prepared to quit the hulk of the *Albion* Kirby took his knife and cut into the mast the bald facts of their ordeal:

ALBION, *Kirby, London, upset February 6th 1810, out March 15th, 3 survivors, 37 days.*

Quite what the quartet in the boat made of the 'poor starving wretches' in those early moments – their excoriated skin, wild beards and emaciated frames – can only be imagined, but they shouted encouragement.

'We are glad we have fallen in with you!'

'Come, my brave fellows, let us have you into the boat!'

'Here is a fine brig and everything you may want!'

It seems strange that Captain Kirby subsequently laid stress on the fact that they were British seamen who had come to their aid when his own second mate was a Swede, his dead comrades represented several nationalities and the ship that had abandoned them was, despite her lack of colours, British. Obviously he would have been relieved that they would be taken to a British port, but he also praised the gentle way in which they were helped into the boat as characteristic of 'true Englishmen'. Was it so unlikely that an American merchantman or a French frigate would have treated them as kindly? But then again, this was wartime, and patriotism ran high.

In the bottom of the little boat they found some squeezed limes, and they crammed them into their mouths and ate the first food to pass their lips since the seaweed. Then they were hoisted on board.

They found themselves greeted by Captain Robert Jackson, commander of the *Shaw* – a Liverpool ship homeward bound from St Kitts – his passenger, Mr Edwardes, and the whole crew. They were offered port and madeira to drink, but all Kirby wanted was water and a little ship's biscuit. Meanwhile the boat was raised and the *Shaw* got under way.

Her complement was kindness itself, and Kirby could not praise them enough. It was three days before his clothes could be changed; they had stuck to his skin, but Jackson and Edwardes undressed him themselves, and the sight that greeted them was shocking. His bones had cut through his skin in several places, and his fingers and toes were frostbitten. The two men treated him, gave him fresh clothes and nursed him through the suppuration that followed – yet by a miracle he lost only one toe and a fingertip.

But what horrified Jackson and the others on the *Shaw* even more than the condition in which they had found the three survivors was the conduct of the master of the *Triton*.

The *Albion* trio were not the only sailors to whom Captain Jackson proved a good samaritan. On 23 January, the *Shaw* came up to the *Nesbery*, which had been struck by lighting two days earlier. The Liverpool-registered brig was taking on water and her fore topmasts were shattered; her master was glad of the reassuring company of another vessel until land was sighted.

The *Shaw* reached Liverpool on 4 April, whereupon Jackson bore his fellow captain off to the warm hospitality of his mother's home. Word of mouth and the local newspaper spread the story, prompting sympathy and aid from a dismayed and compassionate maritime community. The aptly named *Albion*, Liverpool's newspaper, recorded the arrival:

The Brig SHAW, Captain Jackson, which arrived here on Wednesday, brought with it the foregoing melancholy account ... The surviving crew ... were in such an emaciated state that they were not able to get into the boat when the Shaw came alongside ... and were found to be chewing the bark of a spruce spar which had been their principal support ... what added to their misery was seeing their fellow sufferers dying for want.

The *Naval Chronicle* also reported the story almost word for word. Later, the three survivors would swear to the truth of their account, the captain in front of the Lord Mayor of London, but for the moment all they had to do was to recuperate. Kirby was slower to recover than Thompson and Anderson, both of whom escaped frostbite. He, by contrast, was weak, and the consequences of the frostbite made walking difficult, but extraordinary news reached him a couple of days into his convalescence. A ship answering the description of the infamous vessel that had so cruelly ignored them was in Liverpool.

Robert Jackson had him taken to the Queen's Dock, and there she was: the new boards on the stern, the unpainted planks of the cook's house ... Hardly able to credit his eyes or his memory, Kirby sent word to Thompson and Anderson, who came down and confirmed the identification.

The matter could not be allowed to rest, not with nine of the ten deaths attributable solely to the failure of the *Triton* to help. Kirby went to the ship and confronted a man who appeared to be the captain.

There was no apology, or even concern. The captain[7] acknowledged that he had passed a ship in trouble and described the precise state of the *Albion*, but he was totally indifferent to the suffering he had caused, and gave it as his opinion that the men he encountered had only had a few days to live anyway, and there was a gale blowing so he could not have got his boat out. He claimed, furthermore, it looked like an American vessel with a French or Spanish crew – implying, therefore, that it had been captured and was carrying a prize crew. Kirby listened, outwardly calm, as the man told him what he thought of the French and Spanish, and then said:

'So you had good reason for not taking us off: you thought we might take the ship from you?'

The *Triton*'s captain looked at him in contempt.

'Me afraid? No, Sir, I was not afraid. Me afraid? No, Sir, I assure you I never was afraid of anything in my life.'

That was all, and his attitude never changed. For whatever reason, Kirby asked his indignant supporters not to take the matter further, but when he wrote to the underwriters setting out all that had happened to the *Albion*[8] he undertook to identify the captain if they insisted, and he claimed to have documents to prove his case – though what these might have been is unclear.

A report, probably originating from the master of the *Shaw*, stated that they found the *Albion* and her survivors in 37°30′ N, 42° 20′ W. Some time later, out of the blue, Kirby received a letter from Thomas Loer, sailing master of the *Nocton Packet*. Loer had come across the *Albion*, still afloat, on 6 April, and having boarded her out of curiosity he must have seen the message carved on the mast. He told Kirby that that he had found her in Latitude 37° 11′ N, Longitude 42° 24′ W. How long she remained afloat thereafter, and where she eventually foundered or was battered to pieces, is anybody's guess. Wrecked timber carriers were not unknown to wallow for weeks, becoming a hazard to shipping. In 1809 HMS *Virago* arrived in Plymouth after towing an unnamed waterlogged timber-carrier for five weeks. From a note aboard her, they learned that the crew had been rescued two months before the ship had been found.

John Kirby returned to sea, back into the North Atlantic timber trade that he knew. In the spring of 1814 he left Quebec bound for London in the *Whim*.[9] The ship never arrived, and the following April the improvised will he had made back in 1809 was declared valid and executed. Whether the ship went down in minutes, or whether her crew suffered an ordeal like the *Albion*'s, will never be known. Captain Kirby joined the hundreds of thousands of seafarers whose ships foundered without anyone to bear witness to their fate.

The loss of the *Albion* also attracted a brief entry in *Lloyd's List* on Friday 6 April: '*Albion*, Kirby, of London from New Brunswick, upset on the 6th February in a gale. Captain Kirby and two seamen taken off the wreck, by the *Shaw*, arrived at Liverpool. Ten of the crew died through hunger.'

No chill winds blew through the corridors of power as a result of the incident, and no great artist immortalized the *Albion* in oils, though engravings embellished Kirby's account when it was printed in London the same year. Had her name been prefixed with the initials HMS or HEICS, she would have enjoyed at least some posthumous fame; had she been a great passenger liner carrying diamond-studded aristocrats or captains of industry, her celebrity would have been assured. Merely being lost in bad weather rarely counts, and yet the sheer endurance of the survivors, and indeed the ship herself, can hardly be overemphasized. People die of hypothermia when trapped overnight in their cars in a British winter, as do mountaineers when caught out in bad weather, despite the most sophisticated clothing and equipment. Wet, dehydrated, freezing and starving, three very ordinary seamen lasted for 37 days on a humble cargo ship that refused to go down.

Sources and Bibliography

My thanks Peter Hammesley of Churchill and Sim Ltd for his observations on timber stowage, to Professor Cesar N Caviedes, Deptartment of Geography, University of Florida for supporting John Kirby's observations on the excessively low temperatures that winter, and to Dr Peter Goodwin, curator, HMS *Victory*, for his suggestion that the *Albion*'s forehoods failed. I am indebted to Mrs Ellen Kirby for generously putting her family's information about her ancestor at my disposal.

National Archives
BT 107/19 (certificate of registry)
HCA 32/1377 (capture and auction information)

Kirby, John, *Narrative of the Wreck and Loss of the Ship Albion of London*, (London: privately published, 1810; reprinted, Stockton: W Robinson, 1846).
Grocott, Terence, *Shipwrecks of the Revolutionary and Napoleonic Eras* (London: Chatham, 1997; second edition, London: Caxton, 2002).
Hall, Frank, 'Oh Be Joyful', *Manitoba Pageant* 22/2 (Winter 1977); also available online at www.mhs.mb.ca/docs/pageant/22/ohbejoyful.shtml
Gibson, Doug, 'The *Adventure*', *Cook's Log* 3/3 (1978): 87 (also available at www.captaincooksociety.com/ccsu74.htm)
Kirby, John, 'The Will of John Kirby, Ship Albion, Spithead, 24 March 1809' (private collection)

The Albion (Liverpool)
Lloyd's List
Lloyd's Register of Ships
Naval Chronicle
Sherborne and Yeovil Chronicle, 7 August 1809

Notes

[1] She is recorded by *Lloyd's Register* as being Dutch built, but her Dutch captain believed she was built in Denmark
[2] Dutch for *Coffee Tree*. Her name is spelt variously in the Board of Trade and High Court of Admiralty Record – *Coffy Boom* or *Coffe Boom*.
[3] ' Ceiling' refers here not to the underside of the deck but to the inside planking of the floor and sides of the ship's hold – just as the domestic ceiling is nailed to the joists.
[4] Some years earlier, the Hudson's Bay Company surveyor and explorer Peter Fidler, based at York Factory on the frozen shore of Hudson Bay in what is now Manitoba, had recorded the effect of Canada's winter temperatures on spirits. He found Holland gin froze at –17° F (–27° C), English brandy at –25° F (–32° C) and Jamaica rum at –31° F (–35° C), evidence not just of the cold but of the wide variation in the alcohol content of the three spirits.
[5] The identification of the vessel as the *Triton* is conjectural. Kirby listed all the vessels loading at St Andrews, with their captains and, in most cases, their port of registry. The *Triton* is the only vessel listed with neither, which suggests he did not want it identified.
[6] 'Lee', and its opposite 'weather', relate to the position of the ship in relation to the wind at any time. The weather side is exposed to the wind; the lee is sheltered. Therefore a boat would be lowered on the lee side, in this case the starboard, where there would be protection from the wind.
[7] *Triton* is a common name, and the only certain facts about her are that she was a ship in the technical sense: three-masted and square rigged on all masts. Nine are listed in *Lloyd's Register of Ships (Shipowners)* of which one might reasonably be identified with the *Triton* at St Andrews. She is a vessel of 345 tons, the same age as the *Albion* and built in Sweden. Comparing that entry with one in the rival Underwriters' Book for the same year it is clear that she has a Liverpool connection – probably her port of last Lloyd's Survey. Her owner was a J Brown, and her trade was either Quebec or Newfoundland – Canada, at all events. In 1808 she had some repairs made. If this is she, then the villain of Kirby's story is captain J Roallons or Reallons.
[8] This account was published as a pamphlet, though whether by the insurers or by friends of Kirby's is unknown. It was reprinted in Stockton (and therefore probably by a Kirby family connection) in 1846.
[9] 'The Will of John Kirby etc proved by affidavit on 16th March 1815.'

5

The Gorgon's Curse

Méduse

1816

Well, then – our course is chosen – spread the sail –
Heave oft the lead, and mark the soundings well –
Look to the helm, good master – many a shoal
Marks this stern coast, and rocks, where sits the Siren
Who, like ambition, lures men to their ruin.

SIR WALTER SCOTT, KENILWORTH, ch. 17

IN 1740 BYRON AND BULKELY had published their extended narrative of the loss of HMS *Wager*;[1] and in 1795 John Dale – or at least his enterprising publisher – had prefixed his account of the wreck of the *Winterton* with the following statement:[2] 'There exists in the human mind a strong and incessant desire to be acquainted with the misfortunes of others.'

What happened in 1816, however, went far beyond 'misfortune'. Most disasters involve human error of some sort, but this plunged deeply into the realms of inhumanity and criminal culpability. While the *Albion*'s plight rated only a few lines in a couple of newspapers, the loss of a certain French frigate became a national scandal that shook a government. One of the very best documented of all maritime tragedies, it was arguably the first in which the press was brought in as a weapon, and its power to shock and dismay has never abated.

Dramatis Personae

Benoît Barbotin :	midshipman; embarked on the governor's barge
Denis Bellot :	midshipman; embarked on the Senegal boat
Griffon du Bellay :	passenger; embarked on the raft
Monsieur Benière :	army captain; embarked on the longboat
Charles-Marie Brédif :	passenger; embarked on the longboat
Colonel Thomas Brereton :	British governor of Senegal
Monsieur Charlot :	army sergeant-major; embarked on the raft
Monsieur de Chastellus :	passenger; embarked on the yawl
Vincent Chaudière :	ensign; embarked on the captain's barge
Vicomte Hugues Duroy de Chaumareys :	captain of the *Méduse*; embarked on the captain's barge
Monsieur Clairet :	army sub-lieutenant; embarked on the raft
Monsieur Clanet :	ship's paymaster; embarked on the governor's barge
Alexandre Corréard :	passenger; embarked on the raft
Jean Daniel Coudein :	midshipman; embarked on the raft
Monsieur Courtade :	master gunner; embarked on the raft
Monsieur Dupont :	army captain; embarked on the raft
Monsieur La Bergue d'Einville :	commissaire de la marine; embarked on the yawl
Jean-Baptiste Espiaux :	second lieutenant; embarked on the longboat
Monsieur Follet :	chief surgeon; embarked on the captain's barge
Jean-Charles :	seaman; embarked on the raft
Mr Kearney :	British officer in Senegal
Monsieur Kummer :	passenger; embarked on the longboat
Monsieur Lachenault :	passenger; embarked on the longboat
Monsieur Lavillette :	passenger; embarked on the raft
Léon :	ship's boy; embarked on the raft

'Gentlemen, it has been 25 years since I last went to sea. I am not ashamed to admit that my seamanship is rusty. I ask you, therefore, to bear with me and to think of me as a father to you. For my part, I promise to

Monsieur Lozach : army lieutenant; embarked on the raft

Marie-Zaide : passenger; embarked on the raft

Joseph Maudet : ensign; embarked on the Senegal boat

Gaspar Théodore Mollien : passenger; embarked on the Senegal boat

Léon de Parnajon : captain of the *Argus*

Monsieur Petit : army lieutenant; embarked on the longboat

Pierre La Peyrère : ensign; embarked on the pinnace

Alphonse Picard : passenger; embarked on the pinnace

Caroline Picard : passenger; embarked on the pinnace

Charles Picard : passenger; embarked on the pinnace

Charlotte Picard : passenger; embarked on the pinnace

Laura Picard : passenger; embarked on the pinnace

Marie-Antoinette Picard : passenger; embarked on the pinnace

Monsieur Ponsignon : lieutenant colonel;
embarked on the governor's barge

Gustave Poutier : midshipman; embarked on the longboat

Paulin d'Anglas de Praviel : army lieutenant; embarked on the longboat

Sander Rang : midshipman; embarked on the captain's barge

Joseph Reynaud : first lieutenant;
embarked on the governor's barge

Monsieur Richefort : passenger; embarked on the yawl

Monsieur Rogery : passenger; embarked on the longboat

Henri Savigny : junior surgeon; embarked on the raft

Colonel Julien Schmaltz : governor of Senegal;
embarked on the governor's barge

Thomas : pilot; embarked on the raft

Auguste-Marie Gicquel
des Touches : captain of the *Loire*

François-Marie Cornette
de Venancourt : captain of the *Echo*

Note that in this chapter nautical measurements are given as per the French originals, which were slightly different to their imperial equivalents.

look upon you as my children.'

An extraordinary statement on the lips of a frigate captain, but the Vicomte Hugues Duroy de Chaumareys had been perfectly honest as he introduced himself to his officers in the Great Cabin of the *Méduse*, at anchor in the Aix roadstead close to the Île d'Aix, where they were sheltered from the winds of the Bay of Biscay. Jean-Baptiste Espiaux, the frigate's second lieutenant, had glanced at his fellow officers and guessed that they felt as he did. Another command had gone to a returned émigré aristocrat, while the officers who had served France through the revolution and the Napoleonic empire were passed over, or offered smaller ships. Worse, de Chaumareys had also been given the flagship of the division, due to sail on 17 June 1816.

The 33-year-old lieutenant, who had reported to this cabin on many occasions, had more justification than his fellow officers to feel aggrieved. The career of Joseph Reynaud, the younger first lieutenant, had been mediocre. Much of it had been spent in port or on convoy duty, and since becoming a lieutenant in 1806 he had been engaged on uneventful Mediterranean cruises on the *Suffren* or, latterly, land-based at the port of Toulon, where in 1814, aged 27, he got married. The three enseignes, Joseph Maudet, Pierre La Peyrère and Vincent Chaudière, had spent too much of their time as prisoners of war to have accumulated much useful sailing experience. Of course, Espiaux reflected, he himself had been captured, at Cadiz in 1808, but escaped two years later by diving from a British transport, swimming to shore and making his way through enemy territory to the French lines. As a midshipman, he had been at Trafalgar on the 74-gun *Algésiras*, and he had the scars on his foot and arm to prove it. They had been taken by the *Tonnant*, but in the ferocious gale that followed the British victory they had been released to help save the crippled ship, and had rejoined their battered compatriots at Cadiz.

Now he was sailing in peace-time, bound for the former French colony of Senegal, which was to be handed back by the British under the terms of the Treaty of Paris that followed the defeat of Napoleon and the re-establishment of the French monarchy. The beautiful *Méduse*, with her fine sailing qualities, had been reduced to a floating dormitory for the civilian and military personnel required to control Senegal.

Thirty of her 44 guns had been taken off[3] so that temporary cabins could be rigged up with canvas dividers, and with over 169 crew and some 240 passengers, including the soldiers, she was at best unpleasantly overcrowded with people who, for the most part, had never been to sea before. A further 125 members of the expedition were distributed between the other three ships of the division: the *Gloire*, *Echo* and *Argus*. They had spent a fractious fortnight penned up in the Aix roadstead by contrary winds, longing to depart, only to cling despairingly to their last memories of the Île de Rhé melting into the horizon, their final glimpse of France.

There had been little to smile about, but Espiaux smiled to himself at the memory of the young woman who had come up on deck during their first night at sea, when they had run into a sharp squall and been forced to tack to avoid running onto the Roches Bonnes. He only had to imagine the scene below as the *Méduse* surged and fell, heeled and rolled, sails thundering and the wind screaming through the rigging. Better to be on deck than among the wailing and vomiting below.

It was simple fear that had driven 17-year-old Charlotte Picard onto the deck to find the ship 'flying on the sea'. Horrified, she stood deafened by the creaking and groaning of the masts and spars, the crash of great waves, expecting that at any moment the whole vessel would be smashed to pieces. Only at the sight of the other three ships on the starboard she did she begin to understand that this wild scene was both normal and exhilarating to the *Méduse* and her crew. It would take a little time before she and the other passengers came to terms with their new environment.

Chief among those ranked the new governor of Senegal, Colonel Julien Schmaltz, one of those forceful characters who, without any talent or qualification, somehow manage to bluff their way into positions of power and social standing. He brought with him a neurotic wife, teenage daughter and a secretary, plus 90,000 francs of government money in coins. The only other significant family group were the Picards. Charles Picard was returning to Senegal in a legal and administrative capacity; he owned land in the colony and judged it safe for his large and irregular family to accompany him to Africa. Charlotte was his eldest; she and her sister Caroline had been born to his late wife, but liaisons with Senegalese women had given him another three young children before he met the widowed Marie Antoinette Fleury who now passed for his wife. Their son, Alphonse, and a cousin close to the two older girls completed the family.

The largest group were the soldiers – not the formidable fighting units that had given Napoleon mastery of Europe, but a battalion under a handful of French officers, comprising assorted races and nationalities – many recruited from French prisons. Then there were the engineers, explorers and naturalists, men like Alexandre Corréard with his workmen; Charles-Marie Brédif the mining engineer and his friend de Chastellus; and an explorer named Richefort.

Those early days had shown de Chaumareys that he would have to hold his thoroughbred to a canter if the division was to stay together, but he had no intention of doing so. The sailing orders from Admiral François Rosily specified that the ships were to sail in company – either to protect de Chaumareys from his own inexperience or to ensure that the French arrived in an impressive body. The same orders also demanded all possible speed, and Colonel Schmaltz was keen to take up his new post. The corvette *Echo,* under Capitaine de Frégate (Commander) François-Marie Cornette de Venancourt[4] was incapable of hanging on to the *Méduse*'s tail; Capitaine de Frégate Léon de Parnajon's *Argus*, a brig, could not set anything like enough canvas to match the speed of a frigate, and the *Loire*, the transport, was a clumsy, Indian-built tub. There was, however, a compelling reason why de Chaumareys should have resisted the temptation to separate. The night before they sailed, he had expressed qualms about the infamous Arguin Bank, a 1750-square-mile (6000-square-kilometre) shelf extending along the coast of Mauritania, south of Cap Blanc. Lieutenant de Vaisseau Auguste-Marie Gicquel des Touches, command-ing the *Loire*, had taken exception to being treated as de Chaumareys's social inferior[5], but he had discreetly offered to lead the division around the hazard. Nevertheless, on the day they doubled Cape Finisterre at the north-west corner of Spain, the *Méduse* had already parted company for good with the *Loire* and the *Argus*. Even with every rag of canvas set, de Venancourt and the *Echo* fell behind.

That same day provided amusement in the shape of a school of porpoises. Passengers watched, fascinated, from the poop, until a sudden horrified cry of 'Man overboard!' rang out. One of the ship's boys had fallen, and a bungled rescue attempt failed to find him. The disarray was a warning of what to expect on another occasion, and the problems were rapidly increasing. The *Méduse* mirrored all the tensions of France at the beginning of the post-Napoleonic period, not least in the relationship between the captain and most of his offi-cers. Just as Louis XVIII had been imposed on temperamentally republican France after the abdication of Napoleon, so the royalist De Chaumareys had been forced on a group of lieutenants most of whom, regardless of class, had served the republic and empire, and all of whom had more experience at sea. As his weak seamanship became increasingly evident it was one of the passen-gers, Richefort, a former mariner of some sort, who began to offer advice.

On 29 June, 24 hours after a failed attempt to enter Funchal harbour, the *Méduse* anchored in the bay opposite Santa Cruz, Tenerife for just a few hours so that fresh supplies could be bought for Colonel Schmaltz. The boat that was sent ashore was commanded by Reynaud and also contained Enseigne La Peyrère and Midshipman Sander Rang.[6] The young midshipman enjoyed his day, recording that all the church bells were ringing and that Spanish ladies displayed a decided liking for Frenchmen in uniform. In between buying fruit, wine, vegetables and water filters and fending off amorous advances they observed the *Méduse* executing strange manoeuvres. Less amusing was the argument that sprang up over some destitute French soldiers, former prisoners of war on the island, who begged to be taken to the *Méduse*. La Peyrère wished to oblige but was firmly over-ruled by his first lieutenant, compassion not being Reynaud's strong suit.

Their disagreement, however, was nothing compared to what had taken place on the flagship.[7] Richefort had warned the captain that experience told him they would not be safe in the roadstead. A strong wind was blowing: de

Venancourt, who arrived at noon with the *Echo*, chose not to send any boats ashore. De Chaumareys's delegation of responsibility to Richefort provoked outrage from Espiaux and the other officers. It was, they told him, disgraceful to put his trust in this unknown individual; more to the point, they refused point-black to take orders from a man who had no authority to give them, a man whom the mining engineer Brédif called a fool, and one of the army lieutenants, Paulin d'Anglas de Praviel, described as an adventurer.

De Chaumareys ignored them. Referring to his commission issued in the monarch's name, he informed them that he was a king on the ship and it was everyone's duty to obey him. Richefort, he confidently declared, was a good and able mariner. Furious but impotent, unless they wished to face a charge of mutiny, the officers of the *Méduse* had little choice but to watch as Richefort volleyed orders that had the ship tacking back and forth for no other purpose than to demonstrate his alleged skill – even, according to the ever-observant Charlotte Picard, taking them dangerously close to the reefs. The return of the boat with the governor's provisions brought back Rang, La Peyrère and Reynaud, all joking about the strange display of ship-handling they had witnessed. But it was no laughing matter: the most dangerous leg of the journey was approaching. Yet for two nights in succession the crew had to deal with fires caused by the carelessness of the baker, symptomatic of the lack of pride or discipline now reigning on board. Richefort had command of the ship, Reynaud had drawn close to Colonel Schmaltz. The only hope for the *Méduse* lay perhaps with de Venancourt and the *Echo* – if de Chaumareys would wait for her and follow her course. The idea of waiting for the *Loire* so the squadron could take up des Touches's offer to lead them around the Arguin Bank was not even considered.

Early on 1 July they had their first sight of the African coast, when Cap Bojador was identified. Early European navigators, sailing close to the coast, had been terrified of the headland, often lost in mist and always pounded by massive breakers. Before 1434 when Gil Eanes became, if not necessarily the first to pass it, certainly the first to return with his news, it had appeared an insuperable barrier to sailing further south. Now it was merely a landmark on a well-travelled route, and gave a view of the pale shore of the Sahara that had long been predicted by the fierce heat of the wind coming over the sea from the scorching desert.

Although anxious about the ship's situation, passengers allowed themselves to be diverted by the ceremony of crossing the Tropic of Cancer. Notice of it had been given the previous day, but around 10:00 a.m. they assembled on deck. Often thought of as rigid and proud, de Chaumareys participated in the tropical baptism in high good humour, leaving Richefort in charge of the ship with La Peyrère as the officer of the watch. While the entertainment was going on, convinced they were running into danger – and perfectly aware that it was useless to apply to Richefort – the officer changed the long-held south-south-west course a few points to take them further west, away from the savage coast. De Chaumareys was furious, but the storm blew over and the *Méduse*'s bow continued to cut cleanly through the white-flecked turquoise water.

Back in the Aix roadstead, Gicquel des Touches had told de Chaumareys that there was nothing to fear from the Arguin Bank provided a ship kept well out to sea, and this was precisely what Admiral Rosily's instructions prescribed. They were to sight Cap Blanc, heave-to in order to fix its position, and then steer south-south-west for 16 leagues, some 89 kilometres. Having thus cleared the dreaded reef, they could turn confidently south-south-east to Portendick (now Tânît) or St Louis. Rosily knew that the seacharts of the area by the hydrographer Jacques-Nicolas Bellin, dating from 1753 and 1763, were far from accurate, and that so soon after the summer solstice, with the noon sun almost vertically overhead as they crossed the tropic line, it would be difficult to calculate a vessel's position. He therefore specified that all four ships must take great care, increase the frequency of soundings and keep in water deeper than 100 French fathoms (185 metres). Those instructions effectively told the captain that at this point in the voyage the chart was as good as useless and he must not rely on it.

As evening approached all eyes were looking out for Cap Blanc, the land-mark that heralded the start of the Arguin Bank. It lay the end of a long, low peninsula that extended south for some 27 miles (50 kilometres), with the shallow Baie du Levrier cutting back north and west behind it. The captain made had it known he intended to drop anchor a cable's length from it in order to carry out the Admiral's instructions, an inexplicable decision given that a French cable represented a distance of just 608 feet (185 metres).

Around 8:00 p.m., Espiaux, Reynaud and Chaudière thought they should now be on a latitude with, or slightly north of, the cape, although it had not been definitely sighted. Midshipman Denis Bellot, who was on watch with Chaudière from 8:00 p.m. until midnight, stated they steered west-south-west. This was doubtless as a result of the soundings taken, which revealed between 35 and 45 fathoms (65–83 metres), less than half the depth required by the sailing orders. At midnight, as Reynaud came on duty, de Chaumareys confirmed the course before turning in for the night. With a good wind, the *Méduse* was making around 6 knots under topsails and foresail; two leagues behind, the *Echo* followed her track.

Also on deck that warm, star-filled night were Henri Savigny, the junior surgeon, and the army lieutenant, D'Anglas de Praviel. They saw the corvette making signals, and were surprised that Reynaud made no move to answer them, much less inform the captain. Unlike the *Méduse*, the *Echo* had clearly not reduced sail, since she eventually caught up with the frigate on the port side and crossed ahead of her. Both ships were supposedly steering the same west-south-west course, yet a wide angle had opened up between them. Gradually the *Echo*'s dark shape dwindled to a point of light, which soon vanished. When dawn came, she was gone. Given de Venancourt's superior seamanship, the most probable explanation is that he held to his course while the *Méduse* under Reynaud diverged from it towards the south.

Yet all through that watch and into Espiaux's, soundings were taken every half hour, and each time, finding themselves still in shallow water, they steered a little more to the west. Finally, at 7:30 a.m. on 3 July they were beyond the regulation 100 fathoms and out of sight of land. A while earlier, the captain had been called on deck and shown a white cloud to the east. It was, he was told, Cap Blanc. This came as news to the geographer Alexandre Corréard, who happened to be standing by and who, as his friend Savigny put it, 'could tell the difference between a rock and a cloud, having seen enough of them in the Alps where he was born'. Corréard thought his knowledge might be useful, only to be told *sotto voce* that it didn't matter. The cape had probably been passed ten leagues earlier, but the important thing was to make the captain believe that it *had* been sighted, so the observation could be made and the ship's course set west-south-west for the next 16 leagues. Unfortunately, someone mentioned to de Chaumareys that the cape had been sighted the night before, and he chose to believe this.[8] The ship's evil genius, Richefort, had also come on deck to resume command of the course. If Cap Blanc had been sighted the night before, then by now they must have run the required 16 leagues west-south-west. Therefore, they were sufficiently south of the Arguin Bank to turn south-south-east and, he insisted fatally, there was no more need to take soundings.

Most of the officers were on the quarterdeck, and they made a despairing effort to convince de Chaumareys that they were in danger and must steer west. It was like talking to a stone, except that de Chaumareys and Richefort laughed their fears to scorn. Espiaux and his fellows might not have been the French navy's finest officers, and they were hopelessly demoralized, but they were competent and they knew they were right. One of them tore into Richefort, trying to show him up for the ignorant fool that he was. The captain's response was to put that officer, probably Reynaud, under arrest.

All this was within the hearing of the passengers who had entrusted their lives to the *Méduse*. Charles Picard, who was making his third voyage to Senegal and who knew what it was like to be grounded on the Arguin Bank, addressed himself forcibly to the captain and his unofficial pilot, warning him they were in danger. In a patronisingly soothing voice, Richefort replied:

'We each know our own profession. You stick to yours, and don't be afraid; I have passed the Arguin Bank twice before, I've sailed the Red Sea, and you can see that I'm not dead yet.'

Rather than state the obvious, Charles Picard put his faith in Providence and went down to his cabin to try to sleep off his fears. For all the good that it would do him, La Peyrère took soundings during his watch[9] and drew them to the attention of his captain. Richefort maintained there was no danger, and La Peyrère lost his temper.

'You're no more a seaman than my sister is!' he shouted. 'You're going to be the ruin of us all, maybe even today. I don't know what's stopping me sticking my sword into your guts!'

De Chaumareys took no account of the warning, and had the studding sails set. With the wind behind and under a great meringue of canvas the *Méduse* picked up speed. At midday La Peyrère and Bellot handed over to Joseph Maudet and Sander Rang.

Maudet's first task was to work out the ship's position; he sat on one of the empty chicken coops on the quarterdeck concentrating over his calculations and watched by a fair number of the passengers. Latitude was simple to calculate using a sextant; he was probably calculating the longitude by dead reckoning.[10] What he found brought a sharp gasp from him and he went to Richefort.

'Monsieur, the headland that we took for Cap Blanc yesterday … It's Cap Corveiro! Although we steered west-south-west through the night, the course we're on now, south-south-east, is putting us far too close to the bank.' He pointed to the chart. 'Look!'

With the same kindly superiority with which he had dismissed Picard earlier, Richefort merely replied:

'Don't worry: we're in eighty fathoms.'

The headland known as Cap Corveiro (now Cabo Corbeiro) lay some 60 miles (110 kilometres) north of Cap Blanc. The mistake was critical. Maudet should have told the captain then and there, but the whole ship seemed to have fallen under a spell of predestination that they no longer had the will or the energy to fight. The passengers had only to look over the rail to see the evidence of their peril. The rich, dark turquoise of the open sea had given way a couple of hours before to a soft aquamarine wash over a pale base. The sailors who habitually trailed fishing lines had been hauling in dozens of fish. Weeds floated past, and some people thought they could see grains of sand. Yet all this produced only a demoralized, resigned silence. Maudet ordered soundings:

18 fathoms.

Maudet had de Chaumareys called.

The captain came on deck and ordered the helmsman to turn a point to starboard. The port studding sails were taken down; the ship came a little more to the wind.

10 fathoms.

Two more points to starboard.

6 fathoms.

They hauled as close to the wind as they could; the *Méduse* heeled to starboard. For a moment it seemed as if she might answer the helm; then she shuddered to a stop. Perhaps only ten minutes had passed since Maudet had found 18 fathoms.

The initial reaction to the grounding was a stupefied horror. According to the explorer Gaspar Théodore Mollien, 'everyone listened to the captain's orders and tried to read the extent of the danger in his expression and that of his officers. They expressed only a great disquiet'. Brédif remembered: 'the officers gave orders in voices that betrayed their agitation; the captain had completely lost his [voice]; there was terror on the faces of those capable of understanding the danger: I thought it very close and feared the frigate's hull would be holed. I have to confess that I wasn't proud of myself at that moment – I couldn't stop shaking ...'

Sander Rang, by contrast, thought his fellow officers handled the moment professionally, though the conclusion he drew was erroneous: 'Everyone ... tried to decipher his likely fate from the expressions on the officers' faces. I think that they saw composure. I don't think that there was one of us who doubted the frigate would come off the bank.'

It was the sight of the helmsman abandoning the wheel that acted as the cue for recriminations to begin, noisy and confused, but with one fairly general aim: to have revenge, verbal or physical, on Richefort. Only the intervention of a few generous-natured men saved him from being thrown overboard. Taking no pleasure in having been proved right, La Peyrère came on deck and forced his way to Richefort.

'This is where your obstinacy has got us!' he told him in disgust. 'I warned you of it!'

Caroline Picard screamed as, in his own shock, Lieutenant Colonel Ponsignon hit her, probably mistaking her for one of his soldiers. By contrast, Madame Schmaltz and her daughter appeared almost oblivious to the chaos around them. Mollien observed how people formed little groups and those 'who set themselves up as spokesmen competed with one another to offer wild advice which people welcomed because of the captain's ignorance; that was unfortunately all too obvious in that critical moment.'

On the forecastle, Rang was following orders. The studding sails had to be hauled down, other sails reefed and taken in; the topgallant masts were struck and the ship's six boats lowered into the water to lighten the ship. Two officers began throwing heavy items overboard for the same reason, but they were told to desist.

Espiaux took a party of sailors in one of the boats and went out to take soundings. The results of his long search were not encouraging: the ship was in 5 fathoms (9 metres), with deep water a long way out. Half a league away – some 2.75 kilometres – the darkening of the sea indicated the safe zone beyond the shelf. To back off the ship, the simplest method, because it only required the crew to change the position of the sails and then let the wind do the work, was out of the question in such shallow and constantly changing depths. The alternative was to heave her off: to carry an anchor out into deep water and then haul on the capstan to wind in the cable and drag her to safety.

The captain's order to take out the kedge anchor invited only scorn from Mollien: 'instead of running out an anchor strong enough to heave the frigate, they only sent out a kedge anchor capable of hauling little more than a barge.' Espiaux was given that task, and Rang, who remained convinced they would save the ship, was detailed to take out the cable. These two continued to obey de Chaumareys, but elsewhere the lack of teamwork was becoming apparent, while the frightened soldiers, doubtless sensing that they were at the bottom of whatever hierarchy existed on the ship, were running about aimlessly. Mollien made a telling observation that 'one person gave orders; the other criticized them or refused to obey them'.

The crew became exhausted. The captain called a halt to the work so that men could get some rest, but when the time came to heave on the capstan there was only disappointment: the seabed was too soft and the anchor too small to cope with the strain of the frigate. They would have to get out a massive bower anchor, and increase the buoyancy of the longboat with a ring of empty water casks so it could carry the burden. Again they failed: the flukes of the anchor fixed behind the longboat kept grounding, and the wind whipped up. They could not get it out far enough to be of any use.

Meanwhile, with the passengers and soldiers helping to work the pumps, they tried to lighten the ship further. Water casks were staved and spare spars thrown overboard, but the idea of taking off the 14 guns was rejected in case the *Méduse* struck on them. To have done the job properly the guns would have had to be carried out into deep water, and half-measures only were being taken. There was much activity but little achievement. Meals were snatched and baggage plundered.

They had actually stranded in Latitude 19° 53′ N, Longitude 17° 01′ W[11] (Greenwich), 56 miles (91 kilometres) due south of Cap Blanc, though the captain thought they were in Latitude 19° 55′ N, Longitude 17° 13′ W (adjusted for Greenwich). Those 12 minutes of longitude, amounting to some 23 miles (38 kilometres), might have made the difference between safety and disaster because from this point southwards the bank recedes. In those waters, however, a greater margin for error was called for. It is possible that, even if they had known their position correctly, their south-easterly course would have crossed the bank further south.

De Chaumareys remained the captain, but the real decisions were now being taken by Governor Schmaltz, who convened a council during the afternoon.

Two contingency plans were on the table. Their first proposal was to get everyone to the small Île d'Arguin, lying to the north-east and close to the coast; the second, to organize a succession of boat trips to take everyone to the mainland, though whether this implied travelling due east, or south-east to Portendick, was not mentioned.[12] The boats could also be used to transport supplies from the ship, and, once provisioned, everyone would form a caravan to walk to St Louis, Senegal, some 180 miles (290 kilometres) beyond Portendick. But Schmaltz then produced a third plan, which had the approval of the captain: the construction of a huge raft capable of carrying 200 men and provisions, which could be towed by all the boats so that everyone could get to the coast in one flotilla. The best course of action would have been to strip the *Méduse* of all but essential provisions and, once she was lightened, make a concerted effort to get her off.

The soldiers received news of the raft with some suspicion, and were not reassured by the sight of the officers in their uniforms. A fear sprang up that they were going to be abandoned.

That night, a third anchor was run out, but the weather had turned hostile, threatening the lives of those seamen and officers out in the ship's boats. They were simply too far from deep water; the cables could not be run out far enough, and work was suspended for a few hours. Some barrels were jettisoned, but Schmaltz did not want to lose the flour, which was a scarce commodity in Senegal, and, like Admiral Graves before him, de Chaumareys refused to sacrifice the King's cannons. Charlotte Picard commented sarcastically, if not at the time then later, that the frigate also belonged to the king.

By evening the raft was complete and declared a success. Made from some of the frigate's upper masts and spars as well as spare spars, it measured some 65 by 23 feet (20 by 7 metres) – the size dictated by the length of her topmasts – with a low parapet all round. Rigidity had been created by lengths of wood nailed across, while a kind of bow had been formed by lashing two top-gallant yards together. There was no form of safety rail nor any buoyancy aids.

But before resorting to the raft, another attempt was made to drag the ship free. With two anchors out, one astern, the other from the bow, it was time to heave the capstan again. This time, the frigate began to answer. With her stern held firmly in place she pivoted round until she faced out to sea, only her stern aground. Had her cannons been taken off and another, longer, cable carried out, she might well have won free; in the end, she moved perhaps 650 feet (200 metres) before low tide finally grounded her, and a beautiful evening gave way to a savage night.

That combination of weather, darkness and failure took its toll on everyone. The afternoon's work of moving the ship, dragging its hull along the bottom, had finally caused her stout hull to bilge, and torrents poured in through the breach. As the frigate shook and listed and water rushed into hold, overwhelming the pumps, panic brought Charlotte Picard sobbing into her father's arms, regretting they had ever left France, terrified of what lay ahead.

She had good reason for her fears. Schmaltz and his cronies had drawn up, in secret, a list of who was to embark in what craft when the order was given to leave the *Méduse*. Now it was made known, and the Picards had been assigned to the raft along with some of the soldiers, 60 sailors, and a group of workmen belonging to the geographer Corréard. The only officer from the ship's company was to be a 23-year-old midshipman, Jean Daniel Coudein who had been out of action for the entire voyage following an accident to his leg. Roused in defence of his family, Picard confronted Schmaltz in cold fury.

'We are not going to get on that raft. If nobody thinks my family deserves a place in one of the boats, then I, my wife and my children will stay on what is left of the *Méduse*!'

There were deep currents here. Schmaltz had replaced the man who would have gone as Governor to Senegal had Napoleon's escape from Elba not delayed the hand-over. Picard had apparently had been made promises, including the restoration of his pre-revolution rank of captain of infantry, that would not now be fulfilled,[13] and as an existing landowner in the colony he was no more welcome to Schmaltz than vice versa. Fearing adverse publicity, Schmaltz backed down and agreed they could embark in the pinnace.

Some people managed to sleep that night; others paced up and down fearfully as the wind and waves beat on the listing hulk. At around midnight, a passenger approached Picard.

'Are you ready to go?'

'We haven't been told of any departure yet,' he answered, and gradually the fear dawned on them that some of the crew and passengers had made plans to leave the ship under cover of darkness. The same rumour was flying round the soldiers, who seized their rifles and rushed to cover all the exits. Warned of the uprising, Schmaltz came on deck and attempted to defuse the situation. The soldiers, drawn up in ragged order, were in no mood to listen and swore to shoot anyone who dared to make off, and at a hastily convened meeting of officers and senior passengers, Schmaltz solemnly promised that everyone would be taken care of and all would leave together.

The night grew worse, the raft broke free of its moorings, and in the process of recapturing it one of the ship's boats was damaged. At 3:00 a.m., defeated by crashing surf, the *Méduse*'s keel broke and the rudder was unshipped. Held only by its chains, it smashed repeatedly into the captain's cabin.

The order was given to abandon ship at 7:00 a.m. on 5 July. During the interval there were many, even the ship's boys, who drank themselves insensible. Some of the sailors were putting on every layer of clothing they possessed; other people were sewing valuables into their clothes. Brédif divided his gold with his friend de Chastellus, who was marked down for a different boat.

The soldiers were embarked on the raft at gunpoint. Lieutenant D'Anglas sat on the ship's rail, forcing them onto the floating platform. The implication of making the raft without any floats, such as empty barrels, to give added buoyancy suddenly became clear; before fifty people had climbed onto it, the weight had caused it to sink some 28 inches (70 centimetres) under the water. The situation was made worse by the weight of a number of barrels of flour and wine already loaded onto the raft; those containing the wine were quickly jettisoned. More and more men, and a woman, too, were being embarked. All but two of the army officers reluctantly decided to stay by their men; Alexandre Corréard, though allocated a place in a boat, decided that his duty was to stay with his workmen, and Henri Savigny, the junior surgeon, was another who followed conscience and chose the raft. Jean Coudein refused a fellow midshipman's offer to change places, saying that he was the eldest of his class. It was a gallant example, the more so because by the time some 149 persons had been forcibly or voluntarily embarked, the raft was submerged more than three feet (about a metre), and the pain of the water on his injured leg almost caused him to faint. Alarmed by his condition, Savigny called to one of the boats busy filling up with people that it was impossible for Coudein to continue. He was told that another boat would come and take him off, but it never did. The experienced seamen who were supposed to be on the raft were reassigned to the boats.

At the last moment, Lieutenant d'Anglas suddenly claimed that he had left something behind and climbed back onto the frigate.

The *Méduse* carried six boats of different sizes, the largest of which, the longboat, had been given to Jean Espiaux and Midshipman Gustave Poutier. Among those on their list were the two naturalists, Lachenault (who was pushing 60) and Kummer. Captain Benière and some of his men also came on board, and, with his complement in place, the second lieutenant left the frigate. Because of their condition and a total lack of oars they had not been detailed to help tow the raft. Neither had the yawl, at 20 feet (6 metres) the smallest of all the boats and even more feeble than the longboat. Nothing was said of her commander, but those in her included the Commissaire de la Marine, La Bergue d'Einville; Brédif's friend, de Chastellus; and the infamous Richefort.

The Senegal boat, so named because it was to remain at Port Louis for the use of the colony, had been hastily repaired after being damaged by the raft in the early hours. Enseigne Maudet had charge, with Bellot as his second-in-command, and Mollien had begged for a place in it.

The governor's barge, a good, solid boat 27.5 feet (8.4 metres) long, was reserved for Schmaltz, his family and friends and their luggage. It had sailors to man its 14 oars, and Lieutenant Reynaud and Midshipman Benoît Barbotin to command it. Schmaltz had also offered places to the frigate's paymaster, Clanet, and Lieutenant Colonel Ponsignon. Altogether, it embarked 28. For the moment, it stood by the raft, awaiting His Excellency's arrival. A little ahead of the *Méduse*, Enseigne Chaudière held off in the captain's 24-foot (7.3 metre) barge, along with the 26 sailors, two masters, Surgeon Follet and others fortunate enough to have deserved the best seats.

That left La Peyrère's pinnace, another sound, 14-oared craft, which contrary to Schmaltz's agreement rowed away without the Picards.

The raft was overcrowded. There was barely room to stand, but even if there had been space to sit the water level would have prevented it. Everyone crushed together, fearing the edges where there was nothing to prevent them falling into the sea, but it was time to cast off. Corréard hailed the deck of the *Méduse* and asked for Captain de Chaumareys. The latter came to the rail and asked what they wanted.

'Are we in a fit state to depart?' he demanded. 'Do we have charts and navigational equipment?'

'Yes,' the captain assured him. 'Yes, I've provided you with everything necessary.'

'Which of your officers is going to come and command us?'

'Myself. I'll be with you in a moment.'

Around a hundred people remained on the deck of the *Méduse*, including the entire Picard family. Charlotte saw the Schmaltz women in their barge and called down to them; they had, after all, eaten together at the Captain's table and become, if not friendly, at least acquaintances. But Madame and her daughter turned deaf ears, and de Chaumareys, who was still on deck, told her she was wasting her time: the Schmaltzes did not want to encumber themselves with her family. Nor, evidently, did he.

By now La Peyrère's pinnace was so far distant that the Picards were sure they had been abandoned. As the yawl passed close, Picard hailed it and asked it to take them out to the pinnace, but the sailors refused. Raising a rifle he had found on the deck, he pointed it and threatened to shoot anyone who tried to prevent his family embarking. They got into the yawl.

'When we came alongside the pinnace,' Charlotte wrote 'the naval officer who commanded it burst into excuses for having left without telling us as he had been ordered to, and he came out with a thousand good reasons to justify himself. But without believing any of it, we were glad to have caught up with him because it was clear that no one wanted to be burdened with our unfortunate family.'[14]

Once safely transferred, Picard told the yawl's crew he would be eternally grateful to them. They took it for sarcasm, and as they went off muttering, Picard remarked loudly: 'We shouldn't be surprised that the seamen have no shame, when their officers blush at being forced to do the right thing.' La Peyrère affected not to hear the remark, and thereafter concentrated on acting like a gentleman.

Meanwhile, de Chaumareys had quietly got down into his barge, provoking dismay on deck. Lieutenant D'Anglas, who had left the raft only to find himself abandoned on the wreck, took aim at de Chaumareys, but was restrained by Brédif. D'Anglas's army colleague Lieutenant Petit, with greater sang-froid, merely called out, 'Since you are leaving us, please do us a favour and, if you return to France, send word to our families!' before tuning his violin.

However, they then saw that de Chaumareys was going out to the longboat to ask Espiaux to take off the remainder on the ship. It took a tow to bring the unwieldy vessel back to the *Méduse*, and in the meantime the other boats were getting into position.

A couple of pieces of canvas were thrown down onto the raft as an afterthought, and the towropes were picked up. The yawl went ahead to take soundings. Then came the captain's barge followed in line by the Senegal boat, the pinnace and the governor's barge. Each of those four boats was connected to the one behind by a separate rope, the governor's barge holding the raft's rope.

It did not seem to matter that, in the unnecessary rush to disembark, food and liquid had largely been forgotten, or that few of the boats had anything by way of charts or sextants: they were only going to the coast. And de Chaumareys had also forgotten that, in the French Navy, it was a capital offence for a captain not to be the last man off an abandoned ship.

Espiaux had not anticipated having to find space for a further 80-plus angry men, women and even a child, who by now had promised to stay together, elected a leader and started to cook a meal. Swearing he would take everyone off even if it cost him his life, he organized an orderly evacuation, but after one look at the overcrowded longboat three men went and hid; another 14 reboarded the ship. Espiaux's last act was to hoist the French flag on the wreck.

By the time he had caught up with the raft it was 1.5 leagues (8.3 kilometres) from the ship, and Rang, who was in the captain's barge, remembered the time as 11:15 a.m. Anxious to redistribute his unequal load, Espiaux asked to transfer some of his passengers. The governor's barge and pinnace refused. Suddenly the longboat sheered across – Rang ascribed it to bad handling or even gesture of anger on Espiaux's part – and almost collided with Maudet's fragile Senegal boat ahead. To avoid the impact, Maudet released the Senegal's aft tow rope connecting it to the pinnace, and with no drag on them the captain's barge and Senegal boat shot ahead. De Chaumareys and Maudet quickly came back to take up the tow once again, but at that moment Rang heard a sailor shout:

'The Governor has just let the towrope go!'

While they had been manoeuvring, the line between La Peyrère in the pinnace and Schmaltz in the governor's barge had also been released; La Peyrère claimed it was done by the other boat. For a while the only boat doing

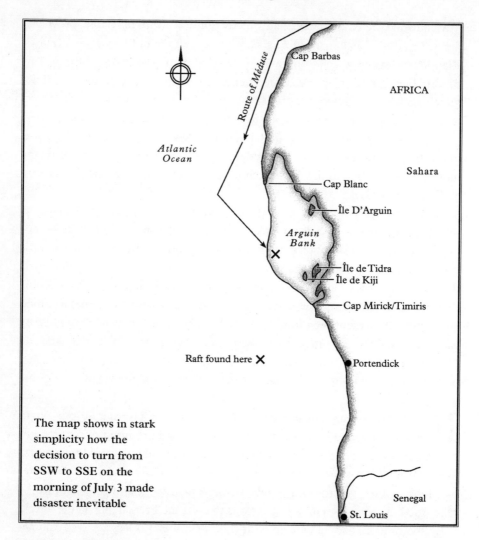

Route of *Méduse*

Cap Barbas

AFRICA

*Atlantic
Ocean*

Sahara

Cap Blanc

Île D'Arguin

*Arguin
Bank*

✕

Île de Tidra
Île de Kiji

Cap Mirick/Timiris

Raft found here ✕

Portendick

**The map shows in stark
simplicity how the
decision to turn from
SSW to SSE on the
morning of July 3 made
disaster inevitable**

Senegal

St. Louis

any towing had been Schmaltz's. De Chaumareys had come within hailing distance of La Peyrère.

'What are you doing' he shouted.

'The tow has broken!'

'Very well then, take it up again!'

At that moment another cry went up.

'We're abandoning them!' At Schmaltz's order, Reynaud released the final link in the towing chain. Clanet, the frigate's paymaster, protested vigorously. De Chaumareys shouted:

'We don't understand.'

'We're abandoning them.'

Those on the raft were slow to comprehend what had happened, imagining that, immediately after the accident, the boats had spotted a ship on the horizon and gone off to intercept it. Those in the boats, by contrast, were all too aware what they had done but, individually, they could do nothing to help. They raised sail and disappeared, the two barges outdistancing the Senegal boat, pinnace and yawl. Only Espiaux made a move, even as he ordered an outraged quartermaster not to fire on the fleeing boats. He tacked, hoping to set an example others would follow, but the sailors opposed going anywhere near the raft in case their craft was rushed.

'I know that, my friends. But I won't go close enough to put us in danger; if the other boats don't follow me, I'll think only of your safety. I can't,' he acknowledged, 'do the impossible.' Realizing his gesture had been ignored, he shouted in a spirit of defiance: 'We're going to sink. Let's show our courage to the end; let's do the best we can! Long live the King!'

Emotionally shattered, Sander Rang saw 'our friends, our companions in misfortune, even our relations, abandoned without help, means of life, far from shore and on a heavy contraption, stationary out in the sea and which they couldn't move or steer … We all wept for our unfortunate companions …' He neither heard nor saw any signs of life on the raft, as if those on it had been utterly overwhelmed by their plight. Torn between guilt and the desire to exculpate himself and his deserting companions, he cited Espiaux's longboat veering across as the initial cause, before adding 'but not all the blame should be put on [it]'. He tried to reason that, eventually, they would probably have had to give up anyway through shortage of provisions: 'It is, then, to cruel necessity that we owe the loss of our companions, but I say it is also to the vile sentiment of selfishness, because perhaps a generous perseverance would have been rewarded.'

From the Senegal boat, Mollien saw things in a clearer and colder light.

… our handsome frigate, lying right over on her port side, and, closer to us, our wretched companions packed onto the raft; only their heads could be seen above the waves. Their cries of distress and the white flag they had hastily raised were an appeal to our humanity to go to their aid – to take them back to the frigate or get them to the coast which was not far off. It's true that a move was made towards the raft; that return to generous feelings only lasted a few moments; with selfishness and cowardice triumphing, those who were in charge of us were inexorable in their barbarous decision.

With 88 people and a leak in it, the longboat rode dangerously low, forcing Brédif and his friends to keep bailing. The other five boats remained in their loose convoy, now heading south-east rather than due east towards the mainland, but Espiaux followed the original plan to make directly for the coast, and around sunset he sighted the high dunes of the Sahara, shining gold and silver. Cap Mirick (now Cap Iouik), almost due east of the wreck, was easily identified as 'like the continuation of a high hill coming from the interior but suddenly rising at its approach to the sea'. The water appeared deep, but it played them false, shallowing to just three or four feet – barely more than a metre – and grounding the boat. Visions of capture and the slave markets of Algiers rose before Brédif's eyes, but he was in good hands. By continuously sounding, Espiaux nursed the longboat out into deep water.

A dark, starless night set in, with a high sea that threatened to swamp the wallowing craft. The skill of the master pilot saved them, steering to avoid being pooped or caught by a broadside. Even so, they partially shipped a couple of waves and had to bail frantically to clear out the water. Under cover of darkness the sailors drank all the liquid that had been put into the boat to hydrate them both at sea and on land.

Dawn found them labouring in a hollow sea with no sight of land, and the lieutenant gave orders to tack. Slowly the ocean calmed, and by 8:00 a.m. they once again saw the shore. By now they had passed the two Angel Hillocks, with their tufted crowns of vegetation. During the night they had passed the westward projecting headland of Cape Timiris and were now just a few leagues from the former settlement at Portendick, which lay about 73 nautical miles (134 kilometres) south-east of the *Méduse*.

After such a bad night, most of them wanted to go ashore, and though Espiaux thought them misguided he agreed to land those determined to disembark. Carefully he ran the boat into shallow water, throwing out an anchor some way from the beach so they could be sure of pulling themselves off again, and 63 men, including D'Anglas, splashed safely onto the burning sands of the Sahara. Brédif remained in the boat; like Espiaux, he preferred to make for St Louis the quickest way.

Those in the Senegal boat had not spent a much better night. Separated from the rest of the flotilla, they had headed south-east from the wreck, and they too had sighted the coast around 6:00 p.m. on the 5th, close to the mouth of Baie St-Jean, some 27 miles (50 kilometres) south of Cap Mirick; despite being 2 leagues (11 kilometres) from the shore, they were in as little as seven feet (two metres) of water. Without an anchor, and having only a compass with a broken glass, Maudet had preferred to spend the night tacking about to avoid trouble. The north-west wind of the morning provided some hope that compensated for the miserable rations, but once it strengthened they had every reason to fear for their poorly repaired boat.

They were, however, hardly any worse off than La Peyrère and the Picards in the pinnace. With only one barrel of biscuit tainted by seawater, and fresh water enough for a glass per day, they and the yawl were struggling to stay with the captain and governor, who had decided to make directly for Senegal. According to Charlotte, de Chaumareys had refused to give them any supplies, and even tormented them by drinking in front of them; but if we are to believe Rang, who was in the captain's boat, he could hardly have been generous with what he did not have.

The previous day's decision to make for Senegal had come as a thunderclap to junior officers like La Peyrère. Some protested that they were overloaded and under-provisioned for such a long journey; others, that to abandon the raft was to betray their honour as Frenchmen. Their words fell on deaf ears. Schmaltz told La Peyrère to anchor and wait for morning.

The Picards' first night at sea in the pinnace was less traumatic than that of those in the weaker boats, and Charlotte's one vivid memory was of a terrified fellow passenger who claimed to see ghosts glowing on the water a league or so away. Charles Picard enjoyed encouraging the man's fears by telling him that Arab sorcerers had set fire to the water to prevent them trespassing on their territory. Dawn came, and the four-strong flotilla resumed its course, though the yawl's chances of surviving the voyage were fading.

By 8:00 a.m. on the 6th La Peyrère faced mutiny, as a number of his men demanded to go on shore and threatened to take over the pinnace at pistol point. The young officer remained adamant in his refusal, but as he lunged to grab a firearm from one of the sailors he pitched forward over the side. Picard grabbed him by his clothes in time to save him, losing his own hat for his trouble. The revolt subsided.

In the meantime, Espiaux was now ahead of the convoy, which had managed to regroup after the alarming night, and spotting them in the distance he gave the order to lower the sails and wait. Remarkably free from rancour, he said cheerfully to his own complement: 'They refused to take any people off us; let's do better, now we are less crowded, and offer to take some off them.'

His appearance produced near-panic in the flotilla. At first de Chaumareys's barge feared it was a Moorish craft and loaded firearms. Espiaux came within hailing distance of the pinnace and shouted that as he had disembarked 63 passengers he could take the Picards. La Peyrère's answer was blunt: 'They would rather suffer where they are.'

The sad fact was that he, and everyone else, believed Espiaux's men had mutinied and were crouching down below the gunwales, ready to leap out into other vessels. Under no circumstances did they want the longboat anywhere near them, but it would be allowed to follow. Espiaux shrugged off the humiliation and raised sail. Brédif, who had constituted himself Espiaux's aide and had been bailing all night, stripped off his clothes to dry them. His purse containing 400 francs had been in his trousers when he took them off. Whether it fell out as he wrung them out he did not know, but the next moment it was gone, and he was heartily glad to have divided his wealth with his friend in the yawl.

They carried on for an hour as the wind strengthened and the sea rose before they saw the yawl hoist a signal and make for them. Torn between fear of the 'mutineers' in the longboat and the conviction that their boat was about to founder, its 15 occupants were forced to ask for assistance. De Chastellus was first in with a helping hand from Brédif, who was convinced that if they had not been able to come to the rescue, he would have watched his friend drown. Certainly the barges would not have offered aid, and Maudet's Senegal boat was no longer part of the flotilla, but it might be doing La Peyrère an injustice to think he would not have shown some compassion, even if did not extend as far as the yawl's most unpopular passenger, Richefort. However, his pinnace genuinely did leak, and the elderly pilot was using lard to try and caulk it[15].

Throughout the day the heat was destructive, and the daily water ration in the longboat extended only to a glass of water. In the pinnace, Marie-Antoinette Picard tried to feed her baby, but her breasts were dry. De Chaumareys' group soaked their linen and covered themselves with it to get some relief from the malevolent red disc of a sun and the scorching wind saturated with fine, red sand from a violent dust storm that was raging over the desert. Rang was encrusted with it; mouths and lungs were parched; Charlotte could barely breathe; and Brédif sucked lead to generate saliva. La Peyrère, probably acting on information from Reynaud (who had charge of navigation for the group), rallied his complement with the thought that they would be in Senegal the following day.

Not until 4:00 p.m. did a north-west wind bring relief from the heat, but towards dusk the elements turned savage, the change branded on Charlotte's memory.

The sky was covered with dreadful clouds. The lovely weather we had just been admiring disappeared completely, yielding to a deep gloom. The surface of the water showed the precursors of a great storm. Along the coast, the desert horizon showed as a hideous, long chain of mountains, piled up together, their peaks belching out fire and smoke. Bluish clouds edged in dark copper broke away from that shapeless mass and came to ally themselves to those above our heads. In half an hour it seemed as if the ocean and the terrible clouds that covered it were one. Not a star was visible. Suddenly a fearful noise came from the west, and every wave on the sea crashed on our frail boat. Consternation gave way to a terrified silence ...

It was a night that, in the captain's barge (where Rang and the master pilot had charge of the tiller) ripped away what little courage remained. Maudet in the lonely Senegal boat feared for the craft's weak repair and lowered the sail. Espiaux's pilot knew that one mistake would see the longboat swamped, and Brédif wondered if it would be better to drown now and get it over with. In the pinnace, Marie-Antoinette lay in the bottom hugging her children; Picard held the girls close. A great wave crashed into them, tearing away the sail and breaching the stern. Off came clothing: shawls, trousers, sleeves torn from shirts – anything to plug the hole – while others bailed for their lives, and for six hours La Peyrère and his pilot fought to keep them afloat in the cauldron.

Sometime after midnight the sea began to fall, and by dawn it was much calmer. The pinnace's compass had broken, and they had to wait for the light in order to steer towards the land. For three of the boats, the voyage to Senegal would shortly end. La Peyrère's men wanted to go ashore, and he took them in close, but as soon as they saw the breakers they changed their minds about swimming and he headed out again, looking for a safer place to land. Picard's youngest ones were crying with thirst. Six-year-old Laura lay almost dying at his feet, and if he had not been told it would be useless, he would have opened up a vein on his arm so she could drink blood.

Brédif awoke on the 7th from a dream of being with his sister in the Alps to the wretched reality of the longboat. At 11:00 a.m. they met the Senegal boat, which had been alone for the past two days and was anxious for news of the others – and desperate for wine. The best Espiaux could do was send over a couple of bottles of spirit; then he took the latitude and worked out that they were 45 leagues from Senegal: 250 kilometres. The two boats sailed together into the afternoon, then the longboat anchored – it is not clear why – and Maudet went on, falling in with the pinnace, which had been alone since losing touch with Schmaltz and de Chaumareys before the storm. Come evening, La Peyrère dropped anchor while Maudet tacked all night, but the latter's crew were starving and mutinous.

By late morning the situation was ugly. To prevent bloodshed, Maudet raised sail and steered the boat onshore through the surf. In vain they looked for water and even human assistance, but there was none; only a mirage that tempted them inland on sand that burned their feet. Returning to the coast they dug holes, but the water was still salty.

Espiaux's men had witnessed the landing and were insistent that he put them ashore. He agreed to disembark them and proceed to Senegal with those who, like Brédif and de Chastellus, wanted to continue. Prepared for accidents, the former stripped off and put a rope round his friend, who could not swim. Then, with swords ready to defend the longboat's small supply of water, they got up the anchor, ready to let it go gently as they approached the breakers. The crew had other ideas, cutting the rope so that the longboat went chaotically into the surf. The first waves crashed over, swamping but not sinking them. Espiaux hastily raised the sails and they were carried safely through the rest, finally sinking in four feet of water, much to the relief of Brédif, though he was furious to find, on returning to the boat, that some of his clothes had been stolen.

They waited for Maudet's party, which had landed a little to the north, to join them. Now it was time to start walking south.

The pinnace was still on the move, but there was no strength left to row and they had eaten their last rations. At around 2:00 p.m., when they saw a group of people from the other two boats waving from the shore, they made the decision. The pilot ripped down the sails, mast and anything that might get in the way before he grasped the tiller and gave the order to row into the break-ers. The pinnace leapt on the waves, throwing the occupants back and forth.

Many of those on land hid their faces; others pointed out places to avoid; some went into the water ready to give their aid. The boat had come safely over two sets of breakers, but the surf ahead foamed terrifyingly high, crashing piti-lessly. And then a wave came from behind, smashing over the pinnace, as Charlotte vividly recalled.

> Our boat groaned, the oars broke; we thought we were on land but we were only stranded, the boat was on its side; a final wave rushed over us with the force of a torrent; we were up to our necks in water; the bitter foam was suffocating. The grapnel was thrown out; our sailors threw themselves into the water and took the children; then came back to the boat and hoisted us on their shoulders, and I found myself on the beach next to my step mother and my little brothers and sisters who were half dead.

Brédif came out of the surf, helping Charles Picard to land, only to find that yet again some of his clothes had been stolen, leaving him with just shirt and trousers. Incensed by the theft he launched into a tirade, which must have had some effect, because the items turned up a while later. The clothing thief was not the only one to feel ashamed. Those from the pinnace had to face Espiaux's pained reproach that they had doubted his good faith two days earlier when he had offered to take some of them aboard. From now on, he would lead them all.

After the storm, the barges of de Chaumareys and Schmaltz resumed their course for St Louis, but while Schmaltz and Reynaud were – relatively speaking – comfortable, the captain and his contingent were reduced to drink-ing urine and sucking lead to eke out their wine. Once again the inescapable heat was unbearable. At midday, when Reynaud calculated their position, they were dismayed to find that they were still 30 leagues – 165 kilometres – from their destination, twice what they had expected. Convinced that the lieutenant must be wrong, all eyes scanned the coastline for a sight of the little Grieuse Wood, a small fertile area by the mouth of the Senegal River. All they saw were a few Moorish tents.

By evening, despair was setting in. De Chaumareys's men wanted to land, but a cooler, quieter night allowed them to sleep and recover from the previous night and the day's labour in the debilitating blaze of the sun. But they needed water badly, and in the morning of 8 July the captain had to beg the governor, who was amply provided. Unfailingly selfish, Schmaltz agreed to part with three bottles of water in exchange for one of wine. As the heat mounted, the crew of the captain's barge grew restless, and the officers toyed with the idea of transferring to the other barge and letting the sailors go where they chose. Rang urged the men to delay a decision until after their position was calculated at midday, and when it showed they had just 13 leagues (72 kilometres) to go there was no more talk of mutiny. At dusk they saw the lights of St Louis and two tiny dark shapes on the sea, one of which proved to be the *Echo*, which had dropped anchor two days earlier on the 6th – the day after the raft had been abandoned.

From the corvette's deck a voice asked who they were.

'Two boats from the *Méduse*!'

There was a silence born of astonishment.

'*Who* are you?'

'Two boats from the *Méduse*!'

'Where is the *Méduse*?'

This time the silence came from the barges. Eventually Midshipman Rang answered.

'Her captain will tell you presently.'

Sensing this was not the time to ask any more, de Venancourt had them brought aboard and dinner was served. Only afterwards did the questions begin, and not until the following day did Schmaltz – not de Chaumareys – order de Parnajon of the *Argus* to load supplies and look for survivors along the coast before continuing to the frigate. It was possible, he suggested, that the people from the raft might have returned there. De Parnajon was also ordered to recover the three barrels of money from the ship. No mention of *looking* for the raft. That same morning Gicquel des Touches finally arrived in the *Loire*.

Colonel Thomas Brereton, the British governor of Senegal, while refusing to hand over the colony to this ragged remnant of an official delegation, and secretly pleased to be able to delay the transfer of power, organized an overland relief party under the command of an Irish officer named Kearney who dressed like a Moor, rode a camel and spoke the local languages.

Meanwhile, under Espiaux's nominal leadership the survivors of the three boats formed a caravan. One of Maudet's men went off and dug in the sand, finding enough water to help their thirst, but they had hardly any food. After an hour's rest by the water they set off, the small children carried piggyback by various of the men, and some of the women dressed in officers' clothes. Away from the coast the sand was too hot for bare feet, so they returned to the shore and took advantage of the cool night to walk until, with their feet cut by shells, they halted at Picard's demand around midnight and slept until just before dawn.

Land was scarcely any better than the boats. In the morning the desert showed them an unending plain of sand without a scrap of vegetation. The only advantage was that by digging they could sometimes find fresh water. They spotted a gazelle on a small hill, but the creature was off before anyone could take aim. On they marched,[16] resting every half hour for the Picard females until the group's cohesion almost broke down. Two of the ship's officers complained that the women were holding up progress, and there were a number who advocated leaving them behind. Warned of the trouble, Picard went straight to the officers concerned and told them precisely what he thought of their selfishness and lack of humanity. A row erupted and swords were drawn on the side of the officers; Picard pulled out a long knife he had acquired on the frigate, and his family rushed to him and urged him not to use it. An unpleasant scene was ended by the intervention of others, led by the relatively elderly Captain Benière. He addressed his soldiers: 'My friends, you are Frenchmen and I have the honour to lead you, and so we will never abandon a family in distress while we have the power to assist them!'

That shamed those who had talked of abandonment into promising to keep the caravan together provided the women walked faster, prompting the officer and his men to point out that good deeds did not come with conditions. Two people decided to split off from the caravan: Kummer and an explorer named Rogery, who felt they would do better on their own.[17]

The lack of food was critical. Searches in the sand dunes found only poisonous plants such as euphorbia, so some of the officers went inland and to everyone's joy returned with armfuls of purslain, a thick-stemmed salad herb. The soldiers and sailors then went off and came back with enough for everyone, but the only water they dug out tasted vile. Once back on the coast they gained some relief from the crippling heat by lying in the water, and there was more food in the form of some large crabs caught by some of the more enterprising men.

Thus far they had met no other humans, but a small expedition sent inland returned with news of a couple of tents. The ground was carpeted with tough vegetation, as painful on the feet as broken shells, but they reached the little encampment and had, for most of them, their first sight of Moors.

Brédif had never left France before, and the culture shock was acute. The sight of the almost naked women revolted him, their tents appeared squalid, and he was equally dismayed that they expected payment for the water, milk and millet they offered, particularly because they had no idea of French currency and valued quantity of coins above denomination. Those with only crowns therefore paid vastly more than those with small change. But what was basic fare in France was rather more precious in Saharan Africa.

With help from the others, Picard negotiated for two goats which, Brédif ruefully joked, cost more than their weight in gold. The women cooked them, but they were too hungry to wait and devoured the meat half-raw. Brédif complained bitterly – and openly – that the sailors ate more than their fair share, while Charlotte protested that one member of the caravan refused to pay his way even though he boasted of carrying 3000 francs.

Having eaten, they rested in the tents until, around 4:00 p.m., a call to arms got them to their feet. Outside stood a mixed party of Moors and native black people who appeared to have captured some of their group. They were wrong: this was a friendly group, come to lead them to Senegal.

They were taken across the blistering sand, and through spiny bushes that tore flesh and clothes indiscriminately, to another camp behind the dunes. Their initial reception was less pleasant: the women pulled the girls' hair and spat in their faces, while dogs nipped their legs and old women snatched at the officers' braid. Their guides rescued them, and then a young Moor went to Charles Picard and said, in perfect French:

'Hello, Picard! Don't you recognize me: Amet?'

He turned out to be a goldsmith whom Picard had once employed in Senegal, and that night the family slept in a tent covered with animal skins raised especially for them by their friend. 'Sweet dreams,' he said before going to his own tent. 'The God of the Christians is also the God of the Muslims.'

Despite their intentions of staying until dawn, an unfounded rumour that they were not safe forced the whole party to leave at midnight with their guides, but they hired asses to carry the weakest. Unable to afford more than two, Picard trailed behind with his elder girls, until the chivalrous Captain Benière realized their situation.

'I will never ride while exhausted girls struggle on foot behind,' he told them. Less fortunate, Brédif walked until he fell asleep on his feet and was almost left behind.

By the time they met the shore again on the morning of 10 July, the asses were hot. One look at the sea and they took off, throwing their riders into the water and then lying down. A brief panic followed while the Picard children were rescued, and shortly afterwards the miracle happened. Out at sea was a sail. It was the *Argus*.

They waved frantically, but they had already been seen and a boat was being lowered. One of the Moors gallantly swam through the surf and brought back a letter to Espiaux, which told them help was on its way.

De Parnajon sent them three barrels, which their guides swam out to retrieve. Biscuit and cheese were shared out, and soon they stopped for a feast on the beach. The alcohol did no one any harm: '… faces began to cheer up, old enemies became friendly, the selfish sought to make up for their egoism and greed; the women grew less sullen; the children smiled for the first time since the wreck,' Charlotte noted. '… I even believe one of the sailors sang the praises of his girl.'

By the end of the day the dunes were lower and, in the distance, shone the

Senegal River that, in Brédif's words, 'made an elbow in this place to run parallel to the sea'. They crossed the stream known as the Marigot des Maringouins and were about to settle for the night when they were approached by men in Moorish dress on camels. It was Kearney, the Irish officer sent by Brereton.

The following day the travelling was arduous in the heat, but Kearney went off to procure an ox for them to eat, and they slept knowing that only one more day remained. Brédif's resolution was beginning to fail; his friends had to help him along the shore. Nevertheless, at 8:00 a.m. on 12 July he was quenching his thirst in the Senegal River, waiting for the boats to arrive. That night they slept at St Louis, many of them taken in by kind-hearted French and English settlers. Not one life had been lost.

The 63 people who had demanded to leave the longboat on 6 July had a worse time, with greater distance to travel. For the first few days the troop, led by D'Anglas and Petit, were on their own, barely able to find any water. Four men died, and so did the wife of a corporal. She had realized she could not go on and begged her husband to leave her; he said he would rather kill her himself than leave her on her own to die slowly. Death did come to her relief, and with it a story that her distraught husband cut off her head and carried it in a bag all the way to Senegal, where he himself died.

Help came from a group of Moors who agreed to guide them to Senegal, but who were themselves attacked and defeated by an enemy tribe. For some days until their captors finally agreed to lead them towards their destination, the French were kept as slaves. Once back along the coast they had the bitter disappointment of seeing, but failing to be seen by, the *Argus,* but at last they fell in with Kearney, who gave them a letter from Espiaux, dated 13 July at St Louis and assuring him they could safely put their lives in Kearney's hands. The second lieutenant ended: 'We have found the warmest of welcomes, our sufferings are already softened, and we are only waiting for the reunion with the unfortunate people with you before we begin the celebrations.'

Those on the raft just did not believe what was happening to them. The accident – the near collision, dropping the tow – they understood, and they saw some of the boats starting to return. Then, from the governor's barge came Reynaud's cry:

'Shall I let go?'

'No! No!' That was Clanet, the frigate's paymaster, but the rope was released, and then came the fatal words, shouted up to de Chaumareys.

'We're abandoning them.'

The shock that robbed the 149 of speech and movement was succeeded by anger and open fear. Swiftly the leaders began to emerge. Savigny, Corréard, Captain Dupont and Jean Coudein said what they could to restore some sort of calm, wanting to believe that the boats had seen a ship and gone for help, and then they took stock of what resources they possessed. They were dismayed. There was no anchor nor navigation equipment: the assurances given at their departure were worthless. In the midst of the anger that exploded, Corréard suddenly remembered that one of his workmen had a small compass, which, until it was dropped through the planks a few hours later, seemed like a promise of salvation.

The leaders had got Coudein, the only naval deck officer on the raft, to the centre to try to protect him, and this became the headquarters from where they hoped to plan some sort of survival effort. They assigned a number to everyone to help distribute the food, which consisted of a wet biscuit in wine. Savigny, the 26-year-old surgeon, raised a mast, using the useless tow rope as rigging, and then set up one of the sails that had been thrown to them, though the design of the raft made it of little use. They were too crowded for any general activity: they passed the time first reassuring one another that rescue would come and then swearing revenge.

The night was horrific. As soon as the sea began to rise, people lurched and fell on one another helplessly. Savigny and a few others rigged up rope handholds, but this was only the beginning. The account by Savigny and Corréard – the only one by those who were on the raft – conveys the awfulness of their situation that night.

> In the middle of the night the weather was very bad; very heavy waves broke on us and often knocked us over brutally; the cries of the people were mingled with the roaring of the waves, while a violent sea kept lifting us from the raft and threatening to wash us away ... All night we fought against death, holding tight to the ropes ... Rolled by the waves from the back to the front of the raft, and from the front to the back, and sometimes thrown into the sea, suspended between life and death, railing against our misfortune, convinced we were going to die, yet still hanging on for grim death against the savage element ...

By morning on 6 July around twenty had been lost, some washed away, others drowned when their feet slipped through gaps, trapping them so that they could not hold their heads above water, which was still well above the knee even to those standing to their full height. Two young men were crying over their father's body when someone realized he was still breathing, and he was brought back to consciousness. In contrast, three men gave up that day and deliberately threw themselves into the sea; others started to imagine they saw ships or land. Griffon du Bellay, the governor's secretary, attempted to drown himself, but Savigny pulled him out. Afterwards he rambled unintelligibly before trying, unsuccessfully, a second time. Most remained relatively quiet, convinced that rescue would come.

It was the combination of darkness and storm that did the damage. 'If the preceding night had been terrible this was still more horrible. Mountains of water covered us every moment and broke, with violence in the midst of us.' They had to rush from one side of the raft to the other to form a human counterbalance to the waves' crazy tilting of their platform. Demented by fear, many lost their heads and broached a cask of wine, gulping it down into empty stomachs. They had one idea: to get rid of their leaders and then destroy the raft. One grabbed an axe and started to hack the cords.

Two camps, armed with knives and swords, had formed almost instantaneously: the leaders and those who wished to save the raft versus a majority who wanted to end it. The axeman was cut down by a sabre; another, trying to sever ropes with a knife, was thrown into the sea. And then all hell was let loose. Captain Dupont was pushed overboard, rescued, seized again by men seeking to gouge his eyes, and saved a second time. Alexandre Corréard came out of a strange trance to organize his team of workmen into an efficient fighting force. One of them had joined the mutineers and been pitched off. Corréard dived in for him, grabbed him by the hair and managed to get him back and patch him up, but he rejoined the other party and was later killed.

The piercing screams of a woman reached them. Marie-Zaide and her soldier husband had been hurled over. Corréard tied a rope round his chest and went in for her; the chief of his workmen, Lavillette, saved the husband.

The revolt was over, for the moment, and while both sides licked their wounds, Marie-Zaide sat with her husband fondly talking to Corréard about her home in the Alps and her 24 years service following the army as a sutler.

Then just after midnight it flared up again. Savigny was bitten and stabbed in the hand; one of the workmen was nearly beaten to death and only saved by his foreman. Sub-Lieutenant Lozach was taken by some men who mistook him for d'Anglas – who had forced them onto the raft and then deserted them – and it took a concerted effort to rescue him. Wounded, injured in the fight for Lozach, and weary, Coudein rested on a barrel, his arms around a terrified 12-year old ship's boy by the name of Léon. Both were thrown into the sea but the midshipman managed somehow to get a hand to the raft and haul them both back. Eventually exhaustion, not reason, ended the hostilities.

Savigny was one of many who began to hallucinate. He imagined beautiful scenery; others said they were going to their hammocks; a few demanded food from their comrades. Corréard thought he was travelling in Italy.

Morning on the 7th recalled them to their senses. The raft was far less crowded now: of the sixty or more that were missing or lay dead around them, perhaps a quarter had committed suicide in the water. Savigny's group had lost just two. Almost as significant was the fact that two of their three barrels of wine and all the water had been thrown overboard. And they were starving.

They got the mast and sail up again, hoping the wind might take them close to the land they could not see, and they used the soldier's tags to make fish-hooks – but the lines caught under the raft. They bent a bayonet, hoping to catch a shark, but the creature bit the blade and straightened it. They chewed leather; one man tried excrement. The only food around them was the flesh of their dead comrades.

Those who resorted to it found it gave them back some strength, but they decided to try drying it to make it less disgusting, less like what it really was. Strips were tied with ropes to the mast for the wind and sun to disguise their reality. Other groups in a similar position – de Lafond's and Inglefield's are two – avoided such a complete breakdown, but the conditions on the raft were exceptional. Everyone was exhausted by lack of sleep, and packed so closely that, to use a modern phrase, they had no personal space. The stress was intolerable. Under such conditions it was impossible for anyone to exert control and maintain discipline. The soldiers were a disparate group who, in general, saw their officers as persecutors rather than leaders, and few had trust in them. Sailors and marine officers – naval and merchant – for whom shipwreck was an ever-present hazard, would have been much better prepared for the ordeal and probably far more optimistic about rescue. As for the cannibalism itself, despair had stripped away taboos very quickly. The officer group – the messieurs, as Rang called them – held out longer, perhaps under the weight of social and cultural pressures.

The night of the 7th–8th was quieter, undisturbed by violence, but still they were still up to their knees in water and could only sleep on their feet, leaning on one another. On the morning of the 8th those unable to stand through the night were found dead. All but one of the bodies was put into the water.

They had some luck that day when they encountered a shoal of flying fish and managed to get a small fire going in an empty cask. Cooked with the fish, the human flesh tasked a little better, and for the first time the officer group ate their share. But the better spirits did not last the night. The survivors still lacked the unity needed for group survival, if indeed group survival was actually possible. There were those who would say[18] that the revolts and the drunkenness were welcomed, even encouraged, by the leaders in order to reduce numbers. People had split into groups based on class, race and nationality, and only formed common cause when it suited them.

Savigny and Corréard blamed the violence that night on a union of foreign European and black soldiers (whether Senegalese or former slaves from the Caribbean is unknown) who, in previous fights, had either been neutral or even allied to Savigny's party. Informers claimed the latter group had promised to help the former to cross Africa, but whether they intended to head for Senegal or make some other life for themselves is unclear. The familiar demand for the blood of D'Anglas had also gone up. Whenever fighting began, the soldiers suddenly became possessed by the idea that he was on the raft. Corréard's foreman, ex-sergeant Lavillette, put up the finest resistance but the officers' group sustained casualties, including the sutler, who had been left with a broken thigh, and her husband who suffered a head wound.

They were down to 30 survivors on the 10th, the day that de Parnajon made contact with Espiaux's caravan. The constant immersion in salt water had stripped the skin from their legs; they were covered in bruises and wounds; the sun baked any bare flesh. Only 20 were capable of moving. Young Léon ran around the raft crying for food and for his mother, treading on his raft-mates who screamed out in pain but could not find it in them to be angry with him. There was, they reckoned, wine for just four days, and very little food. If the boats had gone to Senegal for help – and it was a big if – they would have needed some four days to get there. A ship would have to be equipped, which took time, and then it would have to find them. They had to hold out.

Two soldiers caught tapping the wine cask with a reed were thrown into the sea on the 11th, the same day that Léon died.

> He faded away like a lamp that burns out for lack of fuel. Young and good-natured, he had so many fine qualities, and deserved a better fate. His angelic looks, sweet voice ... the courage he had already shown and the military service he already had behind him: everything filled us with pity ... Neither the wine, which we gave him without regret, nor anything that we were able to do for him could stave off his wretched end. He passed away in the arms of Monsieur Coudein, who had never stopped taking the greatest care of him.[19]

There were two more deaths that day, leaving just 27, only 15 of whom appeared to have a chance of surviving until rescue came, if it ever did. A stark choice presented itself. The other twelve, all badly wounded, were sharing equally in the rations and might drink the equivalent of 30–40 bottles of wine before they met their inevitable end – bottles that could keep the others alive. They confronted a stark choice.

> We argued it like this: to put the sick on half-rations was to kill them slowly. After a discussion dominated by the most awful despair, it was decided that they should be thrown into the sea. This course, however repugnant, however dreadful it seemed to us, would give the survivors six days of wine at the rate of two quarts a day. But once the decision had been taken, who would dare to put it into action? The constant sense of seeing death ready to pounce on us, the certainty that without this ghastly expedient we were finished, everything, in short, had hardened our hearts against anything except our own survival.

Savigny and Corréard's account of the decision takes refuge in the passive mood: *it was decided*. Not, presumably with the consent of the potential victims.

Two sailors and a soldier took it upon themselves to carry out the murder;

the rest of them looked away and wept, particularly over Marie Zaide the sutler and her husband.

A rather different version of events was later related by Thomas, a pilot, to Sander Rang. It shows the officer group in a far more aggressive light.

> A soldier had been despatched and thrown into the sea; they told his wife, the only woman on board, 'since your husband's been thrown overboard, you'll have to join him', and they forced her to jump in herself.
>
> But out of all the abominable deeds committed in those terrible moments, the cruellest is the one I will relate now. It shows to what an extent their hearts were deaf to the voice of humanity.
>
> There was a commis aux vivres [an NCO with responsibility for rations] on board, and his two sons, both aged around 20–22. During the first violence, the father saw that they [the officer group] had designs on his life. He went and hid himself where the lads could not see him and committed suicide by throwing himself into the water.

Later, the two brothers were themselves to be killed:

> They fell to their knees and begged for mercy. The officer refused to listen and repeated his order for them to go into the water if they wanted to avoid a worse fate ... Each of them said 'just spare one of us. You've already killed our father, don't wipe out our whole family. Just let my brother be spared to comfort our poor mother' ... It was all in vain.

Afterwards, all weapons except one sabre were jettisoned. Quite where the truth lies is impossible to establish, but as Savigny and Corréard wrote: 'Readers, who shudder ... recollect that it was other men, compatriots, comrades, who had placed us in this horrible situation.'

On their ninth day on the raft, an extraordinary sight appeared: a small white butterfly fluttering over them. Some were so desperate they would have eaten it; others saw it as a messenger of heaven, an intimation that they were closer to land. Maybe, just maybe ...

They took a few planks from the front of the raft and constructed a platform by the mast, high enough to keep all fifteen of them out of the water. Sitting together there, like Inglefield and his men, they told stories from their past. Surely Savigny looked at the ribbon given him by his girlfriend before he left Rochefort. There was, however, a growing sense that they were finished. The weather had grown hotter and they were drinking urine – Savigny became quite a connoisseur. A few scraps of food were found: a lemon, some cloves of garlic, liquid teeth-cleaner. They sniffed an empty phial of rosewater and sucked their wine ration through a straw.

On the 14th Sub-Lieutenant Clairet, Sergeant-Major Charlot, Coudein and another sailor made a resolution to get drunk and kill themselves. They changed their mind only when a company of 30-foot (9-metre) sharks gathered around the raft. Yet afterwards several of the 15 openly bathed in the sea in the presence of the sharks. They attempted to make a smaller raft, but trials proved it a failure, and they joked feebly. One of them, referring to the Greek legend of Argus and his hundred eyes, said: 'If the brig is sent to look for us, pray God she may have the eyes of Argus.'

On the morning of the 17th Captain Dupont gave a shout: he had spotted the tops of a two-masted ship. Hysterical with joy they straightened some iron hoops from a barrel, tied a coloured handkerchief to it, and hoisted the black sailor, Jean-Charles, up the mast so he could wave it. For half an hour they hovered between relief and fear. Then the ship was gone.

It was too much for them. They took the spare sail and made a kind of tent to shield them from the sun, as if they just wanted to sleep and never wake again. The best they could do would be to carve their names and their adventures on a piece of wood, attach it to the mast and hope one day it would be found after their deaths.

The next day, Courtade, master gunner of the *Méduse*, went out of the enclosure for a pee. He turned back with a shout of joy, pointing out to sea.

'Saved!'

It was the *Argus*, which had failed to spot them the previous day, and the overjoyed de Parnajon, who had taken it upon himself to make the search, was to say to them that not even promotion to commander would have given him as much pleasure as finding them. They were taken straight to St Louis, to be given a rapturous welcome, even by those responsible for their abandonment. Of the 15 who were saved, however, Lozach, Clairet, Courtade and Jean-Charles died shortly afterwards, while Savigny and Coudein were taken in by a French merchant.[20] Most of the ship's officers, including Savigny, went home with de Venancourt, but when the French contingent withdrew south to Daccard (now Dakar), Corréard, the weakest, was left naked in a filthy hospital, visited once by Schmaltz, until his plight came to the attention of the British officers.

Reynaud made three attempts to find the *Méduse* and recover the money. He finally reached her on 26 August – 52 days after her abandonment – but found no money (or if he did it was never made public).[21] What he did find were three living corpses, the survivors of the 17 who had stayed on the frigate. Two of them died at St Louis. The death toll had risen to 159.[22]

Fate, it seems, had always intended the *Méduse* to go down in history, but she missed the chance to become the stuff of naval legend. Built to a design close to that by Antoine Crucy for the *Pallas* class, she was commissioned in 1810 and on 22 November sailed for Batavia in company with the *Nymphe*, carrying Jean-Guillaume Janssens, the newly-appointed governor general of France's possessions east of Mauritius, arriving in April 1811. Learning of the presence of the two frigates at Surabaya, Rear Admiral Robert Stopford blockaded the Madura Strait with his own frigates, HMS *Sir Francis Drake*, *Bucephalus*, *Phaeton*, and *Barracouta*. The *Nymphe* and *Méduse* ran, pursued by the *Bucephalus* and *Barracouta* until the latter found it impossible to stay with them. Only the timidity of the *Nymphe*'s Captain Raoul then prevented the capture of the *Bucephalus*.

The French frigates escaped and, after a long cruise almost to Australia, returned to Brest in December 1811. A less troubled cruise for the *Méduse* down to the Cape Verde Islands in 1813–14 was followed by another to the Lesser Antilles.

In July 1815, a month after his defeat at Waterloo, Napoleon arrived at the Île d'Aix , planning to find refuge in America. The frigate *La Saale* was ready to take him, but outside the roadstead lurked HMS *Bellerophon* – 'Billy Ruffian' to those in the Royal Navy who lacked a classical education. The plan had been simple: while Napoleon sailed to freedom, the *Méduse* would engage the British 74 in a suicidal combat that could have only one outcome. Napoleon decided instead, however, to surrender to the British, leaving the *Méduse* to find her tragic end.

The shipwreck was over; the scandal just beginning. At de Venancourt's suggestion, Savigny sent his story to the minister of marine, François-Joseph Gratet du Bouchage. It was a straightforward account, with no attempt to hide the cannibalism, and it raised a storm.

Savigny could have had no idea of the struggle going on in the corridors of power between the ultra-royalists such as du Bouchage and the opposition supported by the minister of police, Élie Decazes. A copy of his narrative was passed to the latter, who leaked it to an influential newspaper, *Le Journal des Débats*, which published it on Friday 13 September. Summoned to the ministry of marine, Savigny protested that he had had nothing to do with the leak, and the editor obliged him by putting in writing that the document came from the ministry of police.

The *Méduse* affair – politically damaging because it centred on the awarding of the command to an incompetent officer on the strength of his royalist past – could not be hushed up: it was looking worse with every report that landed on the minister's desk. The scale of the disaster was breathtaking, shocking. Du Bouchage sent the captain's reports to Admiral Rosily, together with the evidence of de Venancourt's log and a report by the officers. Rosily provided pages of damning observations and comparisons in rather scrappy handwriting. There was an enquiry followed by a court martial, which considered several indictments: the dispersal of the division; the stranding of the frigate; the subsequent loss of the frigate; the failure of the captain to be the last to leave; the abandonment of the raft. De Chaumareys was found guilty of stranding the *Méduse* and technically guilty of abandoning the ship before the evacuation was complete – a verdict that carried the death penalty. But the president of the court partially accepted de Chaumareys's defence that he had not abandoned the ship out of cowardice but rather to put himself at the head of his people in the various boats. De Chaumareys was sentenced to three years in prison, struck off the navy list and stripped of all decorations, including the Légion d'honneur.

The French government was shaken, and du Bouchage eventually ousted. His successor at a stroke removed all those officers of the *ancien régime* who had been reintegrated into the navy after the restoration. But that was more to do with trying to damp down the ongoing publicity than with the trial.

A copy of the *Times* dated 17 September, containing a translation of Savigny's letter and sent from England, arrived on Schmaltz's desk in St Louis. Determined to avoid the odium of having abandoned the raft, he decided the only strategy was to discredit the young surgeon. His secretary, Griffon du Bellay, himself a survivor of the raft, was instructed to write a letter denouncing the article, and du Bellay complied, afraid that his friends and family would be horrified to think he had been involved in cannibalism and killing. Then Schmaltz put pressure on the remaining survivors in Senegal to sign it. Several did, but Corréard, his health continuing to decline, refused, even though he was warned that he would never be allowed to leave the colony until he agreed to. However, the British were still refusing to cede the colony,[23] and it was a British doctor who insisted to Schmaltz that Corréard must go home, and a British officer who gave him money and advised him to go to London and claim redress from there.

Corréard returned, instead, to Paris and took his request for compensation and employment to the ministry, before du Bouchage had left. Every door was coldly slammed in his face. Eventually he found Savigny, and together they wrote their account of the ordeal: *Narrative of a Voyage to Senegal in 1816*. It was a best seller. The Paris public loved a good scandal.

The two authors went further, obtaining a statement of support from Coudein and retractions from those who had signed Griffon du Bellay's letter while too ill to know what they were doing. Du Bellay himself formally retracted his letter and offered a frank apology for ever having written it, since he knew he owed his life to Savigny. Brédif's uncle sent them the private narrative that Charles-Marie had sent to his sister, and one of the ship's officers (perhaps Maudet) added his (anonymous) observations. This material all went into the second edition (1818), which was also translated into English, and further editions followed.

Among those who played the biggest parts in the drama, de Chaumareys died a broken man in 1841. Schmaltz was recalled from Senegal in 1820 for incompetence and, despite gaining other, lesser posts, died penniless in 1827; he escaped being held to account for abandoning the raft because, as they were still at sea at the time, de Chaumareys was technically still in command and so had responsibility for the decision. Brédif died of dysentery in Senegal in 1818, aged just 31, while Charlotte Picard led a wretched existence there until rescued by a young teacher, Jean Dard, who in 1824 married her and took her back to France. She returned to Senegal as a teacher, and died there in 1862. Richefort's part in the whole debacle was hushed up, and since he had held no official position in the expedition, and exerted direction solely through de Chaumareys's permission, there was no forum in which he could be formally held to account – there was no law or regulation that he had actually broken. He, too, disappeared from view – not even his first name is recorded in the various accounts. It is tempting, but unfair, to blame him for the disaster. De Chaumareys should never have entrusted him with the navigation, but had the captain been able to establish better relations with his officers, he might never have listened to the would-be navigator, and for that the officers themselves perhaps bear some responsibility.

Those officers achieved honourable if unspectacular careers. Reynaud, Coudein and Rang became captains; Reynaud, mediocre to the last, died in 1832; Rang, in 1844, while governor of Nossi-Bé, Madagascar; his fellow midshipman, Coudein, in 1852, having made various long voyages and survived another shipwreck. Promoted capitaine de frégate for his conduct during the *Méduse* disaster, Espiaux died in Buenos Aires in 1835.

Savigny left both Paris and the navy, married his girlfriend, and practised medicine in the village of Soubise – just a few miles from where the *Méduse* had made her last departure from France – where he became mayor, and where he died in 1843. Corréard had a career as both journalist and engineer. He joined the Chevaliers de La Liberté – a secret society dedicated to replacing Louis XVIII by Napoleon II – founded two technical journals and drew the plans for the future Gare d'Austerlitz. Although he lived until 1857, he never recovered mentally or physically from his ordeal on the raft.

The *Méduse* claimed a last victim – one who had never set foot on her. Charlotte Picard thought that their situation would have inspired a Girodet or a David. In fact it was the young Théodore Géricault who immortalized the disaster. He interviewed Savigny and Corréard, visited the morgues and hospitals to see the effects of death and putrefaction, made a life-sized replica of the raft, then shut himself in his studio and cut off his hair so he would not be tempted out into society. The instant he chose to depict was the moment when the *Argus* was sighted, and Jean-Charles was held aloft by the others to wave to it.

When the massive and devastatingly powerful canvas was exhibited at the

Louvre in 1819 under the title *Scène de Naufrage* (*Shipwreck Scene*) critics slated it because they saw nothing noble or inspiring in it, and the government was dismayed at the additional publicity given to a scandal they would have liked nothing more than to bury. Louis XVIII, however, appreciated it, enough to ensure that after the artist's death – and it was the physical, mental and emotional demands of the painting that brought about his early demise – it was bought for the nation. It now bears the title *Le Radeau de La Méduse* – *The Raft of the Medusa*.

Sources and Bibliography

Many survivors of the disaster left their accounts, some private, some for the court martial, others for publication, but few are available in English. Savigny and Corréard provided the most famous version, while Charlotte Dard, née Picard, wrote a very personal account which has as its agenda a defence of her father against those who, in the family's opinion, reduced them to destitution. Rang, Mollien and Bellot are useful, especially in the confidences made to Rang by some survivors of the raft. Particularly engaging is that of Charles-Marie Brédif, written to the young sister he adored. While reproductions of Géricault's painting are easily found in art books or on the internet, none offers anything like the experience of seeing the original.

Numerous documents relating to the loss of the *Méduse* are held at the main archives of the Service Historique de La Défense (SHD) at Vincennes, which are open to researchers. Of particular interest are the volumes BB393 and BB394, and the individual files of the ship's officers. The court martial files are at the SHD's Rochefort archives.
The Roussin-Givry hydrographic expedition file is in the Archives Nationales, Paris, ref 5/JJ/216

Bradshaw, A R, *English–French Naval Terms* (London: Williams and Norgate, 1932).
Corréard, A; Savigny, H; D'Anglas de Praviel, C L; and Rang des Adrets, A, *Relation Complète du Naufrage de la Frégate La* Méduse *faisant partie de l'expédition du Sénégal en 1816* (Paris: Jean de Bonnot, 1986)
Corréard, A, and Savigny, H, *Narrative of a Voyage to Senegal in 1816: Comprising an Account of the Shipwreck of the Medusa*, second edition (London: Henry Colburn, 1818), translation of the second edition of the *Relation Complète*, containing notes by Brédif and an anonymous ship's officer; reprinted, Marlboro, VT: Marlboro Press, 1986.
Dard, Charlotte, *La Chaumière Africaine* (Dijon: Noellat, 1824; reprinted, Paris: L'Harmattan, 2005)
Finke, Jens, *Chasing the Lizard's Tail – Across the Sahara by Bicycle* (London: Impact Books, 1996 (now available from the author at Apartado 542, 8700 Olhão, Portugal).
Gardiner, R (ed.), *The Campaign of Trafalgar* (London: Caxton, 2001).
Gardiner, R (ed.), *Fleet, Battle and Blockade: The French Revolutionary War, 1793–1797* (London: Chatham, 1996; reprinted, London: Mercury, 2006).
Masson, Philippe, *L'Affaire de la* Méduse (Paris: Tallandier, 2000).
McKee, David, *Death Raft: The Human Drama of the Medusa Shipwreck* (London: Souvenir Press, 1975); reprinted as *Death Raft* (London: Fontana, 1976).
Mollien, Gaspar-Théodore, *Découverte des sources du Sénégal et de la Gambie en 1818; précédée d'un Récit inédit du naufrage de la* Méduse (Paris: Delagrave, 1889).
Schneider, Michel, *Un rêve de pierre: le Radeau de la Méduse, Géricault,* (Paris: Gallimard 1991).
Walther, Ingo F, *Masterpieces of Western Art* (Cologne and London: Taschen, 1996).
Woodman, R, *The Victory of Seapower: Winning the Napoleonic War, 1806–1814* (London: Chatham, 1998; reprinted, London: Mercury, 2006).

Marine History Information Exchange Group, http://post.queensu.ca/cgi-bin/listserv/wa?A0=MARHST-L

Triaud-Richard, M. Dominique, 'Pierre, Philippe, Denis Bellot',
    http://dtriaudmuchart.free.fr/bellot_meduse.htm (background on Denis Bellot, by a descendant [in French])

Notes

1   The *Wreck of The Wager*, John Buckley and John Byron (London: Folio Society, 1983).
2   *Marked for Misfortune*, Jean Hood (London: Conway Maritime, 2003).
3   The adverbial phrase used by the French navy to describe such a partially disarmed ship is 'en flûte'.
4   During the late war, de Venancourt had served with the first the Spanish and then the Royal Navy.
5   There was a prejudice among returning émigré aristocrats like de Chaumareys against those of their caste who, like des Touches, had served France during the Napoleonic period.
6   His true name was Paul Charles Léonard Alexandre Rang des Adrets, but he is generally referred to as Sander Rang.
7   There has to be some doubt whether Richefort's manoeuvres took place here, or earlier, during the abortive attempt to enter Funchal. The one eye-witness account is that of Charlotte Picard, whose comment, that on their return from shore the officers joked about the constant tacking, suggests that the incident occurred at Santa Cruz. Sander Rang, however, makes no mention of it, while Henri Savigny, the *Méduse*'s junior surgeon, and Corréard state that the *Echo* moored astern of the *Méduse*. Either way, it was around this point that Richefort achieved virtual command of the frigate.
8   Savigny and Corréard gave the manuscript of their account to one of the ship's officer's so that he could make notes to correct or corroborate their version of events. Unsurprisingly, the officer remains anonymous in the published version, but it is unlikely that they would have expected a midshipman to be able to comment, and impossible that they would have asked Reynaud. Espiaux can be ruled out as the notes contain a eulogy on him. The choice therefore has to be between La Peyrère, Chaudière and Maudet, with the balance of probability favouring Maudet.
9   The soundings that were taken every two hours required the ship to be hove-to; those taken on the half-hour were done with the ship in motion. La Peyrère was able to take such soundings for his own satisfaction even though de Chaumareys would not stop the ship in order to take more accurate measurements.
10 The French Navy was chronically short of chronometers. De Venancourt carried one because he was under orders to carry out a hydrographic survey. In fact, to carry out an accurate survey, a minimum of three chronometers was required to allow for any malfunction or inaccuracy.
11 According to the subsequent survey of the area, longitude adjusted to Greenwich. The log of the *Méduse* was – perhaps conveniently – lost, and her captain gave the stated position from memory, subsequently changing his mind.
12 Anyone studying a modern chart of the area would not understand this reasoning. The Île d'Arguin lay some 68 miles (110 kilometres) to the north-east, while the nearest island to them was probably Kiji, 35 miles (56 kilometres) to the south-east. Neighbouring islands offered easy stages from Kiji to the nearby coast. Even sailing or rowing due east they would have met the northern tip of the island of Tidra. Unfortunately, the Bellin chart was, as Rosily knew, gravely defective. The *Méduse* was out of sight of land, so nobody could make decisions based upon visible features.
13 According to Charlotte Picard, her father had come up with proposals for the colony that had been accepted in Paris and that would have increased his status in the colony. Later those plans were dropped. After Schmaltz was appointed governor, Picard's plans were revived, but others got the credit and Picard lost his chance of advancement.
14 Charlotte's account, like that of others, should perhaps carry a health warning. Her recall of events may well be accurate – discrepancies of time or date are perfectly understandable – but she was writing in a spirit of bitterness, and her attribution of malign motives to some people may overstate the case. However, Mollien, by deliberately identifying only Espiaux among the officers, implicitly damned the others with faint praise.
15 Whatever the condition of repair of the boats, most of them had been out of the water until the grounding on 2 July, and their timbers would have shrunk, leading to leaks when once more immersed. Usually such leaks disappear as the wood swells, but four of the boats were overloaded, and that, with the heavy weather, would contribute to their problems.
16 The various sources used here – Rang (who was not present and may have had his information from his friend Bellot), Brédif and Charlotte Picard – generally agree as to events but rarely on times and sometimes not on dates. Any reconstruction is thus to some degree conjectural.

[17] They eventually reached St Louis with help from the Moors, but only through Kummer passing himself off as a Muslim.

[18] That allegation, though contemporary, only came to light in 1946 with the publication of Sander Rang's narrative, in which he states what he was told by survivors of the raft (though there are understandable discrepancies with Savigny and Corréard's narrative in the dates and times when the outbreaks of violence were said to have occurred). As other writers have pointed out, however, it would have been a risky strategy for the 'officer group' to have put into practice, given that they were outnumbered.

[19] Cynics will argue that Savigny and Corréard included this moving scene in the narrative to gain sympathy; however, they also included a great deal else that authors wishing only to exonerate themselves and others of their group might have wished to play down.

[20] Two of the merchants who took in survivors later presented them with bills for expenses incurred.

[21] The whereabouts of the money has never been proved. Reynaud was a good diver and would have known where to look; nobody could have carried it through the desert or kept it on the raft. It is unlikely Schmaltz could have put it into his barge – and if he had, he would have had no reason to advertise its existence by ordering Reynaud to search for it on the *Méduse*. There are those who like to think it was never put onto the ship in the first place, while other historians believe Reynaud found it and connived with Schmaltz to defraud the government ...

[22] This is made up of 135 on the raft, plus 4 who died after rescue; 4 of D'Anglas's group; 14 on, or trying to escape from, the frigate, plus two of the survivors.

[23] It was finally handed over on 25 January 1817.

6

Worse Things Happen at Sea

Rothsay Castle

1831

... the very rats instinctively have quit it.

SHAKESPEARE, *THE TEMPEST*, Act I, scene ii

THE REAL HEART of the *Méduse* horror is not in the incompetence that led to the wreck, nor the suffering; it dies not even lie in the cannibalism, which repelled and fascinated the public. At its centre lies the cold-blooded, selfish, maybe even premeditated abandonment of 150 human beings whose bad luck was to be on a ship that was doomed from the moment she sailed and whose only crime was to be inconvenient. Such callousness was far from unique. John Kirby had experienced it on the *Albion*, and Poon Lim, the only survivor of the torpedoed *Ben Lomond* in 1942,[1] would not hold the record for survival at sea – 133 days on a raft – if the unidentified ship whose officers studied him at close quarters through their binoculars had shown a fraction of the humanity of Espiaux.

Though what remained of French national pride after 1815 may have been mortified to think that the British in particular were lapping up the *Méduse* tragedy, their victorious rivals across the Channel were in no position to claim moral superiority. Stubbornness and incompetence have no national boundaries. Every navy and merchant fleet has its bad captains, and they are more danger-

Dramatis Personae

Mary Appleton : passenger from Bury

Thomas Appleton : passenger from Bury

Lieutenant John Atkinson : captain

James Brandreth : passenger from Chorlton-cum-Hardy

William Broadhurst : passenger from Sheffield

Ellen Broadhurst : passenger from Sheffield

Margaret Broadhurst : passenger from Sheffield

Sir Richard Williams-Bulkeley Bt : MP for Beaumaris

Tom Charles : passenger from Bury

John Coxhead : passenger from London

John Duckworth : passenger from Bury

Lawrence Duckworth : passenger from Bury

Thomas Entwhistle : passenger from Bury

Ann Faulkner : passenger from Manchester

James Fitton : passenger from Bury

Joseph Fletcher : former passenger

Jane Forster : passenger from London

William Forster : passenger from London

George Hammond : passenger from Leeds

Mrs Hammond : passenger from Leeds

Sam Horrocks : passenger from Bury

Rachel Howarth : passenger from Bury

—— Hughes : son of helmsman

Ellen Jones : passenger

William Jones : steward

William Jones : passenger from Liverpool

Joseph : seaman

Selina Lamb : passenger from Bury

James Leigh : passenger from Liverpool

Elizabeth Lucas : passenger from Liverpool

Joseph Lucas : passenger from Liverpool

Margaret Lucas : passenger from Liverpool

Lieutenant Morrison : expert witness

John Nuttall : passenger from Bury

Margaret Owen : passenger from Beaumaris

Mary Owen : passenger from Beaumaris

Owen Owen : passenger from Beaumaris

John Parry : passenger from Manchester

Frances Payne : passenger from Salford

Elliot Rudland : band member

Catherine Selwyn : passenger from Bath

Henry Selwyn : passenger from Bath

Henry de Souza : passenger from Liverpool

Alice Tarry : passenger from Bury

Betsy Tarry : passenger from Bury

John Tarry : baby, passenger from Bury

Thomas Tarry : passenger from Bury

William Tarry : passenger from Bury

John Tinne : passenger from Liverpool

William Vavasour : mate

William Lewis Walker : resident of Beaumaris

Margaret Walmsley : passenger from Bury

Mary Walmsley : passenger from Bury

William Walmsley : passenger from Bury

James Watson : owner of the *Rothsay Castle*

John West : band member

George Whitehead : solicitor from Bury

James Whittaker : passenger from Bury (son of Robert)

Robert Whittaker : passenger from Bury

Mary Whittaker : passenger from Bury

Thomas Whittaker : passenger from Bury (son of Mary)

John Wilkinson : passenger from Bury

Ralph Williamson : rescuer at Beaumaris

Henry Wilson : passenger from Manchester

Mrs Wilson : passenger from Manchester

Mr Wright : alderman of Beaumaris

ous to a ship than almost any natural hazard because not only are they unable to cope with a crisis, they are quite capable of creating one. Combine that with inadequate legislation and owners whose attitude to safety is at best cavalier, and disaster is in the offing.

It had been grey and breezy at Llanfairfechan. The experienced dog walkers on the wide expanse of Lavan Sands were strategically retreating as the tide turned; a handful of visitors drank cappuccino in the wooden café by the seafront car park, which seemed to be the only place open. By lunchtime in Beaumaris the blustery wind funnelling its way down the Menai Strait had concentrated its power into a gale, edging the tops of the waves with white lace and driving the boats at their mooring buoys into a frenzied dance. A phone call to the boat-chartering company confirmed the inevitable: it was already too rough for the little *Island Queen* to make the trip. A pity to have driven 90 miles in vain, but there was a reassuring irony to the situation. The whole point of the excursion was to see where, in 1831, an unseaworthy pleasure steamer had come to grief all because her captain had been too greedy and too stubborn to call off a dangerous voyage.

The two boys stood with their eyes shining and mouths wide open at the sight of the clouds of steam and smoke that the brisk wind tore out of the tall funnel, and would have been happy to stand there half the morning if James's father had not tugged at their hands. A steady stream of people were filling up the small, brightly painted carriages, and the train was on the point of departure.

For Robert Whittaker of Silver Street, Bury, and his sister it was as much of an adventure as for their sons. The goods line from Bolton to Leigh had just been extended to join the new Manchester–Liverpool railway, and from June 1831 it had been taking passengers. Mary had been up early that Monday morning, 17 August, to make the picnic and get her own son, six year old Thomas ready, then see that his eight-year old cousin, James, was in his best clothes. They had met up with their friend, John Wilkinson, to travel from Bury to Bolton, from where they were now taking the train to Liverpool. Just for a few of days they could escape the maze of soot-blackened redbrick walls, and the constant clatter of the shuttles in the nearby mills, or for Robert, the heat and hammering of his brazier's business. Mary had left her shop in the Market Place to be minded; Wilkinson had laid aside his chisels and saws. It was good to get away occasionally, especially in the summer, though the weather was unpromising.

They would not be the only ones from their town. Selina Lamb, the chambermaid of the *Grey Mare* in Market Place, had got up a party, and gossip had told them the Duckworths were going. Sam Horrocks, who owned the *White Lion*, said that his daughter, Alice Tarry, and her family would also be there.[2]

The engine was now puffing harder; the couplings clanked and the carriage jerked. There was even a cheer as the train began to move. Smoothing down her skirts and tying her bonnet strings more firmly, Mary was glad they had seats, but it was still draughty. The boys were by the open windows, pointing to houses and shops, arguing whether they were going faster than a coach, in love with the speed and the smell of the black smoke. While Mary enjoyed the patches of spreading moor, the fields in the height of harvesting and the green parkland of the great houses, Robert and his friend discussed with admiration the feat of engineering that had cut the line deep through hills and raised it high on viaducts, until the train ran so smoothly and straight that there never seemed to be any gradient.

Leigh was on the left. They crossed the Wigan canal, and now the line was turning south. This was the new stretch, down to Kenyon junction, where they would join the Liverpool–Manchester railway, which had itself been open less than a year. The locomotive slowed to a halt and the boys jumped down to watch it take on water. Then they were off again, through the deep cutting just before Newton, with flecks of soot getting in their eyes. They crossed the valley over the viaduct, looking down on the river and the road to Warrington, before running along the embankment that took them high over the Sankey valley. Some of the people in the carriage with them looked out; others folded their hands and stared resolutely at nothing. Soon they were at Rainhill, where the locomotives had been trialled, gasping with amazement as they were whisked through the tunnel, and with only 8 miles (13 kilometres) or so to go.

The view from the Roby embankment was abruptly cut off by the sheer rock walls of cuttings, and from the comments of more experienced travellers they gathered they were not far from their destination. The train passed beneath a tall, exotic arch and wheezed to a standstill in what could almost have been the courtyard of some gothic castle, except that ahead stood the mouths of two tunnels. The locomotive was uncoupled, and after a short delay to attach cables the carriages began to move slowly into the smaller of the tunnels, prompting the boys to try out the echoing acoustic. The walls were whitewashed, and a rich glow from overhead lanterns produced a reassuring brightness. Ahead gleamed natural light, and at last, less than three hours after leaving Bolton, they were under the canopy of Crown Street station, Liverpool. The holiday had begun, and if the weather was good they would take the packet boat to Anglesey on Wednesday.

As they were sightseeing they ran into Selina's party. Margaret Walmsley, whose father sold china and glass, was with her fiancé, James Fitton, who farmed just outside Bury. Making up the quartet was John Nuttall, the chemist, who had left his wife and children at home. On hearing that the Whittakers were planning a trip to Beaumaris, Selina decided that she and her friends would go, too[3].

More than a hundred other people had the same idea.

William Broadhurst had travelled up from Sheffield on business. His two teenage daughters, Margaret and Ellen, who had been staying in Macclesfield, joined him in Chester and the three of them reached Liverpool in time for breakfast on Wednesday morning at the Wellington Arms. Leaving the girls at the inn, Broadhurst paid a call on an old friend, James Marsden, and they strolled over to the packet office to see about sailing times. Marsden had friends in Beaumaris, and scribbled a note of introduction for his friend.

The attractions of Anglesey were known as far afield as London, from where John Coxhead had travelled with the specific intention of visiting the area, and then there were the residents of Beaumaris and Bangor on their way home. Thirty-three-year-old Dr Owen Owen had been in Liverpool celebrating his appointment as headmaster of Ruthin School by buying furniture, and his younger sisters Margaret and Mary had gone with him, the first time Mary had ever left Wales.

A sizeable group from the Manchester area was woven into the gathering queue for tickets, among them the elderly John Parry and his wife. He had left Bangor 48 years earlier as a young man, and today he was fulfilling an old longing to see the place again. From even closer to home came a handful of Liverpuddlians. Henry de Souza might be Portuguese by birth and had been a secretary to Lord Canning in Lisbon towards the end of the Napoleonic wars, but he had been settled many years in Liverpool and was married to the sister of James Leigh, who had a soap-boiling business in Byrom Street. Leigh's mother lived on Anglesey, and the two brothers-in-law had planned to visit her. On the Tuesday night, however, Leigh's premises were flooded and the trip was thrown into doubt until first thing Wednesday when a good look round showed that that the damage was not too bad. They could go, after all.

For mid-August the weather that morning was disappointing: cold and wet with a stiff breeze whipping over the pier, where Robert Whittaker was not sorry to have his greatcoat with him. From the dock basins rose a dense forest of merchantmen; alongside the pier a small paddle steamer with two masts and a tall chimney amidships fluctuated on the choppy waters of the Mersey estuary. Her name was the *Rothsay Castle*, and she had recently been bought by one James Watson, initially for the Liverpool–Wexford run. An advertisement in the *Liverpool Chronicle* wooed passengers with impressive claims:

> ... This vessel is not equalled by any on the station, both as regards speed and elegant accommodation. Her easy draft of water enables her to run close inshore, ensuring a smooth passage and an opportunity of viewing the scenery along the Welsh coast ... Carriages and horses carefully shipped. A female attends the ladies' cabins. A military band on board. Cabin fare 10/6d [52½p], steerage 5/- [25p]. Apply Wm Watson[4], 21 Water Street.

Fifteen years earlier and just four years after the launch of the Clyde steamer *Comet,* the *Rothsay Castle* had been near the forefront of the steamship revolution. Designed for work on the Clyde and built by A M Maclachlan, she had been lengthened early in her career[5] and her registered tonnage increased from 60 to 73. Her 50hp Duncan McArthur engine was perfectly adequate for her river service, but by the time Watson bought her in 1830, she was old and, in the opinion of Wilson's, the ship-repairers charged with bringing her up to scratch, her bottom was broken and the timbers that formed her frame were too light for the the demands of the Irish Sea. The carpenter who worked on her at the time was of the opinion that she might prove a coffin for someone, but by the time she left the yard, in February 1831, they were confident of the work they had done. Shortly after she transferred to the Beaumaris route in May, she was given new boilers by William Laird's at Birkenhead.[6]

For all that, the *Rothsay Castle* was something of a local joke. It was generally accepted by those 'in the know' that she was unsound. One crewman had supposedly left her at the Isle of Man because he feared for his life; a recent passenger named Joseph Fletcher would one day have good cause to remember the day that he had 'observed upon the craziness[7] of the vessel and expressed reasonable fears in consequence'.

Few of those who boarded her that Wednesday morning, however, were 'in the know'. And besides, they were in holiday mood. Broadhurst came up with his daughters and Marsden, who told him to come and stay with him when he was back in Liverpool. Ann Faulkner tried to persuade her mother to join a family excursion, telling her that the worst to be feared was a bit of seasickness. The older woman was immovable, and in the end Ann's sister stayed behind with their mother while Ann embarked with two of her young children and her maid, having left her husband at home in Manchester with their others.

Whittaker's enlarged group now found themselves greeting even more of their neighbours from Bury, among them William Tarry and family. The 10:00 a.m. sailing time had come and gone, the three-piece band was on deck, but the vessel's captain, Lieutenant John Carr Atkinson RN, showed no sign of being ready to weigh anchor. It is possible that he was having second thoughts about putting to sea given the boisterous weather, which was rough enough that morning to induce an American ship to put back, but on the other hand he was busy taking money from latecomers, and a carriage had just driven up. A footman came on deck and it soon appeared that sailing would be further delayed while the carriage was hoisted on board. Tarry, who had just escorted his large family down into the fore-cabin, told the captain that if he had known there would be this delay he would have gone and had his breakfast. He threatened to write a letter to the newspaper to the effect that the captain was more bothered about getting a couple of extra guineas than running to schedule.

The carriage, which belonged to London lawyer William Forster and his wife, was eventually lashed to the deck. Still no move was made to weigh anchor, and this time it was said that the captain was waiting for a still later passenger. Leigh, the soap manufacturer, told him that if he didn't get going now, he would be reported.

Almost an hour late, and with the band gallantly playing 'Cheer up, Cheer up', the *Rothsay Castle*, with some difficulty, got under weigh. Most of those on board – and there were upwards of 130 – were cheerful enough, and remained on deck; a few who felt unwell or who had small children went below into the two cabins. They anticipated a voyage of six or seven hours, but it would be well worth it. Although a few people were simply going home to Anglesey, most were visitors planning to stay one or more nights on the island, where the annual regatta was scheduled for the following day.

It was not long before they began to suspect that their ship was not quite as fast as they had been led to believe. The wind had lost some of its early-morning strength, but it was still brisk and, blowing from the north-north-west, represented almost a headwind, while the long delay in getting away had also lost an hour of the outgoing tide. For the moment, the deck passengers were more interested in admiring the Black Rock lighthouse, standing 90 feet (27 metres) tall, that warned vessels away from the notorious reef, and also the low fort of the same name standing sentinel on the Wirral at the entrance to the Mersey. Both had been completed only a year earlier.

The tide turned just as the wind freshened, and the ship struggled to make any headway in the roughening sea. This coincided with the band ceasing to play, and for the first time the passengers could hear the engine labouring painfully as it shook the timbers. When the packet finally emerged into the open waters of Liverpool Bay, the sea grew rougher and seasickness set in among the hapless holidaymakers. Auburn-haired Margaret Lucas, who before the start of the voyage had been an arrestingly attractive young woman had gone below quite early, a caricature of usual herself, and was joined by her parents and many of the others, particularly the women and children. They had only covered 5 miles (9 kilometres) and, when not being sick, all that most people could think about was getting the voyage over with and reaching Beaumaris. A middle-aged man from Bath, Henry Selwyn, sat on a bench with his feet over the arm, explaining to Coxhead that it was a way of averting sea-sickness.

Timbers groaning and underpowered engine struggling to turn the paddles on each side, the *Rothsay Castle* made it to the floating light at about 3:00 p.m. Fifteen miles – just 28 kilometres – or less had taken four hours. The captain had gone down to dinner more than an hour earlier, and despite the apparent distress of the vessel had not been seen on deck since. The other ten crew members, including the stewards, were about their business. With the western bank of the Hoyle sands bearing close under the ship's lee, the passengers saw another of Watson's vessels on the Beaumaris route, the *Prince Llewellyn*, already passing them well to windward on her return trip to Liverpool, though they were nowhere close to half-way through the journey. Those on board the *Llewellyn* were taken aback to see the outward-bound *Rothsay Castle* with the sands close and barely able to make headway.

By the chimney, out of the worst of the weather, John Nuttall sat next to William Tarry. Both were silent until Nuttall spoke his thoughts aloud.

'I am sure the vessel will never bear the heavy sea we are in.'

As if Nuttall had voiced his own fears, the land agent got up and went to the cabin stairs, from where he shouted down to the master:

'Why, captain, we are in very great danger!'

Lieutenant Atkinson's response was to laugh and to tell him that if they were to go back they would have to cover all the ground again.

Lieutenant Atkinson[8] was 40 at the time. Born in South Shields he had apparently received a head wound during the later Napoleonic wars, which, according to local gossip, affected his behaviour – if he had been drinking – by turning him stubborn. He had been commissioned lieutenant late in 1815, but, with the war over there was no hope of naval employment. William Watson was to say later that Atkinson had come to him and his brother with excellent credentials. He had successfully commanded the *Rothsay Castle*'s predecessor, the *Ormerod*, and had never shown any fear when taking her out in bad weather.

When Tarry rejoined Nuttall, he looked anxious.

'I have been at Dublin, and the isle of Man, and several other places, but I never was in so rough a sea before.' Uppermost in his mind was fear for his family, the fear that one man could not save six. He was a landsman, and his idea of a dangerous sea would, ordinarily, have amused a sailor. But even a landsman could see that the *Rothsay Castle* was unable to cope with this heavy weather. Her progress was no better than a snail's, and her frail construction, never intended for such waters, was becoming clear. As fear began to spread, the Bury men were drawing together. Tarry turned to Robert Whittaker, pleading for reassurance.

'Good God, Robert, what do you think of this matter? Do you think the vessel can live through such a sea?'

'I do not think it can. I am very much afraid we shall be lost.'

Whittaker later repeated much the same to his friend Wilkinson, who attempted to make light of their position, telling Whittaker he would insure him for a small premium.

'You can't, John,' said Nuttall. 'I am of the same opinion as Robert, that we cannot survive this.'

When one of the younger crewmen showed his face on deck, Tarry suggested to him that they ought to turn back now.

'Turn back?' he echoed incredulously. 'What must we turn back for? We have something else to do than to turn back!'

What the seamen of the *Méduse* had been saying as their ship approached danger is not known, but the officers had made no secret of their disquiet. Such of the *Rothsay Castle*'s eleven-strong crew who had spoken to the passengers, however, were inexplicably, almost aggressively, optimistic.

Far from reassured, they asked Tarry, older than Whittaker by 25 years and used to negotiating, to go and make a formal request to return to Liverpool. They were not to know it, but in addition to dining well, Lieutenant Atkinson had been drinking heavily, and alcohol had given him that stubborn courage that makes men reckless. The same was true of William Vavasour, the mate. The land agent descended into the crowded cabin and faced Atkinson at his table.

'Captain, there seems to be a great deal of danger,' he began. 'I wish you would put back.'

'There's a damned deal of *fear*, but no *danger*,' responded Atkinson. 'If we were to turn back with passengers it would never do: we would have no profit.' His language was to get worse. He swore in front of Mrs Forster, the lawyer's wife whose carriage had delayed the departure and whose early high spirits had soon been crushed by the reality of the voyage. She was deeply shocked by his language and, and after reprimanding the captain for it, Forster took his wife into the ladies' cabin and went up on deck with a grim face.

Later it would be disputed whether Atkinson was a regular drunkard or whether his conduct on this voyage was out of character. If he had put to sea against his better judgement, fearing for his livelihood if he refused, a strong dose of Dutch courage to steel his nerves was credible, if unforgiveable. To have remained in port only to see the *Prince Llewellyn* arrive unscathed would have implied either that his vessel was unseaworthy or that he was afraid, neither of

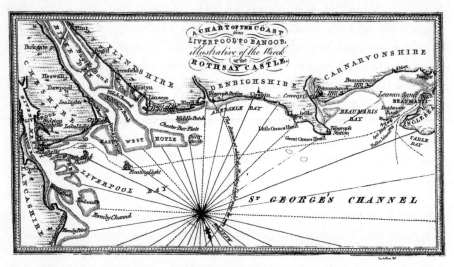

Route of the *Rothsay Castle* in a contemporary map (south is at the top). Shallow sands extending for miles from land already made this a dangerous shore.

which would have pleased the brash young owner, James Watson.

After 4:00 p.m. the captain finally appeared on deck, by which time they had managed to cross the mouth of the Dee estuary, missing the sandbanks more by luck than judgement. The wind, which had been directly against them in the Mersey, continued to drive them close to the shore, and it was as much as the engine could do to keep what little offing it had along the Clwyd coast. John Duckworth heard one of the crew tell Lieutenant Atkinson that the fires of the engine were not being kept up, to which the captain answered, in a repetition of the kind of language that had affronted Mrs. Forster, that he would go and kick the damned devil out of them – whatever 'them' were. By now not one of the deck passengers could stand up without something to hang onto, and they begged him to turn round, saying they would gladly forfeit their fares. Some, well and truly afraid, even offered to pay more if he agreed to give up the trip. But the drink had gone to his head; he brushed aside the offer and turned on one man contemptuously:

'What, I suppose you have committed murder that you are so frightened!' To the rest he asserted: 'I am not one to turn back. If you knew me, you would not make such a request.' He then grew mockingly cheerful, and when the landmark of Great Orme was sighted in the distance, Tarry asked him plaintively:

'How soon will you be able to pass the Orme's head? By ten o'clock, do you think?'

Atkinson smiled reassuringly.

'I bet you a wager we pass it before eight-o-clock.'

Down below, in the ladies' cabin, Mary Whittaker talked with her Bury friends while her son and nephew went on deck with her brother. The voyage was unpleasant, but she felt none of the crippling fear entertained by the men who could see their situation, and some of whom knew enough of steam technology to recognize that the vessel was in serious trouble. A tacit but deliberate attempt was being made to hide the danger from wives and daughters, but it was a limited chivalry. They would have done better to have forced the issue through strength of numbers or threat of lawsuits and obliged the captain either to return to port or put in at the nearest harbour. They were men of standing in their own communities, with a couple of lawyers among them, and could probably have survived any court action that the ship's owner might bring afterwards, yet they watched helplessly as evening fell and the situation deteriorated around them. Steam power was no longer constant. Each time it failed, and the paddles stood still, the foresail was hoisted; once it returned, the sail was taken down. By now 8:00 p.m. was long past, and still they had not reached the great headland, let alone doubled it.

Tarry had brought his youngest child on deck. His wife was in the fore-cabin feeling sick, and the maid, Rachel, had her hands full with the four older girls and boys. Now he sat affectionately nursing the 14-month-old in his arms, sheltered by his coat. John was the first child of his marriage to local widow Alice Appleton less than three years earlier. He already had a boy of 11 and a girl of 12, Thomas and Betsy, from his second marriage to another of Bury's daughters, while Alice had brought her own boy and girl into his family: another Thomas, 10, and Mary, 13. Though not a local man by birth, he had been settled there as a land agent and surveyor for many years; he acted in that capacity for local landowner the Earl of Derby, and was well respected. In his despondancy he was joined by William and Mary Walmsley, whose aunt Margaret – younger than both of them – was with her fiancé, Fitton. Mary looked white and ill, clutching the hand of their little boy, and she decided to seek the shelter of the cabin. Walmsley grasped Tarry's hands and shook his head.

'We're all going to be lost,' he said wretchedly. Close by, Whittaker was putting his greatcoat over little James and Tom who lay cold and sick on the deck. John Duckworth the Shuttleworth bootmaker looked down at him.

'I wish I was safely set down at home or at Holden's in Liverpool.'

Whittaker glanced up bleakly.

'So do I.'

Tarry went down to join his wife, asking the captain to carry John for him as the deck was so unstable. The Lucases had remained down below with John Coxhead, vainly trying to cheer up Margaret Lucas, while the two Owen sisters in their black silk dresses, whom the captain had complimented on their beauty, tried to maintain a brave composure in company. Well aware of the *Rothsay Castle*'s reputation, the family had warned them not to go on her, but Margaret, the younger, had laughed at their fears.

Their brother, the new headmaster, had struck up a passing acquaintance with Broadhurst and sat talking with him on the quarterdeck as the sea ran higher, waves beginning to break over the deck. That position had allowed Broadhurst to observe the helmsman and take an interest in the ship's compass. Although he had no seafaring knowledge, he had no difficulty in seeing that the helmsman did not always carry out the orders given, though whether that was because he was incompetent or the vessel was in no condition to obey the helm is a moot point. Little use was made of the sails, perhaps because the ship – whether the passengers knew it or not at the time – had left two of the crew at Liverpool. Since it was highly unlikely the vessel was over-manned even at the best of time, it stands to reason that the loss of two men was significant in such a situation.

Lieutenant Atkinson was belatedly seen to be taking some kind of action, even if it was only to curse his men for not trimming the ship. A large box full of heavy chains and running on wheels was stowed on the deck; by moving it fore and aft as the conditions required the ship's head could be raised or lowered. Still there was no acknowledgement of danger. On seeing all the frightened faces, Jones the Steward said in answer to a remark from Whittaker:

'How can you be afraid when you see us all so merry?' It was the last attempt to pretend nothing much was amiss. One of the crew came up looking for a colleague, and muttered something that nobody quite understood, but which sounded ominous. When the second crewman appeared from below he was looking very concerned.

'Bless me, I'm knee deep in water,' he muttered. 'Begin and use the pumps.'

Now they knew why the engine power was so intermittent. With water in the boiler room the fires could not be kept going constantly, and now the rising water was slopping six inches deep in the cabins. Nobody believed the steward when he tried to pretend it was bilgewater. The order for all hands to the pump went out, and the passengers stood their turn, three at a time, pumping for all they were worth, but the pumps kept choking up and had to be cleared.

Yet they had passed the Great Orme against all the odds at 10:00 p.m., and were labouring into Conwy Bay with only a few miles left to their destination, albeit dangerous miles. The sinking moon gleamed through gathering clouds to show Puffin Island ahead, off the starboard bow. Some of the passengers recommended putting into Conwy for the night, but the captain retorted:

'God keep me from attempting it.'[9]

Whittaker's suggestion of burning a distress light that would have brought out the lifeboat or perhaps a local pilot was dismissed with the comment that there was nothing to make a signal with, though there was a light at the binnacle so the helmsman could see the compass. Nor did anyone take soundings. Instead, the captain retired to his cabin, preferring to send messages by various passengers urging that the pumps be kept going.

The tide had turned once again and was now ebbing, making the entrance to the Menai Strait even more hazardous than usual. From Llanfairfechan to Bangor stretched the Lavan sands, extending almost to the Anglesey coast at Beaumaris. The northwesterly tip of the sands, cut off from the main expanse by the narrow channel of Penmaen Swatch, went by the name of Dutchman's Bank, and lay right in the centre of the mouth of the straits, some 1.6 miles (3 kilometres) from the Llanfairfechan side and 2.1 miles (4 kilometres) from the north-eastern tip of Anglesey. It was a known marine graveyard. The correct approach to Beaumaris was to keep in the the main channel, Midlake Swatch, between the Dutchman's Bank and Anglesey. A drifting ship had no hope of making that channel, and any other course would lead her onto the sandbanks.

With the pumps failing, one side of the engine fires already extinguished and the other threatening to die, one of the Duckworths called for buckets in the hope of forming a human chain to bail out the water. He was asking for the moon: the solitary pail carried by the ship had already been lost overboard. A resourceful suggestion of using the men's top hats was not tried. The fire spluttered, steam pressure fell, the paddles on either side cranked to a halt. Elliot Rudland, the clarinettist, heard the fireman quarrelling with the captain.

The wind pushed the exhausted vessel sideways, and she struck on the bank, bumped along, stopped, and listed to windward under the weight of the chimney and masts, her bows pointing towards Puffin island.

There was, in Coxhead's words, a stampede up the stairs into the darkness. In the grip of panic over his family Tarry pushed past Coxhead. On the deck, women stood screaming; the men appeared overwhelmed by their predicament. Families clung together beneath the drenching spray as the keel beat on the bank. The bell was ringing a wild plea for help, and her sound reached the shore, but as the ship was all dark, no one on land knew where it came from. John Tinne, from Liverpool's well-known West India merchants, Sandbach Tinne, took over the bell and rang it constantly for 20 minutes, while the ship was dragged by the wind and tide until she came to her final grave.

If there was ever any hope for her it was soon smothered. The captain came on deck, coat buttoned and oilskin hat crammed on his head, and ordered the helmsman to steer hard to starboard, which made no difference. His next idea was to get all the men to run forward to take the weight from the stern which had grounded. A command to reverse the paddles foundered on a lack of steam to turn them, and while some passengers broke out with complaints and suggestions others told them to leave the captain alone. Atkinson reinforced that, saying he wouldn't be spoken to as he had enough on his mind. Someone shouted at him:

'We shall go to the bottom!'

'Damn the bottom!' came his answer, 'we are at the bottom already!'

Amidst all the terror, Rudland went into the caboose to find his precious clarinet, encountering fellow musician John West.

'We are lost, Elliot.'

'No, we'll trust in God and not despair.'

Most of the passengers had given up hope. Tarry shook Nuttall's hand.

'We are all lost. Oh, my poor wife and family.'

'Yes, sir, I believe we shall perish.' They never saw one another again. William Walmsley likewise clasped hands with him, and the same ritual took place with Whittaker, before Nuttall made his way back to Selina and Margaret. The two young Bury women had taken off their bonnets and Nuttall was surprised to find them quietly praying. Dr Owen sat at the stern by Coxhead, hugging his two sisters. One of them was screaming hysterically at the dark sky as if trying to ward off their fate. Having spent the whole voyage below deck the Lucas family had come up, and Mrs Lucas, too, was beside herself, blaming her daughter for their ever finding themselves on the ship.

'Oh my child! Oh Margaret! It was you who persuaded us to come on this journey!'

The girl, equally distracted, tried to defend herself.

'Oh, my dear mother, do not say so!' She turned imploringly to her father.

'Father, was it me? You know I did not want to come!' But the mother was in no state to listen.

'Oh, my children at home! No on left to protect them. Oh, Margaret, this is your fault.'

At the fore end, Henry and Catherine Selwyn were together, she at his feet, her elegant white gown crushed and wet. Forster had his wife in his arms, but he was calm, and when some passengers suggested that having his carriage overboard might ease the listing ship, he agreed, only asking that some of his belongings might be taken off first. Captain Atkinson refused to allow the crew to do it. Forster then asked his footman to bring his cloak, and the man came back with it, draping it round his shoulders. In a last gesture of protection, the husband wrapped the edges around his wife, as if to protect her from seeing the end when it came.

Joseph, a black youth who was part of the crew, went up to Coxhead in tears, recognizing in him one of the few men who retained some sort of coolness. Coxhead found a friendly word for him, whereupon the lad clung round his neck in a way that would have drowned both of them.

'Hold onto my coat,' Coxhead told him.

People were asking in vain for a gun to be fired as a distress signal, only to find the ship did not carry one. Whoever had taken over from Tinne at the bell had rung with such vigour that the clapper broke, and afterwards resorted to a piece of wood that produced a dismal funeral knell all too appropriate for the wretched scene on board. The sea was breaking over the deck; rumours the captain had been swept away were soon confirmed. A group of people scrambled into the one ship's boat, but were told it was useless: it had no oars, and there was a hole in the bottom. All but one, a woman clutching a baby, got out, and John Tinne, a rope wrapped round his wrist, dragged her out before the craft broke from its one remaining davit. A seaman staggered to the lamp in the binnacle and deliberately smashed the only light on the vessel, then complained there was no way of making a signal. Like so much of what had happened, it was an inexplicable moment. Perhaps he too was drunk.

The end was approaching. A huge wave tore off some of the weatherboard on the windward side, snatching maybe thirty people with it. Whittaker was braced by one of the paddleboxes when he was approached by a young man carrying a drum. He might have been the third musician, or perhaps he had found the drum, but he told Whittaker that if they each held onto one side, the drum might save them; he refused to give it up to some nearby women. Whittaker stripped to his shirt and stockings, gave his watch and money to his sister, who was holding her son and nephew by the hand, and told her he would have to try swimming. The drum appeared buoyant, but Whittaker rapidly decided that the disparity in sizes between the two men made it impossible. He told his partner to find someone else, and then watched the pair of them founder within his view.

Close by Mary Whittaker, and with a group of women around him, Nuttall held Selina Lamb's hands and prayed. A huge wave burst over the side, dragging one of the Whittaker boys with it. Too distressed even to know whether it was Tom or James, Mary just grabbed at the child's clothing and somehow hauled him back. At that moment the chimney came down, bringing the mainmast with it, leaving her pressed against the side of the rail, with waves breaking down the weatherboards and dragging screaming passengers struggling into the sea. A moment later an even more powerful wave broke, and the rail gave way. She heard little James screaming for his father to save him, and then she went under. Selina attempted to say something to Nuttall, but she, too, was swept into the water, her words unspoken, and he went in headfirst.

James Whittaker's last plaintive screams reached his father clinging to the remains of the weatherboard, but Robert could do nothing to reach him, and even if he had he could not have rescued him. Seeing other people, including his friend Wilkinson, clinging on to the iron stay that went across the vessel, he somehow scrabbled his way to it and held on for grim death, but the waves were too strong, and each breaker tore more of them away until only the two Bury friends were left.

The casing of the paddlebox yielded to the sea. Whittaker was dragged through the wheel and casing, leaving Wilkinson clinging on and yelling for mercy when the waves allowed him to breathe.

When the chimney and mainmast crashed across the deck, the three Liverpool men, de Souza, Leigh and Tinne, were together towards the aft part of the shattered vessel, which was beginning to break in two.

I observed the vessel parting – the bow with its quivering mast leaning one way, the stern, the other ... There was a bench on the starboard side which I was strongly tempted to seize hold of, but it was secured by another passenger...The two parts of the wreck were separating more and more, and seemed only to be held together by loose tackle. Our portion had now heeled over to leeward. This induced Mr Leigh, Mr de Souza and myself to move over to windward, which was the highest part of the deck. Here they held by the stanchions and railings, whilst I grasped the spokes of the wheel on one side and the end of the maintop-mast on the other – the latter having fallen obliquely across the poop. We were hardly fixed when a wave, larger than any other that had preceded it, came rolling over us, and passing onward to leeward, swept away a whole line of victims together, along with the railings, stanchions and benches; among those were most of the ladies and their friends. Even in this tremendous event I only heard one person shriek ... whilst the others passed away without cry or groan, except what my imagination now fancies ... as a deep drawn sigh from the whole mass at once.

The water in the broken hull was forcing up the deck. Planks split; the remains of the aft end sank lower in the water. Tinne found himself holding onto the end of the mainmast, together with William Jones the Steward and his wife Ellen. She was at the end of her strength, and Tinne feared they would grab hold of him. Now it was case of every man for himself because, as Tinne had earlier observed, helping anyone would only delay the inevitable. He left the mast, swam a few strokes into the sea and dragged himself onto a section of timber. Two men had got there before him; he thought they were his Liverpool acquaintances, but nobody spoke.

The water was as dangerous now from the floating debris of the disintegrating ship as from the violence of the waves. One piece cracked Tinne on the head, nearly knocking him out. Suddenly he saw a huge black wave bearing down on them, carrying with it a great piece of the wreck. From his place at the edge of the raft he waited for it to smash him; but it roared over his head. When his vision had cleared and he could look round, he was alone.[10]

Coxhead was among those who were swept off the listing hulk by that cataclysmic wave, with Joseph holding onto him. In the terrible moment of entering the water he entirely forgot the rope wrapped providentially round his arm until it tightened and saved him from been pulled away. The next wave threw him painfully against the hull. There was no sign of Joseph: the power of the water had been too much. It was the same for Broadhurst, who vainly tried to hold his daughters at the end. Sobbing that it was all their fault for wanting to go on the ship, and telling their father to look after himself, they gathered in his arms when the railing failed, and then all three were separated.

Another wave washed off the mast to which Tinne had left William and Ellen Jones clinging. All that was left on that broken poop, now all but detached from the ship, was what John Tinne had earlier taken to be a dead body, but the form was coming back to life and proving to be another William Jones (not the steward), who had been a passenger on the ship although by profession he was the Liverpool pilot. He was about to have some company.

When Nuttall had found himself in the water, he had no expectation of surviving. A non-swimmer and hampered by his coats, he rose and sank helplessly, and wreckage hit his head. Then he thought of the wife and family he had left behind in Bury, and he knew he owed it to them at least to try to save himself. He struck out, and when part of the ship floated by he crawled onto it, resting there on his knees. A hand clutched at him, clung tightly, and a weight pulled itself onto his back and refused to let go: the 11-year-old son of the helmsman, Hughes. Nuttall grasped a dangling rope and, with the child hanging on, pulled them both up onto the poop to join the solitary refugee.

A little later another sodden survivor, Henry Wilson, heaved himself up to them, glad to have saved himself but distressed by the loss of his wife. They had managed to stay together and to reach a plank that was attached by a rope to the remains of the ship, but they were washed off several times, and the effort of regaining it had sapped her strength. The final time he had seized her right hand with his left but she cried to him to save himself for the sake of the children they had left behind, and the next wave pulled her away from him. A Manchester couple, they had come to Liverpool the night before with their friends from Leeds, the Hammonds, and made the snap decision to go on the Beaumaris trip the following morning not long before the ship sailed.

The children torn from her, Mary Whittaker was carried a good distance from the wreck before she gained the surface, minus much of her clothing but with her wits very much intact. Her reticule, heavy with her brother's watch and money, was still round her wrist, and she instinctively got rid of it, then looked around for something that might save her. In so doing she noticed that her 'exertions', as she called them, were keeping her buoyant, and it that critical moment she realized she could probably swim – a skill not taught to women at that time. She, too, made for the bulk of the wreck, and surprised herself by finding it relatively easy. Eventually she was under the poop, clinging onto a rope and trying to get herself up, but the efforts in the water had been too much; unable to go on she shouted as loudly as she could, terrified of falling back into the sea.

'Will you help me, sir!'

A foot appeared above her, then a leg, and with impetuous relief she grabbed it. An unexpectedly familiar voice told her in so many words to let go or they would both be in serious danger. She obeyed, and John Nuttall, realizing her weak state, unceremoniously grabbed a handful of her hair and pulled her up, onto the poop, where for the first time he recognized whom he had saved. She found herself flat on her back, gasping, and wearing only her shift, corset and flannel petticoat, though most of that had been ripped from the waistband into which it was gathered. Her bonnet hung down over the edge behind her, full of water like a heavy bucket and threatening to strangle her, but Nuttall had been forced to move away. She lay struggling for breath, unable to untie the knot, and finally she gasped despairingly:

'Oh! I'm hanging!'

Wilson heard the pathetic plea for help and reached her. He cut the strings and then got her over to the centre of the poop, telling her to hold the rudder wheel for safety. A while later, by which time she had regained some of her strength, Wilson became aware of someone hanging onto another of the ropes. Together with Mary he reeled in the exhausted and apparently dying John Coxhead. Now there were six of them: Nuttall, Jones, Hughes Junior, Wilson, Coxhead and Mary Whittaker, and for all they knew they were the only survivors.

They were fortunate in having a mariner with them in the shape of the pilot. The poop was sinking until there was water slopping over the surface. William Jones decided they would do better to cut the ropes that still held it to the rest of the stern and then float free of the wreck on their raft, which measured a little under 10 feet (3 metres) on each side. Near the wheel was a hole, and they advised Mary to put her feet through it to give herself a more stable seat; it also enabled her to hold Coxhead's face above the water.

During what remained of the night Wilson was miraculously reunited with his Leeds friend, George Hammond, who, after losing touch with his wife, had floated on one of the spars; Elliot Rudland, the clarinettist, also arrived on a plank. He had been one of those who, like Robert Whittaker, had hoped to find safety clinging to the iron bar that had run across the ship from one paddlebox to the other, but who had then climbed onto the Forster's carriage until it went overboard. Finding the plank, he too had floated around until he encountered one of the trailing ropes from the raft.

The sea was calm now, and the night was at last yielding to the pale light of dawn. There was no sign of the wreck from the raft, nor any other life. Jones recommended that the eight of them make shift to help themselves and start paddling towards the shore, which may have been just over a mile (about two kilometres) away. Seeing they were making some progress, Jones then observed that if they only had a sail they could move even faster. Still holding the almost senseless Coxhead, Mary drew attention to the petticoat that she had torn free of the band and wrapped around her head for warmth. Jones thought it would do very well for them. Wilson protested.

'Don't take it from her, poor thing, she'll be starved[11] to death,' but he had reckoned without Mary Whittaker's pragmatic spirit of self-sacrifice.

'Oh yes. If it will do any good, take it,' she cried, and unwrapped it. A couple of the men held it up to try to catch the wind but, as Jones then pointed out, they really needed a means of tying it to part of the raft. Off came the gallant Mary's garters, and up went the sail. Everyone except Mary, Coxhead and young Hughes stood up to try to make himself more visible.

William Lewis Walker was out for a brisk walk on Beaumaris Green just before 6:00 a.m. when he spotted something odd out on the water in the distance. For a moment he was hardly able to credit his eyes: a sail ... people, on a sinking platform. He ran to raise the alarm and get a crew together.

The sight of a boat putting out from the shore brought joy to those on the raft. For a while they were unsure whether the boat was going to sea on their account or on its owner's business, but once they saw it making for them the celebrations could begin, though they were muffled by the thought of friends and family who must be dead. Then it was alongside, and a cry of 'Help the lady first!' went up. Cold and stiff, Mary was taken into the boat where the crew took off their warm jackets and wrapped them round her.

Leaving some of the men on the raft to wait their return, the rescuers took the first survivors into Beaumaris, where already a crowd had gathered. As

Mary was helped ashore a woman came forwards and put her cloak round her for warmth and modesty, and she was well enough to walk the short distance to the *Bull's Head*, where she was fussed over and put to bed. Only then did she realize how cold and terribly bruised she was; she had been thrown into the sea, buffeted by wreckage and obliged to sit almost naked in cold water for hours, hardly able to move. A few hours of warmth, rest and kindness brought her over the physical effects of the ordeal, while outside the finding of eight people on a raft had turned into a major rescue effort involving many local boats. The regatta was called off.

Among the vessels that put out that morning in response to the emergency was the large private schooner *Campeadora*, whose owner Ralph Williamson was entertaining a group of friends on board. At 8:00 a.m., and perilously close to the breakers off the Great Orme's head, she picked up Henry Jones on a small raft. He had taken refuge in Forster's carriage, and after it went overboard he initially tried to save himself with an empty keg strapped to his body for buoyancy. Foiled in that hope, he reached Lawrence Duckworth on a piece of wood. Duckworth fancied his chances as a swimmer, and in fact did succeed in reaching the shore and survived; Jones stuck with the plank, but had drifted a long way before he was found. An hour later someone on the yacht spotted another man in the water, lying on a plank with a spar held at right angles to it.

'Holloa!' shouted Williamson, and the figure on the length of wood made signs of life and shouted back. It was Robert Whittaker. After being driven through the wheel casing and into the sea he had encountered the plank, and then used the spar to increase its stability.

'Hold on, my boy!' Williamson got into one of the schooner's boats and went to fetch Whittaker, whose first question was when it would be daylight. Astonished, they told him it was broad day. The boat's crew stripped off the wet shirt and waistcoat and one of the sailors gave him his own. Williamson had him taken to the schooner, wrapped in blankets and put to rest in one of the cabins with a hot water bottle and some spirits. They put cream on his eyes and a bandage round them. Only when he was in a condition to be reunited with his sister and the other survivors did they take him ashore. In the meantime, the *Campeadora's* boat rejoined the search for survivors.

John Tinne was one of a few survivors picked up by a small sailing vessel, the first boat to put out after the first survivors on the raft had been picked up. Three seamen were found alive but unconscious after tying themselves to the foremast, which fortuitously remained standing after the broken hull settled on the bottom, holding them clear of the water. One of them was Hughes, the helmsman, whose son's life had been saved by Nuttall. That was to be the only parent and child reunion out of all the families on board the *Rothsay Castle*, and Mary Whittaker was one of just two women to survive. Frances Payne, wife of a Salford draper, lost her husband but was picked up alive from the water, and John Duckworth was another who survived on the forepart of the vessel. His wife's body was recovered up at Penmaen-bach Point. He had been among the last to see the Tarrys, all of whom perished. He had brought some wine with him and

> when we had concluded we should be lost, I begged Mr Tarrey would accept a little of the wine. He took my hand and said:
>
> 'John, I told you all day that we should be lost and that this captain should lose us.' He then took some of the wine, after which he went below, to his family, and brought them on deck.

Later, Duckworth remembered the terrible sight of little Betsy Tarry, thrown backwards and forwards by the breaking surf and uttering piercing screams for her mother and father. His own hands full, he begged Thomas Entwhistle, a Bury neighbour, to try to reach her, but it was too late.

Badly lacerated by a nail sticking up through his tiny raft, William Broadhurst survived, to be found by a boat at about 8:30 a.m.

Twenty-three people were recorded as having been saved, including Broadhurst's friend Marsden – though from Broadhurst's account he was not on board – and an unnamed Irishman believed to be a cattle-driver. The *Bull's Head, Royal Oak, Bulkeley Arms, Liverpool Arms, White Lion* and the *George and Dragon* threw open their doors to receive them; local people were generous with offers of clothing, but the rescue mission swiftly turned into the recovery of bodies. Some were identified by their surviving friends, some by initials in their clothing or by personal effects. The descriptions which appeared in the papers are full of pathos:

> A lady found on the sand, dressed in white gown, Canton crape scarf, dark silk bonnet, gold chain around her neck fixed to a locket; a gold hoop I.L. upon it and gold earrings …
>
> A child about two years old, with red shoes on, found.

During the days that followed bodies were washed up all along the coast; some were never found. People travelled to Beaumaris to identify the bodies, which were taken to the Shire Hall there. George Whitehead, a Bury solicitor, arrived in the town expecting to bring home Robert Whittaker in a 'wooden suit', only to find him and his sister alive and well, his blindness lifted, but both mourning the loss of their boys and their friends. Many families did take their loved ones home for burial. A few bodies, however, lie in the parish church at Beaumaris along with those of the local people lost in the disaster. Relatives of James Brandreth a farmer from Chorlton cum Hardy, had looked vainly for his body, only to learn that it had been washed up at Southport, some 40 miles (75 kilometres) to the north-east, and been identified by the initials on his shirt and the name and address of his watch repairer. William Walmsley also came ashore at Southport, along with an unidentified man wearing wellington boots and a ring engraved with the words 'be trew of harte'.

Two days after the wreck, the inquest held at Llanfairfechan brought in a verdict of accidental death by being wrecked at sea. The jury added a damning rider: 'They therefore cannot disguise their indignation at the conduct of those who could place such a vessel in this situation and under the charge of a captain and mate who have been proved, by the evidence brought before them, to have been in a state of intoxication.'

The jury foreman was the MP for Beaumaris, Sir Richard Bulkeley Bt. He was one of those who had been involved in the rescue, and he was far from finished. On 25 August he chaired a meeting at Beaumaris attended by a number of concerned individuals, including the ship's owner, James Watson. The principal aim was to open a relief fund for the survivors who needed financial help to return home, and to reward those who assisted in the rescue or prepared the dead for burial. Then Bulkeley opened up the guns:

'Having now called your attention to the immediate object of this meeting,' he began, 'I must take the liberty of proposing a measure for the benefit and prosperity of this town and those who visit this part of the country. And in addressing this meeting I hope to be able to keep my temper within bounds and restrain as much as possible the indignation which I feel and which I have no doubt is felt by every man in this room at the conduct of Mr Watson since the catastrophe which has plunged so many families into grief and despair.'

Applause greeted his speech. James Watson himself stepped forward and tried to speak in vindication, but was called to order by Alderman Wright. Bulkeley continued: 'We are not here to discuss with Mr Watson whether the the *Rothsay Castle* was a seaworthy vessel … I shall briefly say, however that the *Rothsay Castle* was known and acknowledged by the inhabitants of this place and Liverpool to have been an unsound vessel.' He went on to propose that the people of Beaumaris, Caernarvon and Bangor should get a proper packet on the station under the command of a competent person, and that they should oppose Watson operating one. The proposition was well received, but Watson got up again.

'I hope, Sir Richard,' he said, 'you do not suppose I am dependent upon a packet to this town?' The statement provoked what were politely described as 'marks of disapprobation' from the audience.

'At least show,' responded Alderman Wright, 'you are not independent of common decency!' He went on to endorse Sir Richard's remarks and to raise a point made at the inquest regarding the lack of a signal gun. Watson claimed there was one, that a sporting gun had been found at the scene of the wreck. Wright stigmatized this as 'the most paltry and pitiful subterfuge ever heard'.

Someone else at the meeting said he understood that people had been employed to recover bodies from the wreck itself, and that in one case they had put a rope round a body and pulled off the arms and part of the head. The arms were quickly reburied in the sand. Under the disgusted gaze of those present, Watson made no reply.

Their anger had been inflamed by letters that Watson and the ship's agent had sent to the papers claiming that the ship was perfectly seaworthy, and by testimonials to that fact from those who had worked on her. Watson had likewise sought to deny claims that the captain was an unfit person to command a ship.

Further examples of Watson's attitude emerged. Lieutenant Morrison RN, who had spoken at the meeting to give technical details of the ship, had travelled to Liverpool on another of Watson's ships, the *William IV*, with two survivors and some relatives, together with the body of the younger Miss Broadhurst. He informed the press that Watson had asked £5 to convey the coffin, and that he had previously demanded 10 guineas to bring Mrs Hammond's body to Liverpool, then come down to 5, and finally, following protests, agreed to do it gratis.

The circumstances of the loss, and the fact that it occurred so close to home, kept it in the public eye in Britain, allowing the newspapers, particularly in the north-west, a feeding frenzy in which the articulate and observant survivors were quite evidently willing to play their part. On 3 September, the *Manchester Guardian* carried a short piece of news from Bury in which local survivors claimed that they had been approached by what they described as 'persons of questionable appearance' who tried to persuade them to say that the accident should be put down to unforeseen circumstances. Eighteen months later the story was back in the press with the libel action of Watson *v.* Colquitt, which was heard in London in February 1833. Captain Colquitt RN had been one of Ralph Williamson's guests on the *Campeadora*: he had participated in the rescue mission for which Williamson – like Walker who first raised the alarm – received a silver medal. Subsequently he wrote a damning indictment of the *Rothsay Castle*, which was published in Liverpool's *Albion* newspaper, and for this James Watson took him to court. Watson lost without Colquitt having to call even one of his 40 defence witnesses.

Just how many were lost on the *Rothsay Castle* is a matter of conjecture. Passengers buying tickets at the office numbered 105, but tickets were subsequently sold on the boat before sailing, and children did not require tickets. Including the crew, musicians and passengers, 132 names can be assembled from the various newspaper accounts, which gives a figure of 109 lost, but that is likely to be below the real total. That was not uncommon. Seventy-five years later a transatlantic liner would sink without anyone knowing how many were on board.

The individual disaster needs to be put into context because accidents involving steam vessels were not infrequent in this period. One reason was that the implications of the new technology were not yet widely understood by those building the wooden hulls that had to bear the stress and strain of the engine and its boilers, nor by those who purchased steamers, particularly second-hand vessels, nor even by many who claimed to be engineers. The wide publicity accorded to the *Rothsay Castle* led to the appointment of a select committee of the House of Commons to 'to take into consideration the frequent calamities by steam navigation and the best means of guarding their recurrence'. Unfortunately, the wheels of government – particularly where vested interests were concerned – turned as slowly as the paddles of the ill-fated packet. It would take more committees, inquiries and commissions to produce adequate safety legislation and standards to protect the public from unscrupulous operators who could tie down safety valves and attempt to repair holes in boilers with anything from wooden wedges to dung.

Two direct consequences of the disaster were the immediate establishment of a lifeboat station at Beaumaris and the construction of the 95-foot (29-metre) Trwyn-du lighthouse on the eastern extremity of Anglesey.

Joseph Fletcher, the passenger who travelled on the *Rothsay Castle* shortly before she was wrecked and who 'observed upon the craziness of the vessel and expressed reasonable fears in consequence', was sometime afterwards suspected of suffering from mental health problems, and was brought before a Commission of Lunacy, whose members had to decide if he should be committed to a lunatic asylum. When the commissioners were told of his comments about the state of the *Rothsay Castle*, however, and the justifiable anxiety he had felt when travelling on her, they concluded that he was obviously perfectly sane.[12]

Sources and Bibliography

National Archives
ADM1/5091
ADM3/224

Talbot, W. Henry Fox, letter to his mother 07 October 1831, document no. 02240, Fox Talbot Museum, Lacock Abbey LA(H)31-003

Adshead, Joseph: *A Circumstantial Narrative of the Loss of the* Rothsay Castle ... (London: Hamilton Adams, 1833).
Hocking, Charles, *Dictionary of Disasters at Sea during the Age of Steam* (London: Lloyd's Register of Shipping, 1967).
Lockhart, J G: *Peril Of The Sea: A Book of Shipwrecks and Escapes* (London: Philip Allan, 1924).

Bolton Evening News
'The Shipwreck that Numbed a Town', *Lancashire Evening Telegraph*, 2 May 2003.
Manchester Courier
Manchester Guardian
'A Holiday Trip Seventy Nine Years Ago', *Manx Quarterly* (September 1910).
'The Manchester and Liverpool Railroad', *Penny Magazine* (March 23–April 30, 1833).
The Times

www.beaumarislifeboat.com

Notes

[1] McCunn, Ruthanne Lum, *Sole Survivor*, Dolphin Book Club, USA, 1985.

[2] Although there is a considerable element of 'reconstruction' in the details of the journey to Liverpool, the Whittakers and Wilkinson did take this route, and did meet their fellow inhabitants at Liverpool. Thereafter all events and quoted dialogue are as given in the various survivors' reports. For obvious reasons, the accounts rarely agree on exact details and times, so in the interests of readability the author has sometimes made choices without detailing all the possibilities.

[3] According to the *Times*, citing an interview with Nuttall, the trip to Wales was all part of an excursion planned in Bury, but other sources suggest it was less organized.

[4] James Watson's brother.

[5] Hocking gives her dimensions as 92ft 5" length; 16ft 1" beam and 8ft 9" depth. This may be her original dimensions.

[6] The ship held the government mail contract and was described as a 'His Majesty's fast sailing War Office Steam packet'; as such she was subject to inspection.

[7] Usually taken to mean 'rickety' or 'leaky' in the maritime context of this period.

[8] The identification of 'Lieutenant Atkinson', the captain of the *Rothsay Castle*, with Lieutenant John Carr Atkinson is circumstantial. The latter was commissioned lieutenant in 1815 and in 1831 was living in Bedford St, Toxteth Park, Liverpool. On 2 September 1831 his widow, Eliza, wrote to the Navy asking to be considered for a widow's pension. Her address was given as c/o Jonathan Wagg, Shilton, Potteries (Staffordshire) and in 1827 John Carr Atkinson had been married in Burslem, another of the Potteries towns collectively known as Stoke-on-Trent. The only difficulty is that the bride's name may have been Jane.

[9] In any case, it would have been impossible.

[10] The account in the *Manchester Courier* states that he dived under the water and shouted to the others to do likewise, but they must have failed to heed the warning.

[11] Dialect, meaning 'frozen'.

[12] This anecdote is told by Adshead, see *Sources*.

7

Death Sentence

Amphitrite

1833

There's tempest in yon hornèd moon,
And lightning in yon cloud;
And hark the music, mariners!
The wind is piping loud –

ALLAN CUNNINGHAM, 'A WET SHEET AND A FLOWING SEA'

HOWEVER DEPRESSING THE REALITY CAN SOMETIMES BE, we want to believe in chivalry at sea, as if the oceans, like the past, are 'a foreign country: they do things differently there'[1]. Noble enemies showing respect and courtesy to one another, the brotherhood of the sea, and, until feminism decreed it to be patronizing, women and children first. That last became a concept particularly dear to Victorian hearts, though the fact was often different. As Dr Lucy Delap puts it:

The convention 'women and children first' in the nineteenth century would have been better stated 'ladies first', followed by white women and children. An account of the loss of the *Kent* in 1825 distinguishes between 'the lady passengers' and the soldiers' wives and children. The former were given precedence, and 'the remaining women and children had to be tied together and lowered by ropes from the stern,'1 during which process many drowned.[2]

Dramatis Personae

Sarah Austin : hotel guest

Mr Barry : hotelier

Ellen Bingham : prisoner; former prostitute

Henry Ducie Chads : retired naval officer

Madame Curtis : hotel guest

James Forrester : surgeon superintendent

Mrs Forrester : the surgeon's wife

Elspeth Fraser : prisoner

Elizabeth Fry : prison reformer

Sophia Gough : prisoner; former prostitute

Pierre Gourney : Boulogne resident

Pierre Antoine Hénin : Boulogne fisherman

John Hunter : captain of the *Amphitrite*

Jane Huptain : prisoner; former prostitute

François Huret : Boulogne pilot

Ann Lewis : prisoner

Lieutenant Colonel Maxwell : British resident of Boulogne

John Owen : boatswain

John Rice : seaman

Ann Rogers : prisoner; former cook

Hannah Tart : prisoner; former prostitute

Louis Tétarde : Boulogne pilot

James Towsey : seaman

John Wilks : journalist

There was just room for the jam: three pots of it, freshly made. Ann Rogers paused, listening for approaching footsteps, then picked up the silk kerchief and tied it round the bandbox. Being the cook gave her a great advantage: she had her own room in the house – hardly luxurious with its narrow bed, but it provided her with the privacy denied to most of the other servants. Through the draughty window the spring chill was sharp; she needed the shawl, and the dull grey-brown woollen would help to compensate for the moonlight. It was risky, but if she was to get her letter delivered to George in London she needed something with which to pay the van driver. By going through the yard gate she could avoid being seen, if anyone happened to be staring out of a window.

Some rooms were lit up; the family had not yet retired for the night.

The footsteps startled her for a moment; she moved closer into shadow as the dull light fell on the shape of Ann Craigie, another of the servants – and the sort of busybody best avoided. She had been with the family for years, not the mere two months that the cook herself could boast, and she looked down on the newcomer.

Rogers kept to the shadow of the wall, then past the stables, her heart beating fast, and soon she was by the carriage drive that led down to the gate, shielded by the shrubbery. She walked quickly now, her skirts catching the low branches; odd hints of fragrance travelled on the still air. The basket was getting heavy, even for arms used to kneading and rolling.

The main gates were shut, but the little side gate opened without even a groan, letting her out onto the turnpike.[3] The ground was dry, and she made haste, panting a little, listening all the while for the sound of wheels and the steady clip-clop of a horse's hooves.

That sounded like it, but better to be certain; she pressed herself against the prickly hedge, breathing in the leaves' fragrance until the covered cart came rumbling up and she recognized the man holding the reins.

'Here, take it,' she whispered. 'Take something for yourself and see the rest delivered.'

She held it up, and just as he was taking the weight from her they both caught the beat of urgent hoofbeats. They froze, Rogers with her hands still offering up the container. A white-shirted horseman was on them.

'Don't touch that!' he shouted, and the driver released his hold as if the parcel had burned him. The newcomer turned to Rogers. 'I've caught you well and truly,' he sneered and sprang to the ground. His horse pulled back on the reins, snorting. 'Craigie thought you were up to no good. Mistress told her to send me after you.'

'Please don't take me back, George!' She was clutching the basket; the carter had whipped up his own horse and was creaking off. 'Say you didn't find me!'

'And lose me own place?' George Eaton, the Podmores' coachman, had no intention of being turned off without references or, worse, arrested as an accomplice or accessory. His hand closed on her wrist. 'You can tell your story to the mistress.'

She was not a frail woman, but she was no match for him, and to do anything but submit meekly would only make matters worse. She went back with him in silence, passing through the doors and into the hall, where most of the servants had gathered. An embarrassed silence fell on them. She looked down at the tiled floor as she was escorted to her room. A few of her fellows had followed. She untied the handkerchief

'Show us what is in the basket,' Craigie demanded. Slowly Rogers put it on the bed and began to lift out the contents: the three pots of jam, the loaves and the cakes, a packet of sugar. She felt the eyes on the letter and hastily tucked it into the bodice of her dress.

'Give me that for the Mistress,' Eaton ordered.

'I won't! It's private.'

He snatched at it; her hands got there first and she pulled it out, cramming it into her mouth, but with one brawny arm round her he tore the paper from between her teeth.

On 10 May 1833 at the Sussex Quarter Sessions the 35-year-old cook was sentenced to be transported to Australia for 20 years. As well as the preserves and cakes she was found to have stolen several pieces of wallpaper from Robert Podmore's wardrobe, left over from the redecoration of the house.[4]

The milk-carrier was on his way home to Holborn when the woman stepped out beside him.

'You look a decent sort,' she said earnestly. 'Do a girl a favour and walk me home. It ain't far. Just down the end of the road, but there's this bloke been hanging around, and I don't feel safe.'

George Day thought of himself as a decent sort and in the limited light of a street lamp the girl looked pretty enough to need an escort. Deptford was part of London's maritime district, which added drunken sailors to the usual mix of law-abiding citizens, hardened criminals and opportunists.

'You're out late,' he remarked by way of conversation.

'Been visiting me mother. Don't the time run on when you're nattering?'

'That's true.'

'I would've stayed with her, but if me dad comes home and finds me …' She chatted on as they walked, flashing him a little smile every now and then.

They reached the end of the High Street, and she turned into Effingham Place where a tavern spilled out laughter and curses; a couple of shop fronts stood shuttered in respectable darkness. She pointed to a door.

'Why don't you come in ?' she said archly.

'I don't know …'

'Special rate for a gentleman like you. Save you walking home …'

He nodded.

'Alright then.'

A woman let them in and the girl led him into a dark room that smelt of stale food and sweat. He wondered if he was being a fool. She lit a candle that cast a glow on the cheap furniture and bedcovering.

'Let's see the money then,' she demanded. He shook his head.

'Afterwards.'

'Money first.' Her voice had hardened. 'You take me for a simpleton?'

'I'll take my pleasure first, then I'll pay you.'

He heard the door smash open; a fist burst against his face and he felt himself falling. They had him on the floor against the cupboard, face down; a shoe pressed hard onto his shoulders; a heavy hand rifled through his pocket. It closed on his watch. Somehow he found the breath to shriek 'Murder!' and he tried to push himself up, but she was raining blows on him.

The next thing he heard came from outside the room. A woman shouted: 'For God's sake! Police! come in or they will murder the man!'

The door blew a draught over him, he was being helped to his feet and somewhere in the room a woman was spitting curses. Dazed, all he could think about was the forty-shilling watch now gleaming on the table. He snatched it up with relief and wiped the sweat from his face. His hand came away covered in blood.

There were two officers, and they had a tight grip on the struggling woman and her sullen male accomplice. Day had been lucky, and he knew it.[5]

Newgate Prison: a dark and noisy shadow in the City, often the antechamber to the gallows. Foetid, crowded cells without proper sanitation, in which the hardened criminal was locked in with the destitute who stole to survive. In the women's cells, young girls were held with older women; mothers had their children with them. Here it was that Ann Rogers and Jane Huptain came together, waiting to be transported to Australia – Huptain for life, and lucky not to have gone to the gallows for the assault.

They were two of just over a hundred marked down for the *Amphitrite*, due to sail from Woolwich in August 1833, the eldest of them 59. There were 12 children, too, three of them belonging to one mother, while some of the prisoners were no more than children themselves: Rosetta Laker, 14, from Marylebone; Mary James, 14, from Bristol, who was convicted on her own account along with the mother who accompanied her; Margaret Knight, 13, guilty of stealing clothing hung to dry over a hedge in Glasgow. They came from across Britain, but the vast majority were from the cities of England and Scotland; most were convicted of larceny, with or without violence. Forty were from London, all convicted at the Old Bailey and sent directly to Newgate. Some were regular offenders, a couple had come from respectable middle-class families but had slipped into poverty and bad company. Two women expected to give birth at sea. There was even a girl from London who had deliberately got herself arrested so that she could be transported; for her, and for some others, it was not so much a punishment as a perceived escape route. They might still be relatively young when their sentences finished, and they could establish a respectable life in Australia.

The Scots were by far the roughest; Scottish justice was, in general, less quick to pass a sentence of transportation than English, so those condemned to be taken to Australia were likely to be further down the criminal road. Elspeth Fraser had been charged with 15 offences.

Public and government charity provided the women with a trunk of clothes and a box of sewing materials to set them up in their new life. Once they reached Australia they would be in demand as servants because it was far cheaper than paying wages for free labour, which was a scarce resource for those who chose to settle on the other side of the world. Convict servants, on the other hand, were only required to be fed and housed. The beginning of mass emigration, sparked off by discoveries of gold in California and Australia, and stoked by crippling poverty in the squalid city back-streets and on the farms of the mother countries, was still a few years off.

The prisoners and their children – some only babies – arrived at Woolwich in groups during the two weeks leading up to the day of sailing, and were embarked on the *Amphitrite*. Not so long ago they might have been marched down to the dock in irons or publicly paraded in open carts for the public to jeer or sneer at, but the Quaker prison reformer Elizabeth Fry had agitated for closed vehicles to take female convicts to their ships in some sort of dignity and privacy. She had also campaigned for matrons to be put in charge of them, but the government was not yet ready to listen.

The vessels in the convict 'trade' were known as *transports* and, like former slave ships, they were privately owned. Unlike the slavers, they were chartered to the government, and many of the owners made a profitable career out of government work, whether it involved soldiers or prisoners. John Hunter, the 33-year-old master of the three-masted barque[6] *Amphitrite*, was a major shareholder in his ship and he had done such work for several years, though this was his first convict run. At 209 gross tons his ship was smaller than the Admiralty had advertised for earlier in June. The original requirement was for a 300-ton vessel with a poop, and the usual procedure was to select two tenders, send the ships for survey and then take up the one that received the best report. After the event, it became known that no other ship had been sent for survey, which meant either that no other tender had been received or that there was some favouritism at work. The *Amphitrite* was also an old ship, only two years younger than her master, and only 93 feet long with a beam of 23 feet (28.3 by 7 metres). There was just enough headroom for the majority of the women to stand upright in their quarters, though they might have had to duck under the beams. The lower deck had been fitted out with bunks, and if the first to embark thought they had plenty of room, they were to be disillusioned. By the time the last woman had come on board, just before sailing, they were three to a bed – and more where children had to be accommodated. Such overcrowding was bad for hygiene and worse for morale. Cooping up so many women bred quarrels and fights, and could bring the best down to the level of the worst.

Every few days until they sailed, they received a visit from Elizabeth Fry and two of her Quaker ladies, who provided religious instruction through reading the Bible. They also taught sewing and reading to try to give some basic skills that would stand the women in good stead on a voyage that could last anything from 4 to 6 months, and give them opportunities in Australia. Patchwork, in particular, was highly prized, and Fry had for some years been obtaining off-cuts of cotton from the warehouses for the convicts to use. Each was also given a Bible to keep. Not all the *Amphitrite*'s women were grateful for Fry's practical compassion. At each visit she was rowed out to the *Amphitrite*, where John Owen, the ship's likeable boatswain, would sling a chair to hoist her up onto the deck, and he well remembered some of the Newgate girls saying they wished she would fall overboard and drown.

While they were embarking, the crew were getting the ship ready for her departure, loading the remainder of the stores that had to keep them and their involuntary passengers in food and water for the entire voyage. There were 14 crew besides Hunter, including young James Towsey, formerly a master's assistant in the Navy, who was working his passage to New South Wales in order to join his brother. He was not the only one seeking to settle in Australia. The one naval officer on board, Surgeon Superintendent James Forrester, was going out with his wife. A haughty woman who had no interest in trying to help any of the convicts, Mrs Forrester acted as if they were sub-human creatures whose existence was best ignored. The only exception was a quiet Nottingham woman of 23 named Poole, who arrived with a lot of her own clothes. Mrs Forrester selected her as her servant for the voyage.

On Sunday 25 August the *Amphitrite* weighed anchor and began her slow progress down the Thames and out into the English Channel. The weather was sultry and oppressive, crying out for a good thunderstorm to clear the air, but allowing the convicts and their children to sit on deck and pass the time sewing or reading in the good light. Most of them gave little trouble. The younger women were largely docile and well-behaved, particularly the three Worcestershire prostitutes Ellen Bingham, Sophia Gough and the aptly named Hannah Tart. After their first night on board two of them complained to Surgeon Forrester that they could not go on sharing their allotted bed with one of the Newgate women because her language and behaviour was intolerable. A change was made so the three Worcester girls could sleep together. Boatswain Owen liked them: they spent their time quietly reading or singing hymns, kept well away from all the others, and one of them was extremely beautiful.

The most wretched case was of a young Welsh girl, Ann Lewis, who spent her time sobbing at the gangway. Sensing a victim, the older women had robbed her as soon as she came on board, and because she spoke no English nobody could comfort her or understand her story. For two weeks all that passed her lips was water, and after that she would only touch an occasional apple or pear.

In total contrast, many of the older women, especially a 17-strong group of the Scots, regularly got into fights and swore like troopers, not caring that there were children all around them. They took advantage of their complete freedom of the deck to make the crudest sexual advances to the crew, who were actually shocked by their behaviour. On several occasions the disgusted Owen, a big man in the prime of life, threw buckets of water over them to drive them off.

Forrester, who had responsibility for the convicts' activities and discipline as well as their health, and who should have kept them away from the forepart of the ship, took no interest in them until they became violent. Then the offender would be brought on deck and put into a tall upright punishment box with just a few ventilation holes. For several hours the inmate was left to calm down, unable to sit and barely able to stand upright – an unpleasant punishment in the heat. Apart from quelling disorder, he left them to their own devices. Their only chore was to bring up their bedding to air every morning, and that was at the captain's order.

On the night of Thursday 29 August, when they were past the Goodwin Sands and through the Straits of Dover, off Dungeness, a storm rose out of nowhere. Thick dark clouds stifled the sunset, and the wind got up strongly from the south-west to lash the Channel and the North Sea coasts as far as Lincolnshire with rain, sleet and even snow. Overnight the wind shifted, blowing at hurricane force from north-west-by-north. During Friday the tempest spread inland and the temperature fell dramatically. It devastated the hop fields of Kent; uprooted laden fruit trees or stripped them of tons of apples, pears, damsons and plums. Violent gusts ripped down chimneys; a section of the cliff at Westbrook crashed into the sea; flying tiles made the streets of Kentish towns and villages lethal. Ships in the harbour dragged their anchors; four barges at Herne were smashed to pieces. It was the worst tempest for 17 years, and out to sea there was carnage as ships foundered in mountainous seas and shrieking winds. Those that could, ran for the shelter of the nearest port or attempted to ride out the tempest while hove-to. The auxiliary steamer *Camilla*, with 70 passengers on board, fought vainly to enter Southampton before being forced to give up and head further along the coast; three ships went down off Skegness; the lifeboat men were exhausted as they snatched crews from death, yet as the Friday night wore on, the intensity of the storm only grew. The brig *Thetis*, bound for London, foundered off the North Foreland, but her crew was saved and brought into Deal. It was the same along the Channel coast of France, where the harbours of Calais, Treport, le Havre and Boulogne were under assault from the elements.

Captain Hunter was one of those who decided to try to ride out the hurricane[7] by heaving-to off Dungeness on the Friday morning. At the onset of the rain the women had been sent below and the hatches battened down. Now they clung screaming to their children, to their friends or simply to the frame of their bunks as the ship was buffeted by great waves that swept her deck, raining through the caulking and the hatches. Every time a member of the crew went down, they besieged him with pleas for reassurance, and the men lied to them and said there was no danger – to do otherwise would have induced mass panic. The weather was not easing. All day they tried to hold their position, but the wind was against them.

Dawn on Saturday 31 August brought no relief; the sea remained wild, but they were at least surviving. By noon they had been driven within sight of the French coast, 3 miles (5.5 kilometres) off Boulogne, and Hunter set the topsail and mainsail to keep the *Amphitrite* away from the shore. It was in vain: however much Hunter fought to get an offing, still she was pushed inexorably towards the land. Three hours later she was in sight of the port, and hundreds of people ran down to the beach to stare at her through the torrential rain. Her flag had been ripped away, but no one was in any doubt that the helpless three-master was a British ship, and for many of the town's residents that only increased their anxiety.

Like other French towns along that coast Boulogne had a sizeable British expatriate population, who enjoyed the inexpensive social life in a pleasant climate that was nevertheless sufficiently close to home to make them forget they were in self-imposed exile from family and friends. At the end of the Napoleonic wars, when ships were laid up and regiments reduced or disbanded, hundreds of British naval officers found themselves on half-pay as reservists. Many of them were younger sons for whom there would be little inheritance, and without their pay and opportunities for the perquisites of war – such as prize money for capturing enemy ships – they were unable to maintain themselves and their families in Society. Retired colonels could sit in their hotel dining rooms reliving their military glory days and asserting their superiority over the French, or join the popular pigeon club and go shooting. Impoverished wives and daughters might give French lessons or remake their dresses into the latest fashion to eke out the housekeeping. Then there were the flashy gamesters who had fled debts of honour, bankrupts evading their creditors and men and women of principle who had fallen on hard times, such as Richard Martin, who as an MP introduced the first animal-rights legislation. A few days earlier this little community had been strolling the ramparts, maintaining their gentility to one another, sea-bathing, or watching their children playing on the broad beaches and enjoying donkey rides. Now the sky was black, the sea whipped to frenzy, and only the hardy were out on the ramparts.

Hunter had no personal knowledge of the approach to Boulogne harbour, even if he had wanted to seek shelter, and no pilot on board to help him or tell him that he was dangerously close to the sandbanks on the edge of the channel. To the watchers on the beach with their telescopes her position seemed all but hopeless with the tide ebbing. If she came any closer she was lost. 'The sea is still raging; it promises to be a dreadful night,' observed one spectator. 'Our fishing boats have returned to port, all but one, number 70, which is thought to have gone down. There's a rumour going round that the London packet which left here last night has also foundered ...'

In contrast to the anxiety on the beach, relative calm born of ignorance prevailed on the *Amphitrite*. Hunter had accepted that the ship was going to ground, and that they needed to make the best of it. On the plus side, her hull was sound and she was weathering the battering very well.

'Just look out for the best berth, and run her up as high as possible,' he is said to have ordered the mate. The orders were roared above the wind to put up the helm. All sails on the main and mizzenmasts apart from the main topsail were taken in, and the yards squared. The *Amphitrite* came round as if at last allowed to have her own way, and swept up. The raging water beneath her bottom shallowed rapidly, and she shuddered to a heavy, groaning halt.

Did anyone tell the women to prepare for the shock of the grounding? Probably not. The crew were getting out the bower anchor, shackle and cable to lighten the ship at the front and to allow her to come afloat on the next tide, swinging round with her head to sea. The maintopsail was set ready for that time. No distress flares were fired, and the ship probably did not run as far up the sands as she might.

For those spectators on the beach and at the seaward-facing hotel windows along the Esplanade, it was an awful scene. They had witnessed it all before, and their only surprise was that there appeared to be no attempt on the part of the crew to take advantage of low tide to abandon ship and save their lives. Not even a ship of the line or an East Indiaman, however strong, would be able to survive that high tide when it came in. However, nobody had made any attempt to warn the crew before she ran aground. Now, from the distant shore, a man was making signals with his hat, clearly indicating they should abandon ship. Young John Rice, one of the seamen, drew Captain Hunter's attention to it, but Hunter just turned his back. If he or any of his crew had been familiar with the tidal conditions at Boulogne during a storm they would surely have abandoned ship or at least showed somewhat more concern, but they had no inkling of what awaited them.[8]

As the vessel had struck, a local pilot, François Huret, raced to get out his boat. Anxious to lose no time he tried to get hold of some horses to pull it down to the beach and over to the best launching place. The owner of the animals refused.

'What am I to do if my horses are lost?' he demanded. 'Who will take responsibility?' Had the British consul been on the scene he could have offered a guarantee on behalf of the government, but he was out of town and did not return until a letter was sent to tell him what was happening.

Without wasting another moment, Huret, his fellow pilot, Tétarde, and their

Huret and his crew launch their boat to go to the rescue of those on the *Amphitrite*.

crew of volunteers[9] picked up the heavy boat and ran with it. They launched it
into the claws of the breakers, hurling themselves aboard and taking up the
oars, pulling with all their strength across the two-thirds of a mile – 1200
metres or so – of roaring fury that separated the vessel from the shore. The bow
rose, then fell into the trough; the man at the tiller held on for grim death.
Drenched and shivering those on shore watched her tossed on the crests and
pitching down, and they clutched their coats, holding their breath as the small
craft struggled until she lay under the bows of the *Amphitrite*. It was 5 p.m.

Hunter had seen them coming, but when Huret shouted up that he was
ready to take them off, the captain refused his assistance, seconded – perhaps
commanded – by the naval surgeon. Most of the crew were below deck getting
their belongings together as a precaution, but those who did know what was
going on begged for the chance to leave. It was refused. There was nothing for
it but for Huret and his comrades to leave the stricken vessel and return to the
shore. He had no idea that beneath the hatches huddled 120 terrified women
and children, three at least of whom told Boatswain Owen that Forrester had
ordered the captain under no circumstances to accept the French assistance.

The return of the pilot boat from its fruitless errand at about 6 p.m. was
witnessed by Pierre Antoine Hénin, the 29-year-old owner of a fishing vessel.
With his curly black hair just beginning to recede at the temples, ruddy cheeks,
square chin, and above all his massive shoulders and biceps, he presented an
impressive figure. His father and two of his uncles had commanded privateers
in the Napoleonic wars, and he had inherited all their audacity, toughness and
enterprise. The immobility of the crew was as puzzling to him as to all the
observers. Were they exhausted? Paralysed by terror? Was the captain naive

enough to think he could save his ship? Others wondered if the captain was drunk and incapable of appreciating his position. Hénin knew there was no possibility of her coming afloat: when the tide roared in the rampaging waves would tear her apart. But the crew could still be saved if they could get a line from the vessel to the shore. His friends, relations and brothers-in-law had all crewed Huret's boat. Now he told the port captain that he was willing to go out to the ship, then ran down to the beach.

Under the blast of the rain, Pierre Hénin stripped off all his clothes, tied a rope around his waist and plunged into the cauldron. To the wonder of those around him who dared not follow his example, he struck out for the *Amphitrite*.

Apart from those on duty, the ship's crew had gone below for the night. Some were at supper, glad to be out of the cascading spray and to wash the salt taste from their mouths with weak beer or a tot of rum. Too tired to eat, others had got out of the worst of their sodden clothes and climbed into their hammocks to warm their limbs and try to get some sleep. The carpenter had reported the hold tight. The situation was not pleasant, but they had no expectation of disaster.

Steadily Hénin battled his way through the waves, each powerful stroke bringing him a little closer to his goal. Twelve hundred metres – perhaps 15 minutes in calm water for a fit and experienced swimmer.[10] Hénin was both, but the sea was violent. His head was visible only occasionally to those with telescopes, but slowly the man on the beach holding the long coil of rope paid out the line. It took almost an hour, and then Hénin was pulling for the starboard side of the *Amphitrite* and hailing the crew in English:

'Give me a line to lead you on land or you're finished. The tide is coming in!' One of the sailors heard him and looked over the side. By then, Hénin had a hand on the hull. 'Go and tell the Captain!'

A few moments later two ropes were swinging in the wind. Hénin managed to catch the one from the bow and, wrapping it round his wrist took a firm hold before setting out for the shore. It was past 7:00 p.m. Time would soon run out. The effort was telling on his powerful frame, but each stroke brought him a metre closer to the shore.

A sudden jerk. The cord was snatched out of his hand. Too short, perhaps, and nobody had thought to bring up another to join to it before it ran out? Fighting his weariness, he turned back towards the *Amphitrite*, shouting for more rope. Hunter and Forrester refused. A tired and disappointed Hénin begged them to haul him on board. Perhaps he hoped that while he recovered his strength they would change their minds, or he could convince them of their peril. Suddenly, exhaustion overwhelmed him. He could do no more. Holding onto his own line he began the laborious swim home, and was finally pulled to safety by his comrades on the shore. Still nobody knew that the *Amphitrite* carried a human cargo.

Hénin catches the rope thrown from the deck

The rope from the *Amphitrite* had probably not failed because it was too short: more likely, it had been jerked back by Hunter or Forrester because it had been thrown without their express authority. It has to be inconceivable that they would have abandoned ship, leaving the convicts behind – inconceivable because it is impossible to think that their crew would have stood for it. Men like Owen, who felt sorry for many of the women, would surely not have consented to murder. But whether or not they were authorized to release the convicts was a difficult decision for the two officers. Their orders were to land them in Australia, not France. If the convicts were let off the ship at Boulogne most if not all would abscond, leaving Forrester and Hunter to account for their decision. The one was used to the navy's strict adherence to the rules; the other must have been wondering whether he would get another Admiralty contract if he made the wrong choice now. Matters were about to come to a head.

Even as Hénin was on his lonely way back to report failure, the pent-up terror below the hatches was too much for the women. For their own sakes, the crew had kept them in ignorance of the situation. Suddenly the ship was being buffeted hard and they could hear water beginning to pour into the hold beneath. With a strength born of fear they forced their way through the hatch and onto the rain-strafed deck, screaming, sobbing, pleading for their lives, demanding that the ship's boats be launched. They could see the reassuring lights of the town calling to them, promising safety. They were desperate.

If nothing else, the efforts of Hénin and Heuret had given Forrester something to think about. He now realized that the ship was doomed, and without reference to Hunter sent for Owen to order him to rig the tackles for swinging out the ship's longboat. It was a sound craft, with room for 60 people. Given that the children were small, it could probably have taken everyone to shore in two trips. The ship also carried a whale boat,[11] but that was less likely to survive the conditions.

All but one of the women went back down to collect their belongings in the expectation of being taken off. Owen saw one girl alone on the deck and asked her why she was not getting her bundle.

'If I can save my life, I don't mind the rest,' she answered; he went down and found her bonnet for her.

Forrester may have given that order to hoist out the boat, but he had reckoned without his wife. She protested vehemently that the convicts would rush the longboat and swamp it, and that her husband's first duty was to ensure her safety. She was aghast at the idea of having to share a boat with such women. An angry domestic row broke out in the presence of Owen and a number of the crew. The surgeon's response was sheer spite: nobody, then, was going on shore that night. The longboat remained where it was.

As the tide raced in, the sea mounted. There was 6 feet – nearly 2 metres – of water in the ship's hold, and the waves began to break over the deck. Darkness was falling early, and the wind whipped howling though the shrouds, smothering screams. The crew took to the spars and rigging; the rest were on the deck, swept by the rising force of the heavy seas. At around 8:30 p.m. the *Amphitrite* uttered a great rending cry and broke in two. A wave gathered up those on the deck and hurled them into the maelstrom.

Young John Rice found himself seizing a ladder that had been washed into the sea. On what remained of the ship, Owen, Hunter, Towsey, three more seamen and one woman clung to the spars of a mast as the seas disembowelled the shattered hull below them. For maybe three quarters of an hour they held fast to their refuge, cold, helpless and afraid, until Owen recognized that the last moment was approaching. Telling his fellows that there was nothing for it but to try to swim to land, he dived in and began to pull towards the lights that flickered like fireflies on the shore.

The whole town was on the alert; people covered the beach: the curious, the ghoulish and those who were there to save life if they could. The Customs men were out, too. Hénin had thought to make another attempt to reach the ship but had been forced to recognize the physical impossibility of a second swim. Other fishermen were there, ready to brave the breakers if anyone came close to land. There were Britons among them, including at last the British consul, who claimed to have arrived at 7:00 p.m.[12] By chance, so was John Wilks, Paris correspondent of the London evening paper the *Standard*, who gained at first hand the scoop of a lifetime. His friend, Barry, proprietor of the Marine Hotel, opened his doors in readiness for what might follow. The French Marine Humane Society had called out hundreds of men with beacons, and set water to boil in its two-room headquarters.

The sea gave them scant warning, throwing a mast at the feet of those closest to the water. Casks rolled ashore, and splintered planks. Then the first bodies: one man, four women. The full extent of the tragedy was about to dawn.

John Owen was still swimming, now by instinct alone. He was exhausted and his lungs hurt, but something, perhaps the knowledge that the Frenchman had shown it was possible, just told him to keep going. All at once something was pulling him; a voice that was not English pierced the wind and the roar of the sea, and he felt himself being dragged out of the water. Then he passed out.

Towsey was aware that there was another man clinging to his plank.

'Who are you?' he asked. An odd question for such an occasion.

'I am the captain,' replied Hunter, before his grip failed and he was gone. Towsey held on, tossed from one wave to another as if the sea played a game with his life. He remembered little but reaching the shore, being picked up and hearing an excited voice exclaiming that he was alive. It was, though he could not know it, Pierre Gourney, one of Hénin's relations. The French gave way to English as John Wilks spoke to him, and he was immeasurably reassured at hearing his own language before he was carried off to the hospital.

Somewhere out there, the tide was bearing a ladder towards the shore with a barely conscious sailor sprawled over it. John Rice was plucked from the sea and carried up to the Marine Hotel, along with Owen. What clothes they had not removed to help them swim had been torn off by the sea, but Sarah Austin,[13] a young Englishwoman staying at the hotel, had no time for embarrassment, let alone hysterics, at the sight of a naked man. Together with Barry she laboured over them, and it was Rice who managed to gasp out the name of the ship and her errand. It made chilling hearing: 16 men, 108 *women* and 12 *children*.

Working alongside Sarah Austin, another young Englishwoman, but of French descent, Madame Curtis, tried frantically to rub some life into a girl who had been carried in naked. For a moment there was hope: a little colour rose in a face that was strikingly beautiful; the girl opened her eyes. That was all. Her body was removed, and another brought in.

Down at the Humane Society it was the same story. Each new arrival was brought in, wrapped in blankets, and the surgeons bled them. One woman made a faint movement, but the hope was short lived. By 11:00 p.m. there were thirty bodies piled up in the outhouse. There would be no more happy endings. Those three men remained the only survivors of the wreck.

Still the dead were coming ashore. One woman was washed up still clutching her baby. People had spread out along the banks. Those who took part in the gruesome work were shattered by what they had seen. The sea had been strangely kind to many of the convicts, sending their bodies to land all but unmarked, as if offering a symbolic absolution of their offences. Whatever crimes they had committed – and most were minor – were forgotten. It was their youth, their beauty and their untimely and unnecessary deaths that the eyewitnesses were to remember. Many corpses would never be found.

O n the Sunday, with the storm over, Wilks dispatched his first report. It would be syndicated across the country.

The following day, the 70 victims who had been recovered were buried. Each was given a deal coffin and placed in one of two long trenches. Wilks attended the funeral, and at 4:00 p.m. filed his second press report. It, too, would be widely printed.

T he recriminations began at once, on both sides of the Channel. Wilks's reports were crisply factual in terms of times and events, but he was no mere observer: he had participated in the rescue effort and his report was highly personal and shot through with anger, disbelief and accusation expressed in emotive rhetoric. Its opening set the tone:

> The shocking event which is announced by the title to this letter ['Dreadful Shipwreck off Boulogne'] has, I assure you, filled the town with dismay, and must lead to a most narrow and rigid investigation. I cannot attempt to describe the affliction, not only of the English but the French, at this most distressing event, and I only express the general opinion when I say that the British public demands that an enquiry be instituted into the conduct of all parties concerned in this deplorable affair.

He had interviewed the three survivors. Rice and Owen were staying at the Marine Hotel; Towsey, who had lost all his possessions, had been taken in by Lieutenant Colonel Maxwell after his discharge from the hospital. There were discrepancies between their accounts, which, in Wilks' mind, boiled down to Towsey seeking to defend his friend the surgeon – with whom he had served on HMS *Alligator* – at the expense of the captain. But they agreed on one fundamental point: that if the British consul had given his authority via Heuret or Hénin to land the convicts, it would have been done. They all, however, had missed the point: nobody in Boulogne had known about the presence of the convicts and their children. The much-vilified consul could hardly have sent an authorization unless he had been told of the situation at the outset, even if he had been on the beach at 4:00 p.m. when the ship first struck.

The other charge levelled against the diplomat was that he should have been out getting rescuers organized – though the French rescuers seem to have done as much as they could in any case – and offering money to fishermen who would put to sea. He might also, for example, have promised the owner of the horses that his government would pay compensation for any injury to or loss of the animals that Heuret wanted to borrow. The consul had unfortunately been at a dinner party.

Wilks took the opportunity to make a scathing attack on a transportation policy that herded women guilty of minor crimes together with hardened criminals. Referring to the testimony of the three survivors, he wrote passionately of

> the deplorable nature of the transport or convict system. Young girls, young women for small offences, females who might have been easily reclaimed and led back to the paths of virtue, were all stowed together with 20 hardened and abandoned criminals from Scotland, whose swearing, whose disgusting language, and violent conduct rendered the ship the scene of constant outrage and disorder. Never was so scandalous a want of attention manifested to the classification of prisoners as that exhibited in the case of the female convicts on board the *Amphitrite*.[14]

The French Customs also found themselves in Wilks's sights, described as 'harpies' for allegedly interfering with the rescue work, even stopping a woman from pulling a man out of the water. His allegation was backed up by a French journalist on the scene. (The most charitable interpretation of the Customs officers' actions is that they might have been trying to prevent pillaging of the bodies, though no explanation was publicly offered.)

Lachlan, the London agent for the ship, had to defend himself against charges from elsewhere that the *Amphitrite* was old and unseaworthy, and that her captain was young and inexperienced. He pointed out that Hunter was 'fully thirty three' and had commanded a ship for at least eight years. He rejected an allegation by the beleaguered consul that the captain and the surgeon had used pistols to refuse French aid, and asserted that the ship had recently undergone a full survey at Deptford, and any repairs had been done to the highest standard.

Sensing an imminent scandal – and one that could also have an impact on Anglo–French relations – the Government swiftly dispatched Captain Henry Ducie Chads RN[15] to Boulogne to conduct a commission of enquiry. Chads obliged with a bland report that praised the conduct of the voyage right up until the point at which the French help was refused: 'For this most deplorable error in judgement they have paid the extreme penalty.' By definition, that laid blame on the captain; at the same time, loyalty to his own service did not prevent him from drawing attention (three times) to the pusillanimity of the naval surgeon in the face of his wife's opposition. Chads quoted verbatim from his examination of Owen.

'... Did the surgeon appear to have any fear of the escape of the convicts?'

'No; he would have allowed them to go on shore, but for the interference of his wife.'

The tricky business of the French Customs was deliberately left out of the report, and Lord Palmerston, the then foreign secretary, wriggled out of questions in the House by saying that high-level discussions would be held on the matter with the French. Two MPs, William Clayton and Benjamin Hawes, had actually presented him with a petition drawn up by the English residents of Boulogne and dealing with a number of questions raised by the disaster.

Owen stayed a full month at the Marine Hotel, where he won the respect of the proprietor and his guests by his behaviour and opinions, as if an illiterate working man capable of fine feelings was a novelty. He talked to Barry a lot about the voyage, and before he left for England – vowing, like Rice, never again to serve in a female convict ship – he let his host[16] record his answers to specific questions. Barry took down his replies more or less verbatim, and sent the resulting document to the *Times*. In a prefacing letter he urged readers to believe that Owen's fine character made his answers fully credible. The detail that appeared through this account fleshed out all that Wilks had written and dovetailed neatly with Elizabeth Fry's earlier demands that a matron should have charge of women on a transport.

Although the transportation of convicts from Britain to Australia had been going on since 1788, the *Amphitrite* was the very first convict ship to be wrecked, and she became a stick that could be used to beat the government whenever a government-chartered ship was lost, or disaster was predicted. In 1837, following an outcry over the selection of the old and much-repaired *John Barry* to carry free settlers, John Russell, the then home secretary, admitted in the House of Commons that only ships holding the highest Lloyd's Register classification, A1, should be used for emigrants, as they were – by then – for convicts.

Comfort was drawn from the courage of Huret, his crew and Hénin, whose conduct won universal and unstinting praise. Individual heroism has always been irresistible. Hénin, in particular, became a celebrity. His portrait was painted, showing him holding the Cross of the Légion d'honneur, which his own government awarded him. With his shirt open and his sleeves rolled up to show his muscles, he looks competent to take on the English Channel in any weather. His next exploit, which also made it into the British press a year almost to the day after his swim to the *Amphitrite*, was the less dramatic rescue of two Frenchmen who found themselves out of their depth after descending from a bathing machine.[17] One of them presented him with 100 francs, which more or less coincided with a somewhat belated award of 300 francs by King William IV. He died comparatively young, in 1841.

The tragedy has been kept alive in a ballad with the title 'The Anford Wright'

Come all ye jolly sailors brave that wear the jackets blue,
While I relate the dangers great and hardships of the sea;
It's of a ship called the Anford-Wright, with a hundred and eight females,
With cargo and crew and passengers too, bound out for New South Wales.

It was on the eighteenth day of June, from the city we set sail,
Leaving our friends behind us, it grieved our hearts full sore.
And as we bore along the shore, till our friends got out of sight,
Saying, 'Adieu unto you blue-eyed girls on board of the Anford-Wright.'

About twelve o'clock on the third day, we were all put to a stand,
When our goodly ship she ran aground, all on a bank of sand;
And the children around their parents flocked and tore their hair with fright,
For to think they must end their days on board of the Anford-Wright.

When our captain found he was aground, both anchors he let go,
Saying, 'Go reef your fore and main-top sails, or soon our fate we'll know!'
When our ship she gave one dreadful reel, and soon went out of sight
And the shriek and cries would reach the skies, on board of the Anford
Wright.

All that reached the shore out of our crew were two poor lads and me;
We reached the shore all on a spar, we swam the briny sea.
One was exhausted by the waves, he died that very night;
That left only two out of our crew on board of the Anford-Wright.

Now the Anford-Wright is lost and gone, both passengers and crew,
Besides thirty-five as brave sailor lads, as ever wore jackets blue.
God grant relief to those poor souls, and to those lamenting quite;
God grant relief to those poor souls on board of the Anford-Wright.[18]

It is hard to consider the plight of the convicts without thinking of those who were abandoned on the *Méduse*'s raft. Two years after the disaster, William Mallord Turner paid homage to Géricault's monumental work in his own painting, *A Disaster At Sea*,[19] which commemorates the loss of the *Amphitrite* and the terrible storm in which she was wrecked.

Sources and Bibliography

National Archives, H011/9/73985 (list of convicts).

East Sussex Record Office, QR/E 916/16 (the case of Ann Rogers taken from the evidence of Eaton, Craigie, Suggers and Mrs Podmore).

Kent Record Office, Q/SBW 134 (the case of Jane Huptain and James Perry, taken from the evidence of George Day and the two arresting officers).

Musée du Chateau, Boulogne.

Chatelle, Albert, *La Ville impériale: Boulogne et son port* (Paris: Guillemot & De Lamothe, 1961).

Finlay, E M, 'Convict Women of the *Amphitrite*', *Tasmanian Historical Research Association Papers and Proceedings* 38/3–4 (December 1991), 119–30.

Pitman, E R, *Elizabeth Fry* (Boston: Roberts Brothers, 1884).

Zurcher, Frédéric, and Margollé, Elie, *Les Naufrages célèbres* (Paris: Hachette, 1872).

Maidstone Gazette
The Times

Notes

[1] Edward Hoare, *Perils of the Deep* (London: SPCK, 1885).

[2] Lucy Delap, '"Thus Does Man Prove His Fitness to Be the Master of Things": Shipwrecks, Chivalry and Masculinities in Nineteenth and Twentieth-century Britain', *Cultural and Social History* 3/1 (January 2006), 45–74.

[3] A turnpike was an early version of the toll-road where users paid a fee for each stretch they travelled, the money being used for the upkeep of the road.

[4] The inference from the quarter session records is that the Podmores, a middle-aged couple with children, had come to live at Clayton not so long before. Who the 'George Meadow, of Fenchurch Street' was to whom the letter was addressed is unknown – perhaps an admirer she had met in her previous employment.

[5] Although some licence has been taken with the events around the arrests, the two women whose stories are dramatized here were convicted of those precise crimes, and the events follow the facts very closely.

[6] A three masted barque carried square sails on the foremast and mainmast but fore-and-aft sails on the mizzenmast.

[7] Possibly under 'bare poles' – that is, with no sails set. Later he set main and topsail, probably on the foremast, which suggests he had nothing set before.

[8] On 3 January 1841, for example, the local people gathered on the pier during a hurricane-force storm to watch a West Indiaman go to pieces at high tide. The crew had offloaded their cargo and walked safely to shore during the preceding low tide.

[9] Among the others were J Coquelin, Dangler, Docarme, Flahutez and Verdière.

[10] At the time of writing, the men's world record for the 1500 metres in a 50-metre pool stands at 14 minutes, 34.56 seconds.

[11] A small open boat, pointed at both ends and steered by an oar rather than a rudder.

[12] Nobody saw him until much later.

[13] Sarah Austin was the wife of John Austin who until the previous year had been Professor of Jurisprudence at the University of London and who was very much a reformer.

[14] E M Finlay (see sources) points out that some of the better-behaved young women were also Scottish.

[15] Chads, then 45 years of age, had a distinguished naval career. As the badly wounded first lieutenant of the frigate *Java* in 1812, he had the unenviable task of maintaining a gallant but hopeless fight against the famous USS *Constitution* after his captain had been killed. Famous for his reform of naval gunnery, he rose to rear admiral in 1854 and was knighted on his retirement in 1855.

[16] The inference has to be that Barry was the sender of the letter that appeared without a name in *The Times* on 16 October 1833, though Sarah Austin is also a possibility.

[17] *The Times*, 7 July 1836. During the summer season, Hénin acted as something of a lifeguard at the bathing station.

[18] From John H Cox (ed.), *Folk-Songs of the South* (Cambridge, MA: Harvard University Press, 1925), contributed by Miss Fannie Egan, 1917. Although the number of convicts has been preserved correctly in the song (108), the date of departure and the number of crew has been changed, presumably in the interests of scansion (or because the original lyricist was unaware of the actual details).

[19] Tate Gallery, London. The painting is unfinished, and, in its impressionistic treatment of the storm, is a complete contrast to the detail and Romanticism of the Géricault.

8

Maiden Voyage

San Francisco

1853-54

One could see human nature to perfection on that wreck.

LUCIA EATON, passenger

BUILDING UNSINKABLE SHIPS has long been an unspoken goal of shipbuilders, unachievable if only because of the compromises that have to be made in order for the ship to be financially viable and to perform its function. Nineteenth-century naval architects sought to overcome the problems of the day, one of which was exemplified in the loss of the *Rothsay Castle*: ocean-going steamers needed a hull strong enough to withstand the worst weather, and to cope with the stresses created by increasingly powerful engines. The engine could no longer to be an add-on, but must occupy an integral part of the design.

Built in one of the world's top yards for a prestigious shipping line, one particular ship boasted a hull that was almost unsinkable, powerful engines and luxuriously appointed staterooms and saloons. She embarked on her maiden voyage with one of her owners on board and the band playing merrily, but, fatally wounded in the bitter North Atlantic, ended by making desperate appeals for help. She predated *Titanic* by more than half a century.

Fort Sutter, California, January 1848

'Sir, I've something important to tell you.' James Marshall was soaked and shivering, but the latter had more to do with anxiety than the torrential January rain. He clawed his fair hair away from his face and rubbed his hands together for warmth.

'What is it?' John Sutter was surprised to see the man back at Fort Sutter so soon, when only a few days earlier he had left for Coloma with supplies for the sawmill he was building for his employer.

'Not here! I need to talk in private. Can we go where we won't be overheard, sir? We mustn't be disturbed.'

Curious, Sutter nodded and led him into his private rooms. He struck a light and the oil lamp flared into life, casting shadows.

'Will you lock the door, sir …'

'If you wish.' His voice still had its heavy Swiss-German accent, though he had been in California since 1839. 'But there's only the clerk here, and he's in his office.' In deference to his visitor's agitation, his hand moved to the door handle, and as it did so a servant came in with a tray. She set it down and went. Marshall was digging in his pocket. Out came a dirty rag; with numb fingers he fumbled to open it. The lamplight scintillated among the folds.

New Utrecht, Brooklyn, December 1853

The curtains were drawn, the lamps bright and the fire crackled quietly, just spitting out the occasional glowing spark . The only other sounds in the darkly furnished room were the occasional susurration of a turning page, or a soft exclamation of irritation from the young woman at the embroidery frame whenever the thread ran out at an inconvenient moment. After a while, she looked up and rubbed her eyes.

'I won't finish this before we leave.'

'It doesn't matter: it won't be all dancing with the officers, Lucia!'

'And what, Julia, makes you think I wish to spend my time dancing?'

Lucia's sister put down her book, but was prevented from replying when one of the servants came in with a letter.

'It's from Lucien.' Lucia opened it; folded in with the short note was a piece of newspaper. 'He writes he found this, by chance – it's dated July 5th – and thinks I will be interested.' She glanced at it. 'It's about the ship.'

'Let me read it.' Julia reached for the cutting and cleared her throat importantly.

This beautiful addition to the steam fleet of the Pacific Mail Steamship Company, lately launched from the yard of Mr. Wm. H. Webb, foot of Sixth Street, has been built in the most substantial manner and with special attention to the trade she is intended for. Her model is very sharp, having concave lines at each end, and it is fully expected she will excel in speed the celebrated **Golden Gate**, *(another of Mr. Webb's construction) which has run from San Francisco to Panama, stopping at Monterey, San Diego and Acapulco, in eleven days and*

Dramatis Personae

George Aspinwall : passenger

Elijah Brown : sergeant

Martin Burke : colonel

John G Chandler : army lieutenant

James Cooper : passenger

Robert Creighton : captain of the *Three Bells*

Dr Joseph Eaton : father of Lucia

Julia Eaton : sister of Lucia

Lucia Eaton : passenger

Mary Fremont : passenger

Sewall Fremont : army captain

William Gates : colonel

Mr Gratton : second mate (crew)

Henry Judd : army captain

Mrs Judd : passenger

Lucien Loeser : army lieutenant

Sarah Loeser : passenger

Edwin Lowe : captain of the *Kilby*

John Marshall : lieutenant colonel

---

four hours, a distance of 3600 miles – beating all competitors from two to three days. Her length on deck is 285 feet; breadth of beam, 41 feet; and she is 24½ feet deep. She has three decks, with a light joiner's deck 8½ feet above the 24½ feet deck, making a covering for cabins, state rooms, and the officer's rooms on the latter deck, besides a clear space above, and forming a splendid promenade fore and aft. She will be rigged with two masts.

'Impressive,' remarked Lucia Eaton with diminishing interest as the text showed ominous signs of returning to technicalities.

'*The hull is remarkable for its immense strength,*' continued her younger sister, confirming Lucia's fears. '*The bottom is solid, and there are double diagonal braces as an additional security for the frame, running from the floor heads to the upper deck, all bolted to the frame and rivetted together at each crossing, and still further*' – she laid mock emphasis on the last word – '*secured by a large iron plate which runs fore and aft over the upper ends of the diagonal braces, to which it is rivetted, and also bolted to the frame. In addition to this, another method of strengthening has been*

Edward Mellus : first officer (crew)

Sarah Merchant : passenger

Valeria Merchant : passenger

Francis K Murray : naval lieutenant

Mr Pendleton : captain of the *Lucy Thompson*

Mr Rankin : passenger

Richard Satterlee : army surgeon

Frederick Southworth : passenger

James Stockwell : passenger

George Stouffer : captain of the *Antarctic*

Mr Strout : captain of the *Napoleon*

Emmeline Taylor : passenger

George Taylor : major

James Van Vorst : army lieutenant

James T Watkins : captain of the *San Francisco*

Charles Winder : army lieutenant

William Winder : army lieutenant

Mr Wyse : major

Mrs Wyse : passenger

introduced into this vessel never before adopted. This consists in having two bulkheads, running fore and aft, one on each side of the engine and boilers, and secured to the bottom and the middle deck beams, and diagonally braced with iron the whole length, rendering it an impossibility for anything much less a complete wreck to start a timber.'

'Don't pretend you understand a word of it!' protested Lucia. 'How do you *start a timber,* anyway?'

'With *a complete wreck,* it says,' answered her sister. 'The next paragraph is more interesting. *The interior is to be arranged with state rooms above and with single open berths, similar to the Hudson river boats, and with open steerage berths below. Having a great number of very large sideports and skylights, affording an unusual amount of light and ventilation, this portion of the arrangements will not be subject to the inconvenience resulting from the want of those two necessities for comfort that render traveling in warm latitudes on board some steamships quite a serious consideration.* So you and Sarah will be comfortable.'

'Julia, this is December! I'd rather we were warm.'

The youngest Miss Eaton turned up the lamp and resumed mercilessly just as their father came in and stood listening. '*The machinery is now being completed at the Morgan Works. It will consist of two oscillating*' – she stumbled over the unfamiliar word – '*engines, with two boilers. The engine will oscillate with a new adjustable cut-off arrangement. The cylinders are 65 inches in diameter, with 8 feet stroke and placed fore and aft in the ship. The wheels, which are fitted with feathering buckets, are 28 feet in diameter, with a face of 8 feet; wheel shafts 18 inches in diameter; one pair of cranks, and one crank pin, and four piston rods.*'

'No more!' Lucia put her hands to her ears in mock horror. 'Father, do you understand any of this?'

'Sufficient, my dear.' He walked over to his youngest daughter, reading over her shoulder. 'If we ignore the boiler dimensions, though you have to admit that a diameter of 13 feet eight inches and a length of 34 feet is not inconsiderable, and also the arrangements for fire prevention, we are left with the fact that, and I quote: *The San Francisco, when completed, will be the finest steamship on the Pacific.*[1] Let us hope so: when they took her out on her last trials she had to be towed back by the tug.'[2]

He was putting a brave face on it. That Sarah would be accompanying her husband, he approved of. He was a military man himself, and if the 3rd Regiment of Artillery was to be sent back to the other side of the continent to protect the thousands of people lured into the mountains in the hope of striking it rich, then Mrs Loeser's place was with Lucien, as the late Mrs Eaton's had been with him. Thirty-five-year old Lieutenant Loeser, who had married Sarah in 1849, was something of a celebrity. A West Point graduate, he was serving with his regiment in California in 1848 when that first gold was found at Sutter's Mill, and he had been entrusted with the task of taking the first sample back to New York to be assayed. For want of a better container he had carried it in a tea caddy. Of course Sarah would go with him, but they had invited Lucia as well, and that was hard on the father who had brought up his six girls ever since their mother's death.

'Was that all Lucien wrote for?' Dr. Eaton enquired.

'No: he wrote he'll be with us for dinner and he wants my last trunk sent up tomorrow on the *Eagle*.'

There was something of finality as the lid was closed on the dresses, linen and bonnets. Once again her life, for the foreseeable future, had been packed away and consigned to a distant place of which she knew no more than Lucien and his army friends at their Fort Wood barracks on Bedloe's Island (now Liberty Island) had told her, or she had read in the newspaper. Not that her packing had been as hard as theirs. Lucien and Sarah were taking everything: bedsteads, carpets, curtains, chairs, glassware, crockery, cutlery, mirrors, towels, as well as all their clothes. Their rooms must look very empty, and that was how she felt, especially since a little voice had begun to whisper everything she had tried not to think about.

Friday dawned in thick, freezing fog; all day she heard the ringing of bells out on the unseen water as ships tried to go about their business in the bay. In the evening the table was set for dinner and a servant had gone down to the pier to meet Lucien, but he returned alone, and with the most unexpected bad news. At 9:30 that morning, on her way to New York, the *Eagle* had collided in the fog with the *Sylph*, bound from the city to Staten Island. The *Sylph* had suffered only superficial damage and had taken off the crew and passengers of the *Eagle*, which had sunk forward of the wheelhouse. There had been several collisions that day.

The accident struck Lucia as an evil omen, a warning that she could not get out of her head and that stifled her enthusiasm for the trip. When her brother-in-law did arrive she was ready to tell him that she would not go. The loss of her wardrobe was reason enough. Unless the trunk could be recovered and the clothes washed and dried there was no possibility of leaving New York on Wednesday. One half of her was relieved, the other disappointed, and under Lucien's persuasion she shook off enough of her misgivings to reconcile her to the voyage. Yet, on the Sunday afternoon, while dressing for church, she happened to glance through the window that overlooked the bay and the scene of the accident. The ill-fated *Eagle,* bow underwater, stern high, was being towed past; the evergreen branches and sprigs that decked her out for Christmas looked more like wreaths; curtains were blowing out of the windows. Suddenly Lucia felt sick, and next day, when she saw the *Eagle* tied up at the wharf, she was no less despondent. The news that her trunk had been recovered and its contents, all 280 pieces of clothing, were being laundered, was no compensation. Whenever she looked up from her sewing, there was the wreck, and on the Monday there, too, was the huge *San Francisco*, out on her final sea trials, but moving very slowly, and the tug was going out to her. The juxtaposition of the two vessels seemed to offer a second warning.

Dr. Eaton had been watching the ship from outside, and he returned shaking his head.

'I do not wish my family to go out in that steamship if she is not perfectly safe.'

He stood at the window with the girls as the steamer stopped behind Fort Lafayette. They expected her to go further, heading for the Hook, but instead she turned, waited for a tug and then returned under tow.

Against her better judgement, but willing to be talked out of what her sister and brother-in-law called her superstitious fears, Lucia Eaton travelled to New York City on Tuesday 22 December, and spent the day making sure her laundered clothing was dry, and then packing it. In the morning, accompanied by Julia and some friends who had come up to see her off, she caught the steamboat out to the *San Francisco*, which after having been tied up at 29 North

River, had been moored further out.

Lucia's parting from Julia and their father, who arrived by another boat too late to do more than reach out to hold her hand, was painful, and the bitter, grey weather echoed her feelings; but she was still young, she had the company of her favourite sister and Lucien, who was more brother than brother-in-law, and there was all the excitement of greeting people coming on board. There were a few private passengers, such as George Aspinwall (who belonged to the family that owned the ship) and Frederick Southworth, as well as a handful of officers bound for other regiments or the naval squadron, but the ship had been chartered by the government to take the 3rd Artillery to San Francisco, and she knew all the officers and their families. A few of them, the more junior ones, arrived early; the troops embarked during the afternoon, and at 3:00 p.m. dinner was served, giving passengers the chance to meet the ship's captain, 45-year-old James T Watkins, who before joining the Pacific Steam Navigation Company (PSNC) had commanded clippers in the China trade. Later, the regiment's colonel, William Gates, brought his wife and three children on board together with fellow officers Lieutenant Colonel John Marshall, Captain Sewall Fremont and the latter's wife, Mary, and family, and they joined Lucia and the Loesers in possession of the chairs nearest the stove. Lucia had lost her fear of the ship: up close she had appreciated the strength of the hull, and nobody seemed to be in the least concerned as the conversation ran cheerfully. Her father had made some enquiries since observing the last trial, and seemed satisfied to learn that the condenser had been renewed. He had told Lucien that the engine problem had been dealt with.

Inside, the ship was beautiful: the saloons at the stern were bright, with thick carpets and gilded plasterwork, and what she had seen of the upper state cabins, furnished with chintz curtains, was impressive. That evening, with some 750 men, women and children on board, the *San Francisco* raised steam and moved slowly down to quarantine at the entrance to the Narrows for the night, while the passengers in the upper saloon carried on with their conversation: complaints about the weather, the difficulty of getting everything packed, the parting with family and friends, and, for those who had experienced it, reminiscences of their last journey to San Francisco. At 9:00 p.m. Colonel Gates got up and said he was going on deck to see to his boys, which surprised those who did not realize that he was referring to his troops, not his children.

Having decided it was time for bed Lucia went down to her stateroom, only to make the unwelcome discovery that compared to those on the upper deck it was poky, and with only a deadlight. It had originally been booked by Major George Taylor and his wife Emmeline, but they had relinquished it for an upper deck stateroom. Now she understood why. But it was opposite her sister's, which made it convenient, and when the sun rose on a bright and crisp morning she was as happy as anyone. The band played on deck, smoke streamed from the funnels, and there was a festive air as the *San Francisco* sailed down the Narrows between Staten Island and Brooklyn on her maiden voyage with her huge wheels[3] churning the frothing water thrown up by her fine clipper bow. As they passed Fort Hamilton, a salute was fired by the 4th Artillery. The officers and men mustered on deck returned a hearty three cheers. Nobody voiced any concern that the ship was grossly overloaded, not in the number of passengers but in the weight of trunks, furniture, supplies and military stores. Her wheels were submerged further than they should have been.

In the first saloon, Lucia Eaton had caught up with Emmeline, who had arrived with her husband just before sailing. Emmeline's health was fragile; it had been a struggle to be ready in time – hence her late arrival. She sat down to dinner with them and with James Cooper, an Episcopal minister, who was taking his family to do missionary work in Brazil. Afterwards, Lucia went up on deck with another friend, and felt sorry for the soldiers. Some four hundred of them, including their families, had been billeted in the forward deck cabin, with some of the officers in the surrounding staterooms, but more than a hundred others were on the exposed deck.

'Some' noted Lucia pityingly, 'were standing by the smoke-pipes trying to keep warm, others stamping their feet and clapping their hands … They were a wretched looking set as they were nearly all new recruits. This was the only place for them and they were obliged to sleep on deck at night. It was very hard.'

The following day, with moderate winds under a cloudy sky, the crew set the studding sails. Later in the day the wind died as the sun went down behind a bank of ominous dark clouds, and, in anticipation of bad weather, all sail was furled and the *San Francisco* proceeded under steam power alone. The sea had been growing rougher as they reached the edges of the Gulf Stream, and one passenger recalled that dinner was sparsely attended. From her cabin, Lucia heard the clatter of cutlery, but she remained queasily in her berth, knowing she would feel worse if she got up. A waiter brought her a light meal of soup and crackers, and she could not even manage to eat all of that.

At about 9:00 p.m., off Cape Hatteras, the wind suddenly came out from the north-west in a fury, raising a heavy sea, and the ship responded by broaching, her head to north, broadside to the waves. Attempts to correct her by setting the fore-spencer and fore-staysail failed. They set the foresail and told the engineer to give the ship as much steam as he judged to be wise; troops were ordered forward in order to trim the ship, but all to no avail: an hour later the wind tore away the canvas and the ship broached-to in a massive sea. She pitched and rolled, labouring in the trough.

Anxious about the exposed troops, Colonel Martin Burke, who was officer of the day, had ordered them into the aft saloon of the upper deck where they were out of the weather but had little more than standing room. Inside the forward cabin, many of the sets of soldiers' bunks had collapsed as the stanchions gave way. Down in her cabin Lucia listened to the heavy breathing of the engines and fancied the note had changed. A waiter came in with a candle and checked that the deadlight was securely fastened.

'What is the matter?' she asked.

'Nothing. I was only looking to see if all was right.'

'Has the engine stopped?'

'It has not stopped since we left [except] on Thursday night,' he reassured her, 'and at that time only to fire up.'

Frederick Southworth had one of the upper-deck staterooms, aft of the wheelhouse, and before he staggered up to it he had actually seen the occasional man or animal – the ship carried meat on the hoof and claw – swept from the pitching deck by a breaking sea; he did not notice any rescue being attempted by the crew. Their attention seemed to be occupied in struggling to haul down all sail, as the huge mainmast twisted and bent like a sapling.

Throughout the night the ship bucked and strained at the mercy of the battering waves, while passengers like Lucia prayed and wished they had never set foot on her. The engineers fought to keep up power until, in the dark, early hours of the morning, the end of the air-pump piston rod broke. The engine was useless. The only power that remained was that which operated the steam pumps keeping the ship dry, and that was inadequate to its task. Parties of soldiers were being detailed to man the hand pumps.

Lucia's door was still open; at seven o'clock[4] that morning, Christmas Eve, Sarah called out to her, 'One of the masts has been carried away!'

Lucien put his head round the door.

'Stay in your berth,' he advised her. 'You'll be quiet there.' A little later – or was it more than an hour? – he was back. 'You'd better come to our cabin.'

Shakily she started to get up, just as a massive wave slammed the side of the ship. Her Bible was thrown off its shelf and landed at her feet. Like the sight of the half-sunk steamer, *Eagle*, it acted as an omen of doom. Her servant handed her a dressing gown and a thick corded skirt, and she put them on over her nightgown before staggering barefoot with Lucien across the corridor into the other cabin, where they both ended up on the floor. Lucia was violently sick.

'There's nothing they can do to save the ship.' The lieutenant saw little point in lying to them. 'Only the Almighty can save us.'

'What's happened?' She tried to stand up, but her legs were like water and the deck see-sawed.

'The rudder chain is broken, and so is the air pump piston. One of the masts has gone and we're in the trough of the sea.' He gathered her into his arms and put her into the bed with her sister. Despite the howling wind and all the groaning of the ship, they could hear Cooper offering up prayers, begging God to spare them.

Berthed in one of the forward staterooms on the upper deck, Lieutenant William Winder, commanding G Company, had been woken in the night by the heavy seas crashing over the ship's broadside. A sloshing and bumping told him that his cabin was inundated and that his pieces of luggage were colliding in time to the roll of the vessel. He was tired, and all he was really thinking of was how to get some sleep. Descending to the lower cabin he found that a group of ladies had set up their mattresses on the floor, so he sat down at the bottom of the stairway, and with his head on one of the treads and a hand on the banister, he dropped into a sleep that was abruptly shattered by a savage torrent of water and debris that poured down the companionway and swept him across the cabin, half-stunned and injured, unaware of the horror that was taking place overhead.

Frederick Southworth and his travelling companion, James Stockwell, had been lying awake in their stateroom berths. They heard the sea bearing down on them; felt the shock as it smashed over the wheelhouse and then the crash of timber breaking all around them. Southworth rolled like a top; salt water filled his face; he was being dragged remorselessly through the icy water...

Ragged timbers, planks and panelling floated around him, their raw ends confirming the power of the sea that had ripped them from the deck. He clutched instinctively at one and looked around. Despite the waves and his low point of view he could see the *San Francisco,* but she must already have been half a mile distant – some 900 metres. A head and shoulders broke the surface beside him, and Stockwell's hand seized the same timber. It began to sink. Southworth relinquished it in favour of another piece and, clutching it for buoyancy, began to swim one-handed towards the crippled ship. There seemed to be a good forty or more people in the water in his vicinity, floundering helplessly, many with blood running down their faces.

The swells that were battering the *San Francisco* gradually brought Southworth back to her, and he managed to catch a rope hanging down over the side just forward of the wheelhouse encasing the now-stationary paddles. For a while he held on to it, rising and falling with the movement of the ship, watching a young man clinging to one of the paddles of the wheel, and plunging under each time the ship rolled. His own strength was going; his cold hands could no longer feel the hemp. He dropped, and as he did so a wave picked him up and threw him against the guardrail. He grabbed it, and when the ship dipped he was able to get higher and crawl, exhausted, onto the forward deck.

It was no place of safety; at any moment another wave could undo the work of its predecessors. The forward staterooms remained intact; he broke into one and half-collapsed, wiping a hand across his face to clear his vision. It came away dripping with blood. But he was alive, and of the 140 people later reckoned to have been swept away in that one incident, only one other, a man named Rankin, regained the ship.

Sergeant Elijah Brown, also of G Company, had a narrow escape when, after the aft hurricane deck was destroyed, he escorted some women down into the second cabin and then locked the doors so they could not go back onto the dangerous deck. Dragged twenty feet overboard by the next heavy sea, he somehow managed to regain the ship.

William Winder recovered his wits enough to reach the main deck, where a savage blast of icy wind burned his flesh through the sodden clothes. In front of him sprawled two bodies, men killed by the wreck of the saloon and cabins; the wheelhouse was gone, too, likewise the boats; dozens of men were struggling in the turbulent seas that swept across the rolling vessel; his blood ran cold at the sight, and there was nothing anyone could do. There were animals out there as well, frantic in their distress, their flounderings hampering those who might have been strong enough swimmers to make it back to the ship.

Officers were holding on to save themselves from being washed over. He struggled over towards the mizzenmast, where Lieutenant Francis K Murray of the US Navy was braced for safety.

'I think she's broken,' the naval man said, and the deck was closer to the water than at any time before. Edward Mellus, the *San Francisco's* first officer staggered towards them with an axe, ready to cut down that last mast, shouting he would try to ease the ship. Murray and Winder lurched to the starboard quarter where some of Winder's fellow officers, James Van Vorst, J G Chandler and Surgeon Richard S Satterlee, all only half-dressed, were huddled alongside Major Wyse, who was with his wife and child. The surf repeatedly drenched them; they looked pitiful, some of them wearing lifejackets. So, Winder thought, this was all that was left of the 700 or more who had embarked on the ship? He declined the offer of a lifejacket: better to get it over with.

It was only when he was able to look down through the skylight into the saloon that he realized there were people in it, mostly ladies, and that the room, while wet, was emphatically not filling. The ship's keel had not broken.

The fury of the sea that destroyed half of the upper deck brought Lucia, Sarah and Lucien out of their cabin in terror, fearing, like everyone who joined them in the rush, that the ship had broken in two. The saloon through which they ran was filling with water; they made for the stairs, Lucien supporting his wife, Captain Fremont guiding Lucia. The staircase was partly blocked with the rubbish that had poured down on Winder, and just as people fought their way to the top, the ship would take on a sudden list that threw them off balance and onto those behind. Many had snatched up life preservers or wooden chairs to keep them afloat when the ship went to pieces. Nobody knew what they were doing, other than trying to save their lives.

The Loeser party made it to the top of the stairs, and eventually found themselves in the little forward galley, through which the water constantly washed. They were soaked and frozen despite the blankets that a soldier had given to them, and which they shared with Captain Henry Judd and his wife, who had joined them. Lucien wrapped a blanket round his sister-in-law's icy, bare feet, and the three of them sat with their arms round each other. There was no glass left in the galley to shield them from the wind; they and the small group with them shivered, or shook with fear. The black waiters stood as if paralysed.

Colonel Burke managed to reach them, badly injured after an iron railing had fallen on his back. He was bleeding, too, from the nose and ears. Lucia had realized that their servant was missing; they had thought she was following them up the stairs.

'We can't stay here,' Lucien said. 'We'll die of cold, if we aren't swept off first.' He got up to attempt some reconnaissance. A soldier approached him.

'Sir, I can try to get you down to the second cabin. It's dry down there.'

They had begun to realize that, contrary to their first thoughts, the ship was still intact, though it was hard to grasp that anywhere could still be dry. What they had not understood was that the saloon through which they had passed was flooded because the deck overhead had been broken, and the water was cascading from above, not rising from below. Other passengers had already gone back down to the saloon, fearing that the Loeser party, whom they had lost sight of, were dead.

The cabin was full of soldiers and some of their wives and camp followers, but they generously made room, and offered what dry clothing they could spare. One of them took charge of the injured Colonel Burke; another brought Lucia a flannel skirt, apologizing that it was all she had. She helped her into it and, for want of pins, fastened the waistband with her own pearl brooch. Moved by her kindness, Lucia looked up and tried to thank her.

'You need not thank me,' came the unexpected answer. 'Your mother was kind to me at Fort Preble, and I would do anything for her daughter.'

Memories of her long-dead mother flooded back. Fort Preble ... she had been born there ... Had this woman nursed her gratitude for all those years? There was another reminder of better days in the shape of an elderly and injured sergeant, whom Lucia remembered from one of the forts in Maine. Then, he had been the band leader, playing at the regimental balls ...

She and Sarah were taken to the bunk-beds, but it took hours to undo the chill they had suffered up in the exposed galley, and they were distressed by what was going on around them. These were not the trained, professional soldiers that the girls were accustomed to, but raw recruits unused to, and resentful of, discipline.

The officers were having real difficulties in persuading many of them to take their turn at bailing or pumping, which was all that stood between the ship and the bottom of the Atlantic. They wanted to get drunk, and though they were allowed to have some spirits to keep them going Captain Judd arrived just in time to stop them breaking into the casks. For all that, and the foul language that shocked the two army daughters, they were kind to their guests, bringing them portions of any delicacies they had filched from the store room.

They had a second scare on what passed for Christmas morning when a massive crash shook the overhead deck. Lucien and Judd rushed up with some soldiers, but it proved to be two iron safes breaking loose, and they managed to get them over the side before they caused any danger. Elsewhere on the ship, rough repairs were in progress. Leaks had to be stopped, and the hole in the main deck above the aft saloon patched and shored up with stanchions. The sleeping places on the forward deck were cut away and attempts made to secure some of the animals. All this in weather so bad that that the men working on deck had to lash themselves to the guard lines, as the ship continued to roll and pitch. In 24 hours the storm drove the helpless wreck some 200 miles (370 kilometres) east-north-east.

Below deck, pumping and bailing continued round the clock. Sergeant Elijah Brown was not to leave his station for five days and six nights; when his ankles became too weak, he continued pumping on his knees until Captain Watkins saw his condition and told him to get some rest. The sergeant's worst moment of that interminable period came when one of the corporals gave a shout of fire that prompted an immediate stampede in the lower cabin, where bailing was in progress. Drawing his revolver, he scrambled onto a table.

'I'll shoot anyone who raises that alarm again!' he warned them, and they went back to work[5]. Other heroes were the three lieutenants, Charles Winder, Van Vorst and Chandler who, whenever the captain needed help, and no matter how little rest they had been able to snatch, heaved themselves off their mattresses and offered their services.

Lucia and Sarah were still in the second cabin when they had a visit from Chandler and Charles Winder. They had no uniforms, pieces of blanket did duty for caps, and they were white with cold and exhaustion. The news they brought was grim. Among the 140 people washed from the hurricane deck that morning were Lieutenant Colonel John M Washington, second in command of the regiment; Brevet Captain Horace B Field, Lieutenant Richard H Smith; the 21-year-old son of Colonel Gates, travelling as a civilian; and Major and Emmeline Taylor. The stateroom of the latter couple had been that which, had not the major pulled rank on Lucien, Lucia would have occupied. Winder and Chandler were also able to relate the miraculous escape of Southworth and Rankin, and a little later Lucia's servant was brought to her, alive and well. She

No illustration of the *Dodington* is known to exist, but this 1755 painting by John Cleveley the Elder depicts a typical East Indiaman in three positions on the River Thames off Deptford.

An engraving after Robert Todd of the 'Distress of the Centaur on the night of the 16th of Septr, 1782 ... passage from Jamaica'.

Bad weather strikes the *Albion*. The ship is on her beam ends.

False hopes of rescue are raised by the arrival of another vessel.

Thirty-seven days into their ordeal the crew of the *Albion* are finally rescued by the *Shaw*.

Constructing the raft alongside the stranded *Méduse*.

Fighting breaks out on the raft after the boats have abandoned it.

Having succeeded in reaching the upper deck of the *Amphitrite*, and with the surf battering the doomed ship, the distraught convicts beg Captain Hunter to launch the boat and save them.

A contemporary portrait (unsigned but believed to be by an Englist artist) of Pierre Hénin holding the insignia of the Légion d'honneur awarded to him for his heroic swim to the *Amphitrite*

The cover of T J Cook's *Three Bells Polka*, showing the *Three Bells* and the stricken *San Francisco*, together with a portrait of Captain Creighton. It was published just a few months after the rescue it commemorates.

As HMS *Victoria* lists to starboard, the crew attempt to get the collision mat into position to stem the ingress of water. Tryon and Hawkins-Smith stand on the chart-house roof.

A portrait of the Serafini family taken shortly before they embarked on the *Sirio*. Back row, from left: Isidoro, Umberto, Felice, Amalia, Silvio. Front row: Ottavia, Silvia, Giuseppe, Lucia and Ottavio. Only Felice, Isidoro and Ottavio survived.

A *siluro a lenta corsa* of the type used by the frogmen of the Decima Flottiglia MAS in their devastating raid on Alexandria.

Leaving New York: Cunard's luxurious transatlantic liner, *Laconia*, before she was requisitioned as a troopship in the Second World War.

Tony Large MBE, who survived the sinking of the *Laconia* by *U-156*, the American Liberator's bombs and the privations of the long voyage towards Freetown in a lifeboat.

Despite their precarious circumstances, Kenneth Dancy (left) and Kurt Carlsen can still manage a cheerful wave from the *Flying Enterprise*.

A line is fired aboard the listing *Flying Enterprise* to enable food and drink to be passed over. Carlsen and Dancy can be seen among the sandbags on the starboard side.

With the *Flying Enterprise* under tow, the destroyer USS *Willard Keith* (DD-775) comes alongside to fire another supply line across. Dancy and Carlsen hang onto the rail to catch it.

The *AS-28 Priz* rescue mission complete, the UK Submarine Rescue Service team pause for a celebratory drink aboard the support ship. *Front row, from left:* Captain Jonathan Holloway, Commander Ian Riches, Alan Heslop, Marcus Cave, David Burke, Peter Nuttall, Stuart Gold; *Middle, L to R:* Will Forrester, Nigel Pyne; *Back:* Charlie Sillett.

The brotherhood of the sea: two of the UKSRS team at last meet some of the *AS-28*'s crew whom they helped to rescue. *Left to right:* Slava Milashevsky, Valery Lepetyukha, Commander Ian Riches, Sergei Belozerov, Stuart Gold, Anatoly Popov.

had been found in the cabin where, after losing her mistresses, she had gone to lie down and wait for death.

A second visit came from Lieutenant Murray, who advised them to rejoin the rest of the women in the saloon, and they gladly agreed to shift. One of the soldiers' women gave Lucia a pair of shoes, and huddled in their blankets the Eaton women followed Murray through what seemed like a labyrinth, passing the engine room where the soldiers were bailing in cramped conditions while the engineers made final repairs to the steam pumps that would spare them the work.

'The lost are found!' was the greeting to the sisters, but they were taken aback by the state of the place. The decoration was soiled, the carpets wet; stanchions probably recycled from the wreck of the upper deck propped up the damaged main deck; some tables were piled with trunks and mattresses were spread across the floor. The crowd who sat or lay on them looked pallid and strained, some calm, others in despair.

Those on the *San Francisco* may have felt themselves alone, but the storm that had wrecked their ship had wreaked general havoc. The *Empire City* was in trouble off Barnegat on the New Jersey coast, and the young *Commerce* was abandoned on her way to London on Christmas Eve. The Portland-registered brig *Napoleon*, which had left Matanzas for Boston, had sprung a leak, seen canvas carried away, and in order to ease the ship had been forced to stave 21 casks of molasses. On Christmas Eve she had sighted the *San Francisco*, but the weather was so bad that it was not until the following day at 3:00 p.m. that she came close and made contact.

Captain Watkins answered that they were making water and requested a boat be sent, but Captain Strout judged that no boat could survive in such a high sea. Comparing the state of his own hull with that of the steamer, he decided that it was safer on the latter than on the *Napoleon*. If Watkins hoped the *Napoleon* would, as requested, at least stand by, he was disappointed, though she did avail herself of some of the provisions thrown over by the crew of the steamer in response to the news that she was short of food. By dawn on the 26th she had gone, noting that on Christmas Day the *San Francisco* had been in latitude 38° 04′ N, Longitude 69° 20′ W. Later that day a second vessel, the *Maria* from Liverpool, vainly attempted to lay by. Her report put the steamer in latitude 39° 18′ N and Longitude 69° 00′ W.

Lucia had succeeded in getting down to her stateroom to recover a dress that her sister had earlier left out for her, as her own trunk had been buried beneath a pile of others. Returning faint and exhausted to her mattress in the saloon she declared that if anyone could get at the trunk they would be welcome to share the clothes.

On Tuesday 27 December hopes rose that the engines were at last in order;

they would soon be underway using emergency steering gear. But before long steam began to pour into the saloon – which adjoined the engine room – until people gasped helplessly for air. The atmosphere became thick and intolerable, and when it was announced that the attempt had failed the primary emotion was one of sheer relief.

In the afternoon a third sailing ship was sighted bearing down on them: the *Kilby*, an old Boston-registered barque,[6] homeward bound with a cargo of cotton loaded at New Orleans. With the weather too bad to attempt more than hailing, Captain Edwin Lowe promised to lay by during the night. Two other ships had let them down, so nobody was surprised when, come dawn, there was no sight of this third and her young Irish master. Soon enough, however, she reappeared, and when she sent out a boat Captain Watkins was able to go aboard to conclude an agreement on behalf of the US Government. Effectively, he was chartering the ship. The terms were simple and written out in pencil: the owners would receive $15,000 to take off as many passengers as possible (a large proportion of the sum being compensation for the cargo that would have to be thrown overboard to make room for them), while Captain Lowe would receive $200 a day from the Pacific Mail Steamship Company for every day that he had to stand by if required to do so for any length of time. Captain Watkins returned with his copy of the paper and consulted with Major Wyse and other officers, who disagreed with the terms. To the sum already agreed they unilaterally added 5 per cent primage[7] and an ex-gratia payment to the captain of $1,000.

Lieutenant Van Vorst took a party across to help with jettisoning the cargo; a hawser was run out to the bow of the *Kilby* to keep the ships from drifting apart, and when the time came to disembark the officers stood with their pistols loaded to ensure an orderly evacuation and no rushing of the boats.

Among the women passengers there was a profound relief that overcame sickness and exhaustion. Lucia was able to get access to her trunk, and as she and her sister possessed the only dry ones, there was some distribution of articles. She gave a saque-gown to a woman who had lost everything, her spring hat to Mrs Wyse, and divided a shawl with her sister, whose summer hat adorned her own dishevelled hair. Even her servant shared what she had with those in need; the one problem was finding anything suitable for the many young children.

While they were waiting for the order to come on deck, someone handed Lucia her Bible.

The evacuation was proceeding. A rope swing had been rigged up, the end tied to the mast. A passenger sat in the swing, holding on above their head, and was carefully lowered down into one of the *Kilby*'s boats, where Lieutenant Murray was waiting to help them slip out and sit down. Colonel Gates, who had been noticeably inconspicuous during the drama of the previous days, now addressed the troops, officers as well as men, asking them to wait patiently until their names were called and promising not to desert the ship before them – though it was clear that there would not be room for everyone to transfer. Then, to the dismay of everyone, and without a word to his second in command, the colonel and his family promptly embarked on the second boat.[8]

Lucia and Sarah endured only a short wait before being summoned on deck, but the time they then spent on a seat, hanging on to the rail as the ship rolled, was more nerve-racking than being lowered into Lieutenant Murray's competent arms. Lucia found herself in the bow of the little boat sitting next to a plump woman who had found the descent somewhat difficult. Her husband had to wait, and she was distraught at leaving him.

'I shall never see him again!' she sobbed, hands clasped together.

'He'll be on the next boat. He'll be with you in a few minutes.'

'My poor mother begged me not to go out in that steamship! She told me I would never get to land. Oh, why did I come, why did I come!'

Lucia, who remembered her own forebodings about the journey, sought to calm her down, and by the time they reached the *Kilby* she was in a more rational frame of mind for the difficult task of climbing the ladder onto the vessel. Lieutenant Murray cheered them all up by telling them that they had been in more danger while being lowered from the ungovernable ship into the *Kilby*'s boats than they had been while aboard the *San Francisco*. He had been a tower of strength during the transfer, and he caught one of Sarah Merchant's younger daughters when she fell out of the swing. Taking on a responsibility that was not his, he had represented to Colonel Gates that they needed to take more provisions aboard the *Kilby*, but the Colonel had ignored him.

An orderly chaos reigned aboard the old *Kilby* as more and more passengers arrived and tried to make themselves comfortable in what was, after all, a humble cargo carrier, while her crew and Van Vorst's party cleared more space in the hold for people, stores and baggage. The conditions were primitive. Lucia found herself in a cabin of some 10 by 12 feet (3 by 3.6 metres) with four further cabins opening onto it. Those four were soon taken, one by the Gates family, but later one was given over to Sarah Loeser, who had been badly bruised in the struggle for the deck. The centre of the main cabin was occupied by a table, which soon had to go, and some hard provisions.

Lucia went on deck with Valeria Merchant to watch the transfers and take a long last look at the *San Francisco*. Then, hearing that they could get a cup of tea in the galley, they reported there and found Colonel Burke who, along with Valeria's father, had been lowered from the steamer in tubs because of sickness or injury.

The very last boat brought Lucien who, as acting assistant commissary, had overseen the transfer of stores for the soldiers. One of the sparse orders that Gates gave was to include Van Vorst, Loeser, Fremont, Judd and the assistant surgeon among those who would be transferring to the *Kilby*, a decision that would leave few officers to support the men left on board the *San Francisco*. By now it was 7:00 p.m., too dark for further transfers, but they hoped that the work could resume in the morning. As the stronger of the two boats was being hoisted in, it suffered serious damage.

The weather was rough all night, blowing a wet gale that veered between south and east. The 41 in the cabin and surrounding 'staterooms', who also included the Brazilian consul and the consumptive George Aspinwall, were packed closely together, and if Lucien had not had the forethought to bring a couple of candlesticks and a box of candles with him, they would have been in the dark, too.

In the night, the hawser parted, and come morning there was no trace of the *San Francisco* on the horizon, not even by the lookout at the masthead. A painful decision had to be taken: hoist sail and make for the nearest port to report the disaster, or lay by and hope to spot the ship. The women were instinctively for staying; the men took a more thoughtful approach and finally resolved that if they did not find the steamer during the day they would have to make for port.

There was no sight of her. With 108 of the approximately 700 passengers and crew of the steamer, the *Kilby* raised sail for Boston.

The *San Francisco* had not foundered. She still wallowed in the trough of the seas, but a new danger had hit those aboard her: sickness in the form of severe diarrhoea, which those onboard mistakenly believed was cholera. In the afternoon of the transfers the first deaths from it had occurred, and they ran at around ten a day – the victims included men, women and children. Some blamed it on the way the soldiers and waiters had broken into the stores and eaten and drunk what they could lay their hands on, but the true reason, as a passenger observed, lay in the combination of overcrowding, cold, and poor diet that the soldiers had endured even before the wreck added terror and despair to their misfortunes. The army surgeons had been sent aboard the *Kilby* – Satterlee was a sick man, and the assistant was probably sent to accompany his family, while the ship's surgeon was handicapped by the loss overboard of all the medicines. Watkins knew that for all the exhausting attempts to rig up jury steering, stem the leaks and get the engines going, there was no possibility of saving the ship, and had put all his hopes on meeting another vessel.

By 2:00 a.m. on Saturday 31 December they had drifted to 39° 18′ N, 65° 09′ W, which was 75 miles (140 kilometres) to the east and some 90 miles (165 kilometres) to the north, leaving her around 550 miles (1020 kilometres) south-west of Sable Island. At that moment, a cry rang out that turned to cheering. A light had been spotted off the bow. Signal guns were fired, and at once the unseen ship answered with blue lights. Come morning she was standing by: an iron-hulled clipper flying the British flag and bearing the name *Three Bells*, port of registry Glasgow, bound for New York and, unbeknown to herself and her crew, a slice of immortality.

The wind defeated Watkins's attempts to shout. As the clipper tacked back and forth, simple messages written in chalk on a board were held up, and the 603-ton *Three Bells* – named after the Bell brothers who jointly owned her – answered through the speaking trumpet. Captain Robert Creighton promised to stand by until the weather improved enough to take off the *San Francisco*'s people, and day after day he kept his word. Not until 2 January was it safe for the clipper to lower her only boat to fetch Second Mate Gratton aboard so he could explain the precise position. Creighton must have been shocked to learn of the deteriorating conditions, and probably by the magnitude of the rescue that was required.

It was still not calm enough to risk abandoning ship. Creighton remained patiently on station

The *San Francisco* experienced a second stroke of luck the following morning, Wednesday, at nine o'clock when Watkins observed the *Three Bells* hoisting a distress signal. It was evident that her lookouts had spotted a sail, and the signal brought the newcomer down to them: the magnificent big clipper *Antarctic*[9] under Captain George C. Stouffer, which had left her home port of New York bound for Liverpool. In addition to her readiness to share the rescue, she offered five sound boats.

Even so, and with moderating weather, it took four anxious days to complete the transfer of four hundred soldiers, thirty women and children, and the officers of the steamship. Not counting those swept overboard in the storm, 59 had died aboard the ill-fated vessel in the days after the hurricane deck was destroyed, and many of the survivors were sick. They were divided between the two sailing ships.

Major Wyse and Lieutenant William Winder boarded the *Three Bells* with 192 men and women from the 3rd Artillery. With them went many of the crew under First Officer Mellus. The total figure varies in the different accounts between 238 and 320 ... Last to leave what should have become the finest steamship in the Pacific was Captain Watkins, who had fought so hard to save the *San Francisco*, only to be disappointed at every turn. He went aboard the *Antarctic*, even though she was bound for Liverpool, joining his third and fourth officers, the remainder of the crew and lieutenants Charles Winder and John G Chandler, who had charge of the second contingent of troops and their families, also numbering 192. Contrary to some reports, the *San Francisco* was not scuttled at the end to avoid her proving a hazard to shipping; her condition was so serious that the captain expected her to founder within 24 hours.

Those on the *Antarctic* were particularly fortunate: although she could carry around 200 passengers, she was almost empty, and her berths could be fitted up for the survivors. When the weary soldiers and crew struggled aboard her they were greeted with a bowl of beef soup, their first hot food in days.

News of the fate of the *San Francisco* was relayed to New York by telegraph after the arrival at Liverpool, Nova Scotia, of the *Maria* on 6 January. The *Napoleon* reached Boston on 7 January and also telegraphed to New York. Her news was encouraging because her captain and mate stated that although there was damage to the upper works, the hull was sound and the paddles intact, which was certainly true. It disguised the fact that the ship was completely helpless, and maybe Captain Strout did not realize that the engines had both failed. Later his conduct would be compared somewhat unfavourably with that of other vessels, particularly the *Kilby*, which could also have pleaded her poor condition as an excuse for leaving the *San Francisco*. The secretary of state telegraphed for a steamer to be sent in search, and all Revenue cutters were ordered on the *San Francisco*'s course.

Looking for one ship after such a storm could have been like looking for a needle in a haystack, but in 1842 Lieutenant Matthew Fontaine Maury of the US Navy, now considered the founding father of oceanography, had been appointed superintendent of the Depot of Charts and Instruments of the Navy Department in Washington. Maury had scrutinized hundreds of naval journals and log books, studying the effect of winds and currents, even asking captains to drop messages in bottles stating the position in which they had been dropped. Finders were asked to write to Maury informing him where the bottle had been picked up. By 1854 he had an international reputation. With his unequalled understanding of the Gulf Stream, he was able to predict the position to which the *San Francisco* would have drifted – it turned out to be the precise position in which the *Three Bells* found her. After the two clippers left the scene, the *San Francisco* was not seen again, and probably foundered before any of the later would-be rescue ships reached the scene.

O n board the *Kilby* all was not well. The ship was in no danger of foundering, but her sails were so old and worn that every time the wind gained in strength they had to be furled in case they were blown out. Most nights she was forced to lie-to: the truth was, they were getting nowhere, and the passengers, almost all without berths, were extremely uncomfortable. Lucia wrote feelingly:

My sister had been very badly bruised and suffering very much wished to lie down. My brother succeeded in getting an old bed tick and had it filled with cotton, a pouch laid over it, and some cotton rolled up in paper from a pillow and a blanket to cover her. This was her bed for sixteen days. It was very hard but she felt thankful for it. Mrs. Fremont and her three little children slept on the floor under my sister's bed. She had an old quilt to sleep on, a blanket to cover her.

The second night after we came on board of the bark we all slept in the cabin.

Mr. Aspinwall, who was ill with consumption: had the sofa. Col. Burke was stretched upon the floor and, as he was still very weak from the injuries he had received, all were obliged to be very careful not to touch him. He was very patient and made as little trouble as possible. Some few of the passengers laid themselves upon the floor and slept being perfectly worn out with fatigue.

There were nine gentlemen, nine ladies and ten children under six years of age sleeping in this little cabin.

That night I sat up upon a trunk. I could not sleep. Miss Merchant sat upon a trunk, also, but she soon fell asleep. Soon a roll of the bark brought her upon the floor and falling upon persons who were sleeping. They awoke in alarm, but she, being perfectly exhausted from the fatigues of the past night and day, did not waken when she fell. I woke her and she took her seat upon the trunk again. At the dawn of day all awoke. Mrs. Merchant seeing me still sitting upon the trunk insisted upon my leaning on her and to try and get a little sleep. I did so and soon was lost to everything around me. I could not sleep long as I was constantly slipping off the trunk.

At nine o'clock the steward brought in tea and crackers, the former being like lye as it was boiled. We had bacon for breakfast for the first time on this morning. It being cut up in small pieces and fried. Our allowance was a cracker and one slice of bacon. The latter was brought in an old tin pan and handed around to those assembled, each taking a piece in their fingers.

Such articles as knives and forks were not to be found on the bark. The bacon and cracker tasted very good to us, and we felt thankful for the repast. The bacon was cut in slices with a large pocket knife which my brother always carried about with him. The soldiers had the same allowance as ourselves. The officers being regularly detailed for officer of the day, each took their turn without trouble, and all was well directed and order established.

Lucia's assertion that all were sharing equally was incorrect. Women, children and invalids were given more generous portions than others, and on the first occasion that Captain John W T Gardiner of the 1st Dragoons was officer of the day he went to Colonel Gates, who had given no orders as to how the soldiers were to be organized or how the officers should arrange their own duties. Gates demanded an additional ration of water for himself and his family. Gardiner was unhappy.

'It will have a bad effect on the men – as some of them are suffering from want of it – if the officers get an extra quantity before the men get any.'

'I don't care a damn for the men! I would rather that twenty of them should die than that my child should suffer,' came the angry reply, and from then on he either demanded to be supplied or simply sent his steward with the water bottles. Gardiner also complained that he demanded more than the daily food ration.

As the interminable days went on the rations of food and water diminished, and the children suffered miserably. One young mother with three small children, two of whom had the measles, lost all hope. To Lucia, who befriended her, she spoke of her pampered and privileged life as an only daughter, how she had never had to do anything for herself until she married.

'Everything comes hard to me,' she said. 'How much better it would have been for me now had I ... been obliged to put up with a few hardships during my childhood, how much better I could have born this trouble.'

On 13 January the *Three Bells* dropped anchor off the Battery, minus more than thirty adults and children who had died on the voyage, of the same sickness that had begun to afflict the passengers on the *San Francisco*. The voyage had been without incident, but part of the cargo had consisted of chloride of lime, and though it had been jettisoned the pungent smell left behind provided an irritant to the lungs, particularly for the soldiers quartered between decks. As soon as it was known she carried survivors of the *San Francisco*, a flock of New York reporters descended on her. Aware that she would be the object of much media attention, William Winder had spent considerable time composing a lengthy statement, which he dictated to the assembled reporters and which was widely printed, along with other reports.[10] The conduct of Captain Creighton in particular was feted. He and his officers were invited to attend a performance of *Uncle Tom's Cabin*, and "The Three Bells Polka" was composed in honour of the ship, the cover of the score embellished with an illustration of the disaster and a portrait of her captain. The poet John Greenleaf Whittier fired off a stirring ballad telling of her gallantry.

The Three Bells
Beneath the low-hung night cloud
That raked her splintering mast
The good ship settled slowly,
The cruel leak gained fast.

Over the awful ocean
Her signal guns pealed out.
Dear God! was that Thy answer
From the horror round about?

A voice came down the wild wind,
'Ho! ship ahoy!' its cry.
'Our stout Three Bells of Glasgow
Shall lay till daylight by!'
Hour after hour crept slowly,

Yet on the heaving swells
Tossed up and down the ship-lights,
The lights of the Three Bells!

And ship to ship made signals,
Man answered back to man,
While oft, to cheer and hearten,
The Three Bells nearer ran;

And the captain from her taffrail
Sent down his hopeful cry
'Take heart! Hold on!' he shouted;
'The Three Bells shall lay by!'

All night across the waters
The tossing lights shone clear;
All night from reeling taffrail
The Three Bells sent her cheer.

And when the dreary watches
Of storm and darkness passed,
Just as the wreck lurched under,
All souls were saved at last.

Sail on, Three Bells, forever.
In grateful memory sail!
Ring on, Three Bells of rescue,
Above the wave and gale!

With her passengers reduced to eating mostly corn meal, the *Kilby* was stuck in contrary winds, unable to make any of the ports from Charleston to Boston, and at one time right on George's Bank. Lieutenant Murray and Captain Lowe were doing their utmost, but as the naval man was to say later, the *Kilby* was a perfect old tub – and they might have floated quite safely in the Gulf Stream for days or weeks – but that they needed a friendly ship or barque to tow them into port. They sighted a sail and also a steamer, but were unable to gain any attention. It was now 60 days since the ship had left New Orleans; her crew were restive, and on the night of Thursday 12 January they went to their captain and said they would run the bark ashore at Barnegat. Nothing that Lowe said could change their minds. Murray went to see them.

'If you run this bark on Barnegat not one person will escape with their life,' he warned. 'You will not be safe, for the bark will go to pieces instantly and you will not be able to get on shore.'

He dissuaded them from precipitous action, but they swore that if the wind remained contrary on Friday they would mutiny all the same.

It was a bad night, the rain lashing down and the fog dense, forcing the *Kilby* to lie-to, ringing her bell dolefully to warn any other vessels of her presence – ironically, warning them to avoid her. The dawn came clearer, and the news went round the barque that a vessel had been sighted. Friday the 13th was not to prove unlucky: within a short time of Captain Lowe having gone aboard the newcomer, Lucia and the others learned that they were to be transferred to the *Lucy Thompson*, bound for New York with two hundred emigrants from Liverpool. Lucia described the scene:

The sea was running very high but we did not feel afraid. We went down the rope ladder, taking hold of the ropes, a man holding on to us to prevent our falling. The sea was very rough and we were obliged to be very careful as we stepped into the small boat. The waves would sometimes send it off a great distance from the bark.

I did not know how very dangerous it was till I saw persons getting into the boat after I was seated. Our boat the first being filled with passengers pushed off. I must say I felt truly happy to leave that old bark. And yet I felt truly thankful that it had afforded us a shelter a place of protection for sixteen days.

There were two hundred emigrants on board of the *Lucy Thompson*, no cabin passengers, so there was sufficient room for all from the bark.

On our arrival at the ship we were taken up by the rope ladder. The sea was running very high and the life boat would be sent by the force of the waves nearly to the bow of the ship, and then, on coming up to the ladder again, the man would take hold with an iron grasp. Often they were obliged to let go, as they would have been dragged out of the boat.

Capt. Pendleton stood looking at us and, seeing how dangerous it was, threw us a large rope letting the men to tie it under the arms of the passengers as they came up the ladder. As he could do nothing more to assist us in getting up, he left the side of the ship. He told us later his feelings overpowered him; he could not stand and look at us miserable looking beings and witness our agony as we made a grasp as it were for our lives at the ropes when we left the small boat and were almost dragged up the ladder.

A camp woman went up first. Mrs. Judd next, myself next, then my brother, sister and others who were in the boat. The emigrants crowded to the side of the ship to see us. As we passed them, they looked at us saying, 'Poor things!' Well they might say poor things, for we were a wretched looking set of people. Our blankets were half on us, our hats hanging off, and hair getting loose hanging in wild disorder. Faces pale as death as we were quite exhausted, having been obliged to exert ourselves very much while coming up the side of the ship.

We passed into the cabin which we found was very clean, roomy, airy and light.

The ship's doctor gave us port wine, which quite restored us.

He turned to me and said: 'Miss, you look worse than any of them.' I replied: 'I have not suffered more than the other passengers, although I may look frailer.'

I cast my eye around on those who were assembled in the cabin of the *Lucy Thompson* and saw Col. Burke, Captain and Mrs. Judd, my brother and sister and myself in the group. We six, the first on the *Lucy Thompson*, had been placed together on the galley of the *San Francisco* on the Saturday morning after the ill-fated steamship had been wrecked. Could we be too thankful to Almighty God for His goodness to us?

They had been extremely fortunate. For the first time since gaining his master's ticket, or so he said, Captain Pendleton had turned over and gone back to sleep after his servant had woken him. But for that lapse, his ship, lying-to until the fog lifted, would have been well on her way to Sandy Hook and never crossed the path of the *Kilby*. Looking at the bedraggled women, he told them that they had seen more in the space of three weeks than he had in his twenty years at sea.

The day after the arrival of the *Three Bells* at Manhattan the *Lucy Thompson* disembarked her unexpected guests into the tug *Titan* off Sandy Hook, at the entrance to New York Bay. That night, Lucia and the Loesers slept under the family roof. They had lost practically everything except their lives. Shortly after the disaster, Captain Mackenzie of the *Amelia* had picked up two floating cases, one of which contained a dozen cane-bottomed chairs and was marked 'Lt. L. Loeser'.

Friday 13th was doubly auspicious for the *Kilby*, on which a number of the *San Francisco* crew had remained as volunteers: she encountered the steamship *City of New York*, which towed her home to Boston. It was only after his arrival at New York that Edwin Lowe discovered the changes made by the army officers to the contract which he had agreed with Captain Watkins – changes that were very much to his advantage. He wrote to Captain Fremont that he did not work for gain, and he insisted it be withdrawn.

The *Antarctic* docked at Liverpool on 23 January, and provided the US consul in the city, Nathaniel Hawthorne (better known as a novelist than for his day-job) with a problem. As his wife wrote: 'Mr Hawthorne has no official authority to take care of any but sailors in distress. He invited the Lieutenant [Charles Winder] to come and stay here, and he must take care of the soldiers even if it is out of his own pocket.' Nor was the consul empowered to charter a vessel. He knew that the Collins Line ship *Pacific* was shortly to sail, but her owners refused to take their fellow Americans as all their places had already been sold. Exasperated, Captain Watkins travelled to London to consult with US Ambassador, later President, James Buchanan. The British recruiting sergeants were highly active (the Crimean War had recently begun), and the Americans did not want their soldiers enticed into the British army. The sooner they were homeward bound, the better. Buchanan, however, could do nothing.

In the meantime, Charles McIver of Samuel Cunard's British North American Royal Mail Steam Packet Company, offered the 1826-ton paddle-steamer *America*, and young Lieutenant Winder took the brave step of signing the £6,500 ($26,000) contract. The *America* sailed on 31 January, and Winder's decisiveness and leadership led to his promotion to captain the following year. At 25 he was believed to be the youngest captain in the army at that time.

There was, of course, an enquiry into the loss of the ship – an army investigation that concentrated more on the conduct of Colonel Gates than on the maritime causes of the disaster. It was not a court martial, but the testimony of Wyse and Gardiner, who did not belong to the 3rd Artillery, showed that Gates had behaved as if he were a passenger rather than the senior serving officer. It would be nine years before he was given another command. Nevertheless, the ship was discussed, both at the inquiry and in the press on both sides of the Atlantic.

Lieutenant Murray disagreed with the theory that the ship had been overloaded, feeling that she was not so deep in the water that safety and performance had been affected. That left the blame on the engines, or at least the failure to ensure they were performing correctly before the ship was allowed to sail. The amount of 'top hamper' – the lightweight saloons and staterooms above the hull – was also criticized as being suitable for the great rivers and the proposed Pacific route, but not for the rougher waters of the Atlantic that she had to navigate in order to reach her intended station. What was obvious, however, was that confidence in the strength of the hull had not been misplaced.

The loss of the ship can be blamed on a simple piston in the air pump, which broke and could not be repaired on board; without power, the ship was then powerless to control her orientation to the waves. Steam technology clearly had its drawbacks if such a small incident could cripple a ship because the crew lacked the equipment or skill to carry out running repairs.

Captain Watkins emerged with great credit from the disaster: his devotion to duty, and his refusal to abandon his ship until all hope of saving her was lost, gained general praise, and he remained with the PSNC, dying on board his ship, the SS *Colorado*, at Nagasaki in 1867. He is buried in Lone Mountain Cemetery, San Francisco. Three months later, the 3rd Artillery made a second attempt to return to California from New York, this time aboard the steamers *Illinois* and *Falcon*. Lucien was in command of the band and four companies that embarked on the latter ship. Hardly had they cleared the port when the engines failed, but they were lucky enough to crawl into Hampton Roads before a storm blew up, and he and his men transferred to the other vessel.[11]

In July 1866 Congress voted to honour the captains and crews of the three principal ships that had assisted the *San Francisco*. The citation read:

> *Resolved by the Senate and House of Representatives of the United States of America in Congress assembled,*
> That the President of the United States be requested to procure three valuable gold medals, with suitable devices, one to be presented to Captain Creighton, of the ship *Three Bells*, of Glasgow; one to Captain Low[e], of the bark *Kilby*, of Boston; and one to Captain Stouffer, of the ship *Antarctic*, as testimonials of national gratitude for their gallant conduct in rescuing about five hundred Americans from the wreck of the steamship *San Francisco*; and that the cost of the same be paid out of any money in the treasury not otherwise appropriated.
>
> *And be it further resolved,* That the sum of seven thousand five hundred dollars each is hereby appropriated, out of any money in the treasury not otherwise appropriated, to the above-named captains respectively, as a reward of their humanity and heroism in the rescue of the survivors of said wreck ...
> *And be it further resolved,* That there shall be paid to each mate of the three above-named vessels the sum of five hundred dollars, and to each man and boy the sum of one hundred dollars ...

A section of Walt Whitman's extended poem *Song of Myself*, written shortly afterwards and published in the first edition of *Leaves of Grass* the following year, alludes to the disaster and to the conduct of Captain Creighton. It evokes something of what it must have meant to those still on the *San Francisco* to know they were not alone. It also looks ahead to that other great American maritime saga, the *Flying Enterprise*, whose final days in just such dangerous weather were eased by the presence of vessels – by coincidence also flying the Red Duster or the Stars and Stripes – which did not give up.

> I understand the large hearts of heroes,
> The courage of present times and all times,
> How the skipper saw the crowded and rudderless wreck of the steam-ship, and
>   Death chasing it up and down the storm,
> How he knuckled tight and gave not back an inch, and was faithful of days and
>   faithful of nights,
> And chalk'd in large letters on a board, *Be of good cheer, we will not desert you;*
> How he follow'd with them and tack'd with them three days and would not give it
>   up,
> How he saved the drifting company at last,

How the lank loose-gown'd women look'd when boated from the side of their
prepared graves,

How the silent old-faced infants and the lifted sick, and the sharp-lipp'd unshaved
men;

All this I swallow, it tastes good, I like it well, it becomes mine,

I am the man, I suffer'd, I was there.[12]

Sources and Bibliography

Long out of print, Lucia Eaton's narrative (contained in Stackpole, along with other contemporary sources) is well worth hunting out. Detailed accounts by many of the survivors, and reports of the military inquiry appeared, fortunately verbatim, in the American newspapers during the first weeks of 1854, and they include lists of the men of the 3rd Artillery as well as the passengers.

Thanks to Janet Schur and Leah Prescott at Mystic Seaport Museum.

Cook, T J, *Three Bells Polka* (New York: S T Gordon, 1854).

Mays, James O'Donald: *Mr Hawthorne Goes to England*, New Forest Leaves, 1983

Stackpole, Edouard, *The Wreck of the Steamer San Francisco* (Mystic, CT: Marine Historical Association, 1954; reprinted, Chester, CT: Pequot Press, 1977).

Sutter, General John A: 'The Discovery of Gold in California', *Hutchings' California Magazine* (November 1857).

Daily Alta California
Liverpool Chronicle
New York Daily Times
New York Evening Post
New York Herald
The Times

www.congressionalgoldmedal.com
www.eastrivernyc.org
www.maritimeheritage.org/ships/ss.html (the best website on the disaster)
www.sfgenealogy.com/sf/gnl/lonecem.htm

Notes

1. Prior to the construction of the Suez Canal and first trans-continental railway, travellers and cargo bound for California faced three choices: the long and dangerous overland route by horse-drawn wagon, a long voyage round Cape Horn or a short voyage to Panama followed by an overland crossing of the narrow Isthmus to embark on a ship plying the route up the West Coast. The *San Francisco* was on a one-way trip round Cape Horn to San Francisco, after which she would remain on that West-Coast route.

2. *New York Evening Post*, 15 December 1853: 'This new vessel sailed around the harbour yesterday on a trial trip, but owing to some disarrangement of machinery, had to be towed back to the city. She is destined for the route from Panama to San Francisco, and will be repaired forthwith and proceed on her passage.'

3. British Admiralty trials in 1845 had shown the propeller, or screw, to be more efficient than the paddle; the latter also had the disadvantage of straining the engine and not being reliable in heavy weather. Nevertheless, there was a significant period of transition before the propeller replaced the paddle definitively. Brunel's *Great Eastern* (1858) had both.

4. Lucia remembered it as 3 am but two of the ship's officers quote 7 am.

5. Lucia Eaton mentions that one of the *crew* attempted to set fire to the ship and had to be confined in irons, which may or may not be the incident to which Brown alluded.

6. Technically, a 'ship' was a sailing vessel square-rigged on all three masts, while a 'barque' (or bark) was square-rigged on the foremast and fore-and-aft rigged on the others. At a later period, ships and barques had three or more masts, but the same distinction in rigging applied.

7. Primage was money, over and above the freight rate, that might be offered directly to the captain as an incentive to take extra care of the cargo. If primage is paid now it goes to the owners unless there is an agreement that some or all should go to the captain.

8. An unnamed officer of the ship stated to the press that Gates disembarked in the *first* boat, and this tallies with Captain John W T Gardiner's initial testimony to the military inquiry; however, Gardiner amended his testimony to say that it was the first boat *that he had seen leave*, but that he had afterwards learned it was the second to complete a transfer.

9. *Antarctic*, 1116 tons and launched in September 1850, was the third ship to be built by the famous East Boston yard of Donald McKay for August Zerega's 'Z Line' of packet ships, which ran from New York to Liverpool.

10. There is little disagreement between the various survivors' reports; anyone consulting them should note, however, that the ship's officers use sea-time. As the day at sea began at noon, not the following midnight, events on, for example, Christmas Eve were reported as occurring on 24 December if they took place in the morning but on 25 December if they happened during the afternoon.

11. After resigning from the army in 1858 Lucien re-enlisted in 1861, as Unionist West Virginia separated itself from Confederate Virginia, and joined the 7th West Virginia Cavalry. After the war he went into civilian life, working for the New York Custom House, and was still employed by them when he died in 1897. He had outlived Sarah by 15 years, and they had no children. There is, unfortunately, no trace of Lucia after her fateful voyage. In 1850, the US Census recorded the family as consisting of Joseph and his daughters: Elizabeth, 25, and Lucia, 23, both born in Maine; Mary, 20, and Frances, 18, both born in New York; and Julia, 16, born in Connecticut. In December 1856, Mary married Lieutenant La Rhett Livingston of the 3rd Artillery at Fort Miller, California, so she must have travelled to join Sarah and Lucien at some stage. Lucia wrote her narrative just six months after returning to New York, when she states that she had fully recovered from the disastrous voyage. By that stage, her brother-in-law and sister were well on the way to California, so the implication is that Lucia did not accompany the Loesers the second time.

12. Text from the ninth ('deathbed') edition of *Leaves of Grass* (1892); the line 'How he follow'd with them ...' etc. was not in the original 1855 version.

9

A Clash of Titans

HMS *Victoria*
and HMS *Camperdown*

1893

It may frequently happen that an order may be given to an officer, which, from circumstances not known to the officer who gave it at the time he issued it, would be impossible to execute, or the difficulty or risk of the execution of it would be so great as to amount to a moral impossibility.

DUKE OF WELLINGTON'S GENERAL ORDERS, 11 NOVEMBER 1803

DURING THE NINETEENTH CENTURY, increasingly large ocean-going steam vessels such as the *San Francisco* were status symbols of the countries whose flags they flew with such pride. Nowhere was this more true than in the world's navies, in which so much national pride was invested, and nothing was more humiliating than naval failure or disaster. The 'wooden walls' that had fought at Trafalgar gave way to iron battleships; chainshot, grape and balls were replaced by huge shells fired from long-barrelled guns mounted in turrets. The Holy Grail was to build the unsinkable and unbeatable warship. In pursuit of this quest, hulls were armoured with thick plating and partitioned into compartments by horizontal bulkheads. Communicating doors could be closed in an emergency so that if water flooded into one compartment, it could not invade the others. But no design was perfect, and nobody was capable of designing out the eternal problems of human error, weakness and greed.

Early afternoon on a fine 22 June 1893; the place is the eastern Mediterranean south of Tripoli, now Tarabulus, Lebanon. Out on a blue millpond sea a fleet of 11 massive battleships, black hulls contrasting with their gleaming white superstructures, steams arrogantly towards the night's anchorage. Spread out in line abreast, they appropriate miles of sea room as only a navy imbued with the certainty that Britannia truly and unassailably rules the waves can. The pungent black smoke of their funnels defaces the cloudless sky.

This is the Mediterranean Squadron of the Royal Navy, the most prestigious squadron of the world's greatest navy, and the man in command is Vice Admiral Sir George Tryon KCB, Britain's most illustrious naval leader of the time. With his thick silver-shot beard, high forehead emphasized by receding hair, and thick, jutting brows that throw his eyes into shadow, he looks not unlike the future King Edward VII. His fleet now cruises on routine peacetime manoeuvres, which have brought them at a leisurely pace from Malta on 27 May via various ports across the eastern Mediterranean, most recently Beirut that morning. The manoeuvres are a training exercise, but they also serve as a spectacular reminder to other countries that here is a nation at the height of its power, a power founded on its naval strength.

From the hills above the Bay of Tripoli hundreds of local Lebanese have

---

Dramatis Personae

The Hon. Maurice Bourke : captain of the *Victoria*

Henry Deadman : engineer, *Victoria*

Felix Foreman : fleet engineer, *Victoria*

Richard Charles Gillford : flag lieutenant, *Victoria*

Herbert Heath : acting executive officer, *Victoria*

Thomas Hawkins-Smith : staff commander, *Victoria*

John Jellicoe : executive officer, *Victoria*

Frederick Johnson : gunner, *Victoria*

Charles Johnstone : captain of the *Camperdown*

Herbert Marsden Lanyon : midshipman, *Victoria*

Albert Markham : rear admiral, *Camperdown*

Gerard Henry Uctred Noel : captain of the *Nile*

Sir Michael Culme-Seymour : admiral

Sir George Tryon : vice admiral, *Victoria*

gathered to observe the fleet, and not out of idle curiosity, nor amazement at this display of British pride, either. A week earlier a local fakir, or holy man, had given them a prophecy:

'Allah, may his name be praised, has resolved to visit the ships of the infidels.'[1]

In the Great Cabin at the stern of the flagship, HMS *Victoria*, the clock showed 2:10 p.m. and Vice Admiral Tryon was discussing the disposition of his fleet with his Flag Captain, the Hon. Maurice Bourke, and Staff Commander Thomas Hawkins-Smith. Tryon was planning to test his captains once again, this time with an elegant manoeuvre to bring the fleet to its evening anchorage in the bay of Tripoli.

'I shall form the fleet into two divisions disposed to port,' he announced. 'The columns are to be 6 cables apart and when sufficiently past the line of bearing with the Tower of Lions we will invert the lines by turning the columns inwards 16 points [180 degrees]. Then when the fleet is back on its line of bearing for the anchorage, the fleet will alter course to port 8 points bringing the fleet in columns of divisions abreast.'

The Staff Commander, middle-aged and with a thick grey beard and moustache, frowned, immediately spotting the flaw in the plan. The turning circle of each battleship in the fleet was at best 600 yards (550 metres) – the *Victoria*'s was even greater – and the proposed spacing of the two columns was six cables: a mere 1200 yards (1100 metres). When the lines turned inwards, each pair of ships would be occupying the same space.

'I think, sir, that 8 cables would be a better distance to form up in divisions than 6 cables,' he said.

The Admiral thought for a moment.

'Yes, it should be 8 cables,' he said.

Satisfied, Hawkins-Smith left the cabin to send down the flag lieutenant to take the signal while Bourke, a clean-shaven, exceptionally handsome 40-year old, strolled over to the door to the stern walk from where he observed the lieutenant arrive, receive the signals and leave to execute them. The first signal was raised to masthead.

Form columns of divisions in line ahead, columns disposed abeam to port.

The other ten ships hoisted the same signal to confirm they understood, and the admiral's signal was hauled down for the second part of the instruction to be raised.

Columns to be 6 cables apart.

Flag Lieutenant Richard Charles, Lord Gillford was awaiting the fleet's answer to his signal when Commander Hawkins-Smith hurried over to him looking a little askance.

'Have you not made a mistake?' he asked. 'The admiral said that the columns were to be eight cables apart.'

For a Flag Lieutenant to make such a mistake was no small matter, and young Gillford – he was only 25 – bristled at the accusation.

'No,' he answered stiffly, 'I think not.' He produced the paper on which Tryon had unmistakably set down the single numeral '6' in his own handwriting. His superior officer was insistent, however, that the distance be checked, so, leaving the signal flying, Lord Gillford returned aft to the Great Cabin. When he informed the admiral of what Hawkins-Smith had said, Captain Bourke, who was still present, concurred.

'I certainly understood from you that 8 cables was the distance agreed upon, sir,' he said.

'Leave it at 6 cables,' the admiral replied, and Gillford scurried from the room to haul down the signal, which was still flying, and thereby execute it.

Bourke was left nonplussed. It was somehow unlikely that after these conversations, all within the space of ten minutes, Tryon was not aware that a 6-cable distance was insufficient for his proposed manoeuvre. Unable to tell a senior officer that he might have made a mistake, Bourke merely remarked to his admiral:

'Our turning circle is 800 yards.'

Nevertheless, the distance was to remain 6 cables. Tryon was widely seen by his officers as infallible, and Bourke himself later said, 'I had confidence in the

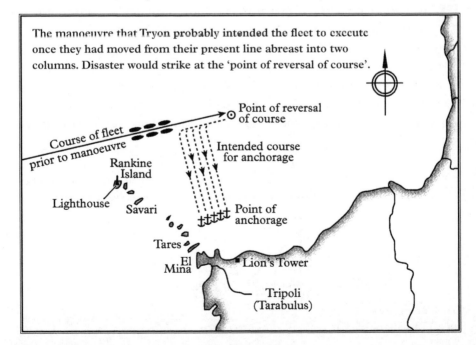

The manoeuvre that Tryon probably intended the fleet to execute once they had moved from their present line abreast into two columns. Disaster would strike at the 'point of reversal of course'.

Point of reversal of course

Course of fleet prior to manoeuvre

Intended course for anchorage

Rankine Island

Lighthouse

Savari

Point of anchorage

Tares

El Mina

Lion's Tower

Tripoli (Tarabulus)

Commander in Chief and no one ever questioned him. I never questioned him.'

Looked at from Tryon's point of view, the signal had been made and it was probably better to leave it than create confusion (and possibly mirth) in the fleet by changing it. It was executed at 2:22 p.m., according to *Camperdown*'s signal log, and there was still an hour before the order to turn inwards would be hoisted. At any time before then he could issue an order to increase the distance between the columns, and no one, apart from Bourke and Gillford, need have any suspicion that, for once, he had almost made a mistake. But if he ever considered doing so, it clearly slipped his mind.

However, when Bourke and Tryon were left alone in the cabin, a conversation took place between them the contents of which would never be disclosed.

Smoothly the majestic ships of the Mediterranean Squadron dissolved from line abreast into two great columns. The First Division was led by the flagship, HMS *Victoria*, and the Second Division by HMS *Camperdown*, the flagship of Rear Admiral Markham. This fleet, though only a single squadron of the Royal Navy, was powerful enough to defeat any other navy in the world. The *Victoria*, commissioned only six years before, was the latest in naval technology; a model of her stood on display in New York for the Americans to marvel at in much the same way that, a hundred years later, the British might marvel at the immense power of a great aircraft carrier such as USS *Enterprise*. Vice Admiral Tryon's personal standing was also immense.

The part that the Royal Navy played in the British popular consciousness of the late Victorian era cannot be over-emphasized. It was a source of national pride, and its doings were followed avidly by the newspapers as today's press follows football teams. Its senior officers were celebrities in a way they had not been since Nelson's day. Unusually for the navy, the young Tryon had come from a wealthy background. Educated at Eton, he came top of his class at the midshipman's examination, was highly regarded during his early service

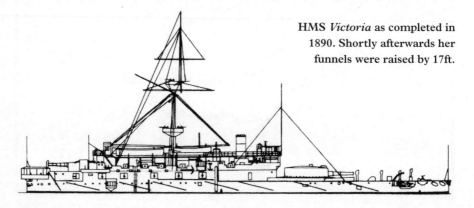

HMS *Victoria* as completed in 1890. Shortly afterwards her funnels were raised by 17ft.

in the West Indies and US station, and joined the Naval Brigade (a regiment of naval personnel fighting as land troops) with whom he fought at the siege of Sebastopol in the Crimean War. He was selected as a lieutenant for service on the royal yacht, the *Royal Albert*, a posting made by the selection of Her Majesty from the most promising young officers, and giving an automatic rank of commander. This accelerated promotion offered him the chance to serve as executive officer on HMS *Warrior* in 1861. The *Warrior* was a revolutionary ship, and is still on display at her berth in Portsmouth for that reason: the first full sea-going ironclad in the Royal Navy. At a stroke her design rendered existing wooden ships obsolete, and made her a plum appointment for any officer. In 1866, at the young age of 34, Tryon was promoted to captain. All through his meteoric rise he served in highly responsible and visible positions both at the Admiralty and at sea, always fully justifying his position and growing reputation as the most accomplished seaman of his age. But the age was one of peace.

Since the arrival of HMS *Warrior* the development of ships had continued, with better armour, bigger guns and more powerful steam engines. But a peace-time navy found itself much more concerned with show than with effectiveness in battle. By 1893 the great warships were showpieces with shining black hulls, pristine white superstructure and highly polished brasswork. Much of this spit and polish was paid for out of the pockets of the officers themselves, and there was understandable reluctance on some ships to create the dirt and damage to paintwork that naturally resulted from gunnery practice. Tryon had prospered in this environment, presumably wealthy enough to pay his share of the paint, bunting and fireworks that were a regular part of public events. He had a reputation for putting on good displays, and his ships were no strangers to royalty, but behind this was something far more professional. He knew that show was no substitute for an effective fighting navy, and he was very interested in the capability of fleets in action. His chance to show his methods to the world came with the naval exercise of 1888.

The Admiralty almost fell over itself courting the press in the run-up to this event, allowing reporters onto many of the ships, and to the public it was presented as a real contest between rival fleets, with press coverage on a par with that of a modern Olympic Games. Primed by the great Spithead revue of the previous year's Golden Jubilee, public interest was at a high pitch. Rear Admiral Tryon, as he then was, was commander-in-chief of a 'rebel' fleet being blockaded in two Irish 'ports' – Berehaven (now Castletownbere) on the south-west coast and Lough Swilly on the north coast – by the main British fleet. Blockading enemy fleets in port was the traditional way the Royal Navy had waged war in Nelson's day, and even the better part of a century later Tryon's attempts to break out must have seemed doomed to failure, 'sunk' by overwhelming (blank) gunfire from the ships at the harbour entrances. Forget that Britain and France had fought together in the Crimea thirty years earlier: it was implicitly understood that Tryon's fleet represented Britain's old adversary who, in time of war, must be contained in port where she could not harm the mercantile interest, much less contemplate invasion.

In the event, showing his usual flair and imagination, Tryon's trapped fleet at Berehaven, in Bantry Bay, probed and worried at the blockading cruisers, creating many false alarms until one dark night the flagship made to break out of the cruiser cordon from the eastern entrance of the harbour.

This was it! The cruiser squadron, in command of one Commodore Albert Markham, turned to begin the holding action that would bring the main fleet out to sea to destroy the rebels. However, as soon as the cruisers began to close, Tryon turned round and hurried back into harbour under the safety of the harbour guns. Meanwhile, at the western entrance, a fleet of Tryon's fastest vessels, their superstructure painted black, slipped unseen out of the harbour and made for the open sea.

Once this powerful squadron had escaped, Vice Admiral Baird, in overall command of the main British fleet, had little alternative but to chase it, and Tryon, who had planned all his tactics very carefully, himself escaped, and reassembled his fleet at sea. Having taken the initiative, he took the rewards. During the next few days the Achill Fleet, as the rebel fleet called itself, cruised the coast of Britain unopposed, 'destroying' ports and cities and holding them to ransom. The campaign culminated in an assault on Liverpool, where a cheering crowd assembled along the waterfront to watch the 'destruction' of their city by a bombardment of blank shells from Tryon's fleet.

There were many who complained of the unorthodox tactics used by Tryon, but the dramatic attacks on targets as significant as Glasgow, Edinburgh and Liverpool had caught the popular imagination. Tryon was a hero. Despite the embarrassment, the Admiralty also much approved of his actions in shaking up the established rules. He had proved just how vulnerable the country had become to a determined enemy, and it became his mission to instil into his captains the same initiative as Nelson had championed a century earlier. They must learn to think for themselves in unexpected situations.

It was in that spirit that, just before the Mediterranean Fleet left Malta for the 1893 exercises, he reissued one of his previous memoranda to the fleet. Prefaced with Wellington's General Order of 90 years earlier, it stated, in part:

1) While an order should be implicitly obeyed, still circumstances may change and conditions may widely vary from those known or even from those that presented themselves at the time orders were issued. In such cases the officer receiving orders, guided by the object that he knows his chief had in view, must act on his own responsibility ...

2.b) When the literal obedience to any order, however given, would entail a collision with a friend, or endanger a ship by running on shore, or in any other way, paramount orders direct that the danger is to be avoided, while the object of the order should be attained if possible.

Given that Tryon was not a man who invited questions and queries, and that he has been criticized for keeping the commanders of other ships in the dark about the object of his orders, the memorandum introduces a certain irony.

Poor Commodore Markham, the unfortunate loser to Tryon's inspired break-out in the fleet exercise, had enjoyed a less star-studded career than his illustrious contemporary. From a financially more modest background, the navy was a means to earn his fortune and an institution with which he was not always wholly in tune. He had a successful early career, typical of the time, mostly spent in the Far East, where he gained some distinction in various brave exploits against local pirates. As a lieutenant he served in the Mediterranean on one of the last three-deck ships in the navy, HMS *Victoria*, a name which, on another ship, he would come to know all too well. In 1868 he was first lieu-tenant of HMS *Blanche*, where he again showed courage and determination in the Pacific, putting down the slave traffic between Australia and the South Seas. Then he created for himself the opportunity to indulge his passion for exploration.

Obtaining leave from the navy, Markham signed on a whaling ship so that he could go north to see the Arctic, which he had long wished to explore. His diaries, which he kept all his life, report with disapproval the drunkenness and foul language of the whaler crew and then later the incompetence of a Norwegian crew he shipped with to the remote Russian Arctic archipelago of Novaya Zemlya. These trips gave him experience that led him to be included in an official naval expedition in 1875. He was in charge of a party that set a new 'furthest north' record, coming within 400 miles (740 kilometres) of the North Pole, but only at the cost of many deaths from scurvy among his men. While being in part responsible for their loss, since he had failed to detect the signs of scurvy soon enough, he showed great fortitude in leading the remains of the party home to a heroes' welcome. He later wrote a book about the expe-dition, *The Great Frozen Sea* (1878).

That leaning towards arcane or academic pursuits such as the Arctic, ornithology and archaeology during his career as a captain gave him a repu-tation as a distant figure who preferred his own company; he also gained a reputation as a strict disciplinarian. In 1891, having had what for the times was a mostly conventional career as a naval officer, if not in his other pursuits, he had reached the top of the captains' list and was duly appointed Rear Admiral, Mediterranean Squadron reporting to Vice Admiral Sir George Tryon KCB.

At 3:20 p.m. Admiral Tryon heaved his not inconsiderable frame up the steps of the bridge and onto the charthouse roof to oversee the fleet manoeuvres to its anchorage. He had just instructed Lord Gillford to raise the planned signal instructing the first division to turn 16 points to port and the second division to turn 16 points to starboard. Gillford, clearly also concerned about the order since his visit to the Great Cabin, had discreetly reminded the Admiral of the 6 cables distance by asking the midshipman to confirm it, but had got no reaction from his commander-in-chief. At 3:27 p.m. the signals were flying from the masthead.

The fleet had passed the Lions Tower on the promontory before the Bay of Tripoli and was steaming at 8.8 knots, past the intended anchorage, towards the coast on the far side of the bay. As the minutes went by, the coast of Lebanon, basking in the afternoon sun, loomed ever closer.

'What are we waiting for?' Tryon asked, and his uncomfortable flag lieutenant replied:

'I think the *Camperdown*, sir.' Lord Gillford then walked aft to check that *Camperdown* was the only one, but Tryon did not wait: he ordered the yeoman of signals to use the semaphore.

All around the fleet the flag signals had been eagerly anticipated; an original manoeuvre to reach the anchorage was only to be expected. This morning the manoeuvre to leave the Beirut anchorage had been executed by the first division steaming out through the second in line abreast. What would the commander try now? Now they had their answer.

The immediate reaction of every captain in the fleet was that the signal was impossible to obey safely; the second reaction of every captain was that since this was Admiral Tryon he must know what he is doing. All the following ships had the luxury of seeing what the leaders would do before their vessels were irrevocably committed, but this advantage was not enjoyed by HMS *Camperdown*, at the head of the second division. Accordingly all ships in the fleet except *Camperdown* responded by confirming the signal.

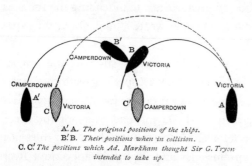

A! A. *The original positions of the ships.*
B! B. *Their positions when in collision.*
C. C! *The positions which Ad. Markham thought Sir G. Tryon intended to take up.*

The manoeuvre at the point of reversal that resulted in the collision, compared with what Markham believed Tryon must have intended.

Rear Admiral Markham had received the signal with some consternation. He and his flag captain realized immediately that the combined turning circle of the columns of ships was 7.5 cable lengths, and if the instruction was to be obeyed there would be a collision between the lead ships. He hesitated to raise the repeat signal which would indicate to his commander-in-chief that he had understood it. Tryon was renowned as a great sailor and tactician in the practical handling of fleets at sea. Much of this present tour of duty had included the practice of complicated fleet manoeuvres as training for the tactics of battle, and it was Tryon's habit to give instructions without explanation. He expected his subordinates to show some initiative of their own in the performance of orders. It seemed inconceivable to Markham that the instruction was simply wrong: maybe his commander knew something he did not.

But still he hesitated to allow his flag lieutenant to raise the 'conform' signal. Instead he instructed him to keep it at the dip which indicated he did not understand it, and called for a semaphore signal:

Am I to understand that it is your wish for the columns to turn as indicated by signal now flying?

Before Markham could send it, however, a semaphore signal came from the flagship. Made specifically to the *Camperdown*, it felt like a direct rebuke:

What are you waiting for?

In his initial report to the Admiralty afterwards, Markham explained that 'it then struck me that he wished me to turn 16 points as indicated by his signal and that it was his intention to circle round the 2nd division leaving them on his port hand'. Their lordships did not in the end accept this interpretation. But perhaps Markham then put his finger on the underlying problem on the day: 'Having the fullest confidence in the great ability of the Commander-in-Chief to manoeuvre the squadron without even the risk of a collision, I ordered the signal to be hoisted as an indication that it was understood.'

At 3:32 p.m. the signal repeat was raised to the *Camperdown*'s masthead; immediately the signal fell from the *Victoria*'s, the cue to execute the manoeuvre. At the speed the ships were travelling they were only three minutes apart.

'Hard a starboard,' ordered Hawkins-Smith. 'Extreme helm.' This last was his own addition, making the turning circle as small as possible; it also signalled his concern, but there was no indication that Tryon noted it.

Majestically, the two lead battleships turned towards each other, but as was his normal practice during a manoeuvre, the admiral was looking aft to see how the following ships were handled. Next in line, HMS *Nile* had already begun to turn inside the foaming wake of the *Victoria*, a deliberate action on the part of her experienced captain, Gerard Noel, to avoid the trouble he could see looming. Could Tryon, watching the *Nile* closely, observe this? At his side, Bourke was increasingly anxious but still he hesitated to openly question his superior. As the ship began the turn he said deliberately to the admiral:

'We shall be very close to that ship.' Then, turning to the 16-year-old midshipman who had only recently left school to join the navy and who had just been appointed as Bourke's aide-de-camp: 'Take the distance to that ship, Mr Lanyon.'

The admiral continued to observe the line of ships behind and if he heard, he made no comment. The midshipman hastily reported 3.5 cables. 'Take it again, Mr Lanyon,' said Bourke, and then, louder, to the admiral: 'We had better do something. We shall be very close to the *Camperdown.*'

Again no reply. Bourke had to somehow reduce the turning circle of his ship further if he was to avoid contact.

'May I go astern full speed with the port screw?' he demanded urgently. By now the two juggernauts had swung past bow to bow and were turning ever closer, churning the water and heeling into the turn. The *Victoria*, being under extreme helm, turned slightly ahead of the *Camperdown* which was now on her starboard bow.

'May I go astern full speed with the port screw?' Bourke repeated more loudly, and Tryon at last turned and saw the danger.

'Yes,' He snapped.

The port engine was telegraphed full astern, but it was already too late for that. On his own initiative Bourke ordered full astern for both engines. *Camperdown* had by now also ordered full astern but only 400 yards (365 metres) separated the ships and the momentum could not be overcome by the engines. The result had a dreadful inevitability. The *Camperdown* had not applied extreme helm as had been done on the *Victoria*, which was consequently further advanced in the turn.

Lt Herbert Heath, the acting executive officer, saw that collision was imminent and shouted down from the forebridge to close all watertight doors and get out the collision mat,[2] then hurried down to the foredeck to see his orders carried out. The officers on the charthouse roof above him watched in consternation as the *Camperdown* inexorably bore down on their starboard bow.

Captain Bourke rushed from his own charthouse deck down to the upper deck to order all watertight doors closed for impact. With violent emotions welling through him, the admiral ran to the starboard rail and shouted across to the approaching leviathan.

'Go astern. Go astern!' But it was a last futile gesture. With a force of almost 18,000 tons per square foot, the *Camperdown*'s bow, all the more lethal for its terrible ram, crashed its way into the vitals of the flagship just ahead of the turret housing the massive 111-ton guns. The *Victoria* was pushed some 70 feet (20 metres) to port. On the mess deck below, the chief petty officer was astonished to see the stem of the *Camperdown* emerge through the iron plates in front of him, twisting and groaning as it crunched into the bulkheads, and cool seawater began to hiss through the gaps.

The ships remained locked together for almost a minute while lieutenant Heath and his men struggled with the collision mat. As the ratings tried to place the mat in position on the forecastle, the effect of the *Camperdown*'s engines, already in reverse, wrenched Markham's ship backwards out of the hole she had made. The *Victoria*'s bows settled at once to starboard; at the same time, tons of water began to roar into the now-unplugged breach. Even before the mat was properly unrolled it was awash, and Heath could see the water rapidly rising. He gave up the attempt and the collision mat was abandoned.

Starting with the starboard flats, Captain Bourke left the charthouse roof to make a rapid personal inspection to check that the watertight doors were closed and see how high the water had reached. He found the starboard doors shut and scuttles all shut, and knew that men must have been trapped and left to drown in the flooded darkness behind doors closed up by their shipmates.

'Is all tight?' he called, and an unidentified voice answered in the affirmative. Someone was ordering everyone to go on deck. Even with the doors sealed, water was still cascading into the ship from somewhere, though he could not comprehend where or why. With his men pouring past him onto the quarter-deck, he headed up to the mess deck and aft to get down to the starboard engine room. There the steam engines still pounded away and the gongs of the telegraph reverberated above the roar. Deadman, the engineer, reported that all doors were closed and there was no water in the engine rooms.

'Is the Fleet Engineer here?' Bourke asked him.

'No, Sir. I don't know where he is.'

Running down the main passage to check on those doors, Bourke encountered Fleet Engineer Felix Foreman going aft, and received the reassuring news that, as far as he could make out, everything abaft the forward boiler room was watertight. On his way back to the admiral, Bourke met Heath and ordered him to assemble the men on the port side of the upper deck while he himself hurried forward again to return to the charthouse roof. As he neared the bridge he could see behind him that Heath must have actually anticipated the order: the men were already in their ranks.

With Bourke below, Hawkins-Smith had been left with the admiral.

'Should we steer to land sir?' he asked. They might be able to save the ship by running her up the beach.

'What water are we in?' asked Tryon.

'Deep water, up to 80 fathoms.'

'Yes. Go astern with the port engine, ahead with the starboard and point her clear of the *Nile*.'

In her desperate manoeuvre to avoid the stern of *Victoria*, the *Nile* had arrived ahead of her and stopped. As *Victoria* cleared the battleship in her path she went forward half speed.

'What speed sir?' said the commander.

'Full,' replied Tryon. 'Go to 7 knots.' The telegraphs clanged the instruction to the engine room.

Lieutenant Gillford was watching the activity among the rest of the ships.

'Sir, the *Dreadnought* is lowering boats.'

'Signal *annul sending boats*,' snapped Tryon.

HMS *Victoria* was moving forward very slowly, though her steam engines were pounding at her maximum 38 revolutions.

'Has the anchor gone?' Tryon was trying to understand what was dragging on the ship.

'No, sir, it is in its place. Not touched' replied the commander, then to the helmsman, 'Helm amidships.'

'I cannot move the helm sir, the pressure is off,' he replied, meaning that there was no steam pressure to work the helm.

'Ring down to the engine room and tell them to keep it on,' Hawkins-Smith ordered. Apart from the steering, they would need it to work the cranes and lifeboat davits.

Tryon was looking over the bridge rail and could see the water was over the foredeck and already washing up to the doors on the great turret. It was a hot day, and all the doors and shutters had been wide open to allow some move-ment of air below decks. Seeing the danger he shouted over the bridge rail 'Close those ports and scuttles.' But it was too late: the water was already rushing in through the entries, and the forecastle sank ever lower in the water. He could only sigh.

'I think she is going,' he told Hawkins-Smith calmly.

'Yes sir I think she is.'

The admiral looked back and saw Lanyon behind him, 'Do not stand there, youngster,' he snapped at the midshipman, 'go to a boat!'.

Delivered at the charthouse rail, that was his last order. Then, almost to himself, he said simply, 'It is all my fault.'

Without warning the ship listed violently and suddenly there was shouting all around.

Behind the two flagships the rest of the fleet, seeing the impending collision, had taken various avoiding actions and were now scattered in confusion around the sea. Captain Noel on HMS *Nile*, the next ship in line to the *Victoria*, had swung his ship around the flagship, narrowly missing her with his stern, and was now stopped ahead of her. He, as well as other captains, had sent out boats, ignoring Tryon's order not to. Noel signalled the *Victoria* that he would take her in tow, but there was no reply. He could see the water three feet deep around the great turret when 'she appeared to fall over to starboard, slowly at first but with increasing rapidity. As she went over the boats and weights on the port side fell to leeward with a terrible crash.'

He watched with horror as, less a minute later, the great ship nosedived into the depths, still under power from her turning screws.[3]

As that final lurch came, everyone remembered the crew formed up in four lines on the quarterdeck awaiting orders.

'Jump! Jump!' ordered Lieutenant Heath, and they broke and ran for the sides. Some who leapt from the stern were annihilated by the thrashing propellers; all plunged into the dreadful maelstrom created as the ship went down.

Gunner Frederick Johnson was one who climbed over the poop rail as the deck tipped away behind him. He staggered down the side of the ship, which continued turning under him until he was thrown back the way he had come to land feet first in the water by the rail he had just clambered over. Sucked down into the depths with the ship he was luckily a strong enough swimmer to fight back to the surface. There he found himself in a terrible circle of troubled water surrounded by around forty other men. The suction of the ship was still pulling at them, while the loose spars and pieces of buoyant equipment from the deck of the *Victoria* below were rising to the surface with the force of missiles, inflicting terrible injuries on any in their way. Johnson grasped at a drifting thwart and was dragged below again by the violent currents pulling water into the ship's vast empty spaces. The water around boiled with the froth from explosions in the deep as water met hot furnaces and boilers. He battled back to the light and crashed his head on some wreckage holding him under. Desperately he clawed free from it and gasped a breath of precious air. He could see many fewer men around him this time, and after a short breath he was sucked back under. Struggling to the surface for the third time he was at last hauled half-choked aboard the *Nile*'s cutter. There were just three or four men left in the water.

Hawkins-Smith was washed off the charthouse roof. He fought clear of the deadly canvas awning, but the suction carried him down. Above him loomed a dark shadow which he thought must be the ship. He struck away from it desperately and at last surfaced, exhausted, supporting himself with two oars until rescued by a boat from HMS *Dreadnought*. Safe in the boat, he checked his watch and saw that it had stopped at 3:44 p.m. Only 14 minutes before, the fleet had been steaming in two impressive columns; now the pride of the Royal Navy was scattered across the bay, and the flagship with Vice Admiral George Tryon and 357 of his 641 men were gone forever.[4] Many of the men lost were the stokers and engineers who were never told to abandon ship. They were all still below in the hell of fire and steam as HMS *Victoria* drove almost vertically and at full power into the mud 460 feet (140 metres) below.

Bourke had never regained the charthouse. He was still on the fore-and-aft bridge when the *Victoria* fell to starboard. Instinctively he clutched at the rail and was sucked down, but he was one of the fortunate ones who reached the surface and evaded the whirling wreckage of boats, spars and gratings blasted up to the surface, before being picked up by one of the *Nile*'s boats.

Tryon's order to Lanyon to go to a boat was not enough to save the boy's life[5], nor did Tryon seem to have attempted to save his own. He was popularly believed to have gone down holding the rail.[6] It was Hawkins-Smith who was with him at the end, and reported his last words. That did not stop some highly improbable legends. According to the *Illustrated London News*, tailoring its coverage to a readership anxious to find a few drops of comfort in a catastrophe that had shocked the nation to its heart:[7]

> The last that was seen of Admiral Tryon was a solitary figure on the bridge, telescope in hand, waving a final farewell to his colleague, Rear Admiral Markham, who from the deck of the *Camperdown*, witnessed the appalling calamity. It is said that a coxswain offered Sir George a lifebelt, and that the answer was 'save yourself'. That was the characteristic chivalry of the old sea dog, to whom his ship was dearer than his life. Every thought during those last terrible minutes were for others – none for himself.

If the story of the fakir's prophecy was not strange enough, at the moment the *Victoria* sank, Lady Tryon was in London hosting a reception at which several of her guests apparently remarked to her that they had just met her husband on the stairs but that he had not spoken to them.

Perhaps the luckiest man that day was the *Victoria*'s executive officer, Commander John Jellicoe, who was suffering in sick bay with a bout of Malta fever.[8] His incapacity relieved him of any liability for the events of the day, which might otherwise have tainted his career. Helped from sick bay by the surgeon, he was picked up from the water and survived to become the Admiral of the Fleet at the Battle of Jutland in 1916.[9]

Like every naval captain before or since who loses his ship and survives to tell the story, Maurice Bourke, as captain of HMS *Victoria*, was automatically court martialled. The Admiralty had moved swiftly to contain the mess and appointed a full admiral, Sir Michael Culme-Seymour, to command the Mediterranean station and conduct the court martial; he arrived there to begin the proceedings on 13 July, six weeks after the collision.

Public expectation assumed that the trial of Captain Bourke would be a precursor to the trials of other involved parties, notably Rear Admiral Markham and his flag captain, Charles Johnstone, but from the beginning Culme-Seymour seems to have had other ideas. His priority as commander-in-chief of the now demoralized Mediterranean Squadron was to get to sea again as soon as possible. The new commander was no fan of Tryon's methods and undoubtedly believed the fleet needed some discipline drilled back into it. There were very real perceived threats in that region, particularly the Russians and the French, who must not be allowed to see any weakness in Britannia's rule of this particular sea. From his point of view, a series of hearings lasting through the entire summer and autumn would be a disaster, and he believed that he had the Admiralty's backing to sort it out as quickly as possible.

Bourke's court martial convened on HMS *Hibernia* at Malta on 17 July, and, together with the reports to the Admiralty of individual officers, established the facts upon which the preceding reconstruction of the incident is based.

There was little room for doubt that Vice Admiral Tryon had made the mistake that led to the disaster. The most likely answer to how the mistake was made was put forward by a contemporary, Admiral Mark Kerr. In his later book, *The Navy in my Time*, he explained that half circles were rarely performed, and sailors more usually estimated the sea room required for 90-degree movements. Kerr also quoted an interview he had with an unnamed lieutenant who had been on the bridge of *Victoria*: 'The admiral told me himself that was the mistake he had made. I could not make up my mind what I would do if I was called as a witness, for we had all been told by Captain Bourke that we were to do everything to preserve Sir George's reputation.'

Kerr's explanation also supports evidence to the court martial given by Rear Admiral Vandermuilen, captain of HMS *Inflexible*, that Tryon had made a similar error previously in manoeuvres off Santorini, but had corrected the order before it was executed.

Bourke may have been the only person apart from Tryon himself to know what was in the Admiral's mind, because of that last conversation alone in Tryon's cabin. At the court martial he appeared very reticent to say anything that would reflect badly on his leader. After first begging permission of the court not to disclose anything of their conversation on the stern walk, even after close cross examination over two days all he had revealed was: 'I reminded the Admiral that our circle was 800 yards. He said the columns were to remain at six cables.'

The general view at the time was that Captain Bourke's reticence was the behaviour of a gentleman. The cross-examination, like the whole trial, had taken place in ferocious heat on the *Hibernia*'s deck, and proved a major ordeal even for such an assured man, yet a sometimes emotional Bourke found time to commend the conduct of the crew: 'I do not suppose there will be another opportunity of saying it, but I think it shows the wonderful command that everyone had over himself, that not one single man fell out to go to the ship's side. Just at the last, Lieutenant Heath gave the order "Jump".'

That the revered hero, Tryon, had made such an error was initially hard for anyone among his officers, the public or the establishment to stomach, but the conclusion was inescapable and fairly soon became accepted. What then became the major source of controversy at home was why, after the mistake was made, another admiral, two captains and various other officers seemed to have done little to correct it.

This may have been Bourke's court martial, but in his desire to 'make one job of this affair', Culme-Seymour widened the scope of the enquiry considerably. Thus, while Markham and Johnstone were not on trial, they gave evidence and were cross-examined upon their actions. Markham's basic contention was that he had received a direct order from his superior and could not disobey it. He assumed that his commander knew what he was doing, and, when quizzed as to what that might be, suggested that the *Victoria* might have been intending to pass outside *Camperdown* on the turn, in which case that was up to Tryon to do. To justify this he requested that the captains in his division should give evidence as to what they thought of Tryon's intentions, and indeed many of them were happy to agree with him. Captain Dyke-Ackland (HMS *Edgar*) thought 'he [Tryon] would have some plan I did not at that moment grasp', while Captain Moore (HMS *Dreadnought*) expected to 'see something unusual in the way of an evolution'. Rear Admiral Vandermuilen (HMS *Inflexible*) went further. He was 'much surprised' to see that the *Victoria* did not right her helm to avoid the collision and when asked why he thought *Victoria* should do this, rather than the *Camperdown,* replied that: 'the C in C made the signal and I thought that when he saw the ships closing he would see that there was not room for them to turn inwards and would take the initiative and pass round the outside of the Second Division.'

It was left for Captain Noel, who in private tended to be critical of Markham and especially of Johnstone, to point out to the enquiry that Markham could equally have turned to port to avoid the collision.

Captain Johnstone also came in for some uncomfortable questions about the efficiency of the *Camperdown*. The court found there had been delays in closing watertight doors, and in carrying out the order to go astern. *Camperdown* had been in serious trouble for a while after the collision. With her own bows badly damaged she was letting in water rapidly, and came close to foundering herself until divers managed to close her bulkhead doors.

Finally, however, the court found in Bourke's favour, which they were bound to do if they were not then to proceed to Johnstone and then, by implication, Markham. The court issued its findings, which were that the collision was due to an order given by Sir George Tryon, and that after the collision everything possible was done by the crew to save life. Accordingly no blame was attachable to Captain Bourke or to any other of the survivors of HMS *Victoria* for the loss of the ship; they had behaved in the best traditions of the service. The findings then addressed the *Camperdown*:

> The Court strongly feels that, although it is much to be regretted that Rear Admiral Albert H. Markham did not carry out his first intention of semaphoring

to the Commander-in-Chief his doubt as to the signal, it would be fatal to the best interests of the Service to say he was to blame for carrying out the directions of the Commander-in-Chief present in person.

Given the evidence presented at the enquiry this was fairly mild criticism of the rear admiral, but it wrapped everything up and Culme-Seymour could get on with more useful business.

Not everyone agreed. After some prompting by interested parties at home, the Admiralty issued a minute two months later, in October 1893, which increased the level of criticism of Markham. Concurring with the findings of the court cited above, it also pointed out that his belief that the commander-in-chief would circle round him was not justified and that he should have ordered reverse screws earlier, given that he distrusted the order he had been given. Furthermore, their lordships specifically criticized Captain Johnstone, who had not actually been mentioned in the court martial's conclusions. These minutes, or at least the views of the Admiralty behind them, meant that both officers' careers were effectively over. They remained in their posts into the following year, after which both left active service. When Markham, by then Sir Albert Markham, died in 1918, the obituary in the *Times* described him as 'the distinguished explorer and writer'.[10]

Condolences had of, course, poured in from the palaces and naval head-quarters of Europe and beyond, and there were understandable mutter-ings around the world about how this great new battleship could be sunk in accidental collision in less than 15 minutes. According to *Le Siècle*, the French minister instructed his naval attaché in London 'to convey his compliments and condolences and all his deep regret to the First Lord of the Admiralty on the occasion of the loss of the *Victoria* and the members of the crew who met their death in the disaster.' Another French newspaper, *Le Figaro*, while sym-pathetic, sounded a note of *schadenfreude* by reminding its readers that:

> Disasters like that of the *Victoria* are, alas, not as uncommon as may be thought; since 1863, there have been 11 of them, including the *Captain*, sunk off Cape Finistère with the loss of 472 sailors, and that of the training ship *Euralia* during a blizzard ... 318 cadets died in that wreck ... If we go back a century we find in 1782 the catastrophe of the *Royal George* at Spithead ...

The *Berliner Illustrierte Zeitung* devoted half a page to a dramatic illustration of the collision. 'National mourning reigns in Old-England', it told its readers. Only a cynic could doubt the sincerity of the international regret for the deaths, but the interest did not end there. The *Berliner Illustrierte Zeitung* pointed up exactly what the Admiralty knew all too well:

> The *Victoria* was among the youngest battleships in the English fleet ... Although
> the *Victoria* appeared to be proof against all the dangers of war and of the sea,
> thanks to the solidity of her construction, the power of her engines and her fear-
> some armament, she has fallen victim to a fatal and unpredictable accident. The
> ship which collided with her and caused her sinking, the battleship, *Camperdown*,
> is in every respect weaker than the *Victoria* was ...

The United States, which was not the military power it is today, found some
justification of its own strategy of building a number of smaller, cheaper ironclads with effective rams as their main weapon. The *New York Tribune* referred
back to the Battle of Lissa (1866, between Austria and Italy), the first large-
scale engagement involving ironclads[11], claiming it 'revealed the power of the
iron ram in modern warfare. The sinking of the shattered *Victoria* ... reveals the
helplessness of the modern battleship when the engines of modern offensive
warfare are brought to bear upon her.' This was not as far-fetched as it may
seem. Though the *Victoria* mounted mighty 16-inch guns, they were still muz-
zle-loading and very slow to operate.[12] In fact, secret tests by the Admiralty discovered that the accuracy of the main armament on these big ships was very
poor at anything other than close range. If they fired and missed, a smaller,
faster opponent could have four minutes or more to close the distance and ram
before the crew could reload.

At home, the *Illustrated London News* published an article by Sir Edward
Reed, MP, laying the blame for the sinking on the insufficiency of armour:

> The *Victoria*'s armour was not touched by the *Camperdown*; the unarmoured end
> only was badly injured. Thus again, clear and public warnings have been disas-
> trously disregarded. It is not a question of subdivision by bulkheads ... The sin has
> lain in the gross disproportion of the unarmoured to the armoured portion of the
> ship ... The enemy has only to badly injure the unarmoured part in order to
> deprive the whole ship of its power to float upright.

Clearly such speculation, whether at home or abroad, was dangerous to the
Royal Navy, continually alert for potential challenges from France and Russia
and, grave though the human element of the disaster had been, the Admiralty
was more concerned by the implications of the sinking for the design of the
ship itself. The Admiralty's controller of construction was asked to produce a
report, the purpose of which was quite clearly to lay these fears to rest. It did
indeed do that for the world at large, concluding that the blame for the sinking
lay with the way the ships were handled and the failure to have more watertight
doors closed. Far better to state categorically that human error rather than
naval design was the problem. Secretly though, the Admiralty and the government were very concerned. Over the next few years expenditure on the navy

grew, and within a dozen years of the disaster, with the launch of a new HMS *Dreadnought*, every other battleship in the world became obsolete.

The conclusions of the report in respect of the watertight doors had a major impact on subsequent ship design, directly inspiring Deptford-based engineers J Stone & Co. to invent what the frontispiece of their brochure in 1904 described as the 'Stone Lloyd Hydraulically Controlled Marine Safety Bulkhead Doors Rendering Vessels Unsinkable'. Note that the word 'unsinkable' is not qualified by 'almost', 'practically' or any other adverb – though it is in the body of the text that describes the system. The same word had appeared a year earlier, in an advertisement-feature in the *Illustrated London News*. In the title of an updated version of the brochure two years later, however, Stone & Co discreetly inserted the word 'practically' before 'unsinkable'.

The system took its name not just from Stones but from the German shipping company, Norddeutscher Lloyd (NDL), who trialled the prototypes on their prestigious liners and who shared the patent. It allowed every bulkhead door to be simultaneously closed and opened by a single switch located on the bridge as soon as danger was suspected or encountered. Individual doors could also be activated from the bridge, and a manual override allowed men trapped in sealed compartments to escape. If for any reason an officer failed to activate the system, 'the inrush of water into the damaged part of the vessel would at once cause a flat to rise which would automatically operate a valve in connection with the bulkhead doors in the vicinity of same. After a door has been closed by this action it cannot be operated from the bridge until the compartment has been cleared of water, but the door can be opened by hand from either side of the bulkhead.' In effect, a ship with one, perhaps more, flooded compartments could remain afloat because water could no longer flow through the ship.

There were four types of door: Vertical Sliding, Simultaneous Cam Action, Horizontal Sliding (Admiralty Pattern) and, most ingeniously, the Isaac's Patent Cleaving Action Bulkhead Door. This asymmetrical door swung flush to the bulkhead, and as it moved into position it swept away coal or other obstructions.

In 1902 NDL resolved to have the system installed on all doors below the water line on all its vessels, and by 1904 it had been fitted to Hamburg Amerika Line's *Deutschland*. The Holyhead–Dublin ferry *Scotia* appears to have been the first British passenger ship to be likewise equipped, although Cunard claimed that honour for the *Caronia*. Stone Lloyd was a major contribution to safety, but as events were to prove, there was still no such thing as an unsinkable ship.

Sources and Bibliography

The standard work on the disaster is Hough's very readable and succinct study. Gordon also deals with the affair in considerable detail in his monumental study of British naval policy in the run-up to the Battle of Jutland.

National Archives
ADM 1/7171
ADM 1/7172
ADM 1/7173
ADM13/204 (proceedings of the court martial and report of the controller of construction)

National Maritime Museum, the Noel papers

Gordon, Andrew, *The Rules of the Game: Jutland and the British Naval Command* (London: John Murray, 1996)
Hough, Richard, *Admirals in Collision* (London: Hamish Hamilton, 1959).
Stone, J & Co, *The Stone-Lloyd System of Hydraulically-Controlled Marine Safety Bulkhead Doors* (London, 1904).

Berliner Illustrierte Zeitung
Le Figaro
Illustrated London News, 7 November 1904
New York Tribune
Le Siècle
The Times

Notes

1 Possibly apocryphal, this story apparently gained currency in the fleet after the event.
2 The collision mat was a refinement of the fothered sail: a piece of stout canvas, threaded with oakum, which was kept ready for an emergency, particularly on vessels that had dispensed with sails.
3 In 2004 two divers discovered the *Victoria* intact, with her bow and about a quarter of her length buried in the sea bottom. Currently she is the world's only known vertical wreck.
4 A memorial, including the names of all who died, stands in Portsmouth's Victoria Park.
5 The *Illustrated London News* claimed that Lanyon had chosen to stay by Tryon to the end. If there is any truth in that story it would make the 16-year-old the only person on the ship who dared to disobey the admiral that day.
6 Tryon's death was parodied in the 1949 film *Kind Hearts and Coronets*, when one of the characters played by Alec Guinness, Admiral d'Ascoyne, also causes a collision and goes down with his ship, saluting to the very last.
7 A poem, *The Loss of the Victoria* , from which the following verse should be sufficient, was composed by William McGonagall, whose lasting fame rests entirely upon commemorative poetry of unparalleled awfulness (most famously 'The Tay Bridge Disaster').

> *The* Victoria *was the flagship of the Mediterranean Fleet,*
> *And was struck by the* Camperdown *when too close they did meet,*
> *While practising the naval and useful art of war,*
> *How to wheel and discharge their shot at the enemy afar.*

8 Now known as brucellosis, 'Malta fever' was caught by drinking tainted goats milk, often while in port at Malta.
9 Strangely, a little after Jellicoe was picked up, a boat from the *Dreadnought* chanced across a chest containing his clothes.
10 Of the remaining principal characters, Maurice Bourke, heir presumptive to the Earldom of Mayo, died just seven years later of TB; Gillford was only 37 when he died in 1905.
11 Four years earlier, during the American Civil War, the ironclads *Monitor* and *Merrimack* had engaged one another at Hampton Roads.
12 The day of breech-loading artillery was coming – they were present on Royal Navy ships even before the *Victoria*.

10

Spanish Tragedy

Sirio

1906

But striking a shoal, they ran the vessel aground;

the bow stuck and remained immovable, and the stern

was broken up by the surf.

ACTS OF THE APOSTLES, 27: 41

M OST DRAMAS PRODUCE A HERO OR HEROINE at whom we clutch in order to restore our faith in mankind. Even when there is no obvious example of conspicuous courage, the ones who did their duty when others failed are cited as an example to the rest of us. The discipline of the sailors on HMS *Victoria* was just about the only crumb of comfort that the public could take from the loss of the mighty flagship and its hitherto-infallible admiral. It proved to be a very nourishing crumb, and it came to the mind of a Spanish naval engineer 13 years later when confronted by a drama off his own coastline – one that also produced precisely the kind of gallant hero beloved of the public.

Over the past half century, European nations have absorbed millions of immigrants, but for the preceding century the traffic – with all its connotations – used to be largely in the other direction. The poor, the persecuted and the disadvantaged left Europe in increasing numbers, some with their eyes open,

Dramatis Personae

José Acosta : keeper of the Hormigas lighthouse
Ángelo Amézaga : first officer
Agustin Antolino : captain of the *Vicente Lacomba*
Juan Bautisto Buigués : captain of the *Joven Vicente*
Vicente Buigués Ferrando : captain of the *Joven Miguel*
José Camargo de Barros : passenger
Rosa Bianchi : passenger
Amelia Camotti : passenger
Ernesta Camotti : passenger
Giovanni Camotti Sr : passenger
Giovanni Camotti Jr : passenger
Zulma Camotti : passenger
Monsieur J Colomer : captain of the *Marie-Louise*
Roberto Eberno : passenger
Ángela Ferrara : passenger
Elisa Ferrara : passenger
Eduardo França : passenger
Julia França : passenger
Martín Hailze : passenger
Mariano Hermoso : passenger
Luigi Lepori : passenger
Pedro Llorca : captain of the *Nuestra Señora de Los Angeles*
Constantino Mainetto : passenger
José Manzanares : captain of the *Francisca*
José Marcondes Homem de Mello : passenger

some out of despair, others lured by propaganda. Lack of affordable land, insecure tenure, poor harvests, compulsory military service in many countries, unemployment, discrimination against the poor, high rents, low wages: all were powerful factors in driving people out. Land in North America, South America and Australia was cheap; when the United States, which needed unskilled labour for its rapid industrialization, begged Europe to send her its poor and huddled masses, Europe responded generously. Those who had emigrated and found jobs in the cities or bought cheap grants of fertile land sent home letters,

Giovanni Marengo : passenger

José Maristany : passenger

Maria Maristany : passenger

José Martinez : captain of the *Cristo*

Juan Martinez : captain of the *San José*

Dolores ('Lola') Millanes : passenger

Brigida Morelli : passenger

Giovanni Morelli : passenger

Boniface Natter : passenger

Giuseppe Piccone : captain of the *Sirio*

Leopold Politzer : passenger

Filomena Scaglia : passenger

Amalia Serafini : passenger

Felice Serafini : passenger

Giuseppe Serafini : passenger

Isidoro Serafini : passenger

Ottavio Serafini : passenger

Umberto Serafini : passenger

Gaetano Tarantino : third officer

Flaminio Turbino : passenger

Francisca Turbino : passenger

Pasqual Turbino : passenger

Emilia Tursia : passenger

Signor Tursia : passenger

Manuel Vinhietta : passenger

Anscar Vonier : passenger

which inspired others to follow them; those who had done less well were often too proud to report their failure. European governments looked favourably on this exodus of the most needy, because it ameliorated a growing social problem. Emigration agents published handbooks that would never have passed the scrutiny of a modern Advertising Standards Authority, but that easily seduced potential emigrants.

Although the most popular destination by far was the United States, South America, in particular Brazil and Argentina, found favour with the Italians,

Spanish and Portuguese, the last two having strong colonial links to the continent. Italians found the language and culture more akin to their own, and they counted for almost half of the immigrants settling in Argentina between 1857 and 1924.

There were darker sides to this emigration.

The slave trade had been abolished in Brazil, but the work still had to be done, and Italian emigrants were the new victims of the rich planters. They readily seized the chance of a free passage for themselves and, most importantly, their families, but in so doing they unwittingly sold themselves into virtual slavery. Once in Brazil they could find themselves treated no better than the darker-skinned slaves they replaced, and were just as much prisoners because, as the planters had calculated, they could not afford to repatriate whole families.

Furthermore, many would-be-emigrants could not afford the price of a third-class ticket, so captains – whose employers may have been running a legal business – were not above making illicit stops to receive such clandestine emigrants in return for cash-in-hand payments. Whether emigration was legal, official or not, close-knit families were broken, often forever, as young people deserted the villages and cities. Many men travelled alone, their object being to send money home; others took their wives and young children, leaving elderly parents behind. Either way, the parting was hard, and for those who waved their relatives goodbye the risks were all too apparent. It formed the subject of many a popular song. 'Mamma mia dammi cento lire' tells the story of a girl who begs to be allowed to start a new life. Her brothers want her to go because there will be one less mouth to feed but her mother vainly attempts to frighten her into changing her mind...

Mamma mia dammi cento lire	'Mother, give me 100 lire
che in America voglio andar ...!	because I want to go to America.'
Cento lire io te li dò,	'I will give you 100 lire
ma in America no, no, no. (× 2)	but don't go to America, no, no.' (× 2)
I suoi fratelli alla finestra,	Her brothers at the window say:
mamma mia lassela andar.	'Mother, let her go.'
Vai, vai pure o figlia ingrata	'Go if you like, ungrateful girl,
che qualcosa succederà. (× 2 etc.)	but something nasty will happen to you.'
	(× 2 etc.)
Quando furono in mezzo al mare	'When it reaches the middle of the ocean
il bastimento si sprofondò.	The ship will sink.
Pescatore che peschi i pesci	The fisherman who trawl for fish
la mia figlia vai tu a pescar.	Will catch you, my daughter.'
Il mio sangue è rosso e fino,	'My blood is red and fine

i pesci del mare lo beveran.	The fish in the sea will drink it.
La mia carne è bianca e pura	My flesh is white and pure;
la balena la mangierà.	The whale will eat it.'
Il consiglio della mia mamma	My mother's advice
l'era tutta verità.	Proved all too correct,
Mentre quello dei miei fratelli	While that of my brothers
l'è stà quello che m'ha ingannà.	Served to deceive me.

All emigrants faced the same dangers: bad weather, unseaworthy vessels, fire, collision and the outbreak of diseases. The loss of ships such as the *Arctic*, *Cospatrick*, *Kapunda*, *Norge* and *Utopia* ended the dreams of many hundreds. One of the most shocking occurred in 1906. The ship at the centre, the *Sirio*, would later become known as 'the *Titanic* of the Mediterranean' or, with bitterness, 'the poor man's *Titanic*'.

They came from all over Italy in their hundreds, possessions stuffed into battered suitcases, arms clutching bedding, many with a staircase of children in tow and tickets clenched between their teeth. Unable to afford a hotel after leaving the train at Genoa, most had spent the night on the warm streets, arriving at the wharf crumpled and dishevelled, parents short-tempered in their weariness and anxiety, children fractious or bewildered. Among the huge crowd queuing at the terminal beneath the hot August sun, Pasqual and Francisca Turbino kept an eye on their young son, Flaminio, as he took the family dog for a last walk on Italian soil; Signor Tursia rocked two-year-old Emilia in his arms. Giovanni Marengo, 29, from Pinerolo, rested his accordion on his baggage. A few days earlier, before leaving Arzignano, the Serafini family had posed in their best clothes for the photograph that would be a last reminder of them to their friends and family. Felice, 43, stood erect with a hand on the shoulder of his wife Amalia who was expecting their ninth child. Around them grouped five sons and three daughters, from 14-year-old Umberto to two-year-old Giuseppe, the four older boys dressed exactly as their father; their sisters and youngest brother in long, patterned cotton dresses.

All were leaving a rural Italy that was the very antithesis of the rustic idyll pedalled to the tourist, a countryside in which many extended families shared a single gloomy room with their animals, where proper sanitation was non-existent, serious diseases such as typhoid were routine and there was little education to offer an escape to the next generation. In the decade before 1900, some 330,000 out of Italy's average annual death-toll of 760,000 comprised children under 15. Full of hope and trepidation, often believing that one day they would return, bringing prosperity with them, the crowd waited for their turn to board the liner whose gangplank was to be the magic bridge to a new world and a new life.

The *Sirio* was a handsome ship; the clean lines of her white hull and the rake of her three masts and two funnels promised a fast, safe and comfortable voyage. She had been built for the trade in 1883 by the Glasgow yard of Robert Napier and Sons, and was a far cry from the *San Francisco*, let alone the *Rothsay Castle*. She had an iron hull and a single screw propeller, and in her early days her beauty had attracted envy and admiration. Nevertheless, new regulations, which should have been in force in Italy in 1906, the year of the voyage, but which had been delayed by the protests of influential vested interests, would have restricted emigrant ships to those with double bottoms and watertight bulkheads. *Sirio* had neither. At 4141 tons and 380 feet (115 metres) long she was much smaller than the modern liners, but with 135 emigrant voyages behind her she had become a regular part of the scenery in her home port.

Much the same could have been said of her Master. Giuseppe Piccone, the most senior captain in the Navigazione Generale Italiana (NGI), had been at sea for 46 of his 68 years, and spent a quarter of a century with NGI shuttling between Genoa and Latin America with only one significant mishap – the loss, under his command, of the *Perseo*. This voyage was likely to be a poignant one; on his return he was going to 'swallow the anchor' – retreat to dry land and retire. He had captained the *Sirio* when she was brand new, and again after she had been modernized in 1891 to keep pace with the newcomers. The shipping lines and shipbuilders had been the big winners in the lottery of life.

Gradually the ship filled up, but not completely: she was to call at Spanish ports, too. The third class, almost all emigrants, went down into large dormitories. There, sanitation was limited, the air would soon grow foul and, with inadequate ventilation and little personal hygiene, diseases such as cholera could easily break out among people living so closely together. But the ship's owners – and they were far from exceptional – had little interest in the welfare of those who were not in a position to complain. It was a different story for second or first class passengers. Among the 13 or so who booked the luxurious and newly decorated first-class accommodation were three influential churchmen. The German-born Father Anscar Vonier from Buckfast Abbey in England had been teaching in Rome for a couple of years and now, at the invitation of a friend and mentor, was travelling to Argentina before returning to Buckfast. The Bishop of São Paulo, Monsignor José Camargo de Barros, had also been in Rome, on diocesan business with his secretary, Manuel Vinhietta, while Monsignor José Marcondes Homem de Mello was returning to Brazil after his elevation to Archbishop of Pará. Dr. Eduardo França, another Brazilian, had brought his wife, Julia, and teenage daughter to Italy while he was exhibiting at the Milan Fair. For young newlyweds Giovanni and Brigida Morelli, the voyage was to be their honeymoon.

Something like 25 travelled second-class, including the whole Camotti family: Giovanni, 52, his wife Ernesta, 38, and three children: Amelia, a strikingly beautiful 16-year-old, Zulma, 14, and Giovanni, 12. The father originally came from Rivarolo; the children had been born in Argentina, so the family were probably on their way home after visiting relatives in Liguria.

For the irrepressible Luigi Lepori, a 17-year-old Florentine, this was to be a special test. He had just passed the entrance examination for Livorno's prestigious Naval Institute, and his father thought it would be a good idea if he went to sea before taking up his studies. Better to find out in advance whether life on the ocean waves was going to suit him.

Leaving Genoa on 2 August, bound for Spanish ports and Las Palmas before the voyage to Cabo Verde, Rio de Janeiro, Santos and Buenos Aires the *Sirio* reached Barcelona the following day. She took on a further group of emigrants, including a family from Olesa de Montserrat who were pulling up their roots and leaving only an elderly grandmother behind. Father Vonier welcomed the old friend from Buckfast, Abbot Boniface Natter, who years earlier had convinced him of his priestly vocation, and in whose company he would travel in Argentina.[1] The lounges were also enlivened by the arrival of three celebrities, all musicians: the conductor and impresario Mariano Hermoso; the popular Catalan tenor José Maristany, now resident in Argentina, who was returning home with his sister, Maria, to get married, and even bringing his bride's gown with him; and the soprano, Dolores ('Lola') Millanes, famous in Spain and Buenos Aires for singing light and comic roles in zarzuelas, a Spanish form of opera. An imposing woman, Miss Millanes came in the style of a true diva, with trunks full of gowns, gorgeous shawls, embroidered linen, lace and personal memorabilia. Yet she, like Maristany, appears to have travelled second class. Both were looking forward to the imminent opening of Buenos Aires's new opera house, the Teatro de la Avenida. Another Catalan musician also boarded at Barcelona, Roberto Eberno, who directed the Sociedad Barcelonesa de Conciertos.

It was not a long stop; by evening the *Sirio* had left for Cádiz, her final port of call before Rio – her final official port, at all events. In fact she almost certainly paused around the mouth of the Júcar River near Alcira, Valencia, in the darkness, and maybe several other places along Spain's Mediterranean coast. A rendezvous with a small boat or two, the clandestine payment of 100 pesetas per head that the ship's owners would never see, and a dozen or two extras could be secreted into the less-frequented parts of the hold. Nobody ever knew exactly how many people travelled on the *Sirio*. As in the case of the *Rothsay Castle*, official figures, in so far as they exist, are meaningless: apart from the illegals, there were many small children and babies who did not require tickets. Estimates, including a figure of 120 or 127 for her crew, aver-age out at a complement of just over 1000, made up of various nationalities.

Saturday 4 August was hot, still, lethargic weather, with the sea intensely blue and the sky just paling a little towards the horizon. As the afternoon wore on, many of the emigrants packed the weather deck to get some air in the shade of canvas awnings rigged up by the crew. In one of the salons, Constantino Mainetto from Genoa decided he fancied a glass of lemonade; Lola Millanes and Mariano Hermoso sat in his cabin, discussing her forthcoming work in Buenos Aires; the Morellis kept to the shade of their cabin; and in another, Martín Hailze and his friends – all Argentinean students – wrote cards. By the stern rail Father Vonier and Abbot Natter were in conversation with a group of fellow passengers. The sun hung low in a flaming inferno as the *Sirio* neared Cartagena.

Stopping to pick up illicit passengers had left the ship behind schedule. Captain Piccone was supposed to be sailing from Cádiz the following day. The *Sirio* was going at a good 15 knots – some estimated it was closer to 17 – in an attempt to make up speed, and steaming parallel to the coast at a distance of just 3 miles (5.5 kilometres). To starboard ran the bar of La Manga, enclosing the Mar Menor, a huge lagoon; ahead, on the low cliff, the lighthouse of Cabo de Palos stood sentinel, its light rising 266 feet (81 metres) above the sea, and off the headland lay an undersea graveyard for ships stretching back to classical times.

The Hormigas islets, in effect an extension of Cabo de Palos, reached out to sea in a scattering of reefs resembling the line of ants after which they were named. Some were dry and formed islands, others were uncovered at low tide. The depths between them varied. There was a channel, some 80 feet (25 metres) deep, that could be navigated with care, but many ships failed the test, and a stumpy lighthouse had been built on the Isla de Las Hormigas as a fur-ther warning to ships to keep well out. Less than 4900 feet (1500 metres), at a bearing of 55° from the lighthouse, lurked the outermost shoal, the Bajo de Fuera, a treacherous peak rising 230 feet (70 metres) from the seabed to with-in 10 feet (3 metres) of the surface.

These were busy waters. The French-registered *Marie-Louise* was bound from Alicante for Oran; there were two other steamers in the vicinity, the French *Poitien* and the Italian *Umbria*, while the local fishing fleet lay on the beach at Cabo de Palos along with holidaymakers and locals. The little two-masted schooner, *Joven Miguel*, was at sea, though her captain was more partial to *smoked* fish: much of his income derived from tobacco smuggling. Vicente Buigués Ferrando had settled at Cabo de Palos in 1885 as a 25-year-old newlywed, having abandoned his malarial birthplace of Moraira in the hope of restoring his health. The move had paid off, and he had fulfilled his desire to go to sea. To a man of his enterprising character and strong nerve, the risks of running contraband tobacco from Oran were acceptable.

From his felucca, the *Joven Vicente*, his fisherman-cousin, Juan Bautisto Buigués, observed the *Sirio* in some amazement.

'She is steering a very strange course,' he remarked. 'Her captain is either an idiot or a superb mariner.'

The *Sirio* had a perfect safety record; Piccone, who was on the bridge and standing beside the officer of the watch, knew the route like the back of his hand; and the area was well charted. But for all that, the *Sirio* carried no charts – just the route map – the captain had chosen a course that was much closer than normal to the coast, and the engines were working overtime. It was a little after 4 p.m.

Quite who was in charge of the ship at that moment is hard to say. It seems to be accepted that it was the third officer, Gaetano Tarantino; later, Piccone gave the impression that it was the first officer, Ángelo Amézaga. Either way, the captain was on the bridge at the time, at his officer's side. From a few miles away, Captain J. Colomer of the *Marie-Louise* had just doubled Cabo de Palos after leaving Cartagena when he 'perceived the Italian steamer, *Sirio*, crossing our course under full steam. I was pointing out the *Sirio* to a shipmate on deck, when I saw that she had suddenly stopped. In surprise I turned my telescope on her, feeling sure that something had happened ...'

She had piled right onto the Bajo de Fuera, and with such violence that her whole keel had been torn off before she came to a shuddering halt. Nobody in the cargo hold or the engine room who survived the impact stood a chance as the water surged in, sending columns of steam through the buckling, cracking deck.

It had all happened without warning, in an ear-splitting crash. Both down in the humid dormitories and higher up in the saloons, people were thrown from their chairs. Those on deck lost their footing; others clutched frantically at the rails, bruising themselves on seats and corners. Julia França and her parents were standing at the bows and thrown back. Ink splattered the wall of Hailze's first class cabin; the pen flew from his hand. Even through the pain he understood that the ship had struck; his friends dragged him onto the deck and into a scene of panic. Joining the rush came the Morellis, clutching the only lifebelt they could find. In the saloon, Mainetto, who had just handed over two lire for his lemonade, thought 'earthquake!', then told himself – wrongly – that earthquakes did not happen at sea. Abandoning his drink, but with enough presence of mind to snatch up his change, he hurried up onto the deck.

The helpless ship was held fast, sloping back into the water. Father Vonier made his way to the bows to see what assistance he could give to the screaming people there – people unused to the sea. Many of them tried to hold onto their numerous bruised and frightened children, while others were struggling to make contact with friends or family in the confusion. Their cries were suddenly lost in a savage explosion as the boilers blew up in clouds of steam and a great eruption of water, lifting the stern until the deck was almost level. Then, as if the ship were a see-saw, the stern slowly went down again until the aft end was submerged, pulling the *Sirio* into a 35° list to starboard.

Passengers drowned in the first class cabins and rooms, which were all at the stern. Terrified, Lola Millanes was begging Hermoso to give her his pistol so she could shoot herself rather than wait for the inevitable end. Her screams were heard, but water was engulfing that part of the ship. Abbott Natter was plunged into the sea. Others like Mainetto were blown from the deck by the force of the explosion. Holding onto to one another, Giovanni and Brigida jumped overboard, clutching the precious lifebelt.

All who had been on deck, or who made it there after the collision, stampeded towards the bows, away from the water. They were frantic for a lifeboat, but even if there had been a place for everyone – and there was not – the angle at which the ship lay precluded launching many of them. The aft boats were underwater; the port boats hung inwards over the deck. Those that remained accessible were rushed, with people fighting one another in the scramble for a place, throwing their children ahead of them or dragging them up over the gunwale. Ignorant of how to perform a launch, crewmen at the ropes let one boat fall. It crashed into the sea, overturning on everyone in it; just two women struggled to the surface. A second boat was launched, only to sink because it was so heavily overloaded. Whole families were pushed into the sea by the rush forwards; parents who could not swim themselves battled to keep their children afloat. Water-soaked petticoats dragged women down; Men and women fought over lifebelts with teeth, nails, fists and even knives. There was no chivalry here, no women and children first. A shocked Hailze saw a big burly man grappling with a beautiful teenage girl, seizing the lifebelt from her and leaving her to save herself if she could. Elsewhere on the deck Camargo and Marcondes, the bishops of São Paulo and Pará, dispensed absolution to a group of monks and passengers kneeling around them. In the water, powerful men robbed women of their lifebelts, hitting them with their fists until they released their hold. Shots were fired in the struggle; an eyewitness saw one man commit suicide after kissing a letter.

Giovanni Morelli fought to stay afloat. The waves around the ship were rough, threatening to overwhelm him and his bride. The lifebelt could not keep the two of them afloat for much longer, but, on her own, Brigida would have a better chance. He let go, and the sea pulled her from him.

With a shock, Brigida realized he was missing. She raised her head, and saw him a short distance away. He raised a hand, waving to her, and he was smiling encouragingly. Then he turned and swam away in the opposite direction.

What of the crew in this crisis? An early report applauded their devotion to duty. Telegrams reaching Buenos Aires and Italy, by an unknown author – probably a journalist – stated:

> The steamer *Sirio* was on its 135th voyage to the port of Buenos Aires, commanded from the first by Mr Giuseppe Piccone, a seaman of well-known ability and experience, and a worthy and educated man who deserves praise from all who know him … Captain Piccone shot himself while travelling in a boat occupied by numerous survivors which was heading for the shore. The calm displayed by the officers has attracted much praise … unlike the conduct of certain passengers who to save themselves pushed aside women and children … This same captain Piccone, while directing the rescue operations, was ready to kill two seamen of the crew who were attempting to save themselves before the passengers. The captain kept his courage and … calm until the last moment, killing himself when all was lost and it was pointless to carry on the work and effort.

The truth turned out to be horribly different. Early in the disaster one lifeboat did get away safely; it contained Captain Piccone and all but one of the officers,[2] and it was widely believed that the contents of the safe went with them. There proved to be no foundation in another rumour, that the officers or crew had physically forced Piccone off the ship against his will – and, as it would turn out, he was still very much alive. Hundreds of terrified, screaming passengers had been abandoned, left to their fate. Let down by their own leaders, more junior members of the crew even took off their uniforms in order to evade their duty and get away at the first opportunity.

The moment Captain Colomer of the *Marie Louise* realized the ship was lost he sent a boat to pick up survivors in the water. One of them was Brigida Morelli. A second vessel on the scene, the *Poitien,* decided that the water was too shallow for her to risk involvement. The fishermen of Cabo de Palos who had seen the disaster with their own eyes were getting their crews together: the *Vicente Lacamba, Pepe y Hermanos, San José, Cristo* … ; the *Joven Miguel* was changing course. The sight of approaching help was too much for many on board, who leapt into the water, even without lifebelts, and began to swim towards their rescuers.

There was no need for anyone to jump: the *Sirio* was not about to founder, because she had not only struck the Bajo de Fuera, but been impaled on it. A good crew could have reassured passengers or issued the lifebelts and, in concert with the rescue vessels, either instructed passengers when to jump so they could be pulled out efficiently, or assisted with transferring them directly to the smaller ships. As it was, nobody had any confidence in the *Sirio*'s crew.

As Bishop Camargo completed a blessing, the listing ship sank lower; water swirled in, sweeping more passengers from the deck. His duty done, he launched himself into the sea. In the fall, his grip on his lifebelt relaxed; the ring landed a little way from him.

Unable to swim and believing the ship was going to slip right off the rocks and sink, Hailze stared at this floating promise of life. The young man who had watched appalled as a man fought a girl for her lifebelt, suddenly found himself thinking that he was young, while the bishop had accomplished his mission in life ... He took his chance. Leaping in, he grabbed hold of it, feeling the blissful sensation of buoyancy holding him above the water. The hull of a ship, a fishing vessel, was coming up: he was to be saved, but left to his remorse at having snatched another man's life-saving aid. Later he would learn that Monsignor Camargo's body had been washed up on the Algerian coast a fortnight after the disaster.

The French boat arrived among the survivors first and pulled out 29, including an Arab man who knew nothing of what had become of his large family, and a desperate Italian father. She took them back to the *Marie-Louise* which, to the dismay of those in the water, and those watching from the *Sirio*, then headed back to Cartagena. It was an inexplicable decision when she could have sent the boat back for many more, but at least the fishermen were arriving.

Mainetto could swim, and even without a lifebelt managed to keep himself afloat. He could see boats around, but they seemed more concerned with those in imminent danger of drowning. He kept going for as long as he could, then, as his strength ebbed he started to shout as loudly as he was able. To his inexpressible relief, he saw one of the craft moving in his direction. He had been spotted in time.

Luigi Lepori, who had been forward at the moment of impact, had been knocked off his feet, but he picked himself up, initially curious rather than afraid. Then it dawned on him that there had been a major accident. Reaching the deck he was aware of people screaming and running around, and a confusion of heads, arms and lifebelts in the sea.

'I saw it all in flash. Intuitively I understood the terrible danger and all I could think about was saving myself. Is the survival instinct stronger than reason? ... I had the idea that if I were naked it would be easier to save myself. Hastily I tore off my clothes, grabbed the first rope that came to hand, let myself down into the water and swam strongly towards a boat which picked me up and took me to shore.'

More water was flooding the *Sirio*; fear was at fever pitch. The *Joven Miguel*, with the long, angled bowsprit that gave her sleek hull the look of a marlin, arrived and managed to lay herself parallel to the liner while Vicente Buigués and his crew of four – all related in some way to himself – took stock. Shouts and cries for help pierced their ears; men and women gestured imploringly. Every moment another person was jumping or diving into the sea, some swimming, others floundering towards them. Somewhere, clinging to a piece of wood, the Turbino family were trying to save not only themselves but the beloved family pet.

Despite the reservations of his own crew, Vicente ordered the boat to be launched, and navigated it himself into the struggling mass. The result was predictable: dozens of hands reached up, grabbing for their lives, deaf to calls to be calm and not swamp the craft. As the boat was pulled over, Vicente pitched into the water and had to swim back to the *Joven Miguel*. He thought quickly. The little boat was floating capsized, so those clinging around it would be safe holding on until more assistance arrived. It was the frightened and despairing passengers still aboard who needed immediate help.

With infinite care he brought the schooner closer until she was partially aboard the *Sirio*, her bowsprit all but wedged between the bridge and deck of the bigger vessel. Her fate was now anchored to that of the *Sirio*. If the liner slipped from the rocks, she would take the schooner with her. For now the bowsprit formed a narrow and constantly rocking bridge to safety along which men crawled. Few women dared to attempt it; they and the children had to be passed one by one.

People already in the water swam to the side and were hauled up on ropes; others, still on the liner, jumped for the deck. Some grabbed hold of the side of the schooner and were dragged aboard but the constant movement of the vessel made it dangerous to approach so closely, and a few who took that risk were crushed between the *Sirio*'s deck and the *Joven Miguel*'s bows. The captain required all his authority to dissuade them. The same movement caused one of the bowsprit stays to chafe against the liner's superstructure. It parted, and the sudden release of tension cracked it across the bows of the *Sirio* like a whip, injuring everyone in its path.

The *Sirio* gave an ominous shiver as if about to settle deeper. The crew of the *Joven Miguel*, nerves taut with apprehension, begged Vicente to disengage. The story goes – it was even repeated in the British press – that he pulled out his revolver:

'While there is a single person left to be saved,' he asserted, 'we do not move from here!'

The perilous evacuation across the bowsprit continued; the *Sirio* remained fast on the rocks. Exactly how many owed their lives to Vicente Buigués is conjectural. Some estimates put it as high as 300. When those who had reached the safety of the fishing vessel refused to go below because they were too afraid, the revolver appeared again so that they would obey and make room for more survivors.

Other fishing vessels were hauling in their unlikely human catch. Agustin Antolino's *Vicente Lacomba* had arrived at the same time as the *Joven Miguel*, and was credited with saving 132. One of them was Eduardo França, utterly distraught at having lost his wife and daughter. Vicente's cousin, Bautisto Buigués, saved 14 in the little felucca *Joven Vicente*, among them the Archbishop of Pará and Roberto Eberno. In the course of that afternoon and evening José Martinez picked up 15 in the *Cristo*, while Juan Martinez came ashore with 20 survivors in the *San José*. The *Pepe Y Hermanos* accounted for 30, Pedro Llorca's *Nuestra Señora de Los Angeles* for 13, and José Manzanares brought 8 home in the *Francisca*. José Acosta and his assistant, who kept the Hormigas lighthouse, took care of those who managed to float or swim to the island, or who were temporarily disembarked there by fishermen making room for more rescue work.

As soon as the sun set – around two and a half hours after the disaster – the wind rose, and to navigate sailing vessels around the shoals, and through waters in which exhausted men and women floated helplessly in lifebelts, was no simple matter in the conditions.

There were some unlikely survivors: a man who saved his quadriplegic wife by swimming with her on his shoulders until he was found; 75-old Filomena Scaglia and her grandson; all five of the Camotti family, and two-year-old Emilia Tursia, whose unhappy face, wrapped in a shawl, betrayed her uncomprehending distress at the loss of her parents. Giovanni Marengo had cause to bless the precious accordion that sustained him until rescue arrived, while Rosa Bianchi wept for the husband and son, with whom she survived for hours in the water until they drowned. Flaminio Turbino's dog proved a good swimmer: it was saved along with its owners.

Maestro Hermoso, José Maristany and the latter's sister were also rescued; the only piece of property the tenor salvaged was the dress he had bought for his bride-to-be. The Austrian consul to Brazil, Leopold Politzer, had a narrow escape. While in the water, he was said to have relinquished his lifebelt to a struggling woman and child, and was himself picked up only just in time.

Despite having been seen swimming powerfully, Abbot Natter became another of the casualties. Father Anscar Vonier, however, was one of those rescued by the fishermen. Ten days after the disaster he was elected abbot, and his blessing took place four days later on the feast of St Luke. The choice of date was significant: St Luke and St Paul had been shipwrecked together off Malta when their vessel hit a reef: 'The bow stuck and remained immovable, and the stern was broken up by the surf.' The similarity with the wreck of the *Sirio*, its bow aloft and its stern sinking, was striking, but the new abbot wrote to his friend, the Abbess of Dourgne: 'There is only one detail that does not square with my situation – Saint Luke reached the shore with his Saint Paul, but I …' he did not need to finish the sentence. For the rest of his life he found it hard to deal with death.

Some of the survivors were taken to Cabo de Palos for the night, a few to Alicante, and then brought by land or sea the short distance to Cartagena to join the rest. Felice Serafini spent a wretched night along with many others at the town's theatre, which had been turned into emergency accommodation. Pitched into the sea he had seen his son, Isidoro, swept away from him just after he urged the lad to save himself. He himself had been saved by one of the Spanish boats, but he knew nothing of the rest. The people around him were in the same distress, fearing the worst but clinging to a fragile hope.

For some there were unexpected and joyful reunions the following day. Ángela and Elisa Ferrara were reunited with the mother they had thought drowned, but who had been put ashore at Alicante. The inconsolable França had spent the night on the breakwater at Cabo de Palos, not knowing that his wife and daughter had been plucked from the sea by the *Joven Vicente*. For them, and everyone who witnessed it, the moment was overwhelmingly emotional.

Others were less fortunate. Serafini was to find two of his boys, Isidoro and Ottavio, but that carefully posed photograph became the last record of the family who had set out for their new life. The Arab man with the large family found himself its sole survivor. Several were reported to have suffered complete mental breakdowns under the stress of losing their loved ones, and the grand-mother left behind in Olesa de Montserrat killed herself upon learning that her entire family had drowned. One man, refusing to accept that he had lost his family, told everyone he met that they were on their way on another ship. Brigida Morelli was another in denial. She still hoped that her husband had been picked up by another boat, and yet she also believed that he had given that last smile so that her final memory of him would be sweet.

The Italian vessel *Umbria* spotted the wrecked *Sirio* within a few hours of the disaster, but still sent a boat to investigate from outside. After returning to report to their captain, they made a second trip, during which they penetrated the interior but found no signs of life – only what they took to be corpses float-ing in the submerged stern – and recovered Piccone's cap and binoculars. A search of the area, including the islands, produced no further survivors, and the *Umbria* continued on her route; her captain would tell the press that he was sure the ship must have been going at full speed when it hit, but also expressed the belief that given their proximity to shore, everyone would have been saved.

The people of Cartagena were generous with hospitality and charity. Even the poorest offered a roof to put over the heads of the bewildered sur-vivors. A charity bullfight was organized at which the nobility gave donations and one of the matadors handed over his fee. Along with the funerals, church-es held requiems and thanksgivings. The Archbishop of Pará officiated at some of these, and with his compatriot Vinhietta he visited the injured and bereaved. Maristany gave a benefit concert for the victims and their families, singing arias from *Rigoletto*, *Tosca*, *Carmen*, *I Pagliacci* and *l'Africaine*. He was unable to offer a repertoire of popular songs because the orchestral or piano parts had been lost with the *Sirio*. That music was not all that was lost. The luggage of all the passengers remained aboard – luggage that, for the vast majority, represented all their worldly goods. On the same night as the ship was lost a tug and a party of divers were dispatched to retrieve trapped bodies, check for any last survivors and salvage the possessions of both crew and passengers. Only the crew were allowed access to the vessel, and, curiously, only *their* baggage was recovered. It was a further five days before the passengers obtained permission to send a ten-strong delegation to oversee an operation that brought off all that could be recovered, and by this time the stern of the *Sirio* had submerged by a further 13 feet (4 metres). At the same time, the authorities had to take steps to recover decomposing bodies in the water around the ship. The delegation arrived to find that every accessible piece of passenger luggage had already been broken open and stripped of anything remotely valuable. A particular target were the trunks of Lola Millanes, which had contained much valuable lace. One was recovered full of theatrical costumes – cloaks, accessories, gowns – as well as the personal possessions, such as photographs and letters. The effects of the water and the heat had rendered it all beyond saving, and it was dumped back into the sea. The body of Millanes herself, identified by the initials on her blouse, was eventually washed up on the beach and buried at Torrevieja.

Including the crew, 669 people were saved from the wreck; how many were drowned is conjecture, but the figure lies somewhere between 242 and perhaps 350. Unlike in many disasters, women and children made up the majority of the dead. For the survivors, the choices remaining to them were stark, and they had little time to decide what to do. The disaster had been bad enough. What followed seemed to add insult to what was already worse than injury.

M ost of the Spanish would-be emigrants simply went home. There was no state aid: they had to bear the cost themselves. NGI sent the steamer *Adria* to Cartagena to bring back anyone who wanted to return to Genoa. The choice of ship was at best unfortunate, at worse, callous. She was more than thirty years old, had a history of minor accidents and the emigrants thought her small and unpleasant. Most of those who wished to go home were simply terrified of trusting their lives to any ship, and wanted to return by train. The Italian consul, who might have been expected to stand up for his nationals, had no compassion, except for Brigida Morelli, whom he had taken into his house. Either they got on the *Adria*, which had docked on Thursday 9 August, or they shifted for themselves at their own expense.

So great were the murmurings over the *Adria*, however, that NGI backed down and instead sent the *Orione* – on which 105 survivors returned to Italy – and then, a week after the disaster, the *Italia* arrived to take 310 people on to

Montevideo and Buenos Aires. On Monday 13 August, the NGI's *Ravenna* picked up a further 72 who were bound for Brazil.

On that same morning, nine days after grounding, the *Sirio* broke in two; her fore half remained caught on the rocks, while her stern plunged 130 feet (40 metres) down. Inevitably, dozens of decomposing corpses were released in the turbulence. For days to come, the tides carried them ashore along the coast, the most poignant being the body of a very young girl still clutching her toy bucket.

Thousands of Italians turned out to witness the return of the survivors to Genoa, leading to scenes of joy, relief and grief. One father came to find out if anyone could tell him anything about the last moments of his son, who had been one of the crew, only to see the young man himself disembarking. Luigi Lepori, whose father was also on the dockside, told reporters that his enthusiasm for the sea was unimpaired: 'I have been so lucky in this my first shipwreck that I am even more keen to go on. It's as if this is a positive omen for my career. After this unexpected challenge I consider myself to be a real sea-dog.' Mainetto was another who was undaunted by the disaster, telling reporters he had only returned to Genoa to collect some more money and clothes and he would soon set off again for Buenos Aires.

By contrast, Felice Serafini disembarked with his two boys in a stupor of inexpressible grief; upon returning home he was advised to take legal action against NGI. He claimed just over 73,000 lire, the overwhelming majority of which represented compensation for the deaths of his wife and six children. The response of the shipping company in its attempt to evade legal and moral responsibility taxes the imagination. They stated that for two days after striking the reef the *Sirio* was still capable of sailing and, therefore, the passengers had abandoned the ship without reason, thus ending their contract. In the face of media attacks, their position proved untenable, and in the end Felice won sufficient compensation to buy some land and build a house for his reduced family.

T he early reports praising the courage and coolness of the crew were soon overtaken by the facts. On 6 August the news appeared in the *Times* via a telegram from Cartagena dated the previous day. It blamed the disaster squarely on the 'imprudence' of the captain, though the *Times* repeated the ill-founded rumour of his subsequent suicide. Two days later the same newspaper published a dispatch from Madrid based upon telegrams from Cartagena including the description of 'a horrible struggle [that] took place between the passengers … and the crew, their knives in their teeth, and officers, revolvers in hand, who fought to make their way by brute force and were the first to save themselves'. The very next day it expanded on the theme, and claimed that 'very grave charges will have to be brought'.

Captain Piccone sought to defend himself from the accusations levelled against him even before any enquiry was held. He asserted that he had been on the bridge at the time of the accident, and in the immediate aftermath of the boiler explosion he was in complete shock. What he said to the Italian newspapers was a contradiction of what the Spanish press had learned from the passengers. He claimed not to have left the ship until it was dark, and when he did leave it was with two of the officers – Amézaga and Tarantino – and a seaman. On his return to Italy, he told the Milanese periodical *Il Secolo* that he had been keeping 3 miles (5.5 kilometres) from the coast and that the disaster was due to 'currents or magnetic influence. This part of the coast is rich in mineral ore which may have affected the compass. At the time we struck, I was next to the compass and Lieut. Amézaga was following the plotted route.' He admitted that Tarantino had advised him that they were too close to the coast, and that tallied with comments by some of the crew that the officers had previously warned him that his navigation was reckless. He also denied suggestions that he was trying to cut a few miles off the route or that he was engaged in an unofficial race against other ships plying the route. Too ill to attend the Italian government's inquiry, he died two months after the disaster.

There was an attempt to throw the blame onto Amézaga, who was in charge of the navigation during that watch – even though the captain had been standing next to him. The company suggested that the ship had hit explosives that had been put into position to aid the salvage of another ship sunk in the vicinity. The inquiry, however, exposed the fact that the *Sirio* had not kept to its prescribed route but had made unscheduled calls along the Spanish Mediterranean coast to pick up clandestine emigrants. That, and human error or negligence, accounted for her close and reckless proximity to the coast. The inquiry's commissioners also went on board the sister ship, *Orione*, to see for themselves how the lifeboats operated. After watching the crew working in vain for half an hour, they withdrew.

There will always be accidents at sea. If the situation is survivable, the immediate response usually determines how many will survive – as was demonstrated by the *Amphitrite*. The *Sirio* carried eight lifeboats and two rafts – sufficient for about half her complement. That was perfectly normal at a time where such equipment was regulated by the ship's tonnage and not by its passenger capacity, though the loss of the *Norge* two years earlier[3] should have concentrated the minds of national governments on that subject. But even though the nature of the wreck precluded the launching of several boats, the fact that only one was successfully launched is a scandal, and doubly so because it was the officers who appropriated it. Their failure to act in the interests of the passengers not only caused the wreck in the first place, but the additional loss of life resulting from it.

A month to the day after the loss, a letter on the subject of organization and discipline was published in Cartagena's *El Eco*, written by Spanish naval engineer Pedro Cánovas Villa:

In the case of the unfortunate accident to the cruiser *Cardenal Cisneros* on the Meixidos reef [near Cape Finisterre, Spain, in October 1905], it took a few minutes for the last man of her disciplined crew to escape safe and sound from the wreck of that handsome ship. In the collision in the waters off Syria of the British battleships *Camperdown* and *Victoria* which resulted in the sinking of the latter, the crew of 500 formed up on the deck without the least hesitation, calm and obedient to the orders of their officers, despite the increasing list, and not a single one jumped into the water to seek his own safety until the exact and final order was given to them by the commander.

In both the cases cited above the organization and discipline were the sole reasons for such firm behaviour ...

In making that second comparison, he could have reflected that the same tenacious adherence to naval discipline had led senior British officers to obey an order which could only end in a collision, but Villa went on to make the point that, while naval discipline could not be expected of civilian passengers, shipowners, especially those involved in the passenger trade, had a duty to ensure the safety of crew and passengers. On that August afternoon not even the most basic 'organization and discipline' had been in evidence.

Villa additionally called for the Stone-Lloyd system of watertight bulkheads, or something similar, to be installed on all passenger ships, and it is fair to say that by 1906 increasing numbers of companies were modifying existing vessels, and specifying the new technology in their new-builds. But, given the absence of both charts and responsible leadership, none of the technology available at the time could have prevented the *Sirio* from coming to grief on the Bajo de Fuera. The only question is how far it could have reduced the death toll.

The Spanish, especially around Cartagena, took pride in the kindness shown to the survivors, and particularly in the rescue work carried out by their fishermen. All the *patrons* were given medals and financial rewards to share with their crews. Chief among them was Vicente Buigués, who was decorated by both Spain and Italy and given an audience by King Alfonso XIII. He returned to his life as a fisherman and smuggler until the Spanish navy caught him running petroleum, and sportingly offered him a financial inducement to abandon the smuggling.

For the Italians, however, the loss of the *Sirio* in such circumstances was a blow to national prestige – and a hard blow given that Italy, for centuries a geographical rather than a political entity, had only become unified in 1871. They were sensitive to pejorative comments about the 'Latin temperament' in the British press, even though British maritime history was littered with examples of equally unedifying behaviour. In Argentina, to which the *Sirio* had brought tens of thousands of settlers during her career, the tragedy has become an important part of the national story, a reminder of just one of the dangers facing those who turned their backs on Europe and struck out for the land of silver.

Il tragico naufragio della nave *Sirio*

E da Genova il Sirio *partivano*	And with the *Sirio* they left from Genoa
per l'America varcare, varcare i confin	to cross America, to cross the border
e da bordo cantar si sentivano	and on board they sing,
tutti allegri del suo, del suo destin.	because they feel happy about their future.
Urtò il Sirio *un orribile scoglio*	The *Sirio* hit a dreadful rock,
di tanta gente la mi-, la misera fin:	for so many people a miserable end:
padri e madri abbracciava i suoi figli	Fathers and mothers hugged the children
che si sparivano tra le onde, tra le onde del mar.	who disappeared among the waves, among the waves of the sea.
Più di centocinquanta annegati,	More than 150 drowned,
che trovarli nessun-, nessuno potrà;	and nobody will be able to find them;
e fra loro un vescovo c'era	and among them a bishop there was,
dando a tutti la be-, la sua benedizion.	who gave everyone his blessing.

Sources and Bibliography

Most of the sources for this disaster are in Spanish, a few in Italian. Special thanks are due to Luis Cortese for so generously putting his work at my disposal, to Buckfast Abbey, and to Andrea David Quinzi for translating 'Il tragico naufragio della nave Sirio'.

Cortese, Luis Osvaldo: *La Tragedia del Vapor Sirio – Un drama olvidado de la inmigración* (Buenos Aires: Ediciones BP, Informes del Sur, 2004).
García Echegoyen, Fernando José, *Los grandes naufragios españoles* (Barcelona: Alba, 1998).
Smith, Dom Leo, 'The Life and Work of Abbot Anscar Vonier', English Benedictine History Commission, Symposium 1996; also available online at www.catholic-history.org.uk/ebc/1996smith.pdf
Stella, Gian Antonio: *Odissee: italiani sulle rotte del sogno e del dolore* (Milan: Rizzoli, 2004).

Caras Y Caritas (Buenos Aires), August 1906
Corriere della Sera (Milan)
El Eco (Cartagena)
El Época (Madrid)
La Nazione (Florence)
The Times

Penalva, Ángel Rojas 'El naufragio del Sirio', www.publimatic.com/hacecuerpo.php?d=elnaufra-giodelsirio&seccion=portada (extensive background on the ship, emigration, the disaster and its aftermath; in Spanish).
Tomás, Andrés Ortolá, 'Vicente Buigués Ferrando', http://club.telepolis.com/ifach/andres/pagi-nas/buigues.htm (biographical page about the principal rescuer; in Spanish).

Notes

[1] Natter was making a visitation of a monastery of French Subiac Benedictines in Argentina, and he had invited Vonier to accompany him as assistant visitor. The purpose of a visitation is to assess a monastery's spiritual and temporal state and to strengthen, encourage and renew its religious life.
[2] Possibly named Padobaglie.
[3] On 28 June 1904 the Danish vessel *Norge* went down in the Atlantic after striking Rockall, and 600 passengers and crew were lost. Her lifeboat capacity was about 250 persons.

11

Almost Unsinkable

Titanic

1912

From out the desolation of the North
An iceberg took its way,
From its detaining comrades breaking forth,
And travelling night and day.

At whose command? Who bade it sail the deep
With that resistless force?
Who made the dread appointment it must keep?
Who traced its awful course? ...

Was not the weltering waste of water wide
Enough for both to sail?
What drew the two together o'er the tide,
Fair ship and iceberg pale?

CELIA THAXTER, FROM 'A TRYST' (1872)

THE TROUBLE WITH THE *TITANIC* is that she has become an industry, a backdrop and a metaphor, the focus of a lifetime's devotion for enthusiasts, a battleground, and the victim of some frankly bizarre conspiracy theories. If everything written about her was laid out, page by page, it would probably cover a greater mileage than the ill-fated ship herself. Anyone trying to write honestly about her confronts a problem not unlike that faced by the conservator of an old and valuable painting: how to strip away the layers of varnish and retouching without damaging the original.

Dramatis Personae

Rhoda Abbott : third-class passenger

Frank Aks : third-class passenger (baby)

Leah Aks : third-class passenger

Thomas Andrews : first-class passenger, designer of the *Titanic*

John-Jacob Astor : first-class passenger

Madeleine Astor : first-class passenger

Marion Becker : second-class passenger

Nellie Becker : second-class passenger

Richard Becker : second-class passenger

Ruth Becker : second-class passenger

Lawrence Beesley : second-class passenger

Bridget Bradley : third-class passenger

Harold Bride : assistant telegraphist

Daniel Buckley : third-class passenger

Albert Caldwell : second-class passenger

Alden Caldwell : second-class passenger (baby)

Cynthia Caldwell : second-class passenger

Ernest Carter : second-class passenger

Mrs Carter : second-class passenger

C. Caussin : captain of the *Touraine*

Selina Cook : second-class passenger

Harold Cottam : telegraphist, *Carpathia*

Ruth Dodge : first-class passenger

Dr Washington Dodge Sr : first-class passenger

Washington Dodge Jr : first-class passenger

It becomes, therefore, tempting to dismiss her as a shipwreck for the nautically challenged, merely a 'stately pleasure dome' for the obscenely rich that got half way across a quiet Atlantic, hit one of the icebergs about which her captain had been warned, and sank in three hours without putting up much of a fight. There are many eyewitness accounts – no comparable set of survivors has been so comprehensively researched. Do they tell a more moving or evocative tale than those of Charlotte Picard, Lucia Eaton, Maurice Bourke, Pierre de Lafond, or John Kirby?

The *Titanic* was far from the first to go down on her maiden voyage,[1] and

Sir Cosmo Duff-Gordon :	first-class passenger
Edith Corse Evans :	first-class passenger
Frederick Fleet :	seaman
Archibald Gracie :	first-class passenger
Benjamin Guggenheim :	first-class passenger
Charles Hays :	first-class passenger
J Bruce Ismay :	first-class passenger
Reginald Lee :	seaman
Charles Lightoller :	second officer
Stanley Lord :	captain of the *Californian*
William Murdoch :	first officer
Alfred Olliver :	quartermaster
John Phillips :	telegraphist
Frederick Ray :	table steward
Arthur Rostron :	captain of the *Carpathia*
The Countess of Rothes :	first-class passenger
Hilda Slayter :	first-class passenger
Edward Smith :	captain of the *Titanic*
Isidor Straus :	first-class passenger
Rosilie Straus :	first-class passenger
John Thayer Sr :	first-class passenger
John Borland ('Jack') Thayer :	first-class passenger
Eleanor Elkins Widener :	first-class passenger
George Dunton Widener :	first-class passenger
Harry Elkins Widener :	first-class passenger

other ships have sunk with greater loss of life. Is she just famous for being famous, or has fame done her a disservice by concentrating minds on her size, her opulence and the inordinate wealth of a small proportion of her passengers? Has her discovery answered outstanding questions for her devotees, or just revealed an unhealthy obsession with the value of the artefacts?

The twentieth century arrived in a fanfare of optimism fuelled by the unprecedented technological and scientific advances of the nineteenth. If the Renaissance put man centre-stage, then the nineteenth century taught him to believe that he could control the world around him through his own understanding and invention. Proof to the contrary – such as the eruption of Vesuvius and the Courrières mine disaster in 1906, or the massive earthquakes centred on San Francisco in that year and in Messina in 1908 – failed to shake that confidence. Shipping was just one industry at the forefront of change. Old ships like the *Sirio* might sink, the thinking went, but the newer vessels being built were bigger, faster and safer – not just for prestige but for profit.

Cunard's famous transatlantic twins, *Lusitania* and *Mauretania*, went into service in 1907. Not only were they the largest ships afloat, but at 25 knots they were also the fastest. The lessons of double bottoms and watertight compartments had been learned, and both ships were fitted with the Stone-Lloyd system (see Chapter 10), leading to the *Mauretania*'s being described as 'practically unsinkable'. *Unsinkable, almost unsinkable, practically unsinkable* … what, in the public mind, was the difference? Even a respected journal such as the *Shipbuilder* was not immune from gilding the lily.

The launch of the Cunarders, which were partly funded by British government money, threw down the gauntlet to US tycoon J P Morgan. In his desire for a monopoly of the lucrative North Atlantic trade for his International Mercantile Marine he had already digested several European rivals including the Oceanic Steam Navigation Company, better known as the White Star Line – though the White Star ships retained their British registration and crews. Since Cunard refused to be swallowed, they would have to be forced out. To build faster ships would be expensive, and larger engines take up lucrative passenger space. Furthermore, as *Titanic* author and expert David G Brown has pointed out, the Cunard twins – and the trio of White Star liners built to compete with them – all took around five and a half days to do the crossing. But a difference of hours is irrelevant to passengers. Only by taking a whole *day* out of the crossing time could any company attract passengers on speed alone. Therefore, White Star concluded, they would continue to compete on size and comfort, not just for first class passengers but for second and steerage.

In 1908 White Star's chairman, J. Bruce Ismay, placed contracts with Lord William Pirrie's Harland and Wolff yard for three huge liners, to be named *Olympic*, *Titanic* and *Gigantic* (the latter launched in the end as *Britannic*). Few vessels can have been so well reported long before they entered service or so eulogized on completion. *Olympic* was launched on 20 October 1910 and *Titanic* followed on 31 May the next year. What she did not know was that her script had already been written.

Ship	Gross tonnage	Length ft/m	Beam ft/m	Funnels	Cruising speed (knots)	Passengers (max)
Mauretania	31,938	790/241.3	88/26.9	4	25	2165
Titanic	46,329	852/260	92.5/28	4	22	2453

Moby Dick, Hornblower, Mr Midshipman Easy, Master and Commander, The Perfect Storm, The Cruel Sea, Captains Courageous ... Those are just a handful of novels and films in which fiction takes its inspiration from life. Occasionally life retaliates by borrowing a text, making a few judicious changes and performing it to spectacular effect.

Former merchant navy officer, Morgan Robertson, published a novella entitled *Futility* in 1898.

She was the largest craft afloat and the greatest of the works of men. In her construction and maintenance were involved every science, profession, and trade known to civilization ... From the bridge, engine-room, and a dozen places on her deck the ninety-two doors of nineteen water-tight compartments could be closed in half a minute by turning a lever. These doors would also close automatically in the presence of water. With nine compartments flooded the ship would still float, and as no known accident of the sea could possibly fill this many, the steamship ... was considered practically unsinkable ...

... She was eight hundred feet long, of seventy thousand tons displacement, seventy-five thousand horse-power, and on her trial trip had steamed at a rate of twenty-five knots an hour over the bottom, in the face of unconsidered winds, tides, and currents. In short, she was a floating city – containing within her steel walls all that tends to minimise the dangers and discomforts of the Atlantic voyage – all that makes life enjoyable.

Unsinkable – indestructible, she carried as few boats as would satisfy the laws ...

This fictional passenger liner left New York one April on her maiden voyage, collided with an iceberg and sank with the loss of all but 13 of her crew and passengers. She was called the *Titan*.

Robertson had imagined a giant liner, but could he have predicted quite how magnificent was the newcomer as she lay berthed at Southampton devouring vast quantities of food and stores? Externally, *Titanic* was beautiful: the elegant round counter-stern that became so iconic during her sinking, and four black-topped, buff-raked funnels – the fourth a dummy used for ventilation – gave her a magnificent dynamism. Inside, however, every effort had been made to suggest, at least for the first-class passengers, that she was a luxury hotel, with reception rooms, writing room in pink and rose, smoking room, lounge complete with musicians to provide popular easy-listening background music, dining room, palm court, veranda cafés and à la carte restaurant. *Titanic* catered for the Edwardian fitness enthusiast with a gymnasium, swimming pool, full-sized squash court and Turkish Bath. Superb panelling and fine mouldings clad the walls and pillars, and the woodcarving has been compared to that of the seventeenth-century genius Grinling Gibbons.[2] Some floors were tiled, others had thick-fitted carpet.

As for the suites and cabins, they were the last word in luxury, all expensively panelled and equipped with electric lighting and heating – some boasted four-poster beds, Adam fireplace and coal fire. If money was no object, a parlour suite on B deck, consisting of two bedrooms, bathroom, toilet and sitting room, could be obtained for a mere £875 each way (equivalent to around £28,500 today) while a single first-class berth cost £30 (just under £1000). Louis XV, Italian Renaissance, Dutch and Queen Anne were just four of the decorative styles on offer. Everything was accessible via one of two magnificent carved staircases designed to show the passengers at their best, and those who did not fancy climbing the stairs could ring for the lift.

In terms of safety features, the *Titanic* had been built with a double bottom, which extended to 7 feet (2 metres) above the keel at the sides, and her bulkheads were fitted with the Stone-Lloyd system of watertight doors. They did not, however, extend all the way to the upper deck.

At ten months old, Frank Aks – or Filly as he was affectionately known – had no way of understanding that his life was about to change. Promises that he was going to see daddy meant nothing because he had never set eyes on him. Samuel, a Jewish Pole who had failed to make a decent living as a tailor in London, had gone out to Norfolk, Virginia, on the advice of a cousin, leaving behind his pregnant wife. In little over a year he was able to send for her and the son he had never seen, and with a £9 7s ticket in her handbag and her strapping baby in her arms, 18-year-old Leah Aks, herself Polish born, set off on the boat-train for Southampton and a third-class berth on the *Titanic*. If she had been on one of the old ships she would have had to take her bedding, crockery and cutlery for the voyage, but White Star were offering everything except sheets in order to lure customers. Nor would she have to sleep in a huge dormitory: most of the third-class accommodation, including her own, was in small cabins, each with heat and electric light and a washbasin filled from a cistern. She could take her meals in the plain but bright dining room, where the tables were laid with white cloths, and there were public rooms and deck space in which groups could get together and organize impromptu entertainment while the children ran about. For the poorer emigrants, *Titanic* offered better conditions than anything they had enjoyed on land. Little wonder that they had travelled not just from across Britain but from continental Europe and beyond.

Up on the boat deck, second-class passenger Lawrence Beesley, off on holiday to the United States and Canada, had discovered the gymnasium and was trying out the bicycle machine when the instructor arrived with a couple of photographers to take pictures. Other machines, operated by electricity, simulated the experience of riding a horse or a camel – novelties or useful accomplishments in those days of Empire. *Titanic* was far from fully booked and, like Leah, Beesley found himself the only occupant of his cabin – No. 56 on D Deck, close to the saloon, for which he paid just under £13. With its panelled walls, mahogany furniture and en-suite bathroom it was as good as first class on many another ship.

There were several reasons for the empty berths: a coal strike had caused serious doubts as to whether she would be able to sail at all; the preference of British 'society' for the established Cunard ships; cancellations (55 of them, quite a few from high-profile passengers); and a slight nervousness among passengers about travelling on a maiden voyage – not necessarily because they feared disaster, but because they didn't want to experience 'teething troubles'.

Given the occasion, Beesley, a former science teacher from Dulwich College, London, had expected something of a theatrical departure, and was surprised at how quiet it was. As *Titanic* slipped down the docks just after noon on 10 April 1912 the crowds of friends, family and sightseers kept pace with her for as long as they could, and the passengers waved back. That low-key tone may have owed something to uncertainty raised by the miners' strike. Slowly the great ship began to pass the liner *New York,* one of several berthed at Southampton. Unable to resist the terrific power of the water pushed out beneath her by *Titanic*'s vast hull, the *New York* snapped her mooring ropes, which whiplashed over the quay. Only some quick thinking by *Titanic*'s Captain Smith and the tugboat that had just cast her off saved collision. A minor mishap – or an omen of doom?

Also settling into second class was 12-year-old American Ruth Becker and her family. Leaving their missionary father in India they had come over on the *City of Benares*[3] for the sake of the health of Ruth's little brother, Richard, and were now bound for Michigan after a few days of sightseeing in London. Mrs Becker expressed disquiet to the purser that they were on a maiden voyage; he laughed off her fears. The first-class passengers were mostly North American, and many of them would join the ship at Cherbourg. Among the richest to embark at Southampton was Isidor Straus, an elderly US self-made multi-millionaire and former congressman. Despite their wealth, he and his wife had two cabins on C Deck, for which they paid £221 15s 7d; the only person yet occupying a palatial parlour suite was J Bruce Ismay who, as the ship's owner, was not required to pay the extravagant cost.

At dusk the *Titanic* was off Cherbourg, where two specially built White Star tenders came out to her. A handful disembarked, and 274 from as far afield as Syria came aboard.

One of the first Anglo-American families to settle in California after the discovery of gold in 1849 were the Dodges, and Dr Washington Dodge, now aged 52, was a 'second generation' Californian, a qualified doctor and a politician. Now he was returning home with his second wife, Ruth, and younger son, also Washington, after a visit to Paris for treatment of a blood disorder. Like the rather more famous and super-rich Benjamin Guggenheim (who was travelling with his French mistress), the Astors and the Duff-Gordons, he booked a first class ticket on the *Titanic* from Cherbourg, and for £81 17s 2d the family found themselves forward on A-Deck, the promenade deck, in the large stateroom A34, close to the first class entrance and a short distance from A-36, where Lord Pirrie's nephew, Thomas Andrews, the designer of the ship, was accommodated. For Andrews, this was a busman's holiday: he liked to observe the ships on their maiden voyages in order to iron out any wrinkles and to incorporate his observations into future vessels.

The close shave at Southampton had delayed their arrival at Cherbourg by an hour, but at 8:30 p.m., in a golden blaze of light, she left the French port for Queenstown, Ireland, her final call before setting out for New York.

Bridget Bradley, 21, was one of seven young people from Ballydesmond seeking a future in the United States. Local farm labourer Daniel Buckley had organized everything, and they joined the 2.5 million Irish emigrants who left from Queenstown (out of 6 million in total) in the hundred years after 1848. Bridget's brother lived in New York, and her sister was a cook in Glen Falls, so she had somewhere to go until she could find her feet. Not everyone of the 113 who embarked at Queenstown was an emigrant, however. Hilda Slayter from Halifax, Nova Scotia, for example, had spent years studying music in Italy in the vain hope of becoming the next Nellie Melba. Finally she accepted both her lack of talent and the offer of a good marriage and went off to England to purchase an expensive trousseau, including a satin opal and pearl wedding dress with all the accessories, costing the equivalent of $4000.

The *Titanic* left Queenstown at 1:30 p.m. on Saturday 13 April with 2228 passengers and crew, and with good weather, the voyage was pleasant. There was no huddling around stoves as the passengers had done on the *San Francisco*: the public rooms, like the cabins, were effectively heated. Beesley observed some of the third-class passengers having fun on deck, playing a lively skipping game accompanied by a bagpiper. Third class was composed of many nationalities, mostly British but with a significant helping from the Scandinavian countries to the north, and from Italy and the Middle East. Few of the foreigners in steerage spoke more than a few words of English.

Beesley and his fellow second-class passengers, who were all quartered on E-

Deck, had a smoking room on B deck and a library immediately below. The library exuded a heavy, comfortable atmosphere: curtains of green silk, brown carpet, solid chairs, a scattering of writing desks, and sofas with mahogany frames and tapestry upholstery. A thin steward with a stoop produced books on request from the glass-fronted mahogany shelves. Beesley, who had never left Britain before, was delighted, and spent much of his time there when the weather was too brisk for the deck, from which he loved observing the elements:

> Each morning the sun rose behind us in a sky of circular clouds, stretching round
> the horizon in long, narrow streaks and rising tier upon tier above the sky-line, red
> and pink and fading from pink to white, as the sun rose higher in the sky ... It was
> a beautiful sight to ... watch the swell of the sea extending outwards from the ship
> in an unbroken circle until it met the sky-line with its hint of infinity: behind, the
> wake of the vessel white with foam ... And each night the sun sank right in our eyes
> along the sea, making an undulating glittering path way, a golden track charted on
> the surface of the ocean which our ship followed unswervingly until the sun dipped
> below the edge of the horizon, and the pathway ran ahead of us faster than we
> could steam and slipped over the edge of the sky-line ...

For passengers with an interest in the subject, the purser posted information about the voyage in the libraries. From 12 noon Thursday to 12 noon Friday, the *Titanic* covered 386 miles (714 kilometres); the next 24 hours, 519 miles (960 kilometres), then 546 miles (1010 kilometres) taking the voyage up to Sunday lunchtime. Beesley was told that she would not be pushed to full speed on what was effectively a trial. In any case, there was no point arriving in New York on Tuesday night, because she would not be allowed to enter the port until the morning and it was safer to be steaming on the open sea than have to spend the night outside. Subsequent allegations that Captain Smith and J Bruce Ismay were trying for the Blue Riband speed record were misguided: the *Titanic*'s 46,000hp could not hope to outsprint the *Mauretania*'s 68,000, and there had never been any intention of trying. But at the same time, they were following the normal procedure of working the ship up, and Ismay had discussed with the chief engineer the possibility of trying her at top speed on the Monday. That would probably have been a little over 25 knots, but achieving it would depend not just on the engines but on the quality of the coal and the set of the currents. Arguably, they had no idea what her precise top speed might be until they put her to the test.

On the Sunday afternoon everyone noticed that the temperature was dropping significantly. The public rooms filled up more than usual as all but the hardiest abandoned the decks. Ruth Becker walked around the lower, enclosed promenade deck with Richard in a pushchair provided by the company.

Beesley filled in his luggage declaration in the library. None of the passengers was remotely concerned, but those in charge of the ship should have been. They had been warned.

As early as 7:00 p.m. on Friday 12 April, the *Titanic*'s two Marconi operators were called by the French vessel *Touraine*, Captain C. Caussin. Giving her position using French longitude (measured from Paris, not Greenwich), *Touraine* stated:

> My position 7pm GMT Lat 49°.28′ Long 26°.28′ W dense fog since this night crossed thick icefield 44.58′, long. 50.40′ Paris saw another icefield and two icebergs lat 45.20 Long 50.09 Paris saw a derelict lat 40.56 long 68.38 Paris please give me your position. Best regards and Bon Voyage. Caussin.

The message was acknowledged.[4] On Sunday the messages increased. At 9:00 a.m. the Cunard liner *Caronia* passed on a warning that west-bound vessels were reporting icebergs, growlers and field ice. Just over two and half hours later she passed on a message from the Dutch passenger liner *Noordam* warning of ice.

At 12:55 p.m. the *Titanic*, call sign MGY, was called up by her stablemate *Baltic*.

> Have had moderate, variable winds and clear fine weather since leaving. Greek steamer *Athenai* reports passing icebergs and large quantities of field ice today in lat. 41° 51′ N, Long 49° 52′ W ...

Just after lunch, at 1:45 p.m., the Hamburg-Amerika line ship *Amerika* asked *Titanic* to pass a message to Cape Race. She also reported having passed two large icebergs that day in 41° 27′ N, 50° 08′ W.

So much ice so far south was unusual, but this was an unusual year and a bad one for icebergs. Only in recent years has the El Niño effect, rooted in periodic rising water temperatures in the eastern Pacific but affecting climate globally, been recognized as a significant factor in world history,[5] and 1912 was an El Niño year. At the same time as it produced the extreme cold in the Antarctic that wreaked havoc on Robert Scott's return from the South Pole, so it created warmer weather in the Arctic, which facilitated the calving of icebergs, some of them monsters capable of travelling a long way south before they melted. None the less, the *Titanic*'s Captain Edward Smith, who like Piccone was in his sixties and for whom this was originally intended to be a last voyage before retiring, did not treat the messages with any obvious concern. After reading the transcript of *Amerika*'s report he handed it to Ismay and did not ask for it back for some hours.

That evening, Washington and Ruth Dodge must have made one of the few decisions required of passengers on a daily basis: dine à la carte in the French-walnut restaurant or go to the huge Jacobean dining room for the usual ten courses.

First Course
Hors D'Oeuvres, Oysters
Second Course
Consommé Olga, Cream of Barley
Third Course
Poached Salmon with Mousseline Sauce, Cucumbers
Fourth Course
Filet Mignons Lili, Saute of Chicken Lyonnaise, Vegetable Marrow Farci
Fifth Course
Lamb, Mint Sauce; Roast Duckling, Apple Sauce; Sirloin of Beef (accompanied
by) Chateau Potatoes, Green Peas, Creamed Carrots, Boiled Rice
Parmentier & Boiled New Potatoes
Sixth Course
Punch Romaine
Seventh Course
Roast Squab & Cress
Eighth Course
Cold Asparagus Vinaigrette
Ninth Course
Pate de Foie Gras, Celery
Tenth Course
Waldorf Pudding, Peaches in Chartreuse Jelly,
Chocolate & Vanilla Eclairs, French Ice Cream

Leah and Bridget had eaten their main meal at lunchtime. The final Sunday meal for third class was a simple high tea.

Lawrence Beesley joined Reverend Ernest Carter and his wife at the purser's table in the second-class dining room. Captain Smith dined à la carte with the Wideners and their other guests, but did not touch any alcohol. Dinner was in full swing when, at 7:30 p.m., the next message was received, so the operator took it to the bridge rather than to the Captain. Sent from the Leyland Line ship *Californian*, call sign MWL, to the captain of the *Antillian*, it warned: 'Lat. 42° 03′ N, Long 49° 09′ W. Three large bergs to the southward of us. Regards – Lord' it was intercepted by the *Titanic*, so when Captain Stanley Lord repeated it for their benefit he was told they had already picked it up.

With no formal entertainment on the ship, many of the second-class passengers, including Beesley, adjourned to the saloon, and were still enjoying an impromptu evening of hymn singing when at 9:40 p.m. the Atlantic Transport Company's *Mesaba* sent out a message to *Titanic* and all east-bound ships: 'Ice report in Lat. 42° N to 41° 25′ N, Long. 49° to 50° 30′ W. Saw much heavy pack ice and a great number large icebergs. Also field ice. Weather good, clear.' Crucially, that message was not prefixed by the letters MSG (Master's Service Gram) to indicate it was for the personal attention of the captain. It was acknowledged by the operator only, and, probably because telegraphist John Phillips and his assistant, Harold Bride, were busy, this message never reached the bridge, to which the captain had returned about 50 minutes earlier. Had it been prefixed with the code MSG there would have been no question of 'spiking' it for later, though whether it would have made any difference if Smith had seen it will never be known.

The second-class passengers had their last cup of coffee around 10:00 p.m. Ruth's family went to bed; so did young Mrs Aks and Bridget. In the smoking rooms some of the men lingered over their games of poker and bridge in easy good humour amid a haze of pipe and cigar smoke. Lawrence Beesley said goodnight to the Carters and retired to his cabin to read. Washington Dodge and his wife had also turned in for the night. Outside, the temperature had dropped to freezing as *Titanic* cut through the quiet black water at 21.5 knots, creating a vicious chill for those on watch in the crows nest. No moon spoiled the brilliance of the glittering constellations across the obsidian sky, or gleamed on the fantastic ice sculptures lying along the liner's route.

In the wireless room, Phillips was working his way through a pile of passenger telegrams to send to the land station at Cape Race. He and Bride were employees of Marconi, not White Star, and so receiving and transmitting messages between ships was only one (and by volume, small) part of his job. Passengers paid to send telegrams ahead of their arrival, and information such as stock market prices was relayed from the Marconi transmitting station at Poldhu in Cornwall to be incorporated in the ship's bulletin. The range of the apparatus was much greater at night – though, perhaps paradoxically, smaller ships with only one operator tended to shut down completely overnight. At 11:00 p.m. the *Californian* came through again.

'Say, old man, we are stopped and surrounded by ice MWL.'

Irritated at the interruption, the overworked and probably tired Phillips responded sharply: 'Shut up. I am busy. I am working Cape Race.' To the land station he transmitted. 'Sorry, please repeat, jammed. MGY.'

Captain Lord's message would never reach Captain Smith; once again, the tantalizing question is whether it would have made any difference. No previous warning had induced him to lower his speed, only to tell Charles Lightoller, the second officer, that if visibility decreased they might have to slow down. No additional lookouts had been posted in the bows.

Lookouts Frederick Fleet and Reginald Lee had begun their two-hour watch at 10:00 p.m. At 11:40 p.m., Fleet spotted the iceberg in their path. Why nobody saw it before is, like much about the disaster, conjecture. Certainly there was no moon, and the sea was so exceptionally flat that no waves would have broken against it. In 1925 Lieutenant Commander Frederick Zeusler of the US Coastguard, who was serving with the International Ice Patrol, calculated that on a clear dark night a berg would be visible at half a mile – about 900 metres. The *Titanic* was travelling at 21.5 knots, at which the distance corresponds to 42 seconds. Fleet maintained to his dying day that the absence of night-glasses was to blame. He rang the bell three times, grabbed the telephone and called to the bridge: 'Iceberg right ahead'.

The reply was a calm 'Thank you'.

'Hard a starboard!'[6] ordered First Officer William Murdoch. That relic of the old days, when sailing ships were steered by a tiller, meant the ship's head would turn to port. 'Full speed astern!'

What happened in those critical seconds is still debated. The popular view – that the *Titanic* swiped the berg *en passant*, tearing a 300-foot (90-metre) gash in her side below the waterline but just above the limited double bottom - is at odds with the experience of those who felt or, more significantly, did not feel the impact, to say nothing of the evidence of the hull, which reveals only six narrow, horizontal slits between the bow and the boiler room. More probable is David G Brown's interpretation, that she suffered an *allision*: that she grounded on a sharp shelf of ice jutting out from the underwater mass of the iceberg, but without losing all momentum.[7] She came off with massive damage to her bottom, which would have fatal consequences for the integrity of the rest of her hull.

Testimony of those members of the crew who were working below, such as Fireman Fred Barrett, bears this out. Questioned during the subsequent inquiries, they spoke of water *coming up* from below. A hatch in the floor, some 60 feet (18 metres) from the bow, blew off. Water did come through the slits opened up on the side, but most came from the bottom, where the real damage was being done by the stresses and strains on the ship's longitudinal framing, which sprang seams and thus compromised the watertight compartments.

Four forward compartments and boiler room 5 were flooded. The *Titanic* had been designed to remain afloat with four compartments flooded …

The Dodges woke up.

The shock to the steamer was so slight, that many of the passengers, who had already retired, were not awakened thereby … I became aware of the fact that the engines had been stopped, and shortly afterwards hearing hurried footsteps on the boat decks which was directly over our stateroom, I concluded that I would go out and inquire what had occurred. Partially dressing I slipped out of our room into the forward companionway, there to find possibly half a dozen men, all speculating as to what had happened ... an officer passed by somewhat hurriedly, and I asked him what was the trouble; he replied that he thought something had gone wrong with the propeller, but that it was nothing serious.

Leaving the few passengers that I had observed, still laughing and chatting, I returned to my stateroom. My wife being somewhat uneasy desired to arise and dress. I assured her that nothing had occurred which would harm the ship, and persuaded her to remain in bed ... We both agreed, however, judging from the nature of the shock, that something had struck the vessel on its side. This however, owing to the slight jar to the vessel, and to our knowledge of her immense size, and unsinkable construction, did not alarm us. I decided, nevertheless, to again go out and investigate further.

This time I went from the companionway out onto the promenade deck, where I found a group of possibly six or eight men, who were gaily conversing about the incident. I heard one man say that the impact was due to ice. Upon one of his listeners questioning the authority of this, he replied: 'Go up forward and look down on the poop deck, and you can see for yourself.' I at once walked forward to the end of the promenade deck, and looking down could see, just within the starboard rail, small fragments of broken ice, amounting possibly to several cartloads. As I stood there an incident occurred which made me take a more serious view of the situation, than I otherwise would.

Two stokers, who had slipped up onto the promenade deck unobserved, said to me: 'Do you think there is any danger, sir?' I replied: 'If there is any danger it would be due to the vessel having sprung a leak, and you ought to know more about it than I.' They replied, in what appeared to me, to be an alarmed tone: 'Well, sir, the water was pouring into the stoke 'old when we came up, sir.' At this time I observed quite a number of steerage passengers, who were amusing themselves by walking over the ice, and kicking it about the deck. No ice or iceberg was to be seen in the ocean.

Not observing any sign of apprehension on the part of any one, nor seeing any unusual number of persons on any part of the ship, I again returned to my cabin ...

No emergency alarm was sounded. Ruth's family on E deck slept through the impact and not until after midnight were they were roused by shouting and people running up the stairs. Leaving Ruth to mind her small brother and sister, Nellie Becker flung on some clothes and asked the first steward she saw what had happened. Reassured by him that the problem was in hand, she went back to bed, waiting for the engines to restart. When they did not, she left the cabin again to ask someone else. She was given the stark order to put on lifebelts and go to the boat deck.

It was Lawrence Beesley's impression that the ship had been travelling faster in the time leading up to the allision, if only because of the increased vibrations felt through his mattress, but that when the ship struck

> there came to me nothing more than a heave of the engines and a more than obvious dancing motion of the mattress on which I sat. Nothing more than that – no sound of a crash or of anything else: no sense of shock, no jar that felt like one heavy body meeting another. And presently the same thing repeated with about the same intensity.

There was no reaction from the other cabins. He went back to his book, until the stopping of the engines a few moments later reawakened curiosity. Dressing gown over his pyjamas, he went up onto the boat deck, slightly embarrassed at what he was doing, and with a steward's indulgent and reassuring words in his ears. There were a couple of men up there in the freezing quiet, but no activity to indicate anything special had happened. Together with a Scottish engineer, he looked into the smoking room, where some card players had felt the impact and even seen the iceberg pass by the window – one of them estimated it at 80–90 feet (25–28 metres) high; it may have been closer to 70–75 feet (21–23 metres), taking it just above the level of the boat deck. Nobody was bothered. Someone gestured to his glass of whisky and asked if anyone fancied getting him some ice for *that*. Beesley returned to his cabin until he, too, heard increased activity. This time he put on his trousers and Norfolk jacket before venturing up to the cold, and now he noticed with some satisfaction that *Titanic* was slowly underway. On his way back down to E deck, however, he realized that the ship was sloping fractionally towards the bows.

> As I went downstairs a confirmation of this tilting forward came in something unusual about the stairs, a curious sense of something out of balance and of not being able to put one's feet down in the right place.

The stewards he met seemed to know nothing, but a few passengers were around. The cabin-mate of one of them was refusing to leave his warm bed. Beesley dressed himself fully and had just got back into his book when the shout came down for everyone to put on their lifebelts and assemble on deck. Still no general alarm had been sounded throughout the vast ship.

What had been happening in the meantime on the bridge will always be speculation. Quartermaster Alfred Olliver testified that orders were given to restart the engines, which tallies with Beesley's memories.

> Senator BURTON: Were the engines reversed; was she backed
> Mr. OLLIVER: Not whilst I was on the bridge; but whilst on the bridge she went

ahead, after she struck; she went half speed ahead.

Senator BURTON: The engines went half speed ahead, or the ship?

Mr. OLLIVER: Half speed ahead, after she hit the ice.

Senator BURTON: Who gave the order?

Mr. OLLIVER: The captain telegraphed half speed ahead.

Senator BURTON: Had the engines been backing before he did that?

Mr. OLLIVER: That I could not say, sir.

Senator BURTON: Did she have much way on?

Mr. OLLIVER: When?

Senator BURTON: When he put the engines half speed ahead?

Mr. OLLIVER: No, sir. I reckon the ship was almost stopped.

Captain Smith must have believed he could get the *Titanic* to Halifax, Nova Scotia, the nearest port capable of handling a huge ship; certainly the Dow Jones News Service testified to receiving a cable to that effect. At the time he gave the order he cannot have understood how serious the situation was, or he would have realized that moving the ship ahead would only increase the rate of flooding and bring forward the moment of sinking.

When loading a ship, particularly an oil tanker or ore carrier, it is vital both to distribute the cargo evenly and to ensure that the operation is carried out evenly, or the longitudinal stress will cause the ship to break its back. The massive weight of water now forcing its way into the *Titanic* caused further strain, and as her bow sank lower, water rose above the level of the water-tight bulkheads – which did not extend to the upper deck. The lower the bow sank, the more water could enter.

Nellie and her eldest child dressed little Richard and Marion, and shuffled coats over their own nightdresses. Without stopping to put on their lifebelts they hurried up one of the staircases and were shepherded into a large room full of women. Some were fully dressed, others far from it; all looked anxious and some were in tears. A couple of stewards arrived and took Marion and Richard while Ruth and her mother climbed the ladder to the boat deck. One taste of the temperature and Nellie sent Ruth back for some blankets. She relied heavily on her eldest.

Down in steerage, Leah Aks had heard a call for women and children to get up to the boats, and had hastily dressed Filly before carrying him towards one of the gates that segregated steerage from cabin passengers so that the former could be health-checked in America before being allowed to go through immigration. It was jammed. Frantically she screamed; one of the crew heard her and came to lift her and the baby over. She ran up the flights, only realizing when she finally emerged into the bitter chill of the crowded boat decks that she had forgotten to put anything on her son's head. Shivering herself, she was clutching Filly when she realized that the beautiful young blonde woman next to her was speaking to her. Madeleine Astor, 18 years old – the same as Leah – five months pregnant and returning from an extended honeymoon in Paris and Egypt with her millionaire husband, held out her long shawl.

'Here, wrap your baby, it's so cold out here.' Wrinkling her nose at the smell emanating from the nappy, she took a bottle of perfume from her handbag and told Leah to keep it.

Many passengers had persisted in believing either that the *Titanic* was unsinkable or that she would remain afloat until long after a fleet of other passenger ships, including the *Olympic*, arrived. Some were, without a doubt, held back by closed gates. A number were believed to have slept throughout.

Captain Smith knew from Andrews that his ship was mortally wounded. In the wireless room young Phillips and Bride were working flat out. The first distress call went out at 12:15 a.m.:

CQD CQD CQD CQD CQD CQD MGY have struck an iceberg. We are badly damaged. Titanic Position 41° 44, 50° 24 W.[8]

A second followed three minutes later.

CQD Position 41° 44, 50° 24 W. Require assistance.

Phillips then changed to a combined SOS CQD call, and was answered by the German ship *Frankfurt*, call sigh DFT.

Titanic to Frankfurt: Come at once MGY.

The puzzling response from the German ship was 'Stand by', but at 12:25 a.m. the Cunard liner *Carpathia*, call sign MPA, came through. Her operator, Harold Cottam, should have been in bed but was waiting for a message from *Parisien*. Finding *Titanic*'s frequency, he decided to tell her that the Cape Cod station had dispatches for her, and was shocked to be interrupted by:

CQD CQD SOS SOS CQD SOS Come at once. We have struck a berg. It's a CQD OM Position 41° 46, 50° 14 W. CQD SOS MGY.

Cottam replied:

Shall I tell my captain. Do you require assistance?

Yes. Come quick. MGY

The exchange was heard by Cape Race, which picked up the correction in *Titanic*'s position.

> 0026 MGY CQD Position 41° 46, 50° W. Require immediate assistance. We have collided with iceberg. Sinking, can hear nothing for the noise of steam.

The Marconi room was close to the bridge and the ship was blowing off the unused steam that was building up now the engines had stopped. It created 'a harsh deafening boom that made conversation difficult and no doubt increased the apprehension of some people merely because of the volume of noise,' said Beesley, likening it to twenty locomotives blowing off steam in low key.

Many ships picked up the stream of distress calls, but few were close enough to be of any practical use. At 12:45 the *Carpathia* called up the *Titanic*:

> We are coming as quickly as possible and expect to be there within four hours.

The Russian *Birma* hoped to be on site by 6:30 a.m. The *Baltic*, too, changed course, as well as the *Virginian* and the *Olympic*. The closest was the *Californian*, whose equipment was shut down for the night.

While the disbelieving radio operators were passing *Titanic*'s distress signals to their no-less-incredulous captains, down in the bowels of the ship the stokers and engineers continued to maintain the power even as the bow dipped lower and the water rose. On the boat deck the first lifeboat to be launched, no. 7, was lowered at 12:45 a.m. from the starboard side, containing entirely first-class passengers. No boat drill had been held on the *Titanic*. One had been due the previous day but the captain hand cancelled it, and to complicate matters the ship did not have sufficient crew to man the lifeboats and launch them. In most steamships, the majority of the crew worked in the engine department, and on a passenger liner a large percentage were attached to the victualling department as cooks, waiters and stewards. Brawny arms and seamanship were in short supply.

The Dodges probably reached the boat deck shortly before the first boat was lowered – Dodge is wrong about the order of launching the boats, and his family went in no. 5, not no. 3.

> At the time that we reached the boat deck, the first boat on the starboard side, No.1, was hanging over the side of the vessel from the davits, and a few persons, men and women, were seated therein. The officer in charge was calling for women and children to fill the boat, but seemed to have difficulty in finding those who were willing to enter. I myself, hesitated to place my wife and child in this boat, being unable to decide whether it would be safer to keep them on the steamer, or to entrust them to this frail boat which was the first to be launched, and which

hung over eighty feet above the water. In the meantime I busied myself with strapping on their life-preservers, and heard the officer give the command to 'Lower away'. This boat was launched with but twenty-six persons in it, although its capacity was over fifty, and about one-third were male passengers.

As I observed this boat lowered without accident, I placed my wife and child in the next boat, No. 3 – boats on the starboard side having the odd numbers. This boat was ordered lowered when it contained less than thirty-five persons. In neither case were additional women to be found. Each of these boats contained at least ten male passengers. As I saw this boat lowered, containing my wife and child, I was overwhelmed with doubts, as to whether or not I was exposing them to greater danger, than if they had remained on board the ship.

At the same time, on the port side of the ship, the elderly Mrs Rosilie Straus turned back from lifeboat 6 to her husband with the now immortal words: 'We have been together for many years. Where you go, I go.' She took off her fur coat and gave it to her maid, insisting that she take it because it would be cold in the boat. She herself sat down with her husband. Neither survived. Second Officer Lightoller was stricter than most in enforcing the unwritten rule of women and children first, but on the other side of the ship, Sir Cosmo Duff-Gordon, his wife, her maid and his secretary were inexplicably lowered away in a boat that could have taken many times more.

The musicians had initially assembled in the first-class reception room, and were playing some light-hearted music that reassured all those gathering there. Only when passengers were ordered to the boat and promenade decks did they re-form outside the gymnasium and continue their performance, fingers growing numb with cold. Beesley recalled:

I was now on the starboard side of the top boat deck; the time about 12:20. We watched the crew at work on the lifeboats, numbers 9, 11, 13, 15, some inside arranging the oars, some coiling ropes on the deck – the ropes which ran through the pulleys to lower to the sea – others with cranks fitted to the rocking arms of the davits. As we watched, the cranks were turned, the davits swung outwards until the boats hung clear of the edge of the deck. Just then an officer came along from the first-class deck and shouted above the noise of escaping steam, 'All women and children get down to deck below and all men stand back from the boats.' He had apparently been off duty when the ship struck, and was lightly dressed, with a white muffler twisted hastily round his neck. The men fell back and the women retired below to get into the boats from the next deck. Two women refused at first to leave their husbands, but partly by persuasion and partly by force they were separated from them and sent down to the next deck. I think that by this time the work on the lifeboats and the separation of men and women impressed on us slowly the presence of imminent danger, but it made no difference in the attitude

of the crowd: they were just as prepared to obey orders and to do what came next
as when they first came on deck.

Leah Aks, Hilda Slayter and Bridget Bradley waited patiently. Washington
Dodge was helping to load the boats. Beesley remained on the upper deck,
looking down over the rail unless distracted by the blinding flare of the distress
rockets whose transient flight briefly lit up the deck and the huge funnels and,
perhaps for the first time, brought home to everyone that the situation was
grave. Nellie Becker's two youngest were being lifted into boat no. 11 just as
Ruth returned with the blankets.

'That's all for this boat,' the officer – probably Murdoch – shouted. Horrified
at being separated from the children Nellie begged him to let her go with them,
and only as she was bundled in did she realize that Ruth was still on the deck.
The 12-year-old had no alternative but to move down to where a group of
people were gathered around boat no. 13. A commotion was breaking out as a
man tried to rush the boat Ruth's mother was in, and was forced back by the
stewards.

Swearing that he would show what was meant by women and children first,
he snatched Filly from Leah's arms and threw him into the boat that was
about to depart. Distraught, Leah tried to scramble after him, but was held
back by the crew, who thought she, too, was trying to jump the queue. She was
still sobbing hysterically as the officers pitched her into boat 13 between
Selina Cook and Ruth. Into the same boat went Bridget Bradley and Hilda
Slayter.

Boat 13 was filling up. The cry of 'Any more ladies?' rang out. None
appeared. 'Very well, men, tumble in,' said Frederick Ray, the table steward
who had waited on Dodge not so long ago. Dodge was the only person from
first class in the group permitted to embark in boat 13. One of the crew glanced
up and called Beesley: 'any more ladies on your deck.'

'No.'

'Then you had better jump.'

Beesley sat on the edge of the deck, threw his dressing gown into the boat
and then allowed himself to drop into the stern. Panting for breath, two women
suddenly appeared, having reached the deck by one of vertical ladders
normally used by the crew.

'Lower away!'

A husband, wife and child materialized. The baby was passed to an Irish lady
in the stern beside Beesley; the mother got in amidships and the boat was
moving as the father jumped. In a last-minute panic, Bridget stood up and
seized one of the ropes, shouting that she would be safer on the ship. She had
almost got a grip of the cold deck rail when one of the sailors in charge of the
boat pulled her back down. Beesley remembered the scene:

Looking back now on the descent of our boat down the ship's side, it is a matter of surprise, I think, to all the occupants to remember how little they thought of it at the time. It was a great adventure, certainly: it was exciting to feel the boat sink by jerks, foot by foot, as the ropes were paid out from above and shrieked as they passed through the pulley blocks, the new ropes and gear creaking under the strain of a boat laden with people, and the crew calling to the sailors above as the boat tilted slightly, now at one end, now at the other, 'Lower aft!' 'Lower stern!' and 'Lower together!' as she came level again – but I do not think we felt much apprehension about reaching the water safely. It certainly was thrilling to see the black hull of the ship on one side and the sea, seventy feet below, on the other, or to pass down by cabins and saloons brilliantly lighted; but we knew nothing of the apprehension felt in the minds of some of the officers whether the boats and lowering gear would stand the strain of the weight of our sixty people.

The 64 in the boat had two narrow escapes in quick succession. As they approached the sea their bow was going to cross the massive stream of water being spewed out of the ship by the condenser pump. Frantic howls of fear reached the crew on the deck, who paused while the boat crew got at the oars, untied them and pushed the bow away from the side of the ship.

They were down safely, one of only a few that actually left the ship full. Still with the ropes attached the boat floated, the current from the condenser pushing it towards the point where boat 15 would land. Looking up, they saw the ominous bulk descending.

'Stop lowering fourteen!' they yelled, not knowing that the boats on their side bore odd numbers. Nothing happened. The boat continued down. Beesley and one of the stokers stood up, and as she came right over their heads they got a hand to her keel and tried to push themselves off. Another stoker was hacking through the ropes that still attached their own boat to the ship. They heard him shout 'One! Two!' Just in time, the restraining ropes parted and they were able to push themselves away. Boat 15 settled beside them, its occupants totally unaware of the drama.

Though some of the boats' crews were so under strength that even first-class ladies had to row – famously, the Countess of Rothes took the tiller of her boat – no. 13 contained around 24 crewmen, including Lee from the crow's nest and several stokers, the latter dressed only in trousers and vest. The Irish lady opposite whom Beesley had sat at dinner distributed various items of clothing she had had the forethought to bring, while at the same time nursing ten month old Alden Caldwell, the baby whose family had only just made it into the boat. Ruth still had the blankets she had brought for her mother and those were given to some of the stokers. One of the latter wistfully remembered the soup that was heating for him on the machinery when the water inundated his compartment and forced him to scramble out before the door came down like a guillotine. Beesley's acquaintance offered him a fur-lined coat, but he refused to accept it while there were women ill-dressed for the bitter chill, and it was given to an Irish girl.

The sea was soft and black, the sky alive with stars. Low-voiced conversations in Swedish and Norwegian mingled with the accents of Ireland, Cornwall and America, and eyes turned towards *Titanic*. Beesley wrote that

> I had often wanted to see her from some distance away ... to take in a full view of her beautiful proportions ... Little did I think that the opportunity was to be found so quickly and so dramatically. The background, too, was a different one from what I had planned for her: the black outline of her profile against the sky was bordered all round by stars studded in the sky, and all her funnels and masts were picked out in the same way: her bulk was seen where the stars were blotted out. And one other thing was different from expectation: the thing that ripped away from us instantly, as we saw it, all sense of the beauty of the night, the beauty of the ship's lines, and the beauty of her lights – and all these taken in themselves were intensely beautiful – that thing was the awful angle made by the level of the sea with the rows of porthole lights along her side in dotted lines, row above row. The sea level and the rows of lights should have been parallel – should never have met – and now they met at an angle inside the black hull of the ship. There was nothing else to indicate she was injured; nothing but this apparent violation of a simple geometrical law – that parallel lines should never meet.

Boat 13 had been launched at about 1:30 a.m. Shortly after, the *Baltic* and the *Olympic* notified that they were on their way; Cape Race asked the *Virginian* to head for the scene. At 1:40 a.m. *Birma* received:

> SOS SOS CQD CQD MGY. We are sinking fast. Passengers being put into boats MGY.

At 1:45 a.m. John Phillips contacted the *Carpathia* for the last time:

> Come as quickly as possible. Engine room filling up to the boilers. TU OM GN [thank you old man, goodnight].

Three minutes later, the *Asian* picked up a faint distress call from the *Titanic*. At 2:00 a.m. the *Virginian* also heard the same. At 2:17 a.m., after detecting another weak CQD, she tried in vain to raise the *Titanic*.

It was too late. Different passengers even in the same boat have different recollections of the ship's final moments. Some heard the strains of 'Nearer My God To Thee' floating across the water. A mile away, Dodge remembered the lights suddenly going out. For Ruth Becker in the bows of the little boat,

It was going down just slowly, not fast at all and the night was dark, no moon, a very dark black night and that boat was just beautiful, all the lights in the boat were on. Just a beautiful sight. But it was going down quietly and the lights were just going under the water as it went down and I remember that very plainly – and I thought it was a beautiful sight and a terrible sight because you could see that the boat was going under the water …

… When the ship broke in half, of course it broke in half between the funnels, the stern stayed up for about a minute or so and then it went down, that's the way we saw it.[9]

What none of them forgot were the cries. Dodge, one of many who believed there had been time to evacuate the whole ship, and who had not realized how inadequate was the lifeboat provision, was shaken.

> Any impression which I had had that there were no survivors aboard, was speed-ily removed from my mind by the faint, yet distinct, cries which were wafted across the waters. Some there were in our boat, who insisted that these cries came from occupants of the different lifeboats, which were nearer the scene of the wreck than we were, as they called one to another. To my ear, however they had but one meaning, and the awful fact was borne in upon me that many lives were perishing in those icy waters.
>
> With the disappearance of the steamer, a great sense of loneliness and depres-sion seemed to take possession of those in our boat.

A few survived the sinking in the water: young Jack Thayer, Colonel Archibald Gracie, Rhoda Abbott and Second Officer Lightoller were among those pulled from the water or rescued from Collapsible Lifeboat A by the couple of boats that did return. Few boats dared, even those with twenty or more spaces in them, for fear of being swamped. The Duff Gordons' boat was all but empty, and nobody was ever sure whether the money paid by Sir Cosmo to the crew was to compensate them for their losses or to bribe them not to go back. Boat 13 was full and did not face that dilemma. They rowed away, trying but failing to sing in order to mask the fading calls for help that lingered for up to an hour.

With the dawn spreading in shades of pink and gold over an eerie landscape of rough ice and towering bergs, Captain Arthur Rostron of the Cunard liner *Carpathia* came to a stop at 4:00 a.m. – the line that White Star's parent company had set out to destroy was, ironically, the first to the rescue. For more than three hours Rostron had raced a deadly slalom course at full speed, firing rockets while his crew made ready to receive any number of people. One by one the lifeboats huddled alongside the *Carpathia*. Too cold to be able to grip a rope ladder, Ruth was one of many women who were hoisted up in slings. Babies and small children came aboard in canvas bags. The early light showed men and women in strange layers of night and day clothes, and even before they were safely on the *Carpathia*, the grateful souls of boat 13 were attempting to return borrowed items to the generous Irish lady who had shared them out.

Ruth was reunited with her mother and siblings; Washington Dodge found his wife and young son, and an acquaintance of theirs who happened to be travelling on the *Carpathia* was one of many, male and female, who gave up their cabins and staterooms to the survivors. Bridget found she had been sharing the boat with one of her Ballydesmond friends, and another, farm-labourer Buckley, survived in boat 4 because Madeleine Astor had thrown some sort of wrap around him so he would not be evicted. Hilda Slayter had survived, but lost her wedding trousseau. The desperate Leah Aks roamed the decks with Selina Cook searching for Filly until she recognized him in the arms of an Italian woman in a black dress – possibly Argene del Carlo, who was pregnant but whose husband was among the dead. The stranger refused to return him, claiming he was a gift from God.

Called upon to make a judgement, much like Solomon, Captain Rostron took both women to his cabin and asked them to describe something distinctive about the child. Leah was able to tell him that her child had a strawberry birthmark and, being Jewish, was circumcised.

The *Carpathia* headed for New York, where anxious and stunned crowds gathered around White Star's offices.

Happy endings were the exception, not the rule. Only 705 had survived out of 2,228. Hundreds of women and children reached New York without husbands and fathers, emotional trauma compounded for many by the loss of the breadwinner. First-class passengers might be bereaved, but they would have families to support them. That was not going to be true for so many in steerage. The survival figures tell a grim tale:

199 out of 325 first-class
119 out of 285 second-class
174 out of 706 third-class
212 out of 885 crew

Yet within those figures lies one interesting statistic. Only 40 per cent of the men in first class made it. The legends are well attested: Benjamin Guggenheim saw his mistress into a boat before changing into evening dress along with his valet. Colonel Astor helped his child bride into the boat and when told that he – the richest man in the world – could not go with her, he handed her his gloves, waved goodbye and then helped load other women before going below to release the couple's Airedale terrier. Thomas Andrews, Isidor Straus, Charles Hayes, John Thayer Sr, all rich and powerful men, stood aside and died. It is too crude to say that money bought survival.

The shock of the *Titanic*'s loss was cataclysmic. The death toll was appalling, but it was the sheer fact of her sinking that rocked the world and shook its faith in the new century two years before the horrors of World War I. She became a warning against human arrogance, her very name synonymous with the 'vaulting ambition which o'erleaps itself'.

Like every other passenger ship of the time, *Titanic* did not have enough lifeboats for everyone, though more than the out-of-date regulations stipulated. After the inquiries in New York and London that followed the sinking, important legislation came into being: 24-hour wireless operation in which safety took precedence, a lifeboat place for everyone on board, and proper lifeboat drills. On 15 April 1912 *Titanic* did what no other ill-starred ship had achieved, but at a high cost.

The UK Board of Trade Inquiry headed by Charles Bigham, Lord Mersey, put the blame for the sinking on the ship's excessive speed under the conditions, but Captain Smith had gone down with his ship and was spared the vilification that pursued similarly reckless captains such as de Chaumareys and Piccone. The ship's speed may explain why the iceberg was spotted too late to avoid contact, but the precise nature of the damage she sustained was hotly disputed for decades. The popular view of the iceberg slicing her open down her length was myth, and until her rediscovery numerous theories were current. David G Brown, proponent of the allision theory, has demonstrated convincingly how such damage to her double bottom would have caused water to enter from much lower down than a gash on the side, and that restarting her engines in the belief that she could reach Halifax forced more water into the hull, overwhelming the pumps and further weakening her seams. But the subject is far from closed.

Nobody wished to speak ill of the dead, but they were all too willing to disparage the living. Men who left the ship in lifeboats – as opposed to those detailed to man the boats or who, like Jack Thayer and Charles Lightoller, were pulled from the water – fared badly in their remaining years. Business problems may have contributed to Dodge's suicide in 1919, but there is no doubt in the mind of his family that he came under intolerable pressure because he survived. Ismay was another who, in the mind of the public, should have done the 'decent thing' and, as the ship's owner, added himself to the death toll. Even the novelist Julian Barnes, in *A History of The World In 10½ Chapters* (1989) allows his narrator to peddle the unfounded theory that Beesley escaped dressed as a woman.

There *was* heroism that night: the stewardesses who remained at their stations; men who put their families into boats and pretended that they would follow them later; the engineers and stokers who kept the fires burning until the last; Captain Rostron of the *Carpathia*, who was knighted for his conduct. But that does not make the others cowards. They did not snatch lifebelts from women and children, or drag them out of the boats: most simply accepted a place in a half-empty boat as it was about to be lowered, and for that they were at best doubted, at worst damned. Despite having nothing against them other than that they survived, none of the *Titanic*'s surviving officers ever captained a merchant ship. The Royal Navy, however, had no cause to regret giving Lightoller command of a destroyer in World War I.

Neither investigation looked into why the death toll among steerage passengers was so high. Lack of English may have hindered many in understanding the seriousness of the situation. Others may have believed the propaganda about the ship's unsinkability. Undoubtedly some found themselves stuck behind locked gates, but was this deliberate, or through an absence of orders to unlock them? Thirty years later, on the *Laconia*, a not dissimilar situation would present itself.

And what of the policy of women and children first? Asked if it was the rule of the company, Second Officer Lightoller famously told the US inquiry: 'No, sir, the rule of humanity'. Where there *were* women and children on the boat deck, they were put into boats, in some cases against their will, regardless of class. For the suffragists this was a difficult moment. It was hard to sneer at the sacrifice made by men without condemning the women who accepted that sacrifice. Edith Corse Evans was one woman who did stand back, giving her friend the last place in the final boat because she had children at home. But for as long as women were treated as weaker creatures, in need of male protection, they could not gain equality. Even the idea that a husband could force his wife to enter a boat without him reinforced male domination.

One important strand has not been covered: the role of the *Californian*, stopped in the ice some 19 miles (35 kilometres) from the *Titanic*, her wireless man off duty. The subject is controversial and complex, and in the interests of justice would be best examined at length, so it will not be addressed here. What is it that has captured the public imagination about this ship, whose life lasted effectively for just four and a half days, and who, unlike her sister *Olympic*, had no time to establish a personality? The quiet dignity of so many hundreds of people; the heroism of those who upheld the code of their class or their profession; the band playing a hymn that raises a lump in the throat, even though nobody agrees on the tune; the palpable sense of the end of an era? Successive films have blurred the reality of the tragedy. But they converge with the survivors' memories, culminating in a single potent image: the great counter-stern rearing dark against the darker sky, and the terrible rending and crashing of internal destruction; the awe-inspiring end of a dream made of steel.

Sources and Bibliography

I am grateful to Shelley Dziedzic and Mike Findlay for information on Leah and Frank Aks, and to Barbara V Dodge for assistance with Washington.

RMS Titanic Inc
Titanic Historical Society

Beesley, Lawrence, *The Loss of the SS Titanic: Its Story and its Lessons* (Boston: Houghton Mifflin, 1912).
Davie, Michael: *The Titanic: The Full Story of a Tragedy* (London: Bodley Head, 1986).
Eaton, J P and Haas C A: *Titanic: Triumph and Tragedy* (Wellingborough: Patrick Stephens, 1986).
Eaton, J P and Haas, C A, *Titanic, Destination Disaster: The Legends and the Reality* (Wellingborough: Patrick Stephens, 1987).
Geller, Judith, *Titanic: Women and Children First* (Sparkford: Patrick Stephens, 1998)
Hustak, Alan, *Titanic: The Canadian Story* (Montreal: Véhicule Press, 1998).
Hyslop, D, Forsyth, A and Jemima, S: *Titanic Voices* (Southampton: Southampton City Council, 1994).
Marine Accident Investigation Branch, *RMS 'Titanic': Reappraisal of Evidence Relating to SS 'Californian'* (London: HMSO, 1992).
Robertson, Morgan, *Futility* (New York: M F Mansfield, 1898).

Dodge, Dr W, 'An Address ... Delivered before the Commonwealth Club, San Francisco, May 11, 1912', http://lodelink.com/titanic/index.html
Hennessey, John M, 'The Titanic Lifeboats Project', www.keyflux.com/titanic/lifeboats.htm
Nielsen, J C, 'Iceberg at The Golden Gate', www.encyclopedia-titanica.org/item/1487/
www.encyclopedia-titanica.org, (massive resource for biographical information etc.).
www.titanic-titanic.com

Notes

[1] Others include the *Lake Fisher*, 1890; the *Andrew Fenwick*, 1875; the *Amazon*, 1852; the *Tacora*, 1872; the *Minnie Breslauer*, 1873, as well as the *San Francisco*.

[2] Panelling from one of the *Olympic*'s state rooms can now be appreciated in the banqueting room at the *White Swan*, Alnwick, Northumberland.

[3] Ellerman Lines, 1902–33, not the 1936-built flagship that was carrying evacuated children when torpedoed in World War II.

[4] It has been stated that at 10:30 p.m. GMT on either Saturday 13 or Sunday 14 April the cargo steamer *Rappahannock*, bound for Liverpool, came within signalling distance of the liner and flashed a Morse code warning of heavy field ice and several icebergs, which *Titanic* similarly acknowledged. Dave Gittens's detailed analysis of this puzzle, however, comes to the conclusion that this story is a nautical myth. *Titanic: Monument and Warning*, Dave Gittens, available on CD-Rom via http://users.senet.com.au/~gittins/index.html

[5] Thanks to Professor César Caviedes at the University of Florida for information on El Niño-related effects in 1912.

[6] It is disputed whether the order was ever given, as no survivors recalled the lurch that they would have felt if such an order had been put into operation. For two fascinating theories on the sighting and avoidance tactics, see Nathan Robison's 'Hard A-Starboard' and Sam Halpern's 'Iceberg Right Ahead' on www.encyclopedia-titanica.org

[7] David G. Brown and Parks Stephenson, 'White Paper on the Grounding of *Titanic*', presented for consideration by the Marine Forensic Panel (SD-7) chartered by the Society of Naval Architects and Marine Engineers at Gibbs & Cox, Inc., Arlington, Virginia, 2001; Captain Erik D Wood, 'Damage to Titanic – a New Scenario', 2004; David G Brown, 'The Last Log of the *Titanic*', 2001

[8] CQD was the grouping of letters chosen by Marconi to stand as a general distress call. 'CQ' was the standard code for 'all stations', and 'D' stood for distress.

[9] While the perception of many was that the ship sank in one piece, Ruth was proved correct when in 1985 the remains of the stern and bow sections were located approximately 2000 feet (600 metres) apart by Dr Robert Ballard.

12

The Sea Shall
Not Have Them

USS *Squalus*

1939

Squalus *was a diesel sub, built at Portsmouth Yard;*
Gearing up for World War II, our crew was pressing hard;
Running her through sea trials, May 23rd 1939,
In a whipping wind we went out again, with fifty-nine men inside.

FROM 'BALLAD OF THE *SQUALUS*', COMPOSED AND SUNG BY JOHN PERRAULT

SETTING ASIDE THOSE WHO ARE SIMPLY CLAUSTROPHO-BIC, people who would rather travel by sea than fly tend to believe that, in the event of disaster, they have some control over their destiny. If a ship catches fire or starts to sink, they have a chance: peacetime submarine accidents send a shiver through the collective consciousness. In wartime, casualties to submariners are high, but have a certain remoteness. An enemy vessel may have existed only as an ASDIC[1] signal, and proof that it had been sunk with all hands often came as a sudden turbulent bubbling and a dark, oily streak on the face of the sea. But how many went down, injured but intact, until the hull could no longer bear the water pressure? Or lay helpless on the sea bed until the oxygen finally ran out?

That remoteness vanishes in a peacetime submarine accident unfolding in

Dramatis Personae

William Badders : diver

Edward Clayton : diver

Cyrus W Cole : rear admiral

Ruth Desautel : fiancée of Sherman Shirley

Walter Doyle : diving officer

Jesse Duncan : diver

Lawrence Gainor : chief electrician's mate

Halford Greenlee : captain of the Falcon

Walter Harman : diver

William Isaacs : relief cook

Charles Kuney : yeoman

James McDonald : diver

Lloyd Maness : electrician's mate first class

John Mihalowski : diver

Charles B Momsen : commander, US Navy

Oliver F Naquin : captain of the *Squalus*

John C Nichols : lieutenant

Joseph Patterson : ensign

Harold C Preble : naval architect

Sherman Shirley : torpedo officer

Martin Sibitsky : diver

Walter Squire : diver

Warren D Wilkin : captain of the *Sculpin*

the glare of publicity. Setting aside the early experimental vessels, the submarine has been with us for 120 years, and during that time, of the 171 known peacetime accidents (there may be others, kept secret for military reasons) only two successful deep-water rescues have ever taken place.[2]

Dover, New Hampshire, Monday 21 May 1939

Mrs Sherman Shirley ... In just a week she would be *Mrs Sherman Shirley*. Ruth Desautel looked at the diamond engagement ring sparkling on her finger and repeated the name to herself. The dress was finished, her trousseau complete. She even had the wedding ring at home in the drawer. Sherman had given it to her before he went off on more sea trials – shakedown trials, they called them – on the US Navy's newest submarine, the *Squalus*.

'Keep it,' the young Arkansas torpedo-man had said before returning to his base at Portsmouth. 'It will be safer in your possession than mine.'

Off Portsmouth, New Hampshire, Tuesday 22 May 1939

Monday's dives had gone well. The 35-year-old commander, Lieutenant Oliver Naquin, had been satisfied with the *Squalus* when he brought her back to a cove on the Piscataqua, the broad river that separates Maine from New Hampshire and provides the Portsmouth Naval Shipyard with its gateway to the Atlantic. Now they were going to make another, quick, dive,[3] popularly known as a crash dive, the escape manoeuvre that every submarine had to be able to execute in 60 seconds.

She belonged to the new generation, the *Sargo* class, all named after 'fighting' fish, though she was perhaps the most aptly named. There was something shark-like in her predatory black hull – 310 feet (94.5 metres) long – as she headed out to sea trailing foam from her bow and watched by the early risers and the green-draped heights. A stiff wind drove the grey clouds across the sun and raised whitecaps on the ocean. Ahead lay the Isles of Shoals, a scattering of low and rocky islands with evocative names such as Smuttynose, Duck and Lunging, and *Squalus* passed within a mile of the stumpy lighthouse on White Island[4] before pushing on for a further 4 miles (7.5 kilometres).

'Rig ship for dive' ordered Naquin from the bridge. His watch read 08:00 Lieutenant Walter Doyle, the diving control officer (DCO), was already at his station in the control room beneath the conning tower, checking the trim, compensating for any changes in weight since Monday's dives. At this point, all the hull openings had to be closed except for the essentials such as the main engine induction outboard valve, which supplied air to the diesels. When the *Squalus* actually dived, it would be shut hydraulically as she switched from diesel to battery propulsion. There were additional valves in the engine rooms that could be hand-cranked shut before diving as an extra precaution against any failure of the hydraulics, but it was a difficult task, and few submarines bothered.

Doyle studied the rigging-board. As each compartment reported 'rigged for dive' by telephone the appropriate light was changed from red to green. That festive combination had earned it the nickname of the 'Christmas tree'. Lieutenant John C Nichols double-checked the compartments forward of the control tower: the large torpedo room, and the battery, which was the preserve of the officers and chief petty officers, and below which half of the boat's batteries were housed. Aft of the control room, Ensign Joseph Patterson, a former Olympic athlete with all the promise of a brilliant naval career ahead of

Outline of a US Navy
Sargo class submarine.

him, was responsible for checking the rig of the after battery, the forward and after engine rooms, and the after torpedo room, where Sherman Shirley was at his post.

One by one the reports came through to Yeoman Charles Kuney's earphones as he sat beside the DCO. One by one the red lights gave way to green. Patterson and Nichols reported directly to Doyle. It was 08:25 when Captain Naquin received the confirmation: 'Ship rigged to dive'.

'Rig out bow planes.'

'Secure radio antenna trunk.'

One blast on the diving alarm.

Leaning against the chart desk, facing forward, one foot on the bottom rung of the ladder and the other on a tool-box so he could see everything that was going on, civilian naval architect Harold C Preble gripped a stopwatch in each hand to time every action, watching the rigging board.

Conning tower hatch indicator, green.

3 and 4 Engines shut down.

5 seconds.

1 and 3 Engines shut down.

7 seconds.

Engine air inductions closed.

9 seconds.

Doyle held up two fingers: two blasts on the diving alarm.

'Pressure in the boat.'

The barometer responded as air was bled in to check the boat was watertight.

Naquin came down into the control room.

'Pressure in the boat, green board,' reported Doyle.

Depth 35 feet.

38 seconds.

Depth 50 feet.

58 seconds.

The *Squalus* was at periscope depth; the change from diesel to battery had produced an illusory silence. As the gauge touched 60 feet and the satisfied Naquin had gone to his periscope, anguished shouts reached Kuney through his earphones.

'The engine rooms are flooding!'

'Take her up! Take her up!'

Never mind the green lights, the main induction valve must be open: icy torrents were cascading into the engine rooms, overwhelming those vainly trying to wind shut the lower valves.

'Blow main ballast!' ordered Doyle. They had to surface, without delay. 'Blow safety and bow buoyancy!'

She was still sinking: however much her bow struggled towards the fading light, the tons of water that had poured into the aft compartments inexorably dragged her down by the stern.

'Shut the after battery door!' Naquin fired the command at Lloyd Maness, who was due to be Shirley's best man. The heavy hatch opened outwards, gravity working against him. Shouts begged him to wait. He managed to hold it open just long enough for seven frantic men to struggle through the rising water, half swimming, half hauling themselves up the angled deck. In the forward battery, barehanded, Lawrence Gainor had gone down into the tank only to find boiling acid as the cells shorted out. If he pulled the switch, he would electrocute himself; if he didn't, the massive battery would explode. He pulled. The emergency lights went out. By a miracle he was still alive.

The *Squalus* settled 200 feet down (60 metres) at an angle of 11°, and with a gentleness at odds with the jets of oil and water spraying viciously into the control room, powerful enough to knock men off their feet. Only when that had been dealt with could Naquin take stock of a situation that had developed in the course of no more than the five minutes since the order to dive.

They feared that many of those aft of the control room must have drowned, but there was no panic in the cold darkness relieved only by a couple of torches. Thirty-three were certainly alive in the first three compartments and, apart from some bruising, uninjured. They had to keep calm, operate the distress system, conserve oxygen, and wait. Their failure to announce their return to the surface would ring the alarm bells at Portsmouth. Water had got into the batteries to create deadly chlorine gas, so after retrieving all the blankets they could from the bunks in the forward battery to keep themselves warm in the plunging temperatures, they sealed off the compartment from the passage so as to keep the gas out.

The first distress rocket was fired. Activated from inside the submarine it would soar up and explode in a thick cloud of smoke that ought to attract any vessels in the vicinity. Then Nichols sent up the marker buoy. Bright yellow and attached to a line, it proclaimed: *Submarine sunk here, telephone inside.* They had radioed their position as they began the dive, so there would be no difficulty in locating them.

What they did not know was that their position had either been mis-transmitted or mistranslated, nor that it would be nearly an hour before their silence would cause concern.

10:40, Portsmouth Naval Base

Admiral Cyrus Cole was finally becoming anxious. USS *Sculpin* was sent out
to look for her errant sister. Assuming a mere oversight, but preparing for a
worst-case scenario, Cole called Submarine Squadron Two at New London,
Connecticut, 200 miles (370 kilometres) away by sea, to put the submarine
rescue support vessel *Falcon* on alert. The news was not good: she was being
serviced, but they promised to get her operational as soon as possible. She was
critical to any rescue, since she carried a rescue chamber developed for just
such an emergency.

Misled by the incorrect longitude, *Sculpin* set course for a point 5 miles (9
kilometres) from the disaster site, and found nothing. It was only by chance
that, around 13:00, a young officer turned from the driving spray-soaked wind
and spotted what could have been a smoke bomb. The *Sculpin* changed course
and picked up the buoy. Long before the voice of Captain Wilkin had reached
Lieutenant Nichols in the forward torpedo room, the familiar thrash of her
propellers and throb of her engine had identified her to the cramped survivors.

'What is your trouble?'

'High induction open, crew's compartment, forward and after engine rooms
flooded. Not sure about after torpedo room but could not establish communication with that compartment. Hold the phone and I will put the Captain on.'
Half a minute later Naquin was there.

'How are things?'

'Consider the best method to employ is to send diver down as soon as possible to close high induction and then hook on salvage lines to flooded compartments and free them of water in attempt to bring her up; for the present
consider that preferable to sending personnel up with lungs.'

He was referring to the Momsen Lung (officially, the Submarine Escape
Appliance), a breathing device especially developed to enable crews to escape
from submarines that could not be raised by other methods. All submariners
were trained in it but none had yet needed to use it. The man who had invented
it was already about to set out from Washington for Portsmouth.

A former submarine commander, Charles B Momsen – nicknamed 'Swede',
although his antecedents were Danish and German – Momsen had been
appalled by the number of submariners killed in peacetime accidents for want
for rescue systems. The crew of the *O-5* in 1923, struck by a steamer in the
placid, shallow approach to the Panama Canal and with a couple of huge floating cranes in the vicinity, had been lucky; that of the *S-51*, rammed by the
merchant steamer *City of Rome* in Long Island Sound in 1925, was not.
Momsen, who had been on the spot, later learned that many of the recovered
bodies were of men who had not drowned …

His proposal for a rescue chamber that could be lowered from the surface
was brushed off by the navy, just before the loss of the *S-4* – off Cape Cod in

1927 – whose despairing crew tapped out their Morse code messages for three days after sinking. Frustrated, Momsen turned to another idea – the Momsen Lung – on which he worked unofficially and tested at the risk of his own life. News reached the press before the authorities, and the work was swiftly endorsed. The prestige he won allowed him to develop his diving bell (officially, the McCann[5] Rescue Chamber) which was now being loaded back onto the fantail of the old *Falcon*, the ship that had been on station above the *S-51* and the *S-4* and which Momsen had used in his own trials. Like the Lung, it had never been put to the test in a real-life emergency, nor trialled at the depth of the *Squalus*.

N aquin had hardly finished his initial communication when the cable parted, but the *Sculpin* had found them and the first reports were feeding back to Portsmouth. Admiral Cole was already on his way on the tug *Penacook*; other ships, including the navy tug *Wandank*, had been requested to make for the area. It was vital to establish physical contact with the stranded submarine, and the *Penacook* dragged first her own grapnel, then that of the *Sculpin*, until she hooked the *Squalus*, attaching the other end of the line to a wooden deck grating to create a makeshift marker buoy.

As afternoon turned into evening and towards night, the *Wandank* achieved contact with Squalus through her oscillator, and *Squalus* attempted to make her morse-code tapping audible to the equipment on the surface ship. It was frustratingly faint, but at 21:45. Naquin succeeded in telling his would-be rescuers that conditions were satisfactory but cold. The latter was an understatement: the temperature was close to freezing and men huddled together under blankets or in bunks; Naquin gave his own coat to a crewman in particularly bad shape. Time lost meaning. Oxygen levels remained low but adequate. For most of the time darkness was total, and all that men could do was to dream of how and when rescue would come.

Despite the weather, the naval seaplane landed safely on the Piscataqua and decanted Momsen and his team, who were taken out to

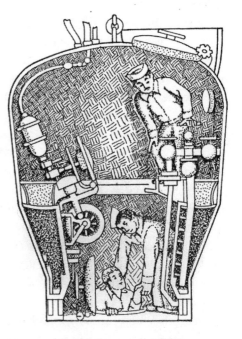

The McCann Rescue Chamber, designed by Charles Momsen for underwater rescue of submarine crews.

Admiral Cole, arriving just as Naquin's message was being made out. Nothing could be done that night other than keep station over the *Squalus* and wait for the *Falcon*, which was steaming around the coast and was due in the early hours of the night. Although Naquin had more confidence in his original idea, the experts preferred to put their faith in the Rescue Chamber.

Back in Portsmouth and the surroundings towns, where many of the crew had their families, Naquin's laconic message that conditions were satisfactory had been widely interpreted as proof that all 59 men on board were alive. By now, Cole had been told that the control room had been unable to raise anyone in the after compartments, but it was only when a group of journalists returned from the site that the news of probable fatalities became public. Wives and parents haunted the naval yard, or shut themselves in their houses. Aboard the *Falcon*, Captain Greenlee's thoughts could never have been far from his son-in-law, Ensign Patterson. Ruth Desautel told reporters she was sure her fiancé was alive.

The *Falcon* arrived in the early hours, bringing more expert divers and a McCann Rescue Chamber (RC), which resembled nothing so much as the barrel of an old siege mortar. In Momsen's succinct words:

> This apparatus is a pear shaped steel chamber, the big end uppermost, seven feet at the greatest diameter and ten feet high. It is divided into an upper closed compartment and a lower open compartment by a horizontal bulkhead which has a water tight hatch in its middle. Surrounding the lower compartment is a ballast tank of a capacity just equal to that of the lower compartment. Inside the lower compartment is a reel with 400 feet of ½" steel wire on it. The reel is operated by a shaft leading into the upper compartment. The shaft is rotated by an air motor. On the bottom edge of the lower compartment a rubber gasket is embedded into a circular groove, so that when the chamber is brought into contact with a flat surface (the hatch ring) a watertight joint may be effected with the application of pressure. Attached to the upper compartment is an air supply and an atmospheric exhaust hose, wire wound for strength. Also electric cables for telephone and light are attached. A wire pendant for hoisting and lowering is shackled into a padeye on top. This wire is also used for retrieving the chamber in case of emergency.

In the morning, the divers were organized. First they had to confirm that the *Wandank* had snagged the *Squalus* and not something else. In his full deep-sea diving kit Martin Sibitsky followed the line down to the bottom. To general relief he reported back that he was on the deck and could see the capstan. Attached to the RC's winch, down came the end downhaul wire, which had to be shackled to a central bar across the forward escape hatch. On the *Falcon*, Walter Harman and John Mihalowski made their way into the upper chamber of the RC.

At 11:30 the RC left the deck and entered the water, where her crew blew the main ballast and flooded the lower compartment before beginning to reel in the downhaul line. The descent began a minute before noon. By 12:02 they were 150 feet (45 metres) down, and paused to relieve the pressure vent. A few minutes later and they had the *Squalus* in their sights. By 12:27 Harman was blowing the lower compartment and checking that the seal was tight before Mihalowski bolted the RC to the rings around the hatch of the submarine. The four steel bolts were a final precaution. Now he was able to open the hatch and shout down.

Nothing. Of course – the crew had shut the lower hatch. But a few moments later he was staring down into upturned faces and passing hot food and drink to them, hearing their cheerful demands to know what the delay had been about.

'Where are the napkins?' someone demanded.

Naquin selected six men – those suffering the most – for the first ascent, including Harold Preble and William Isaacs, the last man into the control room before Maness had shut the hatch. Nichols was dispatched with them to brief the rescuers. At 12:56 the submarine hatch was closed. Now running in reverse, the motor unwound the downhaul line, the RC ascended under its own buoyancy, and by 1:30 the first dazed survivors were emerging onto the deck of the *Falcon*. History had been made, and ghosts laid to rest.

'We tried to appear calm', Momsen said, 'and maybe others were, but to me this was the most exciting moment of my life.'

Within a quarter of an hour the RC was back in the water, with William Badders replacing Mihalowski. This time nine men were brought up without a hitch, including Gainor, without whose raw courage in the battery tank there would have been no one to rescue. Almost immediately the RC was returned to the water. Momsen was anxious to take no chances with the weather turning against them.

Within the RC, Badders and Mihalowski were having minor trouble with the clutch, but in two hours the third batch, another nine men, had had been safely delivered to the *Falcon*. James McDonald swapped places with Badders. One more trip would bring up the rest of those known to be alive.

Naquin observed the captain's tradition of leaving last. At 20:14 they were on their way.

Sixty-five feet and 13 minutes later the RC stopped.

'The wire's jammed on the reel,' reported McDonald via the telephone link. Momsen was prepared for this.

'We'll heave on the retrieving wire,' he told McDonald, hoping that this would force the downhaul wire free. As they did, however, the steel of the retrieving wire strands began to snap – 'like firecrackers' – and they stopped just in time. As floodlights held the closing night back from the *Falcon*, the

RC hung tethered to the *Squalus*. This was an unforeseen complication, and they would have to take the RC back down to the bottom while it was dealt with. As McDonald slowly flooded the ballast tank and began the controlled descent to the floor, Momsen had the damaged retrieving line slowly paid out.

Walter Squire from Washington's Experimental Diving Base now followed the old grappling line down to the deck of the *Squalus*. At the limits of diving capability, under intense physical and mental pressure, and in complete darkness, he found the hatch, but the wire was taut. Momsen had a pair of wire cutters fed down to him, and he cut the jammed downhaul wire that had caused the initial problem.

It was 9:22. Naquin, Doyle, Kuney and their five companions had been in the RC for more than an hour. They had air and light, but they were freezing cold. The silence of the first attempt had given way to singing and discussion of how best to cook steak.

Momsen's next concern was to get a new retrieving wire attached to the top of the RC in the impenetrable darkness. This was a task for diver Jesse Duncan, but the darkness was too much; he found himself tangled in the various lines attached to the RC while trying to hold onto the heavy wire he was bringing down. They brought him up only just in time and got him into decompression.

His colleague Edward Clayton took over. Working 200 feet – 60 metres – down, and with touch alone to guide him, he struggled for more than half an hour to perform the task, his own lines becoming tangled. Momsen brought him up. It was far too dangerous. There was only one option. Momsen gave McDonald his instructions. They were going to hand-haul the retrieving wire, but he would have to relieve the load on it by blowing the ballast tanks as ordered. The dangers were all too apparent. The chamber had to remain just on the negative side of neutral buoyancy. Positive buoyancy would rush it to the surface and under the *Falcon*.

At four minutes past midnight McDonald blew the main ballast tank for 30 seconds. Above, Momsen's men pulled. Not enough. Try another 15-second blow ... Still too much strain. Fifteen seconds again.

Now the wire was hauling easily, the one fragile strand bearing what little weight remained. At 12:23 the top of the RC arrived in the pool of harsh light; two minutes later, and four hours after quitting the *Squalus*, the last seven men staggered free.

The following evening Badders and Mihalowski made a hazardous fifth descent to confirm Naquin's conviction that nobody in the after section remained alive, and found the stern full of water. Of the 26 men who drowned, including Patterson and Shirley, 25 were recovered when the *Squalus* was raised. One body was believed to have floated away during the salvage work.

The cause of the accident was never determined by the inquiry, which convened on 19 June but whose work could not be completed until the submarine had been raised and power restored to her. On 15 September Doyle and Naquin went on board and Doyle tried to close the high induction valve, without success. Once the hydraulic system had been oiled, however, it shut perfectly. Why it had failed two months earlier remains a mystery.

Nobody was blamed, but it became known that another submarine, the *Snapper,* had evaded the fate of the *Squalus* in an identical incident because her crew routinely shut those difficult lower induction valves. A third, the *Skipjack*, had experienced a minor problem with her high induction, and her crew became assiduous in keeping their lower valves well oiled. Neither incident was known to the officers of the *Squalus*.

Modifications were made across the submarine fleet to create a watertight bulkhead and door between the two engine rooms and to replace those difficult hand-cranked valves by spring-driven cut-off valves whose controls were at a distance from the valves themselves.

Commended for his leadership throughout the crisis, but criticized for not ensuring that the crew routinely shut the valves, Oliver Naquin never commanded another submarine. He went on to a successful career in surface vessels, however, while the *Squalus* ...

Squalus sat in drydock, rebuilt and recommissioned;
Engine room they called the tomb, well that's all superstition.
They rechristened her the *Sailfish* but she's the *Squalus* in my dreams;
Every night I go back down inside that submarine.

                                                                (Perrault)

Yet, setting aside the devastating grief of the bereaved families, the *Squalus* incident was hailed as a personal triumph – and vindication – for Momsen, McCann and the rescue team (several of whom received the Medal of Honour), and a seeming assurance that, from now on, a submarine crew trapped no deeper than human diving capability could be rescued. The technology was never kept secret. Then, just over a month later, on her own shakedown trials, HMS *Thetis* went down in Liverpool Bay with the loss of 101 of the 103 crew and civilian engineers on board. Two men escaped from the hatch; the rest drowned or suffocated. In fact, the McCann Rescue Chamber was only ever used on the *Squalus* rescue, and it would be 66 years until a second successful deep-water submarine rescue would be carried out. Within a few months war broke out, and there was practically no chance of rescuing any trapped crew. After 1945 thoughts turned once again to submarine rescue. The Royal Navy's assessment was that since accidents to their submarines were most likely to occur around the UK coast, a static diving-bell design was not the best rescue option, as it requires a virtually perfect sea and weather conditions that rarely prevail in the British Isles. Instead, they invested in escape techniques and equipment such as the Immersion Escape Suit.

Sources and Bibliography

Based on interviews with Momsen, Peter Maas's book is a very readable account not just of the *Squalus* rescue but of all Momsen's pioneering work. Carl LaVO's book is essential reading for anyone who believes that fact is stranger than fiction and wants to find out what happened next. Sincere thanks to John Perrault for allowing me to use excerpts from 'The Ballad of the *Squalus*' and to Commander Jeff Tall, director of the Royal Navy Submarine Museum.

Naval Historical Center, Washington, DC. USS *Squalus* file, World War II Command File.

LaVO, Carl: *Back from the Deep: The Strange Story of the Sister Subs* Squalus *and* Sculpin (Annapolis: Naval Institute Press, 1994).
Maas, Peter: *The Rescuer* (London: Collins, 1968).
Perrault, John, 'The Ballad of the *Squalus*', from *The Ballad of Louis Wagner and other New England Stories in Verse*, book and CD published by Peter Randall, Portsmouth, NH, 2003 (www.johnperrault.com)

Clearwater Sun, 28 May 1973
New York Times
USA Today 16 August 2000

Momsen, Commander Charles B, 'Rescue and Salvage of USS *Squalus*', www.history.navy.mil/faqs/faq99-6.htm (lecture delivered to the Harvard Engineering Society on 6 October 1939). www.seacoastnh.com

Notes

[1] ASDIC stands for Anti- (or Allied) Submarine Detection Investigation Committee. The term was eventually replaced by Sonar, an acronym derived from SOund Navigation And Ranging.

[2] Source: International Submarine Escape and Rescue Liaison Office (ISMERLO). However, in 1973 two men laying a telephone cable off Ireland spent three days at a depth of 1600 feet (490 metres) when their diving bell plummeted to the sea bed. By the time they were located and pulled to the surface there were only a few minutes of oxygen left. The drama inspired one of the two men, former Royal Navy submariner Roger Chapman, to design the LR5 submersible, which is now at the heart of the UK's submarine rescue service. Chapman and Roger Mallinson still hold the depth record for deep-sea rescue survival.

3 *The Fleet Type Submarine* (Navpers 16160, 1946) defines a quick dive as follows:
A *quick dive* is made when the ship is underway on one or more main engines. The bow planers are placed on FULL DIVE and the forward speed results in a maximum downward thrust on the bow planes. As the submarine submerges, the upper surfaces of the hull and superstructure act as planing surfaces and increase the downward thrust. The quick dive is the fastest type and is used in acceptance trials of new submarines, when it must be executed within 60 seconds from standard diving trim.

[4] This lighthouse was once home to Celia Thaxter, whose poem 'The Tryst' (1872) now stands as a portent of the *Titanic* disaster (see p. 248)

[5] Commander Allen McCann USN had worked on it after Momsen, though it was very much the latter's creation. Peter Maas holds the very plausible view that Momsen had ruffled too many naval feathers to be allowed such officially sanctioned fame.

13

The Alexandria Raid

HMS *Valiant* and HMS *Queen Elizabeth*

1941

His valour shown upon our crests today
Hath taught us how to cherish such high deeds,
Even in the bosoms of our adversaries.

SHAKESPEARE, *HENRY IV, Part I*, Act V, scene v

SOME OF THE MOST REMARKABLE and enduring maritime incidents have taken place amid the horrors of the war at sea, and as the mists of propaganda and secrecy disperse they gain rather than lose their fascination. The wartime imperative of unconditional patriotism and maintaining home-front morale tends to stereotype the enemy as monster or coward. National honour and prestige are boosted by an army of insults for the other side: wop, limey, eyetie, frog, kraut, dago, fuzzy-wuzzy ... the list goes on. In stating that 'The Anglo Saxons do not require orders but obey them when they are given. The Germans require orders and obey them. The Italians do not like orders and do not obey them,' an Italian officer of the submarine *Glauco* proved that national stereotypes can also be self-inflicted.

Dramatis Personae

Mr Amin : captain, Egyptian police

Claude Barrington Barry : captain of the *Queen Elizabeth*

Emilio Bianchi : MAS petty officer and SLC diver

Prince Junio Valerio Borghese : commander of the underwater forces of the Decima Flottiglia MAS

Sir Andrew Browne Cunningham : admiral, commander of the Mediterranean Fleet

Luigi Durand de la Penne : MAS lieutenant and SLC pilot

Mr al Fayed : Egyptian police lieutenant

Mohammed Attia Hassan : Egyptian police detective

George Hilton : blacksmith, *Valiant*

Denis Holton : clerical staff, *Valiant*

Einar Leire : captain of the *Sagona*

Richard Long : lieutenant, *Queen Elizabeth*

Antonio Marceglia : MAS engineer captain and SLC pilot

Mario Marino : MAS petty officer and SLC diver

Vincenzo Martellotta : MAS gunner captain and SLC pilot

Sir Charles Morgan : captain of the *Valiant*

Dimbashi el Naccar : Egyptian police lieutenant

Ali Mohammad al Naggar : corporal, Egyptian customs police

Duncan Newson : sub lieutenant, *Valiant*

Ahmet el Sayed Mursim : hotel proprietor

Spartaco Schergat : MAS sergeant and SLC diver

Sverre Thoraldsen : third officer, *Sagona*

Time not only soothes wounds and breeds reconciliation but allows an objective consideration of, often admiration for, a former enemy. In some cases, the enemy does not have to wait for peace.

In 1941 a small group of Italians set out on a mission that, if successful, would give their country dominance in the Mediterranean, change the course of the war, and deal a decisive blow to the unflattering stereotype entertained by both their enemies and their allies at the time. They belonged to the Decima Flottiglia MAS: ostensibly the 'Tenth Light Flotilla', but in practice, a careful piece of linguistic camouflage had taken place. Motoscafo Anti Sommergibile (MAS) technically translates as 'Anti-submersible Motorboat'. In the case of the Decima its acronym stood for Mezzi d'Assalto: assault craft.

The submarine *Scirè* sailed from La Spezia after sunset on 3 December 1941 without fuss or fanfare. Nobody knew her destination, but for months her appearance had marked her out as something special, for instead of a gun she carried three long, cylindrical caissons mounted lengthways on her deck, two just aft of the conning tower, one immediately forward of it. Since the loss of her sister boats the *Iride* and the *Gondar* she had become, in fact, unique – rather like her commander, the dark and handsome Prince Junio Valerio Borghese, a natural leader and a man born either exactly at the right time or five hundred years too late. A committed fascist, with more than a dash of the fifteenth-century *condottiero* about him, he was proud and protective of his men and what they were doing – not just the crew of the little *Scirè*, but those he referred to as his *operators*, six of whom were now aboard the submarine.

Outside the harbour, a lighter made a discreet rendezvous in the closing darkness, and the six operators emerged from the *Scirè*'s hatch to oversee the transfer from the lighter into the caissons of three long objects with strange accretions that made them look like a cross between a torpedo and a small child's conception of a submarine. Each was examined carefully by one pair of men before being lowered gently into its cylinder. After all the caisson doors were secured there was time for a few last words with their commander before brief farewells were made and the six men climbed down into the lighter.

By December 1941 not even its best friends could claim that the Italian Navy was having a good war. In November 1940 the Commander-in-Chief of Britain's Mediterranean Fleet, Admiral Sir Andrew Browne Cunningham DSO, had launched three waves of Swordfish torpedo bombers from the aircraft carrier *Illustrious* that crippled much of the Italian fleet at their Taranto anchorages, the first time aircraft had been used in such a way (something that was not lost on the Japanese observers at the port). Four months later, he again rewrote the naval warfare textbook when he devastated a cruiser fleet off Cape Matapan. HMS *Upholder* sank the cruiser *Armando Diaz* off Malta, and in November surface ships based in Malta disposed of a seven-strong convoy and two destroyer escorts. A captured German airman who told his British interrogators that the 'scenery in Italy is wonderful but the people are horrible, their life consists of singing and eating,' complained that a convoy from Palermo was safer with one [German] Junkers 88 as an escort than 5 Italian cruisers.

Nonetheless, ABC, as the admiral was known, was not having it all his own way in the Mediterranean: Italy's German allies had secured some notable scalps. His fleet incurred heavy losses while evacuating British troops from Crete in April 1941, and in November the aircraft carrier *Ark Royal* and the battleship *Barham* were sunk by U-boats. Nor were the Italians incapable of delivering a sting, as Cunningham recognized in April 1941 when, after the loss of the cruiser *York* in Soúdhas Bay, he warned of possible attacks by motor torpedo boats or midget submarines on British naval bases. From items of captured equipment he had an inkling that the Italians – Decima MAS was not yet in his vocabulary – might have another weapon: human torpedoes.

They may have been colloquially called human torpedoes, but this was not suicide bombing, even if the missions were suicidal. Technically they were *Siluri a Lenta Corsa* (slow speed torpedoes) or SLCs; with exasperated affection their crews named them *maiali*: pigs. In the secluded waters of the mouth of the River Serchio near Pisa, on the private estate of the Duke of Salviati, the frogmen were trained to ride their recalcitrant pigs into the heart of a heavily defended enemy harbour at night, and then use cutters and compressed-air lifts to defeat long metal torpedo nets, and their native wit, discipline and teamwork to foil sentries and patrols. In underwater darkness they perfected the art of hanging the heavy explosive head, 6 feet (1.8 metres) long, from a line secured by two clasps to the keel of the target before detaching it from the body and setting the timer. They practised submerging and surfacing their pigs, turning and trimming, or sneaking with just the pilot's head above the water – at so-called observation level – while his diver relied on the breathing apparatus. They acclimatized their bodies to spending hours immersed in cold water, for this was all about stealth, and the pig could only achieve 2 knots. Then they tested themselves by carrying out dummy attacks against unsuspecting Italian surface ships, running a serious risk of being killed by their own side. All the operators were young, at the peak of physical fitness, hand-picked and volunteers. They liked orders and they obeyed them.

Borghese's conviction that his mission was secret suffered a rude shock when, off the Sicilian coast at night, he was signalled *en clair* by Donath lamp from Capo Peloro, the north-eastern tip of the island. At Messina a letter from Naval Command giving enemy ship movements was brought out to him, along with the verbal warning that a submarine had been sighted off Capo dell'Armi.

Avoiding the danger zone he cruised down the eastern Sicilian coast, running on diesels to recharge the batteries, until, off Taormina and below the sleeping cone of Etna, he spotted an unmistakable dark shape ahead. Moonlight showed him the two guns on its deck. Warily he signalled. Incorrect answer. British, then?

No point in provoking an encounter; he had no gun and, in any case, his success was measured by how many missions his submarine could survive. He calmly resumed his course – as did the Royal Navy boat, running parallel to him for an hour before heading back towards Taormina. He was glad when, on 9 December, they reached the discreet harbour of Lakkíon on the Greek island of Leros in the Aegean, where the Italians maintained a secure submarine base and where the *Scirè*, under tarpaulins to hide her caissons, could berth beneath the high mountains without attracting unwelcome attention. Let the local people think she had limped in for major repairs. The voyage had taken three days. In another eight the real task would begin: to attack the British naval base at Alexandria. Previous attempts had failed, but the lessons had been learned.

The ten men, six of whom who had left the *Scirè* off La Spezia, walked the length of the Sala Mappamondo in Rome's magnificent Palazzo Venezia without too many thoughts of Renaissance art and architecture. Their eyes were focused firmly on the large man in uniform at the desk, which was the only piece of furniture in the room. For Lieutenant Luigi Durand de la Penne, a tall, fair-haired Ligurian whose family was rooted in the French aristocracy and who led the group, it was the second time he had been granted an audience by il Duce. Mussolini studied each of them closely in complete silence before he uttered a word. After delivering a formal speech and questioning them, he wished them luck. Audience over, they departed. Now they had a plane to catch to Rhodes. Thinking over the conversation with il Duce, de la Penne was unimpressed. The Italian leader was completely out of touch with the kind of tactics they were employing and, that being the case, could have no conception of what they might achieve. Mussolini, he concluded contemptuously, was a great buffoon.

That same day, 12 December, they landed at Leros in the guise of engineers, and were taken straight on board the transport ship, *Asmara*, to keep them hidden. Prior to their arrival, technicians of the Decima had been flown in to carry out final checks on the pigs. The following day, Borghese was reunited with his lads, as he affectionately called them, though at 35 he was only 14 years older than the youngest of the main team and barely 6 years older than the eldest. It was time to study the details of the plan and look at the latest information and aerial reconnaissance to reach them.

It seemed an awesome responsibility for the six, but Borghese had confidence in them as being currently the finest of his crews. The 27 year-old de la Penne had been among those who, for 20 hours, had attempted to open the hatch of the stricken *Iride*, torpedoed in 50 feet (15 metres) of water during a previous attempt on Alexandria, and who had personally dragged out the last surviving crewman. He and his diver, Petty Officer Emilio Bianchi, the eldest of the group at 29, had worked together for more than a year. The second crew consisted of a cheerful, easy-going gunner captain, Vincenzo Martellotta from Taranto, who had joined the navy in 1931 as an 18-year-old cadet, and his enthusiastic Petty Officer diver, Mario Marino. Antonio Marceglia, an engineer captain aged 26, was the third pilot: a big man, deep-voiced, and with what his commander described as something stately about him. His diver, Sergeant Spartaco

The Adua class *Scirè* after modifica-
tion to carry SLCs. Built by Tosi, she
measured 197'6" x 21' x 13' (60.18m

x 6.5m x 4.7m), and, submerged, displaced around 860 tons.

Schergat, five years younger, was the son of a diver: he had been born with the gene. Two reserve crews embarked with them, equally keen but younger.

On the morning of Sunday 14 December, after Borghese had firmly refused to hold a training exercise to satisfy Admiral Luigi Biancheri, the five teams embarked on the 620-ton *Scirè*. Their training in the Serchio prior to departure from Italy had been as thorough and intensive as Borghese and the MAS command could make it; the intelligence reports of ship movements and harbour defences at Alexandria were as detailed and reliable as possible. But, even with the promise of coordinated air cover to distract the enemy, it was going to be a difficult task.

By day the submarine ran submerged for safety, her machinery specially muffled to avoid detection. Only at night did she surface and switch over to diesels to recharge the batteries and freshen the air. There was little for the SLC crews to do but rest and save energy for when it mattered: they had no part in the running of the submarine. For much of the journey Marceglia studied the mission, rarely speaking unless to discuss some operational point. Martellotta lay in his bunk, offering a cheerful 'peace and goodwill' to anyone who spoke to him; de la Penne slept his way through most of the voyage, somehow managing to eat a large fruitcake kept in a drawer within reach of his bunk without anyone seeing him wake up. Borghese remembered them as 'really extraordinary fellows, those lads; they were about to undertake action which would require the exploitation of their whole physical and moral energy, and put their lives in peril at every moment, hour after hour; it would be a mission from which, at best, they could only hope to emerge as prisoners of war, and yet they preserved the attitude of a team of sportsmen off to play their customary Sunday game.' The *Scirè* would not be waiting to pick them up afterwards: it would be far too dangerous. Instead, Giovanni Lombardi would patrol off Rosetta in the submarine *Zaffiro* for two nights.

On the 16th they encountered a storm, which forced Borghese to limit time on the surface to the absolute minimum. There was danger in exposing the caissons to the elements – they had spare crews but only the three SLCs – and in any case it was quieter below, where the throbbing hum of the batteries became a gentle soundtrack. Charging through the waves on thundering diesels was no way to relax the teams.

The intention had been to launch the attack the following night, but that would not be possible without good weather and the latest intelligence. They had studied plans of the harbour until they could have drawn it blindfold; they knew where the defences were, and they could pinpoint where their ships would be found, but some previous raids on Alexandria and Gibraltar had failed through lack of up-to-the minute intelligence, which would have revealed that their targets were at sea. Under the circumstances, Borghese postponed the raid, even though it would mean proceeding without air force assistance, which could not be rescheduled. Finally, on the evening of the 17th he received the welcome information from Italian naval intelligence in Athens that the battleships were at their moorings and the sea at Alexandria was calm.

So did Admiral Cunningham, courtesy of the Government Code and Cypher School at Bletchley Park, though it was not news to him.[1]

At the same time, Borghese told his men that the attack would begin on the night of the 18th.

At 10:25 on the morning of the 18th Cunningham issued a general warning to the fleet to expect an attack by air, boat or human torpedo.

The lack of detail in the message had left the Admiral in a dilemma. Previous decrypts had told him that the Italian Navy was taking an unspecified interest in Alexandria; this one pointed to an imminent danger, but how much emphasis should be placed on the mention of the calm sea, which certainly favoured an attack from the water? To black out the harbour would make it very hard for enemy aircraft to identify targets, but give cover to human torpedoes; to illuminate it, on the other hand, would turn those same targets into sitting ducks for aircraft. Cunningham had warned of three possible methods of attack; *Queen Elizabeth*'s captain, Claude Barrington Barry, was concerned about a fourth – 'an infernal machine of the nature of a torpedo … which can be dropped by parachute'. Their response was therefore a compromise, relying on improved vigilance, increased patrols and a few physical measures.

As the *Scirè* closed in on the Egyptian coast, running submerged at 200 feet (60 metres) through the minefield until the seabed began to rise, men from the *Valiant* and the *Queen Elizabeth* were busy installing light torpedo nets parallel to the sides of their ships. The nets extended fore and aft of the ships, but did not enclose them. The *Queen Elizabeth*'s, laid triple thickness, were positioned around 200 feet from the hull, the *Valiant*'s slightly closer. They descended to 40 feet (12 metres) below the surface – the harbour depth at that point was 7–8 fathoms (13–14.5 metres). Captain Charles Morgan ordered the closing of *Valiant*'s deadlights below the upper deck and the taking in of light-excluding scuttles, so as to keep the ships as dark as possible. Ships' companies were told to be alert; copies of the directive were pinned on noticeboards.

The extended defence officer went out in person to check the defence electric lights, and rostered additional officers at the entrance to the harbour. Shore batteries and the long, extended breakwater protected the anchorage, but there was a potential weak point at the southern end where the floating boom controlled access and egress. Cunningham wanted depth charges to be dropped and boat patrols stepped up. They could not shut up shop, so everyone had to be doubly alert. At just after 15:00 the boom was closed to all but small craft.

The *Scirè* was very close, almost skimming the seabed in the clear, shallow water, but darkness was falling, making her less vulnerable to aircraft. The two RAF Dorniers[2] sent up at dusk to patrol the area had headed back to base without spotting her in the failing light, which in the right lighting conditions they would probably have been able to do.

Borghese confirmed the assignments. De la Penne and Bianchi were to take HMS *Valiant*; Marceglia and Schergat, HMS *Queen Elizabeth*, and Martellotta and Marino were to set their explosive under a tanker; all were to distribute some floating incendiaries.

There was a pause. Martellotta's eyes flicked to his diver's face, then back to his commander's.

'Sir, I shall obey your orders,' he said firmly, and added irrepressibly, 'but I should like you to know that my diver and I would rather have attacked a warship.' Doubtless prestige came into it, but there was also a large reward for sinking a battleship. Borghese smiled sympathetically and thought about it. It was, after all, just possible that the aircraft carrier HMS *Eagle* might have returned, and it would be a pity to lose such an opportunity. He modified the assignment: 'Search to be made for the aircraft carrier at its two normal anchorages, and attack to be made on it if found; otherwise, all other targets consisting of active war units to be ignored and a large loaded tanker to be attacked with distribution of the six incendiaries in its immediate neighbourhood.'

The night patrol had begun in the harbour. Between the boom and the passes a volunteer yacht patrol and five little caïques were out on the water.

At 18:40[3] the *Scirè* stopped. She was just over a mile – nearly two kilometres – from the breakwater, bearing 356° from the lighthouse at the western end of the breakwater and in just 15 fathoms (27 metres) of water. The crews began getting ready, zipping up their light Belloni overalls – blue for Martellotta and Marino, who also put on pullovers; greenish grey for the others. They ran through their checklist. Don't forget the essentials: a toothbrush and comb, ID cards, a few British £5 notes and a packet or two of cigarettes. Martellotta took his talisman: a medallion depicting the Virgin and Child. Now came the unpleasant part: getting into the black, rubberized diving suit in the confines of a warm submarine was an uncomfortable, sticky business. Then it was on with the boots or sandals, the weighted belt and anklets; and finally fasten on the oxygen bottles and the breathing apparatus until all that was visible of the wearer was his face and hands. Already they were sweating like pigs and tired from the effort. The pilots strapped on their black-faced luminous watches and picked up their gloves, and supplies of the stimulant Pervitin.[4] They would need it later to help them keep going when the cold and exhaustion started to take their toll.

Borghese turned away from the periscope. It was fully dark above. He gave the order to rise to outcrop level – just high enough to open the hatch safely – and he went up into the conning tower, breathing fresh, salty air for the first time in 16 hours. He looked out. Exactly where they needed to be, and a perfect, still, cloudless winter night, but no colder than the south of Italy There was no hugging, nor even words: they had their own strange ceremony for embarking on a mission. Each bent over, and his commander kicked him in the rear. The stronger the kick, the more luck it conferred. Tonight they would need a lot of luck.

The two reserve pilots went up first: it was their task to open the heavy caissons so that the crews could save their energy for when it was needed. At the front, immersed in the water, de la Penne and Bianchi brought out their pig, started the accumulator battery and moved away, to be joined by Marceglia and Schergat. A little later came Martellotta and Marino, silently cursing the door of their cylinder, which had refused to close and had to be left for the reserves to sort out. Now the *Scirè* descended beneath the waves again to return to the safety of Leros; the six operators were on their own. It was 21:00, and the sky was perfectly clear and moonless.

The boom had been fully opened at 21:00 to let the tug *Roysterer* out so she could give a tow to HMS *Flamingo*, but neither the duty defence officer nor the boom gate officer knew what time they would return, with the result that it was left open. Out on the breakwater, officers and men of the 1st and 2nd Punjabis were on duty. They were considered to have particularly good eyesight. Four Bofors guns were in place.

In formation, the human torpedoes proceeded on the surface parallel to the breakwater, de la Penne in the centre, Marceglia to his left, Martellotta to his right. As the pilot, the officer always sat at the front of the SLC, protected by a screen that acted as a breakwater, and operating the luminous controls in front of him, which were not unlike an aeroplane's. Behind him, but separated by the crash submersion tank, sat the diver, who could use the toolbox as a backrest. Both had their feet in stirrups. Progress on an SLC was never fast: the pig only managed 2 knots, but on a flat sea there was little resistance. By around 23:00 they had covered 7,000 metres and were abreast of the Ras el-Tin lighthouse; the night was so clear that they could make out its structure even though it was unlit. They were ahead of schedule. Time to stop for something to eat.

Some 38 miles (70 kilometres) off Ras el-Tin, the 15th Cruiser Squadron had reported an unidentified submarine on the surface and were asking the Commander-in-Chief if it was HMS *Perseus*. In the harbour entrance, HMS *Trimtoo* was dropping the first of 51 depth charges.

The sudden blaze of light caught the six men by surprise. The lighthouse had come to life, switched on at 23:25 ready for the return of the 15th Cruiser

Squadron. This was no place to sit around; they restarted their motors and moved away from the beam, steadily following the breakwater in about 12 fathoms (22 metres). Just ahead, their track was crossed by the silhouette of a tug towing a destroyer into what must be the harbour entrance. Not so far to go, and the pigs were behaving themselves. The breakwater had taken a turn to

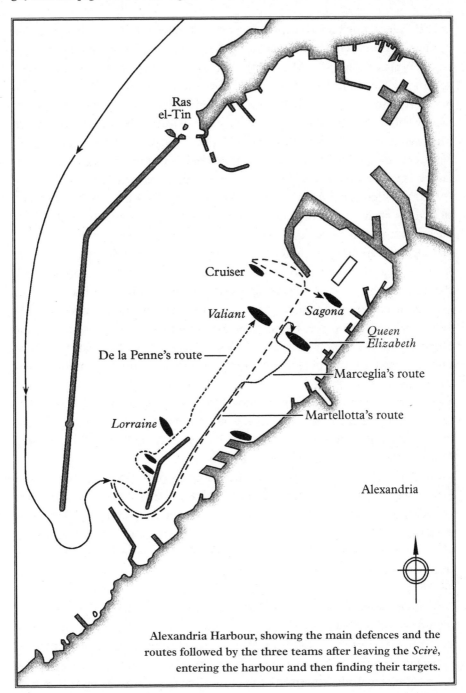

Alexandria Harbour, showing the main defences and the routes followed by the three teams after leaving the *Scirè*, entering the harbour and then finding their targets.

port. They followed it, keeping a little further out, away from the range of its lights. By midnight they were just outside the entrance, submerged with just their heads breaking the surface. The boom was closed.

From the pier above them they heard voices, and could see people walking about, one holding an oil lamp. A large motorboat was cruising in sinister silence.

They were trained not to cry out in pain, but the depth charge that exploded by them sent a violent shock-wave through the pig; the muscles of de la Penne's legs contracted savagely. Martellotta felt as if his legs were being crushed against his craft. He leaned forwards, over the controls and the instrument panel, keeping his torso flat but his head and vital organs out of the water; breathlessly he told Marino to do the same but to turn round so he could watch what was going on behind. It was worse for Schergat and Bianchi because their pigs were being ridden with the rear submerged: breathing through their respirators they took the force of the explosion through their whole bodies.

At 00:24 the signal lights of the gates came on. The three teams grouped close to an obstruction buoy, a sense of anticipation beginning to build. Slowly the boom began to open, but there was too much activity around it for them to risk slipping through yet. Better to wait until eyes and minds were distracted. A motor boat went out. Too small, and the wrong direction. Another depth charge, crushing the legs, tensing up every muscle. Too much of this … Hardly had the effects worn off than the next one came, but now there was more activity on the pier, and noise. It was after 01:00. Something was coming in; the sound of turbines grew louder. The sky was blacked out and a great dark shape came roaring past, sweeping her wash into the group. A couple of minutes later and a second came through.

The arrival was the 15th Cruiser Squadron: the *Naiad* and the *Euryalus* with, some eight minutes behind, the Tribal Class destroyers *Sikh*, *Legion* and *Maori*. By the time the destroyers came up, the Italian leader had made his decision. This was their best chance to get past the boom.[5]

Luigi de la Penne submerged and went forward through the gate as HMS *Sikh* passed overhead, the surge from her bow pushing the pig further down until they were on the sea bed, glad to be clear of the thrashing propellers. Now it was full speed ahead – even if that was only 2 knots – and with *Legion* churning her way above them, they were in. He surfaced, close to the side of the entrance, and the bow wave from the *Maori* threw them against the inner obstruction buoy.

With just his head, black-covered and masked, above water, and Bianchi fully submerged on the back of the pig, de la Penne started to head north, then realized that the *Maori* had stopped and her crew were on deck ready to anchor. He changed course and headed towards the inner breakwater, passed across the bows of two cruisers, and astern of the French battleship, *Lorraine*, one of five[6]

French warships caught in the port at the fall of France the year before. The French admiral had been given a clear choice: fight with Britain, accept internment, or go down fighting. He opted for internment. As de la Penne cleared her he had his first view of the target, the *Valiant* – all 650 feet (200 metres) and 30,000 tons of her, with the eight 15″ guns that had helped destroy the Italian fleet at Matapan. But those huge guns would be of no use against the two men who were about to sink the flagship, as they thought, of the British fleet.

Using their breathing apparatus and maintaining their fore-and-aft lookout, Martellotta and Marino slipped stealthily towards the opening while surfaced. In the next moment, Marino saw a huge black shadow bearing down on them from behind.

'Hard to starboard!' he hissed, thumping his officer on the shoulder to get his attention. Martellotta did as he was told and increased the speed, but a powerful wave caught their craft, pushing it against one of the buoys of the interior barrier. The *Sikh* had come in at some speed, as much as 10 knots, and showing no lights. Chains clashed and clanked on her bows as she made ready to anchor; then the *Legion* was steaming in too, and while the water was turbulent the SLC crew took the opportunity to creep in, still partially surfaced just behind her. They could see no sign of the other pairs. Martellotta was worried. Marceglia and Schergat had been close to them; he had visions of them being caught by the destroyer's bow, as they themselves had so nearly been. But all they could do was go on.

The pair cruised into the anchorage, hunting for the shape of their prime target, HMS *Eagle*, the converted Chilean battleship. She should be easy enough to identify if she was there, though the mask and low viewpoint hindered vision, even on a clear night with the harbour lights shedding bright pools and black shadows. They were moving slowly, parallel to the shore, inside a long detached breakwater; on their right the quay was lined with buildings, while ahead in the quarantine anchorage reposed the magnificent twin bulks of the *Valiant* and the *Queen Elizabeth*. But beyond the *Valiant* Martellotta saw moored a large warship that had not figured in the planning. She resembled a battleship, though scale was hard to judge. The whole outer harbour lay open to view, and there was no obvious sign of the aircraft carrier. This ship was worth serious consideration before they went looking for tankers.[7]

The third crew had been right in the harbour entrance as the *Sikh* had swept in, but they had realized the danger and managed to escape damage and injury. Having recovered and metaphorically, if not literally, taken their bearings, they were able to follow their prescribed route, initially the same as that taken by Martellotta. The harbour was quiet – or at least relatively so. People and small vessels were moving around, but everything was orderly – no suggestion that, as yet, anyone had spotted any unusual activity. And there was the *Queen Elizabeth*, stern to shore, a few lights showing on deck. Marceglia closed in, and came up to the torpedo net. Too much to expect that such valuable ships would have been left unprotected. Marceglia was a torpedo man himself. He had taken a course in armaments and been stationed at two torpedo depots, without ever realizing that within two years of the war starting he would be riding one and calling it his pig. The question now was which way to get past the net? It depended on how far down it extended.

Schergat was the designated diver, although they all had to be experts. With a rope round his waist to guide him back to the pig, the 21-year-old made the exploration and came back triumphant. There was enough of a gap without having to use the lifting gear packed in the toolbox. This operation was going well, and at last he was doing something. He had been a reserve in both the May and September attacks on Gibraltar. For his officer it was a chance to prove himself. Marceglia too had been a reserve in September – when three vessels totalling 30,000 tons were sunk, the first success for the SLCs – and he probably blamed that on what had happened in May. Named as reserve pilot then, he had been drafted in to replace a sick diver only to find himself suddenly struggling for air as exhaustion set in. That was all he remembered until he eventually came round and started vomiting. Not a glorious debut.[8]

At 01:50 the boom had been closed. The *Trimtoo* and other vessels were still dropping their precautionary depth charges on either side. There were additional armed lookouts on the two battleships.

The pig was perfectly safe for depths of 50 feet (15 metres) – 100 feet (30 metres) was the operational limit. Marceglia flooded the flotation tank and they sank into the colder world of infinite darkness, feeling their way down the net. The pressure on their ears and lungs deepened; their diving suits creased against their bodies, pinching their flesh viciously, even through the overalls. The fabric was never waterproof at the best of times; water was seeping in.

They reached the bottom of the net; just a little further, and now they were under it. Time to open the valve and come up to observation level, eyes above the surface, easing the pressure but still reliant on the oxygen. About 230 feet (70 metres) to go, and time was passing rapidly as they made their way along the length of the ship. They were in line with the *Queen Elizabeth*'s funnel; within a few minutes, they were under the bilge keel, once again nipped by the folds of fabric, and Schergat was opening the tool box to bring out the first of what they called the 'sergeants', the clamps that had to be attached either side of the ship. All was going according to plan.

From under the stern of the unknown ship, Vincenzo Martellotta switched on his torch and shone it briefly on the vessel's name to identify her before going any further.[9] It was just as well he took the risk. She was not

British, not even an enemy, but one of the French warships they knew were interned there – one battleship and four cruisers.

Marino was mortified. She had presented such a wonderful opportunity, it seemed unreasonable she should be off-limits. Martellotta warned him to keep his voice down, and swallowing the disappointment they eased themselves around, keeping close to her flank, ready to resume their mission.

The glare on their goggles was dazzling. The light blazed down. A man was standing in the gangway shining a torch on them. Unable to feel even their own heartbeats, they froze, waiting for the alarm to be given.

The silence continued. The French lookout (or so they assumed him to be) made a deliberate sign to them, gesturing in the direction of the British battle-ships as if to say: 'those are the ones you want, lads. Not us.'[10]

The two Italians came slowly back to life. It could so nearly have been the end of their mission and the start of a hunt for the others. They continued parallel to the hull of the French ship and with *Valiant* and *Queen Elizabeth* off to starboard, heading for the petroleum quay. They knew that there should be twelve almost fully laden tankers there, and they only needed to find one. Once again at observation level, they rode the pig at its painfully slow speed for an hour, covering just over half a mile – barely a kilometre – but there at the fuel pier was an oiler, the Norwegian tanker *Sagona*.

By now both men were cold, and Martellotta was beginning to experience the same symptoms as Marceglia had at Gibraltar. His head hurt, and he felt the need to be sick. Probably he was suffering from some form of hypoxia – shortage of oxygen – a common ailment for divers. Once the vomiting started, using the respirator became impossible. Marino realized he would have to do the last part of the task alone.

The third crew of de la Penne and Bianchi took a slightly different route after getting into the harbour. Instead of turning to starboard and going inside the internal breakwater, the pilot took them outside and then round the stern of the French battleship *Lorraine*. He was now looking directly at the *Valiant*.

The distance between was fairly well lit; at observation level de la Penne crept across the half-mile of still water until the front of the pig nosed up against the torpedo nets. That was an unwelcome and unexpected surprise. Marceglia and Schergat had chosen to go under. De la Penne, cold, wet through and recog-nizing that he needed to save his strength, consulted with Bianchi, and the pair of them decided to dismount and push their craft along the net on the surface in search of the opening. During the manoeuvre his suit ripped, exposing him to the full chill of the sea, but by 02:00 they were inside the net, with little more than 100 feet (30 metres) of water left to cross. Bianchi had spent most of the approach submerged; now it was time for his officer to get his respirator on and follow the drill: flood the tank, submerge and steer by compass on the bearing of the battleship's funnel to bring them amidships under the bilge keel.

As soon as he was confident of having reached the hull, de la Penne went to cut the motor, but his hands were too numb and he fumbled the switch. The pig bumped against the hull some 21 feet (6.5 metres) below the waterline, and as he tried to manoeuvre it under the bottom it suddenly plunged down, landing on the harbour floor. Reeling out his guide rope, de la Penne surfaced to check position. He was too far forward – by more than 20 feet (6 metres) – of the no. 1 stack that had been his target. Using the line, he submerged to start the motor and indicate to Bianchi that they would have to move. The motor refused to turn. He felt for Bianchi, and had a shock. There was no trace of his diver.

Hastily de la Penne returned to the surface and looked cautiously around. Still no sign. The decision was made for him: the task had to take priority, and be done quickly if all six lives and all three missions were not to fail. The real danger came if Bianchi were found, so there was no time to lose. He returned to the bottom and examined the propeller. Somehow a length of steel cable had tangled itself around the shaft, impossible to shift. So that explained why the motor was dead. There was no means of making the pig rise up to the bilge keel where the explosive head could be attached. This situation was not in the manual; success now depended upon pure brute strength, and his was ebbing.

A little more than 300 feet away – nearly 100 metres – and still suffering from the effects of his respirator, Martellotta held his pig under the stern of the big Norwegian oiler, just his head above the water, moulded into darkness. There were voices on deck, but he could not recognize the language. Close by came the rhythmic splash of oars, the groan of the rowlocks and murmur of voices. Not British, so probably some of the Egyptians, or maybe men from one of the colonial regiments. Whoever they were, they were unlikely to wish him well if they spotted him.

Afterwards, he realized it must have been an oar that struck him. At the time he was just conscious of the splitting pain and blinding light; he felt himself reeling, hanging onto consciousness, and then he was left with a throbbing head and the old sickness. Marino was definitely going to have to do it, and not by the book, either. Anywhere under the hull would suffice. He himself would remain on the surface and prepare the incendiary devices. In a whisper, Martellotta gave the order.

Two men were required to do the task properly if the clamps were to be used and the device hung under the keel between them. Marino explored the hull below the waterline looking for an alternative. The best option was also the most obvious. He came up and told his officer he would try to suspend it from the propeller. It might not be ideal, but any explosion on a tanker had the potential to be spectacular.

The noise of an engine, parting water and rattling chains came close. Voices echoed from above, and another vessel came and anchored next to the one they were attending to. Martellotta operated the clutch to detach the explosive charge, and Marino went down with it. By the time he rose it was 02:55, and the timer was set for 05:00 (06:00 local time). He looked across to the other ship with satisfaction.

'Let's hope she stays here another three hours and she'll be finished, too,' he whispered to his comrade. It only remained to deploy the incendiaries, mooring them 65 feet (20 metres) from one another and approximately 330 feet (100 metres) from the *Sagona*. These devices were governed by a simple mechanical clock fuze,[11] set to go off at the same time as the torpedo warhead. The detonator would set off the black-powder primer, which in turn would cause a container of petroleum mixture to explode. Any oil spilled by the tanker after the torpedo's explosion would then ignite, turning part of the harbour into an inferno. Cork rings provided positive buoyancy, so that the device floated with just an inch or so visible above the water.[12] Their job done, Martellotta and Marino headed towards one of wooden jetties by the coaling station.

On the deck of the *Sagona* the third officer had been up on deck since midnight to assist with the bunkering operation. The first officer came up just as the Italians departed. Naval gunners had been taking watch by shifts. Nobody heard anything. Nobody saw anything suspicious.

Exhausted, Lieutenant de la Penne paused to rest, struggling to read the luminous compass through the haze of mud stirred up from the soft, sticky bed of the harbour. Impossible to make it out; instead he listened for the pulsating of the alternating pump: the louder it seemed, the closer he must be to the centre of the hull. There was seawater in his mask and he had no choice but to drink it or drown. The hot sweat pouring down his wet body was cooling. Another try. He dragged the pig a few more centimetres. He was so thirsty, yet all there was to drink was more salt water. Each time he stopped to recover it seemed there was less strength left in him for the next heave.

The muffled noise of the pump was louder; the floor of the harbour seemed to be rising. Another effort. Every muscle was straining, heart banging, mouth full of water, harder to breath, the pressure hurting. Time, the vital factor, had ceased to exist. Once more.

For a moment he reeled, a pain shooting through his head. He had hit the hull and must be amidships. That would do very well. He would have to leave the warhead on the floor: he could not lift more than 650 pounds – over 300 kilograms. He used his last strength to synchronize the timer.

Schergat was at the end of his strength as he climbed back onto the pig, but the job had been done to perfection. Now that it was all but over, Marceglia, too, felt the onset of tiredness, and for the first time the cold began to bother him. When his diver indicated an urgent need to surface, he pumped air into the tank and the pig began to rise. Too quickly. Afraid that they would splash out of the water and alert the guards, he had to release some of the air, hoping the bubbles would not attract attention.

The warning of possible attacks had been broadcast throughout the *Queen Elizabeth* the previous evening. If anything happened to suggest a likely assault, the *Alarm to Arms* would be sounded; if it materialized, *Prepare to Repel Small Craft*. The officer of the watch was stationed on the quarterdeck; a second officer on the compass platform; two lookouts on the air defence position on the bridge; two on the hanger top; two armed lookouts with Aldis lamps on both the quarterdeck and the forecastle; one armed lookout on the catapult deck. Barry had his ship well covered. The sound of the breaking bubbles reached the ears of one of the forecastle lookouts.

Marceglia and Schergat surfaced into the direct glare of the Aldis lamp, and instinctively looked down to stop the light catching their goggles. Holding their breath, they remained motionless, waiting and praying. After an eternity of suspense the light went out. Still they waited, then embarked on their escape. On the forecastle, a lookout smoked his cigarette.[13]

When Bianchi, who had fainted, recovered consciousness, he was floating on the surface and there was no trace of de la Penne or the pig. The port side of the battleship towered over him. Reasoning that he had probably been unconscious for only a short time and that his officer must be somewhere down below engaged on the mission, he knew that his most important task now was to maintain secrecy. Ahead, near the bow, floated the *Valiant*'s mooring buoy. He struck out for it.

Precautions similar to those on her sister ship had been taken aboard *Valiant*. On each side of the forecastle a royal marine stood sentry with his rifle and Aldis lamp. There was a Bren gun, too, at his disposal. The harbour was quiet since the 14th Destroyers had entered at quarter to four. The man on the starboard could make out the shape of the *Jervis* heading for the petroleum quay beside the oiler *Sagona*. The portside sentry was leaning over the rail as a sound caught his ears and he stared at the gleaming water. There was something down there. He switched on the Aldis lamp; a man was swimming, making for the buoy. He kept the beam on him, and the other marine hurried to phone the officer of the watch who came at once, bringing with him his corporal.

While the corporal was sent off to inform the captain, the others continued to watch as Bianchi climbed onto the buoy. It was 03:05.

Entirely unaware of what was happening, de la Penne surfaced, tore off his mask and gasped lungfuls of air until he felt capable of swimming. He and Bianchi – if the latter was still alive – would have to make for the rendezvous separately: it was too dangerous to stay in the area now.

The sharp rattle of machine-gun fire caught him unawares. He stopped, looked round, and knew that the adventure was over. Raising a hand, he turned and swam back towards the ship, thinking that the buoy was the best place to await the inescapable arrest.

If he had been shocked to find Bianchi missing from the pig he was no less surprised and relieved to find him on the buoy. Not entirely sure what to do, he went to climb the anchor cable to get on board, but another spray of gunfire warned him to stay still. He pointed to himself:

'Italian!' he shouted. The battleship's forecastle was beginning to fill up as the story went round. Denis Holton, one of the ship's clerical staff, came on deck to watch and share the general satisfaction that, whatever the attempt had been, it had failed miserably. From their perch the two frogmen could clearly hear the contemptuous comments about their nationality. De la Penne nudged his assistant.

'In a few hours time they'll change their minds about Italians!' he whispered, and they waited until a boat came into view. Not so very far away, two heads on the surface of the water spotted the activity, and the hearts of Marceglia and Schergat sank: it looked as if the *Valiant* operation had failed.

The night boat picked up its prisoners, and the quarterdeck sentry searched them before escorting them on board to the quarterdeck, where they were more thoroughly searched, roughly but not violently, and their ID cards and papers taken. The first brief interrogation took place in French, and by 03:30 Cunningham had been informed, and a boat was on its way to the flagship to bring over an interpreter. A few minutes later and the admiral made signal to the fleet that the presence of human torpedoes was suspected. Patrol boats were being sent out to drop depth charges, harbour defences put in first-degree readiness, and tugs ordered to raise steam. Ships were told to pass bottom lines – steel hawsers – to try to remove any possible explosive devices fixed to hulls, but since the *Valiant*'s warhead lay on the harbour floor, and the line passed under the *Queen Elizabeth* snagged on her side, the measure revealed nothing. Destroyers due to pass out of the harbour were detailed to drop depth charges outside.

There were just two and a half hours to go before the warheads were due to explode. Lieutenant Richard Long RNVR came over from *Queen Elizabeth* to act as interpreter, but the two operators refused to answer any questions, and accepted with inward smiles all commiseration on their failure. Morgan had been in touch with the shore establishment and received orders to send them to Ras el-Tin. When they left *Valiant* escorted by Long and by Sub-Lieutenant Duncan Newson it was 03:50.

There, in a small hut by the lighthouse, they were interrogated by an officer whom de la Penne described as an excitable sort of fellow with a revolver in his hand. Bianchi was the first to go in and be questioned; he gave nothing away, and as he was leaving he signalled as much to his leader. Cold, wet, hungry and tired as they were, they had both proved 100 per cent secure, but the parting thrust of the British officer was to promise that a way would be found to make them talk.

They were taken back to *Valiant* by Long and Newson. De la Penne's dignified bearing had already made an impression on the young sub-lieutenant, and his respect grew during the short journey as the Italian told him how he had got into the harbour unchallenged. Ahead, moonlight picked out every detail of the *Valiant*.

'How sad,' said de la Penne turning to Newson, 'that we sailors have to damage such beautiful ships.'[14]

The instinctive utterance of a sudden moment, or a hint that she would soon be 'damaged'? Newson assumed the latter and reported what his prisoner had said. It was 05:00. Only one hour to go.

Long brought with him the order that the two prisoners were to be kept on board the *Valiant*, and informed that they would be 'involved' in anything that might subsequently happen to the ship. In front of Captain Morgan he once again asked the frogmen where the charge was located. They refused to answer, and were taken down inside the ship as far as the sand tank, close to shellrooms A and B and the cordite chambers. They were, they knew, very close to where the explosion would occur.

The petty officers and sentries ordered to take them below and guard them looked rather pale and anxious as they considered the consequences of an explosion, and did their best to get their prisoners to talk, though with kindness rather than threats. They gave them rum and cigarettes, which came as a relief to chilled and exhausted bodies. While de la Penne brooded on his likely fate and took some comfort from the thought of dying for his country, the more pragmatic Bianchi fell asleep.

Having sunk their pig and disposed of their frogman suits, Marino and Martellotta waded ashore near the coaling station – at about the same time as de la Penne and Bianchi were being interrogated ashore – and made their way towards the gates. They were unaware of any activity around the *Valiant*, and had no reason to suspect any higher level of security than they had bargained for.

At gate no. 22, shortly before 04:50, Corporal Ali Mohammad al Naggar of the Egyptian Customs Police was on duty, chatting with three of his colleagues and Mohammed Attia Hassan, a plain clothes policemen. They saw the two men walking towards the gate, and even in the pre-dawn light something about their clothing looked out of place for Alexandria. They glanced at one another. Hassan switched on his torch and ran it over the pair, who stood quietly enough while being inspected. It was the blue of the trousers that alerted him:

not the right shade for British forces. And they were wet. He ran the torch over faces that were typically Italian.

There was no point in resisting arrest. Martellotta and Marino remained calm. Getting home had always been a hope, never an expectation. Bianchi and de la Penne had been lucky in the past; so had Marceglia, but many more were dead or prisoners. That was why all of them had had to put their affairs in order before setting out: families had to be able to carry on if they did not come back. They had the satisfaction of having done the job well. And there was still a chance, if they kept their nerve.

They were taken by Egyptian marine sentries and Lieutenant Dimbashi el Naccar to the outpost office and searched, their belongings set out on the table: the cigarette boxes, bank notes, toothbrushes, combs, wet handkerchiefs, and Martellotta's talisman of the Madonna and Child. Above all, his waterproof Panerai watch with its black face. Second Lieutenant al Fayed, in charge of the outpost, questioned them.

'Are you Italian?'

'Yes.'

'What were you doing here?'

'We are sailors. Our ship was sunk.'

'How did you get here?'

'By swimming to shore.'

No point in denying their nationality when their papers proclaimed that they were Italian.[15] But at least they were in the hands of the Egyptian police, not the British authorities. Martellotta was still answering questions as vaguely as possible when Captain Harrison RN arrived and requested they be handed over to him. On the grounds that Italy and Egypt were not at war, al Fayed refused until he had authorization from his government.

Martellotta kept his eyes on the watch. The hands had reached 04:50 – which meant it was 05:50 local time.

Aboard the *Sagona*, bunkering of the destroyer HMS *Jervis* was proceeding smoothly when two shocks ran through the vessel. To Sverre Thoraldsen, third officer, they felt like depth charges, but he could not determine the direction from where they had come. Down in the engine room the second engineer felt something and decided it was the destroyers – there was one on either side – knocking alongside. Captain Leire woke up and thought there must be some water in the steam line. That sometimes caused heavy strokes. He turned over. The explanation that an SLC had just self-destructed close to his tanker was hardly likely to have occurred to him.

A blacksmith on HMS *Valiant*, George Hilton, recalled how the news began to circulate:

Wakey-wakey had not been sounded off when the unusual took place in the petty officers' mess. The unusual being disturbance caused [by?] low voices, the odd light on and bumping of heads against the hammocks slung like sardines. Things were not quite right. Thus awakened hammocks were being lashed and stowed into the hammock bin, and increasing chatter had it that someone had been discovered by the marine on the forc'sle on the buoy ...

Dawn by now ... It could not be far off 06:00. Perhaps another ten or fifteen minutes left ... There were more than a thousand men on the *Valiant*. De la Penne asked to see Captain Morgan. Taken up to the wardroom, he informed him, through Long, that something was going to happen to the ship and soon, and he advised him to get all his men on deck at once. But he was adamant in his refusal to be more specific. The implication was clear.

The explosion a moment later blew off the tanker's stern, sending a great cascade of water up to the height of her mast, destroying her refrigeration and store rooms and collapsing all the crew's bunks in the stern quarter, injuring the carpenter and the mess-boy. It shook the surrounding buildings, including the police office in which Martellotta and Marino had just found out that they were to be handed over to the British. HMS *Jervis*, the destroyer, caught the fall-out, and Captain Morgan broke off his interrogation of de la Penne to go on deck and locate it. If he had needed proof that the attack was serious, he had it. Returning to the ward room he asked de la Penne if that was what he had referred to, and when he had given him an idea of where it had occurred the Italian told him that there was a possibility of others. Did he mean *Valiant*? De la Penne shrugged. He had done as much as he could to save the lives of the *Valiant*'s crew.

Morgan ordered him to be taken back down below. While he was on his way back he heard the signal for all hands to assemble on deck. Morgan had at last taken the hint and was warning his men that explosions might take place at any moment.

As he descended the ladder into the sand tank he said to Bianchi that things had turned out badly and it looked as though this was the end for them. There was no answer. He looked down as he reached the ground and, for the second time that day, found that Bianchi was not there. On the assumption that de la Penne had gone to tell Morgan where the charge was, his guards had removed him from danger.

De la Penne was alone in the empty hold. A few shackles hung overhead. He admitted to being scared. Would the device go off as the *Sagona*'s had? Would it be a swift death, blown to pieces, or would he drown?

Martellotta and Marino were climbing into Captain Harrison's car when they heard the second explosion at 06:05.

The shock crashed through the *Valiant*. Smoke began to fill the hold; the lights had gone down. The shackles on the ceiling had been blown off, and de la Penne's knee was throbbing with pain where one had hit him in its fall. He could feel the ship starting to list slightly to port. Opening the porthole close to the waterline he wondered whether he could squeeze through it, but it was impossible. He left it open. If the ship sank much further it would start letting in water and accelerate, if only a little, the settling.

Blacksmith Hilton recalled Morgan's tannoy warning and then: 'Hardly had he finished when the for'ard end of the ship lifted with a great shudder with vibrations sufficient to bring you to your knees. Amid many tannoy calls was "Damage Control to your stations".'

Deciding that the tank of a badly holed ship was not the healthiest place to linger, de la Penne climbed the ladder and emerged through the hatch, which had been left unguarded. Everywhere was deserted. He walked aft, and when he did meet a few men they stood up out of respect.

Morgan was on the quarter deck when de la Penne found him. 'Are all your crew safe?' he asked. 'And what have you done with my diver?' The officer of the watch told him to be silent, so he walked further aft and joined a group of officers observing the *Queen Elizabeth*.

For their part, the officers of that ship, including their admiral, were watching events on the *Valiant* from the bows. A minute or so later a massive explosion visibly lifted the *Queen Elizabeth*; the whole blast passed up the funnel, spraying oil and metal everywhere, even splattering those on the *Valiant*. As the deck bucked, hurling him over a metre into the air, Cunningham fought to keep his balance on landing, determined to avoid the indignity of ending up on his backside. All lights went out as the power died. The blast had wrecked A, B and X boiler rooms, killing eight men. The sound easily reached Captain Harrison's car and gave Martellotta and Marino the final satisfaction of knowing that all three teams had pulled off their tasks.

One of the *Valiant*'s officers demanded of de la Penne whether there were more explosions to come, to which he answered truthfully that there were none.[16] He was taken to the officer's mess and reunited with Bianchi, and before 07:00 they were on their way back to Ras el-Tin in the motorboat with Long and two sets of diving gear that had been recovered.

Despite all the activity in the area, Marceglia and Schergat had escaped detection and, having buried their suits, even managed to get out of the harbour in the vicinity of the slaughterhouses. By 7.30 they were at the main railway station in Alexandria and, posing as Frenchmen, they enquired about trains to Rosetta, further east along the coast of the Nile delta. They were in luck: one was due in ten minutes. The problem came when they pulled out a large white £5 note. The station could not accept British currency; they would have to get it changed. Just doing that took considerable time, and not until the afternoon were they able to get on a train. Arriving at Rosetta at 20:00 they decided to find a small hotel. With their sleeves rolled up and the lapels of their overalls turned down, their badges of rank and nationality were hidden, and they had just about dried out.

Ahmet el Sayed Mursim, proprietor of the Farouk el Awal Hotel, spoke only Arabic, which did not worry the French seamen Antonio Doradin and Emile Rabit who signed his register. They were just glad to have somewhere safe for the night, where they would not be questioned, and if the room was, by their standards, squalid, it hardly mattered. It was a chance to make themselves look respectable and get some much-needed rest. Although their trusted *Scirè* had left them and should be well on her way home, the *Zaffiro* was going to be cruising 10 miles (18 kilometres) off Rosetta for the next two nights. All they had to do was take a boat and go out to meet her. For some reason they were in two minds about attempting this, however, and the next morning, the 20th, they made enquiries about trains to Cairo, reasoning that they could get protection from the Spanish consul there until they could make a possible second rendezvous on the 24th.

Whatever their intentions, having left the hotel they walked the seven kilometres down to Izbat Burj Rashid on the banks of the Nile, probably to check the lie of the land and assess the likelihood of being able to steal a boat when the time came.

That afternoon they were arrested by a suspicious Egyptian police corporal, and taken back to Rosetta to be questioned by Captain Amin.

Marceglia did most of the talking: he was evasive about what they had been doing but admitted they had come to Rosetta to avoid being taken prisoner. Amin found him cheerful enough by the end of the interview when he admitted that he very glad the war was finished for him. Although he did not admit his involvement in the Alexandria attack, a subsequent examination of his watch revealed it contained water.

Admiral Cunningham had been left staring at the ruins of his fleet. Aided by the shallowness of the water, Marceglia and Schergat had blown a hole in the bottom of *Queen Elizabeth* some 40 feet (12 metres) across. Three of her boilers were flooded, so she could not raise steam. Her list was corrected by flooding the opposite compartments, but the extra weight left her much lower in the water. Although their operation had not gone to plan, de la Penne and Bianchi had managed to do more damage to their target. Denis Holton remembered the hole as being big enough to drive two double decker buses through, which was a slight exaggeration; none the less, it was 8 feet (2.5 metres) deep by almost 26 feet (8 metres) wide, with the damage confined to one side. What shocked the commander-in-chief as much as anything was the discovery by men from HMS *Euryalis* of the incendiaries around the tanker and the flagship while dropping precautionary depth charges that morning. Two had exploded with a loud 'pop' and burned for a couple of minutes, though without causing any harm.[17] If the *Sagona*'s tanks had ruptured, which by a miracle they had not, and if the incendiaries had ignited them, the result would have been catastrophic. Cunningham gave credit where it was due, obliged to 'admire the cold-blooded bravery and enterprise of these Italians'.

The immediate priority was to keep the news from getting out: to bluff the enemy into thinking the raid had failed. Those who knew Cunningham were aware that he was never at his most genial in the morning. After the events of the past hours, he was particularly crisp that dawn. His flagship might be several feet lower in the water than usual, but the routine would continue – and why were no preparations being made for the 08:00 ceremony of hoisting the colours? A clean ensign replaced the one coated with oil, the Royal Marine guard, bugler and band performed to order, and the colours were hoisted on time. He held his staff meeting at 9.30 and barely mentioned the incident. A photograph was released as if by routine arrangement. But on 28 December he expressed his real thoughts in a letter to Dudley Pound, Admiral of the Fleet and First Sea Lord:

We are having shock after shock out here. The damage to the battleships is a disaster … It is costing a lot, but we must get this harbour really secure. The last few days everyone has had the jitters, seeing objects swimming about at night and hearing movements on the ships' bottoms. This must stop.

We have got all of the enemy operators we think – six in number and I am having them segregated; no communication with the outside world by letter or other means. In fact they will just die for 6 months and I hope give the Italians the impression that they perished in their attempt. Furthermore although the photographic reconnaissance shows the two submarines[18] alongside *Queen Elizabeth* they do not seem to have made any claims of damage to battleships yet. If the RAF will only do their job we may bluff them that only one has been damaged as in a few days I hope to get *Queen Elizabeth* looking like a seagoing ship again and on an even keel …

We are getting badly reduced in cruisers. *Neptune* and party running into that minefield off Tripoli was sheer bad luck … Perhaps we are lucky to lose only *Neptune* and *Kandahar*. We might easily have lost all three … We cannot yet work the 'Dido's' from Malta as there is no 5.25 ammunition … *Ajax* has died on us due to some boiler pinion trouble …

The British now knew a great deal about the Alexandria operation and the Decima MAS, and not just from the equipment recovered. Before the blasts, the two crews that were captured had given nothing away under interrogation.

Afterwards, they appeared to be remarkably chatty. Borghese remarked that it was sometimes easier to ask an Italian to lay down his life than to hold his tongue, and without a doubt the crews were so elated by success that they wanted to talk about it. They were described as 'a fine type of Italian', with de la Penne and Bianchi reckoned to be made of sterner stuff than Martellotta and Marino.

Churchill called the damage to the battleships, and the earlier loss of the *Barham*, as Britain's 'deadly secret', and with reason. Italy was now the power in the Mediterranean, if she only but knew it. Malta could not be supplied or defended, and the whole North Africa campaign was threatened.

Italy did know it. On the day after the attack, while on his way home, Borghese was given the news based on aerial reconnaissance made hours after the attack. The photographs, when he saw them, showed the frantic activity at Alexandria: one vessel sunk to stern level, the other with a list, surrounded by rafts, tankers unloading her … On 8 January the *Italian War Bulletin* announced that one battleship had been seriously damaged; the next day came the announcement of the second success. Yet the two Axis powers inexplicably failed to seize their opportunity. After so many naval failures and disasters in the Mediterranean, were the Italians unable to believe the scale of their success, or was it a simple lack of imagination or will right at the top, made worse by a lack of support by their German allies to assist a naval offensive in the Mediterranean? The British could only be grateful. Not until St George's Day 1942 did Churchill feel able to announce – in a secret session of the House of Commons – that a number of capital ships had been lost.[19]

It was all academic as far as the six heroes of Alexandria were concerned. For some months they were held in Palestine, then the three officers were sent to POW camps in India, their petty officers to South Africa. For Borghese, success meant decoration and promotion, but it was a promotion that took him away from the *Scirè*. He offered to take off her entire crew and assign them to other, far less hazardous positions elsewhere in recognition of their courage and service. They thanked him, but only a few of the seamen accepted. On her next mission, the *Scirè* was lost with all hands.

A month after the attack, Winston Churchill was demanding to know what the British could do to emulate the work of the Italian frogmen. The result was to be a British programme led by Sir Max Horton. But Churchill did not forget the Italians, and on 15 September 1943, a week after the Italian armistice, a letter was sent by his private secretary, Francis Brown, to Clifford Jarrett, Sir Dudley Pound's personal and private secretary.

Dear Jarrett,

I have just had a note from Washington to say that the Prime Minister wished to know what is the present situation of the Italian prisoners who were captured after the attack on our battleships at Alexandria. I understand that Mr. Churchill does not think these prisoners should be treated rough.

Would you please let me have a note which I could show to the Prime Minister.[20]

Churchill's interest was specific, but for some time the Political Warfare Executive had been working in the Italian POW camps with the aim, as they put it, of:

a) securing a body of anti-fascist Italians who might be useful to us at a later state of the war and

b) at generally impregnating as many Italians as possible with a pro-British attitude to post war relations.[21]

In February 1944, Marceglia, Martellotta and de la Penne joined the Allies to fight for the liberation of Italy. Marino and Schergat were released later that year and worked with them. Bianchi used what he described as health-related excuses to remain a POW. For him it was a matter of conscience not to change sides, particularly because Borghese remained faithful to his fascist allegiance.[22]

All six operators at various times received the Medaglia d'Oro, the equivalent of the Victoria Cross, for the Alexandria assault.[23] As King Umberto II stepped forwards with the medal for de la Penne he paused, turned to the high-ranking officer standing by him and said 'Perhaps you would care to ...' He then handed the medal to Admiral Sir Charles Morgan for him to pin to the chest of the man who had put his ship out of action for an important part of the war. Morgan also took advantage of the opportunity to the return to his old adversary the watch taken from him at his capture. Many tributes were paid to the courage of the six men and their commander. Years later, looking back on that dramatic night, Denis Holton told his son, 'we were in awe of the bravery of the Italians'. Churchill had acknowledged at the time that the attack had been carried out with 'with extraordinary courage and ingenuity'.

Sources and Bibliography

Thanks to Clive Holton for sharing his father's recollections, and to S/M Alf Lonsdale and Penelope Lewis for providing a copy of the late George Hilton's unpublished memoir. I am particularly grateful to Dr. Maurizio Brescia for his assistance.

National Archives Files
ADM 199/255 Mediterranean and Red Sea intelligence reports.
ADM 1/14968 ARMAMENTS (11): Inquiry into treatment of Italian prisoners of war who had formed human torpedo team.
ADM 53/11515 1 Log of HMS *Valiant*, December 1941.
ADM 53/114911 Log of HMS *Queen Elizabeth*, December 1941.
ADM 116/4555 Defence of Mediterranean harbours against special craft: reports of attacks, defensive measures, etc.
ADM 178/221 Survivors of Italian ships, submarines and human torpedoes: interrogation reports.
L/I/1/1085 Work of the Political Warfare Executive

British Library
Cunningham papers ADD MSS 52561

Bacon, Admiral Sir Reginald H S (ed.), *Britain's Glorious Navy* (London: Odhams Press, 1943).
Bagnasco, Erminio, and Spertini, Marco, *I mezzi d'assalto della Xa Flottiglia MAS, 1940–1945* (Parma: Ermanno Albertelli, 1991).
Bagnasco, Erminio, and Spertini, Marco, *Decima Flottiglia MAS: dalle origini all'armistizo* (Parma: Ermanno Albertelli, 2005).
Borghese, Junio Valerio (Prince), *Sea Devils*, translated by James Cleugh (London: Andrew Melrose, 1952).
Cunningham, Andrew Browne, *A Sailor's Odyssey* (London: Hutchinson, 1951).
Greene, Jack and Massignani, Alessandro: *The Black Prince and the Sea Devils* (Cambridge, MA: Da Capo, 2004).
Grey, Edwyn, 'A War Crime by Any Other Name', *Proceedings of the US Naval Institute* 130/7 (July 2004).
Hobson, Robert W, *Chariots of War* (London: Ulric, 2003).
Padfield, Peter, *The War Beneath the Sea: Submarine Conflict, 1939–45* (London: John Murray, 1995).
Penne, Luigi Durand de la, 'The Italian Attack on the Alexandria Naval Base', *Proceedings of the US Naval Institute* 82/2 (February 1956). Material quoted by kind permission of the USNI.
Risio, Carlo de, *I mezzi d'assalto* (Rome: Ufficio Storico della Marina Militare, 1972). (Volume 14 of the official history of the Italian Navy in the Second World War.)
Winton, John, *Cunningham* (London: John Murray, 1998).

Corriere della Sera, 18 January 1992
Jane's Fighting Ships, 1941
The Times

Notes

[1] During 1941 Bletchley had made significant advances in the scope and speed of deciphering Italian and German messages encrypted on the C38 and Enigma machines respectively. Information could be passed to field commanders quickly enough to be of immediate use.
[2] The RAF did have a handful of Dorniers in the Middle East, thanks to their Yugoslav pilots, who flew them out earlier in the war. They were used for routine patrols or as messengers. Thanks to Ross McNeil for shedding light on this.
[3] As recorded by Borghese, so quite possibly this is Italian time; therefore 19:40 local time.
[4] Pervitin was the name given to methamphetamine. It was developed just before WW2 and its ability to improve spirits and alertness led to its wide use by the Germans in WW2.
[5] Although none of the three crews mention it, they must have seen the two cruisers come in, *Naiad* at 01:05 and *Euryalus* at 01:07, before there was an eight minute gap to the three Tribal class destroyers *Sikh*, *Legion* and *Maori*. There was a further gap before the Dutch destroyer *Isaac Sweers* entered, and then the boom was closed at 01:50.
[6] The others were the heavy cruisers *Suffren*, *Duquesne* and *Tourville*, and the light cruiser *Duguay-Trouin*.

7 The diagrams left by Borghese and de la Penne differ as to the movements of Martellotta and Marino, and the sketch-map in the British file does not clear up the mystery of where the *Lorraine* was. De la Penne puts her off *Valiant*'s bow, and that has been accepted, but with slight reservation.

8 The May attack failed, in any case, because every British warship they had expected to find in the harbour had been ordered out in the ultimately successful pursuit of the German battleship *Bismarck*.

9 She was probably the heavy cruiser *Tourville*

10 This was told to Lieutenant Richard Long, who interrogated them.

11 The spelling 'fuze' denotes a mechanical device, 'fuse' an electrical one.

12 In the event, none of the incendiaries worked, and there is some doubt as to whether they were all tethered because one was recovered with mud on the bottom, suggesting it had been on the seabed

13 The time given by Marceglia, and reported by Borghese, for this incident – 04:15 local time – is problematic, because it implies that they were the last team to finish, and yet theirs was the most straightforward operation. In fact the two teams assigned to the battleships must have finished at about the same time, because Marceglia reported seeing the activity around the *Valiant*.

14 Letter to the *Times*, 1 February 1992, in response to the obituary of Luigi Durand de la Penne.

15 In the Egyptian police report, Marino is referred to as 'Radiomio Panerei', which must represent confusion with the make of his watch, a Radio Luminor Panerai. Despite its name, the watch was actually a Rolex and had a Rolex movement.

16 His report to Borghese stated that he did not give any answer.

17 Besides the two that exploded near the *Queen Elizabeth*, another was recovered intact some 3 cables (550 metres) off the *Tourville*. One showed evidence of having been buried 2″ into the mud, but that may be because there was not time to deploy them all. De la Penne did not set any around the *Valiant* because he was anxious not to draw attention to his activities.

18 They were providing power to the ship.

19 Both battleships were eventually repaired, the *Valiant* at Durban and the *Queen Elizabeth* at Norfolk, Virginia. They were reunited in the Pacific Fleet in January 1944 and survived the war, to be broken up shortly afterwards.

20 L/I/1/1085

21 L/MIL/5/1069–70

22 The civil war that engulfed Italy after the armistice is far too complex a subject to be touched on here. Suffice it to say that Borghese turned *condottiero* and re-formed some elements of the Decima MAS into a land army fighting in the north.

23 Luigi Durand de la Penne, 1914–1992, widely admired at home and abroad, after the war he enjoyed a naval and political career, rising to Ammiraglio di Squadra. The Italian navy has named a ship and a whole destroyer class after him.

Vincente Martellotta, 1913–1973, returned to his naval engineering roots, becoming a colonel, and in 1947 won the Silver Medal for Civilian Valour following a fire in an explosives depot at Bari.

Antonio Marceglia, 1915–1992, was president of the Fincantieri shipyard, Venice, by the time he retired.

Mario Marino, 1914–1982, gained his commission in 1962, finishing his career as a capitano di corvetto.

Spartaco Schergat retired from the Navy in 1945.

Emilio Bianchi, 1912– , served at the Centro Subacqueo del Varignano, the Nucleo Sminamento di Genova and finally at Livorno's Accademia Navale, retiring as a capitano di corvetta.

Prince Borghese, 1906–1974, after the Armistice and the disbanding of the Decima, fought for the fascists in alliance with the Germans. He was arrested after the war and briefly imprisoned. Thereafter he became a figurehead for Italian neo-fascists, but he died a political outcast, his post-war career at odds with his wartime exploits.

The official Decima Flottiglia MAS is once again a respected arm of the Italian Navy.

14

—

Our Friends,
the Enemy

—

Laconia and *U-156*

1942

1. *Every attempt to rescue the survivors of sunken ships, including plucking men from the sea and putting them into lifeboats, the righting of capsized lifeboats and the distribution of food and water, must stop. Rescue contradicts the prime demands of war with respect to the destruction of enemy vessels and their crews.*

2. *The orders respecting the capture of captains and chief engineers remain in force.*

3. *Therefore, survivors should only be rescued if their statements are important for the boat.*

4. *Stay hard-hearted. Just remember that when the enemy was bombing German towns he did not take account of women and children.*

ADMIRAL KARL DÖNITZ, U-BOAT COMMAND, PARIS, 17 SEPTEMBER 1942

THE '*LACONIA* ORDER' was issued at the end of one of the most extraordinary incidents of the Second World War, which military secrecy and the demands of the Allied propaganda machine kept out of the public domain. It was only considerably later, as those involved began to tell their stories, that the full facts emerged and the searchlight fell on the man whose actions lay at the centre.

Fortunes of War

The air was thick and heavy with heat. The 3000 Allied troops in their desert kit sweated as they disembarked from the *Laconia* at Port Tewfik (now Bur Tawfiq), at the southern end of the Suez Canal, to reinforce the army in North Africa. Forget cricket and warm beer: this was to be killing and warm water, but at least they had arrived safely. The smoky old tub had made it to Egypt's major wartime port. More than a few glanced back at their erstwhile troopship with affection, hoping that she, like them, would get through the rest of the conflict alive.

Epitome of leisure and peace, the passenger ship has never been exempt from war. A century and half ago it was the East Indiamen who were chartered by the government; during both world wars the great liners were requisitioned. Many met their end in the line of duty – the *Lancastria*, the *City of Benares*, the *Montrose* and the *Empress of Britain* are just the tip of the iceberg. And if an iceberg had not put a premature end to the *Titanic*'s career even she would have found herself pressed into service in the first world war. The first *Laconia* had been lost in that conflict, and now her successor sweltered in the Bay of Suez. She had given up her stylish blue hull, white superstructure and red funnel in favour of the dirty grey camouflage dress favoured by the Admiralty, and the streaks and patches of rust showing through the paint left her with the air of a proud aristocrat fallen on hard times. Uniformed lieutenants, colonels, squadron leaders, senior NCOs and civilians gathered in her elegant rococo and neo-classical public rooms or sat on her lyre-back, Chippendale-pattern chairs writing letters and reading. Ye-olde-country-inn smoking room, with herringbone floor and inglenook fire, sustained the illusion of the village pub back home.

In her heyday, shortly after her launch in 1922, the 19,696 ton liner[1] had achieved the distinction of becoming the first vessel to complete a round-the-world pleasure cruise. Now, instead of sun-loungers, her decks sported a motley assortment of defensive hardware, some of it dating back to the first world war, manned by a group of DEMS[2] gunners like Harry Vines, for whom the stopover was no opportunity for extended shore leave. Port Tewfik was vulnerable to air attack so ships were turned around quickly. Less than 24 hours after the *Laconia* had disgorged one human cargo, she took on another:

Dramatis Personae

A J Baldwin : British army lieutenant colonel

Mr Blackburn : RAF wing commander

Thomas Buckingham : third officer, *Laconia*

Ben Coutts : British army captain

A Dickens : Canadian army lieutenant

Karl Dönitz : commander of submarines, Kriegsmarine

James Harden : USAAF lieutenant

Werner Hartenstein : captain of *U-156*

Doris Hawkins : passenger

Frank Holding : kitchen porter, *Laconia*

Claude Jones : baggage handler

Tony Large : naval rating

Mr Lester : naval petty officer

J Liswell : British army lieutenant colonel, officer commanding troops

Signor Major : Italian army colonel

J A McCordick : British army captain

Mr Mercer : British army lieutenant

R S Miller : passenger

Dino Monti : Italian army corporal

J G Mutton : marine

Geoffrey Purslow : ship's doctor, *Laconia*

Sally Readman : passenger (baby)

Marco Revedin : captain of the *Cappellini*

Robert Richardson : USAAF captain

George Rose : junior second officer, *Laconia*

Harro Schacht : captain of *U-507*

Rudolph Sharp : captain of the *Laconia*

Mr Tillie : British army lieutenant

Harry Vines : A/leading seaman, *Laconia*

H R K Wells : RAF squadron leader

Lady Grizel Wolfe-Murray : passenger

John Walker : senior first officer, *Laconia*

Erich Würdemann : captain of *U-506*

200 women, said to be either prostitutes or working against Allied interests; servicemen, including some serious hospital cases; administrative and civilian staff with families attached, and 1791 Italian prisoners captured after the first battle of El Alamein and who had been held at POW camp 321 awaiting transport to a more permanent camp, possibly in Britain which, in so far as anyone knew for certain, was the ship's destination.

That same evening, 12 August 1942, the *Laconia* sailed from Suez and a day later could consider herself beyond the danger from the air, but there remained the ever present threat of U-boats. A blackout was in force: even the night-time lighting of cigarettes on deck was forbidden, but there were greater concerns that could not be dealt with by simple orders. Below the waterline her hull was so thickly encrusted with barnacles and other marine debris that the *Laconia*'s speed had dropped to some 14 knots. More critical was the need to overhaul her engines and boilers to reduce the excessive black smoke that, far more than her size, advertised her presence for miles around.

The POWs were stowed forward, like bulk cargo, in the steel compartments of the hold and on G Deck, below the water line. Their hammocks, hung above the tables at which they passed most of their time, were packed so close together that for once the hackneyed simile of tins of sardines is depressingly accurate. Practically all they brought with them, apart from the few precious mandolins or guitars they had managed to hold on to, were the clothes in which they stood up and which, even before they descended into rags, were designed for action in the hot desert. A few fortunate ones had their army greatcoats and would come to be glad of them. For the present, they all sweltered in the foetid atmosphere, struggling to reach the air vents, where it was easier to breathe. The air, in the words of one British officer, *was foul*, and their complaints that they suffered badly as the *Laconia* went down the Red Sea must have been justified. Their only relief came in all-too-brief periods of exercise on the deck, which Lieutenant Colonel J Liswell, Officer Commanding Troops (O C Troops), regarded as a privilege rather than a right or an essential for health. Any misbehaviour, and exercise was cancelled – not just for the offenders, but for everyone.

After brief halts at first Aden and then Mombassa, where she disembarked the 200 women and some sick POWs, the *Laconia* continued down the Mozambique Channel and called at Durban. Among those who came aboard there were a party of RAF officers and several women, all of whom had sailed from Suez on the much newer and faster P & O liner *Stratheden*. They were not pleased about having to abandon what had been an enjoyable voyage, but the *Stratheden* was routed for North America while the Cunard–White Star ship was for the UK via Freetown, Liberia. Those lately of the *Stratheden* included Lady Grizel Wolfe-Murray and her friend Sister Doris Hawkins, a missionary nurse who had been some five years in Palestine. Doris was taking back to

England a young baby, just 14 months old, the daughter of Colonel Readman of the Scots Greys and his wife. Handing the baby to her, the mother had told her earnestly: 'Never forget, if anything happens and Sally has to go, that you must do all you can to save yourself ... we cannot replace you, and you have work to do.'

A contingent of 103 Polish cadets from a South African training establishment joined the ship at the same time, and were detailed to guard the POWs.

The latter were in an even more pitiable situation. It was much colder now – mid-winter in the southern hemisphere – and instead of frying in the ill-ventilated hold as they had after leaving Suez, they shivered in their degrading prisons and on deck, when exercise included being hosed down or drenched with a bucket of cold seawater, the nearest they got to washing facilities. Their guards then forced them back, at bayonet point if necessary, down the vertical ladders into the bowels of the ship, to be locked behind iron gratings for 22 hours a day on inadequate rations. They had few officers with them to offer leadership and keep up their spirits, and the language barrier was almost solid. Although he had no personal responsibility for them, Third Officer Thomas Buckingham paid a nightly visit to see if there were any who would be better for spending the night in the sick bay.

The allied troops, quartered on E deck, with the water just below the port-holes, complained that they, too, were overcrowded, and that only senior NCOs and commissioned officers were allowed the comfort of the public rooms. They, however, were free to go on deck, even to sleep on deck, as many did when the nights were warm, and their conditions were some distance away from what was happening below them. Their daily rations did not consist of two spoonfuls of thin jam to spread on two slices of equally thin bread, two cups of weak tea and a portion of what passed for soup. As the ship left Durban, the Italians were not even enjoying that: they had been put on bread and water for purloining smoking materials.

Three days out from Durban, on 31 August, Lieutenant Colonel A J Baldwin[3] of the Royal Army Ordnance Corps was asked by Liswell to go with him to inspect the prisoners and offer his opinion on their general conditions.

> I then stated that in my view the conditions were disgusting. Kits had not been tidied and were spread all over the place along with filthy and verminous bedding. Tables and forms which were in the hold were dirty, as also were the food containers. O.C. Troops [Liswell] asked me to take over as Officer i/c Escort from Major Murray. I agreed to do so ...

Co-opting Captain J A McCordick, Royal Artillery, and Lieutenant A Dickens, 48th Canadian Highlanders, to assist him, Baldwin set about changing the regime as best he could.[4] He immediately cancelled the bread-and-water punishment and served everyone a good meal. THE EFECT, he recorded in capitals, WAS ASTONISHING. The toilets were cleaned out, the lice-ridden bedding and kit dealt with; a dozen shower baths were opened up, in lieu of the public spectacle on the deck, and discipline was organized by British sergeants and Italian NCOs. 'After a week, the prisoners quarters were so clean that O.C. Troops sent British personnel down to see them as an example.' Above all, he did what he could to improve the amount of exercise allowed on deck, not easy given the numbers, and increase the ventilation. Collective punishment was largely abandoned in favour of identifying individual miscreants.

While things were beginning to look up a little for the POWs, others expressed grim foreboding about the voyage, which would soon be entering its most dangerous days. Baldwin was told to ensure that in the event of disaster the POWs were to be kept below until O C Troops gave him permission to release them.

The Commander

The lace-making town of Plauen in eastern-central Germany, surrounded by the softly wooded hills of the Vogtland, seems an unlikely birthplace for a naval hero, and Mr and Mrs Hartenstein probably expected their son either to follow his father into business or to become a lawyer. Werner had other ideas, and though he did spend two years at law school, he joined the Kriegsmarine in 1928 at the age of 20 as an officer cadet. Even with the limits on re-armament imposed on Germany after the First World War, the Navy, with its camaraderie, purpose and fine traditions, would have seemed an improvement on a civilian career. Embittered by the humiliating settlement imposed on it at Versailles, burdened by the demand for reparations to be paid to Britain and France – themselves in debt to the United States after the war – and incapable of finding a stable, dynamic government, Germany was mired in all the difficulties that, once the Depression took hold, would make her fertile ground for Hitler's ambitions during the decade to come.

Hartenstein was no political animal, just a conscientious and efficient officer with all the leadership qualities that his ambition required. He progressed steadily through the ranks until, by the outbreak of war in 1939, he held the rank of Kapitänleutnant and commanded a torpedo boat. In March 1941 he transferred to U-boats, and in September that year, now promoted Korvettenkapitän, he was given *U-156*. He had little of the stereotypical German officer about him, and nothing of the Aryan model, either. Of middle height, with short dark hair peaking on the forehead, high cheekbones and a smile that surfaced in his eyes as much as on his lips, there was something elfish about his face. But there was steel in his spine, a duelling scar on his cheek, and he was good at his job. Exceedingly good. His first cruise had proved little more than a transit from Kiel to the great submarine pens of Lorient, on the Brittany coast of occupied France, but in the next two he sunk a total of 15 ships, totalling more than 60,000 tons. Life for a U-boat was not too hard in his early days of command: they had less to fear than would rapidly become the case, and, apart from an incident when the submarine's gun exploded, he had only one close shave. Wounded prey can be dangerous. The British tanker *San Eliseo* had fought back, firing her small gun with disconcerting accuracy and then, despite the two torpedoes in her hull, steaming as fast as she could to ram him. Discretion proved the better part of valour. Hartenstein submerged, and the tanker limped home triumphantly.

On 20 August 1942 *U-156* left Lorient on her fourth cruise, in company with four other submarines – three hunters and one (*U-459*) a much larger, supply submarine. Together forming the Eisbar Gruppe (Polar Bear Group), they were to operate off Cape Town, where Allied ships sailed without escort and were defended at best by a few small guns on their deck manned by a handful of Merchant or Royal Navy gunners.

In contrast to the slow and elderly liner making her way towards Cape Town, *U-156* was a youthful, modern vessel, one of the IX C class and approaching her first birthday. At 222 feet 4 inches (67.76 metres) long, 22 feet 2 inches (6.76 metres) wide and with a height of 31 feet 6 inches (9.6 metres), she was large for a German submarine, much bigger than Borghese's *Scirè*. On the surface her two 2,200hp diesels could take her to 18 knots; even submerged her two 500hp electric motors achieved 7.3 knots. There were two torpedo tubes aft, four at the fore, and a further sixteen torpedoes for reloading. Forward of the conning tower she mounted one 105mm gun, with three 37mm guns aft which, as every Allied naval and merchant seaman knew, were to machine-gun survivors in the water.[5] By contrast with her deadly purpose, she was turned out in soft, pale grey, with the insignia of her group, the polar bear, and the town arms of Plauen as her only decoration.[6]

Werner Hartenstein was still 200 miles (370 kilometres) north of Madeira when, on 8 August 1942, he torpedoed and sunk the *Clan MacWhirter*, with the loss of ten lives. It was all part of a day's work. He pushed on south.

At Cape Town the *Laconia* embarked her last passengers – it is uncertain exactly how many. When she sailed on 1 September she carried a little over 2700[7] people. For veteran captain Rudolph Sharp (a Cunard employee but also a Royal Naval Reservist) these were now anxious days and nights, and he knew all too well the horror of being caught by the enemy. In 1940, during the evacuation of the British Expeditionary Force from France, he was in command of the *Lancastria* when she was bombed by the Luftwaffe. How many were on board will never be known. She was so overloaded – though Sharp was not to blame for that – that the purser is said to have stopped counting after he reached 6,000. Some 2,500 were rescued, but over 5,000 were believed to have lost their lives. It was the worst maritime disaster in British history, and now Rudolph Sharp was in charge of her fellow Cunarder. He steered a zigzag course by day and slept fully dressed. Everyone was ordered to keep his lifejacket to hand. There was no escort, not even the illusory comfort of being in a convoy in which they might not be the unlucky ones. They were on a large, slow and solitary vessel which was making smoke signals for the world to read.

The passengers, military and civilian, passed the time as best they could. Tennis nets were stretched athwartships, garden chairs and shuffleboards littered the deck; camp beds were brought up by those who preferred to sleep *al fresco*. Even the lifeboat falls were used as swings.

For security reasons, *Laconia* maintained radio silence to avoid any enemy interception that would betray her position, but late on 10 September she received an Admiralty order to alter course two hours after sunset the following day. The new course, which may have signalled a re-routing to North America, took her further from the West African coast and brought her smoke to the attention of the lookouts on *U-156*.

Throughout Saturday 12 September, Hartenstein and his young crew shadowed the *Laconia*, at first trying to work out what she was and what she might be doing. She was big, that was for certain – bigger than anything they had sunk so far – and would be a real feather in their cap. It only remained to keep her in sight and wait for darkness in order to make the attack. Meanwhile, as the sun went down, life continued as normal aboard the *Laconia*, and though the blackout remained in force, the occasional illegal cigarette end and porthole light gleamed against the liquorice sea as Hartenstein closed in.

Doris Hawkins had left little Sally Readman asleep in her cabin while she had dinner and then, after checking again on her charge, she went to Grizel's cabin, which was opposite. They talked about torpedoes and submarines, while, down on the mess deck, a young South African volunteer with wavy hair and a gap between his front teeth, Tony Large, wished that Dr Geoffrey Purslow, the ship's doctor, had decided to carry out an on-board tonsillectomy rather than discharge him from sick bay. Harry Vines was on deck reporting for duty.

Born during one war, fighting in the next, Vines had been working in a grocer's shop in his home town of Peterborough in 1939. Three years after Neville Chamberlain had informed the nation that Britain was at war, the 24-year-old, now an A/Leading Seaman, was manning a gun on the *Laconia*.

I had just gone on watch on the on the 6″ guns at 20:00 hours. Also on duty were one Merchant Navy gunner and about 10 RN ratings on UK draft. It was very dark, slight swell and little wind. At approx. 20:15, there was an explosion, starboard side forward, and the ship listed heavily to starboard. This explosion was quickly followed by another on the same side. The alarm bells gave just one ring and then stopped. Being the senior rating I communicated the bridge by telephone and asked if it was action or boat stations. I was told *action stations* and to load and fire at anything I saw.

The first explosion shattered the quiet conversation of Doris and Grizel.

The ship shivered, then stood still; and the air filled with the smell of explosive. It had happened; the first torpedo had struck. I fled to Sally. She was still asleep, and I wrapped her in her woollies, picked up her shipwreck bag and turned. As I did, the second torpedo struck. The ship rocked; we were flung across the corridor. Sally remained in my arms unhurt. Just ahead of me was Grizel[8] ... We were carried on a surging wave of people, some with their emergency outfits, many without ...

The energy loosed by the first explosion threw the ship to port. Hardly had the invading water brought her to starboard than the second again rocked her.

If there was shock above the waterline, as men and women relaxing after dinner were catapulted across the floors of salons and cabins, in the hold there was sheer panic, with the sudden arrival of savage death. When the first torpedo blasted though the hull and exploded in the confines of no. 4 hold, around 400 men died instantly. The few left – maimed, burnt and bleeding in the darkness among the carnage of blood and torn flesh that coated every surface – had no chance as the water rushed in to end their misery. The second torpedo hit no. 2 hold, blowing to pieces another batch of prisoners. Those in the other compartments, like Corporal Dino Monti, surged in terror, begging to be set free as the vessel listed.

In the holds, exits closed, shots rang out. Blood began to flow in the cages. The Polish guards had opened fire, and were driving back at bayonet point those of our men who were nearest the bars; but immediately, while dead and wounded fell, others took their place. The bars bent under our pressure and gave way. People were laughing hysterically, yelling, shouting, cursing. I stood against the bulkhead, trying not to see or hear. Many tried to kill themselves by beating their heads against the partitions. Unconsciously I said a prayer and this calmed me. I told myself the guards would see that the ship was heeling over, that she might sink at any moment, and they would be forced to abandon their posts. Then I should be able to get out, to escape. Our crazed terror gave us extra strength, and at last the bars were broken down, we were through them. Trampling on those who had fallen, my companions and I dashed to the ladders. There was complete darkness ...

Prisoners in the other holds were not so lucky.

'*Aiuto*'

The pain in Tony Large's throat was forgotten in the haste to climb four decks to his boat station amidships on the port side, only to find that the starboard list had made launching some of them impossible. The ship had practised lifeboat drill, but like most safety drills theirs had taken place in good weather and with everyone enjoying a break from routine. At night, on a sloping deck, in the pitch darkness that followed the failure of the lighting, with the lurking presence of an unseen enemy, separated from friends and comrades and with the fear that there would not be enough equipment to go round, the reality was somewhat different, particularly for the civilians and those unused to the sea. The tennis nets and chairs now hampered movement along the decks.

Sally Readman was the only one unaffected by the fear and alarm, quietly murmuring to herself in Doris Hawkins's arms as the earlier steadiness on the deck gave way to turmoil. Free from their metal coffins, the Italians stormed up the stairs, desperate to get to the lifeboats. Doris and Grizel were told that their own designated boat had been lost, but nobody told them what to do or where to go. Finally an RAF officer, Squadron Leader H R K Wells, came to their rescue, carrying the baby and leading them along the deck in search of a boat. The task appeared hopeless: all that could be launched had gone, whether fully loaded or not. Then, some 45 minutes after the ship had been struck, they spotted a lifeboat riding at the foot of a rope ladder. How to get down with a 14-month-old baby? An enterprising officer of the Fleet Air Arm tied a blanket around his waist over his greatcoat to create a pocket between his jacket and coat. Sally was slipped safely into it while he climbed down the swaying ladder. The two women followed.

> We found ourselves on top of the arms and legs of a panic stricken mass of human-ity. The lifeboat, filled to capacity … was leaking badly and rapidly filling with water; at the same time it was crashing against the ship's side. Just as Sally was passed over to me, the boat filled completely and capsized, flinging us all into the water. I lost her.

Positioned aft, Vines stuck to his gun, scanning the water and wondering if he would get a chance to pay back the submarine. Petty Officer Lester had come to take charge of his DEMS men and told Vines to go with him and help make sure that the *Laconia*'s depth charges were set to safe. She was clearly going to sink; the last things the survivors in the water and in the boats needed was for the charges to go off as she went down. Further forward they heard the crack of rifles. Someone said the Polish guards were shooting at the panicked Italians. From his boat, Large heard the same shots ring out, and he, too, was told that the guards, as well as some of the other officers, were shooting at the Italians to prevent them from rushing the boats.

Third Officer Buckingham believed that the Poles had no ammunition which, no matter how easy-going the prisoners were under normal conditions, seems bizarre; others said the British officers had fired live rounds into the mass of people, killing members of the ship's crew as well. Corporal Monti remembered gun butts on deck. Baldwin was the officer on the spot.

...I went straight down into both holds immediately after the impact. The casualties among the Ps/W were very heavy, and they all appeared terrified. I had to use my revolver butt to get out. The Polish Guards manning the entrances were quickly increased by my orders. They had rifles, but no ammunition had been issued and despite the iron gates across the entrances they were quickly rushed by sheer weight of numbers of panic stricken Ps/W. The ship took approximately an hour and ten minutes to go down and during that period I held the staircase at B Deck assisted by Lieut. Dickens and two British sergeants. That was the only way by which Ps/W should have been able to reach the boat deck. Lt Dickens and I had revolvers and ammunition, the British sergeants had only rifles and bayonets until a quarter of an hour before the end when the SMC found and brought us some ammunition. Whilst the ship was settling down I saw O.C. Troops twice and I asked for orders regarding the release of the Ps/W, but I got none. I therefore continued to hold [them] in accordance with the orders ... and also because there were so many women and children to be got away ... Unfortunately, many prisoners of war did get up on the boat deck by means unknown to me ...

That the Italians had gone to pieces under the circumstances is neither in doubt nor, given what they had been through below decks, surprising, though to baggage handler Claude Jones it was unseemly.[9] After the two impacts, he went against the flow to his quarters to find his reefer coat, life-jacket and shoes before heading up to no. 2 station.

The moment I gained the open deck I was caught in a milling mob of frenzied, shouting Italians. I had to avoid being knocked down and trampled on. By a violent effort I broke clear, only to discover No 2 lifeboat, badly damaged, was hanging uselessly from a single davit. I turned back along the darkened deck, evading crazed Italians and refraining from using my torch lest it should be snatched from my hand ... The confusion among the prisoners was serious ... Struggling Italians jammed the ladders, and I took a chance by climbing a stanchion to gain the boat deck near Number 8 lifeboat. It was necessary to keep them at bay whilst the women and children were placed in the boats. I was ordered to help in keeping a space clear. The prisoners came at us like howling dervishes ... We used only our fists and our feet, but elsewhere ... shots were being fired by the Polish guards ...

The *Laconia* was not overloaded; her complement was hardly more than she would have carried in peacetime, and far less than on her outward voyage, but her useable lifesaving equipment was inadequate. Nobody had responsibility for her life-rafts; a number of her wooden boats were leaky – some without even a proper bung – and few had the emergency provisions with which they should have been equipped. The list had made it impossible to launch the lower port boats on A-Deck. Boat 9a fell from the deck, taking those in it to almost certain death. The boats had to be raised before they could be swung out, and that devoured ebbing time.

In the radio room, the wireless operators tried to send out a distress signal. Power was failing and the mainmast had come down when the explosion rocked the ship. The signal was faint. They could only hope someone would pick it up. Someone other than their opposite number on the U-boat.

The order to abandon ship had been given around 20 minutes after the ship was hit. Baldwin had been 'obliged' to retain all the Polish guard for a further 50 minutes. With the ship listing heavily to starboard, and still no word from Liswell, Baldwin gave his own orders to release the prisoners and let down the scramble nets. 'Lt. Dickens and I walked over the side. To my belief, Dickens and I were the last two officers to leave the ship and we left it with the Ps/W.' By that time all the boats had gone.

According to Hartenstein's log, the ship was attacked at 20:07. Just over an hour later Vines recalled:

> … the ship began settling down by the bows and started quivering. The P.O. ordered us to get over the stern into the water. This we did and I got on a raft with P.O. Lester, L.S. Cooper DEMS and two MN gunners, Thompson and Macnamara. We swam away from the ship. A few minutes later, she seemed to break in half, and the stern half stood straight up in the air and then slid under. The suction was terrific and we had a job to cling on. Suddenly there was a violent explosion beneath the surface and it seemed as though we were being crushed. We stayed with the raft until about midnight, when we saw a ship's boat. We boarded this and found it was stove in aft and kept afloat by the buoyancy tanks. The sole occupant was a Pole. Later we helped aboard some British Army officers, Mr Rose, 2nd Officer of the ship, Mr Beatty, Chief Steward, some other ranks and a few Italians, almost 18 in all.

Not all the Italians were so fortunate. In another boat, Frank Holding, one of the kitchen porters, recalled how someone in his boat offered to pass an axe with which to chop off the fingers of any who were clinging to the sides.

Tony Large, who despite his 19 years had already survived the sinking of HMS *Cornwall* less than 6 months before, was another who remembered those early moments.

Numerous rafts and floats in the water. Rowed away from the ship, all the while (the boat was full) being obliged to prevent swimming Italians from hanging onto the oars or gunwales or climbing in … Bailing continuously because of faulty plug … About fifty in boat including 2 RAF officers, four Italians (1 Red Cross), 3 Poles.

Some 2 miles (3.5 kilometres) away, as the ominous noises from the hull were convincing Buckingham that it was time to leave the *Laconia*, Hartenstein watched through his binoculars from the bridge on the conning tower. His duty, provided it did not endanger the submarine, was to collect the ship's captain and chief engineer and take them back for questioning. The *Laconia* was certainly settling – the microphone had picked up both explosions – but she had not yet sunk. He was wary of a trap. The *San Eliseo* had taught him caution. Abruptly his thoughts were broken by news that the ship had sent out a distress signal: SSS, 04.34 South, 11.25 West, and given her name.

Any satisfaction that he had torpedoed a 20,000-ton liner was obliterated by the three letters SSS. Not SOS, a simple recognized cry for help, but SSS, warning of a submarine. He ordered the signal to be jammed at once and for *U-156* to proceed towards the stricken ship. Help would not come immediately, and he had a chance of finding her captain.

In fact, he had none, and not just because of the chaos in the water as hundreds of survivors swam, clung to rafts or held onto overloaded boats. When the *Laconia* made her great plunge she took Captain Rudolph Sharp with her. Unlike most of those who remained on board because they could find no boats and feared the satin water, he had quietly and calmly made his decision to perish with his ship. And Hartenstein had something else to think about. His crew had reported cries of 'Aiuto!' from the water.

It made no sense. He passed Large's boat, and it rowed away as fast as it could from him.

'Aiuto!'

Italian, for *help*. But the *Laconia* was a British ship. Only after he had ordered his men to drag a couple of men out of the water for questioning did he learn that he had sunk a vessel carrying 1800 of his country's allies, not to mention women and children. As well as those in the overcrowded and leaky boats there were hundreds more in the water, at the mercy of the sharks and their own exhaustion. He was right in the middle of them.

Attacks by submarines on merchant ships were regulated by the Naval Protocol of 1936, which restated what had been laid down in the London Naval Agreement in 1930: if a submarine could not rescue the crew, then it could not sink a merchantman. In practice, all sides had comprehensively violated it. Dönitz had instituted the concept of unrestricted U-boat warfare partly on the grounds that since merchantmen were armed they could not claim exemption from attack; the United States had practised the same from the moment it entered the war; in 1940 the British had ordered their submarines to sink anything that moved in the Skaggerak at night. Although the result had dismayed him, what Hartenstein had just done was not out of the ordinary. Unlike what he was about to do.

The sight of the U-boat, with men on her deck and her big forward gun all too evident, struck fear into those in her vicinity. But they could also see that the submarine's crew appeared to be pulling people up onto the deck with ropes. Suspicion remained, but some of the fear diminished.

Hartenstein sent a message to Dönitz.

'British *Laconia* sunk – unfortunately with 1500 Italian prisoners. 90 rescued so far.' He did not clarify that the ninety included a few of the British, and while waiting for a response from the Admiral at his Paris headquarters he went on with the rescue. He also noted in his log that the Italians had accused their erstwhile captors of locking them in the hold as the ship began to fill.

Dönitz could guess what was going through Hartenstein's mind. There was the humanitarian aspect. Having rescued survivors already created a bond: it would be very hard for the men of *U-156* to return them to the death from which they had just plucked them. Then there was the matter of how this incident would play in Rome. There was also, however, the question of duty, and Hartenstein, like any commander, must not risk his vessel.

'Once Hartenstein had begun the rescue operation', Dönitz later told French historian Léonce Peillard, 'I couldn't have given him the order to break it off. The morale of my men was very high, and to give them an order contrary to the laws of humanity would have destroyed it utterly ... My general staff did not agree with me. I remember one officer thumping the table red with fury.'

The admiral's answer reached *U-156* at 01:55. Three submarines had been ordered to head for him as quickly as they could. One, *U-459*, the huge 1700-ton supply sub from the Eisbar Gruppe, decided she was too far away to be of use, but *U-507*, commanded by Harro Schacht, and *U-506*, under Lieutenant Erich Würdemann, set course to join their comrades. Hartenstein would be on the surface and exposed to danger for more than 36 hours before their arrival.

Dönitz wanted more information, and Hartenstein, now with 193 survivors on board and aware that an unidentified ship was transmitting in the vicinity,[10] coupled his reply with a recommendation to turn to the area into a neutral zone. The idea was turned down as unlikely to convince the Allies, but Dönitz alerted the both the Italian Admiral based at Bordeaux, Angelo Parona, and the Vichy French navy in the Senegalese port of Dakar.

Refuge at Sea

Meanwhile, despite having four times her usual numbers on board, *U-156* was preparing for a test dive. Hartenstein needed to be certain it would be possible to submerge in the event of trouble. She performed perfectly, and after she rose, he took a far-reaching decision and broadcast a message in English:

> *If any ship will assist the wrecked* Laconia *crew, I will not attack her, provided I am not attacked by ship or aircraft. I have picked up 193 men, 4° 52 S, 11° West. German Submarine.*

Sent out *en clair*, and transmitted twice on different wavelengths, it was, effectively, a unilateral declaration of neutralization, the man on the spot cutting through all the politics, and Dönitz, in contact with Berlin – where Hartenstein's mercy mission had not found favour with his boss Admiral Erich Raeder, or with the Führer – thought it wiser not to mention that open transmission. For all their misgivings, Berlin did not order Hartenstein to break off and return to offensive duties. The message he received from Paris read: 'Hartenstein,[11] remain on the spot but be ready to submerge. Other boats to take on as many as they can without interfering with their ability to submerge. Neutralization follows.'

From a stealthy killing machine, *U-156* had been transformed into a cross between a mobile soup-kitchen and a night shelter for the vulnerable. Like a sheepdog, the submarine spent the day looking for those in the water, bringing them on board to feed and treat them, and distributing men among lifeboats that were not over-crowded. The commander now knew that the Italian submarine *Cappellini* was on her way, and that the French vessels would also make the rendezvous. The *Dumont-d'Urville* and the *Annamite* would in turn meet with the big French cruiser *Gloire* and take off the survivors. What he had to do, with the help of Schacht and Würdemann when they arrived, was to get all the survivors together in one place. All of them, irrespective of nationality, despite what the Italians had told him of their sufferings on the *Laconia*.

Those Italians who had managed to escape were not vindictive towards their former British captors. The *Laconia*'s Third Officer, Buckingham, who would spend 12 hours in the water without a lifejacket, for much of the time supporting himself on a dead body, owed his life to the 16 Italians in a boat who hauled him on board. The only other non-Italian occupant was an RAF officer, whom they had also fished out during the night.

Doris Hawkins somehow avoided the desperate clinging arms of others struggling in the water, and with the help of Wells she reached the raft that he and Lieutenant Tillie had found just after the *Laconia* went down. She was the only woman among some 10 men, British and Italian, and they put her on top of the raft while the men swam and held onto the sides. Encountering another, all-Italian, raft, they transferred their own Italians. Most seemed to want to be with their own kind, whether that was by nationality or arm of the service, looking for that sense of solidarity.

Tillie became the life and soul of the raft, its leader and its organizer. Every ten minutes a man was allowed onto the deck of the raft to join Doris, and it was only when Tillie himself was sitting next to her that he grew strangely quiet, and she saw the blood on his arm. He died soon after, though not before she had promised to take his watch to his wife. She was cold and wet – they all were; the unstable raft kept capsizing. Some of their number had faded with exhaustion and been lost. The rest had no means of going anywhere: they were dependent upon being rescued. They saw other rafts and people clinging to pieces of wood, and after dawn they suffered, unprotected, in the scorching heat that intensified as the day drew on. They joined up with another raft, which supported two RAF officers and an Italian, and with some trepidation saw *U-156* within some 650 feet (200 metres) of them. Only later, when it was obvious what she was about, did Squadron Leader Wells take the two rafts in tow and attempt to swim with them to the submarine. By that time she was more distant, and then, not having seen them, moved off. The exhausted officer abandoned the attempt.

She came back in the evening, however, and this time the lifelines were for them. All nine were taken on board, where Doris was reunited with the friend she had lost when the lifeboat had capsized.

The German officer took charge of our women (four altogether). Our clothes were taken from us and dried and we were given hot tea and coffee. black bread, and butter, rusks and jam...Four of our officers who were in the worst condition, and we four women, remained in this cabin which served both as sleeping quarters for the German officers and as dining saloon for the whole crew. The Officers gave up their bunks to us, and many of the crew gave up theirs to our men and to the Italians, themselves sitting up all that night and Monday night ... The Germans treated us with great kindness and respect the whole time; they were really sorry for our plight. One brought us eau-de-Cologne, another cold cream for our sunburn ... others gave us lemons from their own lockers, articles of clothing and tinned fruit. The commandant was particularly charming and helpful; he could scarcely have done more had he been entertaining us.

It says much for the atmosphere on that claustrophobic and stiflingly hot vessel, packed with four nationalities, that Doris Hawkins, for all the trauma she had suffered, could not only write with warm affection, but take an interest in the details: what the Germans themselves had for each meal, the lack of anything remotely Nazi – even the small photo of Hitler was tucked away – and the acts of individual kindness. She gained the impression that the Germans took more care of the English than of the Italians, but that may have appeared the case because communication was easier, and she was a woman; and she was keenly aware of the risk that Hartenstein was running.

He was doing his best to minimize it: a large white sheet and some red muslin had been pressed into service, and a giant red cross flag was in preparation, in case they were spotted.

Among the Italians on the boat was a doctor, and the Germans kept him supplied with medical equipment while he treated anyone who needed it. Marine J G Mutton was another beneficiary of Hartenstein's kindness: he was given a shirt after the German saw the state of his sunburn.

Those in the lifeboats were in less dire need than those in the water among the sharks, and were generally left to their own devices that Sunday, 13 September, although *U-156* distributed coffee and other supplies to a number that it had rounded up. Quite how many boats had got away from the *Laconia* was never established, but reports varied between 16 and 22. Some drifted alone on the glittering swell, beneath the blistering equatorial sun; others huddled together for security; a few made the conscious decision to try to make for West Africa. Monrovia lay some 600 miles (1100 kilometres) to the northeast, while Ascension Island was closer, at around 250 miles (460 kilometres) to the south-east, but would be harder to spot.

Tony Large's group had managed to repair their bung, and once the boat had been in the water for some hours the leaky seams had repaired themselves as the wood swelled. But there was little camaraderie aboard it; there were no officers to give a lead, and men sought their own kind, although the 18-year-old Large himself remained in a state of unspoken comradeship with a quiet, fair-haired Italian prisoner he had 'met' on deck shortly after the torpedoes had struck. They sighted the U-boat with a number of lifeboats gathered around it, and they learned that, far from intending to shoot them, Hartenstein seemed to regret sinking their ship. They also found out that a distress signal had been sent.

Vines's boat was so leaky it was up to the gunwales; they, too, washed about listlessly, sighting but not making contact with *U-156*. They had transferred their Italians to a raft tied to them because the boat was too frail for the numbers she contained, but all but one of them had disappeared in the night. The survivor was brought back into the waterlogged lifeboat where he and one of his British fellow occupants died. They were down to seven men including Vines, George Rose, *Laconia*'s junior second officer, Captain Ben Coutts, who had lost his nose at Tobruk, and R S Miller from Rolls Royce. More animation was evident on Boat 9a where Colonel Major, one of the few Italian officers, and British Army Lieutenant Mercer organized co-operation through their common language, French. Boat 14, commanded by Lieutenant Colonel Baldwin, was struggling to contain the violently disturbed chief purser and an army captain who was showing signs of mental problems.

On the morning of Tuesday 15 September the isolation ended for Vines and his companions. Dawn found them close to a group of four boats that had been tied together, and some reorganization took place. Their lifeboat was given over to a group of Italians, and the British divided themselves between two of the other boats, reuniting a number of the DEMS gunners and bringing together four Navy ratings, including Vines and Large, who had no idea what they would go through together. Rose went into the motor boat – unfortunately without any fuel. Large remembered later:

> P O Lester was made coxswain and it was decided we should hoist sails and head for West Africa. We were well stocked with provisions and there were about 50 people on board, We were told from the motor boat, which was equipped with wireless, that they had got about a dozen signals away. Also, that a boat with women and children on board under Mr Walker, 1st Officer, had made for the coast. On board our boat we met 2 other DEMS ratings, Riley and Prince.
>
> The wind was favourable and we made about 4 knots NE. At 10:00 we saw a 4-engined aircraft in the clouds. None of the RAF personnel could identify however. It flew straight on.
>
> Just before dusk the U-boat came alongside towing a lifeboat. On being hailed we struck sail. The U-boat commander spoke in passable English and told us to remain in that position till day-break, when he would give us water and take us in tow, to a rendezvous with three French ships, one cruiser and two gun-boats. He went away and fetched another boat, making three in all. All that night we had to row to keep the boat head-on to the seas, which were rather heavy. The O C Troops was suffering from a gangrenous wound in the leg.

The previous day, before Vines had transferred to that boat, Hartenstein had made contact with it and told everyone to stay where they were so that he could return with supplies. Other priorities had claimed his attention, but he was not pleased to discover that they had disobeyed instructions. This new set had to be obeyed.

Sleep-deprived, anxious for his submarine, his crew and his career, doing his utmost to make up what he had done in good faith in the line of duty, no wonder Hartenstein seemed grim as he stared down at them. This time they would obey him.

> The U Boat commander [recalled Large] was man of about 5′ 9″ in build, dark complexioned and he had what I suppose were duelling scars ... unsmiling, unemotional. I did not see his hair because of a pulled down cap. Spoke good English with a slightly clipped accent. He did not seem a Nordic type.

Another reason for Hartenstein's coldness emerged next day when *U-156* returned. While the slightly oily water ration was dished out – the submarine had desalination facilities – one of the crew expressed disgust that they had filled one boat entirely with Italians. These prisoners were soldiers, without any skills in seamanship. To leave them without a single competent naval officer or rating was cruel. The commander himself made no comment about the incident but gave orders for the two boats to be taken in tow together with two more he had brought with him. It was Wednesday 16 September, and the end of the rescue was at last in sight.

Unfriendly Fire

U-507, Schacht, and *U-506*, Würdemann, had made all speed, and at noon on the Tuesday Würdemann had become the first to heave-to alongside his comrade and share the lonely burden. If Vines had thought Hartenstein unlike the 'typical German squarehead', he would have been even more surprised by the newcomer, a dashing, deceptively young-looking 40-year-old with curly black hair and dark eyes beneath thick brows, who would have looked equally at home on the bridge of an Italian submarine or in a Hollywood film.

Hartenstein had 264 survivors on deck or inside, and Würdemann offered to take 132 Italians, who made up half of them. Hartenstein had already asked the British to put some of their men into the twelve or so boats gathered around him so that he could take more sick or women into the submarine. Squadron Leader Wells had found the necessary volunteers, but Hartenstein refused to allow him to be one of them; the RAF man was not well enough. Transfer completed, Würdemann went off to round up more boats, provoking initial panic in one lifeboat for whom it was their first sight of a U-boat and who believed all they had been told.

Meanwhile, Harro Schacht, far more stereotypically German in looks, was in the area and had come up on the convoy led by Buckingham. Having brought some people on board, including the women and children, he took the boats in tow. Buckingham's own lifeboat was the last to be reached, and the *Laconia* man's relief that the U-boat was German rather than Italian has to be explained by a definite fear of retaliation over what had happened to the Italian prisoners at the time of sinking.

The chance of finding anyone still alive in the water or clinging to a raft was all but over, though Schacht's lookouts spotted a lone, pregnant woman on a raft, and two of his men swam to rescue her. By Wednesday morning the men, women and children of several nationalities were safe in or around the three U-boats, themselves widely spread out but and making for the rendezvous with the French and Italian vessels at about 6 knots. All it needed now was for the Allies to come. Surely the British had picked up the *en clair* signal? There was also, although the Germans did not know it, a new and secret US air base, Wideawake, on the British possession of Ascension Island.

Those aboard *U-156* had their answer in the pristine blue sky that morning. An aircraft was spotted ... Black ... four engines ... the engines snarled in a spirited throb, growing louder ... a Liberator ... long-range ... American ...

USAAF markings. From the bridge Hartenstein ordered the red cross flag to be brought out and spread out over the deadly forward gun. Everyone was to move away from it; the crew lay down behind the conning tower. Let the Americans be in no doubt of the situation.

Hartenstein had a Morse code signal transmitted in English. 'Here German submarine with British shipwrecked on board. Is there rescue plane in sight?'

No response from the Liberator. It continued to reconnoitre the scene down below. Nobody on *U-156* went near the guns. Wing Commander Blackburn[12] climbed up to the bridge and offered to signal to the Americans in a way they would understand. Hartenstein agreed, but the message would be his own.

And so, in the words of French historian Léonce Peillard, 'something happened probably unique in the annals of naval warfare: a British officer on board a German submarine sent a message to an Allied plane'. The message read: 'RAF officer speaking from German submarine. Laconia survivors on board, soldiers, civilians, women, children.'

The encounter had lasted around half an hour, though the other U-boats were sufficiently distant that the plane did not spot them. Although the Liberator crew did not answer the morse message, they flew off, heading south-west. For those staring after their retreating tail fin, actions spoke louder than words. It was returning to base to bring help.

Half an hour of hope passed, before a speck was seen in the sky, growing larger, assuming the shape of the Liberator, coming in low as if on a bombing run, except that everyone expected to see food parcels dropping.

The flaps were open. Frozen horror dawned on every face, including Hartenstein's. Tony Large was in one of the boats being towed behind:

> The plane circled round again and approached from the port beam at about 300 feet, flying at about 150 mph. The submarine still making way and flying Red Cross. Two depth charges which landed about 50 yards ahead and over were released. Charges were silver coloured ... Plane circled again and dropped more charges.

They were contact bombs, but their aim was poor and they went into the water, where they acted as depth charges. One exploded right under Large's boat, hurling it over and pitching 50 men into the water. Another destroyed a laden boat astern of him. Large came to the surface and swam to the upturned craft, heaving himself onto it, watching the plane come in for a third run. One of the U boat's crew had run to drop the tow as soon as the first attack was over and *U-156* was still making way. From the capsized boat Large saw the third assault.

> This time the other two charges fell on each side of the U-boat, which had stopped. The explosion of one covered the conning tower ... [with?] spray and seemed to

lift the ship out of the water. A minute after there was the smell of light oil ...
During the attack the U-boat had made no move to open fire with her AA gun on
the conning tower but had merely held the red cross flag openly visible.

Inside the submarine, Doris Hawkins and the others felt all the fear without
being able to see its cause as the submarine shivered and shook in the grip of
the depth charges. Hartenstein had no option but to put his British contingent
into the water and submerge, and the submarine had to get underway in order
to gain the momentum for the dive. But with gas leaking into the interior, he
also had to put off the 55 Italians he had hoped to keep with him. The British,
he noted, went without a protest. Doris remembered:

> He and his commandant were genuinely distressed. He took us until we were fairly
> close to two of our boats, and then we found ourselves once again swimming for
> our lives. We could scarcely see the boats when we were in the water, owing to the
> heavy seas. One English officer helped Grizel, and Squadron Leader Wells again
> helped me. I am a poor swimmer, and he – a magnificent swimmer but now a sick
> man ... we swam for nearly fifty minutes ...

By this time, Würdemann had not only his 132 Italians but the women, children, Italians and some of the British men from an overcrowded boat he had
come across, plus more survivors pulled from the water: more than two hundred in all. Harro Schacht had found a convoy of four boats led by
Buckingham. These he had taken in tow, transferring 153 to the submarine
itself.

Alone on a Wide, Wide Sea

Most of those whom Hartenstein had been forced to put off never managed to
reach a boat. Some, many of them suffering from shark bites, were picked up
by Lieutenant Commander Marco Revedin in the Italian submarine *Cappellini*
later that day. Revedin had already encountered two boats of British survivors
making for the coast, who told him they were content to proceed under their
own resources.

Doris and Grizel found themselves the only women among 64 Britons and
2 Poles in a single boat. They met the *Cappellini*, which stood guard over them
all night, but, afraid that the Vichy French might fail them – was it any wonder
after what had lately occurred – they set sail for the coast, 600 miles (1100 kilometres) away. An American plane circled them, flashed a message and went off,
but no rescue ever came, only a succession of deaths.

> Grizel became a little weaker every day. She never suffered acutely but she just
> faded ... She spoke often of her family, and her thoughts were constantly with her

husband, fighting in the desert, or with her little sons awaiting her in the homeland
… On 25th September she realised she could not live much longer. She smiled and
thanked me for taking care of her, adding: 'We've had a lot of fun'… This night she
did not shiver, and nothing disturbed her, and in the morning at 6 a.m. she just
stopped breathing while asleep. Dr Purslow held a little service for her, and we
tried to sing a verse of 'Abide With Me', but the effort was pathetic.

Two days later they saw a three-funnelled ship, and burnt a kapok lifejacket
hoping the smoke would be seen, but they were cruelly disappointed, and
depression fell on them heavily.

Dr Purslow developed a major infection that descended into blood
poisoning.

> I stumbled to where he was sitting and tried to speak to him, but no words came,
> he was quite conscious, and in a voice stronger than I had heard from him for
> many days he said: 'As I cannot be any further help, and I am now a source of
> danger to you all, it is better that I should go.' As he heaved himself painfully up
> the side of the boat I found my voice and said: 'greater love hath no man than this,
> that a man lay down his life for his friends.' He said 'Goodbye', and with a long
> look he took that final step backward.

On 8 October they sighted land; the following day a British flying boat passed
overhead and dropped a message that they were 60 miles (110 kilometres)
south of Monrovia and help was on its way. That night, and in yet another echo
of the boats from the *Méduse*, a naval rating held the tiller and brought the little boat safely through the wild white surf that broke on the coast. The welcome
from the African population of the small Liberian village was warm, sympa-
thetic and full of practical help until the promised rescue arrived.

As the *U-156*'s engines roared and she plunged beneath the waves, the
power and suction had all but wrecked one of the lifeboats, which was full
of Italian soldiers. Harry Vines and company managed to right their lifeboat,
discovering that four people had been trapped beneath it and now floated,
dead. Tony Large's Italian companion was also among those who drowned. A
few survivors from the devastated Italian craft swam over but were repulsed by
a boat where it was each man for himself. The boat itself was damaged and
leaking badly, but in the late afternoon help arrived in the form of the
Cappellini.

> About sunset she came within ten yards of our submerged boat [Large wrote] and
> threw heaving lines to those on her …We were given water, a little watered cognac,
> hot meat extract soup, and biscuits that evening, but were warned that if anything

was sighted, the submarine would have to submerge and leave us in the water. We were told the Vichy cruiser was due in the morning and that we could spend the night on deck.

By three o'clock the following afternoon no French ship had arrived. Keeping two officers – one RAF, one merchant navy – on board, Revedin decided to go in search of her. Tony Large's boat had been repaired by the Italian crew, and he and his men returned to it together with 31 British and Polish men whom the *Cappellini* had rescued earlier. The Italians rescued with them were retained on board the submarine.

In the boat there were 51, comprising RN, Army, RAF, MN, Poles and 1 civilian. Wing Commander Blackburn RAF was in charge. We had only 1½ oars, no sail, no gear except an axe and little food and water. One or two of the men suffering from very bad sunburn. We saw no planes that day.

Sept 18th onwards

We drifted about for two or three days, but sighted nothing. We then decided to make a sail. The mast was an oar. The boom a length of wood from the benches and foresail a blanket. The mainsail we made from about 12 shirts and the lining of a greatcoat. We steered with the broken oar. We made about 2 knots NE …

A day or so later, a plane said to be a Marauder or B24 by the RAF circled and flew off to the NE. Next day we saw two Hudsons a long way off. As the days passed we began to get weaker on our meagre rations which were 3 chocolates, 4 Horlicks tablets and 1 spoonful of Pemmican and about ¾″ water in the bottom of a glass. We were now too dry to eat biscuits. We did, however, manage to catch a quantity of fish with a bent nail and a string. These we ate raw and drank the blood. The first man died after about a fortnight. We buried him and kept his clothes for we were very short … next day two more died. It was very hot by day and cold and damp at night. We could not sleep as there were so many of us.

Harry Vines's official report can be read between the lines; much later, Tony Large, who had also made a report, wrote another account of the whole disaster in detail, recalling how in that boat one young man thought he could see Canada, and just swam away; how another, caught stealing water, accepted the rules of the boat and put himself over the side. With grim humour, they had named their boat *Marie Celeste*. More and more died as the days went on, including both Wells and Blackburn. After 17 days at sea nobody had the strength to take the steering oar; many of them gave up in despair when a merchant ship passed so close that they could not believe they had been missed. Just nine were left when the rains came to their relief, and then just four, all naval ratings. In a letter to his parents Large wrote:

There were very dark layers of horizon cloud and one very black spot which might have been something, I called my companion [Vines] and we saw it dissolve into nothing ... we went back into the shelter, rain stopped, he called me out and repeat performance of the dissolving spot. I had a bad knee and went in again. He stayed out and called me again five minutes later. This time I grumbled because it hurt like blazes to move, but eventually I got out. There on our four mile horizon were about a dozen pinpoints of masts sticking up jet black against the grey ... Convoy! I don't know where the strength came from, but I leap up on a thwart to see them better and started waving madly with blue jersey. We didn't dare wake the two sleeping forward because of the general depression it would make if they did pass us by. They were coming towards and across, slowly closer. Harry and I are talking and praying in whispers. Can see funnels and upperworks. One ship turns either towards or away from us. Oh Christ! Pass one of those rain tins, Shorty (excitement thirst). Can see ships signalling to one another. Slowly approaching and at last, when she's about a mile away we can be sure. We waken the other two and they are unwilling to come out. 'Don't joke about things like that.'

They were not joking. She was an Admiralty trawler, the *St Wistan*, and the dozen masts belonged to her convoy, which was only 80 miles (150 kilometres) from the coast, a mere day from Freetown, Sierra Leone. Their 36-day, 700-mile (1300-kilometre) voyage in the open boat, recently rechristened the *Good Hope*, with its echoes of the *Méduse* disaster, had ended on 21 October.

Erich Würdemann, Harro Schacht and Marco Revedin had continued with their rescue work despite being informed of the bombing of *U-156*. On 17 September *U-506*, *U-507* and the *Cappellini* made rendezvous with the Vichy French ships *Gloire*, *Dumont d'Urville* and *Annamite*, and transferred all the survivors they had taken on board, barring Revedin's Italians and four British officers, including Buckingham. The *Gloire* herself had picked up several boatloads. Eventually, she had 1,039 survivors on board. Counting the 4 prisoners retained on the submarines, the 4 RN ratings, including Vines, the 16 in the boat containing Doris Hawkins, and the Italians on the *Cappellini*, 1111[13] were saved. The British were taken to POW camps in Morocco, from where they were liberated just six weeks later by the Americans.

In the wake of the *Laconia*

'All animals', as George Orwell wrote, 'are equal, but some animals are more equal than others'. According to John Walker, the senior first officer of the *Laconia*, 2856 people, including her crew of 359, were aboard when she was hit. Of the 1791 Italian POWs, only around 450 survived, and there is no knowing how many actually managed to get off the *Laconia* before drowning, dying in the boats of exhaustion or succumbing to the bombing raid. The testimony of

Dino Monti states that the men of one hold managed to break down the gate. Of the two holds that were torpedoed, no. 4 was the *Laconia*'s largest and no. 2 the third largest. The combined death toll there could well have been 600, given that that any wounded may have been incapable of escape before they were drowned. Baldwin's testimony, given in response to complaints by the Italian government, makes it clear that the Italians who failed to overpower their guards ended up, like himself, with around 10 minutes to get off the ship.

The British and Poles fared much better. Of 103 Poles, 31 died; of the British, it appears that 558 out of 829[14] survived, though a much larger number left the ship before she went down.

The British inquiry into the loss was nothing short of perfunctory, and it ignored the question of the treatment of the Italian prisoners, preferring to concentrate instead on the poor lifesaving equipment. Ironically, it was Doris Hawkins's recommendation in her short memoir that produced results such as self-righting lifeboats and the provision of fishing rods.

Disasters usually result in official recognition for at least some of the survivors, but neither Cunard nor the Admiralty felt that anyone involved in the whole sorry mess deserved official honours. Someone thought differently, however, and Tony Large and Harry Vines received the British Empire Medal for their gritty endurance in the open boat; their two comrades were mentioned in dispatches. Lady Glasgow, mother of Grizel, took her case for the recognition of Doris Hawkins to Buckingham Palace, and Doris was awarded an OBE. The crew of the Liberator quickly received medals for, as they had reported, sinking one submarine and disabling a second. Hartenstein was awarded the Ritterkreuz.

Despite all the photographic evidence that their three crews brought home, the Germans inexplicably ducked the opportunity of a major publicity coup. Instead, their response to the incident was the issue by Dönitz of the so-called *Laconia* Order on 17 September, so that no other submarine commander would have to make the decision with which Hartenstein had been faced. From now on, U-boat commanders would not risk their boats to *assist* the shipwrecked. But the order did not, as Dönitz's prosecutors claimed at the Nuremberg Trials, authorize or order commanders to *kill* survivors. The Admiral was tried on three counts: Conspiracy, Crimes Against Peace, and War Crimes. The *Laconia* Order came into the third count. He was found not guilty on the first and guilty of the second two, but the judges stated that they did not base their verdict on any breaches of the London Naval Agreement or the Naval Protocol. In the light of testimony from the United States Navy's Admiral Nimitz and the British Admiralty, it was evident that both sides had broken the law. Furthermore, the wording of the *Laconia* Order was ruled too vague for any clear conclusion to be reached as to its intentions. Dönitz received a ten-year sentence which, increasingly, has been seen as harsh.

When it comes to the bombing of *U-156*, the situation is even less straight-forward, complicated over the years by changes in the US response to enquiries about the incident. The Americans had recently established that secret base on Ascension, the barren British possession in the South Atlantic from where they could protect Allied shipping by taking on the U-boat menace with aircraft. They were certainly jumpy, afraid the base would be discovered – indeed, that its discovery was what had drawn the Vichy French fleet out of Dakar. On 15 September they had received information from the British at Freetown that the *Laconia* had been sunk and that they were sending two vessels to pick up the survivors. Crucially, the message made no mention of the German role in all this, yet it is hard to believe that the British mission was not in response to Hartenstein's *en clair* transmission. Possibly they assumed that Hartenstein was only interested in rescuing the Italians, though that is to misinterpret his signal. The Americans, who had a British liaison officer with them, were asked to send a plane to cover the British rescue. Lieutenant James Harden and his Liberator crew accordingly took off.

For the better part of half an hour they reconnoitred the scene, unmolested by a submarine which was making attempts to contact – though unbeknownst to those on the water, Harden and his crew had never been taught how to read signals sent in morse or flashed by signalling lamp. They must have known that Hartenstein could easily have brought them down, yet was evidently refraining. Recognizing the situation was out of the ordinary, they flew off to get within radio range of Wideawake and ask for instructions. They apparently made no mention of the red cross. The response from the 24-year-old Captain Robert Richardson, after consultation with his superior and the British liaison officer, was terse: *sink sub*.

Was it wrong? Everyone in and around *U-156* that day believed so. The Americans, however, reasoned that they would be saving the two British ships on their way to the area, not to mention all the others that might be sunk in future by the three dangerous predators now basking on the surface. Earlier claims that the crew thought the lifeboats belonged to the U-boat and that its crew were, for some reason, abandoning ship, are frankly risible – and since when have survivors in lifeboats been legitimate targets in any case?

The Liberator crew, too, offered differing stories as to the existence of a red cross on *U-156*, yet all the survivors knew how low they had flown. Peillard claims that there was dissension in the Liberator about whether the operation should be carried out or whether they should abandon it and resume their flight from Natal, South Africa, to the Middle East, which had been inter-rupted when an engine fire forced them to land at Wideawake in the first place. Harden is said to have told his crew that if just one of them was in favour of executing the order he would agree to it …

Richardson had no regrets. Twenty years later he admitted to the *Daily*

Express that he had given the order to bomb *U-156*, though he did not know there were British survivors in the boats. He added, however, that even if he had known he would still have issued the same order, regarding it as a military imperative. A quarter of a century further on he reaffirmed the correctness of his decision, laying the blame on poor communications with Freetown and claiming that the British had not told the Americans that the U-boats were on a humanitarian mission. In the absence of that critical information, he concluded that the red cross on *U-156*, which he now said *had* in fact been reported to him, was a ruse and the British would welcome the destruction of the submarine. Despite, or maybe because of, all the military justification, the attack on *U-156* leaves a bitter taste, and Hartenstein remains, rightly so, a hero to those who shared those days in the shadow of *U-156* and came to see the U-boat as a friend. RAF survivor J G Delay put it at its simplest: 'it is true to say that there are many hundreds of us who owe our lives to this man'. Tony Large told this author in 2005: 'I would dearly love to have met him and there are not many days go by that I do not think of him and of the tragedy I witnessed.'

Two days after the *Laconia* Order, Hartenstein torpedoed the British merchantman *Quebec City*, but it did not stop him expressing his regret, discussing with her captain the best course for land, or allowing him to come aboard to consult his charts. In the opinion of survivor David C. Jones, he put his submarine at risk by the delay. Hartenstein expressed the hope that he and his adversaries would meet again in happier times, a fond wish that he would never realize. On 8 March 1943, an American Catalina sank *U-156*. A life raft was dropped for the handful of survivors, but it was never picked up. Schacht, Würdemann and their crews were also among the 30,000 U-boat personnel killed during the Second World War.[15]

Sources and Bibliography

As more survivors of the sinking of the *Laconia* have come forward and papers have been released, a number of books dedicated to the incident have been written, all of which are different, extremely moving and well worth reading for their different emphases. I am grateful to Andrea David Quinzi for his observations from an Italian perspective, and indebted to the irrepressible Dr Tony Large.

National Archives
ADM 199/2142
ADM 199/1142
ADM 199/2144
MT 9/ 3811
TS 13/3280
ADM 136/35
ADM 1/12299

Bellomo, Donatello, *Prigionieri dell'Oceano* (Milan: Sperling & Kupfer, 2002).

Grossmith, Frederick, *The Sinking of the Laconia: A Tragedy in the Battle of the Atlantic* (Stamford: Paul Watkins, 1994).

Hawkins, Doris, *Atlantic Torpedo: The Record of 27 Days in an Open Boat, Following a U-Boat Sinking* (London: Victor Gollancz, 1943).

Jones, David C, *The Enemy We Killed, My Friend* (Llandysul: Gomer Press, 1999).

Large, Tony, *In Deep and Troubled Waters* (Donington: Paul Watkins, 2001).

Padfield, Peter, *The War Beneath the Sea: Submarine Conflict, 1939–45* (London: John Murray, 1995).

Peillard, Léonce, *L'Affaire du 'Laconia', 12 septembre 1942* (Paris: Robert Laffont, 1961); translated as *U-Boats to the Rescue* (London: Jonathan Cape, 1963). The first to tell the story. Extracts published by kind permission of Random House. The 1988 second French edition, not available in translation, is remarkable for the reconstructed account of conversations between the officers at Wideawake and also between the crew of the Liberator.

Trizzino, Antonino, *Sopra di Noi l'Oceano* (Milan: Longanesi, 1962).

War Illustrated, 1947, by kind permission of John Blackwell
Sunday Express, 28 July and 4 August 1963

The Battle of the Atlantic, BBC television documentary series (2002).

www.cronologia.it/battaglie/batta108.htm Quinzi, Andrea David, *L'Odissea della Nave Laconia*
www.u-boot-archiv.de/dieboote/u0156.html
http://wernerhartenstein.tripod.com Based in Plauen and dedicated to the memory of Werner Hartenstein (information in English, Italian and German) this is the site of the *U-156* Society.

Notes

1 She was 624 feet (190 metres) long, and a refit in 1928 had increased her passenger capacity to 347 first class, 350 second and 1500 third.

2 Defensively Armed Merchant Ship.

3 Liswell and Baldwin were both former officers and had been re-employed in 1941 as War Substantives - holding temporary ranks for the duration of the war. Baldwin was in the RAOC; Liswell, a former captain in the Indian Army, was nominally attached to the Herts and Beds Regiment for special employment.

4 Subsequently asked to account for the treatment of the Italian prisoners, Baldwin made the most of his reforms, but did give a list of others who, he felt, would corroborate his story.

5 There was, in fact, only one documented case of a German U-boat committing such an atrocity.

6 Two submarines of the class have survived. *U-505* is in the Museum of Science and Industry, Chicago, in restored condition; *U-534* was raised and put on view at Birkenhead, near Liverpool, but its future is uncertain following a decision to redevelop the land.

7 Léonce Peillard's figure, adjusted to allow for 1791 Italians, not 1800.

8 Doris Hawkins gave her friend the pseudonym 'Mary', presumably because her husband was a senior serving officer; her correct name is used in this account.

9 Jones wrote his account for *War Illustrated* in 1947, the final year of the magazine's publication. His account is likely to be accurate in the essentials, but he thickly varnished it with his own prejudices, which would have chimed with those of the magazine's readership.

10 One of the *Laconia*'s boats had motor and radio and did send out signals. It may have been this that *U-156* picked up.

11 Instead of names or numbers, U-boats were identified in signals by the commander's name.

12 A list compiled in the boat of Tony Large and Harry Vines stated he was an acting flight lieutenant. Other sources have credited him with the higher rank.

13 Léonce Peillard's figure.

14 Based on Peillard's figure of 463 officers and crew, 286 armed services personnel and 80 civilians. But the total would be 953 if one takes Walker's figure of 359 crew, plus 687 'passengers', less the 103 Poles.

15 *U-507* was sunk with all hands on 13 January 1943 and *U-506* on 12 July 1943 with the loss of her commander and all but six of her crew.

15

To the Bitter End

Flying Enterprise

1952

Wild, wild the storm, and the sea high running,
Steady the roar of the gale, with incessant undertone muttering,
Shouts of demoniac laughter fitfully piercing and pealing,
Waves, air, midnight, their savagest trinity lashing,
Out in the shadows there milk-white combs careering,

WALT WHITMAN, 'PATROLLING BARNEGAT'

IN AN AGE in which it is possible to stand on a mountain and dial directly to the other side of the planet from a phone hardly bigger than a matchbox, it is hard to imagine a time when the domestic telephone was a luxury. In those days, exchanges had names instead of dialling codes, numbers might consist of just two digits, and calls were placed through a local operator who had every opportunity to eavesdrop on conversations. In early January 1952 the operator at St Just, Cornwall, became suspicious about telephone calls that were being put through to London. She soon realized that, contrary to Section 5 of the Broadcast Receiving Licence,[1] a subscriber with a wireless had been illicitly intercepting conversations between Land's End Radio, one of the country's best-known maritime radio stations, and ships at sea, and then relaying the information to the *Daily Mirror* at its Fleet Street offices. She passed on her concerns to her superior who alerted Land's End Radio, and on 6 January they asked William Sinclair to sit beside the duty operator and listen

Dramatis Personae

Cyril Bronx : engineer

George Brown : chief engineer

Mr La Buda : seaman

Nikolai Bunjakowski : passenger

Kurt Carlsen : captain of the *Flying Enterprise*

Richard Cosaro : third assistant engineer

Ken Dancy : first officer, *Turmoil*

Nina Dannheiser : passenger

William E Donohue : Captain, USS *Gold Eagle*

Maria Duttenhofer : passenger

Eric Ellis : crewman, *Turmoil*

Baltazar Gavilan : crewman

David Greene : radio operator

Mr Higgenbotham : seaman

Monsieur Huido : captain of the *Abeille 25*

Robert Husband : second officer, USS *General A W Greely*

Mr Johnson : fourth engineer

George Jullien : first officer, USS *General A W Greely*

Rolf Kastenholz : passenger

Michelle McCabe : radio bulletin interceptor

George Miterko : crewman

Curt Muller : passenger

Elsa Muller : passenger

Fred Niederbruening : passenger

Leslie J O'Brien Jr : captain of the USS *Willard Keith*

Neil Olsen : captain of the USS *General A W Greely*

Dan Parker : captain of the *Turmoil*

Mr Pfortsch : captain of the *Arion*

William Thompson : captain of the USS *John W Weeks*

Leonora Van Klenau : passenger

in. He did not have long to wait.

At 13:02 the subscriber asked for Holborn 4321 – reverse charge – identifying herself to the operator as Mrs McCabe, and her telephone number as St

Just 92. Two minutes later she was connected, and she was heard to ask for the news desk. Sinclair, who could have done with a course in shorthand, started scribbling furiously.

> *Mrs McCabe:* Had last information from *Turmoil* to BBC – *Sunday Pictorial* going to be connected to *Turmoil* at 1:30 p.m. The speed of tow 3 knots – tow progressing well, weather fairly good for this time of year – Tug bearing equal strain – tug suggested an increase in speed but Captain Carlsen says quite happy as things are – have done 75–80 miles so far – visibility not very good. No sight yet.
>
> *From Desk:* Will put you over and you can dictate that please – please ring us every even hour.
>
> *Mrs McCabe:* Yes will do that. [*She repeats her report.*]
>
> *From Desk:* Do you mean they have not sighted land yet?
>
> *Mrs McCabe:* Presumably – making for Falmouth but should bad weather come in no-one can hazard again either on *Turmoil* or *Flying Enterprise* – *Enterprise* riding as steady as *Turmoil* – plenty of buoyancy.

At first sight, the activities of a tug and a freighter off England's south-west corner may not appear sufficiently interesting to tempt a nurse and her supposed husband[2] – not to mention others – into breaking the regulations in the hope of making their fortune. This, however, was no ordinary salvage story. Not since the *Titanic* disaster had a merchant-shipping drama gripped the public imagination worldwide so completely, but there were two big differences. The *Titanic* had been a great luxury liner, while this was a humble freighter. And in 1912 the press reported on a story that had already happened on a cold April night far beyond their reach, while 40 years later they followed events as they unfolded, and catapulted three ordinary men into a celebrity they would never live down.

As New Year's Eve approached, 1951 was not giving up tamely. From Boxing Day onwards the weather was atrocious, with winds up to 97 mph (156 kph) recorded on the Scilly Isles. Four fishermen were killed in Cornwall after being swept into the sea at Sennen Cove, and lighting struck three planes in flight. At Shannon a BOAC Stratocruiser ran into water while trying to land at the flooded Irish airport. Fishing vessels went down in Killybegs harbour; communication lines were brought down on England's north-west coast; hurricane-force winds smashed the windows and lanterns of the Skelligs lighthouse; the Fishguard ferry struggled into Waterford 25 hours late. Mountainous black seas tore the propeller off the Panamanian freighter *Wear* bound for Newport. The oil tanker *Mactra* had lost her screw and was holding on for help from the tug *Turmoil*. Two men were killed at Hull while working on a tug; a teenage boy died when a wall came down on him at Dysart, and the owners of a house in Colgrain, Dunbartonshire, had the shock of their lives when the 394-ton coaster *St Kearan* was blown into their garden. Gales damaged the *Queen Mary*'s anchors, delaying Sir Winston Churchill's trip to America. From the British motor vessel *Sherborne* came a radio message that she was going to the aid of an American steamer in trouble 300 miles southwest of Ireland.

Relying on her radar, the *Flying Enterprise*[3] had left a foggy Hamburg on 21 December bound for her home port of New York with a general cargo, 10 passengers and 40 crew under the command of Kurt Carlsen. Danish born but now a naturalized American with a US Master's ticket, the 37-year-old knew his ship well; he had been her captain for three years, ever since she had abandoned the career of a tramp steamer in favour of the New York–Northern Europe trade. She had had her share of minor accidents, but he had always brought her home safely and her owners, Isbrandtsen Lines, had a high regard for his quiet, dogged brand of seamanship. No drama was beyond his competence. When a crew member on his previous command, the *Flying Clipper*, suffered a savage assault on board that left him with a severed artery, it was Carlsen who carried out the rough and ready surgery that saved his life and won the praise of the professionals. Now he kept the bridge almost continuously as the *Enterprise* steamed through the unyielding grey, seeing little of the Christmas decorations and the bright tree whose scented needles filled the dining room with something sweeter and more nostalgic than the smell of diesel.

They had reached the Straits of Dover before the fog lifted, but the respite was short lived. On Christmas Eve, when she was more than 350 miles southwest of Lands End, heading into the North Atlantic shipping lanes, the weather deteriorated. Strong winds and a heavy swell came up, but the *Enterprise* was a sound vessel, one of hundreds of the so-called Liberty Ships churned out by US shipyards during the war to replace Allied merchantmen sunk by enemy action.

Had it remained heavy weather, all would have been well; come Boxing Day it was getting worse, and the weather forecast promised a gale. Carlsen thought of his passengers, most of them middle-aged to elderly, and of the vehicles he was carrying – none of them crated up – and decided to heave-to before he had to. Overnight the wind intensified, screaming across the white superstructure, until before dawn it raged at hurricane force, drawing the sea up into an endless series of savage mountain ranges, tearing past smokestack and crosstrees. As the passengers lay prone in their berths, and the off-watch crew vainly tried to sleep, *Enterprise* laboured and pitched. At about 06:30 on the 27th the roar of the battering wind was abruptly drowned out by a deafening explosion, sharp as a gunshot. The ship shivered from stem to stern.

Even before he investigated, Carlsen knew it was serious. Bent double against the wind he went out onto the deck. The *Flying Enterprise* had broken amidships, from no. 3 hatch, in an irregular line right across her weather deck and down the skin of the ship to the riveting that ran the length of the hull.[4] Serious, but not fatal, though they would have to put in for repairs as soon as the weather moderated. For the moment they would take defensive measures.

Carlsen reduced speed to the minimum and eased her off about four points of the compass into the seas. He ordered the crew to get out some ⅞" wire and take between 10 and 12 turns between the bitts fore and aft of the deckhouse. The bitts were stumpy bollards on the deck, their shape not unlike a cotton reel or a collar stud. Once clamped, the wire pulled the two halves of the deck together, minimizing the gap and taking the strain to prevent the ship breaking her back. Cement was used as a filler, and naphthalene bags were dragged forward of the crack to act as a bulwark against any seas that might wash it away before it had set. The wind had slackened a little, and she was making very little water. A message was sent by radio to the owners, but no distress signal was put out.

For the better part of 24 hours all went well; then the wind gathered itself for a newer and still more savage assault, rolling the ship to either side and blowing a full hurricane from the north until wind and water merged. The waves rose forty, even fifty feet – as much as fifteen metres – and the safest course to steer, the one that minimized the pitching and rolling, was taking them north, away from the shipping lanes. They dared not put themselves out of help's way. Even as he gave the order to correct the course a wave rose up in front of them that appeared like a towering grey cliff blotting out the horizon. As if its whole purpose had been to destroy this one solitary vessel it broke in a cataclysmic, foaming fury, raking the *Enterprise* from bow to stern, tearing away the starboard lifeboat and hurling her out of steering,[5] broadside to the swell. Helpless now against force of the water she rolled some 60° to port. As water cascaded off her she began to right herself, but could not do so fully: still listing 20°, and cracked across no. 3 hatch. Desperate to get her onto an even keel, her captain rang the bell for full steam ahead, and hard right, but the *Enterprise* did not – could not – answer. Carlsen tried the opposite, ordering the wheel hard left, hoping to go the long way round and take the wind on the bow, but again there was no response, and if he had known that her rudder was swinging loose he would have understood why.

Worse was to come. While he planned to try putting the engines into reverse, the engine room rang with the news that the power plant had kicked out because of the list. They could have told him, too, that conditions in the engine and boiler room were intolerable, without ventilation, with oil and water everywhere, but they did not. The chief engineer, George Brown, and his nine assistant engineers and engine crew worked all afternoon and into the evening trying to restore power. The list had caused the generators to lose their oil and lubricant; in the thick, hot, airless atmosphere, men stood over them, hand-oiling the bearings. Carlsen testified that Brown did 'almost an inhuman job trying to recover the plant'. Even so, one generator burned out.

The *Flying Enterprise* was doomed. Without power, her cargo, the greater part of which was pig iron, shifted to port, and she could only drift at the mercy of seas that showed no pity. The crack was opening up. She needed friends, and quickly. Even before he sent the first messages, Radio Operator David Greene was into a very long shift, forced to support half of his weight with one hand while he worked the telegraph key with the other.

The impact of that massive sea had ripped out even the steel furniture fixed to cabin bulkheads, hurling passengers like balls, but there was no panic. Instead of ringing the alarm bell, which he thought would only send them running to the lifeboat stations on the open deck where their lives would be in greater danger, Carlsen asked his chief officer to go and talk to them and explain the gravity of the situation. They were to put on their lifejackets, leave their cabins and make themselves as comfortable as possible in the passage-ways. They were not to move around, but should keep warm, saving their ener-gies for when the time came for swimming. The only boat that could have been launched from the listing *Enterprise* was the starboard, and that had been smashed.

With the exception of 74-year-old Fred Niederbruening from Hopewell, NJ, the passengers all came from Germany, Austria and Eastern Europe, and were emigrating to the United States to escape the grimness of post-war life. Rolf Kastenholz, 27, was a German accountant; Curt Muller, his wife and two chil-dren were Mormons from near Kiel who had sold up to relocate to the heart-land of their faith in Salt Lake City; Leonora van Klenau, 39, a photographer, hailed from Vienna, the widowed Maria Duttenhofer, 45, from Munich, and Mrs Nina Dannheiser from Hamburg. Nikolai Bunjakowski, 54, was one of many classed as stateless persons after the war. They were not the ideal passen-gers for a crisis in which to be young and fit might make the difference between life and death. Muller spent his time in fasting and prayer, convinced that God would preserve his family.

Flocking to the Rescue

Greene's first signal, asking vessels in the vicinity to make contact, was picked up by the *General A W Greely*, an American naval troop ship, which passed it to the Royal Navy at Portsmouth. From there it was sent out to all vessels in the area. The British cargo ship *Sherborne* made contact with the *Enterprise* and reckoned she could be with her within six hours; the American freighters *Southland* and *War Hawk* likewise changed course upon the instant. The *Southland*, which had picked up the SOS at 12:57 and the urgent distress call at 13:30, was first on the scene, followed swiftly by the *Sherborne*, around 19:00. It was too dark and rough even to contemplate trying to transfer anyone. Carlsen asked the two ships simply to 'just plain stand by' during the night, and they were joined before midnight by the Dutch ship MV *Noordaam*. Thus far, the *Flying Enterprise* was just one of several ships in distress in the darkness of the wild winter Atlantic, of keen interest only to a specialist newspaper like *Lloyd's List*, though a source of painful anxiety to the families and friends of those aboard her.

The *Greely* arrived in the morning, as did the *War Hawk* and the Norwegian tanker, *H. Westfal-Larsen*, which was bound for the refineries of the River Thames; all but the tanker put their lifeboats into waves that had barely moderated since the previous day. Carlsen had the passengers escorted up to the windswept boat deck, where a ladder had been rigged down to the port rail. They were to go down, when told, and jump into the sea. To bring the lifeboats in close would be disastrous.

The passengers, still calm, stared at one another and at the heaving grey swell some 30 feet (9 metres) beneath them. The ship was rolling; they had to hold on to keep their footing. The wind howled and screamed. They were afraid, but they did not want to show it. Someone would have to go first. Elsa Muller took a deep breath and stepped away from her children. She would set an example.

A line was thrown up from the *Southland*'s boat, and the crewman who caught it gave it into Frau Muller's frozen hand. She jumped into space, plunging into water so cold that it burned, came up gasping and then felt the precious rope tighten, pulling her towards the *Southland*'s boat. Hands reached down to haul her in, blankets were put round her and as the boat rose and fell on the swell she coughed up the water she had swallowed.

Back on the *Enterprise* her rescue had been watched with all-round relief, but no one was prepared to follow. Chief Engineer Brown approached Muller and offered to jump while holding onto his 19-year-old daughter. Watching the waves breaking against the side, Carlsen was initially unsure whether it was safe to continue. In the end he consented:

'Okay, Chief, go ahead, and God bless you.' That was to become the model: each passenger jumped with a crew member. The *Southland*'s boat headed back to offload her survivors. The tanker circled the site discharging oil to help calm the waves – literally pouring her oil upon waters that were more than troubled.[6]

Not everything went to plan. As the *Sherborne*'s boat came in towards the *Enterprise* it capsized; the same fate befell the *War Hawk*'s, but without injury. Eleven people from the *Enterprise*, who had just jumped into the water in the expectation of being picked up, were left at the mercy of precipitous seas that threatened to smash them against the stricken freighter's hull. For half an hour they were forced to endure the freezing water until the *Southland*'s boat returned for them. Engineer Cyril Bronx had been paired with a woman of generous proportions, 'and what a size she was. She was so big they couldn't drag her out of the sea into a lifeboat and she made the trip to the rescue ship draped half over the side.'

After picking up seven survivors, the *Greely*'s boat, under First Officer George Jullien, was heading away when her motor died. Unable to make headway towards his own ship by rowing, Jullien ordered his crew to steer for the *Southland*, which was closer, and disembarked his load onto her. A wave caught the lifeboat, smacking it hard against the freighter and leaving it unserviceable. A cargo boom was swung out and it was hoisted aboard along with the crew.

Reassured that his men were safe, Captain Neil Olsen launched the *Greely*'s second boat, under Second Officer Robert Husband, into the mountainous seas; another group jumped from the *Enterprise*. To his dismay, Husband saw a wave seize them and throw them back on board in a shower of spume. Before they could take a grip of anything, another great sea washed them off astern, and Husband directed his crew in their direction. Bunjakowski was pulled out drowned; Curt Muller had broken his hand and two ribs; the two crew members were bruised. One woman at least was covered in black oil. Last of the passengers to jump was the elderly Niederbruening, who later told the press he had never been frightened. 'I'm never afraid. Why should I be? When they told us to jump, we had to jump, that's all.' Two crewmen were swept away. Thereafter, jumps were made from the stern of the *Enterprise*.

With seven passengers and eight crew on board, the *Southland* set course for Rotterdam. Carlsen ordered the remainder of the crew to jump, in groups of five, so that everyone would be off by dusk, after which finding people would become difficult. He had planned to go with them, but taking a last look around and casting an eye over the sea, he hesitated. Four of the last twenty men came to find him.

'Captain,' said Third Assistant Engineer Richard Cosaro, 'if you want us to, we are willing to stay with you.'

Carlsen looked at them with pride. With Cosaro were Fourth Engineer Johnson and two seamen, Higgenbotham and La Buda. The last was not even a regular sailor; he had been in the navy during the war, but was now a lorry driver. Occasionally he succumbed to the desire to feel the deck beneath his feet and, in lieu of a conventional holiday, signed on a merchant ship for a single voyage. They were all brave and loyal men, but Carlsen did not want their lives on his conscience. He ordered them to abandon ship with the rest.

Baltazar Gavilan had become separated from the four others who had left the ship with him. Helplessly he was carried away, unseen by the lifeboat, a speck among the oily mountains, with no idea in which direction to swim until suddenly his low horizon encompassed the lean profile of the tanker. He was seen; a rope was thrown down and he struck out for it, managing to grab it as the *Westfal-Larsen* passed by on another of her oil-spreading circles.

A mile or more away – a couple of kilometres – the German-crewed *Arion* was bound for Liverpool from Demerara. Captain Pfortsch, like everyone approaching that area, knew about the rescue drama underway, but there was no need for any more ships to join in. Somewhere ahead, the unconscious body of George Miterko, one of the two crewmen swept from the deck earlier, rose and fell at the whim of the sea.

Carlsen turned and made his way to the radio shack to call up the *Greely*.

'There is only me on board,' he told them. 'Master, Captain Carlsen.'

'Do you intend to stay there with the Captain?' came the answer.

'No, I *am* the captain. The wireless officer has left.' He gave precise details of everyone who had been on board, and one after another the stand-by vessels called in to tell him the names of those they had picked up. His own plan, he told them, was to remain with his ship until a tug arrived. They wished him good luck and all but one prepared to resume their own voyages; the *Greely* decided to stand by. It should have been almost the end of the story, but with Carlsen still on board and the passengers with tales to tell it proved to be just the beginning.

While the *Flying Enterprise* continued to list beneath the unending assault of the storm, a damsel in distress awaiting her knight in shining armour, the *Greely* stood patiently by her, in pre-arranged radio contact every couple of hours and ready to snatch Carlsen from the sea if the freighter started to founder. The US Navy had sprung into action with almost suspicious enthusiasm. A supply ship, the *Gold Eagle*, Captain William E Donohue, relieved the *Greely* on New Year's Day, while the destroyer *John W Weeks* powered through the turbulent seas with a cavalier disregard for the conditions. Smit, the renowned Dutch salvage firm, had their big salvage tug *Oceaan* on her way, but she was about be diverted to help out another of her fleet, the *Zwarter Zee*.

Kurt Carlsen had little to do. The cargo shift had continued; the battered ship was now at an angle of 60°, and she had no more power than the fading supply for the radio. His bed was a mattress in the angle of the deck and the port wall of the cabin; food consisted mostly of pieces of a large pound cake that the ship's cook had intended for a more festive occasion. To drink there was just water and some beer, And after dark the only light came from a torch.

Late on Tuesday 1 January, three days after the passengers and crew had abandoned the *Flying Enterprise*, the tug *Turmoil* reached Falmouth with the disabled *Mactra*, but it was too rough to attempt to enter the harbour that night. Captain Dan Parker knew that it would have to be a swift turn-round in the morning: he had been ordered to go out to the *Enterprise*.

The *Turmoil* was no bustling little harbour tug, but arguably the world's biggest and most powerful ocean-going salvage vessel, built by Leith ship-builders Henry Robb during the war to rescue bombed and torpedoed cargo ships from convoys. At 205 feet (62.5 metres), she was just over half as long as the casualty she intended to bring home, and two-thirds as wide. Like an iceberg, a great deal of her was under water: she drew 17 feet (5.2 metres). The Admiralty still owned her, but she was operated by the Overseas Towage and Salvage Company, and her work was commercial. Whether ploughing through heavy seas or waiting for the next contract, there was something decidedly no-nonsense about her black hull, upperworks in utilitarian buff, squat bridge, stumpy funnel and the raised bow that seemed a permanent challenge to the elements. Her heart throbbed with a steady 4,000hp that could deliver 20 knots or pull just about anything afloat – or even half-afloat. She had all the strength and tenacity of a Staffordshire Bull Terrier. Yet the man who commanded not just *Turmoil* but the respect of all experienced tugmen had spent his pre-war years captaining the huge luxury yachts of the rich and famous. During the war he had been given a trawler converted into a mine-sweeper, and after it, in a very changed world, he went into tugs as a stop-gap measure because luxury yachts were few and far between, and it was not the time, either, to fulfil his dream of one day running a newsagent's shop.

Before he sailed at 08:00 on 3 January, the day after the *John W Weeks* reached the site, Captain Parker signed on two supernumeraries, both experienced first officers in the trade. He already had one of his own, 27-year-old-Ken Dancy, but he had only been with the *Turmoil* for days, and none of his considerable seafaring experience was in tugs.

After the *Daily Graphic* secured a scoop by asking the Air Ministry for permission to put a photographer and a reporter on any Coastal Command Lancaster due to fly over the *Enterprise*, the resulting image had every newspaper scrabbling for its own take on the story. Every radio ham interested in matters marine scoured the wavelengths to listen in on transmissions from the *Weeks*. The US Navy established a round-the-clock press HQ, passing out information as soon as it came in from Captain William Thompson. It was soon augmented by the first account to come directly from Carlsen himself, a broadcast to the *Gold Eagle* that was recorded and brought ashore by Captain Donohue when his ship put in at Liverpool. Carlsen's voice betrayed both determination and weariness as he described the savage battering his vessel had taken, and the evacuation of the passengers. As the German weekly *Der Spiegel* headlined its article: 'Er hängt mit seinen Zähnen dran' – *he is hanging on by his teeth*.

In the meantime, Thompson was fighting to bring his destroyer sufficiently close to the crippled ship to fire a light messenger line across and transfer a few home comforts. The *Enterprise* was helpless, drifting and driven by heaving seas that, though not the craggy monsters of the previous days, were still rough and unpredictable. At any moment she could have smashed into the destroyer. Even firing the line was difficult as the gap between the vessels was constantly changing. Three times they came close to success before the short hours of daylight ended.

The following day, Thursday 3 January, they tried again, and were at last rewarded. Coffee, hot food, newspapers and cigarettes were pulled across the fragile link, and Kurt Carlsen had a welcome change from the pound cake and such dry stores as he could get his hands on.

The Tow

Punching her way through the heavy swells, the unlikely knight errant reached her goal shortly before midnight, to find the *Enterprise* rolling heavily to 80°, her head down and her rudder and screw both out of the water, but with the wind shifting to the north-west and easing to a little over 20 knots, and the barometer rising, there was hope. Thompson reported:

> Position of United States Destroyer *Weeks* Lat. 47° 46′ N; Long 11° 53′ W. The salvage tug *Turmoil* has arrived on scene and preparations are underway for taking the *Flying Enterprise* in tow in accordance with plans formulated during a three-way conversation with captain Carlsen, captain Parker and captain Thompson … Carlsen is very cheerful and grateful for the food and cigarettes and magazines made to him earlier by the *Weeks*. The captain waved his hat as the *Weeks* pulled out of position fifty yards to the windward after passing the food. Carlsen is still determined to remain aboard his ship until it is safely in port. He spent his time today improving the jury rig set up, with the result that communications with him today are excellent. The *Weeks* crew cheered the successful passing today after three heartbreaking unsuccessful attempts yesterday … [Captain Carlsen] is in excellent spirits and is certain that the *Flying Enterprise* will ride it out if the weather does not deteriorate again today.

Work began almost immediately to get the tow across, a simple task in theory, the basis of all those old tales in which the knight rescues the damsel by getting a rope ladder up to her turret prison: fire a light line across, which the casualty's crew grab and haul in. Attached to that is a thicker, doubled line with both ends back on the tug. Get the doubled end over one of the bitts and an 'endless line' has been set up, allowing yet a thicker line to be hauled aboard. When it is time for the main towing line – and Parker was going to use a 5″ circumference 6-core × 37 composition steel wire, with a breaking strain of 74 tons – the tug's engines can take over. As they reel in one end of the intermediate line, the heavy cable is dragged out, attached to the other end. Once the towing line is secured the casualty becomes a tow.

Simple in theory, but it presupposed a few crewmen to grab the line, and hauling requires a minimum of two hands. The wind-lashed, glassy escarpment that was the deck of the tormented *Enterprise* forced Carlsen to hold on at all times by one hand. It was impossible.

They came close. Later it would be said that the task would have been easier if Carlsen had kept some of the crew with him, but that was tempered by the caveat that a captain's decision not to jeopardize the lives of his men must always be respected. He himself had no duty to remain on a ship so close to foundering. His decision to do so provoked questions in the media, which had now transferred at least part of the story to the front page. There were those who assumed he stood to gain financially,[7] a suggestion soon scotched by salvage experts, who suddenly found themselves in demand. What was true was that by having their man on board, the owners could negotiate a contract with a salvage company. Overseas Towage and Salvage had been given that contract (and, like most, it was on a no-cure-no-fee basis). Technically Carlsen could have boarded the destroyer and been sufficiently close to have the same rights, but had the destroyer been called away he would have been obliged to go – and this is the critical expression – 'without hope or possibility of return'.

As well as reporting the events out at sea, the press was busy expanding the story. Carlsen's wife and parents were being interviewed. Journalists dug up Karl Gilman, the man whom Carlsen's 'surgery' had saved on the *Flying Clipper*, who told them he was praying for his former captain. They interviewed the passengers and crew on their arrival in New York; they spoke to the *Greely*'s captain; interviewed Gavilan when the *Westfal-Larsen* docked; went up to Liverpool where George Miterko had woken up in hospital after being brought in still unconscious from the *Arion*. The hardier reporters waved cheque books at any captain who might be willing to take a vessel down into the rescue zone, and the Air Ministry made seats available on scheduled Coastal Command flights.

None of this helped Dan Parker, trying to get that line aboard, watching Carlsen's desperate, exhausting efforts. He kept the tug in as close as he could under the stern, taking as much risk as he dared. The man needed help; he could not do it alone. Captain Thompson requested volunteers from his destroyer even though it would have been suicide to take her so close to the *Enterprise*; not a man hung back. Up on the bridge of the *Turmoil*, Ken Dancy knew that his own captain would not ask anyone to take the risk of going onto the *Enterprise*; for his own part, while he hoped it would happen, he doubted it would be possible in the conditions.

And then, suddenly, the sterns of the two vessels were level; for a moment they crunched together, and instinctively Dancy raced down to the stern, stepped across and grabbed the rail of the *Flying Enterprise*. Almost immediately, the ships parted, and there was no going back. The young man whose parents kept the post office in Hook Green, Kent, climbed over the rail a few feet from where the astonished Carlsen stood, and said:

'Shake hands.'

The popular media loved it. That step became a jump, then 'Dancy's Leap'.

Emphatically he denied that there had been any acrobatics. Other journalists assumed he had been given the task. He rejected that, too, and half a century later he still maintains:

> My boarding was just a split second chance – I was on the bridge of the *Turmoil* when Dan Parker happened to manoeuvre the tug so close that the sterns of the two vessels came together. I rushed from the bridge and before I realized it was on the stern of the *Flying Enterprise*. Typically, Captain Carlsen, after welcoming me, was concerned over any possible damage to his ship!

Carlsen was glad of him, not just for the extra hands and muscles, but for the moral support. This time when the line came over, they were able to secure it to the bitt and, with a hand each, start hauling in the heavier lines. Just when all seemed to be going well, the line broke. It was too late in the day to start all over again; they would have to try tomorrow. Carlsen took his companion into the cabin, which Dancy described as a shambles, the mattress propped in the corner on top of the bunk against the slanting bulkhead. He remembered the books and ornaments in a pile, and the remains of the famous cake. Carlsen spent some time that evening looking for a lifejacket for Dancy, and the best he could come up with – for a man of 27 who stood almost 6 feet tall, more than 1.8 metres – was one that had fitted his elder daughter, 11-year-old Sonja. Dancy noticed that the cabin curtains, already hanging well away from the window, swung further out whenever the ship rolled. They kept their eyes on those curtains as the measure of their danger.

Saturday morning, 5 January, hanging on as the sea tried to throw them off their feet, Carlsen and Dancy watched the line snake aboard again, and again there were the requisite two hands, one ten years younger than the other, to haul it in. Thin it may have been, but it was cold and wet; the length made it heavy, and behind it inched the thicker line. Sometimes it sagged more as the ships came closer; if they moved apart it would rise, but Parker had the skill to minimize difficulties. Working together, Dancy and Carlsen heaved and grunted, hands raw. Scrabbling at the bitt they forced the loop apart and over the metal. They had all but done it, and they could start pulling the thicker lines on board until it was time for Atlas Polar engines on the *Turmoil* to do the donkey work. At 09:37 the signal went out that the tow was in place. The line was secured to a steel shackle, itself held by a steel wire whose ends were wound around the bitts to form a bridle. If the strain became too great, the bridle would break, rather than the towing wire, saving them from having to start all over again from the beginning.

Standing by was the powerful French tug *Abeille 25,* and another newcomer arrived: the American destroyer *Willard Keith*, commanded by Captain Leslie J O'Brien Jr. Undoubtedly Thompson and the crew of the *Weeks* would have preferred to stay and see the job finished, but she was low on fuel. Despite Carlsen's anxiety – 'you are taking quite a beating … your ship is too valuable to risk' – they passed over one final hot meal and left the *Keith* to her watch. Only the presence of the destroyers allowed Carlsen and now Dancy to get a few hours of sleep every night, when it was too dangerous to be on deck.

The *Turmoil* was under weigh, and the *Flying Enterprise* was bound for Falmouth. The choice of Falmouth surprised a number of commentators, for Brest was closer, but, as Captain Huido of the *Abeille 25* scornfully told the French press: 'Those who reckon that the entry to Falmouth is less easy than that to Brest, don't know what they're talking about. Just imagine coming into the narrow entrance to Brest pulling a veering mass like the *Flying*. I'm surprised anyone has raised the question again.' *Turmoil* could have gone faster than her painful 3 knots, but not if she was to bring her badly damaged charge home in one piece, and Parker had to take infinite care. The weather was reasonable but the *Enterprise* was not: she wallowed, snatched, sheared away and rolled like an unbroken filly on a lunging rein, head stubbornly down, protesting but unable to shake the patience of the softly spoken man on the bridge of the tug.

Inside the cabin, Carlsen and Dancy, both quiet men, spent much of the time in companionable silence. Sometimes they spoke of their families, more often the unspoken mutual support was all they needed. They kept a regular eye on the tow, and by day Carlsen maintained his two-hourly contact with the destroyer until the batteries ran low and he knew he had to ration them. They found some dry clothes, and a few bottles of wine. A candle stuck into the remaining hunk of cake made a slow primus stove on which to heat their coffee. All vessels were warned to keep clear of the area: the *Turmoil* was lit up like a Christmas tree, but at the end of the 2000-yard (1830-metre) towing line the *Flying Enterprise* was in darkness, with a list that rolled between 45° and 70°, and capable of swinging violently. The MV *Accra* kept company well off Turmoil's port quarter. Everyone wanted to be part of the drama as it developed. In the morning, the tow was still progressing.

Michelle McCabe carried on passing transcripts of the radio messages picked up by her husband, and as the *Mirror* copied them down William Sinclair scribbled away at the St Just Exchange:

> *Mrs McCabe:* Towing cable greased – Carlsen and Dancy greased towing cable – last night. When this was suggested no grease could be found to grease wire which passes over *Enterprise* – Carlsen said soap would do but after rummaging around they could only find a pound of butter which they promptly used. Dancy and Carlsen are doing alternate watches and getting comfortable rest – they are now used to walking on the bulkheads – they are amidships near the radio room – will

come up immediately if anything goes wrong – *Willard Keith* passed grub over to them this morning ... All on board *Turmoil* very well and hopeful – positive they will get *Flying Enterprise* into port. Had very trying time while standing by – little sleep. Last night there was plenty of snoring heard from the quarters ...

Mrs McCabe appears to be cut off from 4321.

Mrs McCabe: Will you get off this line, operator – I can hear your key going over – I'll report you to supervisor.[8]

1324 Clear down; 1326 incoming call for Mrs McCabe ...

Caller: This is Chambers of the *Daily Mirror* – am in Penzance now – could I come up and see you and perhaps have a little listen?

Mrs McCabe: No I am sorry – I cannot agree to that – this is an approved Home for Young Mental Deficients – I cannot have anyone here.

Chambers: Is the radio in your apartment? Does anyone know of this?

Mrs McCabe: No one knows of this at all – not even servants.

Chambers: Our office would like me to be up there.

Mrs McCabe: It is really not allowed for you to get this information – no one knows about it at all, not even the operators at Lands End.

The *Daily Express* flew Carlsen's parents to London from their home near Copenhagen, a task complicated by the need to obtain passports for them, and at 21:20 Martin Carlsen spoke to his son from the *Express*'s offices before he and his wife travelled down to Falmouth. The *Express* offered the captain $5000 for his exclusive story. Dancy's parents were unable to leave their business, so were besieged at home. All this while Captain Parker was coaxing his unwilling tow, and operator J D Fallow at St Just had taken over the monitoring of the calls. At 22:45 the McCabes had a call from Chambers asking for the latest position.

Mrs McCabe: Position given at 5:30 p.m. from the *Keith* to US Headquarters 020 3 knots 040 and Land's End radio have given a direct gale warning to the *Keith*.

Chambers: Oh dear; let's hope nothing terrible happens. If it does I hope you will contact this office immediately.

Mrs McCabe: I certainly will. I hope to retire on the money made from this story.

Chambers: You ought to do very handsomely.

Early on Monday 7 January, they were 180 miles (330 kilometres) from Falmouth; by dinner time that was down to 120 miles (220 kilometres). The chances of bringing the *Enterprise* safely into port were estimated at 75 per cent by Captain Thompson when the *John W Weeks* had berthed at Plymouth. *Abeille 25* was in company about 1000 yards (more than 900 metres) astern of the *Enterprise*, and the *Willard Keith* had set up a stronger line that allowed the two men to take on board some proper lubricating grease and stout gloves as well us much-needed sandwiches, hot coffee, fried chicken and cigarettes. Cake was becoming monotonous.

By around Tuesday afternoon they were two thirds of the way to Falmouth and hoped to be there in 24 hours, but the weather was deteriorating; the moderate swell rose, and before 18:00 Captain Parker decided to heave-to and take the strain from the *Enterprise*. He gave their position as Lat. 49° 26′ N Long 6° 10′ W, and asked for a wide berth. On one occasion she nearly broke loose, sheering around at right-angles to the tug on her 2000 yards of wire. Calm and competent as always, Parker towed her broadside through the sea, then sent a reassuring message:

'Hello, Captain Carlsen. She took a bad one that time, didn't she. Everything alright this end.'

The *Enterprise*'s situation was worsening: she was still taking on water and when she was not rolling to 80° and more she rode lower in the water. With Dancy and Carlsen confined to the radio room, the seas again broke mercilessly over her, tearing off her port lifeboat as if it were a sheet on a washing line. Visibility sank to 1000 yards. It was almost midnight before Parker dared to resume the tow.

Ashore, plans for a massive celebration were in full swing; nations queued up to pay homage to Carlsen. A congratulatory telegram was prepared in his birthplace, Hillerød; the French minister of the merchant marine awarded him the Officer's Cross of Maritime Merit. King Frederick IX of Denmark conferred upon his former subject a knighthood of the ancient Order of the Dannebrog. French children who had been evacuated from France during the war went to the Danish embassy in Paris to praise Carlsen and beg him to jump into the water quickly if the ship looked about to founder. New York's plans included a ticker-tape welcome.

At 01:30, some 50 miles (90 kilometres) from Falmouth, just as it seemed that despite the weather the *Enterprise* was riding more comfortably, the tow parted. Dismayed but phlegmatic, Captain Parker told Carlsen and Dancy to get what rest they could; nothing could be done until daylight.

It was not the weight of the wallowing ship that had caused the disaster. The bridle was intact, likewise the towing shackle and the quick-release shackle (though damaged) attached to it. Instead, the constant friction of the line chafing as it swung in the heavy seas like a pendulum across the edge of the bow had taken a fatal toll of the tow-line. One by one the 37 individual strands of steel that made up each of the six cores yielded to fatigue, until those that remained could no longer bear the strain.

The tow line was retrieved by the *Turmoil*, which repaired it and gave it a new shackle. Would it be possible for the two men on the *Enterprise* to cut away the damaged shackle and haul the new line aboard? They tried, swept by the freezing spray, hanging on, scrabbling about for purchase on the ski-slope deck, wielding the hacksaw with hands that had forgotten what warmth was. The ragged gash in the metal grew, and at last the shackle clattered away. Then, in Dancy's words – a miracle of understatement –

> an unfortunate sea came up. Captain Carlsen was lower than myself and I really thought I had lost him. Fortunately he managed to cling on and so got back rather drenched. Captain Carlsen seemed to be exhausted for several minutes after this. Thereafter we decided it was too dangerous to make another tow.

The good people of Falmouth were decorating the pier; journalists, dignitaries and the public were descending upon the town; small boats had been standing ready to go out and escort the convoy to port. Messages from his family and US Admiral Robert Carney were being passed to Carlsen who, through the *Keith*, said he was deeply touched that so many people in the world were interested in seeing the little *Flying Enterprise* safely reach port. He was only partially right. They hoped to see the ship come in, but it was the men aboard her and the man who still hoped to tow her in that the world was watching.

Parker hoped that the following morning there might be a chance to connect a tow to her stern, which was far less exposed to the waves, but nobody was taking any chances as the freighter drifted. One possibility was for the tug and the destroyer to take up parallel positions off the stern quarters, run a line from one to the other and creep up on her. If the two men could lower her anchor, the wire could be hooked under it. The manoeuvre was risky: it if failed, the *Enterprise* would be worse off. In the end it was never tried.

Dextrous, the tug in which Parker had established his commander's credentials, had arrived; the big Trinity House lifeboat *Satellite* left Penzance for the wreck site, and before darkness came down the *Turmoil* and the *Keith* had planned what do in the event of a night emergency.

She was still afloat in the morning of Thursday 10 January, her list increasing. Waves as high as 20 feet – 6 metres – broke against her; her rail was constantly submerged, yet even in late morning Carlsen, though forced to take refuge higher up, where he had only a weaker radio set, was not willing to give up on her. Told that the RAF had a helicopter ready, he expressed his thanks but said he did not need it yet.

Nevertheless, early in the afternoon two helicopters took off from Culdrose with the express intention of airlifting the men to safety, only to be forced back by the winds, while, with the ship listing almost to 90°, Dancy and Carlsen kept radio contact with Captain O'Brien of the *Keith* and Parker aboard the *Turmoil*. The last two were trying to convince Carlsen that he could hold on no longer, and in anticipation of the end a rope ran from the cabin door up to the starboard rail.

It began at 15:08, with the curtains at 90° to the window, just as Carlsen was about to reply to a question from O'Brien. A ferocious burst of water smashed the door to the wheelhouse. He and Dancy looked at one another. It was time to leave, and to get onto the side of the deckhouse, where Carlsen waved his hands above his head. The *Enterprise* lay on her beam ends, smokestack pillowed on the swell, exhausted by her struggle. The *Turmoil* flashed a signal with her lamp to say that she was moving in, and then she approached as closely as possible, crowding out the two lifeboats now on station.

From her foredeck, Eric Ellis, 16 years old, watched the two men calmly walk along the funnel.

Then they shook hands. I suppose they were wondering if both would make it. They waited a few moments. A big wave came in and they jumped as it washed out again. Dancy jumped first and swam away fairly quickly. Then he looked back in time to see Captain Carlsen jump. He swam back to the ship a little way and appeared to be helping the captain who didn't seem to be so good a swimmer. My uncle, the chief steward, asked if anyone was willing to go out with a lifeline. We went up to our skipper Captain Daniel Parker and my uncle asked 'is it alright if one of the lads goes out?' But the captain, after thinking for a moment, shook his head. He edged the *Turmoil* closer and we threw a rope ladder over. The two, who seemed to stick together the whole time they were in the water, got up to it. Captain Carlsen got hold of a line we had thrown over earlier and was pulled up the ladder pretty quickly. But Mr Dancy seemed to have cramp. He stayed at the bottom of the ladder, sometimes up to the waist in water until our second mate, Mr York, climbed down and pulled him up.

Dancy went below to get warm. Carlsen, who had observed the captain's right to be last off his ship, stood on the deck and watched the sight he had dreaded and which he later described as the worst moment of the whole drama. It was 15:31. Slowly the stern of the *Enterprise* went down, her bows rose, and still she fought to stay above the waves. Around her, a whole flotilla had come to the funeral, and, as she finally let go, their flares lit up the sky in homage and the requiem of their sirens saluted her.

And shortly afterwards, the captain off the US destroyer, guessing the feelings of Captain Parker, sent a message to the *Turmoil:* 'You have won the admiration of all officers and men of the *Keith* for the outstanding attempt you have made and for the excellent seamanship you have displayed.'

The deck log of the *Willard Keith* recorded the bald facts: '1612 SS *Flying Enterprise* sank in the English channel, latitude 49° 38′ N, Longitude 04° 23′ W bearing 300°, distance 1000 yards from USS *Willard Keith*.' She had been just 39 miles (73 kilometres) from her goal.

Ken Dancy's mother and teenage brother were there to meet him; Carlsen's parents, too, were at Falmouth. Photographs, newsreels and transcripts of the press conference flashed around the world. Along with Dan Parker, the two men sat together, answering questions, their body language reflecting the relationship that had been established, and which had prompted Carlsen, facing the most bitter moment of his career, to say to his companion 'I wish I had ten mates like you'.

Flotsam and Jetsam

Such events, though complete in themselves, leave many ends to tie up. The US inquiry into the loss came to the conclusion that it was caused by 'circumstances beyond the control of the master and crew', and the blame lay with the stowage of the pig iron which formed part of the cargo. 'It is apparent that this commodity is carried on in this manner as a matter of common practice at the present, and this was apparently sanctioned by the shipper, underwriter, owner and master. It is also believed that the empty condition of the double bottoms aft and of the deep tanks in Hold 4 had an appreciable effect on the great degree of list which the vessel suddenly took.'

The General Post Office, which had responsibility for issuing short-wave radio licences, sent out a number of stiff letters to various people who had not simply eavesdropped on the ships assisting the *Enterprise* but who had passed on the information to the media. Ironically, the *Daily Mirror*, as if unaware that the McCabes' actions were a breach of the rules, gave grateful publicity to them – which law-abiding radio enthusiasts brought to the GPO's attention. The McCabes, however, had disappeared.

The owners of the *Flying Enterprise* made an ex gratia payment to Overseas Towage and Salvage, whose 'no win, no fee' contract entitled them to nothing unless they brought the ship in. In response to those armchair critics who questioned Parker's tactics, *Abeille 25*'s captain wrote an emphatic vindication of the *Turmoil's* role. Very few tugs could have done as much; none, more.

Honours and awards, including a Lloyd's Silver Medal, were showered on Carlsen. New York organized a welcome, including a ticker-tape parade, that would have overawed the most hardened media star, let alone a private man. When it came to official honours, Dancy was largely ignored. The view seems to have been, ultimately, that he was just doing his job. The fact that senior civil servants routinely received knighthoods for merely doing theirs escaped the small-minded bureaucrats, one of whom wrote in a memo:

> In my view, Captain Parker did an excellent job in every way … I think recognition of Captain Parker would be welcomed, and I propose to submit his name for consideration of the award of MBE in the [Queen's] Birthday Honours. With regard to Mr Dancy … it cannot be said that there was any real [risk?] at the time

– Captain Parker said that he 'stepped aboard' …On the whole I feel we should not put his name forward.

His colleague, P. Faulkner, responded that

If we put Captain Parker forward we should also put Mr Dancy forward. We cannot alter the fact that in the estimation of the public Mr Dancy's conduct was more meritorious than that of Captain Parker. He went aboard the crippled ship, shared Captain Carlsen's trials and in the end had to jump into the sea … he was in fact in much greater danger than Captain Parker … Unless he was unusually insensitive he must have understood that this was likely to be a hazardous business.

To which came the reply that the MBE was not awarded for courage and that Parker was being recommended for his career as a whole as well as for the *Flying Enterprise* business. And so Dancy received the medal for Industrial Heroism awarded by the *Daily Herald*, and an illuminated citation from the American Institute of Marine Underwriters.

Kurt Carlsen retired in 1976 and died in 1989; Dan Parker died following a fall from the *Turmoil*'s bridge in 1955, but achieved his dream of being buried in an English churchyard. Retired, but far from idle, Ken Dancy remains a little uncomfortable with the publicity that he attracted.

The role of the US Navy taxed the brains of the conspiracy theorists. The arrival of the *Greely* in answer to an SOS, and her help to evacuate the ship, was all perfectly logical. The heroic, always under-reported efforts of the destroyers once they were on the scene was likewise understandable. But why were they dispatched at all, to a simple cargo ship that already had the world's biggest tug to help her, and why did the US Navy foot the bill? It is true that navies sometimes consider the experience gained in certain instances as worth its weight in gold but, in the case of the *Flying Enterprise*, a suspicion arose that she had a cargo worth rather more.

Officially she carried 1270 tons of pig iron, 890 tons of coffee, 55 tons of bone meal, 800 bales of peat moss, 5 tons of columbite ore, 260 tons of onions, plus birdcages, vans full of carpets, some aluminium chloride, animal hair and '71.8 tons of General Cargo'. Salvage work by the now defunct Italian company SORIMA was discreetly carried out in 1953, which recovered some $60,000 in bank notes for an undisclosed client, but in 2001 a new theory was advanced by the Danish filmmaker Lasse Spang: that the *Flying Enterprise* was carrying zirconium for the US nuclear arms programme – specifically for the USS *Nautilus*, the world's first nuclear submarine.

British sub-aqua specialist Leigh Bishop knows the wreck better than anyone and, working with Spang, had initially thought there was a mystery that might be explained by Spang's theory. More recent visits to the wreck, however, changed his view:

> Yes, there were rumours of secret cargo, but I think that the diving that has been made by myself and deep sea detectives John Chatterton and Richie Kholar has put an end to such conspiracies. The last dives we made in September 2005, we explored deep inside the holds ... In the end the research all leads to the fact that Carlsen was a true hero and man of the sea ... The saga of the *Flying Enterprise* is perhaps the last classic tale of the sea where a loyal ship's captain remained with his vessel until the last minute.[9]

Sources and Bibliography

Special thanks to Kenneth Dancy, Leigh Bishop, Barbara Jones, Richard Larn, Jason Bennett of Smit, the National Union of Marine, Aviation and Shipping Transport Officers (NUMAST), John Vernon of the National Archives and Record Administration, John Chenery and the *New York Times* for their invaluable help.

National Archives
BT 100/1155
MT9/5876
BT26/1282
HO 255/97
POST 122/30

US National Archives and Records Administration
Deck Log of USS *Willard Keith*
Deck Log USS *John W Weeks*

Brady, Edward M, *Tugs, Towboats and Towing* (Cambridge, MD: Cornell Maritime Press, 1967).
Brookes, Ewart, *Turmoil* (London: Jarrolds, 1956); as *Rescue Tug: The Story of the Flying Enterprise and the Salvage Tug Turmoil* (New York: Dutton, 1957).
Hancox, David, *Reed's Commercial Salvage Practice*, 2 vols (Sunderland: Thomas Reed, 1987).

Daily Mirror
Daily Express
Lloyd's List
New York Times
Der Spiegel
The Telegraph (monthly paper of NUMAST)

www.deepimage.co.uk
www.lightstraw.co.uk

Notes

1   'If any message, other than a message for the receipt of which the use of the apparatus is authorised, is unintentionally received the Licensee shall not make known or allow to be made known its contents, its origin or destination its receipt or the fact of its receipt (other than a duly authorised officer of her Majesty's Government or a competent legal tribunal) and shall not reproduce in writing copy or make use of or allow the same to be reproduced in writing copied or made use of.'

2   Mrs McCabe was also known as Michelle Quodling. The telephone line, St Just 92, was registered to a Miss A Harvey and a Major Broadley at the Manor Farm, Bosavern, Cornwall, a residential home for children with learning difficulties.

3   Built in 1944 at Wilmington, Delaware as *Cape Kumukaki*, she was 396.5 feet (120.85 metres) long, 60.1 feet (18.32 metres) broad, and of 6711 gross registered tons, with steam turbine machinery.

4   To be precise, according to the US Marine Board report, there were two main fractures. One commenced at the after port corner of no. 3 hatch and ran across the deck and back to the accommodation ladder opening at the side; from there the crack ran down the skin of the ship to the longitudinal riveting at the base of the sheerstrake. This was approximately 12 feet (3.6 metres) down. On the starboard side, the crack ran from the starboard corner of the deck house straight across to the accommodation opening, and from there to down to the riveting on the opposite side. These cracks were estimated at from ⅛″ to ⅜″ in width. A smaller crack, which did not open at all, ran from the after starboard corner of no. 3 hatch towards the side of the ship, and was only about 18″ long.

5   That is, making it impossible to hold the ship on her course.

6   The proverbial expression 'to pour oil on troubled waters', meaning to bring calm to a difficult situation, derives from to the damping effect on waves of water produced by the elastic nature of a film of oil spread across its surface. See O Reynolds (1880), 'On the effect of oil in destroying waves on the surface of water.' *Report of the British Association for the Advancement of Science*, 489–90.

7   Some cited the very different but equally famous case of the *San Demetrio* in 1940, a British oil tanker abandoned on fire after her convoy was attacked in mid-Atlantic. Later, some of her crew re-boarded her, put out the fire and brought her safely to Glasgow. In an uncontested case the participating crew members were awarded the salvage, the judge thanking all concerned for giving him such a pleasant day's work.

8   Mrs McCabe had heard the operator using her lever key. During the setting up of a call the operator would have her key pushed away so that she could speak to both parties. Once the connection had been made, she was supposed to move it back to the centre so that she could not hear the conversation taking place. However, with the key pulled towards her, she could monitor the call without either party hearing her speak or knowing she was listening. When operated, the key, like a light switch, made a click that could be heard by the caller and the call-recipient.

9   Communication from Bishop to the author.

16

The Brotherhood of the Sea

Kursk and the *Priz AS-28*

2000/2005

May the sharks devour us, so long as we don't have to accept your helping hand!

ALEKSANDR SOLZHENITSYN, *THE GULAG ARCHIPELAGO*[1]

THE *FLYING ENTERPRISE* OPERATION exemplified the modern multi-agency, international approach to a maritime incident, involving coastguard, air force, navy, commercial salvers and lifeboat institution. That has become normal where merchant ships of all nations are concerned, but the situation of warships in distress – somewhat less common in peacetime – is complicated by considerations of national security, and no class of vessel is wrapped in closer secrecy than the submarine.

Despite improvements in submarine rescue equipment, including the development of submersibles capable of mating with specially designed hatches, peacetime accidents continued to happen. One of the worst, whether through the circumstances or its freshness in the public mind, occurred as late as 2000. And is it fanciful to suggest that while for Russians the boat's name commemorated the greatest tank battle in history, for English speakers it sounded ominously similar to *curse*? The lessons that had to be learned from it subsequently proved a lifeline for another crew.

Edinburgh, 06:50 Friday 5 August 2005

Giving a last wave to his partner Susan, Stuart Gold pulled away from Waverley Station with just the car radio for company on the daily hour-and-a-quarter

---

Dramatis Personae

Gennady Bolonin : passenger, *Priz AS-28*

Sergei Bolozerov : senior midshipman, *Priz AS-28*

David Burke : engineer, UKSRS

Marcus Cave : naval architect, UKSRS

Ed Dark : flight lieutenant, RAF

Will Forrester : winchman, UKSRS

Stuart Gold : *Scorpio* supervisor, UKSRS

Alan Heslop : engineer, UKSRS

Keith Hewitt : squadron leader, RAF

Jonathan Holloway : British naval attaché, Moscow

Alexander Ivanov : senior midshipman, *Priz AS-28*

Sergei Ivanov : Russian defence minister

Dmitry Kolesnikov : captain-lieutenant, *Kursk*

Alexei Korkin : seaman, *Kursk*

Valery Lepetyukha : passenger, *Priz AS-28*

Gennady Lyachin : captain of the *Kursk*

Lena Milashevskaya : wife of Vyacheslav Milashevsky

Vyacheslav Milashevsky : captain-lieutenant, *Priz AS-28*

Peter Nuttall : *Scorpio* pilot, UKSRS

Nigel Pyne : engineer, UKSRS

Dmitri Podkapaev : Russian naval officer

Anatoly Popov : navigator, *Priz AS-28*

Vyacheslav Popov : admiral

Ian Riches : commander, UKSRS

David Russell : commodore, UKSRS

Charlie Sillett : crane operator, *Scorpio*

Alexander Uybin : midshipman, *Priz AS-28*

journey to work in Renfrew. Concentrating on the traffic, he vaguely heard politics give way to the weather forecast and then the news headlines. The irrepressible twinkle in his brown eyes died abruptly as his brain isolated a single item. A Russian mini-submarine in trouble on the other side of the world. Not again. Please, not another *Kursk*. Five years ago, to the month, to within a few days. It was a disaster that the world at large had not forgotten, and which touched every submariner to the heart, to say nothing of those who, like himself, had been forced to stand by impotently at the scene. Maybe they could not have changed the outcome, but … if only they had been allowed to try, if only they had been called in earlier.

Barents Sea, Saturday afternoon, 12 August 2000

Captain-Lieutenant Dmitry Kolesnikov glanced at his watch and copied the time onto the top of the sheet of paper: *13:15*. He had already written the date: *12-08-2000*. He paused for a moment and then continued: *All personnel from sections 6, 7 and 8 have moved to section 9. There are 23 of us in here. We have taken this decision because none of us can get to the surface.* The words emerged steadily into the dull spotlight cast by the torch. He looked up, nodded , and a voice said quietly, 'Maynagashev'.

Starting a new line, Kolesnikov wrote down the name, then paused for the young, round-faced chief petty officer to dictate his number. One by one, starting with the men from section 6, compartment by compartment, he recorded the simple details of everyone with him, and ended with his own. Inside, the cramped chamber retained a last vestige of warmth. Outside, the waters of the Barents Sea were close to freezing while, 330 feet (100 metres) above, Russia's Northern Fleet continued its exercises in dreadful ignorance of what had happened beneath them.

Compared to the *Squalus* and *U-156* – the *Scirè* does not even register – the *Kursk* was a five-deck monster from another planet, a stealthy, nuclear-powered killer, the biggest and possibly the most dangerous submarine in the world, a target for every superlative. At 505 feet (154 metres), her length equalled that of two jumbo jets and, capable of remaining at sea for months, she possessed luxuries that would have astonished not just Hartenstein, Borghese and Naquin but even cruise passengers from earlier generations: hot showers and a

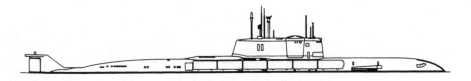

Profile of an Project 949-A *Antey*-class (NATO designation Oscar II) Russian nuclear-powered submarine.

cinema. She could thrash along at 30 knots on the surface and only drop two knots when submerged, while her armament of Starfish and Stallion missiles, plus Shipwreck cruise missiles, was formidable. Her double hull, with a space of 10 feet (3 metres) between inner and outer skins to accommodate the missile tubes, even encouraged a belief that her class was unsinkable. The outer hull was fabricated from steel containing a high proportion of nickel and chrome; the pressurised inner hull was of 3″ (75 mm) steel.

The *Kursk* entered service at the end of 1994 as – officially – a Project 949A *Antey*-class sub; NATO called her an Oscar II; in naval slang she and her huge guided-missile-carrying, nuclear-powered compatriots were *boomers*, and a decade after the end of the Cold War, NATO was still taking a healthy interest in them. British and American submarines played a dangerous game with their Russian rivals, particularly risky because as design improved to meet the challenge of enhanced detection equipment, the potential for collision between vessels increased. Thanks to the composition of that outer hull, the *Kursk* gave off only a weak magnetic signature: she was hard to track but, by the same token, easier to encounter accidentally.

As she pushed her way through the calm waters of the Barents Sea on Friday 11 August, the submarines USS *Memphis* and *Toledo* were 'in the area', detailed to observe the Northern Fleet exercise. Like Tryon's Royal Navy manoeuvres in the Mediterranean, the event was to be a showcase, improving naval morale and tactical efficiency, impressing the people at home and reminding its rivals that it was not to be trifled with. There was another eerie similarity between the two events: no fakir promised the wrath of Allah, but a number of those on board the *Kursk* and their families had a premonition of disaster. Before the *Kursk* sailed from her base at Litsa on the Thursday, one 19-year-old seaman, Alexei Korkin, wrote graphically to his mother about nightmares he had suffered and his fears that the *Kursk*, like the *Komsomolet*s off the northern coast of Norway in 1989, would sink. He imagined his photograph at divisional HQ augmented by a posthumous decoration for heroism, and claimed a premonition that everything was going to pieces.

Together with that foreboding mingled a contrasting consciousness among Korkin and his colleagues that they were serving in the Russian Navy's most prestigious submarine, under an experienced captain, Gennady Lyachin, who was a decorated hero and a leader who knew how to run a highly disciplined and happy ship. On this occasion, there were many more people aboard than just the *Kursk*'s normal crew: 118, all told, including some high-ranking naval personnel who were present as observers. One of them was the chief of staff of the 7th Submarine Division.

From on board the *Kirov*-class battle-cruiser *Petr Velikiy*, Admiral Vyacheslav Popov presided over the exercise. On Saturday, the *Kursk* was to carry out a torpedo attack on the fleet. Her objective was the flagship itself, her weapon a practice torpedo. It carried no warhead and had to be targeted to pass beneath the battle-cruiser. Afterwards, far too expensive for the cash-strapped navy to lose, the torpedo would be recovered so it could be used again. At 08:51 the *Kursk* made her final contact with the flagship. Lyachin had scheduled her attack for 11:30. While the torpedo crew in no. 1 compartment made their preparations, the submarine was at periscope depth, around 110 feet (33 metres), taking a last look at the target.

The particular torpedo selected for the firing was ten years old, one of the class known as *65–76*: introduced in (19)76 and fired from a 65-centimetre (25.6″) tube. It was fuelled by kerosene and hydrogen peroxide, H_2O_2. The latter is a versatile chemical: its use in the beauty industry created the 'peroxide blonde'; other applications took it into domestic gardening and municipal water treatment. Particularly in the concentrated form known as High Test Peroxide (HTP) it is also one of the most powerful oxidants known to science: when mixed with kerosene, it engenders a savagely violent reaction that drives a warhead tens of miles towards its prey.[2] It is also dangerously reactive with certain metals, including copper. It must be segregated in its tank until the torpedo has been fired from the tube by compressed air.

Nobody can ever know exactly what happened during the next 135 seconds, but the most plausible theory is that the torpedo, which had not been used for six years, was suffering from internal corrosion.[3] Just the movement from its bay towards the tube might have been enough to precipitate a fatal leak, allowing the HTP to come into contact with copper wiring and other components.[4] No emergency signal was sent, no emergency buoy released.[5]

The blast ripped backwards through the torpedo room, annihilating everyone instantly, and into second compartment, the control room. If it did not kill all those in it, it would not only have injured them but left them in a state of complete disorientation and shock, probably incapable of operating the buoyancy and directional controls that would bring the *Kursk* to the surface – if those controls were even functioning. How much havoc had been wreaked on the *Kursk*'s controls is at best guesswork, but the damage probably extended as far as the third compartment, because either there was no one capable of sending a distress signal from that section, or the equipment had been knocked out.

As the *Kursk* plunged down, wounded and out of control but, like HMS *Victoria*, without loss of power, the heat turned the forward compartment into a furnace: temperatures soared into the thousands as the combustible contents of the ill-fated test torpedo – half a tonne of Kerosene and a tonne of HTP burned unchecked. It took just 135 seconds before the live torpedoes in their racks, mercifully all conventionally armed, themselves reached combustion point. The effect on the control room behind and even on the third compartment was catastrophic In its own way, it paralleled what happened to the loaded cannons on the French East India Company's *Prince*.

Seismic equipment in Norway, Scotland and beyond had registered a small spike in the Barents Sea, an area not known for geological instability. The disturbance was also picked up by the USS *Memphis*. It was followed two minutes later by a second, larger spike, measuring 3.5 on the Richter scale when, just as the *Kursk* hit the seabed, the warheads exploded. The *Petr Velikiy* trembled; 32 miles (59 kilometres) from the *Kursk* the powerful shockwave hit another Russian submarine, the *Karelia*; analysts on the USS *Memphis* and in Norway were puzzled. If this was all part of the Russian exercise it was unusually powerful, but none of the surveillance equipment monitoring Russian communications had picked up any increase in traffic to suggest that anything was wrong.

Popov knew that the *Kursk* had not fired her torpedo and that she had not made contact to report why, but initially no one was unduly concerned. Such things happened. The *Karelia*'s officers decided that the explosion was part and parcel of the exercise – a detail about which they had not been informed. The fact that no surface ship spotted any disturbance on the water above the *Kursk* presumably indicates that none were close enough to spot it. Only as afternoon drew on did the officers on the *Petr Velikiy* begin to worry, and at 17:00, rather than wait for the next pre-arranged contact at 23:00, they asked the *Kursk* to report. There was silence. It was the report from the *Karelia*, when they radioed to ask for it, that rang the alarm bells. By 20:30 a search and rescue operation had been started, but no announcement, no hint of the disaster was made, and nobody could tell that 23 men were clinging to life.

It says much for those who, in the cash-strapped days that followed the end of the Cold War, designed and built the *Kursk*, that anyone survived the blast at all. But although the massive detonation completely wrecked every compartment forward of the reactors, the most critical bulkhead did not fail. When the initial horror and chaos had abated enough for men to think, the reactors were turned off. Had they not been, they would have overheated and created a major nuclear disaster. Two hours after the explosion, Kolesnikov had constituted himself the leader of the survivors and written his note.

How long they lasted is disputed. They had emergency oxygen replenishment in the form of cartridges that contained crystals of a superoxide. The crystals absorbed carbon dioxide in the damp atmosphere and gave off oxygen, but superoxides need careful handling. If they come into contact with water, as opposed to humidity, they react violently. Without the reactors to power the heating and lighting, however, conditions deteriorated. The temperature dropped to just above freezing; the men put on their thermal survival suits.

At some stage – the second half of the note is undated – Kolesnikov pulled out his precious sheet of paper and wrote a brief farewell to his wife and his mother-in-law. Then:

> *It is dark here for writing but I'll try by feel. It seems like there are no chances, 10–20%.*
> *Let's hope that at least someone will read this. Here's the list of personnel from the other*
> *sections who are now in the ninth and will try to get out. Regards to everyone, no need to*
> *be desperate. Kolesnikov.*

Why did they not attempt an escape themselves? The hull of the *Kursk* was held at normal atmospheric pressure: they could have reached the surface without risk of the 'bends', which only occur when the body comes up quickly after having been subjected to increased pressure for rather longer than the escape would take. Probably they were waiting to be found: survival in the icy waters of the Barents would be limited unless a rescue ship was close by when they reached the surface. Another reason was that the *Kursk*'s hatch was not designed for such an escape, which requires an airlock so that the compartment does not fill with water during individual escapes. Instead, it was designed to mate with a *Priz*-class rescue submersible.

The truth was that the men had realized that their compartment was not tight. Water was seeping in, and as it did the air pressure was slowly increasing. The survivors of the *Squalus* had been under a similar pressure, but not only did they have an airlock, they also had the rope leading up to the marker buoy, which would have helped them make a carefully controlled ascent, avoiding decompression sickness, as a last resort. The only hope for the *Kursk* crew had to come from outside. If not immediately, then certainly quickly.

Not even those authors who have studied the disaster in detail, and with access to official and unofficial channels at a high level, agree on when the end came (see Sources). Peter Truscott believes it was as early as the Saturday night; Robert Moore puts it possibly as late as Thursday 17 August because of the number of used oxygen replenishment cartridges that were eventually found. Nobody disputes the final cause of the death: a flash fire probably caused by dropping one of the cartridges into the rising water, so easily done in the dark with cold fingers and a body numbed mentally and physically by the increased pressure. Some of the crew ducked their faces under the water, but it was a futile gesture. When the fire died out, they emerged to find it had devoured the last atoms of oxygen. Dmitri Kolesnikov died with his note wrapped up and held close to his heart.

News that there might be a problem with the *Kursk* leached into the grim naval town of Vidyayevo, home to most of the crew's families, on the Sunday morning. Nobody told the wives and mothers officially; some were not even sure if their relative was on board. Usually Russian naval wives were stoical, bearing their grief with closed dignity, knowing they would be taken care of if they did not make a fuss, not wanting to jeopardize the reputation of the navy. Not this time.

On the Sunday afternoon Alexei Korkin's mother was in the garden of her dacha when, she says, she heard her son crying out to her.

The *Petr Velikiy* had located what was possibly the *Kursk* on the seabed, but it was not until the Sunday morning, almost 24 hours after the explosion, that the admiral knew for sure that the anomaly was the missing sub. Three members from the search and rescue team that had been called out the previous evening went down in a 20-year-old *Priz*-class submersible that had grossly inadequate power to locate the escape hatch. It is possible that the survivors were still alive, but the *Priz* – which, although compatible, had never been allowed to practise mating with a submarine of the *Kursk*'s class – was unable to make a seal. The submersible's time below was far too limited for the task: the batteries were failing and they had to regain the surface for the long hours of recharging aboard a mother ship that was itself outdated and inadequate. That was the crux of the problem for the Russians. While NATO countries were gearing up for joint submarine rescue exercises in the Mediterranean, ready to pool their modern resources in any emergency, the Russians had not invested in the technology to deal with the loss of their state-of-the-art submarine.

By Monday those seismic readings, coupled with intelligence reports of a vast increase in communications traffic, now told Western governments – and for 'Western', read 'NATO' – all they really needed to know. Norway was the first to offer help: Admiral Skorgen spoke directly to Popov and was politely but firmly rebuffed. The Royal Navy's response was simple. While the politicians debated whether or not an offer of assistance would be welcome or even useful to the erstwhile enemy, and the Russians then debated all day whether to accept the offer that was eventually made that same morning, Commodore David Russell put the UK's Submarine Rescue Service (UKSRS) based near Glasgow, on alert. They were ready to fly from Prestwick Airport with an LR5 and a *Scorpio*-45 – the first, a manned submersible designed to mate with a crippled submarine; the second, a Remotely Operated Vehicle (ROV) that could be used for reconnaissance and for taking down emergency supplies. Both ranked among the most up-to-date equipment in their field.

The Russians mishandled every aspect of the operation. They refused to admit anything had happened until the Monday, and then claimed that the *Kursk* had been in collision with either an American or a British submarine on the Saturday. It was a claim that would be often repeated despite the seismic evidence,[6] strong denials from both countries and the probability that any submarine that had collided with the *Kursk* would itself be in serious trouble. The new president, Vladimir Putin, had just started his summer holiday at Sochi on the Black Sea, and was not informed of the magnitude of the accident, badly damaging his public image by his failure to return to Moscow. Conspiracy theories and wildly improbable explanations abounded. Liaison with the desperate families was a disaster. Reports that the rescuers were in contact with the survivors raised false hopes and brought frantic demands to know how the rescue operation was proceeding. News that Western governments had offered help only increased those demands. On the Tuesday the women did what would have been impossible a decade before, and which had been unthinkable up until that moment: they went public, calling for action, displaying their fear and frustration to the world.

The following day, the Russian Government agreed to ask for Norway's help; then they also gave permission for the British team to fly out. Yet they then refused the British permission to land in Russia: they would have to proceed from Norway by sea. It was eight days before the Norwegian team was allowed to dive on the *Kursk*; the British LR5 was still on the deck of the mother ship, hovering on the edge of the site. By then the tragedy was long over. For Commodore Russell and the British rescue team, which included the *Scorpio*'s supervisor, Stuart Gold, and her crane operator, Charlie Sillett, it was a wretched end to a sorry saga. For the bereaved it was heartbreak, and their anger and grief spilled over into emotional confrontation with the politicians sent to speak to them. Television stations around the world screened the shocking sight of distraught mother Nadezhda Tylik collapsing after suddenly being sedated by injection during a meeting with Russia's deputy prime minister. Subsequent claims that she had a medical condition and that her husband had requested help found few supporters.

The wreck of the *Kursk* was brought home the following year by the Dutch specialist salvors, Smit, and many of the bodies were recovered. Depressingly, the raising of the massive submarine, which required cutting-edge lifting technology, cost Russia far more than would have been needed to update and man its rescue equipment. But two glimmers of hope emerged: an acknowledgement that such a disaster must never be allowed to happen again, and the recognition that international cooperation was the way forward. That optimism would be tested, not in the Northern Fleet's Arctic waters but far to the east, where Russia's Pacific Fleet operates.

FROM THE AIR, the Kamchatka peninsula hangs like a pendant from the north-east coast of Asia, dividing the Sea of Okhotsk from the Bering Sea, studded along its Pacific coast by the craters of some three hundred volcanoes, and dripping a bracelet of small islands down to Hokkaido. It lies along the circumpacific Ring of Fire, a magnet for earth scientists, fishermen and adventurous tourists seeking its extraordinary and beautiful landscape.

The Russians only moved in any numbers into Kamchatka during the nineteenth century, establishing a regional capital at Petropavlovsk, towards the southern tip, where, backed by the huge snow-dredged cones of Avachinsky and Koryarsky, the sheltered Avachinsky Bay formed a natural harbour for a naval base. During the Cold War years the place was off-limits to both Soviets and foreigners; today it remains a fishing and naval town, its drab, uniform architecture from the Soviet era relieved by open spaces and its magnificent setting. Tensions still exist, perhaps less with the West now than with Japan, with whom Russia has disputed ownership of the Kuril islands for the past century, and, some 50 miles (90 kilometres) out, the seabed bristles with a cordon of massive antennae used to monitor foreign submarines. Each antenna measures 330 × 24.5 feet (100 × 7.5 metres) and is fixed about 50 feet (15 metres) from the seabed by 60-ton anchors. They represent no hazard for surface vessels: the waters here are over 650 feet (200 metres) deep. Subsea cables take out the electricity to power them and bring the data back to shore.

Berezovaya Bay, Thursday morning, 4 August 2005

Captain Lieutenant Vyacheslav Milashevsky appears younger than his 25 years; his slight frame, short dark hair, generous mouth and large dark eyes have not quite thrown off adolescence, and belie the fact that he is not only the father of twin daughters but, as second-in-command of the *Priz AS-28*, an experienced officer who has already led half-a-dozen operations. For the last few days, since Captain Vladimir Cheremokhin went on leave, he has again been her acting commander, following in the footsteps of his father, who had commanded her when she was first commissioned back in 1989. He does not lack initiative. His wife remembers how, when she was in hospital giving birth to the girls, he climbed the fire escape in order to beat visiting restrictions.

Just 44 feet (13.4 metres) long and painted in broad bands of red and white, his *AS-28* has all the stealth and menace of a giant cough-sweet, but the *Priz* class of midget submarines was not designed to take out NATO aircraft carriers or launch nuclear strikes. Despite all the shortcomings exposed by the *Kursk* disaster, they have remained Russia's principal submarine rescue vehicle, and they are also used for inspection work.[7] The *AS-28* is due to go in for maintenance around the end of the month, but at the moment, Milashevsky and his crew are on a diving exercise, taking a look at some of those antennae out in Berezovaya Bay. Technically, the exercise should not be going ahead because the *AS-28* is on her own: operating procedures require that the submersibles work in pairs. Her partner, however, is unserviceable. In addition to her usual crew, *AS-28* has on board Gennady Bolonin, a civilian engineer from Lazurit Central Design Bureau, Captain Valery Lepetyukha, from the emergency rescue service plus fellow submariners Alexander Uybin and Alexander Ivanov. Usually it is just Milashevsky, his captain, the navigator Anatoly Popov, and Sergei Bolozerov. But this is a routine task. Soon he will be home, and maybe there will be time to do some unpacking. The family has only just moved into the apartment at Zavoyko on the edge of Petropavlovsk, and a large model of the *AS-28* – he had carved it himself – is cluttering up the lounge. Lena has taken the girls for a break to the family dacha …

Nobody appears to be quite sure when things went wrong. Officially, it was around noon when, quietly manoeuvring along a length of antenna at a depth of 624 feet (190 metres), the *AS-28* blundered unsuspectingly into a lethal web of discarded fishing nets caught on the structure.[8] Her propeller entangled, the cords holding her close to the steelwork, unable to reverse her way out, she was trapped at a depth beyond which the crew could effect their own escape, and beyond conventional diving capability, two-and-a-half times deeper than the *Squalus*.

The SOS was sent at 13:00. More than anyone, Milashevsky's men knew the state of their country's submarine rescue system: after all, they were part of it. They had some water and food – not much, but just enough to outlast their emergency oxygen. The young commander had done the calculation: given the additional personnel, they might have sufficient oxygen for around 80 hours, he reported. But his intention was to ration it more severely than that to give them a greater chance, even though that would make conditions more uncomfortable, and he was particularly concerned for the 60-year-old civilian, Bolonin, and for Lepetyukha, who had had part of a lung removed.

Lena Milashevskaya had a disturbing nightmare on Thursday night, but no word of her husband's plight had reached her at the dacha, though the rumour had spread in Petropavlovsk. Once again, the women refused to wait in stoical invisibility and silence. This was not going to be another *Kursk*. Someone – she would not give her name, claiming only to be the wife of a submariner – rang a local radio station in the city. Within a few hours the story was on radio and TV, where Lena's elder sister became the first in the family to hear it. She phoned her sister. Distraught, Lena returned to the city with the girls, not to her own home – she could not face it – but to her sister's.

The memory of the *Kursk* poisoned the whole atmosphere. Naval assertions that the men were alive and well, that a fishing net was the cause, that it would be possible to drag the submarine into shallower water in which divers could operate, all were regarded warily by the Russian media, which recalled the lies of five years earlier and the inadequacy of the rescue attempt. Yet in another sense the name was a charm. Russia could not afford another *Kursk*.

Some good had already emerged from the earlier tragedy, though not the upgrading of rescue capability so urgently needed. In June 2005, in stifling heat off Taranto, Russia and Ukraine had participated for the first time in the NATO-sponsored Sorbet Royal. What sounded like a sweet temptation from the dessert menu was in fact the triennial live exercise in complex submarine rescue, hosted this time by the Italian navy. Referring back to the *Kursk*, Admiral Sir Jonathan Band KCB wrote: 'International coordination and understanding had come a long way since then. The Submarine Escape and Rescue Working Group … meets annually, and the last meeting was held in St Petersburg.'

United Kingdom, Friday Morning, 5 August

Twelve hours behind Petropavlovsk, the British officially picked up the news around 06:00 UK time via the International Submarine Escape and Rescue Liaison Office (ISMERLO), and publicly on the 7:00 a.m. BBC News. While Russian ships converged on the site throughout that Friday, and the Russian navy expressed confidence that they would be able to secure a successful ending to the emergency with their own resources, the decision had been taken to invite foreign help before the situation became critical. Although President Putin remained silent in public, there was every reason to believe that there was pressure from the highest level to save the men and the country's reputation. Russia's closest neighbours in the region, Japan and the United States, were approached. Both agreed. Japanese assistance would arrive by sea, which would take several days, but at the Deep Submergence Unit (DSU) based at San Diego, California, the Americans prepared to airlift their teams in a giant USAF C-5 Galaxy. The DSU possessed a pair of Super-*Scorpio* ROVs, and they also called up civilian support: two divers equipped with atmospheric suits and another ROV, a Deep Drone, with its civilian operators. Like many other naval powers, the United States had manned submersibles capable of mating with stricken submarines, but the hatches on the Russian vessels were incompatible.

Given the imminent Japanese and US deployment, and with their own base at Renfrew further away, it seemed unlikely that the British would be involved, but at 09:00 the British naval attaché in Moscow, Captain Jonathan Holloway, was on the telephone to Commander Ian Riches of the Royal Navy. News had also filtered through to the RAF base at Brize Norton, Oxfordshire.

Riches had joined the navy as an 18-year-old school-leaver, and submarines quickly became his professional life. Now 47, he had been a little over 18 months as submarine escape and rescue equipment project manager at the navy's Abbey Wood establishment near Bristol. He had heard the same news bulletin as Stuart Gold, and even before Holloway's phone call he had decided to find out whether British resources could be of help. Two-and-a-half hours later he put Renfrew on standby while government authorization was sought. That afternoon in Moscow, Holloway delivered the official offer of help in person. It took just 15 minutes for the Russians to accept. By that time, Riches was on an RAF Nimrod bound for Prestwick Airport, Scotland, and the UK

Submarine Rescue Service's (UKSRS) *Scorpio* ROV had been loaded onto a trailer bound for the same destination.

The *Scorpio*[9] was kept on permanent standby at James Fisher Rumic Ltd, a private company that, among its other operations, managed the UKSRS assets and put together the civilian team to operate them. Bright yellow and black, and the size of a micro-car, the *Scorpio* had all the characteristics of a scaled-up Lego Technics model, but to ROV Ssupervisor Stuart Gold, who had looked after her for 12 years, she had become a much-loved pet rather than a piece of hi-tech equipment. Her task (though she had never been asked to perform it in a real-life emergency) was to locate a disabled submarine (a DISSUB, in the profession's jargon), send back information as to the damage and the surrounding environment, and then take down supplies to sustain the crew until rescue. Her two arms could be fitted with a variety of tools and operated with exceptional finesse from her portable control cabin on a mother ship.

Although the equipment was on standby, the team did not sit around waiting for the phone to ring. People had to be contacted, and Gold's most experienced fellow senior pilot was working in the Mediterranean. He turned to Peter Nuttall, who was supposed to be going to a wedding the following day. There was no question of hesitation. The rest of the team hastily assembled. Charlie Sillett, who was still in Edinburgh, went to Gold's house to collect his passport before hitting the motorway; then there was Marcus Cave, a naval architect with James Fisher Shipping who would oversee adaptations to whatever ship the Russians put at their disposal; David Burke, a project engineer with the parent company; Nigel Pyne and Alan Heslop, who provided electrical and well as mechanical engineering expertise, and Will Forrester, the winchman, who, like Sillett was a mechanical engineer. This was what they had all been waiting for, though they were aware that they would be arriving after the Americans and would at best be the back-up team.

Berezovaya Bay, Midnight Friday 5/Saturday 6 August (UK time noon Friday)

Even before Commander Riches's Nimrod was touching down, the crew of the *AS-28* had accepted that there was nothing they could do themselves to free their craft. Blowing some of the ballast had failed. They shut down power, gathered in the control compartment, put on their thermal suits and lay quietly in the dark to conserve oxygen. From now on, communications with the surface had to be strictly limited. By Milashevsky's calculation 44 hours of oxygen remained, and their lungs were already feeling the effects of the worsening atmosphere. Coughing and nausea would soon set in. The temperature fell rapidly as the titanium hull conducted the chill of the ocean; they shared a few biscuits and a meagre ration of water.

RAF Brize Norton, Friday 5 August

RAF Strike Command contacted Group Captain Ian Elliott, Station Commander, with a simple question: 'If there are no rules, how quickly can you make this happen?' The answer proved to be: *very quickly.* Wing Commander 'Spiv' Gair, commanding 99 Squadron, ordered all personnel who had not been on duty within the past 14 hours to report. The first two crews to arrive would get the mission. Originally scheduled to fly to Iraq and Afghanistan, veteran Squadron Leader Keith Hewitt arrived at the base to find the aircraft, a C-17 Globemaster (RAF registration ZZ173, one of the newest and best transport planes in the air force), already prepared and with the engines started – 'Not something we do even in war, so I knew something big was happening'. At 15:20 UK time, with Hewitt nominated as aircraft commander, Flight Lieutenant Ed Dark and his crew took off for Prestwick. A Hercules was also on its way, with a translator and an RAF police officer to guard the C-17 in Russia.

Prestwick Airport, 16:15 Friday 5 August
(Berezovaya Bay time 04:15 Saturday)

As the RAF team of pilots, loadmasters and other personnel met up with Riches and the UKSRS, and loading began, word came through that the Russians had accorded the flight humanitarian status: they could take the quickest route through Russian airspace. This was a relief to Hewitt whose concerns were for the urgency of the mission and the fuelling of the aircraft. The latter was a major headache.

> It is usual for an aircraft to always have enough fuel for a diversion if required. The maximum fuel weight on a C-17 is 240,000 pounds. However, the total weight of the aircraft, the cargo and the fuel must not exceed 585,000 pounds. With the aircraft and cargo weights on the day, this left me with 20,000 pounds short of what I ideally wanted; we went, anyway. My plan was to have a 'point of no return' at which time if I didn't have a good idea of the weather and have another airfield not too far away as a diversion, I would turn back to a Northern Norway airfield.

Hewitt took off at 20:15 with 25 people on board. They had been asked to take journalists, but the Russians obligingly refused to allow non-essential personnel. While he and his co-pilot monitored the systems, worried about the fuel, and talked to the various air traffic agencies, Riches, Gold and the team made themselves as comfortable as they could on the aluminium floor of the cargo hold, a bare tin can 87 feet (26 metres) long and 18 feet (5.5 metres) wide. Sitting along the side or huddled in sleeping bags, earplugs muffling the roar of the four Pratt and Whitney turbofans on the massive wings, they tried to get some rest, but it was uncomfortable and, even with the lights turned down, too bright. Planning was difficult when they had so little information to go on. Chilled through, even with a fleece and jacket over his boiler suit, Gold read a book, but it was hard for any of them to keep their minds off the seven men who by now must be even colder, more afraid and more uncomfortable, and of what their families much be going through. Experience had not given much cause for optimism: *Kursk, Komsomolets* ...

Half way through the flight they received some unexpected news. They were ahead of the Americans. They were going to get the chance. A surge of excitement ran through them.

Lena Milashevskaya's hope was fading. Her father-in-law had told her he was convinced that his son had only until Saturday night, when the oxygen would run out. Like the other wives, she had heard little from the authorities: her information was coming from the radio and television, and she in turn was giving interviews to the press. The photograph of her holding her two daughters, Sasha and Nastya, remains among the haunting images of those days. She looks a dozen years older than her husband with her short, side-parted, brown hair and narrow-rimmed glasses that are almost too large for her pinched face. Her eyes are averted from the camera, even from the children, imagining a future without Slava.

Berezovaya Bay, 06:00 Saturday 6 August (UK time 18:00 Friday)

During the early hours of the morning, an underwater camera had returned pictures proving that the *AS-28* was undamaged, but reports at around 05:00 that the Russians had succeeded in hooking it in preparation for dragging it into shallow waters had been denied. Their task was badly hampered by the anchor cables holding the vast antenna in place, and not until 07:30 could they be certain that they had a grip on the stricken vessel. Another major problem, admitted only later, was that there had been difficulties aboard another rescue ship, the *Georgy Kozmin*, resulting in damage to its British-built Venom ROV. The regular crew was on leave, and the replacements, under Captain Viktor Novikov, were ill trained in the use of the equipment.

At 09:00, 90 minutes before the American Galaxy took off from San Diego, the cold, gasping crew of the *AS-28* felt the first clanging jolts as the tow began. They, and the whole apparatus around them, jerked forwards. Progress was painful. If nothing else, this must have brought home to them how precarious their position had become. The air was foul, heavily saturated with carbon dioxide. Lepetyukha was in a bad way, and Ivanov was starting to vomit, but Milashevsky was adamant in still being as sparing with the oxygen as possible. By his inexact calculations, less than a day and a half remained. Movement was exhausting: even the most basic exertion, such as getting a new oxygen cylinder or pouring out a little of their fragile water supply, left chests heaving and hearts racing, struggling to extract oxygen. They had been in contact with the surface, confirming that conditions were satisfactory. There was little else they could say, but they were very slowly suffocating.

The tow failed. Something else would have to be tried.

Gennady Bolonin's thoughts were less for himself than the others. He was sixty, but he felt for the younger men, above all for Slava with his wife and two little girls at home. For the commander, the ordeal must be terrible.

Elizovo Airport, 18:22 Saturday 6 August

Well before they reached the area Hewitt had been told that the weather in Kamchatka had deteriorated significantly and the precision landing equipment at Petropavlovsk was unserviceable. This was serious. The landing equipment would have brought him safely to a point just 200 feet – about 60 metres – above the runway, from which he needed only two-thirds of a mile (1100 metres) or about 20 seconds to touch down. Without it, all the figures had to be doubled, and they were in lethal mountainous terrain.

> The good news was that we hadn't used quite as much fuel as we had planned and we had been in contact with Magadan airport on the Southern Siberian coast who had reasonable weather so could be used as a diversion but I would have fuel for only one approach before diverting if we didn't get in. We landed at dusk in fairly bad weather with low cloud and poor visibility and heavy drizzle.

The professionally factual words significantly understate the achievement.

As the C-17's screaming engines died into a whine the *Scorpio* team stretched their stiff limbs, waiting for the aft cargo door to open. Just 24 hours had passed since they had first heard of the disaster, and by some diplomatic and logistical miracle they were now only 50 miles – 90 kilometres – from the submarine. They were joined by Captain Holloway who, having secured the diplomatic deal, had jumped on a civilian overnight flight from Moscow to Petropavlovsk. Now Cave and Nuttall went on ahead by car with him to take a look at the mother ship and organize any alternations.

The team left behind had encountered the first hitch, one that Hewitt had feared: 'The C-17 has a rolling floor and needs a vehicle with a rolling surface to push the cargo on to. The Russians did not have such a vehicle.'

Ian Riches stared in dismay at the solitary fork-lift truck, which was the best Elizovo could muster. As it came up the to C-17, its windows fell out in final mockery. With the greatest of trepidation, Gold allowed his precious *Scorpio* to be unloaded by the truck, but to get the containers off would be at best risky, at worst impossible. Their best hope was still several hundred miles away.

Over an hour had gone by. Frustration shortened tempers. The *AS-28* crew might have only 24 hours of oxygen. Then at last they saw the approaching lights. The ground shook under the deafening roar of a massive transport plane that almost dwarfed the C-17. The Americans had arrived, bringing with them precisely the kit the UKSRS needed. Asked to give priority to the British equipment, which could be offloaded more quickly, they generously agreed.

With relief the *Scorpio* team heard the huge diesel-powered vehicle even before it came into sight. It took a mere 45 minutes to complete the unloading. Then they were into the Russian bus with a liaison officer and heading for the city's port, followed by *Scorpio* and her ancillary equipment on a low-loader, lurching along a road no better than a Baghdad bomb site. Hewitt and his RAF team, however, would have to miss out on the action: after 30 hours without sleep they went into crew-rest with a bottle of vodka as consolation.

'It was very dark, very little light,' recalled Gold. 'Not many people going about. If you can imagine a James Bond movie with pipes and steam, the odd car and some lorries ...'

Petropavlovsk, Midnight Saturday 6 / Sunday 7 August

Fine rain shone dismally in the security floodlighting around the perimeter of the desolate, shadowy docks. The sullen guard with his automatic rifle had apparently received no orders to admit these foreigners and their escort, and declined to refer the matter to his superiors. Echoing Gold's earlier impressions, Riches thought it was like being in a 1970s Cold-War movie. 'I saw the whole thing unravelling' he admitted, as for 20 minutes they stared impotently through the wire knowing that just 50 miles away lives were depending upon them. No less irritating was the realization that Holloway, Cave and Nuttall had been allowed in at least an hour and a half before – but by a different guard who must have gone off duty. When the gates were finally opened they could only wonder apprehensively what would happen next. It had been easier to fly half way across the world than bring their equipment across a few miles of land. In fact, they were about to meet a friend.

Among the Russians who had taken part in that recent Sorbet Royal exercise was Dmitri Podkapaev. Here was someone they knew, who, although he spoke barely a word of English, communicated eloquently by drawing diagrams, and who was in charge on the ground. He stood at the rail of the *KIL-27*, a cable-laying ship that would stand in for *Scorpio*'s mother ship. Cave had a team of Russian workmen already busy strengthening its deck. Podkapaev had a personal commitment to the rescue. He knew three of the crew and, like Gold, he had been involved in the *Kursk* fiasco. Seven was his lucky number, and now it was 7 August.

Three hours later, at just after 03:00 and with all the kit secured, *KIL-27* left the dock. At the site of the incident, the Russian navy, still improvising as best it could, was vainly attempting to lift the submarine. They had two tugs, one either side of the *AS-28*, and were trying to snare her with a sling made of cables. Somewhat further away, Russia's defence minister, Sergei Ivanov was bound by air for Petropavlovsk.

Berezovaya Bay, around 04:00 Sunday 7 August

In the command and control compartment right at the front of the *AS-28*, the foul air was thick, wet and cold, stinking of sour vomit. The sides of the submarine ran with condensation. Some of the men had already prepared their farewell notes.[10] Suddenly the telephone link came to life. Lepetyukha listened to the message with dawning amazement. Outside help was on its way. Not the Americans: the British. They would be here soon. Sergei Belozerov passed round a cup of water, while Milashevsky celebrated the news by opening a new oxygen cylinder. The logic must have been simple. They knew that the British had one of the very best submarine rescue units in the world. If that could not save them, then they were finished: there was nothing to hang on for.

Petropavlovsk, 08:00 Sunday 7 August

An anxious Sergei Ivanov had just touched down at the airport, and was being whisked off to the port where the corvette *Razliv* stood ready to take him out to the site. His arrival was sending a ripple of genuine hope around the tight-knit naval community. There was a distinct belief that no high-ranking minister would have arrived merely to preside over the recovery of bodies; the government would want to be associated with success. The Americans, too, were about to start loading their equipment onto the *Georgy Kozmin*.

In the privacy of her sister's flat Lena Milashevskaya had emerged from shock, grief and anger into anxious but real hope that Slava would be saved. An earlier visit by a naval counsellor had left her furious rather than distraught, by dismissing any hope for the men and telling her that all she could do was pray. Now, although emotionally battered into exhaustion, she was telling journalists how she would get into the hospital to see her husband if the authorities tried to delay a reunion.

Berezovaya Bay, 12 noon Sunday 7 August

The long voyage out to the site had given Dmitri an opportunity to brief the British team at first hand on the situation, which in turn made preparations far more focused. Having seen diagrams and photographs for the first time they could at last say that the job was achievable, that *Scorpio* had the tool-kit do precisely what was needed. One arm could be manipulated to grasp a cable and position it in a cutter attached to the other. A serious difficulty remained, however. Because she was attached to an umbilical, she needed to be operated from a stable platform and if, as here, the water was too deep for conventional anchors, only a mother ship with bow and stern thrusters automatically controlled by a global positioning system (GPS) receiver could maintain its position to the required accuracy of about three feet (one metre). Even a flat calm sea had currents and movement. The *KIL-27* did not have that capability.

Podkapaev had thought it through. With a marker pen he started drawing on the whiteboard of the control cabin. By tethering the cable-layer tightly between two vessels they could hold her steady. It was not ideal, but it was the best they could hope for, and if the sea was calm it ought to work. At around midday they were 'anchored' and began to set up the equipment. Pre-immersion tests gave them a shock. The sonar was out, and only one out of four cameras was working: 40 minutes of Russian roads had done their worst by taking out the electrics to one of the two points supplying the various functions. Heslop and Gold got to work, reflecting only later that *Scorpio* had just been to Italy and back without sustaining a scratch.

At 10:25 Sillett saw *Scorpio* into the water. Under Forrester's steady control the winch paid out the umbilical. The yellow buoyancy compartments, filled with a rigid syntactic foam like a giant Aero chocolate bar, melted into the dark water. Inside the control cabin the rest of the team followed her descent on the screens, watching the depth creeping towards the target of 190 metres. Where was it? A huge anomaly showed up, but no submarine. It was part of the antenna, Podkapaev reassured them. They were in the right place but the *AS-28* was further along. Until they saw that structure they had had no idea exactly how vast the Russian undersea listening structures were.

Now the cameras had picked her up in the glare of the powerful searchlights, there was no mistaking those red and white markings, nor what had snared her.

'Bang into the sub,' Gold recommended. 'Let them know we're here.'

The heavy metallic clang reverberated throughout the submarine, startling the seven crew into joyful hope muted only by their extreme weakness. Dragging himself to the periscope, Milashevsky could actually see *Scorpio*; they all heard the humming of her motors. With only ten hours of oxygen left, they took reassurance from the sound and the activity. She might be a robot, but she was a friend.

In the control cabin she had become part of Stuart Gold, an extension of his own arm, responding to each movement of the joystick. While Nuttall held her steady, Gold reached out towards the first of the hemp ropes with the grabber. Anyone who has ever played the arcade game of picking up a prize with a little crane in a glass case will empathize with an atom of the tension and frustration that faced Gold, and the prize for which he was playing was the lives of seven men. Where the cables were accessible, they were held tight against the submarine's flank; it was hard to get a grip. Time was passing, but in the intensity of their concentration they were all unconscious of it.

Got it! Carefully Gold brought the arm back towards the jaws of the cutter, manoeuvring millimetre by millimetre. It was in.

'Cut.'

A flick of a switch and the jaws, capable of severing 70-millimetre steel wire, sliced through it. Time for a moment of satisfaction, a deep breath to regain the concentration, and onto the next, keeping a prudent distance from that net. It had caught one victim. It must not be allowed a second.

Minutes had stretched into three hours. They had cut the bulk of the web. The cabin was hot; everyone was sweating; few words were spoken. Gold felt a change, a loss of manoeuvrability. The alarm informed him of low oil pressure in the main termination where all the cables came into *Scorpio*. A few moments later, and one of the flanges on the cutter broke. She would have to come up for repairs. Podkapaev feared for the effect on the morale of the Russian crew, but, reassured by the promise that the repair would take just a few minutes, went to get the authorization. In the meantime they began to winch her up.

As she disappeared from sight and sound a depression born of disappointment and uncertainty fell over the trapped crew who had no idea what was going on, only that their lifeline had gone. They lay quietly, hoping, praying, that she would come back.

On the deck of the *KIL-17* the SRS team went into action. The broken cutter flange and the malfunctioning propeller responsible for the loss of manoeuvrability were taken off for repair and the oil restored. Fifteen minutes later, *Scorpio* was on her way back to the water. Her motors alerted the *AS-28* crew to her return, and they heaved gasping sighs.

Once again tension reigned in the control cabin as the last few cords and lengths of net slowly surrendered to the powerful jaws. They had made ten cuts. Just one cord remained, but they could not get at it. For 45 minutes they tried from every safe angle. The only way would be to take *Scorpio* down and under the *AS-28*. It was a risk too far. If she, with her heavy umbilical, became trapped beneath the mini-sub, neither of them would see the surface again and a major rescue capability as well as the lives could be lost.

The pause in activity alerted Podkapaev.

'What is it?'

'We're going to leave the last cable.' They explained their position, reassuring him that the cord was not critical. The submarine was free: if she blew the ballast now she would come up. Nuttall and Gold moved *Scorpio* away so there was no chance of her umbilical fouling the submarine.

The transmission produced no response from the men in the submarine. Contact was now one-way only, and those on the cable layer had no idea whether it was a communications problem or whether there was no one still alive or sufficiently conscious to carry out the task. All eyes were on the screen. Outside, everyone looked at the water.

'She's disappeared,' Gold said abruptly as the candy-striped hull vanished from the screen. With Riches close behind, Podkapaev made for the door.

'She's coming up!' the Russian cried in his own language as he burst onto the deck. Gold and Nuttall would have given anything to go with him, but *Scorpio* was their responsibility and she was still more than 600 feet down. They could only fret. Had she been trapped again, was that last cord tethering her ... Where was she?

Almost everyone had lined the port rail, staring at the water, willing the *AS-28* to appear. Seconds were turning into weeks.

A shout went up, but from the starboard side. The language did not matter: the ecstatic tone said it all. By the time Riches reached the other rail she was floating off the starboard bow, the last water pouring off. Someone thought to look at their watch: it was 16:26, and grown men were hugging one another and tears and vodka were flowing. On the *Razliv* Sergei Ivanov clenched his fists with sheer human joy and relief. Soon he would be a senior politician again. For the moment, he was no different from the crew around him.

But the drama was not entirely over. Someone had found the strength to blow the ballast, but in what state were all seven? A launch was on its way from the big rescue ship to tow the submarine back. Only after reaching the *Alagez* did seven exhausted, haggard men climb out, and back in Petropavlovsk Lena Milashevskaya put the phone down and danced and wept. Soon enough she joined the world in seeing the television pictures of her husband leading his crew ashore. For a moment he paused and raised his right arm in a salute, staring ahead out of large, tired eyes into a future which, for all his assertions to the media that he had always believed they would saved, had so nearly been snatched away.

Aboard the *KIL-27*, the *Scorpio* had been retrieved, welcomed back and packed up, and the UKSRS, too, were soon on their way back to their families. RAF transports cannot sit idly on foreign tarmac, and, fuelled with caviar and vodka, the British contingent were airborne the following morning without having had a chance to meet the *AS-28*'s crew, who had all been taken straight to hospital. The UKSRS team had gone three days without sleep.

There were those in Russia, such as Admiral Eduard Baltin of the Black Sea Fleet, who had opposed the calling in of foreign help in such a sensitive area. Others were embarrassed that their lack of equipment had again been exposed for the world to see. Some worried about the cost, though the British government picked up their own £205,000 bill, a small price for the experience. President Vladimir Putin, however, placed his seal of approval on the decision during his visit to London in October 2005, when he honoured five members of the team. The Order for Maritime Services went to Riches, Nuttall and Gold; the Order of Friendship to Holloway and Hewitt. Unusually, the Queen gave special permission for the recipients to wear their awards alongside British medals. The choice of recipients recognized that, while the mission had been very much a naval operation, success had also depended upon cooperation between four services. Holloway represented the political and diplomatic will that had given the early green light; Riches, the finest traditions of the Royal Navy; Gold and Nuttall, the civilian expertise of James Fisher Rumic; and Hewitt, the Royal Air Force, which had scrambled the C-17 in the interests of speed. After all, as a very senior RAF officer allegedly observed, 'it would have taken a bloody long time to get there in a boat'.

There was plenty of meat for the journalists and professional politicians on both sides: international cooperation, memories of Second World War Arctic convoys, professionalism, humanitarian response. Nor should the willingness of the Japanese and the role of the US team be overlooked; as well as unloading the British equipment, the Americans sent their divers out to the scene to support the Russians, and they were understandably disappointed not to have been the ones to free the *AS-28*. Sergei Ivanov caught the mood most succinctly on the day of the rescue when he referred to 'the brotherhood of the sea'. In human terms, the catch in the voice of Ian Riches when he spoke to reporters expressed the reaction of the whole team to their success. A few weeks later, he and Gold went back to Petropavlovsk for an emotional meeting with the crew and their families. As Gold said later in the BBC documentary *Submarine Rescue*, 'It's not every day that you end up saving someone's life.'

Sources and Bibliography

Kursk

Moore, and particularly Truscott, offer a detailed examination not just of what happened on the *Kursk* but of the rescue attempts, government response and the personal dimension of the disaster. Both are authoritative, easily accessible to the layman, and compulsive reading. Flynn believes that the US and British governments deliberately held back from offering early aid.

American Geophysical Union, 'Forensic Seismology Provides Clues to *Kursk* Disaster', press release, 22 January 2001.
Burleson, Clyde, *Kursk Down* (New York: Warner Books, 2002).
Flynn, Ramsey, *Cry from the Deep* (New York: HarperCollins, 2004).
Koper, Keith D, Wallace, Terry C *et al.*, 'Forensic Seismology and the Sinking of the *Kursk*', *Eos* 82/4 (23 January 2001): 37
Moore, Robert, *A Time to Die* (London: Doubleday, 2003).
Truscott, Peter, *Kursk: Russia's Lost Pride*, (London: Simon and Schuster, 2002).

The Guardian
The Independent
New York Times
The Times

'What Sank the *Kursk*?', BBC *Horizon* television documentary (8 August 2001).
www.bbc.co.uk
www.fas.org
www.wps.ru

AS-28

I am very grateful to Lieutenant Colonel Rory Bruce RMR and Commander Paul Buckland RN at the Ministry of Defence, and to Gregory Clark of BBC Scotland. Particular thanks go to Squadron Leader Keith Hewitt and to Stuart Gold, ROV project engineer/supervisor, James Fisher Rumic Ltd, for their invaluable cooperation.

Daily Telegraph
Interfax
Kommersant
Moscow Times
The Pelican (James Fisher and Sons)
St Petersburg Times
The Times
WPS

www.fas.org
www.ismerlo.org
www.mosnews.com
www.navytimes.com
www.number-10.gov.uk
www.ria.ru
www.sorbetroyal.com
www.thisisevesham.co.uk

Notes

[1] Published by the Bodley Head; reprinted by permission of the Random House Group Ltd.
[2] The gas created by this reaction drives a turbine that turns the propeller. At a speed of 30 knots, its range is about 54 miles (100 kilometres).
[3] Another view, aired in the *Horizon* documentary (see sources) was that the torpedo crew accidentally, or due to inexperience, started the torpedo motor running before it was fired.
[4] The Royal Navy discontinued the use of HTP after an explosion on HMS *Sidon* in 1955 which caused deaths and wrecked the boat. Nobody was certain what had caused it, but concern over the possible role of HTP led to its withdrawal on a better-safe-than-sorry basis.
[5] The buoy had, in any case, allegedly been disabled to stop it accidentally deploying during previous manoeuvres in case it betrayed the sub's presence to US surveillance.
[6] According to Koper and Wallace in their analysis of the seismic date (see sources), a bubble pulse occurred, caused by oscillations of the hot gases that rise to the surface after an explosion. This is characteristic of an underwater explosion, but would not be produced by a collision.
[7] Capable of working at depths as great as 3300 feet (1000 metres), but more usually half that, the *Priz* bathyscaphes can accommodate 20 survivors besides the crew of 3, and with 23 on board they have oxygen for 10 hours (RIA Novosti).
[8] According to some Russian media, Lena Milashevskaya reported that her husband had stated it happened the previous day, but there is no corroborative information.
[9] *Scorpio* technically refers to a class of ROV, but the UKSRS personnel affectionately call their ROV *Scorpio* as if it were her name.
[10] Officially this was denied. There is an element of reconstruction as to events inside the *AS-28*.

Conclusion

*I never saw a wreck and never have been wrecked,
nor was I ever in any predicament that threatened
to end in disaster of any sort.*

CAPTAIN EDWARD SMITH, FIVE YEARS BEFORE HE TOOK COMMAND OF THE *TITANIC*

ANYONE SETTING OUT to create the perfect maritime drama will find a huge list of ingredients from which to choose. Weather, human error, flawed technology, inaccurate charts, limited navigational equipment, hazardous cargo, war and natural dangers such as reefs all stand high among the causes. Some vessels, such as the *AS-28*, come to grief through sheer bad luck or, as in the case of the *Albion*, a single specific reason. Many incidents, however, are due to an unfortunate combination of factors. If the problem of iron bolts in copper-sheathed hulls had been addressed earlier, the *Centaur* and the *Ramillies* might have ridden out the storm and struggled home under jury-rig, and if the *San Francisco*'s sea trials had been more extensive she might not have found herself without engine power in similarly bad weather. Poor navigation and an inaccurate chart put the *Dodington* on a collision course with Bird Island, but in daylight and good weather, her crew would have spotted land ahead with plenty of time to spare. Failing to pass a effective bottom line underneath HMS *Queen Elizabeth* allowed the Italian warhead to remain undetected as its timer counted down. De Chaumareys would never have been given command of the *Méduse* had not a high-level political decision been taken to favour officers of the ancien régime, regardless of competence, over existing officers of greater experience.

The actual wreck of the *Méduse* comes down to human failing, and that is the determining factor in so many disasters. It may be a simple failure of attention to detail, such as trusting that the main induction valve on the *Squalus* would operate correctly, or it may extend to the criminal negligence of running the *Sirio* at full speed through reef-strewn waters in order to make up time lost through picking up stowaways for illicit gain. Several officers might have averted the collision of the *Camperdown* and *Victoria*, but, hamstrung by blind trust and a tradition of unquestioning obedience, they stood impotent in the face of looming disaster, just as the officers of the *Méduse*, the passengers on the *Rothsay Castle* and the captain of the *Amphitrite* did for other reasons.

If, as in the cases of the *Méduse* and the *Albion*, humanity can be shown at its most selfish and incompetent, it can also be seen at its best, from small gestures, such as the doomed soldiers on the *Prince* sparing a kind word for the Indiaman's second officer, or Mrs Astor handing her shawl to the girl standing next to her, to Hénin risking his life in the Boulogne tide, Morelli giving up his chance of survival in favour of his young bride, Coudein defending the boy, Léon, and the bravery of Dancy in boarding the *Flying Enterprise*. The resourcefulness of the *Dodington*'s men in constructing a craft in which they could not merely escape from their island, but actively continue their voyage, may be hard to appreciate adequately today, but however much one may deplore warfare, it is impossible not to admire the ice-cold courage of the men of the Decima MAS in the service of their country. At a national level, the Portuguese took care of the *Prince*'s survivors; the British, Japanese and Americans went to the help of the AS-28; German and Italian submarine commanders risked their lives and boats to help their enemies as well as their allies and compatriots.

One of the strongest themes running through this collection is that of leadership, or the lack of it. How many of the ships that came to grief would have done so with a safer pair of hands on the quarterdeck or the bridge? It is likely that the *Méduse*, the *Rothsay Castle*, the *Amphitrite*, HMS *Victoria*, the *Sirio* and the *Titanic* would not have found their way into a book such as this – or at least not in the same circumstances. Once the crisis has happened, leadership becomes even more vital. Oliver Naquin was commended for his leadership while the *Squalus* lay on the bottom. He kept his men calm and optimistic about rescue with a mixture of firmness – no talking about the men who must be dead beyond the bulkhead door – and kindness – putting his own coat around a shivering crewman, and offering a quiet word of praise to a nervous junior officer. Despite all the disagreements on Bird Island, Jones retained enough authority to keep the group sufficiently cohesive to complete the boat, and the British at Alexandria were struck by the absolute confidence in and loyalty to Prince Borghese expressed by their prisoners, who had followed instructions to the letter and pulled off their mission with flying colours. By contrast, Piccone's desertion and the abdication of authority by Lieutenant Atkinson and de Chaumareys turned crisis into tragedy.

Around half the commanders featured in this collection perished with their vessels, but, on close inspection, one of language's favourite clichés may be more powerful as a metaphor than a reflection of reality. No law obliges a captain to go down with his sinking ship, much less salute from the bridge as the waves close over his head, and nobody would have thanked Inglefield, Watkins or Carlsen for choosing to do so. In a navy the captain was generally supposed to be last off, but having done what he could for the crew and passengers, there was no reason why a captain should not then save himself if possible. Experience and ability are too valuable to discard wantonly.

In the event, however, the shock of seeing his world collapse around him, and the fear or certainty of being blamed for the loss of the ship and of some or all of the lives in his care, may lie behind a captain's decision effectively to commit suicide. Some merchant captains with heavy investments in their ship and her cargo may have preferred death to the stigma of bankruptcy. Rudolph Sharp was no more to blame for the torpedoing of the *Laconia* than the bombing of the *Lancastria*, but two such horrors in as many years amounted to a burden too great to face. If, like Morin, he believed survival to be impossible, why not meet death calmly and with dignity? Whether Tryon likewise embraced death or, like Samson and Atkinson, simply drowned, is speculation. Tryon's chances of survival would have been hampered by his age, size and lack of fitness, all exacerbated by his heavy uniform. Either way, in the words of Shakespeare: 'Thy ignominy sleep with thee in the grave / But not remembered in thy epitaph'.[1]

The links between events separated by decades, even centuries, are striking. Tony Large and Pierre de Lafond could easily understand one another's experience of a long voyage in a badly provisioned open boat in the South Atlantic, though one came from an eighteenth-century sailing vessel, the other from a steam-turbine-powered ex-passenger liner. Charles Lightoller, Maurice Bourke and William Webb all knew the terror of finding themselves on a ship as it went down or broke apart, leaving them at the mercy of the waves and the wreckage. The ships that put up the most gallant fight to stay afloat were not expensive twentieth-century liners or battleships but the insignificant *Albion* and the *Flying Enterprise*. Seventy years separates the merchantmen who waited patiently to take off the crew of HMS *Ramillies* from those who stood faithfully by the crippled *San Francisco*; a further hundred finds a succession of supply ships and destroyers keeping watch over the *Enterprise*. The grief of those who lost their relatives in the hurricane of 1782 is the same as that of the wives and mothers who mourned for the crew of the *Kursk* more than two hundred years later.

In considering that grief, it should also be remembered that it is only through the comparatively recent development of communications, submersibles, deep-diving equipment and complex salvage techniques, that grieving relatives backed by media campaigns can find out what happened and even demand the recovery of the dead. Before then, hundreds of thousands of ships went down without survivors or witnesses to say where or how the disaster occurred. Some, of course, still do. The sea has absorbed and forgotten innumerable instances of courage, ingenuity, suffering, despair, resignation, cowardice and savagery that must have been as remarkable as anything chronicled by those who lived to tell the story.

The Italians have a proverb befitting a maritime nation: *when the ship has sunk, everyone knows how she might have been saved,* and wisdom after the event is certainly a feature of shipwrecks. Everyone seems to have known that the *Rothsay Castle* was unsound, that the *Laconia* made too much smoke, that the *Méduse* was too close to the Arguin Bank, that the combined turning circle of the *Victoria* and the *Camperdown* was more than 6 cables, that the *Titanic* was heading into ice, that there was a good reason for fitting submarines with lower induction valves, and that the Italians were planning something against Alexandria.

The loss of ships, particularly over the past two centuries, has given an impetus to develop new safety measures and procedures in the fond hope of averting the next tragedy. Disasters such as the *Méduse* spurred navies to carry out surveys of important coasts; the *Rothsay Castle* was one of many fiascos that encouraged the construction of additional lighthouses and the expansion of the lifeboat service – not to mention legislation requiring effective condition surveys for vessels. The loss of the *Victoria* brought about the invention of the Stone-Lloyd system, and hastened a whole new class of battleship; the *AS-28* crew owe their lives to technologies developed in the wake of too many submarine tragedies. The real memorial to the victims of the *Titanic* is not the deluge of books, websites and big-budget films on the subject, but the first Safety Of Life At Sea (SOLAS) convention in 1914. SOLAS remains the linchpin of the international maritime community's drive to reduce accidents; in 2006, for example, the 81st session adopted new regulations requiring all passenger and most cargo ships on international voyages to be equipped with Long-Range Identification and Tracking equipment – the marine equivalent of the black box flight recorder carried by aircraft.

The subject of the *Titanic* brings us to that vexed question of why she dominates the popular image of the shipwreck to such an extent. Together with her huge death toll, and the hype that created the erroneous belief in her unsinkability, the ship's name and size has certainly fed the legend. How could the *Sirio* and the *Rothsay Castle*, old and unremarkable, hope to compete in the public imagination with a brand-new floating city, the name of which proclaimed a physical superiority and offered an arrogant, pagan challenge to old-fashioned values such as humility, moderation and modesty? Even the great warships have had a problem in competing with so much glamour. Naval history regrettably remains primarily a male preserve, and when disaster occurs, warships are rather lacking in the women, children and small furry animals[2] whose fate strikes a particularly long-lasting chord with the public; the very discipline instilled into all ranks often seems to make light of a traumatic ordeal. Yet the stories of those who survived are no less moving; the causes and the social-historical background no less interesting.

There is another other factor worth observing. The *Titanic* disaster offers a great deal of sanitized and dramatic appeal for an age that thrives on symbols and image. The prolonged suffering endured by those on the *Albion, Méduse, San Francisco* and *Laconia* is frankly repellent. Frostbite, cannibalism, dysentery, excoriated skin, sunburn and blood-spattered holds do not have the same visual appeal as men in evening dress helping fur-wrapped ladies into lifeboats under the eyes of stiff-upper-lipped officers in immaculate uniforms. Particularly when box-office ratings are an issue. Class and glamour sell in a global market. By contrast with tragedies such as the *Méduse, Sirio, Laconia* and the *Lusitania*, torpedoed in 1915, there is something clinical about the sinking of the *Titanic*. Beesley came close to expressing something of that remote quality when he commented on the reflection of the *Titanic*'s lights in the still water: 'parallel lines should never meet'. That is not to devalue either the suffering or the sacrifices made that night (even though some of the calm can be ascribed to ignorance of the ship's desperate condition), merely to suggest that there are other, perhaps more difficult and uglier stories out there that deserve a sizeable share of the excessive attention lavished on this one vessel.

The pamphlet, the ballad and the collection have given way to the 'popular history' book and the docu-drama, both trying to offer context, illumination and themes. Taken as a group, what is the appeal of the maritime drama? Entertainment? Suspense? Human nature in all its colours? Morality? The vicarious thrill of touching danger from the safety of the sofa? All of those things, plus a reminder of our own vulnerability in an alien element, tempered by a rose-tinted belief in what we might achieve in a crisis. We all hope we would be a Jacob Astor or a Mary Whittaker, a Jean Espiaux, a Pierre Hénin or a Doris Hawkins, but it might be unwise to bet on it.

That is where such stories may have a subconscious effect that is not always healthy – that of encouraging unrealistic expectations – and because of all the attention paid to it, *Titanic* is probably the worst culprit. A dozen years after the sinking of the ferry *Estonia* in the Baltic Sea in 1994 a young dancer who had survived it remained dismayed by the contrast with the *Titanic*: there was no 'women and children first' code, no chivalry – which, incidentally, proves that in an age of gender equality an independent woman can still believe in Lightoller's 'rule of humanity'. What saved her was a raw determination to survive, which gave her the physical strength to claw her way up the staircases past others who hesitated. A young man who was among the last to get off lamented the lack of heroism, not just in others but in himself.[3] Neither had done anything wrong, but gratitude for surviving had become tarnished by an irrational sense of guilt for not having measured up to some mythical standard. Few people will ever be trapped 200 metres down in a crippled submarine or experience the tension and dangers of sneaking into a fortified base to attack a battleship, but almost anyone could find themselves on a passenger vessel in distress, whether it be a luxury liner in the Caribbean, the Genova–Palermo *traghetto*, the commuter ferry in San Francisco Bay or a pleasure boat on Windermere.

Notes

[1] *Henry IV, Part 1,* Act V, scene iv.

[2] Two Pomeranians and a Pekinese were rescued from the *Titanic* by their owners, and one passenger, Ann Isham, drowned because she refused to get into a boat without her (large) dog. However, in his autobiography, *Footprints in the Sea* (London: Evans Brothers, 1959) Captain Augustus Agar, VC RN, makes a point of relating how his men rescued a tiny kitten from the oily water after HMS *Dorsetshire* was sunk by Japanese bombers in 1942 off Sri Lanka.

[3] 'Surviving Disaster: The Sinking of the *Estonia*', BBC/Discovery Channel/Poseidon, 2006.

Glossary

Some terms have more than one meaning. The definitions given here relate to the context in which the term is used in this book.

Aft: Towards or at the stern.

Back water, to: To stop a boat by pushing on the oars rather than pulling on them.

Bar: A shoal or sandbank at the mouth of an estuary.

Barge: A type of ship's boat.

Beam: The width of a vessel, referring to the transverse beams.

Beam ends, on: A list of around 90° from which the ship will not right herself.

Bilge, to: To be holed around the bottom of the hull.

Bilge-keel: The two downward projections from the underside of the hull, one on each side of, and running parallel to, the keel. They provide stability.

Binnacle: The housing for the ship's compass.

Broaching/broach-to/broached: When the ship finds herself broadside to the sea as a result of her head flying up into the wind.

Bulkhead: A partition below deck.

Captain of the top: The rating who was in charge of those sailors – invariably the finest among the crew – stationed on or above the topsail yards.

Careening block: A wooden casing containing one or more sheaths around which a rope is passed so as to gain enough mechanical advantage to pull a ship onto its side so that repairs can be made to the hull below the waterline.

Chains: Chains attached to both sides of the ship abreast of each mast.

Clamps: Planks fitted beneath the lower deck beams to give extra strength.

Course: The lowest sail on each mast (differentiated as fore-course, main-course and mizzen course).

Crossjack: The lower yard on the mizzen mast (on a square rigged vessel).

Crosstrees: Supports for the platforms known as 'tops', where the lower masts are joined to the topmasts, or the topmasts to the top-gallant masts.

Entry port: An opening cut into the side of a ship to provide an entrance.

Flagship: A warship in which an admiral has hoisted his flag, or a merchantman whose captain is the commodore (senior commander) of the company's fleet.

Flat: The large compartments below deck.

Fore-: At or towards the front part of the ship.

Forecastle (fo'c'sle): Technically, the furthest forward compartment. The 'forecastle deck' refers to the raised forward deck which was common before the advent of the flush deck.

Fore-spencer: A sail set fore and aft (as opposed to square) on the foremast.

Founder: Sink while at sea, usually as a result of serious leaks or damage caused by striking an underwater object.

Futtock shrouds: Short shrouds connecting upper rigging to the lower mast.

Grapnel: A small four-pronged anchor.

Gunwale: The very top of the hull, immediately above the sheerstrake.

Halyard: Rope for lowering the sails set above the courses.

Heave-to: To position a vessel in relation to the wind so that, with her sails trimmed, she cannot make headway – effectively, she comes to a halt.

Helm: An alternative word for tiller; a general term for orders relating to the steering.

Jib-boom: An extension to the bowsprit, the forward-most projection of the ship in front of the hull.

Lanyard: A short piece of rope.

Leeward: Down wind (effectively, sheltered from the wind).

Longboat: The largest of a ship's boats.

Main mast: Effectively, the largest mast; a brig has a fore mast and a main mast; a three-masted ship has fore, main and mizzen.

Mizzen mast: On a vessel with three or more masts, the mast furthest aft.

Oakum: Fibres from old rope, used to fill gaps between the planks.

Offing: Distance from the land or offshore hazards.

Orlop: The lowest deck of a ship with three or more decks.

Pinnace: A rowing boat with a de-mountable mast, carried by a warship.

Points of the Compass: The circular card over which the needle of the magnetic compass swings is divided into 32 points, each of 11° 15′ (giving a total of 360°). For example, to turn from north to east is a movement of 8 points, or 90°; east to east-by-south represents just one point.

Poop deck: A raised deck which is both uppermost and furthest aft.

Port: On the left (as viewed from the deck when facing the bows).

Quarterdeck: The raised deck, or portion of the flush deck, forward of the poop. The preserve of the captain and officers.

Quarter galleries: Sheltered walkways accessed from the cabins at the stern quarter of the ship. They were found on larger warships and East Indiamen, and they communicated with the stern-walk, the captain's private walkway behind his cabin.

Quoin: A wedge.

Reef: rocks or coral close enough to the surface (and sometimes exposed at low tide) for a ship to ground on them.

Reef, to: To shorten sail as a temporary measure. A row of short ropes, called 'points' and running horizontally along a sail, could be tied up to the yard in order to reduce the amount of sail on which the wind acted. Larger sails might have two or three parallel bands of points, allowing the sail to be single, double or treble reefed.

Relieving tackles: Blocks and ropes set up to protect the tiller from breaking under the strain of sudden violent motions.

Roundhouse: The large cabin below the poop, opening onto the quarterdeck of a warship or East Indiaman. It gained its name because, by using the quarter and stern galleries, it was possible to walk *around* it.

Sheerstrake: The row of planking level with the upper deck of a wooden ship, immediately below the gunwale.

Sheet: A rope that adjusts the position of a sail in relation to the wind.

Shrouds: The heavy standing-rigging that runs from the side of the ship and helps hold the mast vertical.

Spar: Any pole – mast, yard, boom etc. – making up the ship's rigging.

Spritsail: A small sail set under the bowsprit.

Stand off: To keep at a distance (from land or another ship).

Stand to: To take or maintain a course or direction.

Starboard: On the right (as viewed from the deck when facing the bows).

Stave (in): To break a hollow receptacle – such as a cask of spirit or the carcass of a ship – by force. In the past tense, a cask is *staved* in, but planking is *stove* in.

Steering oar: An oar held over the stern for steering in the absence of a rudder.

Sternpost: A vertical timber attached to the keel at the stern of the ship and from which the rudder was hung.

Sternwalk: A covered, private walkway at the stern of a warship in the late-nineteenth / early-twentieth century for a captain or admiral, outside his quarters.

Strike down: To lower masts or spars.

Swim: In this context, probably to keep afloat and moving.

Tiller: A wooden bar connected to the rudder, used on its own for steering a small boat, but connected by lines to the steering wheel in larger vessels.

Top-gallant mast/sail: The sail/mast above the topsail/topmast.

Topsail/topmast: The sail/mast set above the lower.

Upper works: In this context, the upper part of the hull.

Waist: The open area of the upper deck between the raised forecastle to the front and the raised quarterdeck behind – until the advent of flush-decked ships.

Watch: Period of duty. Over a 24-hour period, the watches changed at noon, 4 p.m., 6 p.m., 8 p.m., midnight, 4 a.m. and 8 a.m.

Windlass: A smaller version of the capstan but mounted horizontally; used for lifting anchors etc.

Windward: The side from which the wind blows.

Yard: The spar, or pole, that crosses a mast and from which the sail hangs.

Yawl: A type of ship's boat.

Illustration Credits

Text illustrations

p.21: *Les Naufrages Célèbres*, 1872; author's collection.

p.49: Map by Stephen Dent.

p.112: Map by Stephen Dent.

p.144: *A circumstantial Narrative of the wreck of the Rothsay Castle...*
London: Joseph Adshead, 1833. British Library Shelfmark: 790.b.6.

p.170: Zurcher and Margollé; author's collection.

p.172: *The Story of the Sea*, vol. 2, London: Cassell and Company, 1896.

p.211: Map by Stephen Dent.

p.212: Conway Picture Library.

p.216: *The Story of the Sea*, vol. 1, London: Cassell and Company, 1895.

p.279: Conway Picture Library.

p.282: Naval Historical Center, Washington, DC.

p.293: Bagnasco, Erminio: Sommergibili della Seconda Guerra Mondiale. Parma, Ermanno
Albertelli Editore, 1973. Reproduced by kind permission of the author.

p.297: Map adapted by Stephen Dent from *Proceedings* of the US Naval Institute 82/2 February
1956. Reproduced by permission of the USNI.

p.368: Conway Picture Library.

Endpapers: Map by Stephen Dent.

Plate section:

East Indiaman: Conway Picture Library.

Centaur: Distress of the *Centaur* by Robert Todd © National Maritime Museum(PY9182).

Albion: Narrative of the Wreck and Loss of the Albion, John Kirby, 1810,
British Library shelfmark B 495.(13).

Méduse: Zurcher and Margollé; author's collection.

Amphitrite: (*The Story of the Sea*, vol. 2, London: Cassell and Company, 1896)

Pierre Hénin: Musée de Boulogne.

Three Bells Polka: Courtesy of the Keffer Collection of Sheet Music, University of Pennsylvania
Library.

Victoria: The Story of the Sea, vol. 1, London: Cassell and Company, 1895.

Serafini family: Publicaciones Digitales El Mercurio. Edita MercurioPress.
© elmercuriodigital.es, Ángel Rojas Penalva.

siluro a lenta corsa: Bagnasco, Erminio: I mezzi d'assalto della X Flottiglia MAS, ed. Albertelli,
Parma, 1997

Laconia, Tony Large: Author's collection.

Flying Enterprise: Conway Picture Library

AS-28: Stuart Gold

Index

North
Atlantic
Ocean

Pacific
Ocean

South Atlantic
Ocean

1 *Prince*, 1752
2 *Dodington*, 1755
3 HMS *Centaur* and HMS *Ramillies*, 1782
4 *Albion*, 1810
5 *Méduse*, 1816
6 *Rothsay Castle*, 1831
7 *Amphitrite*, 1833
8 *San Francisco*, 1853–54
9 HMS *Victoria* and HMS *Camperdown*, 1893
10 *Sirio*, 1906
11 *Titanic*, 1912
12 USS *Squalus*, 1939
13 HMS *Valiant* and HMS *Queen Elizabeth*, 1941
14 *Laconia*, 1942
15 *Flying Enterprise*, 1952
16 *Kursk*, 2000
17 *Priz AS-28*, 2005